To Jacquie,
with friendship
and appreciation,
Ruth

Breaking
the
Earthenware
Jar

In 1994, women, some carrying lighted torches, pause at dusk during a rally held on International Women's Day - March 8 - in Dhaka, Bangladesh. Among other issues, the rally called for equality between women and men, and safety for women while in the street.

Breaking
the
Earthenware
Jar

**Lessons from South Asia to End
Violence against Women and Girls**

Ruth Finney Hayward

Regional Office for South Asia

2000
© United Nations Children's Fund

ISBN No. 92-806-3574-3

The manuscript has not been edited to official publications standards and
UNICEF accepts no responsibility for errors. The contents of this report do not
necessarily reflect the policies or the views of UNICEF.

The designations employed in this publication and the presentation of the
material do not imply on the part of UNICEF the expression of any opinion
whatsoever concerning the legal status of any country or territory, or of its
authorities.

All correspondence should be addressed to:

The Regional Director
UNICEF Regional Office for South Asia
P.O. Box 5815
Kathmandu, Nepal
Telephone: 977-1-417082
Fax: 977-1-419479
Email: lgurung@unicefrosa.org.np

Cover Photograph: Frances Klatzel/Mera Publications

Design: Format Graphics, Naxal, Kathmandu

Printed: Jagadamba Press, Kathmandu, Nepal

Contents

PART III:
Towards Solutions and Gender Peace

PART IV:
Conclusions

Appendices

List of Tables and Boxes

Foreword

"Educating a daughter is like watering a tree in your neighbour's yard."

This off-handed comment, made to me almost in passing by a father in a village in Northern India, epitomises what many men - and unfortunately many women – consider to be the natural order of things. A girl child is worth less, much less, than a boy. Her birth is a time of sadness, not of celebration. And once on the road of worthlessness, too many South Asian girls, especially poor girls, can expect to experience exploitation, abuse and violence on their way to womanhood – a womanhood all too often thrust upon them through early marriage or sexual exploitation.

Violence against women and girls is by no means exclusive to South Asia. It is emerging as a world-wide pandemic. But we live in the region in which SAARC (The South Asian Association for Regional Cooperation) declared the 1990s to be the "Decade of the South Asian Girl Child", yet in 1997, Mahbub Ul-Haq felt impelled to give the region the title of "the most gender insensitive" in the world. It is the only region with a sex ratio of less than 100 women for every hundred men; a region with 22% of the world's population, but 45% of the world's maternal mortality, highest rates of female illiteracy, greatest proportion of girls out of school. And behind these disturbing statistics, lurks a too regular pattern of violence against women and girls – in the home, in the neighborhood, in the police station.

This book turns the spotlight on such violence, and poses challenging questions: How best to address troubling issues like selective female foeticide, child neglect and abuse — including sexual abuse? How to learn more about the realities in the family behind problems related to gender roles and relations, such as beating in pregnancy, incest and murder — including so-called "dowry death," "stove-burning," and "honour killing"? And are there higher proportions of girls and women committing suicide than would be expected? If so, why? These are things we all would prefer did not occur anywhere. But they do.

Of all the forms of violence against women and girls, perhaps the most challenging to eliminate is violence in the family, where it has long been denied or trivialised. No wonder, then, that it may come as a surprise that there is evidence suggesting a high incidence of domestic violence in South Asia. Men appear to be the most frequent perpetrators of violence against their wives. Some also abuse their children, especially their daughters. This goes against many cherished values and beliefs about family life here in South Asia, as it would anywhere.

Behind the frequent violence against women and girls hovers an ugly word: impunity. All too often, men are able to get away with extreme violence against their wives, daughters and female neighbours. Too few people seem to care. Violence in the family is supposedly a private affair, beyond the domain of the law. An honour killing, acid throwing, the violent death of a woman at the hands of a drunken husband - where is the accountability? Where is due legal process? Where is the outrage? Violence against women and girls has major policy and programme implications. The grief and suffering that it causes, and the loss of lives, is a public issue, not a private one.

This book offers an opportunity to re-examine assumptions about family, about care of children, about respect for women and girls — and their human rights. It invites open-minded consideration of problems that appear to exist, with public debate about changes needed, and how to bring them about.

The Fourth World Conference on Women, held in Beijing in 1995, along with the parallel NGO Forum in Hairou, China, put violence against women among the list of critical areas of concern for follow-up by governments, civil society and the international community. This year, 2000, is the year for "Beijing plus 5" reviews of progress — and the distance still to go. What better time to bring forth this 'wake-up call' that amplifies the voices of many South Asians who are working to end violence against women and girls?

The urgency to tackle these issues is also inspired by the many forms of rights abuses that they influence, where UNICEF has major commitments to make improvements with our government and civil society partners. Child and infant mortality, maternal mortality, street children and child labour, uneducated children, sexual exploitation of children, HIV/AIDS: the list of problems where violence in the family, against women and girls, is a likely factor is long.

UNICEF's commitment to the human rights of children and women - as enshrined in the Convention on the Rights of the Child (CRC) and the Convention on the Elimination of All Forms of Discrimination against Women (CEDAW) - cannot be fulfilled so long as violence based on gender is practised, tolerated or excused.

How best to work towards the elimination of gender-based violence, and with which new partners, in civil society as well as government? How best to support more fulsome use of human rights instruments and mechanisms to eliminate violence against women and girls? How to bring in men and boys as partners, not perpetrators? How to focus on prevention itself, not only redress for a few victims?

Part of the answer lies in our taking a closer look at how children are nurtured, how they develop, and what are the critical periods in infancy and early childhood for the acquisition of tolerance and respect rather than a sense of entitlement and superiority compared to others. At what age (3, 4?) does the little girl begin to understand that she is an inferior being, compared to her brother? Parents and teachers, in particular, will need to be supported in their responsibilities to encourage the growth of healthy human beings who respect human rights — of women and girls as well as men and boys. What are the negative impacts of violence around children? Parents and teachers deserve to know, as we must, if we are going to be able to support programmes that reach them as partners for prevention.

While poverty is a scourge, and signals all manner of ills and lacks in human society, it cannot be accepted as an excuse for gender-based violence , which is found in all classes and circumstances. Certainly not all poor people engage in family violence either. Poverty of the spirit needs to be overcome, not only poverty of the purse. Negative attitudes to women and girls have to change. Stereotypical thinking and behaviour need to be given up — as called for in the Beijing Platform for Action and by so many South Asians, as well. We in the development community also need to rid ourselves of any tendency to act as though what we do with and for girls and women matters less than what we do with and for boys and men. Development itself should never exploit those whom it is meant to serve, girls and women among them.

This book is a contribution towards the public dialogue that precedes a commitment to a truly better society, beginning with improved family life that truly protects the rights of all and prepares citizens who will respect those rights.

I thank all who have contributed to this book. I am pleased to say that it is based on research done through this office when the author, Ruth Finney Hayward, served as Deputy Regional Director and took the opportunity to listen to South Asians who were already working against gender violence. I hope that their message, reflected here, will prove useful in this region and beyond.

Nigel Fisher
Regional Director
UNICEF Regional Office for South Asia
Kathmandu, Nepal

Author's Preface

One hundred and eighty South Asians have been living with me for over two years, that's how it seems. Women and men from Afghanistan, Bangladesh, India, Nepal, Pakistan and Sri Lanka — their stories are all over the house, on tables, by the chairs, by the bed and on the rug where I sit on the floor. I have tried to immerse myself in their experiences, their views, to become a means for their voices to be heard. Why? Because each is doing something practical to end some type of violence against women and girls in his or her country.

For me, this book is like a quilt made from their experiences, piece by piece. When I was a child my mother gave me a wonderful quilt: small circles of colourful fabrics were joined, each touching four others, to make a pattern. The pieces each had their own identity, but the connections to the others made for a bigger and more useful result.

That is the way I hope this book will be: something simple and useful that features material from many different sources, many different communities and many different countries. "Who made the quilt?" I asked my mother. "All the women, each contributed, they didn't use their names," she said.

I wondered that something so vital had nameless creators, with such generosity of spirit. Most of the interviews from which this book is created were to have been done on the understanding that results would be presented anonymously, to permit interviewees more freedom of expression. Sometimes, however, interviews are with someone whose identity is singularly clear. How many women can be the first woman to hold a karate black belt in Bangladesh? How many men in India could be the director of the film *Bandit Queen*? How many women in Pakistan did ground-breaking research on domestic violence with outpatients in a Karachi hospital? And so on. The answers are: "Only one," "Only one," "Only one."[1] Except for such people, some others who have given permission to use their names and those who often give their opinions in public about gender violence as part of their professional lives and responsibilities, real names are not used. Pseudonyms or a descriptive phrase introduce the interviewees. Sometimes I have even changed some personal details about individuals who are not named, to reduce any risk to them from their forthrightness. All let their interviews be tape-recorded or notes to be made, and many did not expect this protection. Still, "Above all, do no harm" is a useful motto.

The interviews were arranged through the various UNICEF offices in the countries represented in the project, or by the regional office in cooperation with local contacts and offices. The selection was up to the participating offices and interviewers. There were many interviewers, some hired for the purpose, some UNICEF staff. I only did a few interviews myself. I do not personally know most of those interviewed, although I feel as though I do.

Each office was given a list of various kinds of gender violence they might want to consider when looking for activists to interview. Each received a list of topics to cover with interviewees: definitions and causes of violence; motivation; their own interventions, and models for and results of these; what they would recommend be done in childcare to prevent gender violence in the future; what they knew about and thought of the usefulness of the Convention on the Rights of the Child and the Convention on the Elimination All Forms of Discrimination against Women as tools for change; their priorities and recommendations for action. But some interviewers went their own way and didn't ask all the questions. In any case, interviewees clearly saw the interrelationship between the different kinds of violence, causes, solutions: they usually talked about many different things together. The results do not lend themselves to quantification, but that was never the intention.

There is more material from India than from other countries, and the least from Afghanistan. The proportions don't signify that there is more or less gender violence in the countries concerned, only more or less material available to me. Although each of the chapters does not give equal time to each country, I tried to make sure that in-depth interviews from each country — as well as shorter quotations — were featured in the book.

As with many large projects, this book was written in stages, sometimes with long interruptions between them. The first stage was done during part of the almost five years when I was Deputy Regional Director for UNICEF's Regional Office for South Asia (ROSA) in Kathmandu. In less than six months, part-time, mostly early in the morning, late at night, on weekends, I drafted the first part of the book. And then — almost a year later — there was the reward of a two-month stay at Innocenti, the UNICEF International Centre on Child Development in Florence, for which I am most grateful. Once again, after another assignment of almost half a year, I went back to the gift of Innocenti for a few months to finish even more of the first draft of this book. Then came a period at UNICEF Headquarters in New York City, where additional research was done, consultations made and writing completed. Despite these many moves, I persisted, inspired by all the efforts of those in South Asia working to end violence against women and girls. They shared so much for this project. The book belongs to them.

For those who inevitably will say, as I do myself, "But this and this aren't covered at all or are treated too briefly," my answer is, "Yes, please bring your piece and add it to the quilt, make it bigger, more useful." This book is merely a beginning for questions and ideas, rather than a conclusion. It is meant to reflect and encourage a movement against violence to women and girls, a movement that can be even more powerful than many involved in it might imagine: so many women and men have their insights and energy to add if and when they hear the door is open for them to do so, if and when they know their efforts are needed, if and when they see that good results may follow. (A quiz about the incidence and costs of gender violence can be found in Appendix 3 for the reader who, at the outset, wants to test her or his knowledge about some of the facts to be found in this book.)

Women and men activists from South Asia are the primary audience I had in mind when I wrote the book. In it I hope they will see their efforts in the context of a picture larger than any one individual's or group's experience could show. I hope they will see many opportunities for cooperation. The secondary audience for the book is, of course, all of us who can learn from the lessons of the South Asian experience.

For several reasons, there are only a few statistics about gender violence for South Asia in the book. First, these are relatively difficult to come by. Second, their validity, reliability, methodology and interpretation are almost always subject to question. Third, one can ask for more and more and more facts before accepting that something unpleasant is true and needs urgent action to stop it.

But what difference does it really make if 500,000, 1 million, 2 million or 6 million are affected, before one says it is a problem? The numbers matter more for deciding what resources to allocate, where, for what, and for measuring progress. Let the process of prevention and redress proceed, and more information will be discovered, refined. Statistics never tell us about individuals or even causes, only about patterns, possible connections, probabilities. Case studies check and amplify patterns that statistics summarize. In some ways, case studies fall short; in other ways, they surpass what statistics can tell us. The two are always complementary. Here, the message of both is that gender violence — which targets women and girls simply because they are female — is everywhere, it affects each of us as victim, perpetrator or both unless and until we say "No!" to what has been assumed for too long to be "the way it is." The solution must be everywhere, too, from each of us, who will no longer tolerate inequality and violence at home or in public. Everywhere people are waking up to the extent of violence in their society and the urgency to eliminate it in all its forms.

A regional meeting in Kathmandu, "Ending Violence Against Women and Girls in South Asia," 21–24 October 1997, brought together a diverse group, some 120 women and men (only a few of them among the interviewees for this book), each of whom was working against gender violence. They committed themselves to joint and complementary action. Their "Kathmandu Commitment on Ending Violence Against Women and Girls in South Asia" (Appendix 1) was an important step towards a truly South Asian movement, across borders and boundaries of all kinds. They were determined "to break the silence" about subjects as troublesome as incest and child rape, wife-battering and favouritism of men and boys in the family.

As Carol Bellamy, Executive Director of UNICEF, said in her speech to launch UNICEF's 1997 *Progress of Nations*, which featured an important article on ending violence against women and girls:

> [T]hroughout the world, there is no more pervasive violation of human rights than violence against women and girls.

> It is everywhere in every conceivable form — from assault, rape, sexual slavery and domestic abuse to torture, mutilation and disfigurement — even murder. It affects rich and poor, in every country, every community, every neighbourhood.

And yet the vast scale of this outrage is still not widely acknowledged, much less extensively quantified. Nor are the devastating effects of gender violence on societies truly understood.

In her speech, Carol Bellamy made it clear she wanted to promote more understanding of violence against women and girls as a form of oppression with "corrosive effects on children, and on human progress generally." She hoped that "denial and passive acceptance" about gender violence would be successfully changed. She also urged more attention be given, in particular, to education for girls as a means to ensure the rights of women and to inspire women's and girls' confidence.

As one woman from Bangladesh interviewed for this book put it, "It just takes a little bit of courage to stand up to violence." Her message, and that of the others in the book, is relevant beyond South Asia. Gender violence is pandemic. So is the tendency to remain silent about it, especially in countries that pride themselves on family life, but may not have examined the facts about abuses within it.

I hope that the honesty and action from so many in South Asia will encourage others to face up to and overcome gender violence, particularly in the home.

It is an honour, and it is humbling, to find myself entrusted with parts of this quilt made of so many life experiences that also represent and touch more lives in turn, especially the courage in them. As will be clear in the acknowledgements section, credit is due to all who participated and contributed to this book, to all who challenge wilful exploitation and destruction of women and girls as less than fully human. Men's courage to question standards for masculinity is also deeply moving, and vital; without it, families are not so likely to become violence-free and to be genuine sites of nurturance.

I only put the pieces together for this particular glimpse of so many constructive lives, which are making a new, more equal and just society wherein girls are not at risk simply because they are born girls, and boys are not exalted just because they are boys. As one activist said, "It shouldn't be wrong to be a woman."

---

1   People who are the subjects of the more lengthy interviews featured with their names have agreed that the material may be so used. Most have even read the draft. (Not all their suggestions for additions could be accommodated, however). Others said they didn't need to do so.

Acknowledgements

All those who are working to end violence against women and girls in South Asia are the first to be acknowledged — for their insight, courage and remarkable efforts towards human rights within the family as well as outside it. A special thanks go to the women and men among them who generously agreed to share their rich experience by giving interviews for this book. The interviewers, some UNICEF staff, some not, also deserve credit. I had the opportunity to know and work with only a few: Nadeem Fazil Ayaz, Ruchira Gupta, Thomas Kelly, Karen Kundiyat, Naila Sattar, Vidhya Shrestha and Glory Sodemba. I greatly appreciate their and others' contributions. Those who translated, transcribed or typed interviews also have my thanks. Without their efforts, the wonderful interview material would not have been available for use here.

Turning to the UNICEF family, I first want to thank Carol Bellamy, Executive Director, for the vision and leadership that makes ending violence against women and girls a priority for the organization's work. Her commitment, patience and support during the sometimes frustrating process of completing this book made all the difference. Stephen Lewis, Deputy Executive Director during most of the time when I was writing the book, was one of the first at UNICEF to show interest in this work. More than that, he sustained that interest over several years, encouraging me, which was very helpful. And Sadig Rasheed, Director of the Programme Division, provided support when it was must needed. Thank you.

Among my UNICEF colleagues in the Regional Office for South Asia (ROSA), where I was Deputy Director from 1994 to 1998, there are many to thank. Urban Jonsson, then Director; the late Dr. Mabelle Arole, M.D., then Regional Health Advisor; James Irvine, then Regional Education Advisor; and Anne Skatvedt, Regional Communication Advisor, were very encouraging from the outset, reviewed drafts and shared many helpful insights with me. There would not have been anything for them to read were it not for Glory Sodemba, my secretary for almost five years in Kathmandu. She, Lalita Gurung and Antariksha Roka worked devotedly to help bring this book to life. Bhanu Pathak helped find important reference material; Misbah Sheikh provided some research on the impact of domestic violence on children; Alexandra Cole-Hamilton identified some examples and some prospects for work with youth against gender violence.

The UNICEF Representatives in all the offices of the region played key roles in the effort to bring this project to life, as did the various focal points on gender and communication. They made the topic of ending gender violence an important one for UNICEF support in the region, and gave time to many activities covered in this book. In particular, I would like to thank the following people for their comments, resources or both: Shahida Azfar, Representative in Bangladesh; Alan Court, Representative in India; Kul Gautum, Deputy Executive Director of UNICEF, who was Director, East Asia and the Pacific Regional Office and Special Representative for India when research and writing for this book was underway; Jim Mayrides, former Representative in Pakistan; Stewart McNab, Representative in Nepal; Jim Mohan, former Representative in Afghanistan; Dan O'Dell, former Representative in Nepal; Brita Ostberg, then Representative in Sri Lanka; and Steve Umemoto, Representative in Pakistan. Communication and gender advisors throughout the region played important roles, too, making many vital contacts for the book during both the research and publication phases. They are too numerous to mention by name, but special thanks go to Razia Ismail, then with UNICEF India; Jayanthi Liyanage of UNICEF Sri Lanka; Raana Syed of UNICEF Pakistan; as well as Peter Chen, then with UNICEF Nepal. And Niloufar Pourzand of UNICEF Afghanistan contributed in a number of important ways.

Wonderful hospitality and assistance were given to me during trips in the region by more people than I can name here. I would be especially remiss not to mention the following: Mabelle and Raj Arole; Shahida Azfar; Abha Bhaiya; Kamla Bhasin; Ralph Carriere; Sebha Hossain; Razia Ismail; Olivia Jonsson; Chandni Joshi; Jim Mayrides; Jim Mohan; Brita Ostberg; Raana Syed; and Steve Umemoto.

Among those from the Kathmandu community who contributed in the early stages, Patricia Roberts edited some of an early draft, and Lee Birch kindly gave some advice on design, photographs and publishing in South Asia. Frances Klatzel of Mera Publications co-ordinated final production, and conceived the cover design. Anil Shrestha and his team at Format Graphic Studio did the layout, design and last minute corrections of the book. Thank you all.

Misrak Elias, UNICEF Representative in Jordan and then Chief of UNICEF's gender programme at Headquarters, and Sree Gururaja, Senior Advisor, were encouraging throughout the project and also helped arrange some funding from the Government of Switzerland, for which I am grateful. UNDP and UNIFEM contributed to support some of the interviews, studies or meetings on which this book draws. Accordingly, I would like to thank my colleagues Carroll Long, Deputy Director of UNICEF Regional Office for Asia and the Pacific and former UNDP Representative in Nepal, and Saraswati Menon of the UNDP Regional Office for South Asia. My long-time colleagues Chandni Joshi, Regional Advisor for UNIFEM South Asia, and S. K Guha, UNIFEM Programme Officer in New Delhi, deserve special recognition. Their collaboration, encouragement and support have been indispensable, particularly for the 1997 Kathmandu Regional Meeting on Ending Violence against Women and Girls, from which the Kathmandu Commitment resulted after a session under Mr. Guha's guidance. Their partnership is also acknowledged for the UNICEF/UNIFEM study "The Use of the Legal System to End Violence Against Women in South Asia." Savitri Goonesekere, vice-Chancellor of University of Colombo in Sri Lanka, and member of CEDAW Committee provided the very useful guidelines. Christa Meindersma, an international human rights lawyer, played a very significant role as a consultant to UNICEF ROSA helping me to coordinate that study. Many outstanding lawyers from the region contributed country studies. Those with whom I had the pleasure to work, even briefly, and to whom I owe much gratitude are: Sigma Huda, from Bangladesh; Kirti Singh, from India; Sapana Malla, Yubaraj Sangroula, Shanta Thapalia and Indira Rana from Nepal; Eman Ahmed from

Pakistan; Shymala and Mario Gomez, from Sri Lanka. Also, as will be evident in the text of the book, I have been deeply impressed and inspired by the work of two Pakistani lawyers and human rights advocates — Asma Jahangir and Hina Jilani. I am indebted also to Charlotte Bunch for her pioneering work that brought the human rights of women and girls into sharper focus at the global level, and to Radhika Coomaraswamy, the Special Rapporteur on violence against women, its causes and consequences, for her clarity about the principle of universality vs cultural relativity regarding women's human rights — as well as for the wealth of useful information that she consistently provides in her excellent reports.

A word on the photographs. Most are the result of a 1997 contest for South Asian photographers, "Violence against Girls and Women in South Asia: Prospects for Change." I coordinated it for UNICEF ROSA with the support of photographer Thomas Kelly and his then assistant, Vidhya Shrestha. Judges of prize winners were all from South Asia and included: Shahidul Alam, Director, Drik Picture Library, Bangladesh; Dr. Mabelle Arole, then Regional Health and Nutrition Advisor, UNICEF ROSA; Gopal Chitrakar, Photo Editor, Gorkhapatra Sansthan, Nepal; and Kishwar Naheed, then Director General, National Council of the Arts, Pakistan. I appreciate all their contributions.

I would like to thank all the South Asian photographers who participated, particularly those whose work has been selected for this book. Arrangements for use of photographs were made by UNICEF ROSA or by Headquarters in accordance with contest rules. Photographers Thomas Kelly and S. Paul deserve thanks for the use of some of their photographs.

As for some of the tables, this is to acknowledge with thanks the material I have adapted, with permission, from the UN Statistical Office. Joann Vanek and Linda Go were wonderfully patient colleagues. Other sources are cited in the text, and I acknowledge the very important and ground-breaking work that their various authors have done. Without the World Bank's 1994 discussion papers by Lori Heise, Jacqueline Pitanguy and Adrienne Germain, and WHO's impressive efforts to highlight violence against women and abuse of children as public health problems, there would not have been so much progress in so little time in this field within the United Nations family. Under Noeleen Heyzer's leadership, UNIFEM's campaigns to end violence against women provide continuing emphasis. Ilana Landsberg-Lewis, also of UNIFEM, shared useful details with me. Interagency cooperation on various parts of the work reflected in this book has been outstanding.

Quotations from published sources are all used with acknowledgement and thanks. Care has been taken that individual quotations should not exceed 200 words, and permission has been sought to use any material longer than that. The obvious exception is material from or for UNICEF and its UN or government partners. As for the interview material, quoted sometimes at length, the reader may want to bear in mind that the interviews concerned were conducted specifically by UNICEF for this book.

For the time I spent writing at the International Child Development Centre in Florence, Italy, Innocenti, I have many to thank: Paolo Basurto, then Director, who enthusiastically welcomed and supported my efforts there, as did the Deputy, Bernadette Abegglen; Urban Jonsson, then an Advisor to the Centre, for the proposal that this work merited such support; and Mehr Khan, Director since October 1998, for having me back and encouraging me to write even more than had been foreseen, thus extending my stay. My thanks also go to staff at the Centre. In particular, I want to acknowledge the indispensable contributions of Keith Richmond and Robert Zimmerman: Keith made suggestions for editing; Robert prepared the bibliography. Many helped with the typing: Carolyn Anne Cotchett, Lis-Britt Dalkari and Mara Elsner, in particular, worked diligently to assist me at Innocenti.

My editor, Michael Kaufman, International Director of the White Ribbon Campaign, is a noted author and a leader on ending gender violence, particularly with regard to men's roles against it. Because I wanted to make sure that what I wrote would resonate with ongoing work about men as partners against violence, not only its perpetrators, I contacted Michael, whom I did not know at the time. He reviewed an early draft, said he believed in this project and then took time from his own writing and advocacy accordingly. He was patient, diligent and full of good suggestions, as well as being supportive throughout the lengthy process when, sometimes, I had doubts that it would be possible to finish given various obstacles and shifts in my assignments. Thank you, Michael.

I also drew support and guidance from many wonderful South Asian professionals who interrupted their own very busy lives to give me inspiration or comments. It is for people like these, in particular, that the book is a small offering, in acknowledgement of their own goals and efforts. They include: Meena Acharya, economist from Nepal; S. B. Agnihotri, Special Secretary, Government of Orissa; Kamla Bhasin, activist extraordinaire, devoted to regional identity for women and men beyond borders and boundaries of many kinds; Radhika Coomaraswamy, UN Special Rapporteur on violence against women, its causes and consequences; Shanthi Dairiam, of International Women's Rights Action Watch (IWRAW), Asia and Pacific, Malaysia; Savitri Goonesekere, Vice Chancellor of Colombo University, Sri Lanka, and Professor of Law there; Hamida Hossain, a leading activist from Bangladesh; Shireen Huq, a founder of Naripokko, whose effective support for women's empowerment is widely recognised, Razia Ismail, whose expertise in communication and advocacy as well as the girl-child was extremely helpful; Vina Mazumdar, the doyenne of women's studies in South Asia and Director of the Centre for Women's Development Studies in New Delhi; Shaheed Nadeem, playwright; Rekha Pande, historian, University of Hyderabad, India; Pam Rajput, of University of Chandigar; Rahul Roy, film-maker; and Dr. Shekar Seshadri, M.D., child psychiatrist, National Institutes of Mental Health and Neurological Sciences (NIMHANS), Bangalore. And Monica Sharma's work on maternal mortality has been inspirational.

Those who kindly read and commented on interview material to be used with their name include: Drs. Mabelle and Raj Arole, M.D.s; Kamla Bhasin; Dr. Lubna Bhatti, M.D.; Professor Harenda de Silva; Shireen Huq; Dr. Lohiya, M.D.; Rani Padamsee; Rahul Roy; Dr. Shekar Seshadri, M.D.; Anjana Shakya; Indrani Sinha; Kiran Tewari; and Dr. Aruna Uprety, M.D.

Those activists who read and commented on the entire manuscript deserve particular thanks. They include: Dr. Neelam Gorhe, M.D., President and Founder Trustee of STREE AADHAR KENDRA, Pune, India; Roushan Jahan, Founder Member, Women for Women, Bangladesh; Dr. Shershah Syed, M.D., Director of the Women's Health Forum, Pakistan; Anjana Shakya, human rights activist of INHURED, Nepal; and Mufti Ziauddin, lawyer from Swat, Pakistan.

Without the keen interest shown in this project by Dietrich Garlichs, Executive Director of the German Committee for UNICEF, and Ingvar Hjäartsjö, head of the Swedish Committee, I would not have been able to finish. Thank you both, very much, for your commitment and constancy regarding the importance of ending violence against women and girls, and the worth of this particular contribution towards that goal. Swedish writer and playwright Eva Moberg also made an important contribution through her generous participation in the 1997 regional meeting in Kathmandu, her insightful comments on the book and her encouragement.

In the final stages of preparing the book, I was a Senior Advisor, Special Project on Ending Violence Against Women and Girls, with the Gender, Participation and Partnerships Section of UNICEF in New York. I would like to thank Joan French, Chief of the Section, Sree Gururaja, Margaret Kyenka-Isabirye, Erma Manoncourt, Nicolette Moodie and Sherrill Whittington, among others there for their support and for their comments. Indispensable help came from three UNICEF interns, Lillian Messih, Neesha Nanda and Laura Rótolo, as well as from Rahel Tekle, an intern at UNFPA whose time Pamela DeLargy of UNFPA kindly shared. Rijuta Tooker and Sivanesan Rajan provided much needed secretarial assistance in the final stages. Kassech Alley assisted with solving computer problems, and Lucy Scull provided expertise on budgetary matters. Pat Lone and Elaine Furniss helped guide me through the publication review process. Victoria Haeri consulted on copy-editing needs. Rachel Fudge diligently, expertly and pleasantly did the copy-editing saving me from many errors or omissions, and thus contributing to a better experience for the reader.

Soon after he took over the post of Regional Director for UNICEF ROSA in 1999, Nigel Fisher decided to bring all the hard work of so many to fruition as a publication sponsored by his office. The partnership with him and Anne Skatvedt, who was in charge of seeing the project through under Nigel's leadership, has been the most pleasant part of the many joint efforts on this book. Thank you both for your determination and dedication to help end gender violence and for giving this book a role to play in the movement to do so.

On the home front, my husband, Bob, kindly gave up any traditional gender-role expectations for me, thereby freeing more of my time for the book. He tolerated lost family time on weekends and evenings; he forfeited vacations together; he lived with papers and books everywhere. Without my husband's gift of taking on an undue share of household chores and giving up his own professional work to follow me during my work on the book, I could not have finished when I did. He also made many useful comments on various versions of the drafts, and kept encouraging me. Thank you, Bob, for believing that this book tells a story that can help save lives and for contributing to it in so many ways. I am also grateful to our children Sean, Greg, Wendy and Erica: thank you for your interest, patience and encouragement.

For any worth the book may have, all those mentioned above — and others too numerous to name — share the credit. For any omission or errors, the responsibility is mine alone. Knowing that, I still make this small offering towards gender peace, not gender violence, in South Asia and beyond.

Ruth Finney Hayward,
9 November 1999, New York

On 27 February 1995, the corpse of an infant girl was found near the Bagmati River, at a Hindu temple in Kathmandu, Nepal. A postmorterm examination revealed that she died of a head injury.

Problems and Prospects for Change

PART I

Breaking the Earthenware Jar

"If it is a girl and she survives that vessel, she will not survive the earthenware jar." An old man or woman may say this, looking at a pregnant woman's swollen belly. Some newborn girl, still alive, will be slipped inside an earthenware jar, as though she could easily be returned to her mother's womb and kept there. Then the jar will be buried in the ground.

There are many such stories from South Asia[1] about violence to girls and women done simply because they are female, because they are not valued as such or because they have "misbehaved" according to some norms of the predominantly patriarchal societies of the region. From before birth to old age, girls and women are thereby denied rights, tormented and even killed. Without generally accepted or reliable means for redress or remedy, an abused woman in a South Asian family usually keeps the problem quiet, out of fear, "to protect family honour," "for the children's sake" or because she thinks she is at fault. Perhaps she even thinks it is all normal, inevitable, a "woman's lot" in her family, community and society. And if a girl is abused, there is seemingly little she can do to escape her situation.

The many forms of violence against women and girls based on ideas and condemnations about their gender can be understood as "gender-based violence" or, simply, "gender violence." It is a worldwide problem, but one that is fairly new for open discussion in South Asia.

Why does gender violence happen at all in a region that places great value on family life, includes women among its political leaders and has goddesses as well as gods in some religions? Widespread attitudes towards girls and women as inferior, even as the property of men; systematic discrimination; "traditional practices" and acts in the name of religion; oppression by patriarchal institutions; indifference or collusion of the State — all are involved in denying girls and women their human rights and fundamental freedoms and, sometimes, their lives. Commodification of women in the media and their economic marginalization in the global economy are additional negative forces, along with politics that sometimes build male solidarity around the issue of controlling women.

Vina Mazumdar, one of the most respected scholars and leaders of the women's movement in South Asia, provides perspective on the great difficulty of changing women's generally subordinate position in the region:

> We remembered that this region had thrown up some of the most powerful women rulers in the world. But they did not work for restructuring of the social order, eliminating patriarchal institutions. We have taken pride in their successful defense of national sovereignty and leadership role in defending third world interests in global fora.
>
> But as prisoners of power in hierarchical global and national social orders, they could not be creators or defenders of democracy from below. Nor could they even begin the task of eliminating the subordination of women in the mass. (Mazumdar n.d., page 317)

Where are the stories about the women and the men who are appalled by and active against the customs and practices, traditional and modern, used to stifle or condemn girls and women? Where are the accounts of the many South Asians who surely believe such practices should not be excused by "culture," "tradition" or in the name of religion, who believe anything that denies rights or kills — simply because of gender — does not deserve respect? Where are the women and men who would break the earthenware jar, and all it symbolizes, in order for the newborn girl to live and thrive as a human being equal in value to a boy, with the same rights?

Surely there are many who believe violence against women and girls is simply unacceptable, that it dehumanizes men and boys as well as women and girls, that it debases rather than reinforces the social and political order that should instead protect the human future as well as the present.

The desire to find, listen to and learn from such individuals was the motivation behind the research for this book, which draws on the experiences and voices of some 180 women and men from Afghanistan, Bangladesh, India, Nepal, Pakistan and Sri Lanka.[2] Each interviewee is doing something practical to stop some form of violence to women and girls in his or her country. From their own cultures they may also find as well as forge positive examples for the affirmation of women's and girls' rights and equality. Some risk their lives to do so.

These women and men "activists"[3] and many others like them in often unsung local efforts in South Asia, as elsewhere, are the source from which an unstoppable movement has started to flow and gather force in South Asia. It includes South Asians from all walks of life: farmers, villagers, slum dwellers, professionals, educators, lawyers, physicians, writers and government officials as well as those from non-governmental organizations (NGOs). They were chosen from many walks of life because the problem of gender violence is everywhere and thus its solution must be everywhere. About 40 per cent are men. This reflects an important point of view that is constant in this book: Men are not only seen as by far the main perpetrators of gender violence against women. They are also seen as being affected by it and by the narrow gender role that they play out. Men and boys are vital partners to ending gender violence. They also will benefit from its end.

Why is it so important to end violence against women and girls? First of all, it is important because of the terrible physical and emotional pain and suffering that the violence causes, the needlessly lost lives. Also, women's empowerment and full participation are prerequisites for reaching major goals of the world community — development, equality and peace. When, instead, women and girls are the targets of violence, in its many forms, because they are female, their opportunities and rights as human beings are denied, their participation in development limited. There are both financial and human costs. The quality of family and community life declines.

Children's futures — and that of society — are tainted. When that happens, fear and conflict, rather than self-confidence and peace, begin at home.

Why look at South Asia? The level of violence against women and girls in the region appears to be very high, especially in the family, where a review of studies so far available suggests it may even be the highest in the world. (Chapter 2 discusses related studies of wife-beating.) Patriarchal values and systems predominate in South Asia, with negative effects on girls and women. For example, Urban Jonsson (former Director of UNICEF Regional Office for South Asia) notes that in South Asia "women are excluded, subordinated and exploited more than in any other region of the world. . . . [R]eligious interpretations legitimize the particular form of patriarchy found in South Asia" (Arole 1999, page x).

Leela Dube, in her 1997 book *Women and Kinship: Comparative Prospectus on Gender in South and South East Asia*, provides an analysis that offers strong clues about how kinship and social structure influence the particularly negative outcomes for women and girls in the region. She contrasts the kinship systems and related ideologies and practices about girls and women in South Asia and South-East Asia. In South Asia, kinship systems are predominantly patrilineal[4] and a newly married couple is customarily expected to live with the husband's family. In South-East Asia, kinship systems tend to be bilateral[5] and a couple usually has more freedom of choice about where to live after marriage. A newly married couple is not normally expected to live with the husband's family.

Dube observes:

> It is a peculiarity of South Asia that the female sex is denied the right to be born, to survive after birth, and to live a healthy life avoiding the risks of pregnancy and childbirth. Poverty alone cannot explain this. (Dube 1997, page 144)

She also notes that

> In patrilineal South Asia, one of the manifestations of inequality in conjugal relations is the beating and battering that women receive at the hands of their husbands. This is an expression of a man's right over his wife's person. (page 123)

Dube says that, in contrast, women in South-East Asia also have more freedom of mobility and economic participation, and that if they are beaten, they are more likely to protest than South Asian women are and to find refuge with their natal families or in employment. Women in South Asia, then, seem to face many constraints on their lives and a high propensity for gender-based violence against them, even in the home.

The great challenge for those who would end violence against women and girls in South Asia make their courage and some successes all the more compelling.

In short, there is much to learn from their efforts to create a social order that is more egalitarian than hierarchical, and that does not sanction or accept violence against women and girls.

What the Book Covers

Whatever the problems and their underlying causes, this book is also a story of hope. It takes up various questions and some emerging answers about how to end gender violence in South Asia, drawing lessons to be shared within the region and beyond. The experiences, views and recommendations of South Asian activists form the core of the book, along with related findings and international concerns. References to the problem of gender violence elsewhere and a few important initiatives to end it are included to give perspective on the South Asian situation.

The first part of the book, Problems and Prospects for Change, is about the basic problems that women and girls face due to gender violence. It also explores South Asians' views about such problems. This introductory chapter gives some basics about violence against women and girls — definitions, key international treaties and declarations that form part of the solution to the problem — and discusses the relationship between gender violence and some other human rights issues. The problem of gender violence in the South Asian family is introduced, along with the difficulty of bringing about change in what has generally been considered a private space under male control. Confrontations between patriarchal interests and more egalitarian ones that are compatible with the fulfilment of human rights are under way. Paradoxically, this is happening in the very subcontinent that has the world's largest democracy and a vibrant history of pursuing freedom, rights and equality for its peoples, and which has a strong women's movement.

The rest of Part I goes into more detail about how gender violence affects women's and girls' lives, particularly in the home. Women's and girls' well-being, health and longevity are all at risk from extreme neglect and discrimination as well as physical and sexual violence and traditional practices. Some efforts at prevention are being made, but these are still limited because the problem of gender violence is not yet clearly seen or addressed, even by health care professionals. Many of the women "victim-survivors" concerned are really still girls, although they are wives and mothers. The problems of these "girl-women" are often overlooked. How childhood is betrayed by various kinds of violence in the family is reviewed.

The second part of the book, Excuses, Explanations and Challenges, helps answer the questions "Why?" and "Can it stop?" about gender violence. It opens with a brief chapter on the excuses that are often given for the acceptance of gender violence — excuses that need to be seen for what they are, and dismissed. If the main cause of gender violence is the unequal power relations between women and men based on women's supposed inferiority and men's supposed superiority, then cultural ideology and images can help reveal norms for women's and men's roles and their relationships. These cultural ideals and caricatures are explored, drawing on creative writing, history and research in the region, as well as on some facts about social structure and the patriarchy in South Asia. Men's gender roles are also considered. This part of the book thus sets out the nature of gender roles that predict violence against women and girls, while also offering hope for change by introducing women and men whose lives challenge the stereotypic norms as they strive to end different kinds of gender violence.

The next part of the book, Towards Solutions and Gender Peace, is about where change is most needed and how to achieve it. Here the discussion turns explicitly to the family, the community and the school, as well as the world of work and the legal system. Bringing about new attitudes as well as opportunities and laws; building movements that cut across all sorts of divisions; and focusing on gender violence as a key development and human rights issue — these are portrayed as engines of change for South Asia and beyond. Featured throughout are the experiences and words of South Asians working for change.

Basics: Some Definitions and Related Issues

For those readers less well acquainted with research and discussions on gender violence, some basic definitions follow, for a common starting point.

Definitions Are Broad

What is considered violence against women and girls has been steadily broadening beyond the physical realm alone. Some examples below show the wide range of categories for types of violence against women and girls. Harmful traditional practices are included, as are acts not only of commission, but of omission. Links between violence to women and girls and human rights issues have also been made clear.

The Nairobi Forward Looking Strategies for the Advancement of Women, adopted in 1985,[6] specified only physical and sexual acts of violence, without any formal definition of violence against women: "Violence against women exists in various forms in everyday life in all societies. Women are beaten, mutilated, burned, sexually abused and raped. Such violence is a major obstacle to the achievement of peace and the other objectives of the Decade and should be given special attention."

- Article 1 of the United Nations Declaration on the Elimination of Violence against Women (1993) (the Declaration) contains the first formal definition of violence against women put forward in the UN system. It is very broad:
  Violence against women means any act of gender-based violence that results in, or is likely to result in, physical, sexual or psychological harm or suffering to women, including threats of such acts, coercion or arbitrary deprivation of liberty, whether occurring in public or private life.

- Article 2 of the Declaration lists some forms of violence that are of particular concern:
  Violence against women shall be understood to encompass, but not be limited to, the following:
  (a) Physical, sexual, and psychological violence occurring in the family, including battering, sexual abuse of female children in the household, dowry-related violence, marital rape, female genital mutilation and other traditional practices harmful to women, non-spousal violence and violence related to exploitation;
  (b) Physical, sexual and psychological violence occurring within the general community, including rape, sexual abuse, sexual harassment and intimidation at work, in educational institutions and elsewhere, trafficking in women and forced prostitution;
  (c) Physical, sexual and psychological violence perpetrated or condoned by the State, wherever it occurs.

- Since Article 2 includes "other traditional practices harmful to women," it invites a range of practices to be treated as forms of violence to women and girls. For example, Heise, Pitanguy and Germain proposed (1994, page 12): "In UN parlance traditional practices refers primarily to such practices as genital mutilation and child marriage. . . . We suggest broadening this concept to include harmful practices and behaviours common in industrial societies which are likewise motivated by a desire to make women into acceptable, attractive sexual partners for men.[7] . . . [W]e feel that genital mutilation should be viewed as one point on a continuum of harmful practices motivated by women's desire to conform to socially prescribed standards of beauty and marriageability."

- Acts of omission as well as commission have also been recognized as types of violence against women. Radhika Coomaraswamy, the UN Special Rapporteur on violence against women, observes in her review of the Declaration, "This gender bias from birth which discriminates against women when it comes to nutrition, education and health amounts to violence against women" (UNCHR 1994, page 38). In fact, the definition in the Declaration above, especially when considered along with Article 2 about the forms of violence — which indicates these should "not be limited" — is broad enough to permit such an interpretation.
In the same vein, the European Union used a generic definition in 1986, which specifies acts of omission as violence: "Any act or omission which prejudices the life, the physical or psychological integrity or the liberty of a person or which seriously harms the development of his or her personality."[8]

- The links between discrimination, violence against women and denial of girls' and women's human rights are very strong, if somewhat elastic. For example, the Vienna Declaration and Programme of Action adopted by the World Conference on Human Rights in 1993 states:
The human rights of women and of the girl-child[9] are an inalienable, integral and indivisible part of universal human rights. The full and equal participation of women in political, civil, economic, social and cultural life, at the national, regional, and international levels, and the eradication of all forms of discrimination on grounds of sex are priority objectives of the international community.
Gender-based violence and all forms of sexual harassment and exploitation, including those resulting from cultural prejudice and international trafficking, are incompatible with the dignity and worth of the human person, and must be eliminated. This can be achieved by legal measures and through national action and international cooperation in such fields as economic and social development, education, safe maternity and health care, and social support.

- The Fourth World Conference on Women Platform for Action (UNDPI 1996b) incorporates the definition of violence against women as in the Declaration, and goes on to add two additional paragraphs. One concerns situations of armed conflict and the other emphasizes reproductive rights:
Other acts of violence against women include violation of the human rights of women in situations of armed conflict, in particular murder, systematic rape, sexual slavery and forced pregnancy.
Acts of violence against women also include forced sterilization and forced abortion, coercive/forced use of contraception, female infanticide and prenatal sex selection.

How Broad Should a Definition Be?

The World Health Organization (WHO) notes: "There is no universally accepted definition of violence against women. Some definitions argue for a broad delineation that includes any act or omission that causes harm to women or keeps them in a subordinate position. This would include what is sometimes referred to as 'structural violence,' for example, poverty and unequal access to health services and education" (1996b, page 5).

WHO also observes that "The benefit of a broad definition is that it places gender-based violence in the broader social context (Richters 1994) and allows interested parties to bring attention to many breaches of women's human rights under the rubric of violence against women." The report notes, however, that "far-reaching meanings" may limit a definition's use. In any case, Articles 1 and 2 of the Declaration are already very broad in their implications.

So, finally, what does "gender violence" or "gender-based violence" mean in the broadest sense? I would say this comes close: Any act of commission or omission by individuals or the State, in private or public life, which brings harm, suffering or threat to girls and women, and reflects systematic discrimination — including harmful traditional practices and denial of human rights because of gender.

This book, then, takes a broad view of violence against women and girls, based on United Nations documents. In this context, domestic violence can be understood also to be expressed in a broad range of ways, both through acts of commission — physical, sexual and psychological — and through acts of omission, including neglect. When physical violence is the subject, "beating," "battering" and "physical domestic violence" are the terms used; "wife abuse" or "partner abuse" could include psychological or sexual abuse. Some examples of different kinds of gender violence over the life cycle are given in Box 1.

Box 1	Gender Violence throughout the Life Cycle
Prenatal	Sex-selective abortion, battering during pregnancy, coerced pregnancy
Infancy	Female infanticide, emotional and physical abuse, differential access to food and medical care for girl infants
Childhood	Child marriage, genital mutilation, sexual abuse by family members and strangers, differential access to food and medical care, child prostitution, trafficking in women
Adolescence	Dating and courtship violence, economically coerced sex, sexual abuse in the workplace, rape, sexual harassment, forced sex
Reproductive	Abuse of women by intimate male partners; marital rape, dowry abuse and murder; partner homicide; psychological abuse; sexual abuse in the workplace; sexual harassment; rape; abuse of women with disabilities
Old Age	Abuse of widows, elder abuse (affects women more than men)

Adapted from Heise, Pitanguy and Germain 1994

Some Important Conventions

There are many important international human rights conventions that can help prevent and eradicate gender violence through the protection and fulfilment of women's and girls' human rights. The conventions are legally binding under international law for the nations (referred to in formal language as "States Parties") ratifying them. Two in particular are already widely recognized and supported by efforts of South Asian activists working to end violence against women and girls. The discussion in the book returns at many points to their importance.

The older one is the Convention on the Elimination of All Forms of Discrimination against Women (1979), which is generally referred to as CEDAW.[10, 11] It does not actually mention the word "violence" in its articles, but two general recommendations, 12 and 19, have been given to States Parties as guidance for their reports on implementation to cover violence against women (see IWRAW and Commonwealth Secretariat 1996, pages 72–76). Ivanka Corti, a member and past chair of the CEDAW committee that reviews reports from governments, explains that violence against women is seen as a form of discrimination and is a vital subject for government reports on their progress towards equality.[12] In fact, Recommendation 19 states "Gender-based violence is a form of discrimination that seriously inhibits women's ability to enjoy rights and freedom on a basis of equality with men" (IWRAW, SCA, UNDAW, UNIFEM, UNICEF 1998, page 72). All the countries of South Asia featured in this book, except Afghanistan, have ratified CEDAW, though some have done so with reservations (see Table 1).

The second legally binding convention that deals with violence against women or girls is the 1989 Convention on the Rights of the Child, known as CRC[13]. Article 2 prohibits discrimination on the basis of sex. The Convention explicitly addresses violence against children: Article 19 calls for the protection of the child (those under the age of 18) "from all forms of physical or mental violence, injury or abuse, neglect or negligent treatment, maltreatment or exploitation, including sexual abuse," while Article 34 calls for the protection of children "from all forms of sexual exploitation and sexual abuse."[14] No definitions are included. All the countries of South Asia discussed here have ratified or acceded to CRC, some with reservations (see Table 2).

There is only one legally binding convention in the world specifically about violence against women: the 1994 Inter-American Convention on the Prevention, Punishment and Eradication of Violence against Women, the Convention of Belém do Parà. It applies only to Latin America. As of yet, there is none like it to protect women and girls in South Asia.

While there is no active movement towards a UN Convention to Eliminate Violence against Women are under way, however, an Optional Protocol to CEDAW was adopted by the UN General Assembly on 6 October 1999. This mechanism, when in force, will give women everywhere more protection from gender-based violence if existing remedies in their countries are exhausted.

Mechanisms for Accountability

States Parties make reports on a regular basis to committees charged with reviewing and commenting on their progress in implementation of the conventions. The comments are advisory only: NGO participation in the process of preparing official

Table 1: CEDAW Status in South Asian Countries

Country	Status	Reservations[1]/Declarations[2]
Afghanistan	Not yet ratified[3]	Not applicable
Bangladesh	Ratified 6 November 1984	Reservation to Art. 2 on condemnation of discrimination and commitment to its elimination by States Parties. Reservation to Art. 16(1)c on equal rights and responsibilities during marriage and its dissolution.[4]
India	Ratified 9 July 1993	Reservation to Art. 29(1), which says that disputes between States Parties go to arbitration and later to the International Court of Justice. Declaration regarding: Art. 16 (1) on marriage and family relations; Art. 16(2), which says that child marriages should be illegal and that there should be a minimum age for marriage set in law.
Nepal	Ratified 22 April 1995	None
Pakistan	Ratified 12 March 1996	Reservation to Art. 29(1), which says that disputes between States Parties go to arbitration and later to the International Court of Justice. Declaration that its accession is "subject to the provisions of the Constitution of the Islamic Republic of Pakistan."
Sri Lanka	Ratified 5 October 1981	None

Source: United Nations, *http://www.un.org/Depts/Treaty/final/ts2/newfiles/part_boo/iv_boo/iv_8.html.*
1. According to the Vienna Convention of the Law of Treaties, Article 2(1) (d): "reservation means a unilateral statement however phrased or named, made by a State, when signing, ratifying, accepting, approving or acceding to a treaty, whereby it purports to exclude or to modify the legal effect of certain provisions of the treaty in their application to that State."
2. Statements which are not intended to exclude or modify the obligations of a State under a treaty. Note: while the Vienna Convention on the Law of Treaties does not define "Declaration", the foregoing is the definition in use.
3. Afghanistan signed CEDAW on 14 August 1980.
4. Bangladesh withdrew its reservations concerning Article 13(a), which provides for the right of women to family benefits, and Article 16(1)(f), which grants women equal rights with men regarding guardianship of children.

government reports varies depending on how consultative and open a process a particular government may organize.[15] Governments often welcome NGOs' rich experience in consultations on formulation of policy and action interventions as well as in the review process itself.[16] The accountability issue is addressed at various points in this book; the participation of NGOs in it is a topic in the section. The greater the familiarity of NGOs and women's organizations with the pertinent international treaties and mechanisms for state accountability, the more they are empowered to work as effective partners for women's and girls' human rights.

Table 2: CRC Status in South Asian Countries

Country	Status	Reservations/ Declarations
Afghanistan	Ratified 28 March 1994	Reservations to "all provisions of the Convention that are incompatible with the laws of Islamic Sharia and the local legislation in effect."
Bangladesh	Ratified 3 August 1990	Reservation to Art. 14(1) on the right of the child to freedom of thought, conscience, and religion. Reservation to Art. 21 on adoption.
India	Acceded* 11 December 1992	Declared that it will progressively implement Art. 32(a) on a minimum age to work. (India does not currently have a minimum age for all forms of labor.)
Nepal	Ratified 14 September 1990	None
Pakistan	Ratified 12 November 1990	None
Sri Lanka	Ratified 12 July 1990	None

Source: UNICEF, *http://www.un.org/Depts/Treaty/final/ts2/newfiles/part_boo/iv_boo/iv_11.html.*
* Accession has the same legal significance as ratification. Only countries that sign the Convention are eligible to ratify it. Countries that do not sign the treaty, and wish to join it, must do so through accession.

How South Asian Activists See Violence against Women

Their Definitions

The South Asian activists whose lives are the basis for this book define violence against women in ways that show awareness and concern that it is based on notions about inequality between men and women, as reflected in their prescribed gender roles and relations. Examples of their definitions follow, from one activist in each South Asian country. Their definitions fit well with those in international documents.

> Earlier, my definition of violence was beatings, rape and sexual abuse. Now it is anything which infringes on my rights to be treated as a human being.
>
> *— Indian woman, NGO leader*

> Actually, I think of violence in a broad sense, both mental violence and physical violence. Mental violence includes cruelty against women in the home, including domestic violence. There is also social, religious and legal violence. And in buses, on the street and in factories, everywhere where women and children are, even in our country and society, there is violence against them.
>
> *— Nepali woman, lawyer*

The vital thing which is missing is the recognition of women as individuals. Women are always seen in the perspective of their relationship with men. This is the fundamental violence against women. Women's entity as an individual human being is simply not accepted.
— Pakistani man, researcher

When a woman wants to do something which is her right, but she is not permitted to do so, for which she mentally suffers, then that is violence against women.
— Bangladeshi woman, activist

The general deprivation of women should be [considered] violence. Of course, so is direct hitting or putting any ban on their participation in social and economic activity.
— Afghani man, NGO

Well, violence against women is an extremely broad subject because the manifestation of violence covers so many areas, but I will focus my remarks most specifically on sexual abuse of women and children . . . and also on domestic violence.
— Sri Lankan woman, victim of incest as a child

Gender Violence and Rights

These words echo, in far more vivid language, the same general views and concerns as are found in the United Nations Declaration on the Elimination of Violence against Women (see above).

The South Asians tend to be explicit that, for them, the deprivation of rights to women and girls is itself a form of violence. Throughout this book, then, we will find that the activists are addressing the denial of women's and girls' human rights as the true problem of which gender violence is a part. This is compatible with the outcome of both the Vienna World Conference on Human Rights and the Fourth World Conference on Women mentioned above, as well as the content of CEDAW and CRC.

It is remarkable that the ways in which activists in South Asia, from all walks of life, and some with very little education, speak about rights is so clear, so committed. Their lives seem to have taught them that fulfilment of rights is not assured so long as there is discrimination. Their focus is more generally on social, economic and cultural rights rather than on civil and political ones. In short, they take up the questions about rights in daily life and intimate settings.

Manifestations of Gender Violence

As we have seen from the earlier discussion of Article 2 of the Declaration on the Elimination of Violence against Women, the forms of violence against women and girls vary widely. All have this in common: Women and girls are judged and condemned in terms of what society dictates for their behaviour. And they are supposed to have less power and public space than men have. It is as though women were in a separate and lower caste (see Nabar 1995 for more on this idea). Thus, gender-based violence is directed against women and girls because they are females, and thus found wanting in some way or the other. Or, perhaps, violent acts are an attempt to prevent a woman's future "transgressions."

Manifestations of gender violence range from the subtle to the deadly and are found in many different settings, with parents, husbands, community figures and the State as most likely agents, as the women and men interviewed know all too well. Gender violence is not seen by these activists as the act of an individual deranged male so much as it is a predictable result of norms and inequalities embedded in and expressed through the very structures of society. Gender violence is reflected in institutionalized violence of different kinds. Examples of different manifestations of gender violence follow from interviews with the activists — at least one from each country. The three main sites of gender-based violence — home, community and State, as specified in Article 2 of the Declaration — are all covered. The examples also represent acts of both omission and commission.

Suppression at home

Violence is designed to keep women suppressed in the family and society. It starts from childhood and is a part of the way parents bring up their daughters, for instance, always telling them "Don't speak loudly." According to the prevailing social customs, if a woman is the victim of violence, she is blamed rather than sympathized with.

— Bangladeshi man, film producer

Even if a woman is good and has no fault, her husband troubles [abuses] her on the advice of his mother. If a woman has only daughters, she is troubled.

— Indian man from tribal area

Murder and mutilation by family

Often a girl is lit with trash and burned, or kerosene is thrown on a young teenage girl and she is locked in a room to burn. Many stepmothers have done that to their stepsons also. The girl often cannot go to the home of her parents or has no home to go to. They are burned, or their noses are chopped off, without fearing the consequences because there are no consequences.   *— Pakistani woman, plastic surgeon*

Discrimination in education

Even though they [girls] are clever they have no chance to go to school. They are forced to go to work at an early age, and there is also child marriage. — *Indian man Dalit,[17] activist*

Then they scolded me in very obscene language. "You bitch, devil, whore." I felt ashamed and started to cry. They said, "We will not allow you to escape even though you cry."
— Sri Lankan girl student, victim of "ragging" (hazing)

Work abuse

There is emotional abuse and there is also work abuse. There was a study on the tasks performed by men and women in a rural community. Under men's share there were five tasks and under the share of women there were 36.   *— Pakistani woman, journalist*

I find the harassment of working women appalling, and I am not talking of strictly sexual harassment. They are assigned the worst jobs and virtually no possibilities of self-growth. Their initiative is killed, and generally they are kept confined by an invisible control system.
— Pakistani man

State abuse

When some people say something against some ladies and the government takes them [the ladies] to jail, after that the soldiers are making rough because they believe they are bad women.   *— Afghani woman*

Also there is, in many parts of Nepal, violence by the State. When I say this, it seems so harsh, but when the police rape women and harass women, . . . and then there are stories of a chief district officer who raped someone. We have so many stories like these. All these things are by the State. We cannot say that the State is intending to do that, but it is taken for granted that if it [a violation] happens, there is nothing to do.

— Nepali woman, physician

"But Aren't You Exaggerating?"

In South Asia Itself: Some Facts about Gender Violence

How big a problem, really, is violence against women and girls in South Asia? Some South Asians, particularly urban men, asked me questions like the following after they had heard about the research UNICEF was doing on action to end gender violence in the region. They were talking, in particular, about domestic violence, assault and battery, and the murder of women and girls by men at home.

"But just how common is violence against women and girls in South Asia?"

"Isn't it just a Western problem, imported in films and video, but not of real concern here?"

"Yes, there are some moving cases, but is it a real problem given our family values and the honour for motherhood?"

"It's really the mother-in-law who is responsible, you know, not men. Women do it to each other."

Simply put, the theme of their questions is: "Aren't you exaggerating?" The answer is "Definitely not." The code of silence about violence to women, especially in the family, is only being broken now. It has obscured much of the truth. The next chapter describes how women's lives and health are affected, and covers in more detail most of the subjects introduced here as part of the problem of gender violence in South Asia:

- South Asia is the region in the world where women's life expectancy is least favourable compared to that of men. It is less than men's in two countries and almost the same in several others, in contrast to most regions of the world, where women's life expectancy exceeds that of men (Sivard 1995).
- Compared to demographic expectations, there are an estimated 60 million "missing women" in South Asia, primarily due to discriminatory child-care practices, which kill by neglect, linked to lack of access to health care and education for girls.
- A study of 8,000 abortions performed after amniocentesis tests to determine the sex of the foetus in the Indian state of Maharashtra showed that all but one of the foetuses were female (Narasimhan 1994, page 51).
- In Nepal, 40 per cent of marriages involve girls under the age of 15 years (UNCHR 1994, page 38).
- A woman's group in Bangladesh has publicized data showing that more women die from burns, suicide and injury than from pregnancy and childbirth (N. Huq 1997).
- In India, there were 6,006 dowry-related murders officially registered in 1996, up from 5,092 registered cases in 1995 (National Crime Records Bureau 1999, page 162).
- In Sri Lanka, 60 per cent of women interviewed in a sample survey responded that they had been subject to domestic violence during their period of cohabitation (Coomaraswamy 1994b, page 21).

- An overview of crimes against women in New Delhi from 1984 to 1994 concluded that most crimes against women "were committed more within the confines of a home and not out on the streets. . . . [A] home is no longer a safe place for a woman whether it is the natal home or the marital home" (Hazarika 1995, pages 41–42).
- Research begins to show it is men, much more than women, who are responsible for violence to women in the home. For example, one study of perpetrators of family violence in Bangladesh showed that male relatives were responsible for all but 29 of the 750 instances of violence reported (Jahan 1994, page 50).
- An increasing number of South Asian girls and women are being sold into sexual bondage across national borders. Their own families are often responsible, as has been shown for Nepal (Frederick 1998). In one settlement, for example, "up to 200 families have sold their daughters, mostly between 12–15 years old" (Newar 1998, page 25).[18] Parental involvement in trafficking has also been documented for Bangladesh, India and Pakistan (UNICEF 1999, page 35).

In Other Regions: Some Facts about Violence against Women and Girls

Still, readers in other regions have no reason to be smug, as the incidence of violence against women is substantial around the world. Some examples (all studies cited by WHO 1997 unless otherwise noted):

- In Egypt, a nationally representative sample of women aged 15-49 who are or have ever been married showed that 35 per cent of women said they had been beaten by their husband at some time.
- In a survey in the Kissi districts of Kenya, 42 per cent of women surveyed reported that they were beaten regularly by their spouses.
- In Israel, a random sample of 1,826 married Arab women showed that 32 per cent had been beaten by their partner at least once in the last year.
- From Switzerland, in a study of 1,500 women 20 per cent reported being hit or physically abused by a male partner.
- In the United States, a nationally representative sample of married women or women with partners showed 28 per cent reported at least one incident of physical violence by their partner (Straus and Gelles 1986).
- The World Bank estimates that 30 per cent of the healthy years of life lost to women in rural China are due to suicide (Heise, Pitanguy and Germain 1994).
- In the United States, a rape occurs every six minutes, and it is estimated that 85 per cent of rapes are never reported to the police and that less than 5 per cent of rapists go to jail (Coomaraswamy 1994b, page 20).
- In Canada, one in every four women can expect to be sexually assaulted at some point in their lives (Coomaraswamy 1994b, page 21).
- Every 90 seconds, a woman is raped in South Africa, meaning that approximately 390,000 women are raped each year (Coomaraswamy 1994b, page 21). A more recent — but still controversial — estimate is that a rape takes place every 26 seconds in South Africa. It is also estimated that one in every three schoolgirls in Johannesburg has experienced sexual violence at school (Rape Crisis Center 1999).
- In Peru, a study conducted in the Maternity Hospital of Lima revealed that 90 per cent of 12- to-16-year-old mothers had been raped, the vast majority by their fathers, their stepfathers or another close relative (Stephenson 1996, page 4).

- "Globally, at least 2 million girls a year are at risk of genital mutilation — approximately 6,000 per day. . . . An estimated 85 to 114 million girls and women in the world are genitally mutilated" (Toubra 1995, page 5).

The Question of Culture

What about culture? Although the excuse "It is part of our culture" may be a popular one used to try to justify various forms of gender-based violence, such an argument is unacceptable under human rights treaties. For example, consider Article 5a of CEDAW (1979):

> States Parties shall take all appropriate measures: a) To modify the social and cultural patterns of conduct for men and women, with a view to achieving the elimination of prejudices and customary and all other practices based on the idea of the inferiority or the superiority of either of the sexes, or on stereotypical roles for men and women.

In fact, countries are called on to put cultural arguments aside when these would excuse violence to women. As Radhika Coomaraswamy, the United Nations Special Rapporteur on violence against women, notes:

> Article 4 of the Declaration on the Elimination of Violence against Women states clearly that "States should condemn violence against women and should not invoke custom, tradition or religious consideration to avoid their obligations with respect to its elimination." (UNCHR 1994, page 16)

She observes that, instead, the three are often used to justify violence against women. She goes on to say that

> the spirit of all the world's religions is dedicated to equality, including equality between the sexes. Though interpretations may vary, there is no question at all the world's religions are committed to the pursuit of equality and human rights.

She notes in the same passage that there are certain "man-made practices," as she calls them, characteristic of "fundamentalist" movements, which are presented in the name of religion but actually both misrepresent religions and violate human rights. She points to the important ongoing dialogue between women concerned with rights and persons close to "religious traditions." She observes:

> It is the concern of the international community that the dialogue results in the elimination of man-made practices which violate human rights and the spirit of equality contained in the world's religions. This question should be high on the list of priorities. Religious considerations should never be used to justify the use of violence against women. (page 14)

When religion is mentioned in interviews within this book, a distinction is usually made between the true teachings of a religion regarding women's status and the distortions of these by fundamentalists or those who simply want to exploit and intimidate others. Custom, superstition and tradition are not equated with religion by the activists, as will be evident in interviews and quotations presented throughout. That the core teachings of major religions in the region are compatible with women's and children's rights is made clear also by Mabelle Arole in her 1999 book *Religion and Rights of Children and Women in South Asia.*[19]

Why Violence against Women and Girls?

From a Global Perspective

In her 1994 report as UN Special Rapporteur on violence against women working with the UN Commission for Human Rights, Radhika Coomaraswamy briefly considers the following as causes for violence against women: unequal power relations, sexuality, cultural ideology, doctrine of privacy, patterns of conflict resolution and governmental inaction. Among her observations is the following:

> Violence against women in the family and society is pervasive and cuts across lines of income, class and culture. [It] must be matched by urgent and effective steps to eliminate its incidence. Violence against women derives from their unequal status in society. (UNCHR 1994, page 7)

As the South Asians See It

The South Asian activists' ideas about causes focus with few exceptions on the first three that Coomaraswamy considers, as listed above. They appear to be interrelated. Examples of related statements include:[20]

Masculinity defined at women's expense

> We consider women as valuable property — to be protected from damage and presented to the husband in a prime condition. This morbid obsession with preservation of virginity is at the very root of the behaviour patterns of men in our society. When a man wants real revenge from his enemy, he will invariably try to degrade his opponents' women. He is inflicting irrecoverable damage to the property of his opponent.
> — *Pakistani man, volunteer NGO worker and researcher*

Drunkenness

> Sometimes sexual violence is due to inebriation. Even, say, wanting to protect yourself with a condom — the women are scared to ask the man when he is drunk. The women think that he will get aggressive and shout and beat her up.
> — *Sri Lankan woman, NGO executive director*

No property rights for women

> The root cause of violence against women and girls is their lack of property rights. A woman is born as another's property, not her own. Legally, she has no rights, up to age 35.
> — *Nepali woman, lawyer*

Inequality is taught

> The kind of education that is imparted tends to veer towards discrimination against women. You know, the role models that are portrayed, the kinds of stories that are taught to students — where the man is the bread-earner and the woman is the housewife.
> — *Nepali man, journalist*

Misuse of religion

> Generally, religion is used as a tool to oppress women.
> — *Pakistani man, political activist*

> Of course, all religion is not against women. Even the Christians and the Muslims, they have appreciated women. In Islam, the Prophet Muhammad appreciated women and put many regulations for women to develop them, to develop their prestige in society, while in pre-

Prophet times, it was not so. This very tight traditional society put a ban to women's development. Women were considered second-class and everywhere were subordinated.

— Afghani man, agriculturist

Economic exploitation

Also, upper-caste dominance and capitalism . . . both are leading to more and more violence against women. . . . Basically, dowry harassment by in-laws takes place because they want to extract money, assets. . . . It's very funny, people would rather not invest in their daughter's education and personality development but keep accumulating money for her dowry! *—Indian woman, who works with prostitutes*

Various

Causes of violence against women are: one, the fact that she is a woman; two, society looks at the woman as inferior; three, men's violent nature and culture of male dominance; four, lack of education; and five, the recent phenomenon of women being attracted to vagabonds. *— Indian man, lawyer (who did not explain his point five)*

In general, the South Asian activists who were interviewed seem less preoccupied with possible economic explanations for gender violence than with social facts, such as norms based on the assumed natural inferiority of women and superiority of men and the imbalance that follows in the comparative positions and power of women and men in various structures that make up society. However, many writers and some activists do emphasize economic exploitation, influenced by neo-colonialism, "development," capitalism, structural adjustment and patriarchy writ large, as the main cause of violence to women in developing countries (see, for example, Mies 1986).

Women's unequal status in society both predicts and is deepened by violence against them in its many forms, which are in turn influenced both by global factors and traditional ones. Part Two of this book looks more closely at the unequal status between women and men as the main cause of gender violence and also gives hope for changing rigid norms involved.

The Family as a Site of Struggle

The family in South Asia can be a particularly dangerous place for women and girls. As indicated in references above, millions are abused, neglected and left to die through behaviour in the family. No small number are attacked directly. Something is very wrong with the reality of family life, compared to the ideal, when girls and women are neglected, abused and even killed by family members, the very ones who are expected to protect them.

Even where underreporting does not permit truly accurate projections, the incidence of domestic violence itself would likely be in the millions in South Asia, given the high rates one would extrapolate from the studies and considering the size of the South Asian population. In South Asia there are some 609 million females, well over half of whom are between 15 and 64 (see related data in Sivard 1995, page 40). If even half of those were affected in some way (a conservative estimate given the rates in studies), that would mean some 150 million women and girls between ages 15 and 64 experience gender violence. Violence to girls, of course, starts much earlier, as will be discussed.

Women and girls are more at risk of violence from male relatives than from strangers. In the male-dominated patriarchal family of South Asia, women's and girls' lives are thus in danger from conception onwards, simply because they are female. Their value is considered less than that of men. It lies in their sexual and reproductive services as well as the labour they provide under control of men. Their function is to perpetuate men's family names, their honour and power. The slightest perceived insult to a man's honour and control can be the cause for him to beat or kill his wife or daughter. They may also be denied freedom and access to opportunities for fear their sexuality will be abused, the men in their families shamed.

In a sense, it is not the relationship between men and women in the family that leads to gender violence; rather, it is the relationship between men, struggling to position themselves vis-à-vis one another in a patriarchal society that values powerful men. Where females are considered as property, control over them is a symbol of the man's status and power. To a great extent, men in the patriarchal society are thus in collusion against women. For example, the police are reputed to look the other way or not to take "domestic cases" seriously, even though assault, battery, rape, incest and murder are actually involved. It would appear they do not want to insult other men or lose their own male privilege.

Most men in South Asia, then, seem to have tacit, if not outspoken, support from agents of the State, as well as from family members, to do what they want with females in their own families. There are so many ways to neglect, abuse, torture and kill them. "Justifications" in the name of culture or religion are often made. As will be seen, monetary gain for men may be involved. Sometimes girls and women are like a new crop to be harvested.

The truth that the family is an institution that all too often fails those it should protect comes as a shock because this truth is so very much at odds with cherished values and ideas about family life in South Asia. Fortunately, the shock can lead to strong action to assist those whom the family condemns, to try to improve systems that support the family and improve expectations for family life. New strategies are being used by governments and NGOs alike to expose the problems and the perpetrators, to insist on and win justice. Still, progress is slow. There are powerful forces that promote the status quo. In some cases, they are growing even stronger, in a kind of backlash against efforts to end gender violence and fulfil women's human rights. All the more reason to look the problems in the face, now, and to emphasize solutions while prevention may still be possible.

Based on information so far available suggests that some forms of violence in the family against women and girls are more widespread in South Asia than in any other region of the world. (This is discussed in Chapter 2 in more detail.) Why does this matter? Because action follows assessment and analysis in social change, just as intervention follows epidemiology in public health.

Prospects for Change

Government Leadership

How will governments in South Asia react to increased attention, both at international and local levels, to the problem of violence against women and girls? All the countries but Afghanistan approved the 1995 Beijing Platform for Action in which violence against women is a "critical area of concern" (UNDPI 1996b, page 33). Most have a multitude of laws against various forms of gender violence. All have government machineries and officials dedicated to improving matters; all liaise with women's groups on the subject; all have problems in bringing about change, but still look for some ways to do so. All hear criticism, very strong at times, from many quarters about gender violence, and the press in South Asia constantly features stories about violence to women and girls.

Most of the countries have themselves made strong public statements against gender violence, like the three from which excerpts are shown below (see Boxes 2, 3 and 4) from some statements that were developed for the Fourth World Conference on Women in 1995. But will change really follow? Do successive governments support or even go beyond positions that earlier ones took, or commitments that they made? For Beijing follow-up (as assessment of implementation of the Platform of Action of

---

Box 2   **India: Countering the Threat of Violence against Women**

"Violence against women should be viewed as one of the most crucial social mechanisms by which they are forced into a subordinate position. It is a manifestation of unequal power relations, which has led to men's domination over and discrimination against women. Thus, violence against women, throughout their life, comes to be socially sanctified.

"Acts or threats of violence instill fear and insecurity in women and hamper their striving for equality, development and peace. The social, health and economic costs to the individual and society as a result of such violence could be prohibitive. . . .

"It is being realized that violation of women's rights can only push half of humanity into further depths of degradation, making the goal of a humane social order more distant. Confronting the ideology of patriarchy and removing the fetters of inequality are not only moral imperatives. Without these, women's development and empowerment will remain empty promises. . . .

"As a signatory to the Convention on the Elimination of all Forms of Discrimination Against Women (CEDAW), India is deeply committed to these lofty objectives."

—*Government of India, India National Report, Fourth World Conference on Women, Beijing, September, 1995; New Delhi: Government of India.*

Box 3   **Nepal: Women, Rights and Violence**

"The Constitution provides for equal rights to men and women. Such rights are being widely exercised. Nonetheless, certain specific laws infringe upon the Constitutional provisions. Such laws shall be identified and presented to the legislature for amendment within the next two years. The government will also prepare and present a bill within one year to the legislature providing for equal rights to women in relation to ancestral property. Additionally, legal provisions in relation to violence on women, including those related to trafficking shall be reviewed and the enforcing agencies shall be strengthened. Legal as well as rehabilitation assistance to victims of violence shall be supported on a broader scale. These constitute the second set of commitments."

—*His Majesty's Government of Nepal (HMG/N), Fourth World Conference on Women, Beijing, September 1995; Kathmandu: HMG/N.*

| Box 4 | Pakistan: Violence against Women |

"In Pakistan, violence against women is rooted in the social relations of patriarchy, which are based on a system of male domination and female subordination. Both overt and covert, it is the means by which patriarchy establishes and maintains these authoritarian hierarchies.

"The different instances of violence against women are part of a continuum of violence which underpins all spheres of private and public life. These range from the most extreme forms of overt brutality (like rape and mutilation) to the more subtle and invisible forms (like son preference and child marriage), which cripple the mind and destroy human potential. Any attempt, therefore, to perceive acts of violence as disconnected acts of aberrant behaviour is to misread the phenomenon. Equally, it needs to be understood that unless and until radical changes are effected in the power bases of the social formation, attempts to address the problem will not go beyond the merely cosmetic and, at best, will have a short-term impact.

Institutionalized violence
"The legal system, the law-enforcement system, and the media are some of the major means through which the state maintains its power. In the past fifteen years, discrimination laws, along with the exploitation of religion to control women's sexuality and productivity, have been instrumental in increasing violence in women's lives.

". . . These laws have resulted in an increase, both in the incidence of sexual violence against women, and in the number of women in prison. According to statistics from the Human Rights Commission of Pakistan, 75-80 per cent of all women in jails during 1993 had been charged under the Hudood Ordinances....

"From 1977 to 1988 both the electronic and print media, including school texts, newspapers, the state-controlled radio and television, unremittingly propagated the ideology of male domination and female subordination. Giving new legitimacy to gender-based discrimination, the electronic media was particularly instrumental in increasing women's vulnerability to violence. While some attempts have been made since 1988 to project women in more positive light, many of the old stereotypes continue to haunt women's lives. . . .

Strategic objectives and action
"Any strategy directed towards the elimination of violence against women must first recognize its many facets, and then devise concrete steps to deal with it at both the social and legal levels. Keeping in mind that the family is the basic unit within which the patterns of violence are founded, a major thrust of the strategy must be towards changing the power structures. The media, therefore, must play a critical role in the campaign to eradicate violence, supported by changes in the institutional structures."

— *Government of Pakistan, Fourth World Conference on Women, Beijing, September 1995; Nepal: Government of Pakistan.*

the Fourth World Conference on Women is generally described), commitments are clearly being reiterated.

There are many obstacles to implementation, including vested interests of powerful groups at community and national levels. Many writers also comment on politically inspired gender violence as a problem in the region. (This will be discussed further in Chapter 11.) Laws are not considered enough to bring about change, as will be reviewed in Chapter 10. Attitudes must change — or laws and other vehicles for change will never be used. Growing consciousness about the importance of human rights as the basis for development and good governance is helping. The fulfilment of girls' and women's human rights is indeed a precondition for development to be sustainable and to provide human security. And where discrimination and violence negate and destroy girls' and women's lives, the girls and women, their families and nations all suffer for it. The topic of violence against women as a major rights and development issue is a vital one, which this book addresses repeatedly and takes up in more depth in the concluding chapter. Fortunately, dialogue about gender violence as a human rights abuse is bringing together more and more actors against gender violence who earlier might have ignored it as a so-called private, even trivial, matter.

But what to do? What is the extent of the problem, how best to address cultural and political violence, how to meet victim-survivor's needs and to undertake prevention? These are vital questions. Governments may well feel overwhelmed, because of both the growing visibility of gender violence and the already strained budgets for social needs, particularly in light of the level of military expenditures in at least three countries, India, Pakistan and Sri Lanka. They have high military expenditures: 3.6 per cent, 7.0 per cent and 4.7 per cent of GDP as compared to 3.2 per cent for the world average (Ul Haq and Haq 1997, page 80).[21]

Conventions alone cannot bring change. They can only stimulate and reflect it. Unless the content of the conventions resonates and reverberates with attitudes and practices at all levels of society, gender violence will likely continue or even increase.

Individual Efforts

Efforts by the activists to eliminate gender violence in its many forms range from the simple to the dramatic. These efforts are very much a part of daily life for those interviewed and for others like them. They show that a change in what feeds gender violence can begin almost anywhere; how men and women treat each other every day is a fundamental part of change, and such change can be simple as well as dramatic:

- A husband takes another look at the way he talks to his wife — and corrects it.
- A woman travelling by bus from work publicly challenges the man trying to entwine his leg with hers, and doesn't back down when he abuses her verbally afterwards.
- A man successfully negotiates projects for women in rural areas, even though women there are not supposed to go outside their homes and had once risked beating if they did.
- A boy questions child marriage, despite his teacher's criticism of him for doing so.
- Lawyers, both women and men, work for women's property rights so that women will be supported as more than property themselves.
- A farmer brings a charge of rape against a neighbour who abused his young daughter.
- A girl speaks out against incest, despite being threatened for doing so.
- A woman decides she cannot live with her in-laws and her husband, who beat her and her daughter, so she leaves home, first lives on the street, then makes her way to a better life for herself and her three children.
- Men challenge and beat up other men for bashing or raping women — even when they know there should be another way to get justice.
- A woman under threat of death by fundamentalists for talking about women's

rights shows them relevant scriptures from the Quran and offers up her life if the fundamentalists choose to go against the scriptures.

And there are many, many more examples in the book.

At the individual level, then, there is often great motivation to bring about positive change and it springs from many sources. Examples of what inspired activists to work against gender violence follow.

Why Women and Men Are Stepping Forward against Gender Violence

Despite the obstacles, people around the world are beginning to challenge gender violence, including family and domestic violence, and the fundamental tenets about what women and girls can do and be. From the interviews in South Asia come examples about why exceptional people act to question and change gender violence. The examples allow us to better understand how society's silence can be ended, and how more women and men can become involved in challenges to a punitive and destructive status quo.

Witnessed violence

I have been aware of VAW [violence against women] since my days as a resident pupil in a missionary school. Sometimes we had to visit villages and during one such visit, I saw a woman being beaten by her husband. The woman was thoroughly blood-soaked after the beating. But no one came forward to protest. This hurt me much and after this I was involved.   — *Bangladeshi woman, NGO director*

Was victimized

I think it is very empowering for victims of violence to do something about stopping the violence. Because it is a way of regaining control of their lives, it is a way of regaining control of who they are, because sexual abuse, for instance, is very much about losing control. Your control, your dignity has been taken away so suddenly by the perpetrator without your having had control over that. And I think working with other women, to empower other victims, is empowering for us. So, it becomes almost like a collective healing that takes place. . . . I mean, how are you going to get justice, how are you going to get reparation? So it is a way of getting justice back for yourself, to try to work with others, to find a collective solution to the problem. However, having said all of that, it is not enough to simply have had the experience of violence to do the work. The experience has to be matched by training, it has to be matched by awareness, it has to be an informed activism.   — *Sri Lankan woman, survivor of incest*

Was encouraged by a parent and influenced by religion

I care about my fellow countrymen and women. I was greatly influenced by my mother. My mother taught me to share with people and to reach out to others and help. She was a garment worker in a factory in Dhaka. She was a single mother with three children and had to walk three miles to work every day. Women were paid only two thirds of what men were paid for the same job. She began to grow weaker. One day she collapsed at work. She had been selling blood to feed us. Her co-workers were outraged and together spoke up against unfair labour practices. They were met with threats, intimidation and finally dismissal. She had left her village to work in Dhaka to fulfil both her own dreams and her duty as a daughter. Many other women had migrated from villages to the town. Rural women still migrate as a preferred alternative to working without pay on the family farm or waiting for occasional non-farm jobs. Their success is measured by how much money they send back and how their village homes have improved. She went back to the village and worked on the shrimp farm and took in occasional sewing work to put us through school. She taught me that I am a human being first and a man second, and that as a man I should help women publicly and privately to build their lives. I was also influenced by Islam, which taught me "to serve people." All this made me feel a part of society and taught me to participate in politics and to try and change society. Our family was very democratic so whenever there was a problem, we children could always chip in and say what we thought.

— Bangladeshi man, union organizer who emigrated to India

Learned about non-stereotypic possibilities for women

I had very vague ideas of what it was all about, but I felt that women were a badly neglected group, and I invariably liked being the gallant "hero," joining hands with the "losing side!" During the same time, I met Dr. Sadiqua Shariff, whose affection and kindness for others profoundly changed my attitudes. Most importantly, I learned from her that women could dream, plan and implement big things besides being good at cosmetics, shopping and household chores — so strong was the traditional image of women in my mind. And of course, in the early '80s, it was the courage of Asma Jahangir[22] challenging the naked power of martial law that inspired so many of us. I am no exception.

— Pakistani man, member of an NGO

Inspired suddenly

I watched my son beat my daughter-in-law. One day I saw my granddaughter cower when he came into the house drunk. I knew I had been through it, my son's wife had gone through it, but I decided my granddaughter would not. I loved her dearly. She was full of life and energy. I did not want that energy and life taken away from her. At that time other women were talking about the problems of alcohol and stopping the opening of a liquor shop. I agreed to join them in the march and it changed my life.

— Indian woman, who became a leader of an anti-liquor campaign

Punished for speaking out — and became more determined

In 1992, I was sent to a Women's Development Programme organized by the Rajasthan Government. I was then made a social worker. My life was never the same. At that time the Rajasthan Government had started a campaign against child marriages — the idea was to take the campaign to small villages. I did just that. I spoke about it, went from home to home in the village campaigning against it. The only problem was I was not allowed into the homes of the upper-caste people. And their wives observed heavy *ghunghat* [purdah, the segregation and isolation of women]. So I began to stand outside public places like the temple or the well and talk against child marriage. Men — both upper and lower caste — were very angry; they would taunt and jeer but I carried on. Many of the other Dalit women also told me to stop but with more resistance, I became more determined.

— Indian woman, anti-child-marriage and rape activist

Became aware of gender-based violence as a human rights issue

Here in our country, when we say "women," the problem starts. Before the Islamic revolution, the women had some rights, but after the Islamic revolution, they lost their rights. After the Taliban came to Kabul and other parts of Afghanistan, women's rights were finished. They think women are not human. They hit women who go out of their houses. They close the doors of schools for women and don't let women go to their work and offices.

— Afghani woman, professional

Was moved by a case in the media

In recent years the realization [that violence against women is a problem] has come about due to a process and was catalyzed by an incident. The process has been the interaction with human rights groups. That helped me to see this as a human rights issue rather than a social problem. The suicide of Nurjahan and the media explosion that followed had a profound impact. A case of adultery is committed by two persons, yet it is the woman who is blamed. There was a need to expose this kind of thinking, this double standard, where "a man is just a man, but the woman is bad." The Nurjahan incident brought the whole thing to the forefront.   *— Pakistani man, journalist*

Concerned about the effect on children

Since everything starts in the family, and society is a collection of families, it is vital that in childhood, children are made to value their own bodies/spaces/property. In addition, parental responsibilities should be shared. There should be mutual respect between spouses because they are the role models for children who could end up being either the perpetrators or victims.   *— Sri Lankan woman, activist, researcher and lawyer*

For the sake of society

This is a fundamental issue simply because of the number of persons it involves. If half of the population lives under oppression or is vulnerable to different kinds of harassment, how can you expect such a society to grow? Women are dependent, they are exploited economically and they are exploited sexually. If we can improve the scenario, our society would surely benefit.   *— Pakistani man, lawyer*

Even with all the motivation among activists like those quoted in this book, what are the prospects for changes on a broad basis? That is a question that can be much better assessed at the conclusion of this book, in Chapter 12. Here, suffice it to say that there are important international, regional, national and local, and NGO as well as individual initiatives. Not enough linkages are being made from one locality, one subject, one group to another, but efforts to network effectively and influence policy as well as to undertake practical action are growing.

Still, many activists do not know about each other's work against gender violence, especially in the home. They tend to be isolated from each other at least on this subject. This is particularly true across professional and class lines but also within professions and classes. It is certainly true across borders. More visibility is needed about action against gender-based violence as a professionally worthy subject, important for an individual, a nation, a region to redress — and not only as a private and moral concern. More recognition should be given to those individuals, professionals and authorities who question norms that tolerate or encourage violence to women and girls.

NGO Cooperation against Domestic Violence?

The number of NGOs taking up the issue of violence against women and girls is surely growing. Still, NGOs are not always ready to face the challenges posed by dealing with violence in the home itself.

A possible reason for the relative neglect of domestic violence was brought home to me in 1997 during a month-long regionwide regional training course organized by NGOs and held in Nepal, on Gender and Development: Towards Conceptual Clarity.[23]

Some of the sessions were on violence against women. One afternoon the facilitator included a moving account of her own childhood, when she was a victim of incest and discrimination within her family. Yet the group seemed strangely uninvolved in the session compared to their reaction to earlier ones on structural adjustment, or gender and development training. I wondered why. Walking afterwards up the dark lane to the dining hall, I overheard two young women talking about the session. "A bit long compared to others," one said. "Yes," the other replied. That was all. The group of about 30 women was mostly silent as we walked.

But later, as we sat in a circle around an open fire, I saw one woman crying. She was comforted by a friend, who looked at me in such a way that I understood I should respect the upset woman's privacy, not comment. Another participant began to talk about a young girl who was raped but didn't understand what had happened to her. Years ago the little girl had come to her, twisting her body and blood-stained clothing, then clinging to the woman for comfort. Shocked, the woman asked what had happened. No reply at first. Then the little girl said, "I hurt," and pointed between her legs. On examination, it became clear that she had been brutally raped. The perpetrator had threatened to kill her and her family if she told anyone. The woman near me was letting herself remember. She was angry. She wasn't sure what to do about such cases. Her own work is against girl-trafficking, which often involves girls who have been so violated. She is doing what she can.

As the story unfolded, the woman sitting across from me, on the other side of the fire, continued to cry. Later I was told she was recalling similar violence against her sister when she was a child. It happened in her own family.

"They can't face it easily," my activist friend, a group facilitator, told me. "They lock it away. There is denial. But it will start to come out now. It must." Then I understood the quiet surface after the session on domestic violence. It had been crafted to look like disinterest but really it was a roof, a wall, a door — the outside of a hiding place. The session was helping the women to remember, to come out and face the problem of domestic violence in their own and others' lives.

I expected then that domestic violence might emerge as one of the priorities for regionwide action by the group. But it did not. The priorities included gender training and girl-trafficking. "Why girl-trafficking and not domestic violence?" I asked. An organizer said, "Give them time."

Yes, girl-trafficking is something most people readily agree is wrong. There is the association with exploitation, with innocence lost against a girl's will, with her being made into a commodity. The issues seem more clear-cut than in domestic violence, which many still regard as a private matter, and for which there are so many excuses made: the woman is to blame, she is property, it is tradition, the man is frustrated, etc. Domestic violence will be the most difficult subject for a movement against violence, perhaps the last. It is also, surely, the most important. It is literally closest to home and affects the most women.

An NGO coordinator from India interviewed for this book made these comments about the seeming reluctance of NGOs to deal with the subject:[24]

> First, NGOs need to clarify their own perspective on violence against women. Most NGOs don't like to touch family issues. Women's issues are conflict situations. NGOs avoid these. They are not on their agenda . . . violence against women should become an issue for everybody, not just a few women's groups.

Although many would certainly disagree that NGOs avoid subjects that involve conflict, these words about "family issues" and "women's issues" are still worth considering. Do NGOs and others readily address questions about what goes on in families where so many lives are at stake? If not, what support do they need to do so? Chapter 11, on building movements, will look at some rapid changes in the amount of attention being given to domestic violence, and why. Here some basic dilemmas are brought to life.

Outcome in the Balance:
"Feminist Fantasy" or Responsible Activism?

Is it only a "feminist fantasy" that violence against women and girls can and should be stopped, not only in society in general but in the family itself? It will be, despite all the conferences that have been held, the conventions and commitments that have been made by governments and others, all the studies to come — unless there is more cooperation between women and men, various classes and professions, rural and urban groups, religious scholars and leaders, and among professionals, NGOs and governments, as well as more cooperation across borders. No single individual, no group, no government policy or development programme can accomplish this alone. It requires cooperation across all sectors. Above all, it requires hearing and supporting rural women and girls in their claims for their rights, in the face of local customs and interpretation of religion used to bolster the patriarchy.

For example, there are increasing efforts everywhere for rural women to know that violence against women is being questioned, and that support services are available. Yet this still can involve more risk than safety for them. Over and over again, activists say, "Attitudes must be changed first." They also think this is possible through education, the media, the legal system and by empowering affected women to have less tolerance for violence. The effort required is immense, not only by women's groups, but also through networking among all the parties in the otherwise oppressive system. Growing fundamentalism is seen as a threat to women's advancement and rights, and also calls for an effective strategy to counter its negative impact on women.

Even without a major effort to stop violence against women and girls, and in the face of threats and uncertainties, individuals who hear about possible support on the issue will still come forward, seeking to claim their rights. But they may be very disappointed if more effort is not made soon to develop adequate services and support systems that effectively bring together who and what is needed when it is needed. In addition, treating the subject as an important public policy and health problem, with awareness and advocacy for its prevention, could deter many cases.

Youth Seek Justice Not Violence

What is the result for the young person who steps forward, believing in her claim to rights, which she has heard about?

Two accounts, a verbal one from a policewoman[25] in Pakistan and a story from the *Times* of India, tell about girls who went to the police rather than keep quiet about violence against them at home.

First, the Pakistani policewoman's recollection:

We had a case like this a while ago involving a father and a daughter, which we took to trial. The family concerned lived in a slum area of the city; the girl was about 9 to 10 years; the mother worked as a maid in people's homes; and the father, being on the elderly side, spent most of his time at home with the girl. Once or twice he tried to open the girl's trousers but didn't succeed. When the girl told her mother about the incidents, the mother hit the girl and accused her of lying. She didn't have the courage to even confront her husband. Then one day the father got his way with the girl. The girl waited for her mother to come home from work and then showed her soiled clothes, saying: "Look, you didn't believe me, well, here is the proof." Even then the mother was hesitant to believe her, as she feared for their other children. The girl insisted that they go to the police station, but the mother refused. Luckily for the girl, her maternal uncle arrived at that very moment and after hearing the story agreed to take her to the station. Once she got here, we gave her a full medical exam, found proof of the rape, went and arrested her father and started criminal proceedings against him.

The responsiveness and efficiency of the system as described sound almost too good to be true. It is not typical of what activists say happens in most cases.

More typical, unfortunately, is a 22 June 1997 story from the *Times* of India (see Box 5). It tells about a 16-year-old girl raped repeatedly by her father; she became pregnant, allegedly had an abortion, returned home, was raped by her father again, then brought a complaint but there was no system in place adequate to bringing justice to a girl with a complaint against her own father.

What happened to her? She was living in a jail, even a year later, because no one knew where else she could go.

The courage of such girls is extraordinary. Most victim-survivors, particularly when they have experienced incest, do not come forward. In the past they might simply have been killed for even thinking out loud about challenging a male family member in public.

These girls' actions exemplify part of what the women's movement, the human rights movement and the United Nations seek: the awareness of rights and the expectation that these will be upheld for women and girls as well as for men and boys. In a sense, these young girls' actions are a culmination of the recommendations from the 1995 Fourth World Conference on Women, and all the other international women's conferences and meetings.

Some Obstacles and Hope

In Beijing, as elsewhere, governments as well as NGOs made stirring statements to end gender violence. Some of the most impressive in the world are from South Asia, as the examples below show. But are governments, NGOs and activists united enough to be ready for the girls and boys who expect and are entitled to a future without gender violence? United enough to prevent gender violence in the first place and thus truly to protect and fulfil the human rights of all? State inaction is an obstacle to change, as is any violence against women inspired by politics or accepted in the name of political expediency. One hopes that such obstacles, in South Asia as elsewhere, will give way to more profound commitments with even more resources as the scale of the gender violence pandemic is recognized by more and more people, from political leaders to the rural poor.

Box 5 | **Article from India**

Girl, Raped by Father, Abandoned by Family, Seeks Justice

A sixteen-year-old girl belonging to Loni village was allegedly raped by her father over a period of one year and made pregnant by him. Abandoned by her family and other relatives after she lodged a complaint against her father, for the last four days the girl has been staying at Loni police station.

The girl reportedly filed the report despite pressure from her mother and senior village folk not to do so. With family and relatives turning their backs on her, the girl has been lodged in a room next to the police station chief's office "with a woman police constable."

Station In-charge Rangnath Shukla said, "She has been kept incommunicado so that nobody pressurizes her before she makes her statement before a magistrate under section 164 of Cr. Pc.

He added that the girl had been taken to make her statement, in camera, at the district courts. But on Saturday night police sources said the girl's statement could not be recorded since a "Lok Adalat* was being held."

This means their girl will have to continue living at the police station till Monday at least when the competent court decides on her future address.

The girl's father, meanwhile, is lodged in the district jail. He was arrested and sent there on Wednesday after his daughter filed a complaint with the police under Section 376 of the Indian Penal Code.

The complaint, filed at 5 p.m. on Tuesday says, "My father raped me at knife point about one year ago when the rest of the family was away. Later, I told my mother and she scolded both my father and me."

The girl's report goes on to say that her father kept abusing her sexually. Finally, she became pregnant by him. And, "three months ago, my mother took me to Delhi and got my two month old foetus aborted." The report does not give the address of the place where she allegedly underwent an abortion. Neither has the police investigated this.

In her complaint to the police, the teenager alleges that on Tuesday her father attempted to rape her again. And when she resisted, he allegedly beat her and then threw her out of the house. It was then that she filed a police complaint.

Loni police station in-charge Rangnath Shukla said the girl has been medically examined and X-rayed to verify her age. Mr. Shukla said many village folk as also her mother had tried to persuade the girl not to file a complaint against her father.

"But the girl has now become too rebellious to be persuaded," he said. Of her family and relatives, only her paternal grandfather is willing to accept her. But the girl, Mr. Shukla said, says, "He is like the rest of the family, who beat me for seeking justice." One of five siblings, the teenager has two sisters aged nine and five and two brothers aged 17 and seven."

Local court. | Adapted from the Times of India (22 June 1997)

People in South Asia are noticing distortions of family life, re-examining values and norms, speaking out. This is a time for advocacy to hasten change. South Asians are learning from one anothers' constructive and often imaginative interventions, as can the rest of the world. Their honesty invites the same from other parts of the world for a truly global dialogue on what to do to stop gender violence in all its forms, especially family and domestic violence, which have been most neglected in the public eye. The purpose of this book is to help spread the South Asian experience and promote the exchange of lessons learned in different countries within and outside the region. But the book is only a small part of a rapidly growing exchange, which its preparation reflected and helps to stimulate.

Still Needed: Breaking the Silence

Dr. Saad Raheem Sheikh, former Director of the United Nations Population Fund Country Support Team for South and West Asia, in Kathmandu, speaks eloquently about the first step towards a safer future for all in South Asia: breaking the silence — even, or especially, when it risks offence to those with power and influence who perpetuate discrimination to further their own ends.[26]

If it seems there are more problems than solutions forthcoming, Dr. Sheikh's courage and words remind us to take stock of the true importance of what we are reading from activists' statements. Each person interviewed speaks about what has been forbidden to be known — each such person breaks the silence, opens the way for the flow of action that follows when truth opens the door first.

Dr. Sheikh puts it this way:

> I am going to talk about the conspiracy of silence. Whereas we promote vigorously the education of women and particularly the girl-child, yet even the educated women are subjected to sexual abuse and the most gruesome violence leading to death. We need to focus our attention on the education of society on real issues — the issues that are an anathema to most of the religious groups. . . .

> I ask myself and ask you, what is it in our society that we can be misled to the brink of blindness or coerced to remain silent by illiterate and so-called religious leaders? How much horror and hypocrisy do we have to tolerate? How much damage and destruction of humanity will be done in the name of religion or in the name of God, before we rise from this slumber?

> In our societies, clans and families, we know certain young girls or women, who from teenage onwards have been withdrawn, scared, non-communicative or somewhat strange. The family says she is schizophrenic or psychological. Has anyone ever had the courage to say that she was sexually assaulted? The fact that these assaults came from close relatives, stigma comes in and in the name of family integrity and to preserve the modesty of the girl, the real story is hushed up and the poor girl suffers her whole life. Incidents of incest are increasing in our countries — yet no voice is raised. We are all obedient, we love our parents and family elders, we don't want a scandal in our families, any disclosure will destroy the family fabric. Suppression is best for all concerned.

> [W]e are all civilized people, we love Ravi Shankar[27] and Nusrat Fateh Ali Khan,[28] our artists and writers are winning global prizes and our scientists, financial specialists and doctors are getting world recognition, yet the unfortunate section of our society — the girls and women whom I described above — are being sent to the torture chambers, which may be given the same analogy as the gas chambers of Nazi Germany — What do we do? We are also watching this "Holocaust" in absolute silence!

> . . . [W]e the educated and informed intelligentsia of the world and particularly those who work with NGOs are the conscience of our nations. You are the ones who will launch a

crusade to re-educate our educated people, you will remove forever the lid of secrecy and so-called shame of our societies. This cannot be done by legislation alone, it requires massive education and social awakening among our people.

. . . We need reformers, committed leaders and especially young leaders who will move and shake the religious establishments and guide them to an enlightened leadership where hypocrisy will be banished and societies will accept the realities of HIV/AIDS, drug addiction, abortion due to incest or rape, causes of teenage pregnancies and the like. Because the status of women is so low in many cities and because men want to continue their domination of women, it is going to be a long haul. . . .

This social crusade cannot be achieved in a year or decade, . . . but this struggle will continue for hours, days, months and years, until victory is won; then we can once again call ourselves *human*.

Endnotes

1   The region includes all the countries in the South Asian Association for Regional Cooperation (SAARC): Bangladesh, Bhutan, India, Maldives, Nepal and Pakistan. Bhutan and Maldives are not covered by the interviews and research for this book, and Afghanistan has been added. The latter is part of the area of the UNICEF Regional Office for South Asia (ROSA), which coordinated the work.

2   Most of the interviews were arranged and conducted through various UNICEF offices in the region with whomsoever these offices identified as activists against violence to women and girls. The same basic list of questions was given to each office to be used. It included topics such as definitions, causes, origins of activism and recommendations for action. But the interview material received did not always follow the outline.

3   It is difficult to find the right word to use in the South Asian context: "activists" may carry political connotations with which some don't want to be associated; "advocates" suggests lawyers, etc. "Activists" is used for convenience, but with the disclaimer that it should not imply anything about a particular political position or full-time profession.

4   Descent and related rights are traced through the male line.

5   Descent and related rights are traced through both parents.

6   The Nairobi World Conference to Review and Appraise the Achievements of the United Nations Decade for Women: Equality, Development, and Peace (see UNCHR 1994, pages 6–7).

7   Heise, Pitanguy and Germain (1994, pages 12–13) suggest these include pathological dieting (anorexia and bulimia) and high-risk cosmetic surgery.

8   Council of Europe 1986 (in Heise, Pitanguy and Germain 1994, page 47).

9   See UNICEF (1998a) for a compelling argument in favour of using this term rather than "girl." It is to focus on a girl's value already as a child, and her varying needs at different stages of childhood, rather than her projected value as a woman in the future.

10   Officially it was to be the Women's Convention, and "CEDAW" was to refer to the Committee that reviewed country reports, but in popular usage "CEDAW" is used for the Convention itself and the Committee tends to be called the CEDAW Committee.

11   The full text of the Convention on the Elimination of all Forms of Discrimination against Women can be found on http://www.unhchr.ch/html/menu3/b/e1cedaw.htm. A printed copy of the CEDAW can be obtained at all UNICEF and UNIFEM offices.

12   In her presentation at the closure of the NGO Expert Consultation on Preventing Violence in the Family (Geneva, 9 October 1998), which the author attended.

13   The full text of the Convention of the Rights of the Child can be found on http://www.unhchr.ch/html/menu3/b/k2crc.htm. A printed copy of the CRC can be obtained at UNICEF offices.

14   Judith Karp (1998), Vice-President of the Committee on the Rights of the Child, which reviews reports by States on implementation efforts, has pointed out that other articles are also related to violence against girls.

15   Groups like the International Women's Rights Action Watch (IWRAW), Asia and Pacific, are supporting ways to bring the experiences, views and voices of activists to the review process.

16   See, for example, Forum for Women, Law and Development (1999), "Shadow Report" on CEDAW, for the initial report of the Government of Nepal.

17   *Dalit* (oppressed) is the term used by lower-caste people (often called "untouchables") to refer to themselves.

18   The cited author does not indicate the proportion of families in the community that this represents, but since he refers to a "settlement," one can assume it is a high proportion.

19   However, politics in parts of the region are centred more and more on the issue of men's control of women, supposedly as a sign of religious faith. Politically inspired gender violence is, then, a phenomenon already known in the region. It is unclear whether the tendency will grow or lessen. Jonsson has pointed out the need for more dialogue about how religious interpretations legitimize partriarchy and constrain development (Arole 1999, page x).

20   All interviews were arranged for this book by the various UNICEF offices.

21   Ul Haq and Haq note (1997, page 80): "It is evident that the level of military spending in India and Pakistan is largely independent of their low income levels. . . . [T]he rising defence burdens in these countries continue to

impose prohibitive social and economic costs on their people. Defence expenditure exceeds spending on education and health in Pakistan by about a quarter. In India, defence spending consumes two-thirds as much resources as does combined spending on education and health. On the other hand, the rich industrial countries spend three times as much on education and health as on their military."

22 A Pakistani woman lawyer renowned for her courage and effectiveness in fighting for human rights.

23 The course was organized by Jagori (Awake), an NGO in India, in cooperation with an NGO in Nepal, Shrii Shakti (Women's Power), and some support from UNICEF ROSA, among others.

24 From an interview for this book arranged by UNICEF India.

25 The interview for this book was arranged and conducted by UNICEF Pakistan; name withheld to protect anonymity.

26 Excerpts are from his speech at the opening session of the UNICEF/UNIFEM/UNDP South Asia regional meeting on ending violence against women and girls, which was held in Kathmandu in October 1997 (UNICEF 1998b).

27 The famed Indian musician.

28 The famed Pakistani musician.

The Cost of Gender Violence for Women's Lives and Health

The true size and weight of the burden on women's lives and health from gender violence in South Asia are only beginning to be measured. It is a complex issue because there are costs not only due to the more direct forms of violence and unfavourable practices harmful to women, but also due to neglect. The neglect that earlier might have been excused as an unavoidable result of poverty is now evident as coming from discrimination so severe, at all levels of society, that it causes disproportionate loss of opportunities, health and well-being, as well as lives for women and girls because they are female. There are also costs to society from violence against women and girls, which are beginning to be measured on a global basis, for which WHO plans to intensify efforts (WHO 1999c and 1999d).

Current practices in the family, as well as health policies and practices, contribute to the denial of rights to health for women and girls, as men and boys are customarily favoured and the burden of gender violence has not, generally speaking, been of concern until the 1990s. This chapter looks more closely at the losses involved, particularly for women; the nature of the surprisingly dangerous family in South Asia despite the emphasis on harmonious family life; and some prospects for prevention efforts, better lives and health.

Discrimination Can Kill

The Question of Longevity

Nothing else sums up so quickly the bias in favour of males in South Asia, from birth onwards, than the fact that their life expectancy compared to women's is the longest in the world. Distorted sex ratios are reflected in the figures for the unusual differences in longevity. The preference shown boys and men tends to deny girls and women sufficient health for them to fulfil the normal life expectancy patterns based on biology, which favour women.[1]

In plain words, such discrimination kills. It is a form of violence to women and girls, one with a high and measurable cost.

In her review of women's health for a world survey on women, Arlette Brauer (1995, page 26) describes seemingly ordinary ways in which women's lives are shortened in poorer countries:

Women seem to have a genetic biological advantage which makes them more resistant to infection and malnutrition. . . . The smaller advantage in longevity which women have in poorer countries in part reflects the larger gaps in those countries between men's and women's living conditions. In their work habits and in their relatively greater access to education, nutrition, and health care, men tend to live under more favourable conditions than women in developing countries.

Worldwide, according to Sivard (1995, page 44), women on average tend to live four years longer than men do. In developed countries, the average is seven more years of life expectancy for women. In developing countries, it drops to three more years of life expectancy for women. But, for South Asia, the average life expectancy (according to 1995 figures) for women is only one year more than it is for men. That difference is the lowest for any region in the world.

There are wide variations for women's life expectancy within South Asia that should be noted (based on 1995 figures in Sivard 1995). In Sri Lanka, life expectancy favours women more than it does in any other country in the region. It is four years more than men's, the same as the world average. In India and Pakistan, as well as Afghanistan, the reported difference is also in favour of women, but only by one year. That is the same as the regional average.[2] For Bangladesh, men and women have equal life expectancy, according to Sivard. A local researcher, however, reports that men's life expectancy actually exceeds that for women (N. Huq 1997). Either way, Bangladeshi women have a lower life expectancy than do women in the other countries being reviewed, except for Nepal. In Nepal, life expectancy is the least favourable for women as compared by Sivard to other countries in the region. She reports that women's life expectancy in Nepal is one year less than that for Nepali men.

For 139 countries on which Sivard gives data (page 44, Table III), no others in the developing world show men's life expectancy exceeding or equaling that for women. Only two in the developed world are exceptions and are recent ones at that.[3] It is clearly normal for women to expect to outlive men, other things being equal.

But other things are scarcely equal in South Asia for men and women, boys and girls. Girls are discriminated against from birth, have notably higher rates of infant and child mortality in many places, are married off early, are told to produce sons and to keep trying if they don't succeed right away, and are expected to serve men and make no demands, no matter what. "Education" is a must for being a wife, but not formal education for life beyond that role (education rates for girls in South Asia are among the lowest in the world). It is taken for granted that females will sacrifice themselves to take care of their husbands and sons. "Women," who really are often still girls although wives and mothers, cannot count on anyone putting their needs first, even when they are sick or pregnant. If married girls or women make demands or fail in their duties, they are likely beaten and can easily be replaced, sometimes with dire consequences for them.

In short, the data on longevity for men and women — so different in South Asia than for most of the world — tell us that to be born female in South Asia brings more risk that life will be drained away all too early through a combination of neglect and hardship, low education and poor nutrition, frequent pregnancies and lack of adequate health care.

The above description may sound like one for the female lot in many parts of the world, but in South Asia the situation appears even more difficult for women as compared to men, or their life expectancy would not be so relatively low. (Chapter 3 discusses the related problem of "missing women.")

A Nobel Laureate's View

The 1998 Nobel laureate in Economics, Amartya Sen from India, has urged that the measure of a country's economic success should take into account "a nation's ability to extend and improve the quality of life" (A. Sen 1993b, page 40). He thus points to the importance of mortality data for assessing the well-being of society and national capacity to promote it: "Economics is not solely concerned with income and wealth but also with using these resources as means to significant ends, including the promotion and enjoyment of long and worthwhile lives."

Reduced life expectancy and higher mortality rates for women than for men are among the problems Sen has explored. He is the one who drew worldwide attention to 100 million "missing" women, primarily in Asia. The phenomenon of missing women, he says, "reflects a history of higher mortality for females and a staunch anti-female bias in health care and nutrition" in the countries concerned (A. Sen 1993b).

To help make this point, Sen and a colleague at Oxford examined hospital records in Bombay and concluded that "women had to be more seriously ill than men did in order to be taken to the hospital" (1993b, page 46). And in a study in two villages in West Bengal about nutritional health care, he found "systematic bias in nutritional health care in favour of boys" (page 47).

As for mortality from battering, murder and suicide, Sen did not consider that. So far, direct physical acts of violence against women have not been taken into account as contributing to skewed life expectancy figures.

Other Negative Outcomes

A summary of regional data on life expectancy, adult literacy, enrolment in primary and secondary schools and care in pregnancy helps tell the story of how exceptionally difficult the situation for women is in South Asia compared to the rest of the world (see Table 3). Two measures of gender disparity in development — the Gender-related Development Index (GDI) and the Gender Empowerment Measure (GEM) introduced by the UNDP (1995) and developed in more detail for South Asia (UNDP 1998) — shows that the ratio of female to male achievements in both the attainment of capabilities (GDI) and empowerment (GEM) tend to be lower for South Asian countries than for the world or developing countries on average.[4]

The evidence is strong that the problem of gender-based violence in South Asia is rooted in patterns of gender relations and discrimination so severe that they shorten many girls' and women's lives and rob others of well-being.

But is all this about "gender violence"?

Yes, in part through acts of omission, starting in childhood, that withhold care, opportunity and rights. These limit health and quality of life, which supports good health. There is also the daily prospect of direct physical and sexual violence as well as psychological abuse at home. Although these problems are now beginning to be taken seriously, attitudes of self-sacrifice among girls and women in South Asia are so strong that many of those abused do not seek help, but accept their lot as fate or as though it were an honour to suffer or die early in life.

Table 3: Selected Statistics on Women's Status

	Life expectancy (females as % of males) 1997	Adult literacy rate (females as % of males) 1995	Enrolment rates (females as % of males)		Contraceptive prevalence (%) 1990–98	% of pregnant women immunized against tetanus 1995–97	% of births attended by trained health personnel 1990–97
			Primary school	Secondary school			
Sub-Saharan Africa	106	71	82	82	16	39	37
Middle East and North Africa	104	67	86	83	50	59	70
South Asia	101	57	77	63	39	74	28
East Asia and Pacific	106	84	98	91	75	36	81
Latin America and Caribbean	110	97	97	109	65	57	82
CEE/CIS and Baltic States	114	97	98	98	64	-	93
Industrialized countries	109	-	99	102	72	-	99
Developing countries	105	78	89	83	55	52	55
Least developed countries	105	63	78	60	22	48	28
World	106	81	90	88	58	52	60

Table adapted from UNICEF, *State of the World's Children 1999*, page 121; for names of countries covered, see original source.

Even if women do look for paths other than the ones they may be expected to tread, society and its institutions have provided few alternatives. Despite various public statements of concern about violence against women and girls, and some mechanisms to address and improve women's situation, governments have not yet been able to ensure that their institutions are free of discriminatory attitudes and behaviour towards women victim-survivors. This is seen, for example, when there is an inadequate response to women's health needs from health care systems and those who make policy. The costs of institutionalized and unchallenged patriarchy are high in both human and financial terms, as this chapter will begin to show.

Little Care for Women's Health:
Voices from South Asia

Women's health in the developing world has tended to be considered as only about reproductive health (and even that has been neglected). And yet, as the World Health Organization and others are now pointing out (WHO 1999a, 1999b), domestic violence is a public health problem around the world. What's more, reproductive health itself is likely to be improved through this broader approach to women's health. As Dr. Nafis Sadik, Executive Director of UNFPA, said in her speech to the Fourth World Conference on Women, "Successful action for reproductive health opposes violence to women in all its forms" (UNFPA 1995, page 1).

Voices from a rural woman and a public health worker describe aspects of women's health problems related to discrimination and violence, as well as reproductive roles, and call for more access to health care. Women's limited access to health care, influenced by attitudes and practices inside as well as outside the home, is itself a form of violence against women that shortens their lives and jeopardizes their well-being.

From the Village: Durga's Story

"Durga's" story,[5] from rural India, tells us in a very compressed and immediate way about the lives of women throughout much of South Asia. Like Durga, they learn first-hand and early that women's place in the family and society is often seen as lower than that of men. The results are far from trivial or academic. By sharing this part of her life, Durga shows simply but vividly the connection between the low status of women, discrimination and physical violence and poor health and an inadequate response in care from family and society. Her story reminds us that many women must repeatedly face and try to live through the painful reality of lost opportunities, diminished relationships, powerlessness, violence, disintegrating families and poor health — all this without much, if any, help. And it illustrates well how many of these difficult problems that women face are also devastating for girls.

> My journey has been long and traumatic. I came deep from the village and was illiterate. I did not attend any school and was married off by my father at age 14. I had nine pregnancies in nine years. Five of my children lived. I was always weak and sickly from the constant pregnancies. My husband would beat me if I was too ill to cook for him or have sex with him. I was also considered unprofitable by the local community and by family standards. I could not work on the field allotted to me by my husband due to my closely spaced pregnancies. I was small, weak and sickly. I had only one son among the surviving children. My husband abused me, beating me frequently and taunting me, too. And in the end he forced me to leave my children and return to my parents' home.[6]

Durga urges:

> Many questions should be asked and answers must be found soon. Can Indian men treat their daughters as their personal property to do as they wish? Should girls be married so young? Should the mothers be consulted, indeed, be fully involved in decisions involving our daughters? When will we have access to counselling, education and contraception? When will Indian girls be equal to boys in terms of education and other rights? Why is our society, which is based on the concepts of equality and justice, not doing anything to tackle the pervasive violence against women? How it affects our bodies and minds! Don't they

realize that stunted mothers can nurture their children that much less? I could not pay attention to my children because I was weak and traumatized. Does our society not want to safeguard the future? Who will protect and give our children comfort and warmth? We boast of our culture but unless we change our cultural attitude to women, our children will never learn the values which sustain and nurture society.[7]

From a Member of a Women's Group

Nasreen Huq, a member of Naripokkho (Women's Side) in Bangladesh, has learned through experience in the health field what Sen describes and Durga questions. Huq observes, "Women in general have more limited access to health care," and she gives reasons for this that have to do with attitudes and discrimination in caring practices:

There is a common perception that women do not need as much as men. Women as nurturers are self-sacrificing and eat last and least. Her health is neglected until she can no longer work. Little girls grow up with this role model as an ideal. Nutritional surveys indicate that girls and women eat proportionately less of their [nutritional] requirements than boys and men of similar socio-economic backgrounds.

The image of "woman as nurturer" not only defines her activities but also confines her to the home. The culture of seclusion also limits her access to health services both in terms of going to the service and allowing proper physical check-ups.

And preference for male children puts more and more pressure on a woman to have sons, no matter what the cost to her. (N. Huq 1997, page 2)

From a Health Worker

A woman health worker in Pakistan also expresses concern about women's limited access to health care, due to inadequate budgets, shortage of qualified doctors and disregard for women's rights:[8] "As a woman I am part of this culture and I am very concerned if 50 per cent of mankind is not being treated well. There is a lot of talk about human rights but generally women are not included." She describes food, clothing, shelter and health as four necessities to which women have limited access. She thinks that, for a woman, health

is often ignored till it comes to pregnancy. A woman doesn't have access to medical care. Can she make choices? Over 90 per cent of the women are aware of modern contraception but the use of contraception is only 17 per cent. I assume it is because she doesn't have access. The State is supposed to provide health care, but the budgeting is very disproportionate. There aren't enough qualified doctors in rural areas. Many women still give birth at home. Not enough money is spent on health but the amount of money spent on women's health is even lower.

The health worker also sees the necessity of dealing with social issues and discriminatory ideas and practices for women's health situation to improve:

I have been working in health care for the past 15 years. I have also worked outside Pakistan. Taking [women's health needs] as a medical problem did not work for me. I was assisting the government in setting up programmes to reduce maternal mortality. The problem is not that women are not aware [of the need for care], but what I assumed, and which is true, is that they don't have access [to care]. Poverty, taboos, prevented them from [being] provided good health care.

What about Wife Abuse? Impact on Health

We have heard from some women activists in South Asia and from a South Asian Nobel laureate about the way discrimination against women in caring practices and opportunities, from girlhood onwards, limits their longevity and health. What about morbidity and mortality from more direct forms of violence against women in the home, especially wife abuse, a term that can include physical, sexual, psychological and economic abuse? How serious is it in South Asia compared to the rest of the world? Are major efforts really needed and justified to address it, and what kind of efforts will those be?

I should say at the outset, there are no clear answers about the extent of morbidity and mortality from the various forms of domestic violence in South Asia. That question is rarely asked. However, even without extensive surveys in South Asia, local studies that exist (combined with what global studies already tell us) are enough to indicate that massive prevention efforts are urgently needed against domestic violence, in its direct and physical forms as well as the more indirect ones that withhold care and opportunities.

Some Global Studies

The health burden from gender violence. A ground-breaking World Bank study concludes that violence against women is a significant global health problem even in comparison to diseases already recognized as major concerns:

> At a global level the health burden from gender-based victimization among women age 15 to 44 is comparable to that posed by other risk factors and diseases high on the world agenda, including the human immuno-deficiency virus (HIV), tuberculosis, sepsis during childbirth, cancer and cardiovascular disease. (Heise, Pitanguy and Germain 1994, page 17)

The authors estimated that almost 3.5 million life years were lost to women victims of domestic violence and rape, particularly from effects of intentional injuries, post-traumatic stress and depression.[9]

Incidence of wife-beating. Drawing on Heise, Pitanguy and Germain's 1994 survey of studies about various kinds of wife abuse, the UN Statistical Office has summarized domestic violence incidence rates from the studies they considered the most reliable; a few are national studies, but most are not (see Table 4).[10] Incidence ranges from 17 per cent in New Zealand (a national study) to 75 per cent for a community in India.[11] Although not included in the UN review, national studies from Australia and Malaysia show figures of 50 per cent and 39 per cent, respectively (Abdullah, Raj-Hashim and Schmitt 1995, page 7). Campbell (1992) reviews data on wife-beating and battering from 14 societies around the world and groups them into four levels, from "essentially none" to "high." The only study from South Asia, from India, falls in the "high" category (along with ones from Iran, Taiwan, Indo-Fijian and Bun societies) (see review in WHO 1999a, page 37).

Studies about the demand made on health facilities by women who have been beaten are another source of data on the extent, severity and consequences of domestic violence. Some studies in the United States in 1979–1990 (cited by Ouellette 1998,

Table 4: Percentage of Women Who Have Been Hit by an Intimate Partner

Developed Countries		Asia and the Pacific	
Belgium	25	India	22-75*
Canada	25b	Korea	38a
Japan	59*	Malaysia	39a
Netherlands	21	Papua New Guinea	–
New Zealand	17	Urban	58
Norway	25	Rural	67
United States	28	Sri Lanka (urban)	60*
Latin America and the Caribbean		**Africa**	
Antigua	30	Kenya (Kissi District)	42
Barbados	30	Tanzania	60*
Chile (Santiago)	26	Uganda	46*
Colombia	20	Zambia	40*
Costa Rica	54*		
Ecuador	60*		
Guatemala	36*		
Mexico	34*		

Source: Survey data compiled by the United Nations Statistical Office and cited in Heise (1995).
*Studies based on non-representative samples, which should not be generalized to the country as a whole.
a. Per cent beaten within last year
b. The National Clearinghouse on Family Violence, Canada (1996) refers to "30 percent of Canadian women reported at least one incident of physical or sexual violence at the hands of a marital partner in a large-scale 1993 national survey on violence against women conducted by Statistics Canada."

pages 26–27) show high rates of injury from wife-beating — and these only include those cases that are brought to medical attention:

- Each year more than 1 million women seek medical assistance for injuries caused by battering.
- Of the women who visit emergency departments in the United States, 22–35 per cent are there for symptoms related to ongoing abuse.
- Research suggests that wife-beating results in more injuries that require medical treatment than rape, auto accidents and muggings combined. Families in which domestic violence occurs use doctors eight times more often, visit the emergency room six times more often and use six times more prescription drugs than the general population.
- Battered women are four to five times more likely than non-battered women to require psychiatric treatment.

Perpetrators. An international review concludes, "Contrary to popular expectations, most assaults on women occur in the home and women everywhere are more at risk from husbands, fathers, neighbours, colleagues than they are from strangers" (UN 1993c, page 7). Yet the relationship between a woman and her assailant is rarely recorded in official records, making it difficult to get accurate information. The studies reported here, however, show male partners are the most frequent perpetrators (see examples below).

Battering during pregnancy. "Battering during pregnancy can be defined as repeated physical and/or sexual assault during pregnancy within a context of coercive control"

(Campbell 1995). It is a worldwide phenomenon. The contribution of battering during pregnancy to maternal mortality tends to be neglected, along with that from other forms of domestic violence. One study from Chicago (US), however, indicates that trauma is the main cause of maternal death (Campbell 1995). *The Lancet* reports that there is a two and a half times greater risk of violent death for adolescent pregnant girls compared to young pregnant women aged 20–24. More unintended pregnancies among the adolescents may be a factor (UN 1989b).

A 1999 study in Matlab, Bangladesh, brings home the high risk of violent death for women during or shortly after pregnancy: "[W]omen aged 15–19 who were pregnant, or who have recently given birth, were nearly three times more likely to die from violence inflicted by others as women of the same age who were not pregnant" (UN 1989b). A 1996 review of prevalence of violence against pregnant women based on 13 studies from various developed countries gives prevalence rates of 0.9 to 20.1 per cent, "with most studies falling in the 3.9 to 8.3 per cent range" (Gamazarian et al. cited in WHO 1999a, page 8). The study also notes that violence during the post-partum period may be even greater than that during pregnancy itself.

In the United States and Canada, prevalence of abuse during pregnancy varies from 1 per cent to 17 per cent according to studies as reviewed by Campbell (1995). The percentage of those battered when pregnant who report being beaten before the pregnancy varies from 3 per cent to 10.9 per cent for the same studies.

Pregnancy, then, appears to be a trigger for much of the abuse. There is some indication that income level is not a significant determinant of risk for being battered in pregnancy, nor is ethnicity. One study, however, found that African-American, Latina and white women all had high rates of abuse (14–17 per cent) but that the Latina rate was still significantly lower (McFarlane and Parker as reported in Campbell 1995). The African-American women were the least seriously battered. In a 1998 review, Campbell (1998, page 185) states: "Tremendous progress has been made in establishing that abuse during pregnancy indeed occurs more often than other routinely screened complications of pregnancy (e.g. gestational diabetes, pre-eclampsia) with resulting health consequences that are often severe."

As for studies outside the United States and Canada, a large survey of pregnant women in the Czech Republic, Russia and the UK shows rates from 2 per cent (UK) and 4 per cent (Russia) to almost 10 per cent (Czech Republic) of pregnant women reporting physical violence during pregnancy (Coudouel 1998, page 18). A study from Spain reports that "up to 22 per cent of adolescent pregnant women suffer physical violence during pregnancy" (Lasa 1993). There is also some indication that younger pregnant women are more likely to be abused. Other risk factors include length of interval between pregnancies, with shorter intervals associated with more risk, and whether the pregnancy was planned or unplanned, with unplanned pregnancies associated with greater risk of battering (Campbell 1995). Parker et al. (1993) indicate that over 50 per cent of women in the study who were abused prior to pregnancy were also abused during pregnancy, and in subsequent visits, 8 per cent of the non-abused women and 48 per cent of teenagers reported abuse in the second or third trimesters.

Studies from developing countries are relatively few. They include ones from Costa Rica and the Philippines that report, respectively, that 33 per cent and 49 per cent of battered women are also battered by their partner during pregnancy. One review of studies from the developing world indicates that the share of battered women who report being beaten during at least one pregnancy is 20 to 65 per cent (Shrader Cox 1994, page 124). These rates are notably higher than those from developed countries and call for more investigation as well as heightened screening and other preventive efforts.

Battering in pregnancy also affects the babies being carried:

> [B]attered pregnant women are twice as likely to miscarry and four times as likely to have a low birth-weight child. Their babies are 40 times more likely to die within the first year of life. (Heise 1991, cited in Shrader Cox 1994, page 124)

Despite all these effects of violence against pregnant women, the problem remains relatively neglected. The seemingly universal elevation of motherhood makes it difficult to associate pregnancy with a risk of violent death.

Murder. "Of 8,932 victims of homicide in New York City from 1990 to 1994, 1,156 or 13 percent were female. . . . Nearly half were killed by an 'intimate partner' [almost always a current or former husband or boyfriend]." One third were killed by their husbands, but were not living with them, so male control over women who want to leave a marriage may be a factor in the murders. Fifty per cent of the murders were at home. The percentage of black women killed (52 per cent) compared to white women (16 per cent) was twice as much as the percentage of black women in the female population (25 per cent), whereas the proportion of white women killed was markedly less than their proportion of the female population (close to 50 per cent). The black women, however, were markedly younger (20s to 30s) compared to the white women (almost half over 50), and poorer — so age (and pregnancy?) and poverty may be risk factors compounded with race, at least in New York City (*New York Times*, 31 March 1997, pages B1–2).

Some South Asian Studies

Death due to physical violence. Morbidity and mortality due to domestic physical violence in South Asia has not been systematically studied for the region. Some important studies from Bangladesh point to the need for similar enquiries in other countries. Jahan (1994, page 50) analyzed family violence in Bangladesh between 1982 and 1988 by type, gender and relationship with aggressor. She found that murder was the most frequent type, and that women (N=315) were far more often the victims than were men (N=18). Nasreen Huq (1997) cites 1992 figures from the Bangladesh Bureau of Statistics that show that the category "suicide, murder and burns" accounts for 5.8 per cent of all deaths of rural women (the fifth highest cause of death for women in rural Bangladesh of 13 listed causes and not counting old age or "other diseases") and the fourth highest (tied with high blood pressure) for urban women. For both groups, deaths due to pregnancy-related causes are fewer (the eighth highest cause of death for rural women, the sixth highest for urban ones).

This is remarkable. A great deal of attention is being given to reducing maternal mortality, and rightly so; yet the preoccupation with women's reproductive role and with motherhood and the newborn's well-being may obscure the fact that women have other urgent health needs that are not always considered under reproductive health. Treatment for injuries and trauma from domestic violence is one.

Prevention efforts will be vital to protect even more women, given the human and financial costs of reserving treatment until afterwards, when it is largely unavailable anyway. Prevention efforts will also help reduce maternal mortality, since violence against women contributes significantly to maternal death. For example, a study of rural maternal deaths in 1982–1990 in Matlab, Bangladesh, showed that some 14 per cent were due to injuries or violence. This was the third highest cause of maternal death.

Incidence of wife-beating. It is important to consider all data available from South Asia on domestic violence in the form of wife-beating, limited as these are, to get a better idea about the situation there. UNICEF Regional Office for South Asia carried out a literature search in 1997,[12] which I updated in 1999. Table 5 summarizes the disparate studies, some of which were not available to me in the original. Some studies are clearly more sophisticated than others, but details on methodology are sometimes lacking. Not all the studies measure precisely the same thing: e.g., some cover regular beatings, and others, any beatings. There are both self-reports of beatings and statements about others being beaten. Some studies are from the point of view of the victim-survivor, others from that of the perpetrator. A few studies are designed to focus on determinants of violence more than incidence per se. Some conclusions may even be opinions — although from respected sources. Despite these considerations and drawbacks, the results contain a clear warning: the problem of wife-beating in South Asia is widespread and serious, yet deserves more recognition and public concern.

Scrutiny of the figures available from South Asia in 21 studies reviewed for this book shows a pattern of incidence that is on the high side.[13] Over 70 per cent of women in at least one study (these are local, not national studies) in each of three countries (Bangladesh, India and Pakistan) are reported to be physically abused by their husbands (Afsana 1994; Mahajan 1990; E. Ahmed 1998).[14] None of 34 studies from other regions, as reviewed by Heise, Pitanguy and Germain[15] (1994), and as reflected, in part, in Table 4, has figures over 60 per cent. Five of the studies they review (for Ecuador, Japan, Papua New Guinea, Sri Lanka and Tanzania) show incidence around 60 per cent, and one of these is from South Asia. In addition, four more studies — by Schuler et al. (1998), Naripokkho (1999), Qureshi et al. (1999) and Sonali (1990) — show incidence of wife-beating between 60 and 70 per cent. They also illustrate the importance of how the population criteria and research questions are defined: the first two studies report on occasional rather than frequent violence; the Qureshi study includes only women who perceive themselves as victims.

All in all, 9 of the 21 disparate studies from South Asia (eight if the quite different Saathi 1997b study is excluded) report incidence of wife-beating at 60 per cent or higher among the groups surveyed. As noted earlier, the studies are not all comparable, and some are flawed, but the levels of domestic violence suggested are, nonetheless, an alert that the problem is far greater than may have been assumed.

I hope these observations will stimulate further careful research[16] in South Asia about incidence, determinants and consequences of domestic violence as well as public debate regarding policy and action needed to prevent wife-battering and all the negative effects it has on women, children, men and prospects for healthy personal and family life.

Table 5: Prevalence of Wife-Beating in South Asia

Country	Sample	Sample Type	Findings	Comment
Bangladesh (Afsana 1994)	50 households from Jamalpur district.	Randomly selected households. Data collected through interviews and focus group discussions with husbands and wives.	78% of households reported incidents of physical violence directed towards women by their husbands.	Data collected from both husband and wife. Reasons cited for physical violence are: delay in food, temperamental husband, etc. Incidents of physical violence declined with the increase in age of wife at time of marriage.
Bangladesh (Schuler, Hashmi and Badal 1998)	Unknown number of women interviewed from 6 rural villages.	No details available on sampling method.	Over 66% of women reported having been beaten by their husband on at least one occasion.	The highest levels of violence were found in villages experiencing the most change in gender roles and that had the most women contributing to family support.
Bangladesh (Naripokko 1999)	845 women from 845 households interviewed in two subdistricts (*thanas*) of Dhaka city	Random: households were selected by a PPS sampling technique. The woman to be interviewed in each household was identified by the SRS technique. Structured interviews were conducted with all the women based on a questionnaire developed by Naripokkho. Women interviewed were over 18 years old.	61.8% reported physical violence at some point in their lives.	
Bangladesh (Schuler, Hashmi, Riley and Akhter 1996, in Koenig et al. 1999)	1,305 reproductive-aged women in rural Bangladesh	No details available on sampling method.	47% report having been ever beaten by their husbands, 19% in the past year.	Authors note significant underestimate possible.

Country	Sample	Sample Type	Findings	Comment
Bangladesh (Koenig et al. 1999)	Representative panel of approx. 8,000 households in two cities, Jessore and Sirajgonj.	Followed by SRS since 1982, with Knowledge-Attitudes-Practice (KAP) survey in 1993 to all currently married women aged 14–59 with 10,368 women intereviewed, including questions on domestic violence and determinants. Physical violence was the main focus.	42.1% reported recent physical violence and 78.7% reported verbal abuse; 17.6% reported threats of divorce. Differences were noted depending on community context (e.g. 39% reported physical violence in Jessore and 46.8% did so in Sirajgonj).	Only 2 determinants were statistically significant in both cities: wife's education and landholding (both inversely related to domestic violence). Significant determinants of less violence were non-Muslim households, better-educated husbands, longer duration of marriage (20 years or more), larger number of living sons (less significant) and wife's mobility. Differential effects call for more attention to community context in relation to possible determinants; also a statistically significant random effect means more conceptual work is needed before further analysis.
India (Action Aid 1994)	503 battered women, 16–35 age group.	Availability sample, selected from women seeking help from Shakti Shalini.	64.68% cited cruelty from spouse/in-laws as reason for seeking help from Shakti Shalini.	Authors observe that irrespective of the education status of women, problems encountered by them are "remarkably similar."

Table 5: Prevalence of Wife-Beating in South Asia, *continued*

Country	Sample	Sample Type	Findings	Comment
India (Mahajan 1990, in Heise et al. 1994)	109 men and 109 women from village in Jullundur District, Punjab.	50% sample of all scheduled caste housewives and 50% sample of non-scheduled caste housewives.	75% of scheduled caste wives report being beaten frequently by their husbands. Per cent reported by higher caste wives is not given. 75% of scheduled-caste men admit to beating their wives; 22% of higher-caste men admit to beating their wives.	Self-reports from perpetrators may not be completely reliable; tendency would normally be to underreport.
India (Jejeebhoy and Cook 1997)	1,842 women aged 15–39; Muslims and Hindus in Uttar Pradesh and Tamil Nadu.	No details available on sampling method.	40% of women report being beaten by their husbands.	Incidents of physical abuse had no relation to region, age or religion. Reported wife-beating was a common phenomenon of married life.
India (Narayana 1996; Evaluation Project 1997, in Koenig et al. 1999)	6,700 husbands surveyed in Uttar Pradesh	No details available on sampling method.	30% of husbands said they had beaten their wives. 22% admitted they had forced their wives to have sexual relations.	
India (Rao 1993)	170 women of childbearing age in three villages in rural Southern Karnataka.	100% sample of potter community in each village based on previous census.	22% of women reported physical assaults by their husbands; 12% reported being beaten within the past month an average of 2.65 times.	Informal interviews and ethnographic data suggest that prevalence rates are "vastly underreported."
India (Siram and Bashi 1988; cited in ActionAid India 1994)	617 battered women.	No details available on sampling method; focus group discussions were held.	More than 50% of the battered women surveyed reported regular beatings by their husbands.	10% of the battered women surveyed were assaulted by their husbands with weapons.

Country	Sample	Sample Type	Findings	Comment
India (Visaria 1998, in Koenig et al. 1999)	Community study of 346 women in 5 rural villages in Gujurat.	No details available on sampling method.	66% reported verbal or physical assault; 42% reported physical assault.	
Nepal (HMG/N, NPC and UNICEF 1997)	Survey of 95,752 people and 16,955 households, with focus group discussions in communities.	Violence data based on focus group discussions with mothers in 144 communities in various parts of the country and in both rural and urban situations.	43% of the focus groups surveyed reported that women are beaten often in the community. If the mother does something for her child without permission from other family members: 88% reported beatings; 88% reported scolding and 17% reported withholding of food.	This figure indicates the proportion of focus group women, not individuals, of the opinion that women are often beaten in their community. Children coming from communities where beatings are said to be "often" show 1.5 times more stunting and 1.75 times more wasting than do children from communities where wife-beating is said to be less. (The results are statistically significant.)
Nepal (Saathi 1997b)	1,250 respondents: 50% males and 50% females from 5 districts.	Randomly selected sample.	82% reported they knew of at least one incident in which a woman had been beaten by her husband.	The data are about both women and girls: Note this study is not based on self-reports by batterers or victim-survivors.

Table 5: Prevalence of Wife-Beating in South Asia, *continued*

Country	Sample	Sample Type	Findings	Comment
Pakistan (Bhatti et al. n.d.)	150 married women.	Availability sample of women outpatients in hospital. A questionnaire was given on an anonymous basis.	34% of women report physical abuse by their husband. In addition, 37% of women report abuse by husband, 39% verbal abuse by husband, 64% economic abuse by husband, 94% psychological abuse by husband and 45% physical abuse by husband during pregnancy.	
Pakistan (Carillo, in Commaraswamy 1994)	Sample size not indicated.	No details available on sampling method.	99% beaten by their husbands.	It is not clear if this is based on a study or is an opinion.
Pakistan (E. Ahmed 1998)	Sample size not indicated.	No details available on sampling method.	80% of women are subjected to domestic violence.	Results are from an informal study conducted by the Women's Ministry, which indicate that these findings are conservative and that the actual incidence of physical abuse will be much higher due to the large amount of cases that are never reported to public officials.

Country	Sample	Sample Type	Findings	Comment
Pakistan (Qureshi, Rizvi, Rabbani and Sajan 1999)	108 case studies selected by "convenience sampling" including "all ethnic groups roughly proportional to socio-economic strata in Karachi."	Inclusion criterion were 1) interviewee perceived self as victim of some kind of violence (verbal to physical); 2) gave verbal consent. Key informant interviews and focus group discussions were also held.	66.8% women suffered some form of physical abuse; 13% of these resulted in severe physical injuries; 12.9% reported some form of sexual abuse (always in combination with other violence); 94% reported verbal abuse; husband was sole perpetrator in 62.6%, mother-in-law in 26% (but not likely to use physical violence); violence was "frequent" in 87% of cases.	Cases were selected to assess determinants and consequences of domestic violence in Karachi. Women said likely to be afraid of sharing information. Domestic violence more likely in lower income families and where working women did not control their own income; women's attitudes said to be "very fatalistic...deep unhappiness and depression were evident in victims and their children."
Pakistan (War Against Rape 1992; cited in Marcus 1993)	Sample size not indicated.	No details available on sampling method.	99% of housewives and 77% of working women are beaten by their husbands.	Women also suffer from physical abuse by parents, sons and in-laws but to a lesser degree than by husbands.
Sri Lanka (Sonali 1990)	200 low-income women from various ethnic groups in Colombo.	Convenience sample from low income neighbourhood.	60% of women reported being beaten by their husbands.	51% of women reported that husbands used weapons.
Sri Lanka (WIN 1991)	515 women from different ethnic backgrounds and 4 different locations.	Semi-structured interviews.	32.4% of women reported suffering physical violence from husband.	Study found that women were often ashamed and afraid to admit that they had been beaten.

Perpetrators. Five examples come to mind of studies with information on perpetrators of domestic violence in South Asia. A careful study of who was the aggressor in family violence in Bangladesh shows that, of 750 cases, male relatives clearly account for all but 29 instances of violence. The husband was by far the most frequent abuser (Jahan and Islam 1997). And for India, Karlekar, Agrawal and Ganjoo (1995) found that men in the family are the main perpetrators. A study of domestic violence from Nepal found that 77 per cent of the violence against Nepalese women was reported as being from within the family, whereas only 13 per cent of the perpetrators were from outside the family (Saathi 1997a). From Pakistan, a study by Qureshi et al. (1999) found that the husband was the sole perpetrator in 62.6 per cent of the case, with the mother-in-law next, but unlikely to use physical violence herself. A Sri Lankan study (Deraniyagala 1992) presents cases that are all about domestic violence by men, with no mention of any other perpetrators even though the study is based on a questionnaire that asked about perpetrators, among other items. One logically concludes that there was little if any variation in the answer given — men. Dias and Fernando (n.d.) surveyed 31 cases of women admitted to a hospital after being beaten, over a third of whom were beaten by husbands themselves. (The proportion of other male relatives involved in additional cases was not made clear.)

Battering during pregnancy. In South Asia, as elsewhere, physical or sexual abuse of pregnant women, and its effects on unborn children as well as on the mothers, have not, generally speaking, been taken seriously enough, particularly when it occurs in the family. Only with more knowledge about the incidence and causes of physical abuse against pregnant women can prevention become a reality.

Three studies of wife-beating in South Asia strongly suggest that, indeed, pregnancy is associated with abuse. A small-scale study from Pakistan indicates that a third of the women outpatients who had been beaten were pregnant at the time (Bhatti et al. n.d.).[17] A second study, from Sri Lanka (Deraniyagala 1992, page 30), indicates that some 42 per cent of the women beaten were pregnant at the time. And in Bangladesh, as mentioned above, 13.8 per cent of maternal deaths in pregnancy are reported as resulting from injury/violence (N. Huq 1997).

Because many factors lead women to underreport violence against them, the number of pregnant women's deaths due to various types of direct physical violence is likely to be very much greater than what is currently known. Furthermore, the severe and potentially lethal effects to the child of beating during pregnancy suggests that physical violence to pregnant women in South Asia not only contributes to maternal mortality but also likely contributes to the high percentage of low-birthweight babies, as well as to infant mortality in the region.

Why would men beat women who are pregnant? Does it mean men question whether the child is theirs? Or they resent sharing the wife's energy and attention? A man may beat his wife simply because the food is not ready on time. In some cases, the man may not want the child. For example, if a man wants another wife, the dowry paid to him may be less if he already has a child. Studies of the reasons for beating in pregnancy in South Asia, as elsewhere, could be very useful for prevention efforts. A review in Campbell (1995) of some initial studies mentions examples similar to those suggested above (with the exception of the one related to dowry, which is culture-specific).

Early childbearing means more risks. According to UNFPA (1998c, pages 23–24), "Early childbearing is the cultural practice in the region. About one-third of adolescent girls begin childbearing as early as 17," and a larger share of all births occur to adolescent girls aged 15 to 19. "On average in most of the region a girl has had two children by the time she is 20 (except in Sri Lanka, where she has had one). Available figures indicate that, in fact, over 10 per cent of girls currently 15 had begun childbearing in Bangladesh, the highest known percentage in South Asia" (page 24). Birth intervals are shorter among adolescents than among older women: some 24–26 months is the median birth interval for the former, compared to 38–41 months for women over 40 (page 27). Shorter birth intervals increase risks of maternal and infant mortality (page 27). They also tend to be associated with wife-beating in pregnancy and with unplanned pregnancy (Campbell 1995), both of which are features in South Asia (UNFPA 1998) and risk factors from wife-beating, along with younger age of mother. UNFPA notes that data from South Asia confirm that "children born to adolescent mothers have higher risk of death" (1998, page 37), but the contribution of wife-beating to that outcome is not yet known. Also, the risk of maternal mortality is higher among adolescent girls — for example, about three times as high for 15- to 19-year-olds in Bangladesh as compared to even slightly older currently married women, aged 20–24 (UNFPA 1998, page 38).

The Hidden Pandemic

Domestic violence, from the subtle to the hideous, is usually hidden as the cause of women's or girls' serious health problems and it may not even be considered as a health issue. Through shame, fear and lack of alternatives women themselves often minimize the effects of the domestic violence they experience. What's more, many dismiss its importance, thinking it is very normal. For both reasons, domestic violence is the hidden pandemic. This sounds like a contradiction: How can something be hidden if it is so widespread? The truth is that few have regarded domestic violence as something they could do anything about, so why should they even notice it?

The Hidden Millions

Women who are targets of domestic violence are the "hidden millions." The name is apt for several reasons. First of all, the women and the actions against them are very much hidden inside the home. Second, the attacks on them are not usually taken seriously in the family, the community or by the law. Even health care professionals, in a position to recognize and respond to injuries or psychological problems, tend to overlook their cause. Third, the power of the male culprits in the patriarchal family makes it relatively easy for them to hide the truth. Fourth, in order to avoid blame, shame and more punishment from the abusive men in the family, women themselves do not speak the truth about violence. For example, women who are dying from burns inflicted by their husbands and in-laws will even deny that anything more than an accident happened. They want to be sure that their children will not suffer retaliation, should they die (see, for example, Bhatti et al. n.d.).

Shame and Statistics: Underreporting Everywhere[18]

The number of women's deaths due to various types of direct physical violence is likely to be very much greater than what is currently known, because many factors lead women to underreport violence against them. This is a worldwide problem that prevents us from seeing the true challenge to health policy that domestic violence poses. Miranda Davies (1994, pages 2–3) says,

> It is difficult to estimate the actual incidence of violence in the household. Communities deny the problem, fearing that an admission of its existence is an assault on the integrity of the family, and few official statistics are kept. . . . Statistics gathered from police records and other official sources show that wife abuse does exist, but they are notorious for underrepresenting the problem. Victims are often reluctant to report that they have been violated: they may fail to report abuse because they feel ashamed of being assaulted by their husbands; they may be afraid; there may be a sense of family loyalty.

It seems the extent of the problem is larger than many studies indicate. Shame is a constraint suggested by studies from around the world. Definitions can also influence accounts. For example, a male researcher who worked in Bangladesh wrote to me explaining why a survey he carried out on domestic violence initially showed lower figures than seemed plausible to him.

> Violence against women is so deeply interwoven in the fabric of the society that our society has learned to accept and tolerate it as the norm. This includes women [who are] literate or illiterate, rich or poor. I was doing a very simple survey on multiple marriages and beating of women. I was amazed to see the low percentage of physical abuse. This made me go back and talk to all the negative respondents. What I found was amazing. Their definition of physical abuse was entirely different. Their definition was that "beating" only occurs when the husband picks up an object and repeatedly hits a woman with the object. A "mere" slap, a "mere" hitting with hand, is not beating. You can imagine the [real] extent [of violence]. To me it seemed that most women one time or another have had their share of beating. One study has found that in the adult period of the women's lives the cause of death in almost 30 per cent of cases is related to violence.[19]

Although it will take many more studies to get a precise reading of the extent and nature of the problem, the accounts by those interviewed for this book, as well as some detailed studies, indicate that gender violence is far more extensive than is generally acknowledged in South Asia, and that any level of gender violence should be unacceptable.

For example, a male journalist in Bangladesh[20] observes: "This is a pandemic. Every woman is subject to the threat of violence everywhere — at home, the workplace — and at any moment."

A Pakistani woman[21] says:

> There is not a single woman in Pakistan who has not been exposed to some sort of violence. Not a single woman, because the social set-up is anti-woman. So just from the fact that you are living here you are facing certain sorts of violence because you are in a subordinate position as a woman, so that is violence in itself. Just verbal violence you face on a day-to-day basis, a general harassment, a perception of your position and rights. It happens to most women in the society. It happens in the so-called privileged people class — it is happening to [all] women.

The state coordinator of an NGO in Uttar Pradesh, India, says:

> Violence against women is an all-pervasive thing in our society, especially in Uttar Pradesh. We have the highest number of rapes, and the figure hasn't come down for the past several years. We have the second highest figures in dowry deaths after Madhya Pradesh, and now caste violence against women is increasing. Women are not spared of violence and atrocities across all communities, across all socio-economic strata. Cases that are reported are just one third or even less, just the tip of the iceberg. Most women are ashamed to report the matter and even when some do, you know very well the stand which the police take. The medical authorities give the report and don't want to get involved further.
>
> I remember that during the first three years (of organization) we just had 18 cases, and the present status is about three hundred cases a year, that is almost one case a day [even though] this in a small place. I have dealt with cases involving bureaucrats, police officers, businessmen, all of them are doing it, treating their wives in the most despicable manner and outside they have such a perfect image.

A Closer Look at the Dangerous Family

The process of confrontation has begun. That is clear even from titles of some recent studies and meetings in South Asia about domestic violence: "The Haven Becomes Hell" (Hassan 1995), "No Safe Spaces" (Karlekar, Agrawal and Ganjoo 1995), "Dangerous Homes" (UNICEF 1997b) and "Domestic Violence: A Silent Cry" (Wijayatilake n.d. a) are examples. The silence is being broken by South Asians about what is all too often the dangerous family.

There are many ways to abuse, remove or kill females in a dangerous family. Some are direct; others are indirect and slow. A review follows.

Direct Methods to Abuse and Kill Women in the Family

These methods of abuse inflict physical damage and pain, and can lead to death. For women, they include assault and battery, rape and murder — whether by burning, beating, poisoning, strangling, knifing, shooting, etc. Some murders are linked with customs such as *sati*, (widow immolation), dowry death (women are killed for not bringing enough dowry) and so-called "honour killings". Rape, transmission of HIV/AIDS and botched abortions can also lead to a woman's death. Action by family members has a role in each, as discussed below.

Assault and battery.[22] Milder, more euphemistic words tend to be heard for wife-beating in South Asia. A woman may say that her husband "troubled" or "bothered" her. Terms such as "spousal abuse" or "psychological and physical abuse of women" and "wife-beating" tend to be used by researchers and NGOs. Even under the law, "malicious acts" or "acts to outrage the modesty of a woman" may be found to cover severe physical violence. But none of these terms conveys the idea that attacks on women in the family may be truly serious, even criminal.

However, some studies related to severity of physical abuse show that acts of domestic violence definitely include what appear to be criminal acts under existing laws, when one considers their consequences, apparent motive and weapons.

Torture. At the same time, the category of "torture both mental and physical" is recognized as a legal offence in some countries, such as India. An analysis of the percentage distribution of various crimes against women during 1997 in India shows that the highest percentage fall in the "torture" category (National Crime Records Bureau 1999, page 163). More analysis of the cases involved would be useful for a comprehensive understanding of crimes against women and the effective use of the legal system.

Dowry death. "Dowry death," a category for a legal offence in India, is most often accomplished by burning. Women may be burned to death, or close to it, if the groom and his family feel they haven't received enough dowry. They try to get more by threatening to kill the bride. These deaths are frequently reported in the press and to NGOs. Official figures are generally considered to be low compared to the real number of cases; many are likely reported as suicide. However, in Delhi alone — where an anti-dowry cell was set up in 1983 in the police station — the number of complaints went up from 1,550 to 7,570 between 1984 and 1994 (Hazarika 1995, pages 26–27). From Punjab, India, comes a detailed study of dowry deaths, which have increased from 55 in 1986 to 157 by mid-1999, according to the Institute for Development and Communication (IDC) in Chandigarh (Vinayak 1999). It reports a staggering 17,649 cases of dowry harassment as having actually occurred in 1995, although only 59 cases were reported to the police. IDC estimates that for every reported case, some 299 go unregistered with the police. Official national figures for India report dowry deaths increasing from 5,092 per year in 1995 to 6,006 in 1997, an 8.9 percentage increase (National Crime Records Bureau 1999, page 162).

Widespread in India, Pakistan and Bangladesh, the practice of dowry being paid to the groom's family, with concomitant risks of extortion and dowry death, has also begun in Nepal. Arole (1999) finds that dowry is a cultural practice, without foundation in any major religion. She notes: "[I]t became a practice in the middle of the nineteenth century and has reached shocking proportions in the last fifty years in South Asia. It is practiced today by all religious groups, and even those who used to have bride-price today practice dowry" (Arole 1999, page 58).

Stove-burning. The phenomenon of "stove-burning" has been widely publicized in both Pakistan and India. It appears to be similar in nature to dowry death, but may not always be linked with dowry demands. In Pakistan, a high court judgement "found it strange that most of the victims were daughters-in-law" (Commission of Inquiry for Women 1997, page 80). The Commission of Inquiry for Women in Pakistan also reported on incidence as follows: "Data collected from just two hospitals in Rawalpindi and Islamabad, Pakistan, over a three-year period since 1994 reveal 739 cases of women burn victims which, it was said, do not represent even a small percentage of the actual cases, most of which are not even brought to hospitals. A compilation of newspaper reports from Lahore, Pakistan, over a six-month period in 1997 indicates an average of 15 cases a month, most of the victims being young married women" (pages 80–81). The Progressive Women's Association of Pakistan (PWA) has published a detailed account of 12 cases of *chula* (stove) deaths with details on 185 cases from two hospitals in Islamabad and Rawalpindi. The report observes, "Although negligence, accidents and faulty kerosene stoves are blamed for these deaths, PWA's investigation indicates that most of these deaths were planned murders. Chillingly, doctors note that the patterns of burns on the bodies of the victims are not consistent with what we would expect to see from a genuine stove accident" (Progressive Women's Association n.d.,

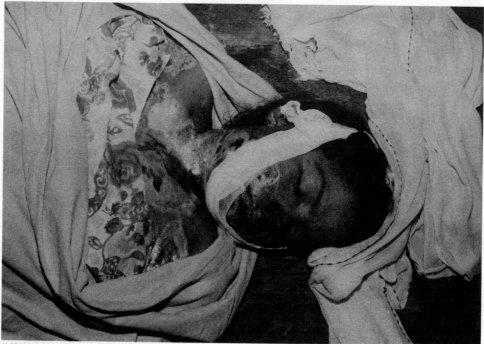

SYED MAJID ALI

Burn victim, domestic violence: Pakistan.

preface). Of some 1,000 cases in Islamabad and Rawalpindi, about which PWA has collected information between 1994–1998, only 0.01 per cent of the victims have survived. Of the 185 studied in depth in 1994, 29 per cent of the victims were under 15 and 47 per cent were 16–20 years old. In the 80 per cent of the cases for which there was information on parental family attitude towards the problem the daughter was facing and had shared with them, none had support from the family. Of 109 cases (of 185) on which there was information about how many children lost their mother, 62 per cent of the dead women left two to three children behind, while 25 per cent had four to five children each and only 1 per cent did not have a child. In 60 per cent of the cases, the husband was the accused suspect (information on perpetrators was given for only 81 per cent of the cases) (see Tables 1–10 of the PWA report).

Acid attack. In Bangladesh and in Pakistan, acid attacks are a relatively new concern not much reported in other South Asian countries. Acid is thrown on a girl or a woman to punish her for faults or because she has rejected a suitor. For instance, UNICEF Bangladesh reports that in Bangladesh in 1996, there were 47 reported cases of acid violence. In 1998 there were more than 200 reported cases, but UNICEF believes that the number of actual cases is much higher (UNICEF 1999a). A few women victim-survivors have been or are being assisted with reconstructive surgery in Spain and the United States. Naripokkho emphasizes the need for training of local physicians in reconstructive surgery and for training of nurses in the proper care for acid-attack victim-survivors. Prevention efforts are also under way.

Sati. Many writers have commented on the phenomenon of *sati*, the practice of immolation of widows in India (see, for example, Narasimhan 1990). In violation of the Sati Prevention Act, 167 cases are reported officially for 1994 (National Crime Records Bureau 1996). The official 1995–1997 figures record only one case in both 1995 and 1997 and none in 1996 (National Crime Records Bureau 1999, page 162). At the same time, some activists observe that cases have been increasing. Arole (1999, page 68), for example, observes that "in some communities the practice of *sati* is coming back. In some cases women may be truly devoted to their husbands (so they want to die with them), while in others they are forced by families to be burned. Yet, some women may feel it is better to die than to have a miserable life, shunned by society." Women accused of being witches are also burned or buried alive, often over property disputes it seems.[23]

"Honour killing." This refers to the killing of a female relative by her family primarily when her virginity or faithfulness is in question; the family is then considered dishonoured and strives to restore respect for its name through murder of the woman or girl concerned. Data from only one district in Pakistan indicate that the rate of "honour killings" there is among the highest so far known in the world, and that more attention is thus needed in South Asia to the scope of the problem and how to prevent it.

A Pakistani lawyer, Mufti Ziauddin,[24] has looked closely into crimes against women in the family and the victimization of women in his district in Pakistan. He found that in seven months 29 women were murdered, 25 of whom could be identified. Given the importance of this information, let me quote him at length from his interview for UNICEF:

> Out of these 25, 20 were murdered inside the home and four outside. Yes, domestic violence. Out of these 20 women who were murdered [in the home], three women were murdered in the house of their parents and 17 in the house of their in-laws. This is very strange for us, that a woman in the house of her parents is safe, but when she goes to the house of her in-laws, she's vulnerable. Out of these 17 women who were murdered in the houses of in-laws, 14 were murdered by their own husbands and the rest were mainly murdered by brother-in-law, followed by father-in-law. . . . Out of 14, two were murdered because there were disputes between the husbands and wives, and mainly because of the mother-in-law and sisters-in-law. They provoked their brother to beat her. These [other] 12 women who were murdered, the charges against them were that of having illicit relations.
>
> Let me tell you another interesting thing. Swat is a small district with a population of 1.2 million. Out of 1.2 million people, within seven months, if 29 women are murdered, the rate is very high.[25]

Even if one considers only 12 of the murders for seven months as "honour killings" — a very conservative approach since spouses are not the only males who carry out such slayings — one finds that the projected yearly killings are 20.5. The projected yearly rate, per million population for that one district in Pakistan, is 17. How does that compare with the figures available for some Arab countries? For example, as reported by Jehl (1999, pages 1 and 8), government figures from Jordan show 25 "honour killings" a year, in a country with some 4 million people. That amounts to 6.25 honour killing per million population. In Yemen, with a population of 16 million, some 400 such killings were reported in 1997, or 25 "honour killings" per million population. The rate per million per year as calculated for Swat, Pakistan, based on Ziauddin's research is 2.7 times that in Jordan — or about 270 per cent greater, and 0.64 — or 64 per cent of the rate in Yemen.

Ziauddin notes that all the murders of women in his district took place in rural areas. He sees the high incidence there as related to their lack of education, employment or services. In short, the fact that women are "confined to household activity" makes them more vulnerable to those men deemed to be in charge of family life.

He says:

In urban areas the women attend schools and colleges. They even go and work outside, most of them in the cosmetic industry prevalent in Swat. We don't have any complaints of women being murdered there.

Rape. Rape is the form of violence that seems to attract the most attention of activists to date in South Asia. This may be partly due to the idea that perpetrators come from outside rather than inside the family. While not necessarily lethal, rape can be, either through the brutality of the sexual attack (see, for example, Sarkar 1996, page 225), or through murder afterwards (see, for example, F. Khan 1994). Murder after a rape obviously prevents the woman or girl from naming the culprit.

Rape, whether inside or outside marriage, is closely linked with unwanted pregnancies, abortion and maternal mortality, also with HIV/AIDS. Some statistics give an idea about incidence: "The Human Rights Commission of Pakistan estimated that, in 1993, a woman was raped every three hours, and at least two were gang raped every day of the year" (UNICEF 1997e, page 19). In India, 13,208 cases of rape were reported in 1994, according to official records (National Crime Records Bureau 1994, page 215). Local reports may give even higher figures. Rape of younger victims, under 10 and from 10 to 16, increased by 15.8 per cent (from 394 to 734) and 17.6 per cent (from 2,105 to 3,244), respectively. The National Crime Records Bureau for India reports a 3.3 per cent overall increase of rape from 1996 to 1997, and a 26.6 per cent increase in rape of girls under 10 (from 608 cases in 1996 to 770 in 1997) (National Crime Records Bureau 1999, page 165).

As for marital rape, most married women in South Asia probably do not have such a concept, as they have been taught to believe that a husband's needs should always be fulfilled by the wife (see, for example, Arole 1995), and no such offence is recognized under the law. Although rape is generally thought of as something that strangers, not family members or even friends, force on a woman, studies around the world indicate that rapists are generally people their women targets know. For instance, 88 per cent of offenders in a study from the Philippines were such (Guerrero and Sobritchea 1997, page 23). This is echoed by data from Pakistan (see E. Khan 1994).

In South Asia, where women's mobility tends to be limited in many cultures, it is common sense that rape is primarily committed by men whom women know, even family members. Domestic servants may also be culprits. One may well ask, however, whether or not servants are blamed in order to give protection to male family members.

Because rape is seen as an insult to the man whose wife, daughter or mother is violated, men will intentionally rape women as an attack on men whom they wish to dishonour, including relatives. Of course, strangers are sometimes the perpetrators, but one should not automatically assume a stranger is responsible for rape. Rape in wartime is another matter. The region has experienced bloody conflicts and war from early invaders onwards, including during partition, in the war between Pakistan and Bangladesh (then West and East Pakistan, respectively) and in Kashmir and Sri Lanka today. Rape has been a common element. In fact, the threat of rape by men from outside is sometimes used by fathers, husbands or sons as a reason to curtail women's freedom and mobility in the name of protection.

HIV/AIDS transmission. It is said that there is a belief in much of South Asia that HIV/AIDS can be cured by sex with a virgin.[26] Obviously, that is not a cure for the man but a transmission of a death sentence to the girl or woman. Married women also are victims. Husbands bring the disease home and then blame wives as the source. The power relation between women and men in the family is such that men are more likely than women to have multiple sex partners and to command when and how sexual relations are performed. The use of condoms with shared decision-making about their use is a goal for many public health workers in the field as well as in prevention policies. Women do not usually influence such decisions. It is even more likely that married adolescent girls do not. For example, UNFPA (1998c) reports that only 11 per cent of currently married 15- to 19-year-old girls "were using contraception in any SAARC country other than that of Bangladesh and Sri Lanka," where one third do. While HIV/AIDS transmission may not be intentional, more responsibility and efforts for prevention should be taken.

The need for prevention efforts is urgent for rural as well as urban areas. For example, an AIDS epidemic update for December 1998 reports that a sentinel surveillance in antenatal clinics in India "shows that in at least five states, more than 1 per cent of pregnant women in urban areas are now infected" (UNAIDS and WHO 1998). They go on to note that in rural areas, "home to 73 per cent of the country's 930 million people," HIV should clearly be a new concern. For example, in Tamil Nadu, "2.1 per cent of the adult population living in the countryside had HIV, as compared with 0.7 per cent of the urban population" (page 4).

As for risk to women, some signs are ominous. For all of Asia, 25 per cent of the HIV-positive adults are women, They need not be those who are engaging in behaviours normally considered high risk. As the update observes:

> The virus is firmly embedded in the general population, among women whose only risk
> behaviour is having sex with their own husbands. In a study of nearly 400 women
> attending STD clinics in Pune [in rural Maharashtra, India], 93 per cent were married and
> 91 per cent had never had sex with anyone but their husbands. All of these women were
> infected with a sexually transmitted disease, and a shocking 13.6 per cent of them tested
> positive for HIV. (page 5)

If women had more control over contraceptive use and husbands were held to the same standards for fidelity as women are, rates would decline. A recent study in Uttar Pradesh, India, notes that sexual abuse of wives is more common among men who have extra-marital affairs (UN Wire, 17 November 1999). It also observes that the abuse "could be the reason for the increase of HIV infection among monogamous Indian women."

Abortions. A 1999 WHO press release[27] estimates that throughout the world some 70,000 women die every year as a result of botched abortions. In the developing world, WHO reports that 1 of every 250 procedures leads to death. For Pakistan, the Pakistan National Forum on Women's Health reports that 1,190 of maternal deaths in that country are due to abortion (UNICEF 1997i, page 17). In Bangladesh, abortion is shown as accounting for 10 per cent of maternal mortality (N. Huq 1997, Table II).

Many people are hesitant to talk about this subject, so these figures can only reflect reported cases. Where abortion is legal, as in India, one might expect the share of maternal mortality rates due to abortion to be less than where it is not. Ritu Bhatia (n.d.) points to a recent study by the Indian Council for Medical Research, which shows that there are twice as many abortions performed by unqualified medical personnel as there are abortions by qualified physicians. She says that in rural areas, given the poor doctor-patient ratio, some 60,000 women die each year from the complications of abortions induced "by poking sticks and other instruments into the vagina." That is almost the total for the figure given by WHO for deaths worldwide due to botched abortions. A study by Fauveau and Blanchet (1989) in Matlab, Bangladesh, observes that abortion, which is illegal there, is common but not usually acknowledged, and that unmarried women (often girls) are at greater risk than married ones, given the value placed on virginity at marriage. Overall, various studies estimate death rates from induced abortions at 7 per cent to 26 per cent. Fauveau and Blanchet (1989, pages 1, 122) find that for unmarried women, 70 per cent of all deaths during pregnancy were "due to complications of an induced abortion, a proportion 2.6 times greater than for married women."

From Nepal comes a more subjective account, from Aruna Uprety, a woman medical doctor. Abortion, illegal in Nepal, was the first issue that drew her attention to social issues affecting women's health. She says:[28]

> After finishing my medical college I started working in a maternity centre. At that time I didn't have any idea of the whole social problems. . . . [W]hile I was in emergency room I found that a lot of women came with problems of criminal abortions. Some women died there. Later on I found that women who have abortions are put in jail, according to our Nepalese law [see, for example, Integrated Development Systems 1982 and Lloyd-Roberts 1999] . . . but the partner, the male, who is never in jail is responsible for this pregnancy. The women do abortion because they cannot talk to their husband or mother-in-law about family planning. . . . Many times there are rape and incestuous relationships. When we put all these things together, I began to think this is really an injustice to women. It is because the women don't have any idea, they don't have knowledge, they don't have power to say "No" to something, that's why they are in the jails, and they have to suffer so much morbidity. But if a woman is empowered, if she is educated, no one can touch her. So very slowly we are working on this. I find that if women are not empowered, no matter how much we talk about health problems, health issues, they cannot be solved.

Indirect Violence That Can Kill

Indirect methods to abuse, deprive and kill girls and women include discrimination in caring practices at home and denial of rights to health care, education and employment, which leaves girls and women more dependent on abusive and murderous men in the patriarchal family structure. Driving a daughter or wife to suicide is another method — although suicide is often claimed by family members to account for cases of women they actually murdered. Then there is maternal mortality itself, sometimes due to direct violence — battering — and sometimes due to acts of omission. This is discussed in a section further below.

Discrimination in caring practices and opportunities. This has already been discussed in relation to longevity, above. Table 1 summarizes regional data on life expectancy, adult literacy, enrolment in primary and secondary school, contraceptive prevalence, immunization of pregnant women and births attended by trained health personnel. It shows that South Asia has the lowest standing of any geographic region on all but two of the seven measures (contraceptive prevalence and percentage of pregnant women immunized against tetanus), a rather dismal picture of women's status in the region.

Suicide. Low status and powerlessness can lead to suicide. Wijayatilake (n.d. b, page 8) describes how a young woman, newly married, attempted to take her life after she was forced to submit to her husband's "bizarre" sexual desires and then felt she had no one to turn to for help . For India in 1981–1991, the National Crime Records Bureau shows that domestic quarrels lead to more suicides among married women than among men. Dowry disputes are said to account for some 4 per cent of these. Dowry demands are also being linked with suicide by women in Terai, Nepal (The People's Review 1997). A study by Fauveau and Blanchet (1989) is an important source of data on suicide for some countries in South Asia. Sri Lanka exhibits one of the highest suicide rates in the world for both women and men. There, death by suicide for girls and women 15 to 24 years old is 55 times greater than deaths due to pregnancy and childbirth.

In Bangladesh, suicide rates for girls and women in the same age group are less than half that in Sri Lanka and less than one third the rate for obstetric-related causes of death. Compared to the suicide rate for girls and women 15–24 years in Japan (the only other country for which data are included in Fauveau and Blanchet 1989), the suicide rate is almost eight times greater in Sri Lanka and slightly more than three times greater in Bangladesh.

Maternal mortality. In some cases, as discussed above, maternal mortality itself can be viewed as a form of murder due to beating in pregnancy or other abuse by family members. In some cases, maternal mortality results from acts of omission by family members. For example, a few interviewers for this book spoke of cases where a man refuses permission for his wife to be taken to a doctor or refuses care for her once she is at the hospital, because it is "inconvenient" for him. "Who will take care of the children? Who will cook dinner?" he may ask. She may not be worth a skipped meal or the "sacrifice" of her doing the cooking and childcare. And if her condition is so serious that she probably will not make it home without care first, he may say, "Let her die!"

The maternal mortality rate for South Asia is the second highest in the world, after sub-Saharan Africa. Country figures from South Asia range from 150 maternal deaths per 100,000 live births in Sri Lanka to 1,700 in Afghanistan, with Nepal and Bhutan close behind, with 1,600 and 1,500 maternal deaths per 100,000 live births, respectively. These are among the very highest in the world. The figures for Bangladesh, India and Pakistan are 850, 570 and 340, respectively.[29] All these figures are in comparison with only some 22 maternal deaths per 100,000 live births in Germany and 12 in Italy, for example. So there are about 7 to 70 times as many maternal deaths per 100,000 live births in South Asian countries as compared to Germany, and about 13 to 133 times as many as in Italy (based on figures in UNICEF 1998f; for 1990, see pages 34–36).

When a mother dies, the care of her children is at risk. For example, Syed (n.d. b) reports a 200 per cent increase of mortality in sons and a 350 per cent increase for girls after a mother's obstetrics-related death.

Cultural attitudes, family decisions against prenatal or even emergency care where it is available and lack of transportation and of emergency care itself all contribute to the maternal mortality in the region. WHO, UNFPA and UNICEF are cooperating with governments and health facilities in a major initiative to reduce and prevent maternal mortality in South Asia. Most governments in the region have recently made commitments to programmes for safe motherhood and in a human rights perspective. Efforts by front-line workers will be discussed further below.

Non-Lethal Ways to Rid the Family of Women

There a number of ways by which a family could rid itself of an unwanted girl or woman without resorting to murder or lethal neglect. Some are reviewed briefly here. One notes that each can bring some economic gain to the family concerned.

Early marriage. Early marriage for daughters can serve to ease the perceived burden of their upbringing. It likely requires a lower dowry payment to the groom and his family than would a later marriage, and it ensures that family honour is protected, as a young bride is likely to be a virgin. (Child and early marriage are discussed at greater length in Chapter 3.)

Abandonment and divorce. These are ways that men can easily rid themselves of unwanted wives without murdering them. Custom gives little protection to women concerned, as not all marriages are registered and maintenance is often lacking. Where dowry is paid to men, "dowry business" can flourish, with men marrying again and again, abandoning (or worse) wives as they go along. Insufficient information on the number of women so abandoned and character assassination prevent development of adequate programmes for them and their children. Economic opportunities are limited for such women.

Institutionalization and incarceration. Having a woman committed to a mental institution is said to be a relatively easy way for a husband to get rid of an unwanted wife in South Asia. A motive to protect property rights is at the basis of many of these abuses (see Honey et al. 1995). Apparently, institutionalization of women can be attributed not only to true psychiatric problems (although of course these do occur) but also to the readiness of society to accept a relative's claim that a women is "mad" or "crazy"[30]:

> In many cases, the woman is sent to a mental institution to rid the family of her. The man's intention of marrying again after getting rid of his first wife is a common reason. Her failure to bear children or bearing only "female children" is another excuse. Greed for dowry and the failure of the woman to fulfil some demand is the ulterior motive. Thus, where families do not murder young brides for dowry, they can achieve the same purpose equally effectively with no criminal sanctions and greater social empathy by declaring her mad. As they cannot be expected to indefinitely look after a woman of unsound mind, the dumping of a crazy bride would not be socially disapproved whereas despite its high incidence, murder of a woman for dowry would be disapproved and criticized. (Dhanda 1987, quoted in Honey et al. 1995, page 93)

Where abortion is illegal, a male may see an opportunity to get rid of an unwanted woman in the family as follows: the husband and another man in the family may plan a rape, hoping she will get pregnant, and then seek an abortion rather than give birth to a child of shame. Then the men can arrange for the police to be notified, to have her arrested, sentenced and incarcerated. The husband is free to marry again.

Women who become pregnant after being seduced or raped are at risk also of being so upset by the consequences, including lack of social acceptance as victims, that they commit infanticide. Even if they miscarry, have a premature birth or a stillbirth, they are apparently often accused of infanticide. The men who raped them are not likely to be charged, according to a ground-breaking study of women in prison in Nepal (Integrated Development Systems 1982).

Prostitution. Some parents even sell their daughters into prostitution to be rid of them as a burden and to make money. Virgins bring the highest price. Some male relatives may choose to "enjoy" the girl first and only then sell her off. A few women report that even their husbands ask them to go into prostitution.[31] Women on their own may be forced into prostitution because of economic necessity and limited opportunities elsewhere. (This topic is addressed in more detail in Chapter 9.)

Psychological Violence and Mental Trauma

As indicated in Chapter 1, the UN Declaration on the Elimination of Violence against Women includes threat and psychological harm, not only physical or sexual forms of violence and traditional practice. An even larger percentage of women and girls have been subjected to emotional and psychological abuse than to physical abuse alone, as will be clear in Table 3, where relevant data are available. These forms of violence should be considered a major health issue in themselves, but they are usually trivialized by government, physicians and health care providers, as well as by the family. In global studies it is noted that some women report that they are more disturbed by psychological than physical violence (Heise, Pitanguy and Germain 1994, page 4). Depression among women is associated with being beaten, as reported by Bhatti et al. (n.d.).

A study from Bangladesh gives an idea of what may be considered mental trauma or torture there:

> Different forms of mental torture were described by women. The most common were threatening to divorce whenever there is a problem or disagreement, particularly related to dowry, not allowing them to talk with any man, demanding explanation for every word, and taunting about her father's house. (Afsana 1994)

And an activist from Pakistan gives his views, urging that psychological violence be given more attention:

> In a workshop one of the participant girls told me that back at home, they could not even laugh. If they did so, the mother would ask whether she had got involved with someone! And if she wept, the mother would ask what she had had [i.e., drink or drugs]! In my opinion, physical violence is not the most cruel. It is the psychological violence which is tormenting. The attitude resulting from a broken personality deteriorates the society even more. Society inflicts so many wounds on her personality that she hardly has anything for a good relationship. They [women who are tormented] do not have a normal behaviour. We produce shadows rather than a personality [in such women].

Why So Much Gender Violence?

The list of possible causes is long: tradition, content of television and movies, unemployment of men (who lose face) or women (who are blamed), poverty, structural adjustment, lack of education, personality disorders, alcoholism, drugs. When one looks at the reasons most frequently given in South Asia, they seem to be about inconsequential things, at least on the surface: in one study, "food not cooked properly" is the most frequently cited reason for abuse (Afsana 1994).

The imbalance of power between men and women is embedded in and supported by definitions of men as superior and women as inferior. These lead to gender violence. In global analyses, this has been commented on by Connors (in UN 1989b), Dobash and Dobash (1992), Coomaraswamy (UNCHR 1994) and others. Miranda Davies (1994, pages 6–7) elaborates on the point. She first lists the various theories for the cause of domestic violence: those that are about individuals and those that are about the structure of society. She concludes:

> Studies show that rather than representing an aberration, violence in the home is widely accepted and tolerated. It is an extension of the role society expects men to play in their domestic sphere. In this analysis, the abuse of women can be seen as a display of male power, the outcome of social relations in which women are kept in a position of inferiority to men, responsible to them and in need of protection by them. . . . [T]he structures of society act to confirm this inequality.

One wonders why in South Asia there might be more gender violence against women in the home than there apparently is elsewhere in the world. There is no clear answer yet. And why even ask when the problem is ubiquitous, anyway? As mentioned in the introduction, it is important to know what kind of problems are occurring, and where and why, so that prevention can be more effective: intervention follows epidemiology.

The South Asians themselves are on the way to finding out the true situation, the reasons for it, and what to do. Patriarchy is constantly mentioned by South Asian activists as the source for much of the problem of gender violence. That means both patriarchy as represented by local institutions and as reinforced by global institutions through "development," capitalism and media. Kamla Bhasin, a very well-known Indian woman leader in the movement of NGOs and women at grassroots as well as policy levels, sees patriarchy as an ideology as well as an institution. She notes that this is the case worldwide and that patriarchy leads to violence against women. The well-known "machismo"[32] in Latin America also reflects an ideology of patriarchy. In South Asia, as far as I know, there is no such popular term to sum up male attitudes of superiority and behaviour. Yet patriarchy is supported, and explicitly so, in many ways in public institutions as well as by families and individuals in South Asia.

Rather than being able simply to infer that there are patriarchal norms and values in South Asia, one hears direct statements justifying these, particularly with regard to custom, tradition and religious interpretations and the importance of maintaining them. Selected texts related to the two dominant religions in the region, Hinduism and Islam, are often cited as justifying patriarchal values and norms. The core values of these religions, however, have been found to be as in tune with human rights and equality for women as are those in other religions represented in the region (Arole 1999).[33]

In South Asia, there has been a swirl of ideas, brought by various waves of invaders, different religions, colonists, economic and development agents and practitioners, and commercial interests. There is a multiplicity of groups from various patriarchal structures, with the men all competing, displaying their power to each other, whether through "identity" politics, communalism, fundamentalism, globalization or military might.

Control of women, and posturing about it, are very much part of the social and political messages men give each other in South Asia. In part, this posturing conveys the idea that groups of men whose women are not "pure" are lesser beings in comparison to those whose women are. Control over their own women is a source of proof for men that they are real men, that their religion is also considered to be protected and strong, according to the purity and honour of the women.

Fortunately, some South Asian men as well as women are looking at questions about masculinity and femininity in relation to gender violence in South Asia, and can thus contribute to the debate about whether and why there is more domestic violence in the region and how to prevent it. The emphasis on imbalance of power between women and men, and underlying ideas of male superiority and female inferiority as a cause of violence, points to the exceptionally strong cultural traditions, structures and political bases that reinforce the idea of patriarchy. All too often, the patriarchal family has become a dangerous place for women and girls rather than a place of safety and protection. The dynamic behind gender violence in South Asia is discussed further in Chapter 5. The promise of change as gender roles are being questioned is taken up in Chapters 6 and 7.

Response of the Medical System to Trauma from Domestic Violence

Despite the high incidence of domestic violence in South Asia, health care professionals may be oblivious to or unconcerned with signs of it in patients. There are many indications that women's injuries are rarely classified as being due to domestic violence. Thus, it is nearly impossible for medical personnel to grasp the pandemic that exists and to become sufficiently concerned to take a public health approach. The first step is to have a system that will register domestic violence as a cause of injuries. A protocol is needed, as are reporting requirements.

It can be done, as indicated by the presence of the one study I found in South Asia, from Sri Lanka, about how injuries from wife-beating are classified and treated by medical personnel[34] (Dias and Fernando n.d.). The Sri Lankan study of admissions to a provincial general hospital describes the cases of 31 women admitted to a female ward during five months in 1995 with injuries that, it was established, were due to domestic violence and required surgical attention.[35] The seriousness of injuries was assessed, along with the women's backgrounds, the identity of the perpetrator and the woman's attitude to her injury and the perpetrator.

The women were aged 18 to 60, mostly married, and around 10 per cent had been pregnant when assaulted. The injuries were serious, including multiple fractures, head injuries and stab and gunshot wounds. Hospital stays were from two days to two weeks.

The authors note that diagnoses of domestic violence as the cause of injuries are often avoided in the medical system:

> The medical system has not been too accommodating to the challenge of domestic violence, even though a hospital is a point of contact to a victim willing to engage in help-seeking behaviour. Theoretically, a hospital not only has the facilities to treat physically-abused victims, but also a capability to diagnose cases and to refer to law enforcement agencies. In reality, the ability of the medical system to effectively co-ordinate such activities is severely limited. (Dias and Fernando n.d., page 1)

This characterization is very similar to the way doctors in most of the world have tended to respond to gender violence:

> While the available evidence suggests that the medical practitioner will be the first formal source of help that a victim of spouse abuse will approach, the response of doctors has, in the main, proved to be unsatisfactory. (UN 1989b, page 75)

There is an obvious danger that the health problems for women that are rooted in domestic violence will not be understood as part of an epidemic — let alone a pandemic — whether they result from acts of commission (such as burning, acid attacks, battering or assault) or acts of omission (such as extreme neglect, withholding food or denying health care), or both, when depression and suicide may result. Because the health system now tends to ignore domestic violence as the cause of trauma, women survivors will likely return to the same situations that were almost lethal — without counselling for them or their families, without legal protection or an alternative place to live or work. For example, only one woman in the Sri Lanka study planned to leave her husband, although in most cases the husband was the perpetrator.

Why is domestic violence so ignored by health practitioners? There are several reasons: women don't report it; if they do, physicians' attitudes to women's complaints may be biased, and women may even be blamed; there is the whole assumption that it is a private matter or inconsequential. And doctors are sometimes hesitant to get involved in reporting cases.

Pressures on Doctors: An Example

There are some types of injuries that are more obviously the result of gender violence than are others: burns by fire or acid, for example. Yet, few women who are burned explain how the injury really occurred. Now, cases are being dealt with more in terms of acute care rather than prevention. The challenge remains to focus on the latter.

Dr. Shahista Effindi,[36] a plastic surgeon who heads a hospital burns unit in a government hospital in Karachi, Pakistan, brings out related issues about burning and acid attacks.

> We get the most severe cases and do not take it upon us to find out about the causes of the burn, but somewhere along the line, the woman chooses to confide in us. If you put anything on fire, it burns. And most women usually burn over 40 per cent [of their body]. And anything over 20 per cent is considered lethal.
>
> We had quite a few women who were burned [intentionally], and they are usually surrounded by family, and they are either so badly burned that they can hardly communicate, but even then they tell our junior doctors or dressers [who change the bandages] whenever they get a chance or they confide in me, and request that we should

not tell anyone because if their husband goes to jail, they are concerned about who will look after their children. . . . So we concentrate more on treating the patient, and, even if they tell us [who burned them], we are unable to report the case. Usually, the husbands and families get away.

Often a girl is lighted with the trash and burned or kerosene is thrown on a young teenage girl and she is locked in a room and burned . . . or their noses are chopped off, without [anyone] fearing the consequences, because there are no consequences [for the perpetrator].

Usually, women don't have the confidence to report or confide that they were deliberately burned, and it is usually via hearsay that one learns about it. Out of all the patients, maybe only 2 per cent have themselves admitted to violence against them by burning. I firmly believe that the actual number of homicides is far greater than one hears of. But you can reach some conclusions by observing the distribution of the burns and find out the cause of the burn.

. . . We usually get the most severe and hopeless cases, but, even with all that, we have a very high survival rate, which is comparable to [the rest of] the world. . . . About 75 per cent survive, and 25 per cent die. The results we get are tremendous.

The results that Dr. Effindi describes reflect well on her training and dedication, as well as that of her staff and the hospital. The rates of survival she reports are exceptional. Of course, the costs for this kind of acute care for extensive burns are high, and are not possible for all facilities to bear. The scale of the problem has been reviewed by the Pakistan Commission of Inquiry for Women (1997, pages 80–81). Among its observations are these:

Over the past decade, murder or attempted murder by stove burning has become more common. Indicative of increasing marital violence and largely affecting the economically under-privileged, these cases are rarely pursued, nor are there adequate medical facilities for the treatment of victims. . . . The problem intensifies when cases are not reported by the hospitals; the police resist recording FIRs [First Information Report]; there are no proper investigative techniques for circumstantial evidence in burn cases, and cases get endlessly delayed. There are only three burn centres in hospitals in the whole of Pakistan, which are totally insufficient to deal with the scale of burn cases prevalent. In Lahore alone, 60-70 burn victims are struggling for their lives at any given time, at a survival rate of under 10 per cent. Many more are treated as outpatients, yet Lahore has only a 10-bed burn unit. The cost of treatment for serious burn cases is also massive, daily costs amounting to Rs. 7– 8 thousand.[37]

The Commission of Inquiry for Women (1997, page 81) made recommendations that cover health as well as legal system response. These include new legislation, new procedures for police, policies for legal support and financial responsibility of the State to be specified.[38] In addition, the Commission recommends, "More burn units should be immediately set up and the existing facilities expanded and improved."

The call for more burn units indicates that the Commission anticipates that stove-burnings will continue, perhaps even increase. They emphasize the criminal liability of manufacturers and the importance of new legal procedures, but not the need for advocacy to change public awareness and work for prevention.

Without an effective public health campaign against stove-burning, the costs to the

State for treating burns will increase, as will the costs for police time, medico-legal reporting and court costs.

Extraordinary efforts are being made by health professionals, like Dr. Effindi and her staff, to provide care to the victims of violence from burns. At the same time, one is reminded of the response in the 1950s to the poliomyelitis epidemic in the industrialized Western countries, devoting increasing resources to acute care and chronic sequelae. But it took a public health approach — prevention (with polio immunization in this case) — to eliminate the health problem. Similarly, a public health approach with prevention as the main goal is needed in addition to the acute care approach for burns if this form of violence is to end, along with its tremendous individual and institutional costs.

Most women who survive burns go right back into the same situation where they were burned in the first place. No attention is paid to the cause. Further trauma, or even death, awaits. Prevention efforts would help reduce cases and costs — now requiring a significant and inordinate proportion of very limited health care resources.

At least some small steps are being taken. For example, according to an interview conducted for UNICEF with Mahboob Ahmad Khan, then Legal Officer at the Human Rights Commission of Pakistan (HRCP), a pamphlet has been issued by HRCP on the subject of prevention of stove-burning: "This pamphlet aimed at educating people on prevention of such accidents. Also it contained instructions and a high court decision aimed at the police conducting such inquiries." If legal follow-up to cases is conducted seriously, that could also serve as a form of prevention.

Burns are only one manifestation of injuries from domestic violence that involve disproportionate costs. Others may not be explicitly acknowledged or calculated as part of the epidemic of domestic violence. Until they are, a focus on prevention, which saves costs as well as lives, will be delayed. Unfortunately, costs in both lives and money are likely to increase for burn cases under the present conditions, and without a focus on prevention.

The Public Cost of Private Pain

Studies of the direct and indirect costs of domestic violence are only beginning to be made in South Asia[39]. They are very much needed to influence public policy and the efforts for prevention.

The Inter-American Development Bank describes some findings for the United States and Canada that indicate that domestic violence is certainly not a private matter so far as its costs are concerned. These compel policy makers to take a new look at their budgetary and programme priorities. For example:

> In Canada, a study has shown that this type of violence costs the country $1.6 billion per year, including medical care for victims and lost productivity. In the United States, researchers have found that losses arising from domestic violence range from $10 billion to $67 billion. (MacCulloch 1997, page 2)

There are different methodologies for defining losses. If one adds the costs for the health system itself, those for the legal system and those to employers and families concerned, the amount races upward.

A study for New Zealand calculated costs of family violence by using three different scenarios: figures based on police involvement only, on five times as many people being involved and on labour-market income also lost because of family violence.

> The results of the analysis indicate that the annual cost of family violence in New Zealand is at least $1.2 billion. This is more than the $1.0 billion earned from our wool exports in 1993/94, nearly as much as the total amount of $1.4 billion spent on the unemployment benefit and around half of the $2.3 billion earned from forestry exports. (Snively 1994, page ii)

Even higher figures would be obtained if the costs were calculated to include those for the effects on children of violence to their mothers. For example, an Inter-American Development Bank study in Nicaragua touches on such costs:

> Children from families in which women are subjected to domestic violence are three times more likely to require medical care and are also hospitalized more frequently. Some 63 per cent of these children repeat a grade at school and on average drop out at age 9, compared with age 12 for children of women who are not the victims of severe abuse. (MacCulloch 1997, page 2)

A compelling study from Michigan (US) — the first of its kind — of the costs of prevention versus the costs of response associated with child abuse and its consequences is instructive. It shows that prevention costs are some 19 times less than the costs of dealing with the consequences of child abuse. The costs of child abuse were estimated at $823 million annually, while the costs of prevention programming were estimated at $43 million annually (Caldwell 1998, page 1). The author does not take into account the relation between the abuse of women and the abuse of children. Since such a relationship exists, the prevention of abuse to women should also reduce several aspects of child abuse, not only direct physical attack.

For the costs of maternal mortality, Rebecca Cook (1997), in a presentation at the regional consultation organized by UNFPA, suggested that, because of their present indifference to maternal mortality, governments be asked "to compare military lives lost in conflict with women's lives lost in pregnancy and childbirth, and to contrast the national budgets for military defence and maternity services."

A comparison of military lives lost and women's lives lost because of various forms of domestic violence would also be worthwhile, since, as we have seen for Bangladesh, the proxy category "burns, injury and suicide" is more frequently the cause of death for women than is "pregnancy-related causes."

While not reaching the same levels of costs in absolute terms as those in industrialized countries (due to various factors, such as much higher spending for health care), the costs for responding to gender violence in South Asia are very high for the countries concerned. If cases were identified by victims, family and medico-legal authorities, costs could be recognized and commensurate efforts made to reduce them through prevention.

Where government fails to respond to women's health needs, discriminatory political choices are revealed. Women's prescribed role to take care of others first would seem to be reflected in decisions about health care policies, budgets and services, given their relative neglect by the health care system. All the more reason to make the incidence of gender violence and its costs far more clear, with a priority for prevention as part of health policy.

Preventing Violence against Women:
The Case of Maternal Mortality

Increased Concern

Fortunately, a major initiative against maternal mortality is under way in South Asia. It promises results that could be important for improving the response of the health care system to other forms of gender violence. Governments and NGOs alike are increasing their efforts to reduce the very high rates of maternal mortality characteristic of the region. For example, the Prime Minister of Bangladesh launched a nationwide Safe Motherhood Campaign in 1997; Sri Lanka hosted an international meeting on the theme in 1998; and Pakistan held a national meeting on women's health the same year and took up the problems of both maternal mortality and domestic violence. All this recognition that maternal mortality is neither natural nor necessary has been long in coming. It coincides with questions that challenge narrow definitions for women's gender roles. At the national level, results of the various campaigns will not be known for some time. At the local level, however, there already are some results from work started earlier by dedicated individuals and organizations. The pioneers tend to see the problem of women's health as having to do with much more than obstetrics, as linked with violence and negative attitudes to women that need to be changed.

Maternal Mortality as a Form of Domestic Violence

All too often, a maternal death represents a disguised form of murder by beating or by an act of omission where a family could have sought available care in time to prevent the pregnant woman's death. One of the activist men interviewed in Nepal for this book told how he fought a husband and finally tied him up so that his pregnant wife could go to the hospital. When the husband insisted that his word be followed because "She is my wife!", the man helping her said, "But she is like my sister." More often than not, however, no one would interfere.

Some cultural factors. A Nepali lawyer working in a girl-trafficking community described the way he saw the problem when I asked him if maternal mortality was considered an issue there: "No," he said. "It is seen as a natural thing. They don't question it. We have to start at the root: discrimination against girls, lack of affection for daughters. We have to cut that. Then, they can question maternal mortality and do something to help stop it."

Pregnant women also contribute to their mortality risk by accepting the norms that limit their care and treatment. Shireen Huq, Nasreen's sister, works against gender violence also. In her interview for this book,[39] she recalls a telling incident in rural Bangladesh when she was working there as an interpreter with a documentary film team conducting interviews. The crew set up to film an interview with a rural woman in the courtyard in front of her hut. They had the right lighting, wanted an intimate mood, allowed time for an unstructured interview. A woman was in the background, on the veranda cutting vegetables. Shireen recalls, "At one point she wanted to get up and I requested, 'Until we finish, could you please stay in the frame, otherwise there is a problem of continuity.' And she stayed."

But when filming was over, the woman didn't leave. She wanted Shireen to ask the cameraman to go first. Shireen continues,

So I said, "Yes," and asked him to step outside for a minute. And she said that she had been bleeding. She had been sitting there bleeding, and it was horrifying. . . . Obviously, what had happened was that she had been miscarrying, sitting there quietly. I was shocked. I was just 18, and I didn't know what to do, but my immediate response was to rush her to the health centre, which was two miles away. We had our Land Rover, so I said, "No problem: we will take her to the health centre." They [people in the village] said, "No, no, she cannot go, her husband is not here." I said, "Why can't she go? It doesn't matter. Why does her husband have to be here? See, she needs medical attention." And they said, "No, absolutely not, she is not going without her husband's permission," etc.

Then I had to negotiate with her sister-in-law, with others, that she should go. I said, "We will take her, and anybody else who wants to go with her," etc. So they finally agreed. . . . We had to walk half a mile. I have not seen so much blood in my life. She was wearing a white sari and it was all dripping red. We took her to the health centre. There was a male doctor, and she just froze. So I had to sit there; I had to sit there and counsel her until she relaxed. And the only thing she did was cover her face: that was one way she could protect herself while we examined her. This was in 1972; things have changed now.

The situation is all too similar to that in the well-known fable "The Emperor's New Clothes," in which people exclaim about the Emperor's splendid raiment as he passes. After all, an Emperor must have fine clothes. It takes a little child to say that the Emperor really doesn't have any clothes at all. In South Asia most people will insist that they honour "Motherhood," even while many women are dying during pregnancy and childbirth. It took the voices of NGOs and some enlightened physicians to call out the truth like the honest child, to say that mothers are dying from neglect by their own families and governments.

Part of the explanation lies in the powerful stereotypes that govern expectations for behaviour of women in the family. Wives and mothers are generally expected to take care of others in the family before they take care of themselves. Their own health needs very likely suffer as a result. Any health problems they have may not even be acknowledged or considered important enough to justify spending scarce time and money on them. Nor do family members want to forgo services they expect from a wife and mother — which they would lose temporarily if she went to the doctor or hospital. Women have internalized these values and rarely complain.

High maternal mortality rates also represent hypocrisy in a society where people claim they honour and value motherhood. Why the discrepancy between values and slogans about women's place of honour in the family and the abuse and neglect they, even mothers, experience there? Again, part of the explanation lies in the powerful stereotypes that govern expectations for behaviour of women in the family. There is the idea that motherhood is natural, woman's work, and needs no assistance. No one talks about killing pregnant women, yet that is what happens when women don't get the care they need — even where it is available. This is no doubt due in large part to the fact that girls and women are considered disposable by so many, with the life purpose of supplying sons.

As the public health worker from Pakistan points out:

Violence against women is very cultural. Violence is often related to a woman's health, especially her reproductive health. Childbearing forced upon her by family is violence. Over 50 per cent of women, when they have three children, do not want more, but in reality the mean number of children they produce is over six, so the extra three children they produce are not because of their free will. There is pressure and coercion, to maybe have more boys.

Even more opportunities for prevention. Very significant efforts are clearly being made in South Asia to reduce maternal mortality, as called for by many who are concerned with the present high rates. As noted earlier with reference to the problem of stove-burnings as a health problem in Pakistan, the benefits of a public health approach — prevention — can be usefully emphasized: it is better, cheaper and more effective to prevent than to treat.

Two entry points readily available and appropriate for an inexpensive, effective intervention against battering are antenatal care and mother and child care after birth. Campbell (1998) points out the importance of adding questions about physical abuse at various stages of pregnancy and also check-ups of babies, given the connection frequently observed between wife-beating, beating in pregnancy and beating of children themselves when mothers are beaten. With high rates of maternal mortality reported due to beating, and increasing concerns about child abuse, it would seem inevitable to add these kinds of questions. Benefits for children as well as women are likely to be dramatic, especially since it has been reported that there is an increased chance of miscarriage and 40 times greater likelihood of death of newborns in the first year when mothers are beaten in pregnancy (Shrader Cox 1994).

Towards Prevention at the Village Level

Interviews from the Village

Excerpts follow from interviews with Durga (a continuation of her story) and Dr. Aruna Uprety[40] from Nepal, who works in rural areas, also for women's health.[41] Both want to prevent violence against women, of which maternal mortality is one part. They see access to health care, knowledge and decision-making about contraception, and changing outmoded negative attitudes and practices as priorities, along with more commitment from government for prevention of violence to women. The success of efforts like theirs to mobilize support locally for women's health can help inspire national and regional efforts to prevent domestic violence, which influences it. And the two can be successfully linked in prevention campaigns, as examples of two abuses of women's rights to life and health, both gender violence, which must not be tolerated.

Durga's story: Continuation. After her husband sent her off to her parents' house without her children, Durga's brother helped her to leave home, go to a city and get a job as a domestic. Her husband did not allow her to see her children. But Durga learned from a former neighbour that her husband was "negotiating the marriage of my 13-year-old daughter with his friend's son. The boy was 35, and my husband would be given Rs. 10,000 instead of having to give a dowry. They never sent my daughter to school."

Durga could not prevent the marriage. But with her employer's help, she was able to get her three youngest daughters, ages 6 to 10, to come and live with her. Her son also came. He told Durga that his 13-year-old sister had gone off crying with her new husband. Durga tells us the sad story that followed.

She was his third wife. As she was his newest wife, he took her to town where he worked. She looked after him, cooked, cleaned and entertained his friends. She also had a baby at age 15. A year later she lost her husband. She lost her baby, got married again, had two more children. Her second husband left her. Then she was with an Army officer with whom she had another baby. Later she was with a government driver who left her with a four-year-old. She died while delivering her sixth baby.

After all this, Durga changed her life.

That is when I decided to leave my job as a domestic servant and go back to my village and prevent other girls from this kind of violence. My employer was a doctor. She taught me about contraception and safe delivery methods. I felt girls in my village would really benefit from this knowledge. My daughter's death made me feel that I should go back as soon as possible. No one talks about the violence practised against young girls used as reproductive machines.

She teaches contraception to the women in the village:

They will have more control over their bodies and husbands will not be able to abuse them at will. Now I know most of the girls and women at least by face, if not name. I can go into their homes, talk to the younger husbands as my sons, talk to the older women as a contemporary. I can deal with them at a personal level. If it became a big institution, no one would listen. They would think all these ideas and concepts are for somebody else. Women would not be able to discuss their reproductive health at all. Government efforts are not personal and therefore not effective. Also the government is not sincere. After all, most positions are occupied by men. How can they understand what we have to go through?

Durga's campaign has spread to many blocks in her district. She now has three girls assisting her. She sees the links among girls' and women's low status, violence against them and health problems for them and their families. She calls for changes in attitudes to women and girls, to lessen health problems and inspire development itself. She also talks about the pervasiveness of violence to women and girls and about the need for it to be named as a public, social problem, not left as a private matter.

Violence is an act of aggression. In this sense, forms of violence are widespread and against women and girls. It cuts across caste, class and gender. The use of a girl or woman as man's personal property has led to man taking out his anger and frustrations on her. He can use or abuse her. Children watch their mothers being traumatized and either grow up with low self-esteem, primarily in girls, or become aggressive themselves. Because of this, violence is rising in India. . . . Physical attacks on unprotected women are common. Violence against women at home is considered a peripheral matter. It is treated as a family matter in which outsiders should not interfere. So women can be forced to keep bearing children in spite of illness or weakness and no one will question the ethics. India has been a feudal society. Without accepting it publicly our society has sanctioned violence against women.

Aruna Uprety, M.D.: "Women are treated like buffalo." Dr. Uprety has worked in the Far West of Nepal, on primary health care, women's health and gender issues. She is helping to strengthen a resource centre on maternal care and childcare. She says:

Because of the [low] status of women, there is a very high mortality rate. Even though there is no statistic showing how much mortality there is, so many women die. And in those parts a special word is given for delivery, "Jatkal." It means second life. After every delivery, if you live, it's not your life, it's second life.

. . . I would like to see the health problems of women with morbidity made better. A lot of women suffer from nutrition-deficiency diseases. Not only because they are poor. Women are treated like buffalo: If there is something that they can eat, OK; if there isn't, it doesn't matter.

This attitude hampers the whole family life. If woman is sick and cannot work, the husband and whole family will suffer. Woman is the centre of the family. And if the centre is weak, the whole thing will be weak.

So in those parts [the Far West], I am helping women during pregnancy and delivery. They should get some help. Very simple things. We shouldn't think about modern medicine and things like that. If women will not be put in the cowshed after delivery I think that it will be a big achievement.

It is thought that the woman is unholy at that time, so she should not touch anyone, she should do everything on her own. . . . She is not given nutritious food to eat at that time. She shouldn't be given meat, yoghurt, milk, because it seems that [according to them] if she is given milk and yoghurt, the god of milk will be angry and she will not produce milk. Stupid things. I think that it is violence.

Where I am working, women were never given green vegetables, lentils or good food after birth. But now they are being given [nutrition] education and very slowly they are starting to give [new mothers] all this good food, and I think that is good.

Asked about what should be changed for violence against women to stop, Dr. Uprety was very thoughtful:

This is a very difficult question. The most important thing that society needs to change is the attitude towards women and womanhood. . . . The women in village areas are only taken as a labour force. In order to do physical work they don't need literacy or education. So from the very childhood the parents send the boy to school and girl to work. The base is here, the attitude towards women, from the very first day of birth. There are so many proverbs which say that women are like shoes that you can change any time. And in the western part there is a common phrase that says that if there is a boy baby, the women can have meat, but if there is a girl she should have pumpkins. From the very beginning there are so many taboos. Girls are breastfed for five or six months and boys are breastfed for a long time. So from the very first day of birth, and from childhood and adolescence, there are so many problems because of the attitude towards women. And I think [public] education should have played a great role to change this.

As Dr. Uprety says, "When women are empowered, they will be able to have the health care they need." She adds: "I think that health problems cannot be solved till women are empowered. . . . Mostly, I want to see that men and women are equal."

Both Durga and Dr. Uprety see the interrelationship between women's relative lack of status, violence against women and maternal mortality. Both want to prevent violence against women, particularly, but not only, as connected with reproduction. Dr. Uprety speaks out on the neglect, in particular, of violence against women and what she sees as the State's lack of concern.

Women's Right to Health

Both CEDAW and CRC include articles related to the right to health: CEDAW Article 12 addresses the need for States Parties to eliminate discrimination against women in the field of health care. Article 14, about the particular problems of rural women and their significant roles in family survival, calls on States Parties to take measures to eliminate discrimination against women in rural areas and in rural development; access to adequate health care facilities is emphasized.

CRC Article 6 calls on States Parties to "ensure to the maximum extent possible the survival and development of the child" while Article 24 deals more explicitly with health and health services and calls on States Parties to ensure that no child is deprived of his or her right of access to such health care services." The article also covers the need for measures to develop, *inter alia*, preventive health care, to "ensure appropriate pre-natal and post-natal health care for mothers," and to abolish traditional practices "prejudicial to the health of the children." While CRC does not directly mention the fact that adolescents are often themselves mothers, Article 24 indeed provides the basis for particular attention to be given to the health care for young mothers.

Public Health Campaigns against all Forms of Domestic Violence

How to have successful public health campaigns against domestic violence? For the most part, such efforts have been focused on single issues and responses rather than on a holistic approach to prevention. Big campaigns that cross borders and sectors have been more against rape and girl-trafficking. Acts of violence by family members against their own are less likely to be taken as an important public health issue. They tend to be left as private matters and are relatively neglected so far as actual programmes in the field are concerned. UNIFEM initiated an advocacy campaign to end domestic violence in 1999, and also has some funds for follow-up with field projects, but — as important as these are — they are limited compared to need.

Before domestic violence will be taken seriously at national or regional level as a public health issue for prevention efforts by governments, silence about it obviously has to be broken. Incidence, severity and costs have to be measured and made better known at different levels of society. Otherwise, rates will increase and expensive acute care — sometimes not even labeled as dealing with domestic violence cases — will be the only recourse in the health field. And there are likely to be repeat cases, with additional costs so long as there is silence about the cause of the injuries and about the urgent need for prevention. (This is especially evident in the case of burns described above.)

Is domestic violence really taken seriously in South Asia now, even as a health issue, let alone as one of enough significance to justify prevention efforts within a public health model? This remains to be seen.

Dr. Uprety did not think violence against women was approached as it should be:

[E]ven human rights activists do not talk about women's problems. They never talk about violence against women as a human rights violation. They always talk about violence against only prisoners, political prisoners. But 51 per cent of the population is having problems with domestic violence, social violence, religious violence, but they don't talk about this. Personally, I feel that maybe out of a hundred, 0.01 has happened, and that is that people are talking about it at the policy level.

She also sees a direct but neglected connection between improving women's status and the health and development of the country as a whole:

> I don't think that some drastic thing will happen if changes are not made soon, but women will be suffering. That will have a negative impact on the whole country's development. Our country is suffering so much because 51 per cent of the population is behind. Women cannot only work physically, they can work mentally, too, and can work very well. But that resource has not been utilized. If we do not use this in one year, nothing is going to happen, but the situation of the country is going lower and lower. Now the problem, especially in big cities is with alcoholism and drugs. . . . Now there are problems with AIDS, with sexually transmitted diseases.
>
> We know that all these problems are there because women cannot say anything themselves. Women's role in the family has been minimized. A woman cannot say that her husband or her son is an alcoholic. She cannot say anything [to criticize men in the family], and this has a negative impact.

A View from Pakistan

The view from Pakistan seems more optimistic. In its report, the Pakistan National Forum on Women's Health made the following statement on gender violence in a health perspective (UNICEF 1997e, page 18):

> Violence is a public health problem and there is an epidemiology of violence as there is an epidemiology of poliomyelitis and that by learning to understand the causes or effects of violence, we can arrive at ways to govern it — the means of prevention in terms of health. The time is ripe to examine its effect on women's health and to limit the harmful consequences.

And the report also sees that violence is more than a problem for women alone:

> In Pakistan, the problem of violence against women would not have existed, had it not been for the fact of a patriarchal culture, which has led to women being seen as primarily in their biological role. These are major national issues and must be seen as such, not only in the context of women's physical, emotional and mental health but also in their sociological consequences.

One of the most immediate is the devastating effect on children, as we will see in the next chapter.

In summary, the examples from South Asians so far introduced tell us the following: violence against women is an epidemic in the region, part of the global pandemic. It reflects structural inequality, based on gender, in society. Gender violence obviously affects the lives and health of millions of individual women; nevertheless, it is often disregarded or treated as trivial, particularly in the case of domestic violence. Gender violence also affects the health of the community and its future, as a place where children can grow up to have their human potential and rights fulfilled. Looking at the effect of gender violence on women's lives and health is important in itself. It also invites awareness about the immense cost of gender violence — domestic violence in particular — to women, to the family and to society as a whole. And most important will be the much-needed attention, through multi-sectoral approaches and networks, linked also with policy levels, to prevent violence against women and girls at home. A family should be a safe place for all its members.

A Voice from Sri Lanka

A woman activist[42] from Sri Lanka, a victim-survivor of incest as a child, puts well the need to understand the costs of domestic violence, for an emphasis on prevention, rather than just making available some services for a few victims here and there:

> Well, I think first of all, violence against women and girl-children has to be seen as a serious threat to the public health and safety of a nation. It has to be prioritized in the same way as one prioritizes ethnic violence, civil war, you know, poverty, hunger, those kinds of things. There has to be an attitudinal shift definitely, in families and in society and in government, in other words [recognition] that this violence is being carried out solely because women are women. It is a gender-based violence, it is not coincidental. And to also . . . look for resources to deal with this issue . . . to allot them to deal with violence against women. In other words, to prioritize it and not deprioritize violence against women. And also to view, I think, women and girls as a very valuable part of one's community and society so that the value placed on women and girls is not going to be less than the value placed on men and boys. And to actually see violence against women and girls as a serious physical, emotional and financial burden on a nation because of the victimization. . . . I don't think that people look at the cost of violence against women and girls, and if they look at the cost of violence against women and girls, I think that people would want to eradicate it.

Endnotes

1   Shireen Huq of Naripokkho (Women's Side) in Bangladesh observed to me that although the life expectancy gap was closing, excess mortality for women remained (personal communication, August 1999, Bangladesh); however, it would seem that longevity gaps that favour men and excess mortality of women would co-vary.

2   Elsewhere in the world, such a small advantage for women's life expectancy is reported only in Guinea, Yemen and Zambia (Sivard 1995, pages 44–45).

3   According to Sivard, only two other countries in the world, Finland and Luxembourg, show women's life expectancy not exceeding men's. The dynamics behind this likely reflect changes in both women's and men's roles, since men have gained more in life expectancy since 35 years ago, when data showed that women outlived men by 10 and 6 years, respectively, in the these two countries.

4   The exception is Sri Lanka's standing on the GDI: its score is above that of both world and developing country averages. The worst scores from South Asia are on the GDI and the GEM for Nepal and Pakistan. Attainment in capabilities, as indicated by GDI, are with regard to life expectancy, education and income. Attainment in empowerment, as indicated by GEM, are with regard to political and professional participation and per capita income. The interested reader may wish to consult UNDP (1998) for more details on the methodology and about its application in South Asia, particularly from the point of view of the situation in Nepal. (Intracountry analyses by district are also available.)

5   "Durga" is a rural Indian woman interviewed for this book by Ruchira Gupta, award-winning Indian journalist and documentary film producer, who translated the interview into English from the woman's own language. Her name has been withheld to protect her anonymity.

6   It is generally considered unusual for a wife to be accepted in her natal home.

7   Durga speaks of her own country, but her words could apply equally well to other countries in the region and many outside it.

8   Interview arranged for this book through UNICEF Pakistan; name withheld.

9   The study includes a useful methodology for estimating the healthy years of life lost ("disability-adjusted life years," or DALYs) due to domestic violence and rape. The concept of DALYs "is based on the estimates of the share of life years lost to premature mortality and morbidity that can be attributed directly to gender-based victimization of women and girls 15–44" (Heise, Pitanguy and Germain 1994, page 48). Of some 58 million DALYs lost to women due to conditions that domestic violence and rape influence (that is, STDs, HIV, abortion, depression, post-traumatic stress disorder, unintentional injuries, suicide, homicide and intentional injury), a 6 per cent share is said to be attributable to violence and rape. This means almost 3.5 million life years lost for women so abused.

10   The data from Heise, Pitanguy and Germain (1994) covered various kinds of abuse, from psychological to economic, depending on the study concerned. The UN Statistical Office chose the most representative and comparable studies for its summary.

11 Studies from Heise, Pitanguy and Germain that are not about physical abuse have been excluded.

12 With thanks to Bandana Shrestha, researcher at UNICEF ROSA, who reviewed the studies.

13 It is possible that a few studies referred to as from different sources may be the same one, presented in different analyses by the authors.

14 A study from Nepal (Saathi 1997b), which indicates that 82 per cent of respondents know of at least one incidence of wife-beating, is not included here.

15 One reported for India includes two figures, 22 per cent and 75 per cent. Both are from self-reports by men about their wife-beating. The lowest figure is for upper-class men, the higher one, for lower-class men (Heise, Pitanguy and Germain 1994). Self-reports by perpetrators are likely to be self-serving and thus to underestimate violence against women

16 The International Center for Research on Women (ICRW) and The Centre for Development and Population Activities (cedpa), both in Washington, D.C., are supporting a number of studies worldwide as part of a programme Promoting Women in Development (PROWID), funded by the Office of Women in Development (G/WID) at the United States Agency for International Development (USAID). India is one of five countries in which there are PROWID research projects. The results are expected to provide more rigorous data on a number of aspects about violence against women.

17 This is discussed in more detail in Chapter 6 about women who speak out.

18 A 1999 report by Samya Burney for Human Rights Watch observes that the Pakistan Commission of Inquiry for Women has reported that violence against women is on of the country's most pervasive violation of human rights, yet the government has not responded to the problem in an serious way (back cover).

19 Personal communication, 1997; identity protected. See also Davies (1994), page 27. The definition of "acceptable" versus unacceptable domestic violence varies from place to place and time to time. For example, the "rule of thumb" was used in 18th-century England: so long as the rod a man used to beat his wife was no thicker than his thumb, his action did not count as abuse.

20 Interview arranged through UNICEF Bangladesh.

21 Interview for this book arranged through UNICEF Pakistan.

22 In law, "assault" is often considered as an act that threatens physical harm to a person (whether or not actual harm is done); "battery" refers to an act inflicting unlawful personal violence to another. However, people tend to use "assault" to mean "a violent physical or verbal attack" rather than a threat. Assault and battery in everyday parlance are rarely used to describe attacks on women by relatives in the home, but are reserved for those against whom criminal charges will be likely.

23 Personal communication with Kamla Bhasin, New Delhi, 1997; see also Narasimhan (1994), pages 43–51.

24 Interview arranged by UNICEF ROSA, in cooperation with UNICEF Pakistan.

25 If the incidence was roughly the same for 12 months, that would predict some 50 murders of women per year — predominantly by their families.

26 Sree Gururaja, Senior Advisor on Gender for UNICEF, adds that the same belief prevails in Africa (personal communication, 2 September 1999).

27 WHO (1999), "Abortion in the Developing World." WHO/
28. *www.who.int/inf-pr-1999/en/pr99-28.html*, 17 May, Geneva.

28 Comments are from an interview arranged and conducted by UNICEF ROSA. Name used with permission.

29 Countries do not necessarily agree with these figures, as I learned during my almost five years in the UNICEF Regional Office for South Asia.

30 This echoes the analysis made by Phyllis Chesler in *Women and Madness* concerning the United States.

31 Based on accounts referred to in some UNICEF conducted interviews for this book.

32 "Attitude of arrogance on the part of men with regard to women; sexual morality favourable to males," according to Espasa-Calpa 1989 (translated by Laura Rótolo, intern at UNICEF Headquarters).

33 This publication is based on the meeting "Religion, Ethics and the Rights of Children and Women in South Asia," 26–28 March 1996, which was organized by the UNICEF Regional Office for South Asia.

34 An interregional study of hospital responses to cases of domestic violence is currently under way. It includes some hospitals in New Delhi. See reference in Heise (n.d. b).

35 Cases with complications from rape or criminal abortion were excluded, as these were directed to the gynaecological ward.

36 Interview for this book arranged by UNICEF Pakistan.

37 These figures are for Lahore, where the cost of living is presumably lower than it is in Karachi.

38 A report by Sonya Burney for Human Rights Watch observes how the findings of the Commission of Inquiry for Women "were brushed aside by the Sharif government. As a result of such dismissive official attitudes, crimes of violence against women continue to be perpetrated with near total impunity" (Laura Rusu, personal communication, 20 October 1999).

39 For example, Times of India refers to a study by the International Centre for Research on Women in seven cities of India, which estimates that each "Assault on a housewife costs the family a loss of Rs 2000." (see Times of India 24/2/2000, Page 11.)

40 Arranged by UNICEF Bangladesh.

41 Interview arranged for this book and conducted by author. Name used by permission.

42 There were only four interviews dealing with maternal mortality in the entire 180 conducted for the project that is the basis for this book. This was so despite the fact that the topic was included in a list of types of gender violence for which interviewees were sought. This gap may be because maternal mortality has been generally accepted as part of the status quo, because it has not been looked at as a problem of gender discrimination and violence, or because there are other priorities for activists.

43 Interview arranged by UNICEF Sri Lanka.

Children Betrayed: Violence at Home

Imagine

I magine you are a child who looks to your mother and father for comfort, food, help, protection, love. Now your mother is screaming. Your father is beating her. She is bleeding. You want them to stop. There is nothing you can do. It will happen again and again. Still, you try. You run to them, pull at your father's clothes, trying to stop him. He hits you, too. Afterwards your mother is sad and afraid. She doesn't pay as much attention to you as she did before. She worries that your father will hit her again. About what — and when — she isn't sure.

If you are a girl, one day when your mother isn't home, your father, or uncle, or brother or cousin does something that hurts very much, that makes you bleed, that you don't understand. He says he will kill you, or your sister, or even your mother if you tell. This can all happen to a boy, too. If you tell your mother, she hits you, calls you a liar. Or, if you are bleeding so badly that she finds out, then she gets angry at your father, or blames you. He is angry, too, and beats you both. Or she wants to just take you and go. She doesn't know where. She may even have to leave without you, leave you with your father, who hurt her, who hurt you.

Worse, he can kill her — and you. Is it your fault?

If he brings a new wife, no one may care about you because your mother was thrown out, or left home, or is dead.

You have to work so much at home. You want to go to school but father says no, or he only lets you go sometimes. He or the other man still hurts you. You can't sleep, you don't get enough food or just can't eat like you did.

You keep seeing what happened to your mother and to you. Loud noises make you startle in fear. How can you stop it? Sometimes you just stare into space to make it stop, at least in your mind, for a bit. You try not to feel.

Where to go? There is no safe place. Father may ask you to go to the city with a friend or uncle, to work in someone's house and help send money home. But everything turns out so differently, so painfully. There is no escape. And even later, when you have a child, whose father's identity is uncertain, that child will be witness to all the suffering you must still go through.

If your father doesn't send you away like this, he tries to get you married to someone as soon as possible. You are still a girl. You don't want to get married and be tortured like your mother was, and have your own children hurt like you do. You are afraid, but have no choice.

As an older child — a young woman, a girl-woman — you think that you must have done very bad things before this life or in it for all this to happen. You may lose your temper and beat your child, too. You don't want her or his life to be like yours. You'd better hit the child again to stop her or him from being bad, like you, like the father. If that child is a girl, maybe she should just die early . . . as sometimes you wish you had.

If you are a boy and see your father beat your mother over and over, and feel powerless to stop it, you may learn to treat girls and women the same way. Or a deep and fierce sense of protection, frustrated for now, may lodge in your mind and heart, waiting, in conflict, for its chance to surface. You may want to kill your father, and you fear you might really try.

If you were hurt in a secret way, your sense of shame, your anger and frustration grows. You may want to do the same to other boys, so others will feel hurt, too, so you will be like your father — the one in control. Or you may want to fight the horror, yet wonder who and what you really are. You scream inside and sometimes do wild things. Alcohol or drugs may be a way to escape.

Whether a boy or a girl, you sometimes think about ways to escape — running away or even suicide.

Or you may be determined, even with everything that happened, to have a better life, somehow.

Maybe you can even help others like yourself.

Reality

For millions of children in South Asia it does not take an act of imagination to picture themselves in one of these stories. In one aspect or another, this has been their life. It is, however, a story only now being told. "Millions" may sound like an exaggeration, but it is not. We do not have all the information needed for exact figures, but we have enough for informed and compelling estimates, as this book will show in more detail in the conclusion. The extent of our surprise at the likely high numbers of those affected shows how much adjustment is needed, urgently, in our understanding about the scale of the problem and in setting new priorities to confront it.

At the global level, WHO has recognized child abuse as a major public health problem. It estimates that 40 million children ages 0 to 14 "suffer from abuse and neglect and require health and social care." Studies of sexual abuse from around the world are said to indicate a prevalence of 7 per cent to 34 per cent among girls and 3 per cent to 29 per cent among boys (WHO 1999d). Figures go even higher in some studies. For example, the National Clearinghouse on Family Violence, Canada (1997, page 2) reports that "the most extensive study of child sexual abuse in Canada . . . indicates that, among adult Canadians, 53 percent of women and 31 percent of men were sexually abused when they were children." (Obviously, incidence will vary depending on how "sexual abuse" is defined.)

A report about women on welfare in the United States (DeParle 1999) shows that the incidence of childhood sexual abuse is markedly higher among them than for the general population in the United States, with a median figure of 33 per cent based on six studies from welfare populations, compared to 18 per cent based on a 1994 review of 19 studies in the general population. Incidence of 20–25 per cent is currently accepted by experts, the author notes. Also, he quotes a clinical psychologist who says that the abused children who heal quickest are those whose stories are believed. "But when the victim's mother sides with the abuser . . . you're talking about multiple trauma" (page 28).

If we were to add the numbers of girls and boys affected by witnessing violence at home, the need for urgent action would be even more apparent. Far too little attention has been given to acknowledge and ameliorate the impact on children from witnessing violence and abuse while growing up, let alone from being its direct target. As for witnessing violence in the family, the possible effects — including post-traumatic stress syndrome — are becoming better known. Knapp (1998) explains that silence about the problem is due to the lack of physical scars as well as little awareness or even denial that witnessing violence affects children of all ages. She points out that children younger than two can be affected by witnessing violence and that

> there is the assumption that the very young do not intellectually register what they have witnessed. Yet some case studies show that children nonverbally express effects of exposure to traumatic events by 16 months of age and that post-traumatic reactions occur in children fewer than 2 years of age that can be profound, long-lasting and seem similar to reactions of older children and adults. It has been suggested that profound and perhaps permanent brain changes can result following [witnessing] violent trauma in the first three years of life. (page 355)

From studies in various parts of the world, it is already known that when a child grows up in a violent home, her or his nutrition, health, behaviour at school, emotional well-being and self-esteem are more at risk than they would be if the child came from a peaceful home. In later life, children from violent homes are at greater risk to be addicted to drugs or alcohol, to be involved in crime, to commit suicide, to be recruited as prostitutes, to have difficulties in their sexual relations and to be violent themselves with partners, peers and children. (See Hennes and Calhoun 1998 for a review of related research primarily from developed countries and Sheikh 1997 and Hayward 1997a for reviews that also touch on South Asia.) Violence at home in one generation is multiplied in the next: it has been reported that boys who observe a father's violence against their mother have a 1,000 per cent greater risk of repeating abuse with their own future spouse, while girls who are exposed to parental violence are at higher risk of finding themselves in a future violent relationship (Knapp 1998, page 359). National Clearinghouse on Family Violence, Canada (1996) also reports links between children's witnessing violence and learning to be violent. Their review points out that "children from violent homes are being taught that violence is an effective way to gain power and control over others." Also, it observes that they are more likely to excuse violent behaviour as well as to engage in it in both childhood and adulthood (with girls affected more by accepting violence towards them than by being violent) (page 4).

In South Asia, girls, especially, are sometimes themselves objects of sexual abuse in the family, even by the father and other close male relatives. Girls may also be sold into sexual slavery by family members. Girls who run away to escape abuse at home risk becoming prostitutes if there is no safe haven for them.

A less dramatic form of child abuse that hurts girls in particular is neglect. One might well call these girls "the twice neglected" — once at home and again by society.

Neglect kills millions, slowly, simply because they are unwanted girls. We tend to overlook them because they die quietly, and because the first reports about them were usually presented in terms of missing millions of women based on statistical analyses of sex ratios in the population structure without desegregation by age or compelling details of individual cases. More detailed analysis, along with increased interest in the related work of 1998 Nobel laureate Amartya Sen, is creating more interest in and acknowledgement of the problem, however.

Foeticide after sex-determination tests takes the lives of some girls before they are born; infanticide kills others, again simply because they are unwanted as girls. Negative attitudes towards girls seem to be linked with the idea that girls are not an asset but an economic liability.

Among girls who live and grow up are those who are married when they are still children. Afterwards they live a very limited life, with a greater chance of being abused as young wives than do older brides, according to some recent findings in South Asia.

In South Asian families, then, there are at least six kinds of violence against girls in particular:

- sexual abuse, incest and rape by family members;
- recruitment by family members into prostitution;
- neglect by family members, even to the point of death;
- foeticide and infanticide;
- dowry demands;
- wife abuse — of girl-women, within child marriage.[1]

This review starts with the most dramatic cases the South Asian activists address: incest and rape of girls in the family. Then it moves through an account of the other types of family violence in the natal home that are directed primarily at girls. Then it turns to the marital family. Abuse of girl-women who are married when under 18, the legal age of marriage in CRC, is the last topic regarding direct violence against girls. The less acknowledged but troublesome effects of witnessing family violence are also discussed.

Activists' efforts are featured throughout the chapter.

Anyone who knows about any form of abuse to children in the family but who does not act to stop it can be seen as an accessory, "a passive perpetrator," as one activist called himself before he spoke out. It is negligent or worse to ignore the violence, whether it is direct or indirect, through acts of commission or omission, with immediate or long-term effects. Fortunately, some parents, professionals and even children are saying "Enough!" and breaking the silence about gender violence at home, and the ways it hurts girls in particular. Here, we feature and build on the voices and work of some of the courageous South Asians who question what happens to children in families. They do so precisely because they believe that breaking the silence is the first step towards diagnosing present weaknesses and determining what is needed to strengthen family life. One of the most urgent, and difficult, problems to reveal is sexual abuse and incest of girls at home. In fact, a group of 65 South Asian activists identified sexual abuse, particularly of girls from ages 5 to 14, and by family members, as the most frequent form of child abuse needing attention in the region (UNICEF 1998b, pages 94–95).

Sexual Abuse, Incest and Rape of Girls

Definitions

"Child sexual abuse" refers to a range of activities: touching and fondling of a child's genitals, forcing a child to touch and fondle another person's genitals, penetration of the child's vagina or anus by a penis (referred to as rape and sodomy, respectively), with or without ejaculation. When an object is used, or the hand, people may not take it so seriously. In most cases, a legal definition of rape requires evidence of penile penetration. Incest is, in effect, rape by a close relative, which is obviously difficult to claim or prove in male-dominated families. When they talk about sexual abuse, rape and incest, activists and others do not always use the terms precisely. "Molestation," "sexual assault" and "outraging the modesty" are additional terms that are sometimes used without definition, introducing even more ambiguity. Shekar Seshadri, an Indian child psychiatrist working in Bangalore with the National Institutes of Mental Health and Neurological Sciences (NIMHANS) points out that it is not customary, even among psychiatrists, in South Asia to talk precisely about sexual abuse. The lack of language for discussing the subject of child sexual abuse properly makes diagnosis, treatment and other interventions problematic. The context of what is said often makes it clear, however, that incest is involved even if it is not so stated.

A legal approach and anatomical descriptions do not capture the impact or magnitude of the problems for children. Some of the activists and studies of sexual abuse or child rape from Bangladesh, India, Nepal, Pakistan and Sri Lanka begin to do so.

Some Examples from South Asian Activists

An Indian woman,[2] who is a lawyer and activist, states bluntly:

> I have rescued many girls. An 11-year-old girl became pregnant after she was raped by her uncle. Another girl was thrown out of her home by her stepmother. Many people believe that venereal diseases can be cured by having sex with a virgin. This is leading to more cases of rape. Contrary to what people think, it is not outsiders who rape, but relatives within the family, neighbours, friends and even servants.

It is a reality repeated over and over again. Another Indian woman, a psychiatric social worker, reports:

> I'm disturbed by the sexual abuse of young girls. This destroys not only their childhood, but a whole part of them. The reason is that this sort of violence is hidden and covered, so she is denied therapeutic help to undo the harm. She lives with it and deepens the hurt with time.

> My own experience is that I was assaulted when I was 16 years old. I felt that there were many more girls like me. I know of a three-year-old child who was raped by her father, and I had to deal with the mental breakdown of the mother and the stupefied shock of the child.

An Indian woman NGO leader[3] commented about a different incident:

> Cases like this where girls are being raped by their own cousins or uncles in their very homes are also quite common. A girl is unsafe, even in her own home because [the men]

think they will get away with it. Nobody will come to know. The girl, out of shame and family honour, will not disclose it to anyone.

From Pakistan, a woman psychiatrist[4] points out some of the difficulties she has encountered when trying to deal with sexual abuse of girls in the family:

We are presently dealing with a seven- or eight-year-old girl who has been a victim of sexual abuse. Because of this, she has gained an unnatural interest in sexuality inappropriate for her. The mother . . . is taking out her anger more on this child, blaming her and [only] at times blaming the father.

There was another case when the stepfather was attempting to assault his 13-year-old stepdaughter. The mother was trying to get her daughter married off, instead of getting rid of this man. We have to try to work with the family and keep the child's best interest in mind. If we take the child away, we don't have safe shelters where we could place the child for a few weeks or months. In this great big city we lack any such facilities.

Dr. Shershah Syed, Convenor of the Pakistan National Forum on Women's Health, gives an account of three girls, ages 2, 14 and 15, who were sexually abused in their families. Two were pregnant and victims of incest, one by the father, the other by her uncle. Dr. Syed points out that none of the girls or their female relatives were willing to discuss the matter with family or police. They were afraid of being victimized even more. He says that there are many more of these kinds of cases but that "the society does not want to acknowledge this situation. There is no mechanism available to help these unfortunate victims of incest" (Syed n.d.).

The countries of South Asia are not the first to have to deal with the reality of incest, child sexual abuse and child rape. Nor are they the first to deal with denial about it. The first publication in Europe on sexual abuse, including incest of children, is said to be Ambroise Auguste Tardieu's "A Medico-Legal Study of Assaults on Children," published in France in 1857 (Masson 1984). The book describes 32 cases of extreme abuse of children by their caretakers, including their own parents. Masson indicates that between 1858 and 1869 in France, some 11,576 cases of rape or attempted rape were reported, including 9,125 of children (primarily girls it seems) under 16, with the majority from ages 4 to 12. But the courts rarely took seriously testimony and evidence that would implicate male relatives. In the England of the 1800s, judges regularly threw out cases with incest charges as an affront to public sensibility. Children were not to be believed if they claimed men violated them (Clark 1987). Judith Lewis Herman (1981, page 10) describes how even Freud could not bring himself to state publicly a belief expressed in his private correspondence that an "essential point" in "hysteria" or claimed neurosis among females was childhood sexual trauma caused by incest. He knew the stories of incest told to him by patients were true, but he chose to spare men rather than address the real problem. Herman goes on to point out that, to this day, physicians and judges are often influenced by the frequently held view that girls who describe incidents of incest cannot be believed; they therefore dismiss evidence that might otherwise help indict important men — or any men at all (pages 11–12).[5] Masson (1984) points out that Freud actually had given a paper about incest in which he acknowledged its importance in the aetiology of hysteria. The reaction was so negative, however, that Freud later disavowed his earlier views and said that memories of incest were based on fantasy. Furthermore, Freud was of the opinion that when seduction of children did occur in the family, it was by mothers rather than fathers. Masson finds this strange since Freud very likely accompanied Tardieu to the morgue for some examinations of child victims of sexual abuse, rape or incest, and murder.

The examples and discussion so far point to the importance of our giving more attention everywhere to preventing and bringing to justice cases of sexual abuse of girls (and sometimes of boys) in the family. As Tardieu wrote in 1857, "The executioners of these children showed more often than not to be the very people who gave them life — this is one of the most terrifying problems that can trouble the heart of man" (Masson 1984).

Some Research from South Asia

- A survey of child sexual abuse in Bangladesh all too easily found numerous cases. Of more than 150 persons interviewed, half admitted experiencing some form of child sexual abuse. "It appears that no age is a safe age. Children as young as five/six years have been abused," the study says (Breaking the Silence Group 1997, page 3). Children ages 10 to 14 were the ones most frequently abused, among both girls and boys.

- For 1991–1996 in Bangladesh, the official figure for rape is 5,738, "as quoted in the parliament by the Home Minister himself. . . . [T]his may be taken as only the tip of an ice-berg. The most shocking part of the information was the fact that 933 of the victims of rape i.e. 16.26% were minors. This points to the extent of social failure to protect girl children from such horrible violation" (Jahan and Islam 1997, page 8).

- Figures from Delhi are equally grim: In the first six months of 1994, nearly two out of three rape victims were children. In 1993, out of a total of 321 victims, 197 were minors, of whom 35 were less than seven years old and 119 were between 12 and 16 years old. Meanwhile, in the small city of Maharashtra, India, was the so-called Jalgaon scandal involving 500 girls under 16 years of age who were sexually abused and then photographed to blackmail them later (Mehra and Chattoraj 1995).

- The *Crime in India 1997* report shows that "of all the victims of rape cases in 1997, children alone accounted 28.8 per cent share. The cases of Rape of Children below the age of 10 years were on a rise every year in the country except in 1996 since 1993. . . . [W]hen compared to the figures of 1993, the victims in the age group below 10 years increased by 21.4 per cent while those in the age group 10–16 years increased significantly by 32.1 per cent" (National Crime Records Bureau 1999, page 178). The total of child rapes officially reported for children below 10 for 1997 was 770; for children 10–16 years, 3,644.

- There is a new motivation for child rape in South Asia, since some men with AIDS will opt for what they think of as safe sex, for the belief is considered widespread that intercourse with a virgin offers a cure for AIDS — such as a reported case of a 22-year-old police constable in Delhi who raped and killed a nine-year-old girl. "He believed that if he had sexual intercourse with a young virgin girl he would be cured of AIDS" (Manchanda 1994, page 137).

- Within the family, incest and sexual abuse of children is being rated as having a greater incidence than would have been thought, as references in this section indicate. The noted psychiatrist Sudhir Kakkar has estimated that at least some 600,000 to 700,000 Indian children are likely to have experienced sexual abuse, most from a family member (Kakkar 1996, page 15).

- One study from Nepal reports that more than 50 per cent of all victims of rape are girls under the age of 16, most of whom are raped by relatives (Pradhan 1996, cited in Sheikh 1997). And a survey on domestic violence found that 13 per cent of the respondents knew about at least one case of child sexual abuse (Saathi 1997a, pages 9–10).

- In Pakistan, a 1990 survey of 120 female students 16 to 18 years old at St. Joseph's College, Karachi, showed that 6 per cent reported disturbing childhood sexual experiences with a relative or a servant. In a 1992 study of 220 females ages 17 to 19, at four sites in Karachi, 15 per cent reported "disturbing sexual encounters" in childhood (Khan 1994, regarding the 1994 Bedari Workshop in Islamabad).

- Scrutiny of nine national papers in Pakistan from January to September 1997 showed 354 reported cases of child abuse. Of these, 97 were gang rape (Saifullah 1997). Another Pakistani study (Mehdi-Barlas 1997) finds that, based only on reported cases, one can calculate that a rape incident involving a woman/child occurs in Pakistan at least once every three hours on average. In one 10-day period, 50 cases were reported in Punjab alone. More than 20 victims were minors, the youngest being eight years old.

- The 1997 Report of the Commission of Inquiry for Women, Pakistan, includes additional information on child abuse, from a variety of sources:

In 1994, two psychiatrists in Karachi did separate informal studies with identical findings, indicating an incidence of child sexual abuse similar to the West. According to their studies, 20% had suffered uncomfortable sexual experiences as children, 30% knew someone who had been abused as a child. A 1994 study conducted by a psychologist from Punjab University of 9000 low-income girls from 26 cities showed 5–15% who reported child sexual abuse.[6] . . . The experience of an organisation working on this issue in Islamabad indicates that at least 80% [of] people know someone who has been sexually abused, the only lower figure coming from a group of doctors and nurses where 38% said they knew victims, most outside their professional lives. The indication that cases of child sexual abuse may be on the rise or is getting reported more often comes from the medico-legal department in Karachi which reported an average of 34 cases of rape and abduction of girls under 15 for a six-month period in 1992, 73 for a similar period in 1994. (Commission of Inquiry for Women 1997, page 84)

- A report by Simorgh, an NGO in Pakistan, draws attention to a problem that mentally disturbed or retarded children and adults face:

Those women and girls who fall into this category are extremely vulnerable to rape as the rapist has no fear that the victim will be able to identify him or be believed if she does. Dr. Khalida Tareen who has been working with retarded children said that many of them were sexually molested and raped by relatives, friends of the family or domestic servants. The rape of mentally retarded girls is so frequent that Dr. Tareen recommends a hysterectomy so the girls are spared the trauma of pregnancy. Again the girl seen as a potential victim pays by having a part of her body removed.

Stories of rape in mental asylums abound. There too hysterectomy is a standard procedure in the absence of adequate protection for women. (Simorgh 1990, page 48)

- From Sri Lanka, ground-breaking retrospective research with advanced secondary and university students revealed that 12 per cent of girls said that they had experienced sexual abuse as children, and that even more boys — 20 per cent — said they had. Girls avoided divulging their relationship (if any) to the perpetrators. Boys most often said it was a family member (Harendra de Silva 1996).

Underreporting

As horrendous as official statistics and newspaper reports are, studies indicate that reported figures severely underestimate the extent of the problem. For example, Kirti Singh (1998, pages 30–32) writes:

The fact that, sexual assaults against children is one of the most underreported crimes in the country, has been highlighted by several women's groups apart from government statistics. In one background paper distributed by one group, it was estimated that for every reported crime against children there are 100 which are not reported.

Child abuse, within the family, cuts across class and caste divides and is equally prevalent amongst both the poor sections of Indian society as well as upper classes, where both the criminal and the vulnerable victim reside.

Reporting of child sexual assaults may be even lower and less accurate in smaller cities and towns, where shaming mechanisms are stronger than in urban centres. For example, in the Delhi figures for rapes reported in 1993, as mentioned earlier, 61 per cent were of minors. All-India figures for 1990 show that of 9,863 cases reported, 2,484 were of children below the age of 16, that is, 25 per cent of all reported rapes — still a high number but far less than that for Delhi in 1993.

One reason for low reporting of sexual abuse and assault is the personal shame that comes with it. Unlike most other crimes where the survivor can seek public justice and can state that the other person was at fault, sexual assault is likely to lead to blame of the victim. Even if victim-survivors know they aren't to blame, their sense of disgust and dirtiness, their fear of retribution by the perpetrator, of social ostracism, their knowledge that the justice system will likely not treat the offence seriously, their fear of not being believed — all these are so overwhelming that most survivors choose to stay silent. (Even in confidential surveys many people won't admit to having been assaulted. Some people will say they know someone who was assaulted rather than admit they were assaulted themselves.)

Yes, a Family Affair

Perhaps the most prevalent reason for low rates of reporting is that, contrary to popular myth, most sexual assaults are not committed by strangers. For example, Wijayatilake (n.d. a, page 7) in a paper on domestic violence in Sri Lanka, says:

There are many incidents that go unreported or undocumented where the innocent victim is in a custodial position. When a member of the family, such as a brother, father, grandfather or uncle is the offender, the victims themselves as well as their family members fear humiliation and of being ostracised by the rest of the community. As a result, such offence go unreported and no redress is found for the victim, who could be a child or an adolescent who would be mentally and physically scarred for life.

She described the unreported case of a six-year-old girl who had been raped by an uncle while her grandmother, with whom she lived, was at the corner hawking vegetables:

[S]he found the child tearful and bruised. When questioned little Ramani haltingly by related how the uncle, had hurt her, of course Ramani did not realise that she had been raped. Later when her medical officer at the municipal medical clinic examined the child, he informed the grandmother that the child had been raped. But the old women did not want to report the matter to the police, since she feared them arresting her son, as a result of her protective feeling towards her son, the offender went unpunished. The crime was unreported, hidden and "covered up."

Also, the Bangladeshi study cited above found

that most of the abuse takes place at home and by those who have ready access [and are] members of the [allegedly] safe circle [of family and close friends.] Strangers who abuse are few and far between. The report also finds that the abusers continue to maintain links with the family, even after committing abuse. The family circle is kept intact even at the cost of a family member being abused. (Breaking the Silence Group 1997, page 9)

As Fawad Usman Khan of War Against Rape (WAR) in Lahore, Pakistan, observes, "Many educated people in Pakistan refuse to accept the existence of incest in our society simply because such horrendous cases rarely make it to the press" (Khan 1994, pages 27–28). Psychiatrists point out that child molestation and sexual abuse are far more common than is believed.

Jasjit Purewal (1995, page 6), from India, writes that

the family can rarely cope with the public ignominy that it will lead to. Since the child cannot negotiate its own safety, the family often decides against making the crime public. The argument is for "keeping the family together." The child and her future [are] sacrificed to the public image of the family.

Also from India, the comments of Mehra and Chattoraj (1995, page 137) on incest, or "rape cases within the family," are worth reporting at length. Figures on rape in India, they say:

reveal only a tip of the iceberg. Rape cases within the family are rarely reported in India. The finding of a ground breaking study (1994) recently conducted in and around Bangalore by [SAMVADA, an NGO and] NIMHANS [the National Institutes of Mental Health and Neurological Sciences] furnished the first disturbing indications that a significant proportion of Indian girls suffer sexual abuse as minors. And more often than not the perpetrator is a member of the family. 348 girls from 12 Bangalore schools and colleges were interviewed. Researchers found it particularly difficult to break through to the survivors of childhood sexual abuse at the two rural colleges. But the statistics that emerged from the study told an eloquent if shocking story. Three out of every 20 girls interviewed [15 per cent] had experienced serious forms of sexual abuse including rape, and [for] one third of these [1 in 20 girls] it occurred when they were less than 10 years old.

> Five out of [every] 10 had been molested or had been targeted for sexual overtures as children, while 8 out of 10 had been victims of physical abuse like breast squeezing and bottom pinching, at an early age. Most survivors had been left with long lasting scars such as depression . . . and a deep-rooted distrust of men. But perhaps the most upsetting finding was that as many as 55 per cent of the men responsible for abuse were family members, brothers, cousins or close relatives. In a culture which places great importance on female virginity (equating it with purity, virtue and honour) the trauma of an abused girl child is aggravated by a sense of worthlessness.

Surveys on child sexual abuse by Indian psychiatrist Dr. Shekar Seshadri,[7] reported in an interview for this book, found that "almost 55 per cent of this abuse occurs within the family, not necessarily the first-degree relatives but cousins, uncles and so on. A substantial portion of it actually occurs before the girls reach puberty, before the age of nine. It's not as though it is anatomical sexuality that serves as some kind of provocation for an abuser."

How does prevalence of child sexual abuse compare with other countries and cultures around the world? It is impossible to say with certainty at this stage. Khan suggests that rates of child sexual abuse in Pakistan are similar to those elsewhere. Dr. Seshadri thinks that "the prevalence of child sexual abuse in India is not substantially higher than in other countries. It's about the same, about 15 per cent [of children], neither abnormally higher nor abnormally lower."

These opinions are either comforting or disquieting, depending on whether one focuses on the gravity of the problem or is primarily reassured that it is apparently similar in South Asia and other parts of the world. But the truth is, it is still too soon to state the actual prevalence of child sexual abuse in South Asia with certainty. Millions of children are affected and their problems are, in general, being neglected.

More studies — and social services — should be encouraged. Few studies are available and these have relatively small samples; also, they use a wide range of methodologies, some more precise and scientific than others. And it matters what terminology is used. Different answers to the question of what constitutes sexual assault can lead to wide-ranging data on incidence. For example, in some studies and some areas, sexual assault is deemed to have occurred only where penile penetration occurs. As Dr. Seshadri points out in his interview:

> The Indian Penal Code speaks about rape on the one hand and the outraging of modesty on the other. There is an entire grey area in between. If a child doesn't satisfy criteria for penile penetration or if it's digital, or penetration by some other object, then it doesn't fit, as there is no space and legitimacy for the child in the law where psychological harm is caused. You can document a bruise or a vaginal tear, but how do you document psychological trauma?

First of all, one has to be able to admit that it exists. Here, again, Saad Raheem Sheikh's words challenge us:

In our societies, clans and families, we know certain young girls or women, who from
teenage onwards have been withdrawn, scared, non-communicative or somewhat strange.
The family says she is schizophrenic or psychological. Has anyone ever had the courage to
say that she was sexually assaulted? The fact that these assaults came from close relatives,
stigma comes in and in the name of family integrity and to preserve the modesty of the girl,
the real story is hushed up and the poor girl suffers her whole life. Incidents of incest are
increasing in our countries — yet, no voice is raised. We are all obedient, we love our
parents and family elders, we don't want a scandal in our families, any disclosure will
destroy the family fabric. Suppression is best for all concerned.[8]

The power of the family to abuse — and suppress the victim-survivor along with any
discussion of the matter — is indicated by South Asian activists' answers to written
questions about the main causes of child abuse put to them at a regional meeting.
Choices made most frequently by some 65 activists were "patriarchy/power relations
within the family" (N=28) and "a parent or caretaker abused when young" (N=24).
Economic reasons and lack of education followed. The most frequently recommended
interventions were improved services, such as counselling, medical and legal (N=44),
along with police and government agency action (N=43), followed by "prevention"
(N=23) (UNICEF 1998b, pages 94–95).

Psychological Effects of Sexual Abuse

Girls suffer from a sense of abandonment as well as violation after abuse. Although
South Asian studies about the impact of sexual abuse on girls are relatively few, what
has been carried out reveals, first of all, the deep psychological impact on both mother
and child. Purewal (1995, pages 157–158) suggests that:

> Mothers are often unable to take action against family members abusing the child,
> particularly when the abuser is the father. Economic dependence, low sense of self, lack of
> power within the family, incapacity to accept the responsibilities of a single parent and the
> moral shame of the act keep mothers quiet. The sense of guilt and blame that the mother
> feels is accentuated by society which categorically hints that the mother's sexual
> inadequacy has led to her daughter's abuse. These sad and complex pressures on women
> per se often make the mothers silent and tragic spectators [of] the abuse of their own
> daughters, often denying it vehemently.

In countries where there has been more extensive research, we can see clear
conclusions about the psychological impact. For example, research in the United States
shows that sexual abuse has a significant and lasting detrimental effect in up to two
thirds of victims. One fifth of all child sexual abuse victims evidence serious and
permanent psychological effects, but for almost all children there are effects that last
for years. Female incest victims feel abandoned by their mothers and emotionally
abandoned by both parents, and they develop negative images of their mothers and
themselves. They also report problems in interpersonal relationships, feelings of
isolation and mistrust of men. Early victimization leaves women more vulnerable and
may increase the chances of future victimization (Heise, Pitanguy and Germain 1994,
page 20).

> Like women, men who are abused as children also feel they are unfit human beings. Filled
> with shame, they experience themselves as profoundly defective and horribly toxic. (Rauch
> and Jones 1995, cited in Sheikh 1997, page 6)

They suffer from anxiety, depression, hostility, anger, impaired relationships, low self-esteem, sexual dysfunction, sleep disturbance and suicidal ideas and behaviour (Hopper 1997).

A study in New Zealand points to low self-esteem, anxiety and difficulty in school for abused children and, later, in adult relationships. Interviews with 497 children revealed that childhood abuse, in any form, is associated with higher rates of psychopathology, sexual difficulties, decreased self-esteem and interpersonal problems (Mullen et al. 1996).

Segolene Royal, then Minister for Schools in France, suggests that "many of the 800 annual suicides by French youngsters occur . . . because they are subjected to sexual aggression that destroys them" (quoted in Dahlburg 1997).

Studies in the United States link sexual victimization with excessive drug and alcohol use, unprotected sex, prostitution, teen pregnancy and later adult health problems (Zierler et al. 1991; Heise, Pitanguy and Germain 1994; Sheikh 1997).

Saad Raheem Sheikh, from Kenya and Pakistan, part of whose 1997 speech made at a regional meeting in Kathmandu appears above, has called attention to the likely but ignored psychological affects of sexual abuse on South Asian girls.

The Family and Prostitution

Some girls in South Asia are sold into prostitution even by their families or are so abused that they leave home and end up as prostitutes. One of the most infamous communities said to be involved in trafficking is Sindhupowlchuk in Nepal (Frederick 1998). Considerable efforts have been made by NGOs and the government, including the police, to change the ethos of Sindhupowlchuk about its daughters. Many Nepali girls are trafficked to India, Bombay in particular, but community efforts like that in Sindhupowlchuk can help cut the flow. Nepal is not the only source for girl prostitutes. Bangladeshi girls and women are said to be trafficked through India to Pakistan (Ali 1997). Girls from Bangladesh may also end up working in Calcutta, closer to home. And this is to say nothing of those from India itself.

A woman social worker[9] in a brothel area of India, who works with Bangladeshi immigrants as well as locals, reports:

> The violence on these children is astounding. They are raped and beaten if they don't listen. A 10- or 11-year-old is expected to take on 10 to 12 customers a day. It is worse than rape. She knows that if she protests she will get more clients and also be beaten up over and above all this. So she doesn't make a noise and meekly accepts. So these are some of the worst kinds of violence that are taking place regularly. I cannot dream of anything worse.

Once girls are dragged into this, many lose their will to escape. "Culturally, our girls believe that once the body has been violated, they will never get pure again — so why not continue with this profession and get some money which is needed?"

In Nepal and India, practices of some groups can lead to child prostitution. These may involve dedicating girls to temples as a religious offering. An example is described by Kiran Tewari,[10] who was an activist in the Child Welfare Society in Nepal at the time:

In the Far West, there is a place called Baitadi. There are women there that we call *Devakis*. There girls are offered to temples by relatives who want their prayers to come true. So they promise the goddess of the temple that in order to have their prayers answered, they will give their daughter to the temple as an offering. It started a couple of hundred years ago. The goddesses are very powerful, and people would give their own daughter so that their wishes would be fulfilled. They used to provide for their daughter in these temples, but later what happened is that people used to promise to give a girl to the temple. So they would buy girls from poor villagers and leave them in the temple as an offering.

Now people buy and give girls to temples for any reason: winning elections, buying land, anything. And these girls, once they are given to temples, cannot marry because there is a superstition that misfortune will fall on whoever will marry this girl. And nobody provides for them, so they have to turn to prostitution for money. Ninety per cent became prostitutes. In the early days they used to go to Burma for prostitution. There were several attempts to do something about them to stop this practice. Now there are 112 *Devakis*. They have children from their sexual encounters, and their daughters are called *Devis*. The mother is so poor, and so, if someone wants to buy the daughter to give to the temple, she sells her. I was in Baitadi to talk to the villagers about this. But they did not want to discuss the issue. It is their tradition. We talked to the women and to others who support this, so there was a lot of opposition.

Such practices are also well-known and documented in India, although former *Devadasis* (women dedicated to the goddess Yamuna) are being organized to work against its continuation. (See, for example, *Voices of Change*, a 1997 video from UNICEF ROSA directed by Thomas Kelly and produced by this author.) Changing such traditions is not easy, especially when some people stand to benefit from them. The concept of the best interest of the child has not, in general, taken hold compared to the power of tradition. But there are those who have come to understand, through pain in their lives, and who are determined to make a difference despite cultural prescriptions to the contrary.

A story of a former Nepali sex worker[11] is a poignant cry for prevention as well as rescue. More than that, it shows the strength and capacity of victims to survive and prevail, to help others and to go beyond their own suffering:

I will tell you my life story and you will understand. My father is a farmer in Nepal in a small village. One day when I was nine years old, my uncle came to the village and asked my father if my sister could accompany a family with two children back to Bombay. He said they would pay Rs. 800. My father agreed. However, I went instead of my sister, because she had a one-year-old baby. I was taken in a truck. I vomited on the way. Then I was taken in a train, a steamer and then a taxi. They had told my father that the family lived on the ninth floor of a tall building. Instead I was taken to a wooden two-storied *chawl*.

My uncle left me with a woman. When I asked him where was the tall building and where was the family, he simply said there was a change of plans. My father had told me that there should be no complaints. So I kept quiet. My uncle never came back and the woman told that my father had sold me for Rs. 3,000. A lot of girls were in the house. They used to sleep in the morning and put on make-up in the afternoon. They told me to put on make-up, too. I kept saying no. But they made me put on make-up and do everything. A man parted my legs and two of the women told me what I should do. I cried so much that the man went away without doing anything. But he came back the next day and said he had paid the money for me. I did it there. He was very big.

For three years different men would come and go, sometimes four or five in a day and sometimes 20 or 30. I would collect about 9 or 10 rupees a month, with which I began to buy cigarettes. There was one man who began to visit me regularly. He would just sit and talk to me. Later he spoke to my *gharwali* [madam] and began to take me out for drives. He would park the car and sing for me. One day he gave me a lot of money and told me to run away. I just started crying. Then he took me back and told the *gharwali* he wanted to marry me. She said she wanted Rs. 50,000. He said he would get it in a week's time. Meantime, there was a *seth* [rich man] who owned the building I worked in. My *gharwali* used to tie *rakhi* on him [consider him like her brother; refers to a specific ceremony usually between brother and sister]. He came and told her he wanted me. He used to get me drunk and rape me. One day he got my *gharwali* drunk and took me away. He locked me in a small room and kept me there for three years. I had his baby. I knew he was already married and his wife had thrown him out. He would go out in the day and come back in the evening.

All day, my baby and I would stay in the room. We only went out when he took us out. In the evening he would drink till late. He also began to get other girls home and have sex with them in front of me. He began to kick the plate of food aside I would cook for him. I did not like that. I protested and he pulled out a knife and threatened my son. There was a small balcony outside my room. I was on the first floor. One day I jumped out with my son. To feed him I went back to the brothel. But he was completely traumatized there and become speechless. I was 17 or so then.

Sometimes the men would stub their cigarettes on me. I wanted to go out but the madam told me she would tell the *seth* where I was. One day a man called Vinod Gupta came to rescue another girl from our brothel. I left with that girl and I took my son. I told Guptaji[12] I wanted to work with him and save other girls. He was very happy and said I was a courageous girl. That is what I do now. I am 35 and have worked with him for about 15 years now. My son is an adolescent, about 17. He dropped out of school, cannot concentrate and will not do a job. He feels he is not a part of society. I don't know what to do about it.

It has been estimated that there are some 250,000 girls from Nepal in prostitution in Bombay, as mentioned earlier; girls are also trafficked from Bangladesh to Pakistan. Chapter 9, "Work and Gender Violence," takes up the subject of girl-trafficking in more detail. As of yet, there has been very little attention to the children of those trafficked, who also need help.

Who Cares? Neglect and the Missing Millions

Violence against children is not always dramatic, even when the results are. A particularly insidious form affects nutrition and health. Then it quietly kills, taking a dramatic toll, but for years this scarcely roused much public or policy concern. It is neglect, which has led to missing millions of women, who seem to have died, primarily when they were girls. An Indian economist and an Indian demographer cared enough to make us notice. A connection has also been made between the missing millions and negative attitudes towards girls, which are translated into differential care. Negative attitudes towards girls also influence infanticide, foeticide and the spread of the practice of dowry into groups that did not have it before (Dreze and Sen 1995).

Here is the story, briefly.

A great many more than one hundred million women are simply not there because women are neglected compared with men. If this situation is to be corrected by political action and public policy, the reasons why there are so many "missing" women must first be better understood. We confront here what is clearly one of the most momentous, and neglected, problems facing the world today. (A. Sen 1990, page 66)

In the late 1980s, it was economist Amartya Sen, who won the Nobel Prize for Economics in 1998, who coined the term "missing women" to describe those who should have been alive given natural sex ratios, but who were simply not there as shown by a comparative analysis of census data by sex.[13]

According to Sen, the world average for the sex ratio of women to men was 990 per 1,000, based on 1981 census figures. The highest ratio, 1,064 per 1,000, was reported for Western Europe. The phenomenon of missing women was seen most clearly in Asia, where the ratio of women to men fell to 953 per 1,000. That is 111 fewer women per thousand in comparison with Western Europe, and some 37 fewer women per thousand in comparison with the world average for the sex ratio (A. Sen 1993, cited in Agnihotri 1995).

In Bangladesh, India and Pakistan, the ratios were particularly low, 939, 931 and 929, respectively. Even compared to the world average (990 women for every 1,000 men), this is some 51 more missing women in Bangladesh, 59 more in India and 61 more in Pakistan for every thousand men. Compared to Western Europe, it is 125 more missing women per thousand men in Bangladesh, 133 per thousand for India and 135 per thousand for Pakistan.[14] The reader may find it useful to recall the biological fact that more boys than girls are born but die soon thereafter so that the sex ratio approaches unity early in life. Also, there is usually an advantage for women in the later years of life, as males tend to die at higher rates than do females from adolescent onwards. As Harvey B. Simon (1999, page 107) puts them, these are some of the important details:

Indeed, the longevity gap makes its first appearance in embryonic life itself. Sperm cells that contain a Y chromosome can outswim sperm bearing an X; as a result, 115 males are conceived for every 100 females. But for reasons that are not entirely understood, male embryos are more likely to miscarry than females, so boys outnumber girls by only 104 to 100 at the time of birth. The excess of male deaths continues in infancy and early childhood, but the difference is small until adolescence, when testosterone kicks in and boys start behaving like men [with three times the female ratio of violent death]. . . . By age 25, females outnumber males and the gender gap keeps widening with each subsequent decade of life.

Why Are Women Missing?

Sen concluded that there were more than 100 million missing women who should have been alive. He said this was due to discrimination, particularly in health care, employment and education opportunities for women. Without saying so directly, he thus focused attention on abuses of women's social, economic and cultural rights — abuses that had been overlooked, but which were so extreme that they led to untimely death. He did not himself bring up infanticide, selective abortion or murder as possible contributing factors to low sex ratios of women to men. It is presently impossible to calculate the incidence of infanticide and abortion because there are few pertinent studies. What little data we have are indeed alarming, but Sen's focus was more on unintended than intended deaths and the enormity of that neglected problem.

No one wants to believe that more than 100 million women and girls have been killed through State and family neglect and discrimination, let alone by intention. Thus it was natural that, in the more than 10 years since Sen first published his work, it had been largely ignored or severely questioned before he won the Nobel Prize. Only a few have built upon it.[15]

Why? Some critics said that the census data Sen used are faulty, that the "missing" females were really there but were not seen and not counted in censuses because they were confined at home or because male household heads did not mention them. Migration, whether in-migration of men or out-migration of women, is another factor brought up to try to account for the relative lack of females in parts of the world. It has even been argued that the low ratios of women to men are due to biology, that in some parts of the world even more boys are born compared to girls than is usual. If so, this has not been explained. As mentioned earlier, nature's way is for more boy babies than girl babies to be born, but for more girls to survive, given equal care. Thus, sex-ratios that strongly favour boys over girls in the early years suggest cultural, rather than biological, reasons behind them.

Satish B. Agnihotri[16] is one person who took the problem of the missing millions very seriously. In his work he is adding new elements of analysis: a focus on the younger age groups, on differences between tribal groups, scheduled castes and the general population, on trends over time, and all at the district as well as state levels (Agnihotri 1997b; see also UNICEF 1998b, pages 85–86). He is calling for closer attention to the phenomenon of missing girls, in particular by district, to design policies for interventions that target high-risk areas. Based on the 1961, 1981 and 1991 census data, he has analysed the sex ratios of zero- to four-year-olds and five- to nine-year-olds at the district level by the groups above. The results show that the sex ratios are declining, that is, *the problem of missing females is getting worse, not better.* He also finds that there has been less discrimination against females in the tribal groups and scheduled castes than in the general population, but that even in these groups, there is a recent tendency towards lower sex ratios. In a band of districts and states in the north of India, the female-to-male sex ratios are lowest. They fall as low as 840 females per 1,000 males in some cases. And at subdistrict level, in areas known for foeticide and infanticide, they fall even lower, as was described earlier.

Agnihotri (1999) emphasizes[17] how unusual it is to have low female-to-male sex ratios for such young ages:

> [W]hat really sets South Asia apart is that the discrimination affects the survival of the girl child below the age of 5. Or that's what my research shows. Pre-industrial Europe, 19th-century USA, Meiji-era Japan were also societies where discrimination against the girl child existed. Excess female mortality was documented through historic demographic research. But in most of these places, the slight excess of female mortality was occurring above the age of 10.

At a 1997 UNICEF/UNIFEM/UNDP regional meeting in Kathmandu on ending violence against women, Agnihotri commented on the relative influence of biology and culture:

South Asia is showing the interesting trend that even during infancy there is excess girl-child mortality, that is something which is not biological at all. It is a good rule of thumb to know that excess male child mortality is always attributed to biological causes. I have not come across any single incidence so far where it is related to behavioural causes. And excess female child mortality is almost always related to behavioural cause. So when people say these ratios in South Asia are in cultural conformity and so on and so forth, just say, "Give me a break." Biological causes we can understand, but when behavioural causes are creating sex ratio distortion, then the cultural excuse should not be accepted. And culture is for us to change. (See Agnihotri 1999 for a more detailed explanation.)

He pointed to a district map of India to show us areas where the sex ratio of girls to boys in the five-to-nine group is less than 800, something that has been overlooked by many analysts. A district-level analysis for all of South Asia would help pinpoint more areas where interventions would best be targeted. In India, a comparison of census data from 1901 to 1991 shows that the sex ratio has dropped from 972 females per 1,000 males to 927 (Raju et al. 1999, page 84) with some 35 to 90 million affected.

According to Agnihotri (1997b), one strong predictor of the female-to-male ratio is women's participation in the labour force. He found that where participation is higher, there is also a higher female-to-male ratio. The reason seems to be that the value of women is enhanced by the anticipation that they will not be an economic liability. Likewise, where dowry practice — in which a woman's family must provide money and/or material goods to her new husband's family — is not rampant, the female-to-male ratios are higher. Agnihotri's work points towards a conclusion that where women's labour-force participation is high and dowry demands are non-existent or low, there is less abortion of female foetuses and less infanticide of girl newborns.

For rural south India, a study by George, Haas and Latham (n.d.) in 12 villages of Tamil Nadu found that 10 per cent of newborn girls in half the villages were killed soon after birth. More boys than girls were in those "femicide" villages, while more girls than boys were in the others. The victims were almost all higher birth-order girls. Neglect of the girls born later in families was also apparent in the femicide villages, as indicated by higher rates of stunting (low height for age). The authors point out that the villages where girls are more accepted are lower caste (*Harijan*[18]), ones in which women actually have greater freedom and social status than they do in the other castes, in part because their labour and productivity are valued (George and Dahiya 1998).

Harijans have not traditionally followed the custom of dowry. They would seem to exemplify, at least to some extent, the connection between female labour-force participation, low dowry demands and more value on girls as suggested by Agnihotri. The connection between poverty and femicide is not supported. Dreze and Sen (1995) report, in fact, that there are more girls and women in the population at district level where there are higher levels of poverty. Raju et al. (1999) observe that "economic growth and the reduction of poverty may initially put women and girls at a greater disadvantage." This is probably because the customs like dowry and limited mobility or employment of women, more characteristic of the better-off castes, begin to be copied as poverty lifts.

Raju et al. (1999) observe that where more girls and women survive in India, there also are more women workers in agriculture and in paid work and who are literate.

Foeticide and Infanticide[19]

Agnihotri suggests that in the more extreme cases of low female-to-male sex ratios, abortion and infanticide may indeed be contributing factors. For example, one often-cited study of amniocentesis in Maharashtra state found that of 8,000 aborted foetuses, 7,999 were female. "The exception was that of a Jewish mother who wanted a daughter" (Narasimhan 1994).

R. P. Ravindra (1993) describes his chance discovery of how sex-determination tests (SDTs) spread to rural India, promoted by doctors and quacks who used amniocentesis after the fourth month of pregnancy. Since then, tests have proliferated widely, with the use of ultrasound units also. Ravindra traces the history of a campaign against such tests that began in Bombay in 1982, and led to the organization of a Forum against Sex Determination (SD) and Sex Preselection in 1985, with members from a wide range of backgrounds. Surveys of SD centres were made; a spectrum of new reproductive technologies was considered with regard to their probable use and risks; connections with the media were forged for publicizing the practices and risks; and legislation was proposed to amend the Medical Termination of Pregnancy Act to make sex-selective abortion illegal (except where it was therapeutically justified). A group called Doctors against Sex Determination joined the campaign, but the main national organizations of doctors avoided comment on it or the issues concerned. The campaign was partially successful and the Maharashtra Regulation of Prenatal Diagnostic Techniques Act 1988 was passed.

There were many problems in the content of the new law, its implementation and monitoring. One problem was that women were punished for undergoing the tests. Another problem was the licensing of the private sector for use of prenatal diagnostic techniques. At the same time, groups in other states were calling for a nationwide law against prenatal sex-determination tests with limited exceptions on medical grounds. Ravindra worried about what would happen if the national law were enacted with the same provisions regarding punishment of women taking the tests and licensing in the private sector that he thought plagued the Maharashtra law.

Ravindra (1993, page 92) referred to Barbara Miller's (1981b) observation in her book *The Endangered Sex* that the sex ratio was dangerously low in one third of the rural districts in north and west India, which she attributed to the neglect of female children there. Ravindra noted that, while Miller had utilized the 1971 Census figures, the 1981 census showed that the area involved was expanding and spreading:

> This rapid imbalance in sex-ratio was caused by the neglect of daughters. What will happen if the twin mechanisms of neglect of daughters and selective elimination of daughters before birth operate simultaneously is anybody's guess. Looking at the proliferation of SDT clinics, a serious imbalance in sex ratios across a very large territory of India cannot be ruled out. No one knows exactly what might happen then. One thing is certain, it would make women's lives more insecure, restrictive and less dignified. It would make human life more miserable and violent. . . . The question is, should we allow the situation to deteriorate or shall we work systematically to confront this challenge now? (Ravindra 1993, page 92)

George and Dahiya (1998) are among those who have documented the rapid spread of sex-determination tests into the countryside and their effect on the sex ratio. They found:

Ultra-sonography is abused for sexing foetuses. More doctors are buying ultrasound machines and some are taking it in cars to villages. The only difference after the national law banning the test was passed in 1994 was that cost of the test doubled. Almost everybody, including women MCH (Maternal and Child Health) doctors felt that selective abortion of female foetuses would increase the status of women. They were unanimous in the positive role of ultrasound in normal pregnancies. The only dispute between the radiologists and the obstetricians of MCH was on the issue of who was most competent to do the scanning! (page 2194)

The authors report that ultrasound has become the most widespread method for sex determination since early in the 1990s, and that multinational companies import and even manufacture the equipment in India for the growing market. Portable models are available, along with credit and service — and they promise "considerable financial gains."

George and Dahiya note that female foeticide occurs in many cities as well as the countryside of India, that it increases with birth order, that it is more likely where a family has one son and that even the first child may be aborted if it is a girl. George (1997) estimates that some 1.2 million girls were "missing" in India between 1981 and 1991 due to sex-specific abortions and female infanticide, while some 4 million died prematurely due to neglect.

When I met Dr. George in Delhi in 1999, he told me how he learned about the problem of infanticide when he went to work as a researcher on nutrition in the villages of Tamil Nadu in the south of India. He said that he heard about cases every two to three months but had to struggle to get other professionals to believe him, especially because even Indian demographers denied their existence. Villagers told Dr. George that female infanticide in their area actually went back at least several generations. The methods for killing girls were the same as in other distant parts of India from which the practice may have been carried long ago.

Dr. George told me that it was the Chief Minister of Tamil Nadu, Ms. Jayalalitha, who first publicly acknowledged the practice of infanticide, in 1992, and set out to have it eliminated by the year 2000. Among other things, she started a scheme to care for unwanted infant girls. Dr. George said that already by 1995, claims were made by government that the practice of female infanticide had been eliminated, at least in districts of particular concern. Dr. George said that coverage of cases by the media was then discouraged. At village level, he found, however, that the practice was actually continuing although disguised: a murdered baby might be registered as a stillbirth, or the murder might take place outside the village area, where the remains would be disposed of secretly.

The study team interviewed over 1,000 women regarding pregnancy outcomes for five years: 41 per cent of the early neonatal female deaths are said to be due to female infanticide, even though official mortality data do not confirm this. Dr. George thinks that 8 to 10 per cent of infant deaths in 1995 could have been due to female infanticide. Public Health Survey data show a rate of 900–920 girls per 1,000 boys in several districts.[20]

Preventing Infanticide: Viji Srinivasan's Work

Viji Srinivasan has been working for over 10 years in Bihar. Adithi, the NGO she helped found, is named for a Hindu goddess from the Vedas who is associated with motherhood. The NGO selects villages thought most likely to practise infanticide (given low female-to-male ratios and without notable selective out-migration of women) and tries to bring the practice into the open. It promotes alternatives to the practice and motivates community members to set goals and establish monitoring systems to eradicate it. Srinivasan has investigated gender discrimination in five villages (all from Dumra Block in Sitamarhi District) of Bihar with the lowest sex ratios of females to 1,000 males, for zero- to six-year-olds as indicated by the 1991 census. She says the range in the villages concerned is from a low of 401 to a high of 658 girls per 1,000 boys aged zero to six[21] (Srinivasan 1995, page 20). This compares with a ratio of 882 for Sitamarhi District as a whole (Raju et al. 1999, page 118).

In two villages, she and her team compared the number of children alive and dead, by sex, for various age groups up to age 18. She reported unusually high ratios of girl-child deaths per 1,000 deaths of boys for ages zero to three: 1,820 in one village and 1,571 in another.

The most frequent reason given was *"saurighor* death" meaning "dead in the room where born." Srinivasan reported that respondents did not admit to infanticide, despite the evidence. But interviews with local birth attendants and medical people revealed otherwise. According to her, the husband is always asked first. Based on personal knowledge, one birth attendant estimated there were about 50 to 100 girl infants killed in four years in her village area alone.

Srinivasan presented her findings on infanticide in a workshop with local women. First-hand accounts of female infanticide were given. Lively discussion and many recommendations followed. One idea is to have the shared goal of violence-free villages that will monitor their own incidence of different types of gender violence and work to end infanticide, dowry and beating, accordingly.

> From my experiences of my patriarchal family and of the areas I have worked in, the men are supreme. They may pretend all they like that it is not they who want dowry, it is their wives (the mothers-in-law); or that it is not they who want to kill the girl babies, it is their wives. But the fact remains that it is the men who have the power, even within the families. If the husband was to say to his mother "my wife should not be ill-treated," there is no way the mother-in-law can continue to subject her to repeated ill-treatment. Similarly, if the husband (or the father-in-law) was to say "I don't want my baby daughter (or grand-daughter) to be killed," who will dare to kill her? But in my experience with female infanticide, the men never killed a baby girl themselves. They hide themselves from the crimes! (Srinivasan 1995, pages 11–12)

In its report, Adithi comments, "the women and girls have shown great courage, commitment and strength, the men and boys much less so, and many a time [act] obstructively. Clearly, there is a deep divide in Sitamarhi district between the sexes which begins at about [age] 7" (Adithi n.d. a, page 3). It also observes that:

> The protest of women against domestic violence has increased. They resent, hate and collectively protest. Definitely the men do not like this, but an increasingly large section of men are reconciling themselves to the new situation. (page 5)

At the same time, increased violence against women is noted in some of the villages where "sense of belonging and unity among the women is developing and this undoubtedly does not fit in the patriarchal structure" (page 5).

Negative Attitudes behind Dangerous Acts

Whatever the scale of foeticide and infanticide of unwanted girls, clearly the problem deserves more attention. Efforts at community and policy level are needed to change negative attitudes and practices that kill females by intention or neglect. An example from Bihar shows how deeply entrenched are the attitudes and practices that lie behind the phenomenon of missing women and girls.

In a society of male superiority and control, at an early age, boys begin to learn at home and in school that they are more important and valued than girls. Negative attitudes towards girls and women are deeply ingrained. This was underscored in an unusual study about the attitudes of both males and females towards girls in the family carried out by an Indian NGO. This NGO has worked for over 10 years in various infanticide-prone villages of Bihar from four districts[22] where sex ratios as reported by Srinivasan are astoundingly low — only some 230 to 700 girls per 1,000 boys, age zero to six (1995, page 20). In this study, some 200 married men and women were asked whether or not they thought girls were a burden to bring up, and whether or not they thought girls should die, or be got rid of after birth — even by killing them (Hurdec 1997). Among the men, 96 per cent said that girls were a burden on parents; 46 per cent of the women had a similar opinion. When asked if it would be best if girls died at birth, 97 per cent of the men said yes, compared to only 2 per cent of the women. As for getting rid of baby girls, even by killing them, 65 per cent of the men agreed, but only 8 per cent of the women agreed.[23]

In a related study, in Sitamarhi District of Bihar, a woman birth attendant who was interviewed in depth by the NGO Adithi about infanticide admitted to accepting money to kill some baby girls. Her preferred methods were to break the neck, to fill the throat with black salt or to stuff the girl infant into a clay pot and cover it. She said that it was men who gave the orders, and everyone involved in the murders received money from the family. The view of many birth attendants and quacks practising in the villages is said to be: "What is the problem? It is not at all difficult to kill a baby girl. And she can be buried or cremated anywhere. In the burial ground there is never any attendant, nor is any certificate[24] required" (Parinita 1995, page 29; Srinivasan 1995, pages 27–28).

The August 1999 draft of a report from the Indian Women's Movement has some sharp comments on such gaps and their negative implications for girls:

> While civil registration of births and deaths has been mandatory in India for over 30 years, nobody bothers. The arrival and departure of infant girls goes unreported. In many health centres and hospitals doctors and workers are believed to collude in recording "still births" so that neither unwanted birth nor hurried death are put on file, and unwanted formalities of truth are avoided altogether. (Indian Women's Movement 1999, page 100)

The Connection between Infanticide and Dowry

One of the main reasons given for the negative attitudes to girls, and for killing them, is the growing cost of dowry. Like Agnihotri, Srinivasan sees an interrelationship between dowry and infanticide, as well as a link between infanticide and low skills and few opportunities for girls. Consequently, she has helped set up centres for girls' literacy and campaigned against dowry as part of her effort to end infanticide. In her important book, *If Indian Men Wish* (1995), she calls on men to become more active against the discriminatory and lethal practices derived from patriarchal attitudes.

In particular, Srinivasan emphasizes the importance of efforts to end dowry. She dismisses excuses like "We are getting dowry, we are not demanding but they only want to give gifts to their daughter." For Srinivasan, the concept of dowry has roots in the subordination of women and should not be accepted. "I think it is time Indian men take a stand on dowry, female infanticide, on all the violence on women and girl children. It is time to stop perpetuating the myth that women are women's worst enemies" (1995, page 12). She is asking men's groups such as Lions, Rotary and Jaycees to begin a campaign against dowry.

Dowry Demands and the Disposable Bride

Traditionally, dowry, in the form of jewellery, other goods or money, was meant to ensure a bride's future well-being. In-laws were supposed to record her dowry, keep it for her and return it to her if she needed it for her maintenance in the future. Today, dowry has become a way for the groom and his family to make money and acquire a variety of modern consumer goods, from clothes to cars. The bride's life is threatened if her parents will not comply. A one-time agreement and payment is not necessarily enough. Extortion can continue for years. Despite laws against it, in Bangladesh and India, for example, the practice persists. It is said to be spreading from the upper and middle classes to the poor, in both rural and urban areas. Tribal people are adopting the practice, which was not followed traditionally. It is also starting in areas where it was not practised before, such as Nepal.

In some cases, the bride's parents make promises that they cannot keep, or perhaps demands are increased over time and beyond their means. Those whose families do not provide enough dowry to satisfy such demands are most at risk to be burned to death, driven to suicide, killed in some other way, abandoned or divorced. Quick cremation of these women obliterates evidence. If a bride who is a poor money-maker for her in-laws is got rid of before she has a child, all the better. There will not be a child as a liability to take care of and the husband will most likely be able to get a higher dowry for his second marriage if he doesn't yet have a child by his first.

The abuse of dowry, which now imperils the lives of girls and women, is well illustrated by a study from Bangladesh that shows that dowry business is flourishing. Parents of young boys start planning what they will get from dowry while parents of newborn girls start worrying about how they will pay. Not only can the prospect of ruinous dowry demands lead to infanticide, but the age of marriage for girls may also shift downward, with more school drop-outs or complete non-attendance, because dowry demands are less for young brides. This makes it more attractive for families to get their daughters married off when they are still quite young.

Monwara's Story

"He is very good looking. His hobby is to marry again and again and take money from the bride's parents." These are the words of Monwara, a 25-year-old Bangladeshi woman slum dweller with three children, one of 500 women who participated in a study of dowry as a development issue, for the United Nations Development Programme in Bangladesh (PromPT 1996, page 13).

Monwara was married at 15 to a man who already had two wives, unbeknownst to her. Her parents gave him money, clothes and household goods as dowry. Later, he secretly took a fourth wife. Monwara later filed a case against him with the police but he had her threatened until she dropped it. He also demanded money from her earnings as an employee at a garment factory. She gave it, he deserted her, moved and has married again, four more times, for eight marriages in all.

Monwara is one of an apparently growing number of girls and women in South Asia who have become like crops to be harvested, or worse, decimated, due to dowry abuse. They are disposable brides. Monwara is actually one of the luckier women in this study: not only is she alive, but she has her children, she is employed and she hasn't been forced into prostitution or theft by extortion or desertion.

Earlier, more general studies showed that poor people in Bangladesh rated dowry as the third most important problem they faced. But when this research team went to five urban and rural areas to discuss dowry, local people made it clear that dowry was "the most important problem they are facing right now" (PromPT 1996, page 4). They called for government action to be taken against dowry business. They said that everyone knew, through media and NGO contacts, that "dowry laws exist," but that "there is no possibility to use the legal system" (page 16). They claimed this was so due to high costs, corruption and bias in favour of male litigants.

Findings from the study make very clear the alarming nature of the relatively new problem of dowry demands as a kind of extortion used to advance a young man's status. Before Bangladeshi independence, the groom gave gifts to the bride's family, said to be required under Islamic marriage law, and he also paid for the wedding. Dowry seems to have started only after independence and has increased dramatically since the late 1980s.

Regarding dowry-related abuse, the study reports:

> The incidence of physical and verbal abuse of wives due to non-fulfilment of dowry
> obligations by their fathers is so high that it is almost considered a norm. It occurs in at
> least 50 per cent of recent marriages. (page 4)

In 1 of 10 households in the PromPT study, there is a deserted wife. In 1 in 20 in the slum areas, there is a divorced wife. The proportion of divorced wives falls to 1 in 40 in rural areas. The study finds that the divorces in the rural area all are due to dowry matters.

Fathers who cannot afford dowry demands keep "over-age" girls at home, a practice that poses an economic problem for them and is distressing for the girls, who are likely to be the subjects of rumours. Land and assets may be exhausted to meet dowry demands, while money lenders charge up to 120 per cent interest for loans. To cut down on costs and avoid expenses at home, some fathers force their daughters to marry married men, elderly men or illiterate boys.

The report describes the new dowry-related pressures on families in urban slums:

> In urban areas the teasing is particularly explicit and the girls suffer harassment from boys

and musclemen. Adolescent girls and parents from the slums told us that sometimes boys throw acid at the girls or burn them with cigarettes in attempts to make them yield to their dowry demands. Some urban girls told us that neighbours and relatives of the prospective groom sometimes start rumours to purposefully smear the reputation of the girl so that the boy can demand higher dowry. (page 9)

Over-age girls, deserted or divorced wives may be pushed into being servants for others, a life as a prostitute or theft. At the very least, their welfare and that of their children is likely to suffer markedly. A recent report of a study in a Bangladesh village subdistrict close to Dhaka shows that marriage disruption caused by divorce was associated with lower chances of survival for children below five (Bhuiya and Chowdury 1997). The presence of an intensive Mother Child Health and Family Planning programme in the area did not alter the risk, nor was it different for boys and girls.

In India the problems of dowry have received attention, but to little avail, for some time. Fears about dowry demands have been exploited by clinics touting the economic value of sex-determination tests: "Better to spend Rs500 today [on sex determination and abortion] rather than Rs500,000 at the time of the girl's marriage [on dowry]" (Narasimhan 1994, page 51).

"I Won't Pay Dowry"

Those few people who decide not to give or accept dowry are not only an exception, they are an inspiration to others. However, they pay a consequence: he or she may not be able to arrange a marriage, even where dowry is against the law. The choices are too often cruel ones — marriage with dowry, future extortion, even murder; or no marriage, with threatened shame, exclusion and economic burdens for the girl and her family.

"Someone has to take a stand against dowry," said "Abha,"[25] a well-to-do Indian woman with a beautiful, educated daughter in her early 20s. The mother saw the link between high dowry demands and the possible murder of females as infants or earlier, through neglect or direct action. She believed that families were influenced to kill or neglect daughters in order to avoid future economic hardship from dowry.

And so Abha decided not to pay dowry as both a matter of principle and to set a good example. She told me, "The example of saying 'No' to dowry starts with me, as it must also with others. It is especially noteworthy that I refuse to pay because my family is well-off."

Because of her decision, Abha had already lost three seemingly good marriage prospects for her wonderful daughter. Abha said that when discussing possible wedding arrangements, she always made it clear from the start that she wouldn't pay dowry. The prospective future in-laws always agreed, saying things like, "Those who give the daughter have given everything."

She was misled.

"I thought I could believe them," Abha told me, "but I was stupid. The boy and girl concerned liked each other. That misled me. When I asked the boy what he would like to have from me, he said, 'Nothing.' " But when she sat with the parents, they insisted on an auspicious dinner for at least 250–300 guests, expensive shawls for many family members, cloth for 26 men's suits (clothes for the boy for the rest of his life), saris for the women, jewellery for the groom's mother, a big engagement party and a big wedding.

Abha said, "I can afford it, but I won't pay it. And how cruel it is for a family without a good salary. I think of a man with three daughters. It is more than his life's salary. To get that money depends on corruption, bribes, intimidation, depriving someone else's rights. The practice of dowry has actually increased, despite the law against it."

Abha tells what happened when she tried to explain to her prospective in-laws the reasons not to give dowry.

> I told them, "I hope you understand infanticide and foeticide. I don't want to give parties to murderers. There should be equality between us. I believe that my daughter is no less than a son. We also have dreams."
> He said, "But you are not killing anyone when you are giving dowry."
> "Yes, I am," I said, "through bad examples about girls as commodities."
> He replied, "That will only change with the revolution."
> And I said, "When will that begin and who will bring it?"
> "Society," he answered.
> "But," I commented, "who is society, if not us?"

Abha told me more about why she thought it was so important to say "No" to dowry:

> The whole idea of dowry has become vulgar. Before, it was really meant to be a property for a girl, a kind of insurance for her future. But now, it is like a payment to the in-laws. The idea seems to be that it is some kind of compensation for the girl to be in her in-laws' house, to pay in some way for her eating and for the opportunity even for her to work there. My logic is different. Both husband and wife contribute.

The boy's family strongly disagreed. The prospective mother-in-law called Abha's daughter and complained: "Your mother takes decisions in the family. Houses run by women are not good houses. I cannot lift a piece of paper without my husband's saying so."

Abha's daughter said, "But I believe in joint decisions about my future life with a future husband." She was influenced by her father's as well as her mother's example. He had not asked for dowry when he and Abha were planning their wedding. Abha described what happened: "My husband never started his married life thinking that I am less. When he proposed to me — our marriage was not arranged — he said, 'I want to marry an individual, not someone who wants to bask in my glory.' "

His elder brother had not asked for dowry, either. Abha concluded, "I cannot degrade my own daughter now by paying dowry."

What happened? Her beautiful, well-educated daughter then lost her fourth marriage prospect. The girl said that she is never going to marry if dowry is required. That is her part of the revolution against degrading and killing girls. More need to join it so that girls can safely be born, grow up and safely choose to marry or not.[26]

Wife Abuse of Girl-Women

Another form of direct violence to girls that has gone relatively unmarked is abuse of wives. It is all too easy to forget that millions of wives are "girl-women," still legally girls due to age but sociologically considered as women. They are overlooked because they don't fit neatly into the category of either child or woman and the "sanctity" of marriage closes them in. These are the girls who are married off while still clearly children, or the girls married off as young teenagers. Those married off at a young age are robbed of their childhood. In the family, they are more susceptible than are older wives to rape and other forms of physical and emotional abuse. Arole (1997) has commented on the tendency for rape on the wedding night in India. From Pakistan, the NGO Simorgh shares some more specific comments regarding marital rape, including that of girls:

> A young woman leaves her husband who has been mistreating her and goes to live with her parents, taking her three-year-old daughter with her. Her husband, a week later, climbs in through the *roshan daan*, knocks his wife and daughter unconscious with chloroform and rapes his wife.

> A 16-year-old girl, totally unprepared for what is to happen to her on her wedding night, is violently raped by a man whom she has never seen before but to whom she is married. The girl has a nervous breakdown. The boy's family ask for divorce as they say the girl is mad and, therefore, not fit to be married.

> A young woman is married to a distant relative. Over a period of a month, her husband tortures her mentally and physically: he inflicts cigarette burns on her and rapes her brutally.

> A nine-year-old girl is given in marriage to a 50-year-old man in exchange *wata-sata* [a practice whereby females are exchanged between families] for his providing his sister as a bride for their son. The little girl, who does not even have her period, is raped by her "husband" on her "wedding night."

Simorgh asks: "Consider: Is a *nikahnama* [a marriage ceremony/certificate] a carte blanche for brutal sexual assaults on a child's or a woman's body? Can we countenance the use of *nikahnama* to protect child abusers and rapists?"[27] (1990, page 44).

Young brides are highly unlikely to continue in school or learn a trade. They will experience a higher maternal mortality rate, and their children will have both lower average birthweight and a higher possibility of infant mortality. And women having sexual intercourse from an early age have a higher likelihood of developing cervical cancer (National Institutes of Health 1996).

In spite of all this, as early marriage is a norm, particularly in villages and rural areas, the situation of girl-women remains overlooked. Few social agencies address or even recognize the special plight of these individuals. Whenever one reads "women" in descriptions of violence at home in South Asia, remember the girl-women and their rights and lives denied.

Child and Early Marriage

There are many different measurements for age of marriage, including: the average age at first marriage for currently married women of all ages; the proportion of girls and women who marry at such-and-such an exact age; the proportion of girls and women in a certain age range who are currently married or cohabiting, etc. And there are many different sources for data, and from different time periods. Government sources, international ones and micro studies do not necessarily agree so far as figures are concerned, yet all indicate that there are vast numbers of girl-women in South Asia. UNICEF (1998j) data on the per cent of males and females age 15 to 19 who are

Table 6: Percentage of Women Aged 20–24 Who Were First Married by Specified Age (selected SAARC Countries)

Country	Percentage of women who were first married by exact age			
	12	15	18	20
Bangladesh (1993–94)	7	47.2	73.3	82.1
India (1992–93)	11.8	26.1	54.2	71.4
Nepal (1996)	NA	19.1	60.3	75.7
Pakistan (1994–95)	2.2	33.4	71.9	86.3
Sri Lanka (1993)	NA	1	12	24

Adapted from UNFPA 1998c, Table 9.

currently married or cohabiting show figures for females that range from a low of 7 per cent in Sri Lanka to a high of 48 per cent in Bangladesh, and for males, from 1 per cent to 7 per cent respectively.

A more detailed picture emerges in Table 6, on the percentage of girls and women currently aged 20–24 who were first married by exact ages (12, 15, 18 and 20) in selected SAARC countries, reported by UNFPA (1998, page 17) . Of particular concern, for the purposes of this discussion, are those who clearly married when still only girls, at ages 12 and 15: for Bangladesh (1993–1994), more than half married then; for India (1992–1993), some 40 per cent did; for Pakistan, about 35 per cent are said to have done so; and for Sri Lanka, only 1 per cent are so reported.

The high percentages are in contrast to the reported legal age of marriage (see UNFPA 1998c, page 18), which is 18 for females in the above countries, and 18–24 for males (although in Nepal it is legal with consent of parents for females to marry by age 16; for males, by age 18).

The tendency for early marriage appears to be even greater in rural than in urban areas. For example, Ravindra, an Indian doctor working against foeticide, observes:

> The average age of marriage for girls in the rural areas of India is fourteen or fifteen. She experiences her first pregnancy around the age of sixteen. Eighty per cent of rural Indian women are anaemic. This pregnant girl lying on the table in the next room must have been one of them, a mere number in statistics. Pregnant at sixteen, [sex determination] test in the fourth month, abortion — either natural or if the child happens to be "female"; next year next pregnancy; again test and so on, the cycle would continue. If anything went wrong, one could always blame the dirty work on dust and garbage.

> In India the mortality rate for young women, especially during pregnancy, is one of the highest in the world. (Ravindra 1993, page 55)

In fact, South Asia has the highest proportion in the world of married 15- to 19-year-old females, some 40 per cent (UN 1995, page 7). There are some 30 per cent more girls than boys aged 15 to 19 who are married. This is the widest gap for any region in the world.[28] It highlights the practice in South Asia for younger females to be married to markedly older males .

The practice of child marriage is a particular concern. Strictly speaking, it would include any marriage of a girl under 18, but it tends to mean marriage of girls before the onset of menses, while early marriage refers to girls who marry after menses but before legal age. Neither the Vedas nor the Quran prescribes child marriage; still, it is often defended as part of tradition and linked to religion. *Manusmriti* (The Laws of Manu) and the Sharia are cited by some Hindus and Muslims, respectively, to justify it.

There are also practical concerns. Child and early marriage usually require that less dowry be paid by a girl's family. And where bride price is required (from the groom's family to the bride's), it may be waived if a girl from the groom's family is given in exchange for the new bride. In this regard Goodwin (1995) tells a particularly moving story about Maria, an 11-year-old Afghani refugee in Peshawar, Pakistan. Her father, a security guard for Goodwin, forced Maria to marry an old man in exchange for a new bride for himself. Maria, who wanted to continue her schooling, was instead isolated in purdah and said to be pregnant before she was 12.

Some idea about the tradition of child marriage is indicated by the 1921 census for pre-partition India. It shows 612 widows less than one year old; 2,024 under five; 97,857 from five to nine; and 332,024 from 10 to 14 (Nagi 1993). Laws against child marriage were won through great effort in pre-partition India, but the practice is still followed in various parts of the region. Through it, even one-year-old girls may be pledged to other households, which they join near puberty. In some cases, they leave home much earlier, are more like servants at first than wives, and then are expected to provide sons as soon as possible to continue the male line. Sex may be forced even before reproduction is possible.

In pre-partition India, the issue of possible sexual abuse of child wives was raised but not taken very seriously by the courts. Sarkar (1996) recounts a few cases mentioned in newspapers of the 1870s — a child wife beaten to death by her "elderly" husband when she refused his bed, and a girl of 11 killed for similar reasons. Both men received only light sentences. We are also told of a girl, Philmonee, about 10 years old, who was "raped to death" by her 35-year-old husband in 1890, when 10 was the statutory age limit for marriage. The defence challenged the court as to how many men present "were not in some way complicit with the practice" of cohabitation with a pre-pubescent wife. The husband was exonerated.

Meanwhile, the British were embracing the view that "our native fellow subjects must be allowed the fullest possible freedom in deciding when their children should be ceremonially married" and that this was "a matter with which no Government could meddle and no Government ought to meddle" (Sarkar 1996, page 227).

Under the law, girls married as children had the right as adults to repudiate the marriage if it had not been consummated. For example, Sarkar reports that in 1877, a young woman named Rukhmabai refused to live with her husband on the grounds that as an adult she could then repudiate her child marriage. Although threatened with imprisonment, she was spared "only after considerable reformist agitation and the personal intervention of Queen Victoria" (Sarkar 1996, page 213). Obviously, the case gave a lot of attention to child-marriage issues. And in 1891, the minimum age of consent for girls was raised from 10 to 12. The reaction from revivalists in West Bengal was that obligatory rituals in Hinduism should be maintained and protected regarding purity of brides and men's responsibilities to their ancestors. They claimed that the *garbhadhan* ceremony, or the compulsory cohabitation of husband and wife immediately after the wife had reached puberty, would be undermined by the new amendment should a girl reach puberty earlier, which was said to be likely given the hot climate. At stake was the purity of offerings to ancestors made by the sons of marriages polluted by the absence of a proper *garbhadhan* ceremony. Consequently, it was said, "generations of ancestors would be starved." At the same time, Hindu revivalist-nationalists were spreading dramatic accounts like this one about the likely negative consequences should the Hindu custom of child marriage be challenged: "The day has at length arrived when . . . jackals, hares and goats will have it all their way. India is going to be converted into a most unholy hell, swarming with hell worms and hell insects. . . . The Hindu family is ruined" (Sarkar 1996, pages 235–236).

In contrast, "forty-four women doctors brought out long lists of cases where child wives had been maimed or killed because of rape. From the possible effects of child marriage on the health of future generations the debate shifted to the life and safety of Hindu wives" (Sarkar 1996, page 225).

Although these pages in history were turned long ago, attitudes have not necessarily changed throughout the region. Dominant men in patriarchal communities that practise child marriage may see it as their right and their obligation. It is sometimes used as a means to create or maintain alliances between different male lines and to protect the purity and continuity of these lines. To have a post-menses, unmarried girl in one's house may still be considered to invite the possible destruction of the male line should the girl fall prey to a male other than the one her father chooses for her. If incest occurs, pollution and destruction of the male line is at risk. And if the girl victim-survivor of incest conceives, her father's male line may be taken as destroyed, along with the souls of those in it. Where there are beliefs like these, it is considered urgent for girls to be wed before puberty, so that they already "belong" to another line when they menstruate, and cannot pollute their own. The historical material helps us see how strong beliefs may be despite laws against child marriage. Offences will not likely be reported when such beliefs persist, along with their practice.

And in Pakistan to this day there are a number of mechanisms for exchange of women — often young girls — between tribal groups, to make alliances or settle claims. "honour killings" in response to real or alleged sexual relations outside of marriage may be compensated for by "payment" of a girl or girls, for example. It is recognized that a man may even kill his sister, daughter or wife, supposedly to protect family honour after her alleged defilement. He can claim compensation in the form of a girl or girls he desires from the family of the alleged perpetrator — who then is spared. (See, for example, Commission of Inquiry on Women 1997 for further discussion.)

E. Ahmed (1998) writes that, far from being unusual or necessarily tied in with honour killing, "the practice of child marriage is common in all parts of Pakistan, in particular in the poor and rural areas" (page 25). She also points out that the existing law against child marriage[29] sets the legal age of marriage for girls at 16 — but that the penalty is only Rs. 1,000 fine, a month imprisonment or both. "Furthermore," she writes, "a conviction under this law does not make the marriage null and void" (page 25). Only if the marriage has not been consummated can a girl who was married off under 16 repudiate it before she is 18. As for prevailing attitudes about the law and child marriage in Pakistan, Ahmed tells us:

> This law has met with much resistance by the clergy who state that Islam puts no age-limit on marriages and thus the law is not acceptable. The justification given for child marriages is that the parents would like to see their daughters settled in their lifetime. However, this is

a weak excuse given the ease with which men can divorce their wives. (page 25)

Where women are younger than men at marriage, they would seem to be more at risk of being abused, especially if the age gap is wide and the marriage takes place in a patriarchal culture that emphasizes male control of females. For example, a small but important study from Bangladesh, involving wives as young as five at first marriage, shows that the younger wives are, indeed, more often abused (Afsana 1995, page 151). Among 50 "women" interviewed, of those who are wives at age five to nine (a total of eight in the sample) close to 88 per cent were assaulted; for those aged 10 to 14 (a total of 34), the proportion was about 82 per cent; for those aged 15 to 19 (a total of six), the share was some 67 per cent; only two of the wives were aged 20 to 24, and neither reported an assault. Another example comes from Pakistan, from a man who recalls his uncle's advice to him for a successful marriage: "The night I got married, my uncle advised me to soak my leather shoes overnight and give my wife, who was then 10 years old, a taste of these shoes [to beat her] first thing in the morning. He said that she would be fixed for life if I did so" (Hassan 1995, page 39).

Of course, early marriage, meaning post-menses but under the legal age for adulthood, is more prevalent than is child marriage. Even very young brides will probably have been taught that motherhood is a sacred duty, along with services to the new husband and family. A contradiction exists between the stated value given motherhood and the actual treatment for pregnant women, especially when they are young and uneducated. Again, low birthweight babies, greater child and maternal mortality are all associated with young motherhood, as is increased risk of cervical cancer.

Young brides are also likely to be school drop-outs or never to have attended school. Illiteracy is greater among women in South Asia than it is among women in any other part of the world: about 64 per cent, compared to 53 per cent in North and Western Africa, about 24 per cent in the rest of Asia and Oceania, only some 15 per cent in Latin America and the Caribbean, and less than 10 per cent in developed countries (Goodwin 1991, page 95). Also, Bangladesh, Pakistan, India and Nepal are among the 25 countries listed by UNICEF as having large disparities (10 per cent or more) between enrolment of boys and girls in secondary school (UNICEF 1998, page 26). For India and Nepal the disparity reaches 20 per cent or more, a gap shared with only three other countries in the list (Turkey, Togo and Yemen).

On the basis of available information, UNFPA (1998c) indicates that "about one in three to one in four adolescent girls of Bangladesh, India and Nepal and one in 10 of Pakistan has begun childbearing as early as 17." The figures they report show that of girls currently 16 years old in Bangladesh, Nepal and Pakistan, 23.4 per cent, 11.8 per cent and 6.1 per cent, respectively, had began childbearing. For India, they report that among ever-married 13- to 16-year-old girls, 36.1 per cent had begun childbearing. The high percentage of married girls aged 15 to 19 in South Asia reflects decisions by families not to send girls to school at all, or to take them out early. Again, patriarchal values are reflected in decisions like these against equality for girls. Both child and early marriage are first steps to denial of rights, including the likelihood of physical and sexual abuse at home, and of early pregnancy.

One must take into account the fact that the young, uneducated bride who joins another family risks being seen more as a servant to her husband and his family than as an equal. She will be expected to work long hours for the benefit of the new household and not to complain. She is less likely to have access to contraception and, unfortunately, the young wife may be molested or raped by her own father-in-law or brother-in-law, not only her husband. She should not complain for the sake of family honour, and also to save her own life. A husband who hears about his father's, uncle's or brother's alleged misbehaviour is more likely to punish his wife than confront his male relatives. For example, a young woman in Gujarat had her nose cut off by her husband when she asked him to protect her from his father, who she said had raped her.[30] The reason: she dared to dishonour the father who headed the family.

Indirect Abuse: Witnessing as a Form of Violence

Witnessing family violence has very harmful effects on children that are not generally recognized. These affect both girls and boys and are no doubt widespread given the high rates of spousal abuse in South Asia and the likelihood that children either hear or see the beatings.

There appears to be no South Asian research and few testimonies on the impact of witnessing abuse. And so, if we are to alert ourselves to the likely gravity of the problem in South Asia and the need for prevention, it is useful to draw on research done elsewhere, bearing in mind the high rates of spousal abuse and the fact that children are often present when it occurs.

In their book *Islands of Safety*, Joy Osofsky and Emily Fenichel (1996) argue that witnessing violence is a traumatic event for children. Osofsky writes:

> Many people, including parents, members of the law enforcement community and journalists, think that infants and young children who witness violence are "too young to know what happened." They "don't take it in." They "won't remember." In fact, infants and young children can be overwhelmed by their exposure to violence, especially — as is likely to be the case with very young children — when both victims and perpetrators are well known and emotionally important to the child and the violence occurs in or near the child's own home. (Osofsky 1996, page 7)

Osofsky enumerates the factors that influence the severity of a child's response to witnessing violence: intensity; proximity; familiarity with the victim, perpetrator or both; the developmental status of the child; and frequency of exposure. The net result is "devastating to the social and emotional development of young children, who learn, from what they see, that violence is a usual and acceptable way to respond to other people" (page 8).

Charles Zeanah and Michael Scheeringa, in their essay in *Islands of Safety*, "Evaluation of Posttraumatic Symptomalogy in Infants and Young Children Exposed to Violence," point out that parents and caregivers "may be unaware of how affected children may be from experiences of violence, particularly chronic domestic violence" (Zeanah and Scheeringa 1996, page 9). The total impact is a form of "traumatic stress disorder" (Zero to Three 1994). Symptoms of traumatic stress disorder include re-experiencing the traumatic event (in play and nightmares), numbing of responsiveness, hyper-arousal (such as exaggerated startle responses, tantrums, sleep problems) and fears and aggression (towards self and others).

It has been estimated for the United States alone that 3.3 to 10 million children witness domestic violence each year (Knapp 1998, page 356). Also, it is estimated that 60 per cent of the children witnessing domestic violence are multiple victims who themselves experience physical or sexual abuse from a perpetrator in the family (page 357). Studies in Canada as reported by the National Clearinghouse on Family Violence, Canada (1996) estimate that the proportion of "the abused children who witness the violence range from 40 to 80 percent" (page 2). A 30 to 40 per cent overlap between children witnessing wife assault and being the target of direct physical abuse is reported (page 2).

All this is made worse because a distressed caretaker will find it difficult to care for a distressed child. Those who directly experienced the abuse will often be unable to help those who were witnesses.

Added to this is the likelihood that a home where a woman is battered is also a home where children are battered. According to US studies cited by Betsy McAlister Groves (1996, page 30), "in 60 to 75 percent of families where a woman is battered, children are also battered." Janet Carter, the Director of the Violence Prevention Fund, gives a 50 per cent figure,[31] and a report from Canada shows the range from 30–40 per cent (1996, page 2). The subject is not often addressed in studies from South Asia; but in one from Sri Lanka, of 200 women, it was noted that some 60 per cent reported being beaten, and of those, 29 per cent reported their children were also beaten (Deraniyagala 1992, pages 4–9).

It isn't clear if underreporting is involved or not. Rates in other countries in South Asia, where indicators show women's status to be much lower than in Sri Lanka, could vary widely — probably on the higher side since women might then have less voice about the husband's actions.

Groves (1996, page 30) notes that "when violence occurs in the home, children have no refuge. . . . Here, one parent is the perpetrator and the other is the terrified victim. To whom does the child turn? The child has no one." Such violent "households become organised around the abuser." The parenting of the mother is affected. "Mothers may become desensitised to the impact of violence on their children, and their judgement about protecting their children from exposure to violent or traumatic material may be impaired" (page 31).

As for the effects of child abuse, 65 South Asian activists against gender-based violence listed the following as being of particular concern (UNICEF 1998b, page 94):
- depression (33)
- second-generation abuse (32)
- school problems (20)
- health problems (17)

In a brief but useful review of some recent studies on the impact of domestic violence on children, Sheikh (1997) cites a wide range of effects on children of witnessing domestic violence:
- The psychological impact on children of witnessing violence can be just as severe as if they had actually been victims of physical or sexual abuse themselves.
- Children who witness violence, like abused children, display emotional and behavioural disturbances as diverse as withdrawal, low self-esteem, nightmares, self-blame and aggression against peers, family members and property.

- Many child witnesses to violence have a difficult time trusting people and learning problem-solving skills.
- Different age groups also suffer differently. Infants do not sleep well, may not develop as fast and may always have a fretful reaction to a loud voice. Toddlers often exhibit frequent illnesses, severe shyness, low self-esteem and trouble in school. School-age kids may steal, lie, have eating problems, poor school results and turn to drugs and alcohol. Overall, though, the younger the child, the greater the threat to healthy development.

Repeating the Violence

The only study from South Asia that I know about that collected data on second-generation violence is that of Professor Harendra de Silva (1996), who reports: "28/474 (69%) of males [in the study] admitted having abused children. . . . 20/28 (71%) of them have been sexually abused during childhood." Professor Harendra de Silva stresses that "today's abused children become tomorrow's abusers."

Nutritional Impact

Differential feeding practices for girls and boys in South Asia have been observed by a number of researchers. The extent of their negative impact on girls is widely discussed, although not always agreed upon. Nutritional outcomes connected with child abuse and wife-beating have become evident in some recent studies in South Asia. A study in Karnataka, India, concluded that children who were beaten were more malnourished and received less food than children who were not abused (Rao and Bloch 1993). Perhaps withholding food was another conscious form of abuse, perhaps this resulted from an abusive attitude and disrespect for the children by either parent, perhaps it was caused by intimidation of the mother by an abusive father — but, in any case, the results are the same.

This dovetails with other research that looks at the nutritional results of wife assault. Since, in some cases, the same households will be scenes of violence against both the mother and her children, then the problem is a compounded one.

An imaginative and excellent Nepali study used 144 representative sites in a sample of 16,955 households drawn by the Central Bureau of Statistics (HMG/N, NPC and UNICEF 1997). It found that in communities where women were beaten often (as indicated by community focus-group discussions in villages), children aged 6 to 36 months had a higher risk of stunting (1.5 times) and wasting (1.75 times) than did children in communities where frequent beating is not reported. (No analysis was made for any possible differences for girls versus boys.)

These findings are in line with the conclusions of Vulimiri Ramalingaswami, Urban Jonsson and Jon Rohde (1996), who suggest that the status of women predicts nutritional outcomes for children. Specifically, they say, greater emphasis on the wife role rather than the mother role in South Asia (as compared to sub-Saharan Africa) limits women's nurturing behaviour towards children and favours that towards men. The result, they speculate, is that caring practices for children are more limited in South Asia and, thus, nutritional status is negatively affected.

Another explanation could be that women who suffer and fear beatings are more anxious and depressed and thus give less attention than they otherwise would to the child. If there is greater incidence of domestic violence generally in South Asia, that could lead to reduced caring practices due to the extent of depression presumed among women who are beaten.

What Happens When a Mother Tries to Leave Home

The above are but preliminary indicators of some of the results of direct or indirect physical and sexual violence against children and the violence against their mothers. When mothers do try to protect themselves and their children from abuse at home, the results are not easily in their favour and even divorce itself may prove impossible, or very negative for the woman and her children, given the strong social norm for women to be married.

Custody Issues: Possible Further Loss for the Child

Our interviews highlight the anxiety that a woman in a violent home in South Asia likely has about the result for her children if she leaves her husband's home. For example, one Nepali woman says that even after a woman has obtained a divorce to get out of a violent situation, "the man still has control over her because he keeps the child. For a mother not to have her child is his way of tormenting her through the child." And a Pakistani woman social worker says that many women stay in abusive relationships not only because of social taboos associated with separation but out of fear of losing their children. She described the case of a woman who

> was in the marriage for about four years and was going through physical abuse from her husband and was emotionally abused by her in-laws. It was a difficult choice to leave her husband with two kids. She still hasn't been through divorce, because she is afraid he will take custody over the kids, since he is economically secure and she is not.

Even a woman with relatives and a shelter to help her can have difficulty keeping her child if the father wants custody. (Or if she manages to get custody, he is unlikely to pay maintenance costs for the children.) To make matters worse, many children are even more at risk when a new woman is brought home, as bride or mistress, by the man. A new round of ill-treatment might come from the new woman. Mothers fear to leave home or to get a divorce, even with extreme provocation because the alternative might be for the children to suffer even more with a stempmother and father — while the mothers could lose all contact with their children.

Some choose to leave and pay the consequences. Such consequences are not only an agonizing loss for the woman; they also are a tremendous loss, a sense of confusion and a feeling of abandonment for the child.

A Bangladeshi woman activist[32] tells her story about what happened when her son was four years old and her husband beat her in front of the child:

> I was extremely upset and insulted that my husband treated me like this in front of the boy. My husband also said that if you go away now, you will suffer and one day you will have to come and fall at my feet and beg forgiveness.

Despite the threat, she moved in with her brother, who was, in turn, pressured to send her back. But after a while the woman says her husband,

> asked me to try to patch up things and give one more chance for the sake of my son. So I went back to my in-laws' house. I had hardly been there for a week when he went back to his old ways and started beating me violently and on a regular basis. Then I took a final decision that I would leave him forever and not come back ever again. So I went back to my brother's house.
>
> My young son was very attached to his paternal grandfather (my father-in-law). In my absence he would be looked after by him and my son looked up to him a lot and did not bother about his parents.
>
> One day when I had gone out to give tuition, my father-in-law came and took the boy away from my brother's house. He promised to bring him back after a week. Since my son was attached to him he went along willingly.

Her brother tried to get the boy back but he was first put off and then later threatened with an attack by the neighbourhood *dadas* (toughs). She says, "Naturally I was upset by this threat and told my brother not go there anymore."

For her to get custody she would need a steady, regular income as well as a stable place to live. But she had left her brother's house for a women's hostel. And even if she had her own place, who would look after the four-year-old if she went out to work or to shop? In the end she decided not to seek custody but rather to obtain visiting rights, which she successfully did.

Unfortunately, neither her in-laws nor her ex-husband agreed to the visiting rights. After pressure from lawyers, he agreed to weekly visits, which were conducted in a meeting place he dictated. This went on for a year.

> After that, when he saw that my son was getting attached to me and getting to be friendly and free with me, he stopped these visits. I was seeing my son after four years and he was eight by then. When the boy started opening up to me, my husband made various excuses not to bring him to see me. Then I tried sending many letters to the boy but did not get any replies to my letters. If I wrote 10 letters I got a reply to only one.

The husband had moved many times and wouldn't give her the address. About three times a year she got a phone call from her son, but these,

> completely stopped over a year ago. During this entire period I managed to fix up and see the boy twice but he was extremely quiet and withdrawn and would answer only when questions were asked.
>
> Then suddenly this year, about two months ago, he called the office where I work three times to give the news that he had passed his Class 10 exams and had done very well. Twice I was not there and then my colleagues asked him to leave a message and give a time to call. I was of course delighted and insisted on fixing up a time to meet him. He agreed reluctantly and then I went to meet him and waited for three hours but he never showed up at the railway station where he had agreed to see me en route to his aunt's house. My colleagues repeatedly asked the boy to leave a number or an address where he could be reached but he was very unwilling.

There has been no news after that.

The Impact of a Mother's Suicide or Murder

A woman in complete despair about domestic violence towards her and her children might kill herself. Or, as accounts elsewhere in this book tell us, many women who are said to commit suicide have actually been murdered with the murder quickly covered up. There also are outright murders of women who are mothers. And where suicide occurs, the women involved may be in despair because of domestic violence and limited support or alternatives for them.

The impact on a child survivor of his or her mother's violent death is devastating. Yet the children affected are scarcely mentioned. How many children are left behind after a mother's suicide? How many are there who lost their mothers in dowry deaths, stove-burnings or "honour killings"? If there are statistics available, these are rarely publicized. An exception is the study by Progressive Women's Association of Pakistan of victims of stove-burnings: of 109 cases for which information about children was available, only 19 per cent were of childless women.

A murder case reported in an interview from Afghanistan[33] dramatizes the problems that can follow a wife's murder and how the child's voice and interests may be overlooked entirely because of laws and customs used in decision-making:

> The husband killed his wife in the room where the children were. Because the father killed his wife, the children were [placed] with the mother of the wife. When the son became seven years and the daughter was younger, the man came and said, "Give me my children." When they brought the case to our office, we asked them to bring the children. On that day we were asking the children, "Where do you want to go?" They were crying and saying, "We don't want to go to our father's house, he killed our mother." We sent this matter to the *Shura* [local body that makes judgements of cases in the name of religion] of the mullahs, but they wrote that the children must be with the husband/father.

The *Shura* ruled that,

> under Islamic law, the children will be with their mother's family only up to seven years for the son and up to nine years for the daughter. At that time, the son was seven years.

> Before [the mujahedin came to power], we had another guideline from the government for these kind of cases: if the mother was killed by the father and the children didn't want to go to his house, you could ask the children where they would prefer to live. If they chose their mother's house, they could stay with her.

That practice has apparently changed. What do we know about happens to children of murdered mothers in other countries in the region, and the effects on them of having to live with the murderer, where that is the case?

Glimmers of Hope

We have already met some South Asians who stand against the various forms of gender violence that affect children. More such initiatives are needed concerning all forms of gender violence that affect children. The girl-child and girl-woman are particularly vulnerable to parents and extended family, husbands and in-laws. Parent education and husband education for better family living and fulfilment of rights could be tried with reference to reducing gender-based violence.

In some areas, professionals and social workers offer support, inspiration and hope. This chapter closes with some examples of those working against child sexual abuse both outside and in the family.

The Indian social worker quoted earlier about her work with prostitutes and their children in Calcutta quickly came to the conclusion that part of her responsibility as a social worker in a brothel area was to help eradicate trafficking of children:

> For this we are going to the police and talk to them — to find if the children are arrested; [we] go to the courts, and so on. Now we also have to find out what is done to the people who are doing this and if they are caught how they are dealt with. The police let them off and usually complain about lack of witnesses. We have to see that this does not happen and that they are taken to court, and given some punishment. We also need to network with organizations working in Nepal, Bangladesh, even the rural areas or villages of the source areas.

Like the young Nepali woman who escaped prostitution in India, there are abused children who, against the odds, are starting to say, "Enough." And some of them are choosing to do whatever they can to get others and their own children out of abusive relationships and lives.

As for family violence, sometimes the abused become tomorrow's healers. For example, Afshan Chowdury, who talks openly about having been sexually abused as a child, organized research about sexually abused children in Bangladesh (Breaking the Silence Group). Professor Harendra de Silva[34] from Sri Lanka recalls experiencing domestic violence at times and physical and emotional trauma at school. Both model for others the importance of breaking the silence. They show that one can use even negative life experiences in positive ways. It is Professor Harendra de Silva who says that he began to consider himself a "passive perpetrator" of violence against children if he did not admit that some cases he saw in his paediatric practice were actually the result of family violence. He began to take action, starting with the research mentioned above, with university entrance-class students who were asked to recall and report incidents of sexual abuse in childhood. Later, his work generated so much concern about child abuse that he was named the head of the Child Protection Authority under the office of the Presidential Secretariat of Sri Lanka.

Dr. Shekar Seshadri is another pioneer working to bring the issue of child sexual abuse into the open. He says that prior to 1993,

> There was no system where the inquiry about child abuse considered the whole issue of sexual abuse. There was an assumption on our parts that sexual abuse didn't exist because we didn't ask and we didn't know how to ask. None of us was taught how to take the sexual history of a patient even though it was assumed that we were supposed to be skilled in these areas.[35]

Consequently, he and his colleagues began to ask questions and turned to the professional community for answers: "Many thinking people in activism, journalism, the women's movement and voluntary counselling agencies came together on a common platform and we found that sexual abuse was a fairly collective experience."

They wanted to do personal safety workshops in the schools but were initially prevented because schools feared these would arouse children's sexuality, and because they were asked for data to show that child sexual abuse really was a problem. So Dr.

Seshadri and colleagues at SAMVADA (an NGO) designed a survey, which came to be known as a combined interactive workshop, and a surveying system to collect retrospective data from students in colleges.

As a result of the SAMVADA and NIMHANS work, a network of specialists and activists meet periodically and a help line has been set up. This has led to a steady increase in the number of children referred at the clinic or hospital level. Meanwhile, an umbrella organization, Forum against Child Sexual Exploitation, has been started in Maharashtra with some 27 organizations as members.

Two of the critical new things being done in this area, according to Dr. Seshadri, are work with adult survivors of incest and work in the schools. A particular feature of this work has been cooperation between government and NGOs:

> We are trying to framework this under a life-skill format within which gender, sexuality, violence, AIDS and conflict resolution are included. There should be a common programme that binds all these concerns for the government and the non-government sectors. Among other things, the programme uses innovative teaching devices such as theatre.

Dr. Seshadri points to the need for further work to reform laws and the legal system with regard to child sexual abuse. He says that since the mid-1990s, "there has been a definite movement of looking at both reformation and trial procedures." Both are important since even the best laws can be subverted by an unresponsive justice system.

Overall, perhaps, one of the key objectives is to give a voice to the children and to the survivors of child sexual and physical abuse, in all its forms. Dr. Seshadri says, "There is an assumption that girl-children are automatically subsumed in the women's movement. But that's not true. We need to create some sort of space and legitimacy for children within this system as well."

In the end, it is hard to separate the forms of family violence that affect girls and women. Partly this is because many girls have women's roles; partly it is because what happens to women now affects daughters now as well as the vision and reality of their future as women. The rights of both girls and women are irretrievably linked and must be protected together.

Endnotes

1   "Child marriage" refers to marriage before the onset of menses; "early marriage" usually means post-menses but when still legally a child. Under CRC, those under 18 are still considered children.

2   Interview for this book arranged by UNICEF India. Name withheld.

3   Interview for this book arranged by UNICEF India. Name withheld.

4   Interview for this book arranged by UNICEF Pakistan. Name withheld.

5   Such an attitude has a similar effect to that of the older tradition in European law courts according to which "the violated woman [has] lost her credibility as a prosecutrix along with her chastity" (Clark 1987, page 47).

6   The Commission points out this is most likely an underestimation, as family members were present during interviews and some interviewees were men.

7   Dr. Seshadri is a psychiatrist at the child and adolescence services of the federal Government of India's post-graduate teaching hospital, the National Institute of Mental Health and Neuroscience (NIMHANS), in Bangalore.

8   From address at the October 1997 UNICEF/UNIFEM/UNDP-sponsored Regional Meeting. Dr. Sheikh was Regional Director for UNFPA at the time.

9   Interview for this book arranged by UNICEF India. Name withheld.

10   Interview arranged by UNICEF ROSA in cooperation with UNICEF Nepal. Name used by agreement.

11 Interview arranged for this book by UNICEF India. Name withheld. Similar cases have been documented in the prize-winning film by Ruchira Gupta, *Loss of Innocence*.

12 *ji* is an honorific added at the end of a name or used by itself.

13 Before him, as early as 1961, others had described the phenomenon of imbalances in sex ratios in India for many years, but without systematic analyses. For an excellent summary, see Miller (1981a).

14 Figures cited by Raju et al. (1999) from the *United Nations Demographic Yearbook 1996* vary somewhat compared to the figures Sen originally published, but show the same general problem.

15 For example, see the review of the literature by Onishi (1996). See also Miller (1981a).

16 Until recently, Agnihotri was Secretary to Government, Department of Women and Child Development in the State of Orissa, India.

17 Interview with Dr. Satish Agnihotri by UNICEF Nepal during his visit to Kathmandu.

18 "Beloved of God," a term introduced by Mahatma Ghandi for the "untouchables." The term *dalit* (oppressed) is often used by the people themselves.

19 The focus in this section on India should not be taken to mean that foeticide and infanticide only occur there; rather, the problems have been brought into the open there, compared to the situation in other countries. For example, some case studies from Nepal can be found in Integrated Development Systems (1982), but concerning women in prisons, not the general population.

20 For a very detailed study that covers the likely differential effects on sex ratios of foeticide, infanticide and neglect, see Das Gupta and Bhat (1997).

21 One notes, however, that Census figures are for children ages zero to five. All the same, the Census figures confirm that one of the states in a belt running across north India is where the official female-to-male sex ratios at district level are among the lowest in the country. In fact, the change in the number of women and girls for every thousand men and boys in Bihar from 1901 to 1991 is 143, the second highest shift, for the worst female-to-male sex ratio in the nation (Raju et al. 1999, page 84).

22 Sitamarhi, Purana, Bhagalpur and Gumla.

23 George reports that women in Haryana were also reluctant to have infant daughters killed; one even absconded with the infant in order to save her. Fortunately, she was received back in her natal home.

24 While a certificate is legally required, the speaker apparently finds that legality is not enforced in practice.

25 Interview arranged by UNICEF ROSA for this book and conducted by the writer. "Abha" is a pseudonym used, as requested, to protect anonymity.

26 In 1999, Abha told me her daughter had been married into a family that would not accept dowry.

27 They point out that "Rape in marriage is absolutely not recognized in our society or by our legal system. In theory, it is possible for a woman to file a complaint against her husband for violence. She cannot, however, file a complaint of rape against him because the marriage contract is interpreted as having given the husband an absolute unqualified right over his wife's body as far as sexual intercourse is concerned."

28 In sub-Saharan Africa, the gap is some 25 per cent, and dramatically lower elsewhere in the world.

29 Child Marriage Restraint Act (1929).

30 In 1997, in Kathmandu, I saw *The Hills Are Shaking*, produced by an NGO in India in 1988. Unfortunately, I no longer have the name of the NGO. Also note a similar incident in which a husband cut off his wife's nose and her hair for complaining to his mother after he beat her for not doing some domestic chores. See "Husband arrested for chopping off wife's nose," *The International News*, 27 September 1997, pages 1 and 8. Goodwin (1995, pages 52–55) describes the cases of two young women who were gang-raped and then had their noses cut off. She explains, " 'To cut off someone's nose' is a figure of speech in Pakistan that means to humiliate someone. The attacks in both cases were reprisals aimed at the women's brothers. In neither case did the police conduct an investigation."

31 In her presentation "Service and Interventions: What Has Been Practiced and Unmet Needs?" Global Symposium on Violence and Health, 12–15 October 1999, Kobe, Japan, WHO Centre for Health Development.

32 Interview for this book arranged by UNICEF Bangladesh; name withheld.

33 Interview for this book arranged by UNICEF Afghanistan. Name withheld.

34 Interview for this book arranged by UNICEF ROSA and conducted by author.

35 From statement at the Kathmandu Regional Meeting, 21–24 October 1997; see UNICEF (1998b).

In 1995, passersby watch as a man beats his wife in Dhaka, Bangladesh.

Excuses, Explanations and Challenges

PART II

No More Excuses

Excuses abound for violence against women and girls. They are all too readily made and accepted. But what could anyone possibly say to try to excuse sexual abuse of children? Denial that it could even happen is the most frequent response. A study done in the Pacific region shows that offenders actually do try to make excuses as follows (from Davies 1994, page 106):

- I was giving her (or him) some sex education.
- All fathers do this.
- My wife is frigid (or ill or pregnant).
- I was just showing affection.
- It's our special game.
- I didn't do any harm.
- The child's mother is to blame, she should have known about it (or stopped it).
- It was the child's fault. She (or he) led me on.

The Pacific report goes on to say: "There is no excuse for child sexual abuse. Never. These excuses are wrong. . . . The adult is responsible — not the child" (page 106).

This is clear, but what about excuses for abuse of women and attitudes about them? They seem more readily made and accepted by society as, over and over again, men are excused for violence against women. How do some men justify it? Why do some women accept it and even help perpetuate it? Why don't communities and governments do more about the problem? How is this violence explained and widely understood? Would the statement above, from Davies, still be accepted as obvious if it were about abuse of women in the family?

"There is no excuse for abuse of women. The man is responsible — not the woman."

If gender violence is to be stopped, if advocates of change are to work successfully with women, men and children in cities and villages across South Asia and beyond, then answers are needed for these questions. Some of the activists suggested that I try to put the excuses for gender violence all together, as a kind of checklist that could be added to discussions about why gender violence is so widespread and why its acceptance should be questioned.

Based primarily on the interview project, this brief chapter charts the excuses, justifications and popular explanations given for acts of violence to women in South Asia and their acceptance of it, as well as for the State's "blind eye" on the subject.

The list of the accumulated excuses is very long. That tells its own story quickly: This is just too much; why haven't people noticed before that these are all just excuses; see them for what they are; don't accept them anymore.

Popular Excuses for Men's Violence to Women

"It's His Role, It's His Wife, It's His Business"

In interview after interview, we received the same response: violence to women is accepted. It is part of tradition. It is what a man is supposed to do. When a Nepali man interviewee had tried to stop another man from beating his wife, the husband told him that as she was his property, he could even kill her if he wished, and this was nobody else's business.

Shireen Huq,[1] a Bangladeshi woman active in the NGO community, tells this related story:

> When I was 19 or 20, one of the women who worked in our home lived in a kind of low-income housing area, not very far from our house, and we had gone to visit her for some reason. When we were leaving — you know the houses are very close together — a woman was screaming. So I ran to this hut, actually without even thinking what it was, and I just walked in [and saw why] this woman was screaming. Her husband was beating her. But there were a lot of other people around.

> Nobody was doing anything so I said, "What is wrong with you people?" I asked this man, "Why are you doing this? Why are you beating her?" He was shocked to see me. "Who's this woman?" he said. "Why is she in our home?" Not only that, the woman who was being beaten suddenly sat up and looked extremely shocked. And suddenly both of them turned toward me and asked, "Who are you?" "Why don't you mind your own business?"

> I realized that was the norm, that was the practice. [There were] all these women around, and they thought I was odd that I should get so agitated about a common thing such as a husband disciplining his wife. And that is what they told me: "He is disciplining his wife. She had been naughty."

A Man's Ego

In Sri Lanka, a woman director of an NGO finds that many men feel they must prove their superiority:

> Unless they feel [superior], I think they tend to take it out on the women. [Where a woman has more education, or is richer, or is perceived as being "Western-cultured" there can be violence.] My brother-in-law had an inferiority complex. That is what it all boiled down to.

Jealousy

She also gives jealousy and possessiveness as "reasons" for violence to women:

> A woman I know tells me that when they go out for a party or dance she is so scared that someone will come and ask her for a dance. She is mortally scared because [her husband] is so possessive. That might in itself be a precipitating factor for violence.

Lust

In India, a woman member of Parliament is appalled at the acceptance of rape. "Rape is not seen as violence against women but as an offence [born] of man's uncontrollable lust. Men must learn to discipline their lust."

Lack of Education

A Nepali woman activist expresses this view:

The main reason [for violence against women] is lack of education. When people are uneducated, their minds are full of evil things. Then they are unemployed, the whole day they have no work to do, and in the evening they drink. When they come back home at night they start to victimize the family. In this society women are the most victimized people. That is why in our country women are looked down on by the male counterparts. If they were educated, then they would have been more conscious and more aware of such things. But because they are not educated their behaviour shows that they are like animals.

Poverty

Poverty is sometimes given as a reason for men's violence against women, again with the implication that the men's frustration is simply taken out on the women. Nafisha Shah, a journalist in Pakistan, notes: "Men are frustrated with the economic condition and vent their frustrations on women."

Alcohol

The woman director of an NGO in Sri Lanka sees alcoholism as a major factor:

Generally, it is by their late 30s and early 40s — quite late in the marriage — that the abuse really heightens and the women really suffer, since that is the time that the men really drink a lot.

In Nepal, a man social worker also notes widespread abuse of alcohol:

With infrastructure development, with the building of roads, alcohol of every kind is very readily available in the villages. But there is no development, no work, no industry, no nothing. So, what the men do is that they take what little money they or their families make, or take loans, and get drunk. Then they abuse their wives, not just by beating them, but by not contributing to the family's income and wasting scarce resources. Alcoholism is a problem.

Women's Assertiveness

In Pakistan, a woman police officer notes that talking back to one's husband can trigger abuse: "This one man from a well-off, educated family was brought to the station because he was beating his wife. He complained that his wife would back answer him a lot."

Journalist Nafisha Shah, also from Pakistan, whom we met above, notes:

The language women use in rural areas is very abusive. Often because of such bad language they use, men get angry at them and beat them up. It is part of the culture. Women are advised by other women not to speak so much. To be quiet, because talking leads to more violence against them. Women have their own mechanisms to cope with these pressures. One is talking non-stop, the second is wailing. Even if a distant relative dies they will wail non-stop. It is very loud and is sing-song. It has a rhythm to it. They will praise the dead. They wail so loudly, that it seems to me that they are not wailing for the dead, but for themselves.

Alleged Promiscuity of the Woman

A woman lawyer/activist in Sri Lanka recalls when a well-educated woman, a music teacher, was being beaten by her husband, a journalist: "Even though he accused her of being promiscuous and having other men's children, she still went back to him."

A man lawyer from Pakistan recalls:

Once when I spoke about the case of a 13-year-old girl who had been gang-raped, married to and tortured by a police tout, and almost sold into forced prostitution, one of the audience replied, "A 13-year-old is old enough to enjoy sexual relations." And of course, almost everybody agreed that the girl must have had a boyfriend or two, was therefore of a loose moral character, that she was quite capable of consent and probably deserved the abuse that she got. I was advised not to lose sleep over the case, but to dig in and get some juicy details.

A woman activist in Pakistan says:

Any woman who thinks and who has confidence to be a human being is a prostitute. That is something thrown at women. If you talk in a certain way, walk in a certain way — you are just a prostitute. It is simply said to you.

"Women Dress in a Provocative Way"

"Olu," a woman secretary in Sri Lanka, recalls:

He [her husband] just talks — saying that I wear see-through clothes to show off to men. He does not allow me to wear anything that is [even slightly] transparent or without sleeves. So, like that he will find some excuse to harass me.

"His Mother Asks Him To"

An Indian man literacy teacher observes: "Even if a woman is good, and has no fault, her husband troubles her on the advice of his mother. Because a woman has only daughters she is troubled. Violence starts from birth."

"He Is Better Off without Her"

It happens that men are attracted to women other than their wives. They may have sexual relationships with these women or might decide to marry one of them. The wife becomes an impediment. In such cases, the man may really want to drive the woman off or even to kill her. When she is pregnant and he beats her, this can be an attempt to cause miscarriage. In countries where the man is paid dowry by his wife's family, it is said that for a second marriage the man will receive a higher dowry if he does not have a child.

"For Anything, No Reason Needed"

A woman NGO worker in Uttar Pradesh, India, notes: "We have a saying in our region that you don't really need a reason to beat a woman. Even if she is moving while making the dough, that is reason enough to beat her."

"It Isn't Really Violence"

A man social worker in Nepal recalls:

> We received a call from a Nepali woman. We visited her house and found her lying on the floor with big bruises all over. Her husband had beat her over and over again. She had to be hospitalized. But, when we asked the husband why he beat her, he said that he didn't beat her. He said that she was talking too much, so he just slapped her a couple of times to stop her.

Women's Acceptance of Violence against Them: Explanations and Excuses

Fear

In Bangladesh, a development worker believes: "The women do not want to talk about their problems or admit the torture because they are afraid of the society they live in."

In India, an activist says: "In ignorance they are afraid to get out and admit violence and torturing, and [so they] end up in suicide."

Karma (Destiny)

The secretary in Sri Lanka says: "I am so sick of things. I must have done a great sin in my past birth to suffer like this."

A woman lawyer in Nepal says:

> We need to move away from the idea that it's our karma, that it is OK for us to be beaten, because it isn't. In terms of adults, until they change, in terms of respect for women, boys will think that it's OK to dominate women and to violate them, and girls will accept this as their karma.

"We Grew Up with It"

A Pakistani woman journalist recalls:

> I have been exposed to the problem in my own family, but it was never considered violence. It was something women grew up with. We had men marrying three times, because of problems like not having children or family pressures. These men were marrying again and again and leaving the women behind to fend [for]their own. We had relatives that would beat up their wives everyday and you would hear them scream, and we saw toothless women who had lost their teeth by being abused by their husbands. We grew up with it. It was so much part of our family that one never thought of it as something that did not happen anywhere else. We thought it happens everywhere. It was so much part of us.

"Because of the Children"

Sometimes women accept violence to keep the family together and to be able to continue seeing their children. One woman, "Shalini,"[2] the director of an NGO in Sri Lanka, talks about the repercussions for a woman who left an abusive man:

> You don't want to deprive your child of two parents. My domestic is a super woman. She had left her husband and he had prevented her from seeing the children all this time. One

child had an accident and when she went to the hospital the husband would not allow her to even see the child. He threw her out.

Dependence

Shalini also observes: "If you are not economically independent, then you might not want to move out because you have no other option."

Stigma of Divorce

Shalini's sister stayed in an abusive marriage: "My sister had been conditioned by my grandmother so much as to not think in terms of divorce, whereas I was more influenced by my stepmother."

"No Support System, Nowhere to Go"

Shalini also notes that victims of domestic violence often have no one to turn to: "When you go to the police station to report wife-battering, policemen will say, 'Just go home and try to get along.' They don't even take the statement down."

And when there is nowhere to turn, sometimes there is a tragic end. As one of the activists notes: "Some women commit suicide rather than suffer further violence with no place for refuge."

"So Many Things, and Feelings of Inadequacy"

Olu, the Sri Lankan secretary, stays with her violent husband despite his threats to kill her and her own lack of self-esteem:

> He will never let me have the kids. He says for me to go, but what about my two sons? The elder is 11 and the younger is only four. I can't leave them. Where can I go? My parents are dead and I have only one unmarried sister in Sri Lanka. He has shouted at her too. He is so violent, sometimes he has threatened to kill me. I don't have any savings since he gave up his job last year. I have to manage everything on my salary. Now he even beats me up and asks me for money for his cigarettes and bottles. I feel so shy.

"He Really Is a Good Man"

She also makes typical excuses for her husband's abusive behaviour:

> The problem is that he is quite a good father most of the time. My elder son loves him and is very close to him. Even the younger. I don't think the baby is aware of anything. But, definitely, my older son knows. He has seen quite a few drunken scenes though he has not actually seen me being hit. My husband is too clever for that.

"He Was Drunk"

She adds:

> He is like a different man when he is drunk. So boisterous and loud. He says hurtful things, like how I didn't bring enough money into the marriage. He says that I am fat. Sometimes he says that I am ugly. Then he punches me or kicks me and tells me to leave the house.

"He Is Weak, He Needs Me"

Finally, she adds: "Even now he is dreaming of going off to the Middle East. Earlier, he wanted to get into politics. Before that he dreamed of opening a pastry shop. But, he is not a man who can do things."

"He Is My Husband, He Loves Me"

A physician who helped start an NGO in Maharashtra notes:

> Some believe that beating is an expression of love. One husband stopped beating his wife. The wife started suspecting that he had started a love affair with another woman. There are some rare incidents where the wife demands beating. When asked why the husband beats the wife, she replies, "He is my husband, why should he not beat me?"

A Woman's Reputation

An Indian woman activist explains: "Women may also fear that their character will be maligned and they will be known as prostitutes or bad women whose husbands have rightfully thrown them out."

"Sisters, Parents Could Be Hurt Otherwise"

Another says:

> Some women fear that if their marriage doesn't work out their sisters' chances for marriage will be ruined. Also their parents may be shamed. In some cases parents will suffer economically if they have received dowry from the husband.

Women Tolerate It

A woman lawyer in Nepal observes: "As long as women tolerate violence, things will not change."

The Stresses of Conflict

A staff member in the UNICEF Afghanistan office says that Afghani women may excuse violence by men against them on account of the stresses of conflict that affect the men, who take it out on women who "understand."

Self-Blame

A Nepali woman, co-founder of Saathi (Friend), an NGO, notes succinctly: "It's the self-blaming attitude of the victim."

Excuses for Women's Violence to Other Women

Women's violence to other women is occasionally mentioned. Three excuses are given.

"It Is What Already Happened to Them"

One of the activists has this important observation:

> When these women become mothers-in-law, they mistreat their own daughters-in-law, because they were mistreated and they want to mistreat someone else now. It is about

power. We think power is a male thing but it is very prevalent with women, too. My own friends who are from urban areas and are married are also mistreated by their in-laws. Violence is not in one form, it is everywhere.

Revenge

A Bangladeshi woman activist recalls: "One of my relatives was mistreated by her in-laws because one of the in-law's long-dead family members herself was mistreated generations ago. She was taking revenge."

"They Are Men's Agents"

A man researcher in Pakistan notes:

Women who become grandmothers are given a very special status, which I consider to be extremely derogatory. They are seen as figureheads of institutionalized violence against women. Ostensibly, men are supposed to be seeking their advice when denying their family women of their due rights in the name of custom. In essence, the elderly figureheads are merely being exploited by men to perpetuate their stronghold on women. Previously, some of them may even have gathered some satisfaction [to compensate for] all the violence that they themselves have endured through life.

Excuses for Society's Acceptance of Violence against Women

A Private Matter, Male Solidarity, Men's Vested Interests

Over and over again the reason given for looking the other way is that the violence against women is a private matter between husband and wife. This view accepts woman as man's property and completely governs women's human rights. It probably also reflects male solidarity about the importance of their control over woman, and the property, income and sexuality women could otherwise control. For example, women in Nepal trying to change the property rights are accused by men of wanting to ruin and destroy society. A former Prime Minister's close associate told me that although men will pretend to support a bill in Parliament for women's property rights,[3] they would never let it pass because it would cause them to lose some of their personal holdings and power.

A Taboo

A renowned Indian dancer and theatre personality believes:

Violence is everywhere, yet violence is taboo. It must be dealt with but we are afraid of its power — the power that violence will unleash if we touch it or try to unravel it. It might consume us.

"A Side Issue, Not a Human Rights Issue"

The failure at the policy level to take up domestic violence is well described by a Nepali doctor:

I am so sorry to say that from the policy level, it has not worked at all. Nothing has happened. One big achievement is that now at least they are talking about violence, because before, there was nothing. But from the policy level, they are not doing anything.

That's why when I talk about all this, the government is always angry with me. They are not sensitized. They don't think that women's problems are in the mainstream. They think that it is a side issue. They talk about different issues like human rights activities but even human rights activists do not talk about women's problems. They never talk about violence against women as a human rights violation. They always talk about violence against only prisoners, political prisoners.

Honour of the Community

A Pakistani woman journalist says:

Previously, my experience was limited to my family. There is wife-battering, which is physical abuse, and there is also mental abuse. Later, when I started probing into other areas, I found out about *karo kari*,[4] which is slaughtering of women. It is called *karo kari* in our area but it occurs in all areas of Pakistan. Murder of women happens everywhere in the world, but to have a ritualistic protection and celebration is unique to this country. If a woman is suspected of adultery, it is not only OK for me to kill her, but the whole community should go and do it together. It is a ritual to protect the honour of the community.

Alleged National Interests

In Nepal, a man in human rights work says:

There is the concern that by giving the daughters equal property rights, much of our land is going to be in the hands of Indians. I feel that all these arguments that are forwarded against giving women their property rights are just excuses, however well founded they might be.

Oppression by the State

A man lawyer in Pakistan says:

But the most disgusting incident was the one about an intelligence agency. There was a person detained by one of several intelligence agencies in our country. They showed him a film video of his daughter going to school and followed that with a porn video showing a violent rape scene. My heart sinks when I think of that. Oppression is disturbing. Oppression from the State is outright demeaning.

Taken for Granted

In Nepal, the woman physician mentioned above says:

There is, in many parts of Nepal, violence by the State. When I say this, it seems so harsh, but [this is what happens] when the police rape women and harass women. And then there are stories of a chief district officer who raped someone. We have so many stories like these. All these things are by the State. We cannot say that the State is intending to do that, but it is taken for granted that if it happens and there is nothing to do.

Lack of Laws

She notes: "We do not have a law against domestic violence."

"Respect Motherhood and the Family"

One excuse for lack of intervention is that a family is a sacred and private institution that must be preserved at all costs. But although motherhood is seen as sacred, most of the women who are beaten are mothers. Is gilded motherhood a prize for the surrender of rights, in exchange for protecting others while being submissive?

In the Name of Religion

Many of the Pakistani interviewees refer to the change in the laws against women under General Zia, when the Hudood Ordinances were introduced in 1977 in the name of religion. One observes:

> The laws also need to change. Even though the Hudood Ordinance has not been applied that much, it is still a handy tool that can be used against women. These laws reflect the way the State thinks and you have to change that perception. The State is a provocative body and you need to control it in a certain way. We also have parallel legal systems,[5] which need to be abolished.

Box 6:   **Afghanistan: In the Name of Religion**

Five Afghan female employees of CARE International were beaten by the religious police in Kabul on Saturday, 24 May 1997. The women have been employed by CARE with the written authorisation of the Taliban authorities to conduct monitoring and survey work for CARE's emergency feeding programme for widow-headed households. The beatings were conducted in public and without any legal proceedings. The incident reflects the gulf between the more moderate Taliban leadership which run most of the ministries in Kabul, and the less-disciplined members of the religious police who work under "Amr bil-Maruf wa Nahi An il-Munkir," the directorate to promote virtue and prohibit vice.

At 7:30 a.m. on Saturday morning a CARE mini-bus picked up five women monitors at an intersection near the Ministry of Public Health. All five were wearing the chadari, the tent-like garment mandated by the Taliban as a cover for women in Kabul. Two pickups from Amr bil-Maruf wa Nahi An il-Munkir started following. The leader of the religious police used his loudspeaker to order the mini-bus to stop in a very crowded area on the main road to airport. The police then got down, surrounded the bus and ordered the driver to get out. The driver complied and explained that this was an NGO bus and the CARE flag was clearly visible on the back. The police said that they knew that.

The police leader then used his loudspeaker to announce to the crowd that all foreign NGOs were bad, everything about them was bad and that those women were bad, [that] they were prostitutes. [They said that people] should get their salary and food from God, not from foreign NGOs. In a high-pitched voice he ordered the "prostitutes" to get out of the bus and ordered his men to whip and beat them. The religious police beat the back and shoulders of the first woman to get down four to five times with a meter-and-a-half long whip made of metal and leather. The next woman was beaten two times, the third one on the ankle. The last two women pleaded and were beaten lightly on the lunch baskets in their hands. The police leader motioned for them to go away. They managed to escape through a wheat field and later taxis.

The CARE mini-bus and driver were taken by the religious police and released later in that day. All police involved in the incident were wearing the armband which identifies them as members of Amr bil-Maruf wa Nahi An il-Munkir.

— From a press release issued by CARE International in Afghanistan, 26 May 1997.

Perhaps the most extreme current example of policy against women's equality — in the name of one interpretation of religion — comes from Afghanistan. Take the case of five female CARE staff who were beaten by religious police, even though they had permission to work with CARE outside their home and were correctly dressed in garments that cover them totally (see Box 6). Additional examples can be found in Physicians for Human Rights (1998).

"Conflict Situation"

Denial of women's human rights to education, health care and employment among others may also be "justified" in terms of the alleged need to protect them in times of armed conflict by limiting their mobility, exposure to and risk from "strangers." For instance, in Afghanistan, authorities have claimed, from time to time, that restrictions may ease once the conflict situation is over.

"In the Name of Custom"

The failure by the Pakistani Parliament to pass a bill against honour killing was "justified" in the name of custom itself.

"There Isn't a Problem"

A woman NGO member in Nepal says:

> A lot of people don't want to admit it. And because they themselves don't admit that they are victimized, it is not acknowledged by society as being a crime. Even the existence of violence within the home isn't acknowledged.

Beyond Excuses

The interviews quoted above give a new perspective to violence against women and girls: the fact that it is commonplace and often excused does not make it acceptable.

A closer look at the main cause of violence against women and girls, taken up in Chapter 5 below, also points to the very realistic possibility of ending it as women and men question norms for their relationships.

Endnotes

1 From an interview for this book arranged by UNICEF Bangladesh. All the other quotes are from interviews arranged by the UNICEF office in the countries concerned. Names of interviewees withheld.

2 Interviewees in Sri Lanka were given pseudonyms by the UNICEF office there.

3 In Nepal, a woman must be 35 and unmarried before she can, by law, inherit. If she marries, she then gives up the inheritance. A bill was introduced in Parliament in 1996 to change this, giving women the right to inheritance. So far, it has not been passed.

4 Women suspected of extramarital sex, whether by force or not, are *karo*; the perpetrators, *kari*. The woman may be killed for the sake of family honour. The man may be killed, or spared if his family pays compensation in the form of a woman or girls to the family of the allegedly violated girl.

5 This probably refers to the co-existence of both a legal system for decisions at local level based on the Quran and the federal legal system based in the hands of a nominally secular judiciary. There also are the Hudood Ordinances, mentioned earlier, which can be evoked.

Shadow and Sun: Femininity and Masculinity in South Asia

Unequal Power Relations as a Cause of Violence

"The ideologies which justify the use of violence against women base their discussion on a particular construction of sexual identity. The construction of masculinity often requires that manhood be equated with the ability to exert power over others, especially through the use of force. . . . The construction of femininity in these ideologies often requires women to be passive and submissive, to accept violence as part of a women's estate. . . . It is important to reinvent creatively these categories of masculinity and femininity, devoid of the use of force and ensuring the full development of human potential." (UNCHR 1994, pages 15–16)

The main cause of gender violence is the unequal power relations between women and men based on definitions of "feminine" as inferior and "masculine" as superior, as well as the broader cultural ideology and social practices, which reinforce these.[1] In short, where gender roles are constructed with an emphasis on men's entitlement to power and women's submission, gender-based violence likely follows.

It is important, then, to look more closely at some ideas about power in idealized relationships for women and men in South Asia. Are there possibilities for equality and for shared power in gender relations, according to traditional as well as modern examples? Or is the emphasis on men's power over women?

In pre-partition India, E. V. Ramaswamy had already criticized the notion that men should control women, and that men were inherently superior:

Unless women destroy the philosophy of "manhood" there is surely no liberation for women. It is "manhood" that has enslaved women. Qualities like freedom and courage have been attributed to "manhood" in the world. Men have decided that only men have these qualities. Moreover, women must fully realise that Hindu religion grants them no liberation or freedom in any respect . . .

[T]he Hindu religion states that god has created woman as prostitute by birth and that she cannot be free at any time and that she should be controlled by the father as a child and by her sons in her old age. (Indian Association of Women's Studies 1995, page 49)

A less radical way of saying it is that there should be more than one model for masculinity, more than one for femininity.

This chapter first looks, then, at how power is or is not to be shared in idealized relationships between women and men according to some historical and current literature, taken as a source on cultural ideology. Literature and popular culture often exaggerate reality, making it larger than life, and thus let us see the "ideal" more clearly. To suggest the inherent flexibility to be found in South Asian culture, and the promise of finding new models for masculinity and femininity, we start with examples of the powerful feminine, thus turning the more usual depiction of male-female relations upside down.

The Powerful Feminine

In the cultures and religions of South Asia, is there any more fearsome and powerful a manifestation of feminine force than that of the goddess Kali, venerated by Hindus? Kali first sprang into the human world from the forehead of the goddess Durga, after men and gods were unable to defeat demon forces. Ajit Mookerjee (1988, page 54) describes what happened:

> Holding a skull-topped staff, skull garlanded, wrapped in a tiger skin, emaciated, wide-mouthed, lolling-tongued, with deep sunken red-eyes Kali filled the skies with her roar. Laughing terribly, she devoured the demon army, flinging the elephants into her mouth along with their riders, crunching up their chariots and horses with her teeth, crushing others with her feet, striking with her sword and beating with her staff until the army was laid low.

The triumph of Durga and Kali, of good over evil, is celebrated in a major annual holiday in India (*Dassera*) and Nepal (*Dashain*). According to Mookerjee (1988, page 54), Kali's mythic role is to destroy the aggressive, ego-centred force usually associated with the male principle. She is best understood as representing that feminine force, *shakti*, which does not depend on the power of any male relative but is primordial, creative, preserving and destructive in turn. In fact, without *shakti* to awaken and support them, it is said that the male gods turn lethargic and passive, and can be defeated.

One re-occurring image of Kali shows her standing on her god-husband, Shiva, who lies supine and listless under her. Kali is also depicted astride her god-husband initiating and controlling sex between them. Feminine wrath and sexuality are shown as unpredictable forces that can reach beyond men's and even gods' easy control.

This echoes some concerns about female sexuality and power said to exist in the Muslim world. For example, according to Geraldine Brooks (1995),[2] it is widely believed among Muslims that 9 of the 10 parts of human sexual desire were assigned by nature to the female sex. Where this belief about insatiable female sexuality exists, a man's ability to control a woman's sexuality will always be threatened.

From the Muslim world also come images of women in battle, defeating men. These are portrayed in a story[3] based on the life of Shah Bano.[4] In her girlhood, Shahinshah is said to have learned about images of women, supposedly written by men for men and forbidden to girls. She even read the tales of legendary women — Amir Hamze and Tilism-e-Hoshruba — to her playmates, friends and cousin-sisters:

> The girls would listen to these strange tales in astonishment. These are girls who gratefully ply their boats through the rivers of patience. All have been brought up in the maelstrom. Prisoners of the zenana.[5] When released from there they will inhabit the graveyards.

Whereas the universe of Tilism-e-Hoshruba is quite else. Here women reign supreme. They gallop their steeds in the fields of war. They subdue men with the sword, the arrow, magic, incantations. Then flinging their burden on the backs of horses they carry their captives home. They make love, are jealous, are the ornament of gatherings. Queen Lighting Sword, Queen of the Clear Vision and Dignity, Queen of the Flaming Vision, Queen of Tremendous Magic, Queen of Commerce and Caster of Spells. These are princesses and weavers of magic, whose names have established traditions and whose commands are obeyed from the earth to the heavens. (Hina 1994, pages 111–112)

Shahinshah's husband in the story, Dulare Mian, burns all her books after they wed and forbids her to read or write. She had never forgotten the occasion when, after their marriage, "her God-on-earth, Mustafa Ali Khan, alias Dulare Mian, had for the first time seen her with a book in her hand. The next moment, in four pieces, it had been flung out of the door. Then the trunk full of books was dragged into the courtyard and set ablaze" (Hina 1994, page 113).

Fortunately, there are other very different examples of how men should regard women's abilities and power. Here it is worth recalling that Aishah, who is usually seen as the most beloved and favourite wife of the Prophet Mohammed, was under 10 years of age when they married, but she was not then oppressed. According to Mahnaz Afkhami and Haleh Vaziri (1996, pages 85–86):

[Aishah] is praised for her genius. She had learned to read and knew numerous poems by heart. . . . She was one of the first Muslim women to claim a political career and the right to participate and lead in public domains traditionally reserved for men. She led some thousands of men into "the battle of the Camel," a reference to the camel ridden by Aishah, the only woman on the battlefield.

In South Asia, some men not only allow or support women's power, they emulate it. For example, in *shakti* worship, there is a practice of ritual transvestism, the name for which means "to unman men." Men devotees, even today, wear women's clothes and jewellery and "observe a few days' monthly retirement period." This is because the doctrine for the followers of the god Vishnu who engage in the practice do so in the belief that "all souls are feminine to the Supreme Reality" (Mookerjee 1988, page 26).

In truth, the bedrock of cultural ideals about femininity and masculinity in South Asia is found in the pre-Aryan period, when goddess worship is thought to have prevailed throughout most of the region.[6]

The Controlling Masculine and the Submissive Feminine

Images of female power and male submission to it, like those described, contrast markedly with more common ones of the controlling male and of expected female submission. For example, in Hindu culture, *Manusmiriti*, the Laws of Manu, are a popular source for standards for men's behaviour towards women in marriage and adult life. A frequently cited injunction is: "Dogs, drums, low castes and women are to be beaten."[7]

A Nepali man journalist[8] mentions another saying he credits to the same text:

There is another quote in the *Manusmiriti* that says a woman is the shadow of her father, then the shadow of her husband, and then the shadow of her son. She has no identity of her own.[9] She is always "in relation" to someone else. She does not stand up on her own.

Because of that, I suppose, men feel justified in being violent towards women. There are various other sayings in Hindi and Nepali, to the effect that women are dust from shoes.

The shadow image for women is apparently also current among Muslims in some parts of the region. For instance, Rama Mehta, the Indian woman author of the novel *Inside the Haveli*, tells the story of Geeta, an educated girl from Bombay who is married into an aristocratic Muslim family in Udaipur, where the women still observe purdah. A brief scene between Geeta and Pari, her mother-in-law, captures the easy acceptance there of the idea that woman's rightful place is in shadow: " 'May you live in your husband's shadow for a hundred years,' she said when Geeta touched her feet. There was no rancour in her voice, no change of expression in her kind eyes" (Mehta 1996, page 107).

The notion of women's total dependence on and submission to men comes out also in what a Pakistani man[10] working in Sindh told us:

We historically belong to *Ariya Samaj* [the community of Aryans], where man is always the ruler and woman is the subordinate. Therefore the man has never given her individual freedom or rights and considers her a property like land or money. Our religious teachings also tell us that because woman was made from the rib of the man; therefore she does not have any wisdom and she is weak. And hence it is her duty to obey the man. In our society a woman is considered an object, a saleable thing. So she is confined in four walls and she is protected like any other property, or like gold, which people keep in bank lockers. Moreover, a woman may work in fields or in an office but she remains dependent on her man who controls her income. It may be her father or her husband. Even for her own needs she has to look towards him. Girls are married off without their consent. After marriage she is considered a machine to make babies.

In general, the ideal for womanhood in India is similar. It is epitomized by Sita, the wife of Lord Rama and heroine of the *Ramayana*, a major Hindu epic taken by many as a guide for values and behaviour today. It had a wide following when made and shown as a television serial in India recently.

Sita is depicted as the dutiful wife — the model for Hindu girls. Abducted by a Demon King, she is rescued unscathed by Hanuman, the Monkey King. Afterwards, the people in the kingdom whisper rumours that she has lost her honour and, thus, that of Lord Rama. She withstands a test of fire.[11] Finally, when her husband, Lord Rama, challenges her again, she asks the earth to swallow her up if necessary to prove her innocence. The earth opens and she disappears.

The fact that Rama lost Sita because of his unfounded suspicion, unnecessary doubt and relentless testing is rarely, if ever, brought home to boys, let alone to girls. Instead, Sita's purity and dutifulness are stressed as a model for girls. Boys learn from the story that if they are to grow up to be like Lord Rama, they should doubt, suspect and control women who may otherwise stray, no matter how seemingly pure they appear to be. Boys learn from Lord Rama's example that their own honour in the eyes of the community depends on a woman's purity and honour (*izzat*). This same idea prevails in Muslim communities in South Asia.

Men's penchant to control, however, gets expressed in patriarchal societies as something a woman needs, not as a man's insecurity. For instance, in Bapsi Sidhwa's novel *The Bride*, set in Pakistan, a man says to his younger brother about the latter's new wife: "You know, she requires a man to control her" (Sidhwa 1984, page 170).

Immediately, the younger brother becomes harder in his attitude and behaviour towards the girl so he can look the older brother in the eye, like a real man, in control of women.

In Muslim cultures, some of the interviewees tell us, notions about men's and women's relations are derived from folk tradition as much as if not more than from the Quran. For example, a Pakistani man[12] who does social research comments:

> In connection with our research, I was looking into Punjabi proverbs on women and could hardly find anything positive. Most of them referred to women as unfaithful, unreliable, of low caste — like a shoe which can be changed at will, a conspirator, and forever rebellious if not controlled. The positive reference was on the sturdiness and hard work of a Punjabi woman. I doubt if even the Sufis have said something positive about women in his (this refers to author Data Gunj Baksh) famous work *Kashf-ul-Mahjoob*, relates women to evil. In complete contravention of Quranic verses, most Muslims believe that Eve was created out of Adam's rib, which is why she is supposed to be rigid.

Equal Power

Few images from traditional sources in South Asia come to mind about male and female sharing power equally and without conflict. From ancient times, in what are today Bangladesh and India, stone figures have been found that combine both male and female physical characteristics. Ardhanarisvara, "representing the equilibrium of the feminine and the masculine aspects that make up a single human being,"[13] and Kamakalavilasa, "female and male conjoined,"[14] are examples, along with various hermaphrodite figures dating from the 11th century. There are examples, at least from India, of males doing activities thought of today as typically "feminine," such as milking a cow or carrying a child, both to be seen in Mahaballipuram, near Madras.[15] From modern-day Nepal, the work of Nepali woman artist Ragini Upadhyay goes so far as to show a popular and beloved male god, the elephant-headed Lord Ganesha, as female: this is the artist's way of saying that the feminine is equal to the masculine.[16] And in one variant of Mahayana Buddhism practised in Nepal, figures of male and female in sexual union are meant to symbolize the ecstasy and bliss that come from the union of compassion and wisdom.[17] The male figure represents compassion and the female figure, wisdom — a reversal on what might be expected. This reversal adds characteristics to both the male and female gender role that normally are excluded, at least in stereotypes. Both female and male capacity are thereby increased and strengthened, not diminished.

Norms for Femininity and Masculinity: The Antecedents of Gender Violence?

Even though there are antecedents for gender equality in South Asia today, popular images of femininity and masculinity are decidedly not equal. What are the images of ideal femininity and masculinity that most women and men in South Asia strive to fulfil and to have their children fulfil? How strongly are relationships between women and men influenced by the images and the attitudes about them? Do social institutions, norms and values in South Asia reinforce and reflect ideals for gender roles that actually predict violence against women? Who challenges the system, doesn't accept the prescriptions for femininity and masculinity, and what happens to them when they do?

These are important questions. Stopping gender violence requires looking at and challenging the particular social and cultural norms for femininity and masculinity that influence inequality in the power relations between women and men. Where women are supposed to submit and men to dominate there is likely to be gender violence — especially if it is assumed that women have a source of unpredictable power within them that should be suppressed and controlled. Where men and women both accept norms for their respective superiority and inferiority, and these are reflected in shared cultural or religious beliefs, social organization and practices, it is likely that gender violence will be even greater than it is elsewhere.

It must be stressed that "gender" differences and roles are not synonymous with whatever psychological and behavioural differences there may be between women and men as determined by biological sex; rather, gender roles are learned. They reflect socially created and socially sanctioned cultural norms for the attitudes and behaviour of women and men, girls and boys. In truth, "femininity" and "masculinity" simply mean "like a woman" and "like a man." The ideals for each one can and do vary dramatically from culture to culture and era to era. Still, power imbalances that are supposed to exist between women and men are usually codified in ideals of femininity and masculinity. It is typical that these are posed in contrasting sets, as they are in South Asia, such as yielding/controlling, passive/assertive, innocent/worldly, weak/strong and shadow/sun for the female and male, respectively. Furthermore, the way in which gender is constructed is often considered to be synonymous with supposed dichotomies between the sexes that are "given" by biology. That means they are often erroneously considered to be beyond question.

According to descriptions from interviewees, as well as a wide range of literary and other sources, it appears that the ideal girl in South Asia is most often considered one who is married when she is still a virgin, is dutiful to her in-laws and husband, and gives birth to sons. She is obedient, quiet, hard-working and modest. Her sexuality, emotions and intellect are seen as potentially dangerous characteristics that must be controlled — by herself, her parents, her husband and her in-laws — if the ideal is to be fulfilled. This ideal seems to apply for Hindus and Muslims alike, although the details of the prescription vary. Proponents of Buddhism often claim that the religion is more egalitarian with regard to expectations for females compared to males. However, even in Buddhist Sri Lanka, many of the characteristics mentioned above are seen as ideal for girls.

The ideal boy? His position at birth, as fixed by the class or caste of his family, is likely considered as more important even than his personal characteristics.[18] One who comes from a more wealthy and powerful family, which has status and prestige, would be a parent's preference for their daughter to marry. He should have some property, be able to control it and count on other men for his endeavours, and also to do his duty to those who may be even more important than he. He should control the women in his family and thus preserve family honour. He must have sons to carry on the lineage.

A complex of cultural ideals and expectations — especially regarding socialization, marriage practices and the structure of the family — are part of the social system in

South Asia that allows and even promotes the idea and practice of female inferiority and male superiority. These reinforce men's violence against women and women's acceptance of it. Indeed, the construction of gender can limit potential and separate each of us from our full humanity. At worst, the process creates opposites, half human beings — literally dehumanizing women and men. Then "femininity" and "masculinity" become very restrictive categories, representing a dualistic world. The two halves, of course, are not equal. The female half likely counts for far less with regard to self-esteem, treatment and rewards, especially but not only in marriage and the family.

How women are counted as less than men and less than human, really, is suggested in a study from the United States done many years ago. (One hopes the results would be less extreme if the study were repeated today.) In the late 1960s, Broverman et al. (1997)[19] studied who —whether women or men — is seen as normal and healthy, and who is seen as mentally disturbed or unbalanced, the lesser beings. The research design was this: Mental health professionals from a number of fields — psychiatry, clinical psychology and psychiatric social work — were asked to describe the normal healthy man, woman and adult. A questionnaire was used, with a long list of bipolar adjectives such as very submissive/very dominant, not at all aggressive/very aggressive, very aware of feelings of others/not at all aware of feelings of others, unable to separate feelings from ideas/easily separates feelings from ideas, very illogical/very logical, and very gentle/very rough.

The 79 mental health professionals were divided into three similar groups made up of both men and women; each group was given a different task. Each person in group one, say, was asked to pick the item from each pair of phrases that best described the "normal healthy man." Those in another group were to describe the "normal healthy woman." And finally, another group selected phrases to describe the "normal healthy adult."

The alarming thing about the conclusion was that the description of a normal healthy adult was more or less identical with that of a normal healthy man, while the description of a normal healthy woman could be considered more like that of a disturbed rather than healthy adult.

The authors pointed out that "clinicians are more likely to suggest that healthy women differ from healthy men by being more submissive, less independent, less adventurous, more easily influenced, less aggressive, more excitable in minor crises, having their feelings more easily hurt, being more emotional, more conceited about their appearance, less objective, and disliking math and science" (Broverman et al. 1997, pages 4–5; also see Broverman et al. 1972 regarding further research).

The researchers point out that this reflects the sex-role stereotypes — which today would be called "gender roles" — that constrict equality of opportunity and freedom of choice for girls and women, and, to a lesser extent, for boys and men. They concluded "the cause of mental health may be better served if both men and women are encouraged toward maximum realisation of individual potential, rather than to an adjustment to existing restrictive sex roles" (Broverman et al. 1997, page 7).

Some Factors behind Restrictive Gender Roles in South Asia

In South Asia there are restrictive gender roles and many practices that reflect the idea that a woman is less than a man, even less than human, and that she should be dominated, especially in marriage. Five "limiting factors" will be discussed briefly here:

- socialization that favours boys;
- early marriage for girls;
- isolation of women after marriage;
- separate spheres for women and men;
- domestic violence.

Definitions of masculinity and femininity both fuel and are maintained by each of these limiting factors. The influence of the patriarchy on gender roles and relations, and specifically on domestic violence, is also considerable and will be discussed. It is a challenge to understand why men don't give more thought to gender violence as a problem and why many women seem to accept violence against them as a matter of course. And why do some mothers-in-law even help perpetuate the norms for femininity if they themselves suffered when fulfilling them?

For the most part, the answers lie in the nature of patriarchy and how it influences definitions of masculinity and femininity, as well as the practices to shape and control behaviour and attitudes so the ideals will be met. In the patriarchy, and the predominantly patrilineal and patrilocal kinship systems of South Asia, one can find the basis for the factors taken up first below, before the discussion of patriarchy.

Socialization That Favours Boys

One song captures the sentiment that is true in most of South Asia:

> O father, you brought up my brother to be happy.
> You brought me up to shed tears.
> O father, you have brought up your son to give him your house,
> And you have left a cage for me. (Dube 1997, page 89)

"Boys preferred here." The birth of the boy is celebrated. The birth of a girl is dreaded. (Many avoid it by any available means.) The process of gender socialization that sharply favours boys begins at birth. Much of the focus is on training the little girl to turn her into suitable material to be a proper wife, and the little boy to grow up to dominate her. For the "ideal" girl, socialization means, then, learning to have a submissive attitude, and for the "ideal" boy, it means learning how to get his way easily. It is useful to recall a statement made in Bangladesh in 1996, at a national workshop on ending violence against women that was attended by some 250 women's groups:

> The deeper causes of violence against women and children are found in a psychological and cultural context which favours boys and men while suppressing and devaluing girls and women. Many girls are brought up on the idea that they have less worth and are less capable. Many boys are brought up protected and spoiled, "not seldom" without the necessary survival skills to fend for themselves. They get their way by throwing tantrums rather than through discussions, negotiations or compromises. Perhaps this is one reason why, as adult men they often react to discomfort with violence rather than words.
> (Carriere 1996, quoting Jahan and Islam 1997, pages 64–65)

Such a process of differential treatment is described by Sri Lankan writer Punyakante Wijenaike in her novel, *Amulet* (1994), which explores the roots of family violence and incest.[20] It is significant that this novel comes from Buddhist Sri Lanka, where the indicators of women's status are higher then elsewhere in the region.[21] In spite of this, we see a description of attitudes and norms that are all too typical for the region. The fictional heroine, Shyamali, describes her upbringing:

> From childhood I understood this difference between my younger brother and myself. Mother saw to my basic needs but never was I held close in her arms, never was I fondled the way she did my brother. Mother convinced me that bringing up a daughter was like manuring and watering a plant which would, one day, be up-rooted and re-planted in a husband's garden. So she confined me to being a potted plant, occasionally taken out of the house for a watering. She never permitted me to send deep roots into my family soil. She made sure father's house and estate was written early in my brother's name. . . .
>
> I was not permitted to grow strong in personality since I was stifled, pruned down, restricted to requirements of the household, kept in the background until the proper time came to bring me out as a bride. "A good housewife, a mother. A woman must learn endurance and patience," my mother said. She did not encourage too much achievement in school, stopped me from sitting for the senior exam. But she did encourage me to learn cooking, piano playing and sewing. Even my desire to draw sunsets and landscapes she discouraged. She refused to buy paints, paper or canvas. (Wijenaike 1994, pages 2–3)

How different from the treatment of her brother. Their mother "devoted her life to him, personally bathing, feeding," says Shyamali. "She entrusted him to the care of no hired woman, like she did me" (page 16).

And girls are not as likely as boys to be sent to school, in part because of beliefs that formal education would undermine their tractability and marriageability (to say nothing about the risk that they might lose their virginity). As Shyamali's mother says, "A woman's mind must not perceive anything further than the handle of a spoon" (pages 2–3). Instead, they are taught how to serve their future husbands. Boys are taught to be served.

Translator and editor Samina Rehman from Pakistan (1994, pages 10–11) says that for many women, the only books they are allowed are:

> *Bahishti Zewar (Heavenly Ornaments)*, a book of etiquette for Muslim women by the religious scholar, Maulana Ashraf Ali Thjanvi, that, along with the Holy Quran, formed a part of every educated middle- and upper-middle-class girl's dowry. The Maulana reinforces the concept of the husband as, literally, God-on-earth, offering prescriptions for developing unquestioning obedience and loyalty, sacrifice, denial of the ego and the art of pleasing the husband in every conceivable way.

In Zahida Hina's (1994) short story, "The Earth Is Ablaze and the Heavens Are Burning," in Rehman's (1994) edited collection, we see a husband using the *Bihisti Zewar* to intimidate his wife, whose father, apparently, had not done a proper job in educating her for marriage. From the content as described, *Bihisti Zewar* seems to be a primer also for what boys must learn about their own importance:

> Listen to what Hazrat Ashraf Ali Thanvi, the Blessed one, has to say. "As far as possible try and hold on to your husband and follow his slightest command. If he were to order you to stand the whole night with your hands folded, it is better in the interest of the here and the Hereafter, that you suffer a little discomfort in the here and vindicate yourself by earning a place in the Hereafter. Never say anything at any time that contradicts his mood. If he calls the day night you must follow suit.

Listen Shahinshah Bano, do away with the devil in your mind. A woman's status is so low, so humble, that man is forbidden to even perform his ablutions or bathe in the water left over from her ablutions or bath. We have been made to rule the women, have you understood?

That night was the first night that she was convinced that no prescription for the salvation of women had descended from above. All the books, all the writings, all the sayings were there simply to acquaint men with ways of imprisoning women in the seventh degree of hell. (Hina 1994, page 116)

According to a Pakistani business executive[22] who participated in the interview project for this book, many families in Pakistan still give their daughters *Bihisti Zewar* as a gift at marriage. He points out, "And the irony is that the women are not allowed even to read Holy Quran."[23]

Kiran Tewari, a Nepali social worker[24] explains how girls in his country learn low self-esteem, while boys know early that they are the ones in charge:

When she is a child in her father's house, her brother takes over, because he feels that his father's property is his. The girl has no power to ask for anything because her family says, "She will be going to someone else's home. She's not ours, so we won't spend too much on her."

She loses her self-esteem. I think that is mental torture. Also, when she is married, they use the term *kanya-daan. Daan* implies gift, relinquishing of rights. *Kanya* means virgin. So the parents literally give their [virginal] daughter to the in-law, and they have relinquished all their rights on her, and she on them. Now she is the property of her husband and in-laws. Routinely, daughters are told not to return from the in-laws' home unless they are dead.

A process of differential treatment for boys and girls is a powerful mechanism for the establishment of separate — actually opposite — gender norms in South Asia. Other practices reinforce these norms.

Early Marriage for Girls

A seemingly sure way to guarantee both the "purity" and the pliability of girls is to insist on their early marriage, as does "a learned Brahmin," cited in B. S. Nagi's *Child Marriage in India* (1993, page 4):

A damsel should be given in marriage before her breasts swell. But if she has menstruated before marriage, both the giver and the taker fall into the abyss of hell; and her father, grandfather and great grandfather are born insects in ordure.

Nagi also notes that some Hindu teachings enjoin parents not to keep a girl unmarried even at the age of eight. Indeed, *Manusmiriti* promises parents the reward of heaven if a daughter is given in marriage by age nine and hell if she is given after her puberty (Arole 1999, page 54).

For Yubaraj Sangroula, a Nepali man lawyer,[25] the prescription of child marriage is linked to religious beliefs and stereotypes about a girl-woman's underlying nature:

Nepali society is very traditional and follows orthodox Hindu philosophy. Parents feel it is their responsibility to give the daughters in marriage before the first menstruation. There is vested interest. If the parents can perform the daughter's marriage before menarche, while she is *kanya*, a virgin, then the door to heaven is open [to them]. That is the belief.

The mother may say marrying young will be difficult for the girl, but the father does not pay heed. Most families believe that an early marriage will help the girl adapt to difficult situations more easily. If the marriage takes place later, the girl will be more aware of who she is and her status as a human being. She may protest about what happens to her in the name of society and traditions. But if she is married at an early age, she will not question. She will adapt to and accept any kind of injustice.

The general belief is that a woman belongs to another family. It is considered her luck, her fate. If she had done good in her past life, then she would have been male in this one! Another reason is families used to be very big and having many children was common. If daughters could be given away early, family size would be reduced. The grain or the income that the family had could support more and expenses would be less. This is still valid in villages. The main reason, though, is religious.

Arole observes that the early Vedas "suggest that prior to the 4th century BC, females entered marriage at about 15–16 years of age." She says child marriage was "frowned upon" and "women had the right to choose their husbands" (Arole 1999, page 53).

Among Muslims, there are strong historical precedents for child marriage but not the same religious prescriptions. Arole cites Asghor Ali Engineer regarding the lack of any direct reference to child marriage in the Quran. In fact, verses of the Quran about marriage refer to the importance of marrying true believers and the need to deal justly with them, not to a recommended age for marriage (Arole 1999, page 54). One recalls that, whereas Aishah was a very young bride, the Prophet's first wife, Khadija, was 40 when he married her.

That much said, the actual practices in the region often mean the marriage of girls at quite a young age, for both predominantly Muslim and predominantly Hindu countries. The gap between the age of first marriage for males and females is a useful indicator of how likely it is that the female is expected to be submissive and the male to control her. In South Asia the gap is the second widest in the world, with an average of 5.2 years for the region (UN 1993). It ranges from only 3.5 years in Sri Lanka to 7.5 years in both Afghanistan and Bangladesh. In contrast, the gap in East Asia and the Pacific region is almost half that in South Asia: 2.7 years; only Africa surpasses the gap in South Asia, and barely, with an average of 5.7 years.

For over 100 years, child marriage and child widowhood have been a focus of social reformers in much of South Asia. Cohabitation and consummation of marriage have been addressed separately. In 1860, the Indian Penal Code prohibited intercourse with a wife under 10 years of age. The effort in India to raise the minimum marriage age even to 12 was protracted, due to fears that a girl would menstruate earlier, inviting shame to her family if she had not married beforehand. The Hindu Child Marriage Act, which raised a girl's age of marriage to 12, was passed only in 1927. In South Asia today, 18 is the legal age of marriage for girls in all the countries covered in this book, while 18 to 24 are legal ages for the marriage of boys (UNFPA 1998, page 18). In reality, a sizeable proportion of girls, in particular, marry earlier (see Chapter 2).

Marriage at any age makes a woman the property of her husband and in-laws. Within such an arrangement, women, especially when young, become particularly vulnerable to domestic violence.

Isolation of Women after Marriage

It is easy to understand that isolation, both physical and emotional, contributes to the likelihood of a girl-woman's submissiveness after her marriage. A man's ability to control her is enhanced by the dependence on him that her isolation helps to create.

In much of South Asia, marriage requires that the bride go to the home of her in-laws and that she not come back unless dead (see, for example, Agarwal 1994a). Any visits are under the control of her husband and new family. These would most likely have to do with her giving birth, or a parent becoming sick or dying. It is not automatic that she will be given permission. For instance, the fictional character Shyamali was not allowed to visit her home when her mother died.

Purdah is another form of isolation and control to which women in some cultures are expected to submit, usually after the onset of menstruation or marriage, whichever is earliest.[26] Like early marriage, purdah ensures that women have a limited vision of and participation in the world outside the home. This is quite literally the case for women who wear all-enveloping clothes from head to foot. Agarwal (1994a) notes that the origin of the practice of purdah in South Asia is obscure, and that its history includes examples of protests against it by both individual women and men.

Even where purdah is not observed, a separation of the private and public worlds is expected, the former for women, the latter, for men. This is explored further in the next section.

The emotional isolation of women by men in marriage is illustrated by the way the wedding night tends to be described. For instance, in Wijenaike's *Amulet*, the character Shyamali says: "He acted as if I was another possession. . . . He was quick and brutal with me. He ignored my cry of pain and performed his act of penetration as if it was something he had to accomplish that night and when it was all over he left me crying, turned his back on me and went to sleep" (Wijenaike 1994, page 24).

It is a fictional story, but it is also the reality that many young women in South Asia have experienced. Most of the women interviewed by Mabelle Arole for her 1995 book, *Voices of South Asian Women,* said that the first time they were beaten by their husband was on their wedding night.[27] The fictional Senani's experience in fact summarizes what many men in the region, even in predominantly Buddhist Sri Lanka, have learned: their masculinity is confirmed by their ability to conquer and control. Controlling women depends on the man's turning away from a woman's feelings and emotions, as well as from his own. Where women are considered as objects, men do not need to waste time or emotion on them.

Separate Spheres for Men and Women

The reduction of a woman to the domestic property of her husband, a means to express masculinity and carry on the patrilineage, mirrors one aspect of the ways that gender divisions are not only stereotypes for proper behaviour but are actual divisions of power. Such divisions are reflected in the division of physical and social space: between the supposedly private, domestic sphere, to which women belong (but where men still wield power) and the public sphere (in which men are triumphant and, traditionally, unequivocally in control). Dividing the world into domestic and public space, with women confined to the former, which is less valued, is another way of isolating women and reducing their potential power.

Where the range for prescribed behaviour of women and men is narrow, the reaction against any deviation will most likely be stronger — in part, because the prescribed behaviour is set out as natural, embedded in the sex of the being, from nature and god. And in a dualistic world, where the domestic world is the female realm and the public world is the male realm, females are expected not to be seen or heard outside their realm, and males are expected to be little involved in the details of the domestic world. Through the rigid separation of the two, men and women are, ultimately, unknown to each other. This in turn reinforces the notion that we are essentially different beings, isolated by nature and circumstance from each other.

In Khalida Hussain's (1994) story from Pakistan, "The Fairground," the woman narrator has a recurring dream of meeting her nameless husband in the market. He doesn't recognize her in public.

> My dream is that I am going down the alley and the alley is silent and empty, all down its length. Nobody is visible even at a distance. I am afraid and then I see him approaching, in his white clothes, racquet in hand, dripping with sweat. I feel reassured on seeing him but he doesn't notice me even as he is looking at me. This surprises me, and I lift my burqa [a black garment that covers a woman from head to toe] so that he can take a look at me but even then he doesn't recognize me and passes me by. I want to call out to him but I lose my voice. Then I run after him. At the sound of my footsteps, he turns around to look but his face has changed. He is someone else, an unknown person. I am frightened, and begin to have doubts about my face and wonder if it has changed as well. I want to search for my house, but all the houses in the street are the same. . . .

> I have always known that he is somewhere else outside of these stairs and this alley. People look at him and know him in some other way, a way in which I cannot see and know him. That is why, even when with me, he is actually away, outside this alley, and I don't know the person who exists outside the alley. He knows all this and he wants to keep things the way they are. I often sense his body as just a body and I am afraid. But these are things he knows as well, and knowing them, he wants to keep them the way they are. (pages 95–96)

Thus, the separation not only produces partial human beings and reinforces the gap between women and men. Especially in the type of public space described in this story, it is the complete erasure of the woman's identity. The narrator of this story says, "in the black burqas nobody had an identity. It was not possible to tell one from the other. I began to feel ants crawling on my back and the black emptiness in my belly started growing" (page 100).

Near the end of the story, she can't find her son. He has gone off with someone else in a burqa, someone whom he thought was his mother or aunt. Stepping out of the separate spheres brings with it punishment for the woman: she will lose herself and possibly even her child.

A story by the Rajasthani writer Vijaydan Detha (1997) further explores this separation of spheres and its crippling impact on men as well as women. His story is based on a folk tale.

Growing up, two boys pledge that when they are men their children will be wed. The problem is that the children are both girls. Never mind. One simply declares his daughter to be a boy, brings her up that way, and marries her off as a bridegroom to his friend's daughter. The two are happy. A ghost chieftain is entranced by the sight of the girls' lovemaking and lets them share his ghost palace, from which men are banned.

But one day, the "husband" becomes a real man. Immediately, he looks at things and his wife very differently. He wants her to nap, while he takes a walk to the village. She is surprised at the notion of being left behind, in the private not the public space. That night, their lovemaking is very different. The man looks back on their earlier lovemaking this way: "How many days we wasted, just fooling around." But the woman says, "What do you mean, wasted? Those joys cannot be forgotten, not even after death." This leads to his "realization" about how powerful he is and how frail is the woman. The next morning, "the husband's eyes opened, the sun had already climbed into the sky. Its rays shone into the room. Seeing the rays, pride awoke in his heart, telling him that it is man's heat and power which rises in the heavens in the form of the sun. Woman is merely his shadow."

Before, the two of them owned the palace equally. But this chafed against his assumption of superiority. "Who owns this palace," he demands, "you or I?"

Teeja, the female still female, wonders how he could have changed so much in a single day and now loathes their palace and their relationship. She thinks, "How had this 'I' come between them in the course of a single night?" She says that the palace belongs to the ghost chieftain. "He," the female-turned-man, accuses her of having a lover and swears he will build a palace and fort, have a harem greater than that of the ghost chieftain and diminish her importance. He beats her senseless.

But later, sitting alone, he somehow remembers what he has lost. He so yearns to return to the earlier relationship that the ghost chieftain changes him back. Once again, the women take up their unsullied relationship, itself a fantasy, with the ghost chieftain's blessing. No man can enter.

The story suggests that the relationship between woman and man in marriage within a dualistic world immediately corrupts even the basic good nature of the man, given the stereotypes of masculinity and femininity, the male preoccupation with sexual possession of the woman as property and his concern for "status." In this bleak vision, where there is such inequality, such a separation of spheres, the possibility for love and connection is spoiled. Women become chattel. And for men, the domestic sphere is not a place of precious relationships and connection, but of supposed mastery and control, partly for posturing in front of other men. But in such mastery, he is unable to be simply human.

Domestic Violence

The high rates of domestic violence in the region have already been discussed. Violence towards women and girls about control of their person and sexuality starts even before marriage. Sometimes it is used to force girls to marry or to punish them if they will not. Crimes of kidnapping and abduction, said to be often for purposes of marriage, are among the most frequent of all crimes against women in the region; for example, in India they are the third most frequent offence against women, with 15,617 cases reported in 1997, up 5 per cent from 1996 (National Crime Records Bureau 1999, page 162). Abduction is also used to force a girl to marry in Pakistan and Bangladesh. Acid thrown in a girl's face when she resists a proposition is a problem of grave concern in Bangladesh. Thuggery is used to intimidate parents if dowry is not enough in Bangladesh (PromPT 1996). And from Buddhist Sri Lanka comes a story, as told by an interviewee[28] to Maithree Wickramasinghe for this book, of a girl's being raped and then forced into an unhappy and abusive marriage to avoid facing shame. When she was 18, the girl was raped by a boy she had known since she was 12. He kept her underwear to shame her into marrying him. Even when she threatened suicide he would not stop threatening and abusing her. Her mother shouted at her and beat her for not getting married. The interview continues: "Finally, one evening when he approached me at home to talk to me, I threw kerosene oil from the lamp on myself and set myself alight." "Were you not scared to do such a thing?" Maithree, the interviewer, asked.

> I think I was so angry and frustrated and desperate at the time. I was not scared. I was in the hospital for one and half months as a result of the severe burns on my hands and other parts of my body. After that, my aunt looked after me.

> After I came home, I was virtually forced to marry him. His mother kind of brought the proposal. When I felt the baby in my stomach, I felt really scared and finally decided to marry him even though I truly believed that I would *aattaraman wenewa* [become lost] by doing that.

Only after 17 years of beatings did she hit him back and leave him.

Once married, even the most willing and gentle girl may still be subjected to intimidation and violence. Shyamali, the Sri Lankan heroine of the novel *Amulet*, is an example. She is given in marriage, with a generous cash dowry, to Senani, who revels in controlling her and avoiding emotional intimacy. (He has secretly killed his own sister, with whom he had a long-term incestuous relationship, at first forced on them as children by their nanny.) Whatever restrictions the character Shyamali felt in her childhood made her vulnerable to a terrible marriage:

> My restricted life, my inhibitions, made me an easy victim to my husband. Father and mother did not know the man they gave their daughter to, the daughter they had reared like a delicate golden bird in their home. They only knew that there was a man of status. . . . He was marrying me for my prestige as the daughter of an aristocratic family, a genteel lady. . . . I would then become mistress of my husband's property, a masterpiece hanging on his wall. . . . I was nineteen. (Wijenaike 1994, page 5)

The fictional husband, Senani, an architect with a home in Colombo, recalls his motives for choosing Shyamali:

> I wanted a wife who was simple, almost naive in her outlook. . . . Shyamali had come from a sheltered home with a limited knowledge of life and people. She was also uncertain of what she wanted out of life. She was mine and mine to make and mould. I could wear her like a medal to boost myself up the social ladder. A young, fair, respectable wife from a good family. Untouched, unspoilt. . . .

> I do not want to lose control over my wife. The structure of my marriage, my very life, is based on control and power. I do not want to be like father. He lost control of the situation. (pages 115–116)

His father had failed, in Senani's view, to keep his own wife from killing herself when she discovered that he was having an affair.

Over time, Shyamali discovers a diary left by Senani's sister, whom he killed, which tells the story about Senani's mother and father, which he wants to hide: for him it is about his father's failure as a man, his own potential failure. Shyamali takes refuge in the same attic where Senani's mother died. She meditates and strengthens her Buddhist faith. As she prepares, finally, to confront Senani, he is on his way upstairs, contemplating killing her.

This story helps us see that domestic violence in South Asia is very much a part of men's seeming need to control women, for them to confirm their own masculinity in terms of cultural ideals.

The Fragility of Masculinity

Senani's is a model of masculinity that carries with it a constant threat to the man himself. Such masculinity is a surprisingly fragile construct and, ultimately, impossible to maintain. It rests on measures of power and control that are always threatened and never secure. It does not matter what a man has achieved in the past: in his future there is always a chance of losing power and, hence, losing manhood.[29] This is compatible with what Michael Kaufman, Canadian author and leader of a movement for men against gender violence, writes:

> It is, of course, impossible for any human being to be all-powerful or like the sun blazing at the centre of the universe. And, so, this creates a problem for men, especially in relation with women. Faced with a woman and her own strength and power, some men become fearful of her independence, her intelligence and her power. They do so because they believe that any manifestations of such things represent a loss of honour and power for them, especially with other men.[30]

The Question of Sexuality and Power

Michael Kaufman also notes, "Such a loss of power is often equated with sexual impotence."

Tiloka, the fictional husband in Rajinder Singh Bedi's (1994) novel from India, *I Take This Woman,* makes a similar observation: "Only the impotent are scared of their women" (page 21).

Women have different power. Power from Mother Earth, the moon, the dark, their equality with nature and giving birth, which men cannot do. Goddesses abound. Men worship them. But as Ragini, a Nepali woman artist, shows in her paintings, goddesses seem to benefit men more than they do women. For example, Laxmi[31] is the Hindu Goddess of Wealth, but who is rich? Saraswati is the Goddess of Learning, but who goes to school? The Kumari, known as the living goddess, ensures the well-being of the Kingdom of Nepal. The King seeks her blessing. But once she menstruates or bleeds from a cut, she is replaced; she cannot then lead a normal life. Men avoid marrying her, fearing they would die an untimely death. Real women's power isn't so worldly as is men's, it seems. But their underlying mystery and unexpected behaviour remain, as in the example of the goddess Kali, and prompt men's effort to try to control what cannot be known.

The emphasis on controlling women seems to be fed, in part, by men's perception of women's supposedly powerful sexuality and emotionality. Because of this, or because men lack confidence in their own prowess and fear that of others, some husbands imagine sexual affairs should wives even be around other men. And outside of marriage, men may justify molestation, rape, even gang rape, on the grounds that women really want it and "ask for it," no matter what women may say in words, no matter if they are unaware of any sexual connotations in their behaviour. Women who go outside the home, whether for defecation, chores, education or work, are thus suspect. They are temporarily away from the physical control of male relatives. They are thus often seen as "fair game." In addition, men who attack such women insult those male relatives who fail to control "their" women. Through violating such women, men assert their own superior masculinity as defined through their control over the women. Masculinity is thus experienced as a key part of what determines hierarchy among men and power struggle among them.

For a woman, any expression of sexuality outside of marriage, whether by choice or not, can bring death. For example, fatwas — rulings by local Muslim religious and village leaders — are given in villages in Bangladesh against women who have become pregnant as a result of rape, incest or consensual sexual union (see Alam and Ahmed n.d.; for a study of fatwas in India, see Shourie 1995). A fatwa can lead to many outcomes, including public flogging and death by stoning. Fatwas bring shame and dishonour to the woman's family. Many women opt to commit suicide rather than subject themselves and their families to such disgrace. The fatwa is ostensibly against the woman. It also can be seen as a condemnation of the man, who should have controlled her, and an indictment of his masculinity in the patriarchy. In short, the patriarchal context exaggerates male violence against women and women's submission.

In Michael Kaufman's words[32]:

> The simple equation is this: To be a man is to have power. This includes power for men over women and power over at least some other men. To be a woman is, supposedly, to not have worldly power. Thus if a woman has such power, it can only be power she has "robbed" from the man — taking on "his" attributes.

> Not only, then, must a man be powerful (in order to be seen by himself and by other men as a man) but such power is a zero-sum equation: the more that women have it, the less that men have it. The more "his" woman is powerful and in control of her destiny, the less power he feels he has, the less he is a man. It is, of course, the strange logic of relations between the sexes in a patriarchal society.

Masculinity in the Patriarchy

It is within this total framework that we can now clearly explain men's violence against women as an expression of the demands and contradictions of masculinity in a patriarchal order. Here we can follow Kaufman's typology of the fourfold sources of men's violence against women. It would seem to apply in South Asia as well as the West.[33]

First, as many women have noted, gender violence is a means, used by men, consciously and unconsciously, to limit and control women's potential power and independence. It is a way to tame them.

Second, it is an expression of men's sense of entitlement to privilege and power.

Third, in apparent paradox to these first two, it is an expression of men's own fears of weaknesses and powerlessness, of not being "real men." In Bapsi Sidhwa's (1984) novel *The Bride*, the newlywed man, Sakhi, is terrified that news of his attempts to appease his bride will have spread through the village. "What must they think of him, he wondered" and changes his ways immediately (page 171). He is further challenged and his shock and rage increase when his pants are accidentally loosed in a public struggle with his wife, and he is exposed. Literally and symbolically, she has uncovered his manhood and shown it to be vulnerable, not all powerful.

Fourth, many men, forced to suppress a range of emotions that are deemed to be inconsistent with manhood, channel a range of feelings into one emotion that is socially validated for men, that is, anger. The newlywed, Sakhi, is "quick to anger," and soon he is burning "with an insane ungovernable fury" about his shame in front of other men. He explodes and almost beats an ox to death before he is interrupted by his elderly mother and his bride. He beats his mother almost to death. Zaitoon, the bride, is also beaten. After her own beating and further humiliation, she learns to submit.

> She grew immune to the tyrannical, animal-trainer treatment meted out by Sakhi. In his presence she drifted into a stupor, until nothing really hurt her. He beat her on the slightest pretext. . . . At night she acquiesced docilely.

And as for Sakhi, "On the whole he was delighted. He looked his brother in the eye" (pages 172–174).

The violence by this individual man against this individual woman seems to be more about his relationship with other men and his own insecurities about his manhood than about his relationship with his wife per se.

Finally, the young wife, Zaitoon, runs away. This is taken as a collective affront to Sakhi's whole clan. He picks up his rifle and says he is going after her. The other men follow:

> One behind the other, they emerged, eyes ablaze in fanatic determination. The crowd of tribals dispersed in a hushed understanding, each to get his own gun and prepare for the hunt. Not a word was said. They identified with the man's disgrace, taking the burden on themselves Collectively, they meant to salvage the honour of their clan. It would poison their existence unless they found the girl. There was only one punishment for a runaway wife. (page 190)

Michael Kaufman comments on such norms for masculinity and femininity and the related imbalance of power between men and women:

> One way of seeing all this is that men are defined as essentially human, while women are defined as something else, as an offshoot of Adam, in the Judeo-Christian-Islamic tradition. Women live in men's shadows, and they are dust compared to stone.

> One of the strange things about this, however, is the extent to which men are themselves but a shadow. While they are supposed to be the sun, the sun itself doesn't cast a shadow. It only provides the light. Men might try to pose and pride themselves as the source of light, but it is a pretense that cannot be maintained.

As I read this it strikes me that in many of the South Asian short stories described in this chapter, the men characters do not have a vibrant individual presence, at least not while at home. Theirs is more a negative space. They are simply missing as real people so far as full emotional relations with women are concerned.

And in a strange way, even the supposedly superior man is actually reduced to a portion of his potentially full self. For example, consider how Ismat Chughtai, the path-breaking woman author who wrote in the 1940s in Urdu in Pakistan, characterizes what really matters in a man. In her story "Sacred Duty," a young man working in Dubai with a monthly salary of "12,000" (currency not specified) is married off:

> The match had been arranged over the phone. He was not all that good looking, also just a trifle short, but does a girl have to put up her husband for rent? One doesn't bother with a man's physical attributes; its his qualities that count. And in this case qualities numbered twelve thousand and total comforts even more. (Chughtai 1990, page 20)

Michael Kaufman has also provided the following useful summary, based on our discussion, about some ideas covered so far in this chapter:

- Gender definitions and stereotypes are norms for behaviour that have powerful implications. Women are assigned traits that encourage them to submit, while men are assigned ones that encourage them to exercise power, dominance and control.
- Such stereotypes are an expression of the very real power inequalities between women and men. Stereotypes aren't isolated qualities, but expressions of unequal relationships.
- There is a system of rewards and sanctions for both women and men that teaches and reinforces the stereotypes and the relations of power. There is the threat to both sexes that stepping outside the norms will inevitably be met with punishment.
- Such stereotypes coexist and are promoted by systems of beliefs that encourage us to accept these norms as natural and eternal, thus discouraging questioning and challenge.
- No one fits fully or without struggle into a norm or stereotype. Some women and men rebel, or at least feel a sense of loss, perhaps despair.

I would recall here that in Chughtai's "Sacred Duty," the parents of the young Muslim girl who runs off to marry a non-Muslim say, "There is only one thing to do: let's go to Allahabad and shoot them both" (1990, page 22). In fact, the young couple outwits the murderous parents, and both young woman and man are portrayed as questioning individuals, not just as stereotypes. But theirs is more the exception than the rule in a patriarchal society.

The Patriarchy: Source of the Problem

This book has repeatedly referred to "the system" and to "patriarchy." And indeed, since patriarchy is the heart of the matter, it is useful to look at the evolving institution of South Asian patriarchy and its relation to violence.[34] Patriarchy refers to a system of control or governance by men, whether in the family or state. Interlocking systems at all levels of society, controlled by men in hierarchical relationships, are commonplace. In its pure form, in the family, the place and word of the father (patriarch) are supreme. In societies such as traditional South Asian ones, a senior, venerable man (patriarch) may be looked to for guidance and decisions when there are conflicts. His authority may be religious as well as political, or these functions can be separated. Institutions, including the family, are constructed in patriarchal societies on the basis of gender inequality.

Control by men of female sexuality and reproductive function is essential. This is to ensure the continuity of the male line (patrilineage) and the relationships in and between male lines. The distribution of property (patrimony) and the recognition of a man's family name (patronymic) and authority are based on a man's relationship to senior males. For a woman, the emphasis on purity as a testimony to her father's, brother's, husband's or son's honour foreshadows various kinds of violence against her in the family. In highly patriarchal tribal societies, for example, "honour killings" of girls and women accused of illicit relations are to be expected (see also Chapter 2); confinement and beatings to prevent such relations are commonplace; and, as has been discussed, marriage of girls at a young age is usually considered desirable, the easier to control a girl's or woman's fertility and person.

In the contemporary South Asian patriarchy, female sexuality is suppressed compared to male sexuality, in the interest of social order under men's control. Of course, to do so means limiting women's freedom, spirit and knowledge. Since a woman's sexuality and reproductive function cannot be separated from her person and soul, it is also considered that these need to be beaten down into manageable size in the patriarchy. That way, a woman will not, and cannot, have the sense of self or rights to contest male control over her body (Jayawardena and de Alwis 1996). Male relatives seek to control, protect and exchange with other patrilineages their own daughters' and sisters' reproductive function. They do so in order to build and strengthen alliances that would ensure continuity and aggrandizement of the power, privilege and property of their own patrilineage and its patrimony. It would be unheard of in such a system for a daughter to expect to have a voice against her grandfather, father, uncle or even her brother. All related men share interests in safeguarding and benefiting from family property; girls and women are considered only one part of this property.

Between families and classes, the principle that men are defined as superior to and responsible for controlling women can be used to measure the men's relative social success and deserved standing. If their women are at home and do not need to work or complain, the men are seen as successful in this context. Poor men are vulnerable to the criticism of more well-off men that their poverty makes them less than real men because their women are seen working or heard complaining. In short, poverty can be interpreted as a type of social emasculation (Hart 1997).

In short, male power over women in the household may be exhibited in an exaggerated way as part of the effort by men to show other men how strong they really are and how weak other men are. Women's subjugation in the household is thus cultural, political and social, as well as economic. As cultural, political, social and economic change occurs, the patriarchy may be threatened; yet it apparently recasts itself in new versions, which may appear different on the surface, but which still have control and domination of women at the foundation (see, for example, Sharabi 1988 and Mies 1986).

The "Language of Gender Violence" in the Patriarchy

Violence against women in the patriarchal family occurs for many reasons. Whatever men's intentions, and whether these are implicit or explicit, conscious or unconscious, their acts of violence fall into a number of categories, sometimes overlapping, sometimes not. I see these as punitive, preventive, opportunistic, compensatory and symbolic. For me, the physical acts of domestic violence can be seen as a kind of language between the perpetrator, his victim and others. The wife is not always the one to whom a man sends his main message. Other men are the real audience. The message is, "I'm a man." Sometimes the perpetrator is really reassuring himself.

The following are the main types of violence, by purpose:

Punitive violence is to punish a wife for real or alleged actions that are deemed by a man to constitute misconduct.

Preventive violence is to keep a woman intimidated and controlled enough so that she will not do something. Potential extramarital relations are of particular concern. Everyday abuse can even be seen as a preventive. For instance, at a meeting of the women's wing of the All-India Medical Association, which I attended, a woman speaker referred to a supposed joke that goes something like this: A man is beating his wife. She asks, "Why are you beating me? I didn't do anything." He says, "I know, that's why I'm only beating you. If I knew what you'd done, I'd kill you!"[35]

Opportunistic intentions are ones that would create a new opportunity for the man through the elimination of his wife's spirit, presence, status or life itself. For instance, a man who is tired of his wife can falsely accuse her of having a bad character. He might then even beat or kill her — both widely considered within his authority if she is unfaithful. In this way, he is free to carry on openly with another woman, even to marry again and receive dowry, as well as to maintain his position in the community. He may even gain some sympathy. Discrediting one's wife can be useful to maintaining and enhancing a man's reputation, options and opportunities.

Compensatory intentions behind gender violence are less likely to be explicit. This can be in the sense of emotional compensation for a man's frustration about his status and achievements in one sphere; accordingly, if a man loses his job, he tries to make himself feel more important by beating his wife. Or the compensation may be taken in monetary and physical terms, rather than psychological ones. For example, there are culture-specific forms of violence, such as *karo kari*, that are opportunistic and compensatory: A daughter is accused of having illicit relations with someone. She is killed. He is likely to be killed. The boy's family is given "blood money" and/or a girl in return. This practice lends itself to misuse as a way to get rid of a male enemy at the cost of a girl in the family, and with considerable monetary and social gain. It can also be used to trade in an unwanted daughter for a desired bride. *Karo kari*, practised in parts of Pakistan, is one of a variety of types of so-called "honour killings". Women's sexual virtue is considered to represent the honour of the family and community.

Symbolic violence. Intentions to assert one's masculinity no doubt lie behind most acts of gender violence that are not hidden from others. The point is for them to be known, for the perpetrator to be seen by other men as a real man who deserves his place — or an even better place — in the hierarchy of the patriarchy. Too often, male solidarity is reinforced by acts of domestic violence that are made public. Until definitions change for what it means to be a real man, domestic violence is unlikely to decline.

Such symbolism rests on definitions of manhood in patriarchal systems that are based on one's ability to have authority over others, male and female; to have male heirs and property, as well as respect for one's name. Men must control their women in order to be real men in the patriarchy. In patriarchy, built on the need to control women's reproductive function, women are constantly checked and challenged to assure that their sexuality is controlled. A man's doubt and need to signal others that he is in control can make life a torment for even innocent girls and women. Taken all together, such things signal that a man is truly worthy of recognition, respect, property and advancement in the patriarchy. On the other hand, family shame in such a system challenges the male's strength, control, virility, power and advancement.

Why Do Women Submit?

What can possibly keep a woman from experiencing her own power and intelligence, from wishing to control her own destiny? From protesting and refusing to be beaten? One asks such questions just as one asks, What can keep a man from wanting to know and show who he is as a human being, not a "type"? In part, it is systems of practices and beliefs like those outlined here. Through these systems a woman might come to say, as does the woman narrator in one story from Pakistan, "I am an ordinary Muslim [or substitute the name of another religion] woman. . . . A slipper on men's feet. I was born only so I could be married to a man. Obey his every whim" (Hina 1994, page 12).

In this context, it is not so difficult to understand why so many women submit to gender violence: Often, there has not been any other choice. Usually they cannot return home, they lack resources, they fear the loss of their children and they have no place to go if their parents will not accept them back in the natal home, there are few shelters, and most neighbours and officials are unsympathetic. They do not see a choice, then, except, perhaps, suicide, licentiousness or begging.

Some Forces That Have Strengthened the Patriarchy in South Asia

Militarism, colonialism, nationalism, revivalism-cum-fundamentalism, even British feminism, and development itself: Each has strengthened the patriarchy in South Asia whether this was intended or not.

Militarism

In South Asia, the process of colonialism was acted out on the pre-existing terrain of masculinity and patriarchy. For example, in her analysis of "martial and imperial masculinities" in 18th-century North India, Rosalind O'Hanlon (1997, page 9) writes about "codes of martial masculinity":

> A man was most a man as a soldier, in the company of other men. . . . [Their] qualities were displayed in very direct and physical ways: in the splendour of men's physiques, the dazzle of equipage, the grim efficiency of their weapons and the magnificence of their fighting animals. Here, allies, troops, patrons and rivals continually weighed and judged, challenged and affirmed each other's possession of the manly qualities and competence deemed essential in the successful ruler, ally, military commander and warrior. Ridicule and failure always loomed as possibilities, as the qualities of the inner man revealed themselves to this audience of his fellows, and were appraised by practiced eyes. Here . . . men constructed and sustained masculine identity very much in relation to their peers.

O'Hanlon refers to the "shared codes" between Hindu and Muslim culture, the "shared ideals about bravery and correct manly behaviour in warfare, games and hunting." Such martial masculinity, she suggests, was one constituent of a complex and competing process "to establish a hierarchy of higher and inferior forms of masculinity"(page 16).

Early warfare was fought on a tribal basis, the most pure form of the patriarchy. There also were cases in which men from a variety of backgrounds came together to serve their rulers. In turn, the ruler became like a patriarch, demanding loyalty of the men under him, as though they were his lesser relatives in the patrilineage. Martial models are still played out among groups of men, as defined by politics, religion, caste or class, neighbourhood as well as family. In their struggles for ascendancy in the hierarchy of masculinities, women are seen as fair game and as tokens in a game to prove ever higher forms of masculinity.

In Afghanistan, "the Kalishnikov culture" that prevails in the late 1990s signals the importance of the male role as warrior and protector, with females secluded. In this context, women who do not obey the various edicts are severely punished. Men are thus encouraged to be even more strict with their families, supposedly for protection of the family and for the sake of Islam, and also to proclaim that they are in control. The threat of rape or of women's possible promiscuity are sometimes given to justify the extreme edicts and control.

Colonialism and Nationalism

Paradoxically, colonialism and the nationalist response against colonialism in South Asia have each strengthened the patriarchy and its control over women in the home (Sarkar 1996). In both cases, the idea of the family as a completely private sphere under male authority has been used, often for political purposes. The privacy of the family was linked with the privacy of religion and culture, in which practices regarding women's roles were often in conflict with their rights. Both to demand and justify the state's disinterest in women's situation at home, colonialists and nationalists alike evoked and exaggerated stereotypes about women and men. The fulfilment of rights for women under the law was thus severely limited. Under British colonialism, in some ways this gap was meant to compensate local men for the loss of their honour and rights in the public arena. A form of male solidarity, one might say.

At the same time, nationalists cited some of women's stereotypic qualities, such as an alleged capacity for self-sacrifice, as the basis for involving them (in the short-term) in causes men defined and led. Once the nationalists met with success, the women were expected to return to the home, and to stay under male control. This process of temporary release for women from traditional roles, for men's political purposes, is said to be typical in many, if not all, liberation movements (Mies 1986).

Colonialism and Revivalism

One well-known case for the defence of patriarchy for South Asia was the rallying call of militant Hindu nationalism in Bengal in the last few decades of the 19th century. In short, the Hindu domestic sphere was projected as under threat from colonialism, which had to be rejected. And Hinduism had to be asserted by revivalists/nationalists. According to Tania Sarkar, an Indian historian, practices of child marriage and *sati*, along with women's purity and willing subjugation to husbands, were exalted. She explains that militants "chose to tie their nationalism to issues of conjugality which they defined as a system of non-consensual, indissoluble, infant marriage" (Sarkar 1996, page 211).

Colonial legislation, they claimed, was invading and controlling intimate domestic space. State intervention in that arena was to be resisted. Sarkar sees women's condition under the control of men as what the nationalists actually wanted to maintain. Thus, the Age of Consent Bill (which, in 1891, raised the legal age of consent for girls from 10 to 12) was the focus of intense debate and public opposition by revivalists. "The link-up between anti-colonial patriotism and Brahmanical patriarchal status quoism provides the larger political context for understanding the storm over the Age of Consent Bill" (Sarkar 1996, page 212).

Sarkar points out that, because of revivalists and their "recently acquired notion of the colonised self," legal initiatives proposed earlier by reformist Hindus to improve women's status were rejected (page 214). She writes: "The household, consequently, became doubly precious and important as the only zone where autonomy and self-rule could be preserved" (page 215).

Unlike Victorian middle-class situations, then, the family was not a refuge after work for the man. It was their real place of work. "The household, generally, and conjugality, specifically, came to mean the last independent space left to the colonised Hindu" (Sarkar 1996, page 215). While colonial law focused primarily on "public" issues, it was also the space left to Hindu and Muslim law, which covered "personal" issues to do with family and religion. And there was apparently a tendency in the late 1800s for arguments by English-trained Indian lawyers about Hindu norms to be taken seriously by English judges (Sarkar 1996, page 216).

Victorian Feminism

Near the end of the 19th century and the early 20th century, Englishmen in India were divided about changes in England in rights for women in marriage, divorce and property. Sarkar says, "They turned with relief to the so-called relative stability and structures of Hindu rules. . . . They found here a system of relatively unquestioned patriarchal absolutism which promised a more comfortable state of affairs after the bitter struggles with Victorian feminism at home" (page 217). In addition, the tradition of case law and common law procedures in England led English judges in India to honour custom, usage and precedent.

Fundamentalism about Women

The media, meanwhile, portrayed the male and female very differently in colonial Bengal. Sarkar shows the extent to which Hindu pride came to depend on extreme interpretations of women's submission as a source of men's strength, even if women had to die or deny their own personhood (page 218). She says the male body was often portrayed in the media as feeble and diseased: "the visible site of surrender and loss, of defeat and alien discipline." The female body was, instead, one "ruled by 'our' scriptures, our custom." For revivalists and nationalists, woman, who had been portrayed as victim, became "a repository of power, the Kali rampant, a figure of rage and strength." Also, "[t]he Hindu woman's demonstrated capacity for accepting pain and harsh discipline" was seen as the last measure of hope and greatness for a doomed people" (page 219).

Sarkar quotes a description of *sati* that makes the point:

"Her face is joyful. . . . The flames burn higher; life departs, and the body is burned to ashes. . . . When I think that only some time back our women could die like this, then new hope rises up in me, then I have faith that we, too, have the seeds of greatness within us. Women of Bengal, you are the true jewels of this country." (page 219)

Through such means, Sarkar shows that love and pain were made the basis for Hindu women's self-realization. The first was of a specific type, the union of two souls, from infancy beyond death. But this raised questions of consent, mutuality and equality that could not easily be answered. The Rukhmabai episode referred to in Chapter 2 challenged the idea of love and pleasure as characterizing Hindu marriage. Force and pain then had to be admitted, even extolled, for women in marriage. Even the government was called upon to assist in women's submission: "A good Hindu wife should always serve her husband as God even if that husband is illiterate, devoid of good qualities and attached to other women, and it is the duty of the government to make Hindu women conform to the injunctions of the Shastras" (Sarkar 1996, page 223).

Even though some of the images are different in Islamic society, here too the State has often played a role in supporting the subjugation of Muslim women to the patriarchal family in response to fundamentalism and its proponents. This was highlighted, for example, in 1985 by the Shah Bano case in India. Divorced by her husband, Shah Bano sought maintenance in accordance with the Quran. The Supreme Court agreed. Fundamentalists agitated against "unacceptable interference in Muslim personal law" (K. Singh 1994, page 385). The government then introduced the Muslim women's Act, as fundamentalists proposed (Ibid). She lost her case.[36]

In Pakistan, Muslim women's subjugation to the patriarchy, writ large, was institutionalized under General Zia, who introduced laws that discounted women's testimony as legal evidence and made legal judgements of rape almost impossible. In the laws about *zina* (adultery), part of the Hudood Ordinances introduced in Pakistan in 1997, adultery rather than rape is the verdict unless there is evidence of penetration and testimony from four male witnesses, all of whom must be in good standing as Muslims. The woman's testimony has little value. And if her claim of rape is not accepted, she will likely be judged as an adulteress (see, for example, Zia 1994).

Efforts were undertaken by then Prime Minister Nawaz Sharif in 1998 to establish Sharia as the law of the land and help unite men from various parties based on a common agenda — control of women — in what can be thought of as a political patriarchy. Buddhists, on the other hand, often pride themselves on having more egalitarian practices towards women. Yet in Sri Lanka, a Buddhist country, problems of gender violence are emerging, too, at the household and community levels as well as in the ethnic conflict situations. However, family violence does not appear to be directly related to religious fundamentalism.

In conclusion, these examples illustrate how both fundamentalism and political expediency may be used in South Asia to reinforce the importance of patriarchy, centred on the control of women.

Development

In some ways, the development process itself has also strengthened the patriarchy by working with and through male household heads, and dealing with women primarily in their roles as reproducers, not producers (see Rogers 1981). Assumptions about households wherein an enlightened head makes decisions and benefits all members, as used in most economic theories and models basic to development practice, have proved misleading (see Hart 1997). Only recently is this tendency, which has been detrimental for women, being corrected. The movement within the development world for attention to "women in development" and, later to "gender and development" has promoted important changes, but development practitioners are not always receptive.

Then there is the larger question about development as an exploitative process that marginalizes the poor and commodifies women, with an increase in violence against them and the environment. People's movements, with space for women's voices and leadership, are seen as necessary to counter, correct and provide alternatives. (See, for example, South Asian Declaration on Food Safety n.d. and A. Roy 1999.)

Escaping from Hell

Gender norms, stereotypes, expectations and unequal power are not just ideas. They are the lived realities of women and men throughout South Asia and the world. Both learn to fear the consequences if they do not conform in this life and the next, however it may be imagined. For example, a woman who does not bear sons may expect punishment, as expressed by a Pakistani woman to Misbah Sheikh during the latter's work in the countryside.[37]

> "I wanted to know quite simply," she repeated, "if I will go to hell."
> "What have you done that makes you think you will?" I responded.
> "Well," she continues, "You know that this is the month of Ramadan. And here, it is the wife's duty to have the evening meal ready for her husband when he returns from the fields. Unfortunately, ever since the birth of my fifth daughter, I am not so quick anymore. Yesterday, especially, I was overtaken by those unbearable pains I told you about earlier and didn't have dinner ready on time. When my husband came home and saw that the *chappatis* [unleavened bread of wheat or flour] weren't made, he began beating me. But that's not why I'm complaining, you see. If I didn't do my duty for him, then he has every right to beat me. However, what did bother me was that he started screaming at me, calling me horrible names and said that because I hadn't borne him a son, I would go to hell. Is this true?"

Where is the collective answer of "No" to this beleaguered voice? Where is the challenge to these many norms of femininity and masculinity and the inequalities of power between women and men?

We have had glimpses of the emerging figures and heard briefly the voices to change negative practices about and restrictive roles for women and men throughout South Asia. Their fuller stories (some of which are in the next two chapters) shatter stereotypes and unmask institutions in order to strengthen them as places where rights and equality will prevail. Their stories are all the more impressive given that it may be more difficult for South Asians to challenge stereotypes and norms, because of the relatively narrow space for individuality left within the narrowly defined gender roles and the practices and norms supporting these.

But the seeds of opposition, rebellion and reconstruction are also in the system. Otherwise, we would not be witness to the testimony of the many from South Asia who question tradition and forge new paths.

Fortunately, South Asian men are among those who want change, away from patriarchal values, institutions and hierarchical relations between women and men. Their role will surely accelerate change in patriarchal values and gender violence used to maintain them.

For example, Imran Aslam, editor of the *Karachi News*, Pakistan; Nadeem Fazil, also from Pakistan; and Rahul Roy and Anand Patwardhan, both film-makers in India, shared the following strong and encouraging opinions.

Imran Aslam[38]

It is time for a men's liberation movement in Pakistan. It is only when they are allowed to express all the facets of their personalities, rather than having to suppress emotions, fear and love — while being allowed to and encouraged to express hatred and frustration in the form of physical violence — that they can become part of the solution rather than the problem. (Aslam 1997, page 29)

Nadeem Fazil

Efforts to combat violence against women have been strengthened by a new approach, where instead of alienating men by blaming and accusing them for being cruel to women, they are increasingly being involved in the struggle to minimise the menace . . . This new role for men calls for a "new definition of masculinity." . . . Perhaps there already are some individuals in our midst who subscribe to this undertaking. Their numbers have to grow, now that a start has been made. (Fazil 1997, page 29)

Rahul Roy[39]

Violence is the language of communication between the two genders. . . . I feel that ultimately what we are looking for is a genderless society. I don't believe that gender is one of the necessary ways in which society has to be organized. I think the point that we always get caught in is this whole thing — that men are not feminine enough, or that women have to break stereotypes, and identify with more masculine symbols. . . . But masculinity and femininity are cultural constructs, and I think those have to be destroyed, for any gender equality, [and] for violence between the genders to disappear.

One of the ways society has been organized is around notions of patriarchy, a power system which is very important for the way we approach our social and political lives. . . .

The point is that the power that is experienced by both genders, or the powerlessness that is experienced by both genders, has to be removed. . . . We know what we have to dismantle: all 'round throwing away of patriarchy.

Easier said than done, but the point is that at least we have a fair understanding of it now — we know that that is the way we have organized ourselves. We know what we have to dismantle.

Anand Patwardhan[40]

I think we have to break down this masculine-feminine thing completely — these are constructions which people have been socialized into. . . . We have to discourage and laugh out of existence those ideas of manhood and masculinity which are perpetuated by advertising, perpetuated by everything we read, the posters that we see, everything. So that's why *Father, Son and Holy War* [an award-winning film he made, which covers "communal" violence between Hindus and Muslims, as well as the problem of fundamentalism and its ties with masculinity] tried to show you what popular culture has done with this as well. One has to basically re-understand what it means to be a human being, and forget about male and female. . . .

Is Gender Violence Inevitable?

An optimistic answer is that intelligence and culture may be used to modify man's tendency towards aggression in general, if people are aware and committed enough to try. That is the view of anthropologist Michael Ghiglieri (1999) in his book *The Dark Side of Man: Tracing the Origins of Male Violence*. Ghiglieri argues that human aggression has been shaped by the evolutionary process of natural selection and is programmed by DNA. But so is the potentiality for cooperation and human survival.

Which way the balance will shift, towards aggression and destruction or towards mutuality and survival, can be influenced by a multitude of factors. These include the balance between resources and population (Turnbull 1972); the social structure (Dube 1997), the strength and reliability of the social contract giving the State rather than individuals authority for punishment of wrongdoers (Pinker 1997); as well as security or threat in the environment; mental health and well-being or not; morality; and what children learn from the many influences on them during socialization — which include parents, peers, school, media and "culture." Where prejudice based on differences such as sex, race, ethics and religion is accepted, the ground is surely prepared for justifying violence against "the other." Notions about inferiority of women and girls, then, tend to predict violence against them. That is not likely to end unless and until factors that support ideas of male superiority and female inferiority are questioned and changed, along with violent acts themselves.

There is evidence that culture does ameliorate the expression of male violence in general and of gender violence in particular. For example, murder rates of men by men have been shown to vary widely (Nisbett and Cohen 1999). This can be taken to mean that biology is not the only determinant of violence, although it is a powerful one. As for why men would murder or harm women partners rather than male rivals, Pinker (1997) shares some insightful reflections in his *How the Brain Works*. In part, it is to try to ensure that his genes survive and prevail — at least this is the view based on sociobiology and taking into account the neurological inheritance humans are thought to have. According to Pinker, a man's preoccupation with controlling women's sexuality and reproductive capacity gives him a greater chance of passing on more of his own genes and of lessening chances for other men to do so. This may be particularly compelling for a man whose woman partner did not choose him as her mate. The implication is that she might prefer another partner for passing on her genes, if given a choice. He notes:

The largest cause of spousal abuse and spousal homicide is sexual jealousy almost always the man's. Men beat and kill their wives and girlfriends to punish them from real or imagined infidelity and to deter them from becoming unfaithful or leaving them. (Pinker 1997, page 489)

He also points out that "[I]n most social milieus, a man's reputation depends in part on the maintenance of a credible threat of violence" (page 496).

In this context, one sees that men's violence towards women not only controls them but can also serve as a threat to other men, without the same risk to the perpetrator, which aggression against men might produce.

Furthermore, where women's morality and character are considered to be degraded or weak due to a particular ideological system, they are not likely to be trusted. Male solidarity is then a means both to control potential male rivals and to control women.

Enter the patriarchy and patrilineal kinship systems. Dube (1997) also notes that patrilineal systems of descent and social organization, with patri/viri local residence put women and girls more at risk of various forms of oppression than do other types of kinship systems:

Patrilineal systems function and survive at the cost of women. Women's peripheral membership of their natal group, their transfer to their husband's group, and their purely instrumental value as bearers of children for their official groups all have definite implications. The absence of rights over property, over the means of living and over their children makes women vulnerable to oppression of different kinds. (page 156)

Agarwal's work (1996) describes a patriarchal belt stretching from East to West across the subcontinent, with more restrictions of various types on women than are found in non-patriarchal areas, such as Kerala. It would be interesting to know if rates of violence against women in Kerala and other areas outside the patriarchal belt are lower than elsewhere. Would one, then, expect to find less gender violence, especially in the form of beating, battering and murder, where strong patriarchal forms of social organization and ideology are absent, where women's status is higher, where women can inherit property, choose partners, find employment, work outside the home, be considered moral beings all the same? Theory points in that direction, as do Dube's related observations. And Pinker's observations, based on sociobiology, would also predict less violence to women in kinship systems that permit women to live in or near the natal home. "Women fare better when they stay near their relatives and the men move around, because they are surrounded by fathers, brothers and uncles who can come to their aid in disputes with their husbands" (1997, page 432).[41]

While the Declaration on the Elimination of Violence against Women rightly acknowledges that gender violence "is pervasive, cuts across lines of income, class and culture," this does not mean that there are no determining factors concerning the degree of gender violence to be expected under different conditions. For example, percentages of wife-beating in studies as reviewed and reported by the UN Statistical Office (UN 1993a) are generally lower for developed countries than for developing ones. Available data on wife-beating in South Asia suggest that incidence in the region is particularly high. There could be many explanations. Wherever there is a culture with strong and explicit patriarchal values and norms, particularly high incidence of wife-beating could follow. In much of South Asia, for example, the risk of wife-beating may be higher where girls and women move away after marriage from their blood relatives into groups dominated by non-blood male kin, and thus lose some chances for protection from an angry husband. Far more attention is needed, then, to the nature of patriarchy, its various forms and manifestations, both its costs and possible advantages, in terms of fulfilling children's and women's human rights, along with those of men.

At the same time, what the South Asians are telling us throughout this book is that culture must not be overlooked as a positive force for change. There are those who treat culture as something that does not and must not change. But human history is one of cultural change as people adapt to new habitats and situations. It is unavoidable to challenge arguments that cite culture as a justification for abuse or violence towards women and girls, if one wants to challenge that very abuse or violence. As Nafis Sadik, Executive Director of UNFPA, says:

> We must be courageous in speaking out on the issues that concern us: we must not bend
> under the weight of spurious arguments invoking culture or traditional values. No value
> worth the name supports the oppression and enslavement of women. The function of
> culture and tradition is to provide a framework for human well-being. If they are used
> against us, we will reject them, and move on. We will not allow ourselves to be silenced.
> (UNFPA 1995)

The culture we forge is up to us and our vision of the human future. All the more reason, then, to encourage a socialization process that keeps in view the goal of human security, rights and fulfilment for all, lest ease disappear from family and community life. Questioning the supposed inevitability of gender roles that assign inferiority to women and superiority to men is at the heart of questioning the inevitability of gender violence. The women and men in the next two chapters do exactly that and show that a standard for humanity, rather than stereotypes, moves and guides them.

Endnotes

1   Economic forces that are exploitative have particularly negative impacts on marginalized people, including women. The commodification of women increases the likelihood of gender-based violence towards women and girls in the region. This is discussed further in Chapter 9.

2   Geraldine Brooks, *Nine Parts of Desire: The Hidden World of Islamic Women* (New York: Anchor Press, 1995).

3   In this chapter, I use stories by South Asian women and men to bring out the norms for femininity and masculinity, especially because creative writers both dissect and compress reality to enable us to see more clearly how we order our worlds. Fortunately, all people do not follow the norms, although most are well aware of them. Some of those people who strike out in "new" directions first seem to go through a stage of "negative identity," still centred on the norm but defined in terms of its opposite.

4   Shahinshah Bano is the name of a real woman, divorced after years of marriage, whose property and maintenance rights were then denied her by law, in a famous case, despite Quranic sanction in the opposite direction.

5   Women's section of the house, where purdah is observed.

6   For a useful general summary on the origin of patriarchy in South Asia, see Bhasin (1993), pages 35–39; for details about various Hindu goddesses, see Kinsley (1986); for an account of the important role of goddesses in pre-colonial South Asia, see Benard (1994); for some comments on various Islamic views of women in both tribal and more modern societies of Pakistan and Bangladesh, see Soban (pages 63–80) in Moghadam (1994).

7   The accurate translation, according to Arole (1999, page 61) is "a wife, son, slave, pupil and own brother should,

when they have faults, be beaten with a cord or bamboo-cane."

8   Interview for this book arranged by UNICEF ROSA in cooperation with UNICEF Nepal.

9   The accurate rather than popular translation apparently is: "In her childhood (a girl) should be under the will of her father; in her youth of (her) husband; her husband being dead, of her sons, a woman should never enjoy her own will" (Arole 1999, page 60).

10 Interview arranged by UNICEF ROSA through WAR, Lahore, in cooperation with UNICEF Lahore.

11 Although set alight, she doesn't burn because of her innocence.

12 Interview for this book arranged by UNICEF ROSA in cooperation with WAR, Lahore, and UNICEF Lahore.

13 Vikrampur (Bangladesh), circa 12th century (Mookerjee 1988, page 28).

14 Nepal, 18th century (Mookerjee 1988, page 28).

15 Personal observation.

16 Personal communication from the artist, Nepal, 1997. The painting is in the private collection of the author.

17 See Robert A. F. Thurman and Marilyn M. Rhie, *The Sacred Art of Tibet: Wisdom and Compassion* (New York: Tibet House, in association with Harry N. Abrams, 1991).

18 See, for example, Vikram Seth's *A Suitable Boy* (London: Phoenix House, 1993) and Tehmina Durrani's *My Feudal Lord* (London: Gorgi, 1995).

19 My reference is a photocopy I received in 1997 of an article published in 1970, from which the title and bibliographic information are missing. Unfortunately, the senior author is deceased and the library of Worcester State Hospital, Massachusetts (US), where one is directed to request copies, told me that a fire had occurred in 1992, destroying the part of the collection that had the article (personal communication, Edward Hay, November 1999).

20 Also interviewed by the author for this book, Punyakante Wijenaike preferred that her work rather than comments convey her views. By writing as she has, she has made a major contribution to breaking the silence in Sri Lanka on domestic violence and incest.

21 For example, 50.1 per cent of Sri Lankan women graduate from high school and 43.9 per cent from university, compared with only 20 per cent and 2 per cent, respectively, in Pakistan. The corresponding figures in India are 37.89 per cent, and 14.3 per cent in Nepal. But neither more education nor the tenets of Buddhism (which stresses non-violence) seems to have prevented the extensive domestic violence in Sri Lanka or the high rate of suicide among women that often accompanies physical and sexual abuse.

22 Interview arranged for this book by UNICEF Pakistan.

23 Yet Metcalf (1992) describes *Bihisti Zewar* as a work based on the assumption that women and men are equal and inspired by the idea that women should be educated in their religion. It was written in northern India in the early 1900s as part of a reformist movement.

24 Interview arranged for this book by UNICEF ROSA in cooperation with UNICEF Nepal.

25 Interview arranged for this book by UNICEF ROSA in cooperation with UNICEF Nepal.

26 See F. Mernissi (1991), pages 85–101, for her account of the origin of *hijab*, the veil. She describes how the prophet lowered a curtain to separate himself and his new bride from a male guest who had not yet left the prophet's home long after the wedding feast. She comments on how this simple act, and the pronouncement the prophet simultaneously made about his need for privacy, came to be misused as the basis for veiling women.

27 Personal communication, Mabelle Arole, Kathmandu, 1997, when she was Regional Advisor for health.

28 Interview arranged for this book by UNICEF Sri Lanka in cooperation with CENWOR.

29 Many of the ideas in this chapter on men and masculinity draw on Kaufman (1993). See also Kaufman (1987), Brod and Kaufman (1994) and other publications listed at *www.michaelkaufman.com*.

30 Michael Kaufman and I had the opportunity to meet and to discuss and work on parts of this chapter together. I try to note in the text his main contributions regarding masculinity.

31 For more information on Hindu goddesses, see, for example: David Kinsley (1987), *Hindu Goddesses: Visions of the Divine Feminine in the Hindu Religious Tradition* and John Stratton Hawley and Donna Marie Wulff (editors) (1982), *The Divine Consort: Radha and the Goddesses of India*.

32 Based on a dialogue about this book at the UNICEF International Centre on Development of Children, Florence, Italy, 1998.

33 Ibid.

34 "Patriarchy" and "patriarchal" are terms commonly used by South Asians from most countries of the region to characterize values and practices that strongly favour men in their families, societies and institutions. Some use the terms with pride, others with dismay and a commitment to make changes. Patriarchy is one of several English words, derived from Greek, with the prefix "patri-," which pertains to the father: e.g., patriarch, patriarchy, patrilineage, patrimony, patronymic, patria. *Webster's Ninth New Collegiate Dictionary* defines patriarchy as a "social organization marked by the supremacy of the father in the clan or family, the legal dependence of wives and children, and the reckoning of descent and inheritance in the male line."

35 The occasion was the Third All India Women Doctors Conference, Patna, 27–28 September 1997. See also Hayward (1997c).

36 This is the story fictionalized in Hina (1994).

37 Misbah Sheikh, personal communication, Kathmandu, 1997.

38 From interview arranged by UNICEF ROSA for this book, during his 1997 visit to Kathmandu.

39 From interview for this book arranged by UNICEF ROSA during his 1997 visit to Kathmandu.

40 From interview for this book arranged by UNICEF ROSA during his 1997 visit to Kathmandu.

41 This does not seem to take into account "honour killings" by male relatives, however. Whether or not they are the exception that proves the rule remains to be seen. It may also develop that men from the natal home behave differently towards a female relative, in terms of protection offered or not, depending on whether or not she is married and where she and her husband live.

The Woman Who Would Not Be Beaten

"New" Models: Sources in Traditions and Modernity

A new model of femininity — what should it be? A woman who is strong? Not dependent on men to take care of her? A woman who doesn't accept abuse? One who knows her rights and how to use them? A woman who is loving? An equal partner in a family? An example for equality between women and men, girls and boys?

"Feminine" qualities have long been considered those that are supposedly pleasing to men. Words such as "quiet," "docile," "sweet," "pretty" and "petite" likely came to mind in the past. But "feminine" really means "like a woman."

In what "feminine" includes, then, there is ample room for qualities such as strength, independence and self-confidence, as well as being a loving and cooperative equal. There are many good reasons why these qualities should be among the most important ones for women as well as for men. They indicate mental health, self-esteem and the ability to cope with many situations. Also, equal rights for women and men will not likely be achieved so long as opposite behaviours are expected of them, with women to be weaker and more dependent beings. Furthermore, in homes and nations where rights for women are respected and protected, children's rights will more likely be respected, protected and fulfilled. As one woman activist from India said, "A child who watches his mother being deprived of her rights grows up with a distorted perception of equality and justice. This affects society as a whole."

And to be fair to men, it should be recognized that many would prefer an equal partner with whom to share their lives, not a dependent, weak one.

In development circles, women's empowerment has become commonplace both as a goal and as a means for development. However, there has been relatively little concern about domestic violence as an obstacle to the empowerment of women. What woman is truly empowered by this or that project if her husband or male partner beats her when she goes home — and then takes the money she may have earned? Ending violence against women is a precondition for their true empowerment, as it is for children's full development as healthy, happy and secure individuals, most able to benefit the community and nation.

Where will the models for empowered womanhood be found and featured? The previous chapter pointed to the role of religious traditions and texts as well as literature and stories in promoting a vision of a femininity in South Asia that is usually submissive. Within many of these traditions, however, there are already some alternate models, such as Durga and Kali, but their characteristics as goddesses are not often anticipated in real women. And there are other overlooked examples. As a woman doctor in Nepal says:

> No one ever talks about women who were very brave, like Draupadi or Kunti [characters in the Hindu epic the *Mahabharata*]. Everyone always talks about Sita [from the *Ramayana*] who was the ideal wife, very docile. I always say, "What about Draupadi, who had five husbands? Or Kunti, who gave birth before marriage, and [who], because her husband was impotent, had three children from three different people?"

A man from Pakistan, who does social research, also laments the loss of empowered women as models for women and girls:

> Our folk heritage [in songs and stories] is rich with examples of women who asserted themselves and stood up to subjugation and tyranny. They are all protests against social violence, but we have disowned them.

As for the Islamic tradition, Chapter 5 already showed that while there are both historical and legendary women figures in Islam, their lives are not necessarily presented within South Asia as role models for women and girls.

But change is coming to support various models of empowered women. Efforts are being made to reclaim historical women leaders in both Islam and Hinduism (Mernissi 1993; Kumar 1993). Development work increasingly features women in positive roles rather than as victims.[1] Local women's groups, through solidarity and cooperation, work to advance women's and girls' position. Women's wider political participation is occurring in many parts of the region, although it is being curtailed in others.

In everyday life, many women emerge as models of empowered women. They resist abuse of their bodies, minds and rights, even under difficult conditions. If abuse occurs, they also keep it in perspective rather than letting it destroy their value as a woman and a human being. They see themselves, obviously, as more than the sexual property of a man.

Their lives show us that we need not look only in history, myth, tradition or literature to find models for empowered women. In this chapter, we meet six such women. Each has a strong character; each speaks and acts for rights and opportunities for women. Each is compassionate and caring; each is truly empowered. The women come from different walks of life and different countries, and have different ages, religions and family situations, but all share the same courage. Their stories were chosen to represent the kinds of changes women are making in their daily lives to stop gender violence — changes in their identity, how they define family and earn a living, their study and interpretation of religion, their work with men, in how they present themselves and their claims for their rights. Some face great risks as they help redefine "femininity," others have more supportive situations.

Rani Padamsee,[2] Bangladesh: Karate Black Belt

One of the most dramatic examples of a new kind of femininity is Rani Padamsee, a black belt Shotokan karate instructor in Bangladesh. Rani is the first woman to hold a black belt in Bangladesh and one of the first women in the world to set up her own dojo, her centre for teaching karate. By excelling at a discipline usually considered "masculine," she defies stereotypes.

Where did she get her inspiration and support, this woman who married at 17 and became a mother at 19? Within her family, there were two main influences, her mother and her brother. Her mother's example was that of a strong woman. As Rani puts it:

> I would say that maybe I was always very different because I always fought for whatever I believed in. My mother was also like that. She never treated my brothers and sisters differently. She was the one who always taught us that if a guy could do something, so could we. She taught us that when we were young. Although we had servants in the house, my mother would tell us to wash our plates after dinner — not only myself, but my brother, too. I think the strength came from there. My mother was not so educated. She was only three years old when she [was] married to my father, and he was 14 years older than her. She left her parents' house when she was nine. My father was in the government service and he was so involved in his work. He used to give us time but not as much as she did. She was the backbone of the family. She was the one who gave strength to everybody. She is the one who made us what we are today.

Her brother inspired her interest in martial arts. Watching him was "my first realization of what you can do with your body. You do not even need so much strength." And, later, her husband and in-laws supported her interest in karate, although at first none took her very seriously, and her husband and mother worried that she might get hurt and lose her good looks.

Her Japanese instructor played a significant role in her success. He took her interest seriously, training and promoting her professionalism. When she went to the federation to take her black belt exam, she was the only woman but had the highest grade of all. Her instructor "was so proud that he took off his belt and gave it to me. There is no honour greater than that."

She continued to get his support and talks about the time he allowed her to teach the class:

> The men were not used to a woman as leader. On the first day [of teaching,] everybody showed up for class but they did not take part. They stood on the side and out of 20 students, about five attended the class. The others watched what I would do. They were very surprised. The second day more students came and more the third. When the teacher came back, he wanted a full report of what really happened in the class. I told him that a lot of people did not take part and they probably felt that I would not be able to teach well. When they did show up when he was there, he kicked everyone out. He said that if he knew that one of them was more capable to do the job, he would have given it to them.

Some of her own students have become teachers. "One is teaching in Gazipur. He is teaching some *Garo* [tribal] girls also."

The way in which Rani is raising her own children provides a model of child-rearing based on equality, not norms and stereotypes for how "proper" girls and "real" boys should be. Her daughter may well be the second-generation girl to follow in Rani's mother's footsteps. She has her brown belt; her older brother has his black belt. Rani says this about her daughter:

From the very beginning, I brought her up very differently. Regarding marriage, if she gets mentally abused, forget physical abuse, I do not think that my daughter will stand around and take it. She will fight back and if she and the guy do not see eye to eye, she will walk out. And she knows she always has a home to come back to. I am not one of those parents who would kick her out and send her back. I will listen to both sides.

Rani teaches karate to other children, too:

I would also love to teach the street children self-defence. [But] martial arts is more than self-defence. Once they learn the art, their way of thinking towards violence will change. When they learn self-defence, we will be conditioning not only their minds but their bodies. They will become so confident that they may not be doing what they are doing on the streets. They will start thinking more constructively.

Rani observes that karate is very useful for children she teaches, particularly the girls:

Many of the children who come to me are very shy and some cannot even talk when they first come. If they are asked a question, the parent will answer before the girl can answer. They have been taught not to speak in front of the parent and not to answer certain questions. When they learn karate, they will start learning about themselves, that they have inner strength as well. This does not come initially, but from many years of karate. You will start feeling the physical strength first.

In families, boys have more privileges, which makes them more confident. When the girls first come to me, it takes a minimum of three to four months before they come to realize about themselves and their bodies that they can do whatever the boys can do. Just this small realization can make them do a lot more. I keep telling them that this is just the first step and that they can do anything in the future: If a boy can get a green belt, so can she. This realization that they can be as strong as the boys or that they can do these small things gives them the strength to go farther and farther.

I have had girls who were hunchbacked when they first came to me. I feel that especially at the puberty stage, when girls are just growing up, they feel that they are physically growing and want to hide and do not feel confident, and do not want to talk. But today, I think they speak more than I could. They are the ones who are constantly talking, asking questions, screaming and shouting. I would not even see them smiling when they first came to me. And posture is something I did not even tell them to fix. It just happens by itself. I always tell them that if they walk into a room, the way they carry themselves will tell everything about them. If you are hunchbacked and if you look down at the floor and walk, the boys will know that you have absolutely no confidence. They know that they can really hassle you. Whereas when a girl walks with her chin held high in the air and her shoulders square, people will think twice before [bothering] her. Forget about physical abuse, the person will even think twice before he opens his mouth in front of her.

I feel that my contribution is just a drop in the ocean, but I get a lot of satisfaction. God forbid, if they are attacked, they will know exactly what to do.

Rani also teaches boys:

I know that boys are also being abused, which is why I teach them as well. This is very common everywhere. Maybe it is not so open in our country, but it is happening.

Rani talks about the importance of women doing something for themselves:

Among my friends, I encourage every single one to do something for themselves. Maybe they cannot earn money and work, but I tell them to join exercise classes, learn typing or computers, or even to play golf. A lot of women do not want to do karate. They do not want to cut their nails and they think they will not look nice. So, I introduced exercise classes. It took me two years to convince them to take weight training. They feel that they will get muscular and that their husbands will not like it. I tell them that I have been doing weights for more than 15 years and I do not look like Arnold Schwarzenegger. Over 180 ladies signed up in a period of just two years.

This small realization of going out and doing something for themselves will change their whole thinking. And while I am teaching I talk to these people about a lot of things. And it is really funny that now, if they have a problem, they call me to ask what they should do. Imagine, these people are very rich, but the wife has no clue what the husband is doing. They do not even have a joint account. Some of them do not even have an account. And these are all educated women. They do not have any assets for themselves, apart from buying clothes, jewellery, travelling and spending money on beauty care. I tell them that beauty fades after a while — it does not remain with you forever. Life is something that nobody can give surety of except Allah — it is in His hands. Anything can happen at any time. God forbid, if your husband drops dead today, you do not even know what he has. If you are educated, you are lucky, but if you are not, then what would you do? These small things like coming out of the house, taking a small step by yourself, I keep telling them about.

I do not want them to revolt. I do not want them to start bullying their husbands or their families. But I want them to stand on their feet. For the girls who come to do karate, I tell them that karate cannot be a career for every one of them. Everyone is not going to be as lucky as to have a husband or a family like I did. I tell them that they can learn from this and that they can go for something that they are able to do and that they must stand on their feet before they get married.

As for the married women, she said:

I encourage them to know their husbands even better. I want them to get independent, do something for themselves. Just this bit of coming out changes them a lot. They get a little aware, they see other people around them. I always tell them to look at me. I am not very highly educated but I am standing on my own feet. I have done something for myself. It does not take that much. It just takes a little bit of courage. You just have to hang on. You have to fight your way through. If you are lucky, if you have an encouraging family, a good husband, then you can succeed in this life.

In 1998, Rani's husband died unexpectedly. She kept her dojo but was considering what more to do. She did not want to be secluded at home as many widows are. Again, she was breaking stereotypes, while always showing great respect for her religion, her family and herself.

Stereotypes of femininity still limit her friends' and some pupils' choices more than they do Rani's. She pushes them towards self-confidence and more choices in life, beyond stereotypes. She has related ideas about how to attract more women to karate:

The reason why I did not start a class exclusively for women was because I wanted to prove that I could teach both men and women. [But now I want to do] classes for the ladies. There are a lot of men teaching men. I feel that the way I can teach a woman, no man can do that.

Rani takes into consideration the extra privacy that Muslim women require:

> They would come wearing burkas — the black chador ensemble that conservative Muslim women wear. I have curtains for the exercise classes. I pull the curtains and lock the door. Then the ladies can wear whatever they want. A lot of the ladies for the upper classes also cannot wear tube tops and stuff in their homes. They wear all kinds of adventurous things in my exercise class. And I encourage them. These women would only wear saris and here they would wear tights and T-shirts. It is quite exciting for them. In that one hour they just forget where they came from.

One of Rani's most important points that goes against stereotypes is her affirmation of karate as an appropriate sport for a Muslim woman:

> I consider myself to be a very good Muslim and if this was non-Islamic or against the religion, I do not think that I would have been there [at an exhibition in another country]. Others were surprised and told me that they had a very wrong idea about the Muslim religion. . . . Violence is not part of any religion. I tell people that I am not teaching violence but discipline and self-defence, which everyone needs, irrespective of religion. I may be a Muslim woman covering my body, but I am sure there are people on the streets who would love to rip my clothes off to see what is underneath. I have to protect myself.

She comments on the place that the Quran gives women:

> It's just that people have twisted the religion now. If you really go by what the Quran says, Allah has not made us inferior in any way. He has given women a very high place.

Kusuma,[3] Sri Lanka: Refuses to Be a Victim

A young woman in Sri Lanka challenged the idea that women who are raped should be ashamed, should remain victims, weak and silent. The 21-year-old, whom I will call "Kusuma," is the youngest in a middle-class family of two boys and two girls. They live in a remote village in the North Central province, where her father is an instructor for the government and her mother is a housewife. One of her brothers is a graduate student while the elder sister is married. They own the house they live in and just under 10 acres of paddy land. She attended the village school up to grade 10 and then trained in shorthand and typing. In 1995, she was working in a pharmacy in town and travelled to work on a bicycle. Kusuma told her story to Kamalini Wijayatilake, a Sri Lankan woman lawyer:

> A man named Ajit ran a garage close to the pharmacy. Whenever I went past the garage, he made comments. I ignored him and did not respond.

With effort she went on:

> I went to work as usual on the morning of the 16th of October. I had to pass a stretch of forest on my way to work. The time was about 7:20 a.m. Two men jumped onto the road from the forest and dragged me into it. I struggled and screamed as loud as I could. Because it was a lonely spot, no one heard me. While struggling, I bit into the hand of one of the men and the other man's finger. Three other men who were already hiding in the forest joined the other two and dragged me further into the jungle. I couldn't see their faces since they were masked with handkerchiefs. As I continued to scream and struggle, they shouted filthy words at me and assaulted me with swords and knives.

She showed some of the scars on her calf and arms, and then continued:

> They stuffed pieces of cloth into my mouth and continued to drag me. When [we] came to the middle of the forest one of the men tied my hands together. As I continued to struggle, they assaulted me severely. I had bruises on my thighs as a result of this for quite a while.

Kusuma paused for a while, obviously collecting her thoughts and struggling to hold back tears. Falteringly, she continued.

> Then they began to rape me. . . . They all raped me . . . it was about six or seven times . . . I was in so much pain. I was shivering with fright . . . it was terrible . . . my mind was blanked out.

> At about 1:15 in the afternoon they untied me and released me near the edge of the forest. I stumbled onto the road where I met a woman who happened to be a neighbour. One look at me was enough for her to realize what had happened to me. She took me with her and informed my parents.

> I had attended a legal literacy programme and remembered what steps to take. So, without delaying further we went to the police station. The time was about 3 p.m. From there I was sent to the hospital where a male doctor examined me. Since I had severe bruises, cuts and abrasions, I was sent to the hospital. He told my parents that my hymen was torn. He also offered to repair my hymen surgically since I was unmarried. My parents agreed to have the surgery done.

> Due to my awareness gained through the legal literacy programme, I did not go to the toilet till all medical examinations were completed that day, which was at about 10:30 p.m. I was treated at this hospital for 29 days.

> In November I went to the Magistrate's Court for the identification parade. There were 45 men. All of them were residents of the area. My attackers were masked. So how could I identify them now without masks? But I saw the bite marks on one of the men and identified him as one of the attackers. The police also held four others on suspicion. However, all of them were released on bail.

> I have had to attend court on several days. But although so much time has passed, I still do not know if the culprits will be charged in the high court. Each time I attend court I go through the trauma. The defence lawyer even said that I knew the accused very well and that I myself lifted his sarong! The police are prosecuting, but I feel they are not competent enough.

> I feel betrayed and let down by the system. The culprits get away. Soon after the accused was released on bail, he was working at the garage as if nothing had happened. He can do the same thing to another woman, can't he? Honestly, I feel so angry and frustrated at times. I assure you, if no justice is done through the courts, I myself will knife him in open court.

> The culprits have used their influence on the police, and my case is being dragged on. I have also received threats. So my parents thought it was no longer safe for me to live in the village. That is why I am staying at the crisis centre now. See, I can't even live in my own home with my loved ones any more. But the culprits can go on without any disturbance to their lifestyles. Is there justice in this world?

Kusuma spoke about the attitudes of her family members and others in the village:

My family has not rejected me. But sometimes my parents say that it would better if I had died because of all the mental agony I go through. The villagers gave me their full support. But still the incident haunts me. I still have nightmares. I haven't been able to have a proper sleep since the incident. Earlier I had only heard or read about rape cases. When I learnt about rape at the legal literacy sessions, I never for one moment thought that I would be a victim myself! But when it happened to me . . . my head feels so heavy even when I think about it.

She decided to go ahead with the case despite the lethargic attitude of the police, because she did not want to have a similar incident happening to any other woman: "If rape victims come forward and prosecute without hesitation, I am sure something can be done to make the public aware of what is happening."

However, due to the distance from the capital city and high legal fees, Kusuma has found it difficult to obtain the legal assistance she deserves. Yet she is undeterred in her effort to see that justice is done. Critical to her has been the support given by the women's NGO that runs the crisis centre.

Earlier I went to the courthouse accompanied only by some of my family members. The public used to look at me in a derogatory manner. I felt so humiliated and ashamed. The mothers and sisters of the accused used to scold me within the court premises. I used to feel helpless. Even my parents felt powerless. But now, each time I have to attend court, the women members of the NGO come with me. They all come dressed in white and troop into the courthouse. They sit on the benches and wait till the case is called. I feel through their silence alone that I am not despised. Even the relatives of the accused no longer taunt and harass me when I come to the courthouse. Although my case has still not been brought before the high court, these women give me the strength to go on.

Kusuma said that a high penalty alone is not adequate to combat this type of crime:

I think the time has come to make the perpetrators of this kind of crime accountable. Having strict laws alone is not enough. They will somehow find loopholes in the law. They retain clever lawyers and get acquitted. Since the police handle the prosecution during the preliminary stages, the victim does not receive expert legal services. I don't think the policemen are sufficiently trained to pit their strength against a clever lawyer. In addition, the police do not think that crimes of violence against women are important. According to most of them, "the women have asked for it." They are already biased. In fact, they have made up their minds that women sometimes like the use of force on them! Don't they also have mothers, sisters, wives and daughters? What if something like this happens to their women?

Police have to be given a thorough training on how to deal with this kind of crime. They don't even know how to talk to a woman victim. Their very tone and speech terrifies me. Having women police officers to attend to this type of crime is not enough. The policemen, too, should be given to understand that this is a crime against society.

I would like others to learn from my experience. I am glad that I had at least gained some knowledge through legal literacy training. I think legal literacy with a special emphasis on issues like violence against women should be conducted for everyone. Even men should be exposed to such programmes. Awareness-raising at all levels — among the public as well as among the police — is a must. Until this is eradicated, no woman is safe.

The lawyer who interviewed Kusuma, Kamalini Wijayatilake of the Centre for Women's Research (CENWOR) in Colombo, comments:

After the gang rape, she found it difficult to stay in the village and her family felt [the same]. She was receiving threats by perpetrators of the violence since she had taken enough courage to go to the police, which was unusual for a girl in her social context. What usually happens is they would not go out into the open. They could think of the shame that would be attached and they would just immerse themselves in grief and would not seek out assistance, particularly in that village context.

But this girl thought, "No, let it be a lesson for other women, too. I will bring this to people and I will seek revenge through the proper channels." And since she had attended some training programme conducted by this particular women's centre, she came to them and they gave her refuge and counselling [and] supported her when she went to the courthouse. They went in white saris, sat together with her, their silent protest obviously manifested, particularly in the context of male-dominated courthouse. The judge is a man, the prosecutor is a man, the policemen are men and the majority of the people in the courthouse are men.

She said that women like Kusuma "are strong characters who don't bow down to the social pressure, particularly patriarchal perceptions of what you should be and what you should not be when you are a woman."

Sugani,[4] India: The "Witch's Daughter" Who Heals

In India, a woman I will call "Sugani" has risen above what would have been literally unspeakable not too long ago. Her compassion has also led her to forgive the men in her village who originally blamed her for what happened when she challenged stereotypes for women's behaviour.

Sugani, a 45-year-old midwife in Madhya Pradesh, set up a small maternity hospital in her village so that women would not have to walk for several days to receive prenatal or postnatal care. She combines modern medical practices with traditional medicine, an accomplishment all the more remarkable because her mother was sacrificed as a witch.

Sugani told her story for this book to Ruchira Gupta, an Indian journalist. It is a story of how she was forced to take a stand.

The history of my life is not just a personal story, it is part of the history of my tribe, the Santhals, a history of tragedy and at the same time a history of promise. It has been difficult for me, as an indigenous woman, to speak publicly, particularly as we were raised to believe that the role of women was to maintain a household and to bear children. If you broke with this role, you were seen as abandoning tradition and you would lose the respect of people.

We were born into poverty. I am from a remote village in Madhya Pradesh. We lived on roots and greens, and often our only hope for going into the market and returning with a handful of salt or onions was our ability to find mushrooms or *jamuns* [a citrus fruit] we could sell. When we were growing up we would go to the mines to see how iron ore was brought out. That is how we spent our childhood.

It is 13 years since my mother was burnt alive for being a *yogini* [witch] in our village temple. I had no father and my mother had struggled for 22 years for land and for a document proving that she owned the land. It was a *bigha* [approximately one acre] of farming land given to her husband by the government under a scheme for giving land to tribal people. Her name was not mentioned in the document. So when he died she did not get it.

My mother had been a midwife and knew of many herbal cures for other ailments as well, collected from her mother and grandmother. She was accused of being a witch when she cured a little girl declared dead by her parents. She was tortured, kidnapped and assassinated as a sacrifice at the village temple to appease the gods who had caused drought in our village for seven consecutive years.

I was already 32 by then. I had learnt midwifery and the use of herbal medicines from my mother. It hurts me to repeat the story again and again in public. But I believe that personal stories must be shared with moral courage and dignity by those who have been victims. Often we forget our history but sometimes our history is all that is left.

My mother had made sure that I attended a missionary school. There I was taught to forget my language and culture. I had to learn Hindi. What I knew was ridiculed and treated as folklore. I was treated like a ruin, not as somebody with rights and a future. More often than not I was desperately poor. But I also learnt about the world outside. I had access to magazines and books. I grew up different. I began to lose respect for my mother. I was frustrated in my work as a helper. I did not want to marry anyone from my tribe. My mother did not insist. It was only after she died that I realized how many gifts she had given me.

A slow anger began to burn me. Why was my mother sacrificed? Did it appease the gods or [was it for] the men in our village threatened by her knowledge? My mother was a healer. She always gave herbal balms and leaves to women after they were battered by their drunk husbands. She also had remedies for forced sex, and traditional methods for contraception. She taught me all this. When she was killed I was determined to carry on her work — not secretly, but publicly. I took help from the missionary school where I had studied. They sent me to a hospital where I got trained as a nurse.

I came back and began to run around for the same piece of land which had been denied my mother. It was occupied by a local policeman's relative. I kept running from pillar to post, from the Block Development Officer's [BDO] office, to the court, to the police station.

I was taunted, abused and heckled everywhere. I was a woman, and a tribal at that. The BDO asked me to come to his home to look into the matter. He called me at 10 at night. I refused to go. After that he would not even look at my file. His clerks would pass many remarks at me after that. They used to call me a whore, a witch, and make rude remarks about my body. I filed a case in court against the BDO.

One night some policemen came into the village and raped me and three other women. The men in our village protested. They were not allowed to even lodge a FIR [First Information Report]. They [some of the village men] said I had done wrong to complain against the BDO. After all, I was a woman [they said]. I should have stayed in the background. I deserved what I had got.

I was shocked by this tacit support of rape by the men in my village.

I finally decided to do something about this constant subjugation, marginalization and violence. I organized the women in my village to lead a march to the police station. Years of conflict with the local authorities had given us the moral and political authority to demand peace. Our march was mentioned in the local papers and I was finally given my plot of land.

With the help of the women in my village I set up the maternity hospital. It is a *pucca* [modern and strong] house with 20 beds.

Now even villagers outside our area respect us. No one thinks I am a witch. The struggle for equality has cost us so much thus far and it is going to cost us even more to forge a lasting equality.

Now the fact that I managed to set up the maternity hospital has raised incredible hopes for women, the poor, the oppressed and, above all, for those who are indigenous. For the first time we have achieved something. We have been heard. We are respected. At times being heard is enough for us because as a rule we have been the object of study but we were not listened to. Now we are no longer the object of study. We are making history. We are deciding on our own development methods.

It has given the women of our village confidence for the next project. We will set up our own school, which will also teach our culture and also take on the issue of respect for women.

Sugani talks about the effect on children of violence against their mothers:

Children, at least for the first five years, tend to be more dependent on their mothers. If they watch the life-giver being abused or treated badly in some ways, it confuses them. Their mother's poor health makes her irritable and since her child is the only one below her in the pecking order, she takes out her anger and frustration on him with shouting and beatings. A child who watches his mother being deprived of her rights grows up with a distorted perception of equality and justice. This affects society as a whole.

In spite of what she experienced — or, one might say, perhaps because of what she experienced, — Sugani believes that men must become involved in changing the status quo:

Men and women have to cooperate. Otherwise how will our races continue? In the beginning I was very angry with all men after my mother was sacrificed. I also looked down on the men from my tribe. But after I was raped I saw their genuine anguish and helplessness against the State and I began to connect with them again. My friends' sons or my relatives would go with me to the court and to the police station after that. It was a male journalist who wrote about the case. Also, when I was working with their mothers or wives in the maternity hospital, I noticed many of the men were genuinely concerned. Trapped by their upbringing and poverty, they were not able to do much. If told about what their wives went through when they shouted and abused them or forced sex on them, they did try to mend their ways. Also, younger men have begun to come to me for advice.

Women have also begun to strategize within their families. They try to educate and feed their daughters. I have explained to the men that our tribe is locked in and we must jointly, men and women together, challenge the exploitation by the outside world. That has built a kind of solidarity and respect between partners.

The future should, and can, be different, she believes:

My concept is that there should be an ideal family in which the backlash against unemployment and growing inflation should not be against the women, but these issues should be tackled jointly by the husband and wife. If men and women share and struggle together they will learn to respect each other. We are now part of an industrialized society where man is no longer the only breadwinner. Women's empowerment through the Panchayati Raj Bill [that sets a quota for women's membership in local governing bodies] will definitely change the role women play in the community. With their participation in politics, power relations in families will change, too. Women will begin to challenge religious tenets which keep them disempowered, in case most of the religious texts are interpreted by men to their own advantage.

She would like to intervene in changing public policy at the national level:

> I would like the people at the top to acknowledge the exploitation and systematic marginalization of my people. Something must be done. We are displaced all the time, from jobs, from education, from health and from land. Women are the lowest in the pecking order, [and] so the most vulnerable. I would like to have policies which deal with this.

> I learnt most of the traditional medicine methods from [my mother]. Women with knowledge and intelligence are considered witches by the men in our tribe because they feel threatened. I wanted to prove that sacrificing her was not the solution. Women are more vulnerable than men. I had a hard time convincing my tribe that we were getting fossilized and must not stay locked in. To respect a woman's body and mind is integral to the development of our community. The fact that I have been able to set up this maternity hospital and people come here from other villages too has given my tribe a sense of pride.

> My battle, which began with the violence against my, mother, is slowly but surely being won.

An Exceptional but Unnamed Woman,[5] Pakistan: Fighting Back

This story begins with Lubna Bhatti, M.D., in Pakistan. As a medical student, she helped conduct some of the first research in her country on domestic violence. It was for a student team project, and she says that she didn't really expect to find out very much. Instead, she and her team had results that broke silence, commanded attention and brought to light an unusual woman who fought back.

In three Karachi hospitals, the medical student team in which Dr. Bhatti participated interviewed 150 married women outpatients about their being abused (Bhatti et al. n.d.). The women outpatients waited until relatives could not overhear them, and only then spoke about domestic violence. Dr. Bhatti thinks the fact that they spoke at all was a step forward. It is the first and most difficult step, to face the intimate violence in the home itself, to bring it into the light, away from men's control. She explains the reason and method for the study, and some findings:

> There are not much data available here in Pakistan. Because there are not many figures available, there is not much awareness on this topic. The best thing would have been to do a community survey, but that would have been very difficult because the safety of the women would be jeopardized. So we decided to go to the outpatient department of two private hospitals and one government hospital, because [women outpatients] are most likely not accompanied by husbands and it is easier to interview them.

> . . . [T]he interviews took about 20 minutes to half an hour. The questions were basically, "What are the reasons for conflicts? Why do these things happen in your home?" Our questions were related to psychological abuse, verbal abuse, physical abuse, economic abuse and so forth. We also questioned the women on their attitudes about it: "What did you feel is happening to you?" "Why is it happening to you?" "What are the things [you] can do?"

Regarding the prevalence of abuse, Dr. Bhatti and her colleagues report that of the 150 women surveyed, 94 per cent (141/150) were subject to psychological abuse; 64

per cent (69/150) to economic abuse; 39 per cent (69/150) to verbal abuse; 37 per cent (56/150) to sexual abuse; and 34 per cent (51/150) to physical abuse.

> We also looked at the consequences of the abuse, including physical consequences and psychological consequences, and looked for depression and anxiety. We used the Aga Khan University Depression Scale. Then we compared depression in abused and non-abused women. The mean score of depression was higher for abused women than non-abused women, for all forms of abuse.

Dr. Bhatti notes that depression follows domestic violence, affecting children as well as women:

> It depresses the children. Even the husbands who were beating their wives, the majority of them thought it was not a good way to do things but that is what has always been happening. The main thing that holds the family together is the mother, and when she is depressed, the children don't get educated well and various things. The whole cycle continues.

Dr. Bhatti and her team also found that, "During pregnancy about 45 per cent (23/52) of women admitted to being physically abused," and "a third (8/23) of these women also reported a subsequent miscarriage following such abuse."

What were the women's reactions and thoughts, other than depression?

Most of the women (94 per cent) did not think physical abuse of wives was acceptable, although seven thought it was a husband's right. Of the 51 women being physically abused, 19 (37.2 per cent) said they tried to stop the beating. The student authors of the report note: "Nine had threatened their husbands with physical abuse. One managed to hit back at her husband." This was in contrast to the great majority (90 per cent) who "said that they try to bear with the physical abuse and the best they can do is weep about it."

The research showed that social norms were so strong that "sexual abuse — like marital rape — was not considered abuse by these women."

Dr. Bhatti said that no women from these interviews sought professional help. Only one went to the police.

Who was she? What was exceptional about her background or family situation, as well as her character? Remember, of the 51 who were beaten, she is the only one who complained outside her family.

What evidence is there that women in Pakistan challenge domestic violence? Dr. Bhatti predicts that a movement against domestic violence is likely in Pakistan, although it will lag behind action in some other countries:

> It will emerge from the homes. Women will take a stand or the children will take a stand against the father. The movement will [be started by] the rich people who are satisfied and know that there are others who are not. Some of them might have gone through abuse or have seen others going through the abuse.

Dr. Bhatti talks about the example of women's action against violence in India:

> In India they did a study in some rural areas and found out that 70 per cent of men admitted to physically abusing women. Some women decided to put a stop to the abuse. To accomplish this, whenever they heard of someone being abused, they would go to the home of that person and start banging on the door.

She says this was not yet happening in Pakistan because the women "underestimate themselves." She also noted that "purdah, the four walls and so forth" play a role in confining women. "She sees the possibility of retaliation by women in Pakistan, first as individual — from of frustration, and later as a movement".

> Women are starting to retaliate now. You hear of more episodes in which the wife even kills the husband [not recommended]. This frustration is going to come out one way or the other. When you see that someone else has taken action, it gives you courage to take action.

Dr. Bhatti sees the media and education as two main sources of change:

> Use public media to make them aware and educate women. They should get educated and get degrees even if they never plan to have a job, because at least they can get out of something [the difficulties or abuse at home].

> The awareness is growing, but due to the political conditions and the unsafe environment, priorities have changed for a while. But when things get settled, something will happen. The Saima case[6] brought by Asma Jahangir, a renowned woman lawyer and one of the most inspiring leaders for human rights, was hyped up and more cases will come up. You have to have media publicity.

> Women are doing more things now. More women are financially independent and that gives them more confidence. We are at a plateau phase right now, but we will see a steep increase. Things have changed for the better.

To date, women activists in Pakistan have focused primarily on gender violence at the state level. (This is discussed further in Chapter 11.) The introduction of the Hudood laws under General Zia in 1977 saw women take to the streets to confront the military. Their courage inspired other women and men to fight dictatorship and extremism for rights of women.

I am still thinking about the nameless women from Dr. Bhatti's study, especially the one who fought back and the one who went to the police. There is no information on their backgrounds, their husbands. We don't even know if they are the same women. I like to imagine so.

This exceptional but unknown woman is a symbol and harbinger for the change in women's lives that Dr. Bhatti predicts will come in Pakistan, despite the obstacles.

There are signs that change will not be smooth. Indeed, on 6 April 1999, Samia Sarman of Pakistan was murdered by a hit man allegedly hired by her family. She was seeking a divorce from her husband, who allegedly had beaten her over the years. This happened in the office of Hina Jilani, Asma Jahangir's activist sister, herself a renowned human rights lawyer (for more information, see *www.sigi.org/alert* and Abbas 1999).

Both Hina and Asma received fatwas (judgements in the name of religion) against them, calling for their deaths. Through an e-mail site against gender violence, women around the world called for pressure on the government to protect the two lawyers, who may already have had bodyguards provided.

On 3 August 1999, however, there was a new development, one that exposes many women to great risk. As reported by Zaffer Abbas (1999) in Islamabad, for the BBC, the Senate failed to pass a resolution "condemning the growing incidence of murder of women in the name of family honour." Samia Sarman's murder had prompted human rights groups to ask for "honour killings" to be condemned. According to Abbas, it did not happen, due to political opposition:

> People's Party [the opposition] Senator Iqbal Haider, who had drawn up the resolution, later described it as a sad day for democracy in the country.
>
> He said in order to win the support of some tribal leaders, the [then] governing Pakistan Muslim League had endorsed one of the most reprehensible customs — killing women in the name of honour.

Since then there has been an international outcry in support of Pakistani women — and surely many men — who want to end honour killing. More and more women will struggle with whether or not to break the silence and ask for change, as did the exceptional women in Dr. Bhatti's study, as Samia Sarman did before she was killed. There are risks for women as they try to change their lives and societies. These are also risks if they do not. That is the story that Dr. Bhatti's work helps to tell.

Lalita,[7] Nepal: The Woman Who Would Not Be Beaten

This is the story of the transformation of a docile girl to a woman whose self-esteem and sense of justice compelled her to stand for her rights — and her children's rights. She is, literally, "the woman who would not be beaten." To become that, she first had to be willing to give up everything else — her home, her husband, her livelihood, even her children. She told her story for this book to Glory Sodemba of UNICEF Regional Office for South Asia in Kathmandu. "Lalita" is not her real name.

Lalita confronted the patriarchy at every turn, and almost lost. The first time was as a girl in North-East India, where she grew up (although she was born in Nepal). Her father wanted her to marry an older man, but she refused. Instead, she went off with a young Nepali man to a country she didn't really know. Her father's authority was publicly challenged. He rejected her:

> My father was a very strict man. But he used to love me a lot. When I suddenly did what I did, he was hurt very badly. He feels, and vowed, that I am no longer his daughter and that I died for him. But he still cries thinking of me. My mother reads my letters when no one is around. I won't say he is still angry with me. But it hurt his prestige in the village when I eloped.

Lalita has not been back to her parents' home for over 15 years. Her mother and her uncle, a Buddhist priest, finally came by bus all the way from beyond Simla, near Tabo in North-East India close to the border with China, through Lumbini in lowland Nepal, and up to Kathmandu, where they stayed a few days to see her. Lalita gave her gold necklace to her mother, which seemed to make her mother very proud of her, after all.

But for years Lalita had to live through many difficulties because of the marriage that her father had wanted her to avoid. She started married life in a Nepali village, where her husband left her with his parents most of the time:

> My in-laws harassed me for not bringing enough dowry. I had already given what I had to them. From where am I supposed to bring some again? I was a very naive and a timid girl. I could not speak out. And I couldn't even speak Nepali properly. I used to speak Tamang dialect mixed with Hindi. My in-laws used to say that I used magic, *tuna muna* [hocus-pocus], on their son.

I used to sleep in a small shed and they used to come in the night and beat me, drag me out of my bed or throw my bed out. They used to beat my child, also, who was just starting to walk and talk, and once broke her leg. I was also eight months pregnant with my second daughter. When things like that happened, I used to feel like committing suicide.

I used to think, why do women commit suicide? It always used to pinch me. Now I know the reason. They have to go through so much of hardships and torture that some cannot stand any more of it. . . . Sometimes I felt like killing myself with *khukuri* [a Nepali knife, the curved style used by the Gurkha soldiers]. Some commit suicide when very angry; or when they have thought it over fully and that is the only solution available. I, myself, took poison once. But he [her husband] gave me lemon juice and something else to make me vomit and take the poison out.

If my parents had been near I could have asked them for help but there was no one.

Lalita worried about what her husband might do to their daughter:

The men in my husband's place do not hesitate to sell a daughter or wife to the brothels of India and enjoy the money received from it. My daughter was very beautiful and I could not leave her to them to be sold to the brothels of Bombay. If it were to happen she would suffer more than I would, with AIDS and lack of food. I thought if I had to, I would rather kill my daughter and bear the sin of killing her than let her live in sin. And the child I was carrying would die when I died.

I decided instead that I would live for my children. I was about 23 or 24 years old. After seven months in the village I decided that I am not going to live in this house. I had torn cloth, no shoes, lice in my hair, and my in-laws used to beat me with stick.

She went to Kathmandu with her husband. They had a son. She says she didn't know about family planning and considered killing him after he was born. Her husband spent more and more time in Bombay, and then tried to bring home a prostitute, while he kept calling Lalita one.

Her husband began to beat her when her son was six months old. The owner of a factory where they lived encouraged her husband's abuse:

The master was the kind who looked down on women. Whenever I had a fight with my husband, the master used to blame me for not keeping quiet and for answering back to my man. He did that instead of having a man-to-man talk with my husband for his wrongdoings. He never used to see fault with men. I used to get angry and run away sometimes with my kids or alone and stay at others' houses.

She had no intention of returning to her husband. She said, "If I reject someone then I will never go back again. I was determined that I would rather die than go back to my husband."

She expected to be left in peace although with hardship. In her parents' village, a couple can separate if the man misbehaves with his wife — "then the neighbours will try to put some sense in his head," she said. "But over here, once the man marries a woman he will not let go of her easily [if she wants to leave him]. He will pursue her no matter where she goes. Either he doesn't look after her well or he will kill her."

Once [my husband] beat me to such an extent that I fainted. He woke me up by pouring water on me. . . . He knew that if I had died he would be caught. If he is so scared of that then why does he beat me so! If he doesn't want me he should let me go but he doesn't.

Lalita said her husband caused so much trouble for her friends who tried to help her that she went back to him. Again, she decided to leave, no matter what, partly because she saw the power of men being used against her:

> If I stayed there, my husband would always get support from the master. Wherever I went, the master used to send my husband with his own car to get me. After that we used to get along for a couple of days, then the whole thing would start all over again.

> At first I used to tolerate his beatings but later on it was too much for me. I started to hit back. I could not ask for help from others and even if I did, people would think that it is between husband and wife and not get involved. If people did intervene, he would ask, "What is it to them? She is my wife and I can do anything to her. Or did you have any relationship with her?" . . . So, no one will come for help. You have to learn to defend yourself.

> I was getting tired of this whole issue so whenever my husband would hit me once, I started to hit him back 10 times. There was nothing [else] I could do, he wouldn't leave me and there was never peace at home. I used to climb up the grille of the window and kick him.

One day, when her husband stood on her hair and beat her in the face, Lalita took the saucepan in her hand and hit him violently. He called her "Durga," "Kali," and begged for forgiveness. She went on a rampage through the house, tearing his clothes, and left — without the children. He "bothered" her many times afterwards. She survived and even prevailed after many difficult experiences, even living on the streets.

> I left my husband. He did not let me take my children. It was seven years ago. Democracy had just come to Nepal. After I left my husband I went to work for an Indian family. I was employed there to do washing, cleaning, cooking, everything, for Rs. 300.

But even then her husband would not really let her go:

> My husband did not leave me alone. . . . He told the mistress of the house [where she worked] that I was a woman with a loose character, and a prostitute. He said that I would stand naked in front of her husband and destroy the peace and stability of the household. Hearing this, anyone would be scared, so the mistress of the house gave me Rs. 250 and asked me to leave her house at 11 o'clock in the night.

Lalita sold some jewellery she had from her mother, asked friends for food, and finally found another job. She tried to get her own children back. She argued about their rights being abused:

> I went to the Home Ministry many times to lodge suit against my husband to get my children back. I repeatedly told them that the children are being deprived of their education rights by their father.

> But not a single law could help them. Once my husband came and took the *lungi* [sarong] I was wearing, making it impossible for me to go anywhere. I even begged the law for my security but it did nothing and it will do nothing. So now I feel that first you yourself have to be capable. And you must have someone in power to knock on the door of the law.

Lalita has noticed that many women are abused. She also blames male peer pressure, alcohol and male pride:

[The man] gets drunk and starts beating and scolding his wife. Most women bear with this torture. Most men drink alcohol. You can't stop that. The other thing will be the friends he keeps around him. Some of them might say, "Can't you even control your wife? Why don't you give her a good beating?" So, he starts to think that he must use force to keep his wife under his total control.

But he must think before he starts to beat his wife, why he is doing so? He must ask that question himself. Now my husband tells me that he used to do so because his friends used to tell him.

Lalita said her husband never imagined that she would be able to take care of herself and better than he ever did.

Lalita tries to help other women who suffer from domestic violence. She has learned enough about patriarchy to use the "hierarchy of masculinity"[8] herself, to help keep some men in line:

There are quite a number of young boys between 20 and 25 living nearby. They respect me for what I am and they know that I am someone they cannot tease and make fun of. My best friend was having problems at home with her husband, who used to beat her, and she was always nervous of him. She didn't want to divorce him. So I [told] these boys I needed some help from them. They were ready to help me and I asked them to beat up her husband. My friend did not know anything about it. Afterwards he was in bed for a few months and he blamed my friend for putting those boys to beat him up. Later he mellowed down a little. He is in service with the Nepal Army. I have a friend whose grandfather is a high-ranking army officer. I threatened my friend's husband that if he misbehaves with his wife I will report it to the officer. Since then he treats his wife well. He knows that if his misdeed is reported he will not have any chance of promotion. Now he looks after her well, gives her money and the children go to school also.

Lalita eventually got her own children back. She tries to get them to think well of their father:

Just a few days ago I took my younger daughter to visit a few places. While we were in the taxi she said that she prays to God not to let anything bad happen to them. She said she wants to study a lot, and that she will do this and that to her father. And I told her not to say such things. After all, he is her father.

Lalita's husband still wanted her back. The girls discourage this, saying it would be a living hell. She is sorry that they saw her being beaten.

It is just my fault that I did not know him very well before, but I do now and I am living a happy, free life. I cannot keep him under my control and he is a human being and he would not like to live under anyone's control. Since then they haven't asked me such questions or said anything.

My [older] son stayed with his father for a long time. He has been fed with all nonsense words. He has been told that I work at a foreigner's house and earn a lot of money. He asked my son to steal the money from me and give it to him.

Whatever happens, society still tends to blame the woman, Lalita points out:

"Hamile sochyo bhane samajle sochnu parne kura ho!!!!" Once you leave your husband, it is the women who will start gossiping about her, saying that she left her husband and she had relationships with many men.

She wishes she could do more to help other women:

> If anyone is a victim of violence and comes to me asking for help, then I will try to help as best as I can, either by talking to both parties or trying to solve the problems the best way. But the problem will be we don't have resources to carry out the job. And another drawback is lack of education. If I had education, maybe I could go to the right place to do the right thing. If I was educated, I would have treated my husband differently. I don't think I would have let the law turn its back on me when I was fighting against my husband. It was due to my lack of education and wealth that he was able to treat me the way he did. You need three things in life: first, education; second, wealth, property, this is something for which you can even work for; and third, people must try to understand us.

Lalita hopes for change:

> The law should protect and support [women] and they should also fight for their rights. For example, a woman gives an interview like I have done, then she might be scared what her husband and family say. Why should she be scared of anyone in this life? She must be bold enough to speak or she must not say anything. What is the use of talking in the front then hiding behind later on?

Lalita wanted me to use her real name, she is that strong. I didn't, to protect her children as well as herself. In 1997, two of her daughters were in a shelter to help prevent their father from selling them into prostitution. The older son was with his father, but Lalita paid the school fees and tried to guide her son's path somewhat. She alone provides for a young son. By 1999, she had a new job, again as a domestic. She had some new skills, though: She managed to get an e-mail message to me in New York. She knows much more about the world and the possibilities it can offer.

Lalita's story is one of self-respect, principle, determination and success. Always she thought of her children's well-being:

> But I am sad to say that my children saw everything. I was beaten right in front of them. They even talk about it these days. But I have never told them that their father is not good, or speak against him to them.

Perhaps some in Nepal would say, "Ah, but she broke up the family." Yes, a family that was so destructive, it almost killed her and betrayed her daughters' future. Until women are willing to break up such families, children and women will suffer unduly. That is the truth that Lalita learned. She stopped protecting her husband's weakness and found her real strength, which she uses as best as she can to help others as well as herself.

And her own father apparently was proud of her: He died in 1998, asking to see her. She learned too late to reach him in time.

Nilufer,[9] Afghanistan: "If You Think She Is Not Good, Let Her Become Something As a Bad Person"

"Nilufer" has achieved a great deal in her profession as a lawyer in Afghanistan, against great odds. She has worked to clarify and promulgate the true position of Islam on women's education, and she has risked her life to do so. Here is part of her story, from somewhere in Afghanistan.

> As it was mentioned by Asifa Jan,[10] it is the circumstances that influence a person. Firstly, I belong to a military family, my father was an officer of the army of Afghanistan. As you may

know, army officers are very strict people. Among our relatives I am the first one who attended school, and I opened the way for the others, until I reached the university. After completion of grade six they wanted me to get married, after grade nine they wanted that again, after completion of grade 12 they wanted that to keep me in the house. I started crying and shouting. I went to see my uncle and requested his intervention in my favour. I had to promise the family that "I won't be a bad girl, I will be a useful person for the community, I will earn you pride." Every day I had to convince my father or my uncle or my brothers, one day by crying, the next by some other way.

The family allowed Nilufer to continue her education, but outsiders were critical:

You see, it is because of our culture and traditions, when I went to the university some people sarcastically told my father in front of the mosque: "You have put your daughter in the government's care. You cannot feed your child and you are not a Muslim, you gave your daughter to the king's soldiers."

Despite the opposition, Nilufer's struggles paved the way for her sisters also to attend university and become professionals. Yet strict family discipline remains a way of life for women in their society:

You may know about our society. If my cousin and my father are sitting in a room, we cannot enter that room freely. Girls have no right to choose their husbands. Without the permission of her family, a girl cannot attend the school and educate herself. Another problem is inequality between brothers and sisters in the family, because sons are given superiority in everything, because male members of the family impose injustice on females.

This leads to further injustices against women.

That's why fathers have less attention for their daughters, because they believe a daughter is the "property of others" [meaning the daughter will get married and leave the house while the son will remain as a continuation of the patrilineal family and with the property].

Parents sell their daughters. They demand a huge dowry ["bride price," paid to the girl's family, is the custom in Afghanistan; elsewhere in South Asia dowry is usually paid by the bride's family to the groom's family. That is not the case in this example.]. That's why girls sometimes remain unmarried for years.

They even put their children up for bidding. Those who offer more money will win the girl, regardless of the age of the man. They don't care about the right and future of their daughters. Another thing is the issue of second, third and fourth wife. . . . A divorcee will be considered a bad person.

Nilufer has seen little change in the past 20 years:

During the revolution of the Communists, as they call it, these things were not as bad as now in the urban areas, but in the rural areas it was like this. We don't think it was a cause for the Islamic revolution, it is simply because of low awareness of our people, low education rates and economic backwardness . . . a poor and illiterate country cannot be better.

Imagine. I am a professional with a high position. I have a higher education, but still if there is a suitor for me, I cannot tell my father that I wish to marry with this person. I do not dare to say so.

She never married. She said it was hard

to find a person to understand my wishes, who understands me. I am worried he will keep me in the house. When I wanted to marry someone, my family did not allow me, and when they wanted me to marry someone, I didn't want him. The problem is, I don't want to be so bold. [I don't want to create] a feeling that educated girls are so insolent.

The general lack of education perpetuates the situation, she believes. It is difficult for even an educated man like her father to change things:

I must say, one of the major contributors to this situation is the low literacy rate. Old traditions and superstitions that have deep roots among the people play major roles. What can my father do in a community with no literate members? The only thing he could do was to allow me to have my education completed, and he allowed my sister to become a doctor and treat the family. Still, we are faced with disagreements. If someone comes with a jeep vehicle to take my sister to see a sick person, we cannot allow her to go, because we fear that they may take her away. In the area where we live the people do not tolerate a woman doctor.

Nilufer uses her own education to try to accomplish change:

Whenever I have had the chance to meet women, or participated in their meetings, I have always kept inquiring about their problems. I have always tried to support them legally. I usually go to the courts, but I am also interested in outside work. Concerning the human rights issue, there was a seminar two years ago on women's human rights. It might not be sufficient, but I have done whatever I could. I have provided guidance to women according to my knowledge and understanding.

Nilufer has also helped establish an independent commission on human rights, in conjunction with the United Nations Commission on Human Rights (UNCHR) and has managed to get some Islamic religious authorities to support women's rights for education. Because of her work, some authorities see Nilufer as a threat. She explains why:

I have explained the fundamental rights of women from the Islamic point of view: women have the right for education, women have the right in judiciary, women have the right to have property. I have explained these things on the basis of Quran, and emphasized that a woman cannot be a fifth or sixth wife. A man, a woman, cannot be sold. When they heard the things which I have mentioned, they did not like it. But later on, despite their decision to kill me or terrorize me, I went to see them and I asked them to hear things from myself directly. I presented to them my papers and showed them those verses of Quran and Hadiths [judgements based on the Quran], and urged them to check. "Then you can kill me. If you deny the Quran and Mohammed's religion, it is up to you." When they listened to me, they did not say anything to me and became satisfied. They said, "This time, no problem, but try to avoid talking in the future."

There is still real danger, she feels:

No one can predict what will happen, because of this situation, I never dreamt that they will treat me so badly that spring, even the Shura [local religious authority] had accused me as a *kafir* [infidel] and decided that I must be executed.

I myself also feel unsafe and I worry if one day a jeep vehicle will come and take me somewhere.

A friend of mine, jokingly, told me that some commanders were commenting about me, saying, "Who is this brave girl, give us her address, who is she?" These things, and my own special feelings for oppressed women in our country and my own struggle, made me to believe that I may have some impact. Look, I am young, but you can see how I look older. I sometimes work, washing clothes until late in the night. I bear such things to make things at least better for my sister or her children in the future. If we continue such a miserable life, and if we do not sacrifice ourselves, who else would do so? If they abolish one, two, three or more of us, no problem, it will pave the way for the future generation.

[My brothers] quarrel with me and argue that under ongoing circumstances, if some of these commanders are unhappy about something, one of them will come and loot the house or kill our father, our mother, or kidnap me or another sister. My brothers argue. They are worried about the safety of the whole family because there is no law and justice.

The family attitude toward Nilufer has changed . . . somewhat.

Now my father is an old man, and he has seen that during my life I have never tried to earn any negative points for my family. My father has accepted me now, he cooperates with me to some extent, he reads my articles, but concerning my brothers, it is still difficult for them to accept. When they see me talking, or when they hear from other people about me, they feel uneasy. But since my father is alive, he protects me, and says during his life he had never seen anything wrong from me and he tells them, "If you think she is not good, let her become something as a bad person."

Inspired by those South Asian women who have become prime ministers, Nilufer has set a high goal for herself: to someday become Afghanistan's first woman Prime Minister. If that happens, she would take steps to end violence against women and help bring about equality:

I would introduce a law on the basis of the true spirit of Islam to ensure equality of men and women in such a country. And during the four years of my term of office as Prime Minister I would try to ensure budget allocations to make half the population literate. It sounds like a dream.

Indeed, the news from Afghanistan about what Physicians for Human Rights have called "The Taliban's War on Women: A Health and Human Rights Crisis in Afghanistan" (1998), and subsequent reports in the *New York Times*, including comments by the UN Special Rapporteur on violence against women, do make Nilufer's hopes seem like a very far-off dream.

Diverse Lives, yet Common Concerns

Although the six women in this chapter come from diverse backgrounds, their outlook and struggles are similar. Their religious backgrounds are varied: Animist, Buddhist, Christian, Hindu and Muslim. Some of the women are upper or middle class, some are poor. The youngest is 21, the oldest, 45. Four have children. Their education ranges from first grade to university. Some spent their early years in the countryside, others lived in the city. Most of their mothers were housewives, and several had been married off very young. Some acknowledged their own mothers as important role models, others did not. Some followed their fathers' advice, others defied their fathers.

Some Shared Concerns

The misuse of religion to strengthen tradition and custom as overseen by men is a common concern for them, whatever their religion. "Violence is not part of any religion," Rani says. Sugani's mother was killed and Nilufer had her life threatened in the name of religion. Both Rani and Nilufer explain tenets of Islam that support rights and behaviours of women that others would forbid or punish severely.

The effects on children of gender-based violence trouble them. Whether Rani's desire to train girls and boys to defend themselves, or Sugani's to build a village school where respect for women will be taught; Nilufer's disapproval of girls being sold to the highest bidder, or Lalita's regret that her children witnessed her beatings, most of these women expressed strong concerns about the impact of violence on children in their society or family.

Some of the women are living on their own, more than would be expected in South Asia. Some know that their choices will prevent them from being married, some have left abusive relationships, some have left their villages. In the absence of a man's daily protection — and concomitant abuse — these women have turned to women's groups and friends.

These women have a sense of solidarity with other women and look beyond their own personal lives to help them. Rani wants to help other women become more self-confident; Kusuma wants to help prevent rape; Sugani seeks to provide better maternity care in her village; Lalita counsels friends not to accept beatings; Nilufer defends rights of women as in the Quran, and helps her sister with chores. Just as they support other women, they recognize the support they have received, such as the confidence Kusuma draws from the "women in white" in the courtroom.

They see and know the power of the patriarchy. They challenge it. Still, the women tend to talk about cooperation with men as the ideal for family and society: Even those who have been so deeply hurt, such as Sugani, talk about the men who have given support or about the importance of men finding more empathy with women, and men and women finding more forms of cooperation. Some, like Kusuma, talk about the importance of training for the police and judges. Lalita involves men, both young ones and those highly placed, in her efforts to help other women.

They talk about rights in clear, direct ways, with no doubts, no confusion. Claiming rights seems natural to their kind of spirit. It doesn't depend on book-learning, either.

They have also turned to the legal system, assuming it is a means to respect, protect and fulfil rights, and that they, too, are entitled and able to claim these. They use the legal system more than many women would think it possible to do, or even consider: These women have fought the odds and have taken their cases to court or to the police. They represent well those who have fought for and won rights to land; those who have hired lawyers to get custody of their children; those who have productively challenged religious authorities. Some have learned, in a very painful, even violent way, the faults in the system. In some cases they have suffered grave consequences, such as when Sugani dared to file a case against the Block Development Officer and was raped by policemen. And in Pakistan, a woman seeking to divorce her husband was murdered when she tried to use the legal system to escape family violence.

They see the benefits for their communities and countries for development based on women's advancement. Sugani says, "As a rule we have been the object of study but we were not listened to. Now we are no longer the object of study. We are making history."

In short, these women have chosen a path of claiming women's rights as a way to serve others as well as to improve their own situations. They are living examples of the diverse possibilities of what it can mean to be a woman in South Asia, as elsewhere. All show the courage that is needed for women to break gender-role stereotypes and patriarchal constraints that limit their human potential and rights.

Endnotes

1   In that, spirit, this book talks about "victim-survivors."
2   Interview arranged by UNICEF ROSA in cooperation with UNICEF Bangladesh. Name used by agreement.
3   Interview arranged for this book by UNICEF Sri Lanka; pseudonym given by that office.
4   Interview for this book arranged by UNICEF ROSA in cooperation with UNICEF India. Pseudonym assigned by interviewer.
5   Interview arranged by UNICEF Pakistan.
6   Saima Waheed married without her father's permission. He took the case to court, where it was ruled that she needed

permission. Her appeal to a higher court was upheld, leaving the status of her marriage unclear.
7   Interview arranged by UNICEF ROSA; Pseudonym given by that office.
8   O'Hanlon (1997) refers to the way in which men position themselves vis-à-vis each other according to their degree of perceived masculinity.
9   Interview arranged by UNICEF Afghanistan. Pseudonyms given to all Afghani interviewees.
10   This is a source known to the speaker but not to this writer.

Men against the Patriarchy

Here we meet seven men whose lives go beyond the stereotypic masculine as they work against violence to girls and women in society. So far as we can tell, they also try to stand for gender equality in their own families. These interviews provide the first glimpses of the wide array of men's efforts to end violence against women and girls in South Asia. The interviews were chosen to represent a range of men's efforts, from preventing abuse in one's own family and community to working against abuse supported by the State and by religion when it is distorted and altered due to political or military interests.

What sources do they draw upon for challenging the norm that women are inferior and that men should stand together against women, not in solidarity with them? These sources vary, from childhood insights to sudden realizations as adults when confronted with a particularly troubling or inspiring incident. For some of the men, change and analysis came through a slow process, almost without their awareness until later reflection. In the end, all the men question the usual idea that girls and women are worth less than boys and men. They do what they can to encourage others to work for equality, and not to accept gender violence.

Kiran Tewari,[1] Nepal: Make Decisions Together

People ask me, "Don't you want to have a son?"
I say, "We have Laxmi, she's everything for us."

The speaker is Kiran Tewari, then Secretary of the Child Welfare Society in Nepal, who was interviewed by Vidiya Shresta. He promotes democratic family life for the benefit of children and society.

He says,

When I talk one to one, many men don't agree with me because they believe that women's roles are [and should be] very different than men's. For instance, I want to emphasize joint decision-making in the household where the husband, wife and children, both boys and girls, make decisions together about what affects their lives. This is very uncommon in Asian society, where males make all the important decisions.

Kiran traces his concerns back to his youth, when girls were not consulted, even on major events that affected them.

When I was 16-and-a-half, my 15-year-old sister was married off, and I wasn't even informed. I was so shocked when I found out. I was here and it was right in Kathmandu. My father said they received a very good proposal that they couldn't refuse.

The practice continues today. Even now I get invitations to weddings of 15-year-old girls and their parents say the same thing. These are daughters of well-educated, prominent people. They believe that if they wait, something bad may happen to the girl. She may get romantically involved with someone and bring shame to the family. I think that we are too narrow. Openness is very important. Once we discuss issues, we get to make a decision that everybody can live with.

I try to use this type of thinking at home as well as at the office. We all, male and female staff, sit down and discuss issues. It doesn't matter what their professional level is. We throw ideas around. It takes a long time, but we are all content with our decision. The same should happen in the family.

Kiran explains how he became involved in the effort to end violence against women:

Basically, Nepali society is still feudal; we still think that males should be the providers, the females should be in the house. This belief is actually pervasive throughout society, only the magnitudes vary. Because of this, we need change. From the outside the society looks very harmonious, very cultural. But inside, if you can see into communities, into houses, you'll see suffering. Actually, this exists in my own family also. Females are being treated unequally even though our Constitution says that men and women are equal. Of course, laws discriminate, and in the family, gender differences affect family dynamics. From birth, boys and girls are treated differently. The amount of food given to boys is more than what is given to girls. I think that in our society we need to form groups and work together to speak out against these injustices. Not just mass advocacy; we need to speak to individuals as well. We need to help victims, and speak to others so that they are aware of these problems, so that they respect women's rights. Because I noticed all this, I thought of getting involved.

In his view, attitudes are an underlying cause of violence against women and girls in South Asia.

The biggest problems are our attitudes — that's where the real problem lies. We believe that men should always be outside, women inside. Men should be allowed to move up, to progress, but not women. Women should be directed, guided. It's OK for a man to walk outside alone at night. If a woman goes somewhere to get something at night and something happens to her, society will ask, "Who is that woman? Why was she out at night?" They will not ask, "Who is the person who has committed this act? Why did he do it?" They always look negatively at the woman, even if she does something good. We choose to look only at the negatives. Men are excused and society finds justification for their actions. This is why attitudes need to change.

Another thing that has to change is our values. Our country is Hindu-dominated, with some Buddhism also. There are many positive things — Ram, Sita, Radha, Krishna[2] and when we worship the Devi, Bhagwati,[3] they are very powerful. And girls are symbols of them. We are trained at a very early age to respect and worship them. But our values undermine and dominate women. Women are treated as being inferior, and incapable of being leaders [and] should not take part in decision-making. So when we have this kind of feeling, when women try to come in, they have problems. Women have problems in every sphere. They cannot buy, sell, inherit property, cannot make decisions about their lives or those of their children without the consent of males. When men are displeased by women's actions, they beat women, torture them mentally.

Political rights are different from human rights. When we speak of human rights, we must talk about quality of life, the right to live one's life decently, the right to feel safe. Women have been made to feel afraid. They are always thinking, "Maybe I am doing this wrong." Even mothers treat daughters differently from sons. That needs to change.

I feel that our current value system is the biggest problem. Also, there is the way the society looks at girls. From the moment a son is born, parents immediately begin planning his future — he'll be a doctor, engineer, politician and so on. When a girl is born, parents pay no attention to her because she'll go to another person's house; she won't be theirs, so why waste money?

A boy notices these differences. So, when he grows up and becomes a responsible adult, he will treat his wife and daughter the same way that his mother and sister were treated. And his son will be given good treatment. It will take a long, long time to change this.

Another problem is that women have no economic power. [He then explained that they are considered gifts, or *daan*, to in-laws.] I dislike the term *daan*. If a women is given more rights, she will have much more power. She should be given more economic freedom, so that she can have more respect. She won't be tortured.

And now in Nepal, the dowry system is coming in. We read in the newspapers that girls are killed by their husbands and in-laws because their fathers couldn't give the motorcycle that was promised at the time of the wedding.

Kiran is also concerned about the abuse of girls by parents, relatives, sex-trade traffickers and factory owners:

[A girl is] made to work and to give up her things for others. She may be sexually and mentally abused by her relatives because her parents have no respect for her and treat her so poorly. She has to work all day in the kitchen and do other things for the household and other family members.

Many girls run away from this kind of torture. People can take advantage of them very easily by saying nice things, promising to marry them and to take them away from their families. So they are very easy targets for traffickers and other dishonest people.

Everybody is now talking about child labour in carpet factories. But that isn't where the real problems are. In factories they work in groups, and factories are cleaner than the streets. Yes, there is sexual abuse in the factories, but the degree is much less than in houses where girls work. In carpet factories protecting girls is easier because that sector is more organized, and offenders can be stopped.

He would like to see more attention given to the lot of child domestic workers:

Almost every family has a girl working for them [at least in the city]. She works almost 12 to 14 hours a day, she serves children as old as herself or older. Some families are nice, but others are not. When she is about 10 or 11 years old, they often physically and sexually abuse her. A boy servant the same age would leave and stay on the street even, if he were physically abused, but a girl has nowhere to go. For a girl, she is not safe everywhere. And people are unsympathetic to street children. They say, "She has a bad character, that is why she is in the street." They don't ask why she is here. Girls cannot challenge the situation they are in. More than 70 per cent of all domestic servants are deprived of basic human rights — food, clothes, shelter, etc. Most are mentally tortured. They are kept in an unhealthy physical environment. They are sexually abused. Mental and other skill development is minimal. They depend on their masters for everything. So when they leave the house, they may not even be able to go back home because they don't have money, or their parents won't accept them. If they are lucky, they will marry someone. Otherwise, what will they do?

And, at the other end of the spectrum, is abuse suffered by widows:

In many cases, widows are deprived by their in-laws of their husbands' property. They are very frequently raped and tortured by their brothers-in-law. They become pregnant. If they choose to give birth to the child, they will be ostracized from society. So [a widow] has to force herself to have an abortion. In Nepal, abortion is illegal — it is equal to murder. So, she is caught and sent to prison for 20 years.

Although he cites attitudes as a source of the problem, he also points to economic causes:

I think it is economic pressure in the family that leads to violence. There is violence in both cities and villages. These days, violence is more common in the village. Wives are beaten by their husbands, girls are sold by their families. It's because men get rid of their frustration this way. Another is that with infrastructure development, with the building of roads, alcohol of every kind is very readily available in the villages. But there is no development, no work, no industry, no nothing. So, what the men do is they take what little money they or their families make, or take loans, and get drunk. Then they abuse their wives, not just by beating them but by not contributing to the family's income and wasting scarce resources. So alcoholism is a problem.

And the heart of the solution lies in the family, but the money economy has exacerbated existing patriarchal tendencies and brought new models and temptations, too, for both rural and urban families.

When a man and woman marry, both should take responsibility for keeping the family healthy and strong, and for earning enough to feed the family. There was a survey that showed that what a woman makes goes to buy food and education for her family. And a man's income goes towards buying alcohol, gambling and prostitutes. Very little goes to the family. This tendency is increasing these days.

For Kiran, violence against women is much more than a women's issue. He talks about why and how he became involved:

What is very important is, in our society we say that violence against women is a women's issue and only women should get involved. But I believe that this is an issue that is of concern to all of society, not just to males or females. It is our concern. To tell you the truth, even in my own family, I have seen my mother cope with and accept many injustices. And her view always was, "Well, I was born a female, and this is my fate. I must accept it." I see young girls who are seven to eight years old. They should be as free as butterflies, playing, singing, going to school, enjoying their childhoods.

Females, especially young girls, are our society's most voiceless members. There are women who are doing a lot of work in the public to raise awareness. But in households, women and girls still have no voice.

[My] real involvement began when I went to university. I started an adult literacy programme for women. It was all very new then, in 1972. We had night classes for them. This was in the Far West, as part of my university degree. The women used to carry torches to their classes because it was so dark in the evenings. The whole village was quite surprised. Then we tried to make all this public. We used to ask the women to speak about the good things in their lives when they get education. We talked about health issues and other issues. I was there for six to seven months. Now many NGOs in that and other areas are doing this kind of work. But in those days I started this on my own. This is how it all began. We had no help from outside. We made our own blackboard, bought the paper, everything. And the villagers accepted this. You see, when you are committed and you have a good idea, people will support you because you are sincere. There was a little opposition, but on the whole they were very supportive.

In the Far West, women are much further behind those in other parts of the country. They are very conservative. We tried to give some education to women in the *mela* [a rural trade fair], but the people said that kind of thing might work in a city like Kathmandu, but their area is different. You see, I believe that people everywhere should have access to information. Social justice everywhere should be the same. Women and children there should have the same freedom as women and children here in Kathmandu. Many people think that when we say "freedom," we mean bad things like what we see in rock music videos, and complete lack of responsibility. That is not what we mean. We should try and uphold our Asian values, and within these Asian values, there are many good things, and if we keep them, we can be a model for the world.

But we had a lot of support because people saw that we were educated, sincere and wanted to help. We involved local leaders. We convinced them, and it was possible.

It was Kiran who talked, in Chapter 2, about the practice of offering girls to the temples. Most become prostitutes.[4] Kiran points to the related work he became involved in:

With the help of UNICEF and a group of law students, we went there to make them aware of their rights and what the law says. According to the *Muluki Ain*, the Law of the Land, selling daughters or sons is a crime. Offering children to the temple is a crime. Nowadays, the Children's Act also doesn't permit this. We explained this, and the people know. But obviously there's still a lot of reluctance to accept what we say. . . . We have found sponsors for some of these girls and they are studying in Kathmandu schools.

He calls on women themselves to take a stronger role:

One cause is tolerance [by] the women themselves. They are so tolerant. They must speak out. Our social values discourage speaking out and they are victimized. And our attitudes are reinforced over generations that men are superior.

Kiran Tewari realizes he must also remember to listen to his own daughter:

We make decisions so quickly that we can't always listen to her. There should also be someone to check and correct us. Sometimes I say to her, "Let's sit down and have a conference." Both my wife and I try to share information with her. But, sometimes, like other parents, we lose tolerance and have no time. That's very harmful for her.

Dr. Lohiya,[5] India:
A Pioneer against Violence to Women in the Community

Dr. and Mrs. Lohiya live in a village in rural Maharashtra, India. Twenty years ago they set up a shelter for women, through which they sensitize community residents about problems and teach alternatives to domestic and economic violence against women. In this interview with Karen Kundiyet, they share their insights. Dr. Lohiya begins:

> I came from an orthodox Gujar family where the women have to cover their heads completely. When my brothers got married I insisted my sisters-in-law uncover their heads and should be treated as equals. While I was in high school I belonged to Rashtra Sewa Dal movement, which was established to bring about social change. One of the things that was stressed in the meeting was the equality of man and woman. Every meeting had to have at least eight women and they should sit in front and fully participate in proceedings. This made a deep impression on me. My mother was a social worker, especially working for family planning. At that time I observed that many women coming to our house did not want children. Wife-beating was very common. It was accepted. The wife of one of our workers said, "My husband is not beating me. If he is not beating me how can I say that he is loving me." There are cases like this.
>
> We started Manavlok [human-world] as an NGO to serve people, especially in villages, including both sexes, men and women. When we are working against injustice, it may be economic or exploitation. [When] there is an injustice, so far as the women's section is considered, it is our duty to fight against it.

At first, women were hesitant to approach the organization, which includes seven subcentres. Each centre offers general and family counselling. Once a woman's domestic problem is verified, she is trained in sanitation, literacy and basic skills that can enable her to live on her own if no solution is found within six months. The experiences of the 200 women who have taken shelter there during the past decade provide insight into the nature of family violence. Many cases involve dowry disputes. Of 15 cases filed in the courts, only one has been won. The violence is manifested in many forms, Dr. Lohiya says:

> I don't actually feel that only beating means violence. A sort of exploitation can be violence. Suppose [the husband and wife] are working in the family. [The wife] is working more, she is taking care of the children, she is taking care of the house, she is taking more care of husband. Then she is working, say, 8 hours, 10 hours, 15 hours. Sometimes her husband is working only for four to six hours.
>
> There are cases of beating, there are cases of rape, there are cases of taking advantage of one's profession. One doctor tried to rape the patient, who was a wife of someone he knew from a good family.

Beatings are common. Mrs. Lohiya recalls one such incident:

> I work in a college. Even one of my colleagues was beating his wife. Around 8 or 9:30, our principal came with that lady to me. She was with us for a night. She was horribly beaten. But we told her, "Don't leave the house. He can bring many women by giving money. But your children will not get [a] mother, so it is your duty not to leave the house."

It took nine years to resolve the case. The wife kept the house and the husband remarried. There was widespread support for the woman — yet the husband's family and friends continued to stand by him.

The Lohiyas feel that violence is increasing, even in rich families:

> [E]ven those who are rich expect something from their daughters-in-law and they give trouble to her. For rich families, what I have gathered is that if someone says, "I won't take dowry," it means people think that there is some physical defect in him and he is not demanding money. This is one thing. Another thing is if the father does not give much dowry to another party his social status is very low, so dowry is always related with social status.

Dr. Lohiya explained that according to a survey conducted by Manaswini,[6] there are fewer cases of violence in labour-class families where husband and wife work together on the land than in upper-class families. Money is often the cause, due to the low economic value accorded to housework. When housewives are asked about their work, they tend to say they are idle, even though they are actually managing the entire house:

> It means the work done in a house has no economic value. That is why we feel that the work women are doing should be counted in our national survey. When I get salary I say my income is so much. But the housewife doesn't get a salary although she works hard.

Dr. Lohiya says that cultural tradition has led men to believe they are first in the family and women, second. He believes men need to become more sensitive to the status of women.

> In Marathi [the predominant language in Maharashtra] we say *vanshacha diva*. It means, "I want to continue my family." The female can't continue it, only the male can continue it. That impression should be washed out. We have gone through the studies and we have seen that 75 per cent of the world's work is done by women. This is the fact that should reach all males in the society. This should be taught. There are no lessons on this in the curriculum. We read something about history or geography but nothing is mentioned about relations between man and woman.

Dr. Lohiya sometimes confronts his colleagues about violence in their homes:

> My colleague was from a backward community. He was on our executive committee. I went to his home. I realized that something had gone wrong with his wife. Then in one meeting I asked the villagers about it. They said, "Your friend beats his wife." Then one day I told him, "If you want to be a member of this organization, you stop beating, because that is our criteria." He has stopped. Now he is very happy.

This is a good example of how one man, making clear new expectations for another man's behaviour, can bring change. Pressure from a male with authority over another was particularly effective in this case.

Dr. Lohiya believes that increased awareness can bring social change:

> No social change will come because of some rules and regulations. To govern a country and to change a country are two different things. If we want to develop a society in which woman leads a life nicely and peacefully, we have to create awareness.

> It will be naturally created. Now things are changing so fast. The worldwide scenario is different and there will be change when the villagers, farmers, boys and girls look at the TV,

watch the international sports and they see all these things — the girls in different dresses, and so on.

There will be changes and I think women will carry their own lives without even the support of men.

He believes support can come from many different religious and social groups, including women who have left abusive relationships and re-established their lives. Some abused women the Lohiyas worked with have returned to their husbands or to their parents' homes; others live independently. Very few have remarried.

If a woman has children, she will not remarry. She will say, "If the food is not cooked in one pot, probably it will not cook in the other pot. If I have a bad experience with one husband, how will it work with another one? Instead it will be better to give education to my children." After all, a woman is more interested in her children. Her aim is to bring them up.

Namal,[7] Sri Lanka: "More Men Should Be Involved against Rape"

In Sri Lanka, rape is considered one of the gravest forms of violence against women. Under legislation (Penal Code Amendment Act No. 22 of 1995), rape is said to be committed by a man who has sexual intercourse with a woman as follows:
- "against her will even if she was his wife and she was judicially separated;
- with her consent which has been obtained through force, threats or intimidation, or through fear of death or of hurt, or while she was in unlawful detention;
- with her consent obtained while she was of unsound mind, intoxication induced by alcohol or drugs given to her by the man or another person;
- with her consent when the man knows that he is not her husband but where she believes him to be her lawful husband;
- with or without her consent when she is under sixteen years of age, unless she is his wife over twelve years of age and is not judicially separated from him."

Despite this broad definition of circumstances and stiff penalties imposed through legislation, the incidence of rape is frequent, although seldom reported to either the police or the press. It often remains a "shame factor," not to be discussed in public. But, more recently, people have come out into the open to take a stand on the issue. Even victims of rape sometimes go public despite the humiliation they may receive at the hands of an insensitive society. Several activists, organizations and concerned groups have lobbied and attempted to raise public awareness of the issue. Such actions have sometimes succeeded in enabling survivors of rape to obtain redress through the legal process, despite unlawful interventions of interested parties to protect the culprit.

A man I will call "Namal," interviewed by Kamalini Wijayatilake, works at a development NGO. He is in his late 30s, is married and has a young son. His wife is also employed. He says:

I first became aware of the issue of violence against women through [the NGO where I work]. I have been working in this area for about five years now. Prior to my experiences through this organization, I had not been confronted with the issue of rape, even during my adolescent years. I may have read of it in the newspapers. However, in those days, rape cases were not reported like [they are] now. At least not with this frequency. I am not saying that there was no incidence of rape then, but that I was not personally aware.

When taking into account the number of rape cases that come to our attention in our work at the NGO as well as the media reports, I consider rape as a grave problem. I think the media is responsible to a certain extent. All the violence that is unleashed in the electronic media, to which most of the people have access, is undoubtedly a contributory factor. At the same time, society considers women weak and vulnerable. Women become easy targets for the men. However, one cannot say that only one level of society is affected by this type of crime. Like domestic violence, rape is also committed against women in all strata of society.

I have targeted the media as a crucial factor in this issue. Through the media committee of our organization I have tried to raise awareness of violence against women. We address villagers and schoolchildren as well as persons in authority. We hope to create awareness of this issue among a greater section of the public through our programmes.

I also join in lobbying on issues of violence against women, particularly rape of women and children. However, I am ridiculed for my work in this sphere by my male peers, even by some of my women acquaintances. Sometimes I find it difficult to articulate myself in an open forum, due to the stereotyping which limits and restricts me. There seems to be an invisible line which we men are not supposed to cross when we attempt to work along with women activists. This is a barrier imposed by society, which seems to say that men have no business in a women's area! But I think it affects both women and men alike. If men understand the problem, there won't be incidence of rape. I think it benefits men also to be involved in lobbying, advocacy and awareness-raising on these issues. However, I discuss with my women colleagues and share my knowledge with them, so that they can go forward and lobby.

Namal doesn't simply cast the media in a negative light but believes that it has an important role to play in bringing about a change. He feels that more media programmes — both print and electronic — should be developed to address the issue of rape as well as other forms of violence against women.

I also see the insensitivity of media reporting about the incidence of rape as a problem. Even children should be made aware of these issues. Their perceptions should be changed from the beginning. Schools should conduct special programmes on this so that the children can be made aware.

On the challenges that women and men like himself face, Namal says this:

Raising awareness is a slow process. Outsiders don't understand what we are trying to do. If we are not sensitive to the perceptions of others, our efforts can be counter-productive. They sometimes think that our initiatives are not genuine and class us as fanatics!

We can present our case better when we conduct awareness programmes if someone provides us with adequate information. Right now there is a lack of sufficient data even from the law enforcement authorities. It is better to be backed with more facts.

Bai Sab,[8] Policeman, Bangladesh:
Devotion to Professional and Religious Duty

In Bangladesh, a policeman speaks to a representative from Naripokkho (Women's Side), a women's organization that works vigorously to highlight violence issues and improve women's situation in general. He admits that his outrage against violence to women once overcame his professional ethics. He rejects any social standards for male behaviour that would allow abuse of girls and women. He visualizes the possibility of men being much more favourable and supportive to the advancement of girls and women, not only their protection. Clearly religious, he sees work against violence to women as compatible with his religious belief, as well as his professional duty and personal motivation.

> In our country, there are many types of violence committed against various persons. Violence against women is not so widespread compared to the total number of violent acts. However, it is true that many cases of violence against women are not reported and I am not considering those. I am comparing with only those reported.

> Rape is one [form of violence]. Here a woman's helplessness is taken advantage of. If she is not safe with me, as I am a male, then what is the difference between me and a beast? It is an onslaught on women.

> I got involved in anti-VAW [violence against women] activities right from the beginning of my professional life. Once I witnessed a rape being committed and I forgot about my professional ethics and inflicted rigorous punishment to that criminal. That rapist was a Moulavi [religious leader], who used to teach children the Holy Quran. He raped a minor girl on the pretense of teaching her. I influenced a criminal punishment on him. I know that it was a violation of my professional ethics, but for the sake of the girl's helplessness, I punished him inhumanely. Henceforth I have been conscious about violence. Lack of women's education and economic freedom, improper education and poverty are the factors leading to VAW.

He believes that adherence to religious teachings, self-reliance of women, greater awareness and legislative reform offer the best hope for change:

> All religions are against violence. Those who do not obey the religion and religious bindings carry out various types of violence. To change this situation of the woman, they must be made self-reliant. The best way is to increase awareness among the men and motivate them to play the leading role. Because even if the mother desires her girl-child to have education, and the father does not permit it, then it is not possible for that girl to have education.

> Formal laws must be changed and amended, particularly those relating to rape. It is a distressing fact that a woman herself has to prove that she has been raped. During trials, the victims are cross-examined in such a manner that they would rather die than face the court. For this reason the abused woman does not seek justice, and suffers by herself. A change in the law is a must in this respect.

> When a girl is oppressed, society looks down on her. Other female members of her family are also affected psychologically. They develop bitterness towards all males. There is no social rehabilitation system for victims of violence against women. This has to be set up. The girl is not accepted in the family [nor] the society, especially in cases of rape, abduction and kidnapping.

He believes there have already been some improvements.

> The situation of women is better than in the past. Now they are more conscious, more advanced. Women workers of garment factories do not hesitate to return home at night

alone. These women don't want to be maidservants; they are earning independently. Women have become more easy and free in moving about. Today, you [a young Bangladeshi woman] are asking a lot of questions to a [senior] police officer, but 20 years ago you could not do so. Hence, the situation is improving.

Concluding, the policeman says this:

> I will join your ranks and dedicate myself to your cause, if the almighty Allah permits. I will work to help distressed girls in obtaining proper shelter according to existing law. My professional acquaintances will help me in this respect.

Shaheed Mehmood Nadeem,[9] Pakistan: From Prison to Plays and Public Affairs

Shaheed Mehmood Nadeem, 49, was imprisoned in Pakistan early in his career as a human rights activist. During a period of exile in London in the early 1980s, his work with Amnesty International included advocacy for the human rights of imprisoned women and children, as well as victims of rape and torture. He has organized international campaigns to improve the situation of women, and he has also written plays on the subject. This interview was conducted for this book by Fawad Usman Khan, from War Against Rape (WAR), in Lahore. Shaheed recalls how women themselves once resisted his representation of Amnesty International in their delegation to the 1985 UN International Women's Conference — because he is a man:

> In the Amnesty International office, I think 60 per cent or more were women. Some of the feminists were very offended that it was a women's conference and Amnesty was sending a man there. Our deputy secretary was a woman, the head of the department was also a woman. There were some senior managers who were women. So they had a meeting and they submitted a petition signed by 50 women. They said if a man were sent to Nairobi [for the conference], it would give a wrong signal. The higher officials discussed this matter and said, "No, we must send a person who is responsible for this work. We don't have to send a woman as a token to prove that we have women in higher positions. We work here for human rights."

> They accepted the argument. I did not offer myself; I was nominated because I was responsible for that desk. I went to Nairobi and I represented my organization and I spoke at various workshops and meetings. I was quite busy there and it was good to see women's reaction and it was very positive. They were delighted to have a man, firstly because there were only 50 men out of 10,000 participants, and secondly, they appreciated that we should not go for tokenism and we should go for substance. So this is how I got involved in women's issues.

Shaheed speaks of the broad psychological effects of violence against women, particularly when crimes are initiated by relatives, such as husbands, brothers or fathers:

> [A] very horrible form [of violence] is acid-throwing, distorting the face of a girl. Some of the stories are really horrifying, such as if a girl scolds you for teasing her, or you want to get married to her and she or her family refuses, in retaliation you go ahead and disfigure her.

> Then there are stove deaths, which can also be accidental but in many cases they are bride-burning cases due to dowry issues. What I consider also a very heinous crime is the

physical maltreatment of women in police custody because that is where one goes for protection and justice and if it happens there, one of the state institutions becomes involved. That is something which should never be allowed to happen.

When it comes to sexual abuse, the crime of incest or misuse of authority in family situations by men leaves a lot of scars. In our society it is not being talked about, so there is no way of preventing it or providing some kind of psychological treatment for victims. That makes it even more difficult to identify, detect or do something positive about.

The Ajoka Theatre, where Shaheed directs plays, became active in 1983–1984. At that time, Shaheed's wife, Madiha, asked him to write a play about the suffering of women in Pakistan under the fundamentalist policies of General Zia-ul-Haq. He wrote a play called *Barri* (Window), which is the story of a woman activist who learns about the plight of suffering Pakistani women from three women prisoners. This controversial play, subsequently renamed *Neelay Haath* (Blue Hands), has been videotaped for use by NGOs to initiate further discussion and debate on women's issues. Shaheed comments on his inspiration for the play:

We live in a male-dominated and sexist society which discriminates against women on the basis of sex, class and social and economic basis. Especially in our society where fundamentalism is on the rise, women are very oppressed. Society is discriminating against women and other weaker sections of the society. That actually has a multiple effect [on some people].

It is not true that if women are subjected to any oppression then men remain unaffected. You cannot run away from this, because a man has to be borne by a woman. So if a woman is oppressed then somehow that injustice is bound to have an effect on you.

[T]he first target of Zia's regime was women. The way women resisted that and fought back became a source of inspiration for the democratic forces. Women were really in the forefront of the movement against tyranny. Although they were few in number and limited to the urban centres only, their significance far outweighs the actual numbers. And that shows how much the fundamentalist dictatorship was frightened of women. That inspiration was behind [my play] *Neelay Haath*.

What response has he received to his play and other work?

There is much appreciation of our work even in the remotest corners. A woman activist from an NGO told me that in Cholistan, gypsies in a tent had a small black-and-white TV. They were sitting very close to that and watching *Neelay Haath*. They refused to move until the drama was finished.

The most inspiring thing is when women comment, "You have just said what we had in our mind." For example, there were two short plays, *Dhee Rani* [name of a character] and *Sharam Di Gal* [A Matter of Shame]. We performed *Sharam Di Gal* in the YMCA on Women's Day. Later, Tahira Mazhar Ali told me that there were women who were crying and saying that this is how it happens, that is how the system treats women in such cases: how police deal with the case, how journalists are so insensitive and how the family behaves and responds. They said that it was the first time that someone had said what they could not express. On the issue of rape, understanding a women's feeling and presenting it is quite difficult because of the sensitivity of the issue.

He believes that widespread acceptance contributes to the problem:

[Violence against women] is not even recognized as a violation of human rights or as against the dignity of the individual. Somehow we treat it as if it were the fate of the women. Even women themselves say that, "Yes, this happens," or that if the husband beats the wife every day, there is nothing wrong with it.

Firstly, it should be recognized as a problem, and then it needs to be talked about because when we start discussing these things women are willing to share problems with others. When men and women are able to discuss this problem together in public, then I think half of the problem can be resolved. Obviously there are mistaken notions that these things are sanctioned by religion or by customs. I think no religion, especially Islam, would allow any degradation of women or men. A system which degrades women or children or in any way humiliates them can't be religion. So it is a mistaken notion and it is used as a justification to satisfy people's egos.

There are some kinds of litmus tests of a society [to show] whether it is ready to grant equal rights to women. I think one would be when we accept women's right to choose a partner. I think that is very important. It should not have been an issue but it has become so because of the fundamentalist backlash. Even the courts, where things have been taken for granted, are now opening up to these issues.

I would like to have open discussions on incest and solutions found. It does not mean that these issues should be discussed openly in seminars, or publicly, but there should be some mechanism by which these issues can be resolved and preventive measures can be taken.

He finds incidents reported in the media disturbing:

The news related to feudals[10] in which women are forced to parade naked have a very disturbing effect on me. Also acid-throwing, especially a case in Multan, where the face of a poetess was disfigured. She is a very good poet and she used to be very pretty with a good educational background. A boy used to tease her when she commuted in the city. She told her brother, who scolded the boy, and he threw acid on her in retaliation. Her face became horribly distorted. It is an example of a man's ugly side, the beast inside a man who cannot simply accept any woman saying, "No." [The] male ego wants to destroy everything.

He also is disturbed by what he learns from family members and personal acquaintances:

Every man in our society would have some kind of personal knowledge of the discrimination against women because at least you have a mother if not a sister. So from a very young age you can see that mothers do not have the same power, authority or status as fathers. Obviously, the first-hand information comes from your family members, your relatives, like sisters, cousins or aunts. You see around you women who are beaten, scolded or abused by their men, by husbands or fathers. Then comes your peer group and you see the girls who can't play with boys, who are not supposed to eat before the boys. They are not given the same kind of treatment, benefits, toys, pocket money or presents.

Another source of information is when the women who work as domestic servants [speak out]. I remember some cases of women coming to my mother, and later to my wife, and sharing their problems and sometimes showing marks of torture. I know several victims who had worked in our home, who were the breadwinners and who were actually running the household, and still they were beaten up by the husbands regularly, [men] who were good for nothing, drunkards or addicts, and who forced their women to go out and work the whole day and then look after the family, cook the food and at the same time would beat them up to get money from them. This kind of situation I have seen very often in our society.

Yet in some cases, there have been improvements:

> I was asked to talk to women police officers in Lahore about two weeks back and it was a heartening sight to see these young women police officers in uniforms. The image of women in our society, as weak or fearful, was totally negated.

> These things are helping change the image of women: a women being the Managing Director of Pakistan Television Corporation, women police officers, women editors. That makes a lot of difference. I think especially in cities things have changed, and in the more liberal or enlightened circles men have changed remarkably in a decade or so. Even in villages, because whatever is happening in Pakistan or in the world is now having an impact on the villages as well. So I think things are moving in the right direction but obviously the forces of conservatism, or vested interests or retrogression are still there.

In the process of change, the State will play an important role:

> The [most] dramatic impact would come from a change in the State's attitude, though the work is needed at all levels because attitudes cannot be changed by decrees or laws. But I think the signal has to be given by the State, which represents the people, guides the society and protects the citizens. In our society a lot of people and institutions take their signal from the State and therefore the State has to make it very clear that they are serious about protecting the rights of the women.

> [As it now stands] much of our legislation is still biased in favour of men and against women, especially Hudood Ordinances, Law of Evidence, Law of Inheritance. All of these need overhauling and reforms are overdue. The present Administration [in 1997] has taken some steps, but due to the political problems they have not been able to do what they would have wanted or what should have been done. International standards of women's rights should be implemented.

> The State will not move unless it is forced to move. So the NGOs, the media, the activists will have to push the State in that direction. At the same time, awareness-raising at grassroots level is equally important.

Shaheed helped formulate the Convention on the Elimination of All Forms of Discrimination Against Women (CEDAW):

> It may not have an answer to everything, but as an international standard, it is a remarkable document. This is a very good basis on which we can aim to build a just society which treats its women in a non-discriminating way. We should not think that this is too radical for a country like Pakistan. I think all its clauses are applicable without any major problem if the will is there.

Shaheed closes by expressing his optimism about the possibility of change:

> As far as resources are concerned, a lot has been done in the media. During the past few years a lot of work has been done on TV. Many discussion programmes which are very bold are on the air. I myself have conducted some programmes. I did a talk show on violence against women two or three years ago in which rape, violence and all these things were discussed. As far as theatre is concerned it does not matter what the State policy is. We have to carry on. We have had a tremendous response.

> We can see the cracks, but obviously there is a long way to go, especially the feudal attitudes are too entrenched. One has to keep attacking. But the base is very weak now.

Feudal values and [the traditional] attitudes have become very weak, though they might seem very powerful or impregnable. I think if we pursue and persist, we will see dramatic results in a few years.

Mohammed,[11] Afghanistan: "No Such Things Exist in Islam"

"Mohammed," a teacher in Afghanistan, believes Islamic women have as much right to education as men. He also believes he should help them claim it. He has read about women's past achievements and status in Afghanistan, as well as in other countries. He believes that supporting opportunities for women will help to save his country.

> I believe, and I have always said, that if the well-being of women and children is ensured, Afghanistan will become a progressive country. If we save mothers and children, Afghanistan will be saved.

> Before now, I had this mentality to help women individually. Even when I was a student at the university, I was interested in helping the women and helped my classmates. Now I am very interested in helping women because, you know yourself, the situation of women in Afghanistan. This is the responsibility of all people who really [want to] promote the status of the woman as a human being. This is completely my responsibility to work on this.

Mohammed believes there should be continued discussion of the problems:

> With the head of the women's Shura, I said that they should establish community organizations for women so that they could come and meet each other and discuss [things].

Economic independence for women is critical:

> It is not [a problem] in all families in Afghanistan, but in most. The man is making most of the decisions. This is mainly [because of] the lack of education. And when the education situation and the economic situation are improved in Afghanistan, this will also change. But this will take a long time. It is not an easy job. The problem is also common in some educated families.

> But from the economic point of view, if women are not educated, their active role in the production will decline. Thus, from the economic point of view, women will eventually and inevitably become dependent on men. They belong to the man because they have no economic rights.

> The first way to find a solution is to involve men and women in production and then the division or solution will come later on. The women do not have their basic rights in the society and are not equally involved in production or any kind of work. This is a cultural problem, a traditional problem and an economic problem. It is also the mentality of the different authority [Taliban] who have come [to power].

Mohammed speaks about the role of religion and the importance of education:

> Beliefs have always had effects in the life of women. When a belief becomes a tradition it changes into superstition. Here we face an extremism, compared to the original principles of religion, whereas no such things exist in Islam. We have to differentiate between religion and tradition. Since religion has been diverted into a superstitious tradition, women have been considered as "inferior creatures."

> The general belief is that women should stay at home. This is the belief of the majority of people, who themselves are not educated.

> Without better education for both women and men, then, both sexes will become "traditionalists" and susceptible to superstition.

He has watched complex changes during the past two decades:

> A war has been going on in Afghanistan over the last 20 years. [For a time] women's condition in Kabul and some other places improved. For instance, 70 per cent of Kabul University's students were girls. And because boys were recruited in the armed forces, then there were no obstacles for girls. But still there was no significant change in the status of women over the last 20 years.

> During the short period of Communists, they gave priority for women's freedom. There was a woman member of the Political Bureau. Women were members of the Central Committee and there was a women's organization. Women had the opportunity to go for higher education to foreign countries.

> After this Islamic revolution, even the opportunities for the boys are limited. Kabul University has been closed. Actually, I am trying to contact the head of labour and social affairs, the head of the women's association and also the one woman who is the leader of the Wahdat Party. I am trying to work with them to publish a book about the stories of the active women in Afghanistan.

Mohammed has encountered resistance from some of his colleagues:

> Actually, some of them who are educated and good people are jealous. They are suspicious of my motives for working with women. Maybe they think I like the women. (I like women, but maybe they think I want relationships with them?) This is the darkness of the opinions of people. But there are other people who are helping me and supporting me.

Mohammed explained the importance of education in his family and for other Afghans in order for there to be a change in attitude of women and about women:

> I have already mentioned that we have to change the mentality and attitudes of the people. This is the dominant belief in the society from the religious, cultural and traditional point of view. [Some of us] were liberated from such things because we are the sons of those fathers and grandfathers who did not want these things. We were educated and now we allow our daughters to be educated.

> Women in Afghanistan feel themselves dependent. If you tell them, "You are free," they will not believe it. or they don't know their rights are rights. We need to educate the trainers, that is, women who can lead others.

The future outlook is not encouraging at this time:

> In Afghanistan, war is going on right now. [Before anything else] the fighting must end. Here men have no rights, let alone women. I cannot speak freely. I have no rights; women have no rights; no one has rights. When there is peace and a legal system is restored, then we can do something.

> But as individuals now, we can only fulfil our moral obligations, we must separate religion from superstitions. Firstly, the religion of Islam must be explained.

Shared Views

There are similarities and differences among these men who are bravely making a difference against gender violence. Here we consider some of their views and concerns.

Orientation to Women's Economic Roles

On the whole, these men seem more concerned with violence against women outside rather than inside families. They address violence connected with the State more readily than do the women interviewees. In short, their enlightened views still reflect the tendency for men to give more attention to the public than to the private sphere.

Most of these men recommend providing women with economic opportunities as a direct link to ending violence. Kiran talks about reducing girls' workloads; Dr. Lohiya suggests counting the economic value of women's work; the Bangladeshi policeman cites the lack of economic freedom, along with lack of education and poverty, as reasons for violence against women; and Mohammed stresses economic change as well as improved education as important routes to change. As a group, they gave far more emphasis to the importance of women's economic roles and women's employment than did the women interviewees. The women were more preoccupied with personal relations than with economic independence (although Rani certainly recommended her clients learn more about family finances and that her children learn to stand on their own feet).

Benefits for Family and Country

Some of the men interviewed link questions about women's status with gains for the country and development as a whole. For Mohammed, the stakes are high: "If the well-being of women and children is ensured, Afghanistan will become a progressive country. . . . Afghanistan will be saved." Shaheed sees the link between protecting women's rights and protecting rights for all. Kiran sees higher income levels in villages as a likely outcome of better education for both girls and boys, although he also points to the danger of the money economy.

Effects on Children

Almost all the men interviewed address the effects of violence on children. They are particularly concerned about the plight of girls.

Misuse of Religion

This is a cause of concern for these men. Several talk about the misuse of religion or the negative effects of fundamentalism. They do not accept the equation that male honour depends on female purity and men's control over it. Nor do they accept that honour is the main value for a woman.

Their Family Life

Compared to what the women tell about their personal lives, the men provide far less information about themselves and their family life (either when children or as adults). The comparative lack of personal details fits the reality that men generally disclose less about their private lives and emotions than do women. Even names may not usually be revealed. For example, one notes that for Dr. Lohiya, it is apparently customary to use his professional title and surname only. None talk about how their fathers earned a living, and only two mention their fathers' views and behaviours on gender relations. Only three of them even mentioned their mothers. This outcome is in spite of questions about family life and background.

As for these men's class backgrounds, whether they grew up in a rural or urban setting, the influence of siblings, etc. — we cannot learn any of this from these interviews. We hear only a bit about their marital status (most are married); only with Kiran, Dr. Lohiya and Mohammed do we learn anything of their relationships with their wives. No one but Kiran and Mohammed mentions any children of their own.[12]

What Got Them Involved

We do hear a bit, however, about the roots of their interest and efforts. For most of them, this developed in the course of their own work, or as a result of their education, rather than because of their family dynamics or their childhood, or dramatic experiences in personal life as adults. Kiran and Dr. Lohiya organized their work to fulfil prior beliefs and motivations about women's empowerment in both private and public life. Both were also inspired by images of progressive women and men they saw outside the family. Others were also affected by images of progressive women, such as the women who challenged martial law in Pakistan.

Solidarity with Other Men

Most of these men clearly distinguish those men on their side from those men who are perpetrators of violence or the attitudes that breed the violence. Some men successfully confront abusive friends or strangers; others suffer ridicule for their views and actions on behalf of women. Some have the support of friends. Some don't mention the support of other men at all, as if their isolation is very great, or perhaps doesn't even matter. In one way or another, each of these men lets us know that he is aware he is different from many other men, and he is willing to be so.

A sense of gallantry, of wanting to help the "weaker" sex, comes through somewhat in the interviews. But there is more than that, given the men's commitment to women's advancement and their economic roles.

Beyond Stereotypes

Most of the men featured here refer to and then discard stereotypic expectations for women and girls. They also go beyond those for men. They promote cooperation between women and men by example through their work: Kiran and Dr. Lohiya both organize mixed discussion and action groups. Although ridiculed by his peers, Namal promotes men's involvement in lobbying, advocacy and awareness-raising. He experiences some difficulties with "an invisible line which men are not supposed to cross." He feels he is less articulate than he would otherwise be "due to the stereotypes which limit and restrict him."

The willingness of these men to participate in our interview project on violence against women, and share as much as they have, is to their credit. Their openness and deep concern about gender-based violence is a promising sign for even more effective movements against violence to women and girls in South Asia that will involve men as well as women. More and more men are re-examining gender-role stereotypes as cracks appear in these.

Interview with Shekhar Kapur, India: "I Had Never Grappled with My Own Attitude to Violence"

The process through which a man becomes involved against gender violence may come as a surprise to him; he may not be seeking it at all. The way in which he expresses his new insights may be highly individualized and personal, or he may share his new views in the public eye.

A world-famous Indian film and theatre director, Shekhar Kapur, agreed to an interview for this book with Indian journalist Ruchira Gupta about the making of his film *The Bandit Queen*, based on the life of Phoolan Devi. I am adding his interview here because it shows, in such a human way, the complex process of learning first-hand about the effects of gender roles on our lives and about the various forms of violence against women that are involved. His interview also underlines the importance of using the media, and of having related media policies, against the perpetration of gender-based violence. More than that, it is an example of self-discovery, which others are likely to follow given the changes in gender-role stereotypes that are under way.

The Bandit Queen is one of the more controversial films of the 1990s in India. The film's release sparked off a controversy on the image of women as depicted in Indian cinema and about men's violence against women. As one learns from the interview, some Indian feminists apparently accused Shekhar of creating voyeuristic rape scenes and of further exploiting the exploited. However, he disagrees with this characterization of his film and describes the feminists as often being self-serving and hypocritical.

The interview highlights the power of media to challenge stereotypes and to encourage more gender equality, changing individual lives on gender issues. In this case, the director's own life was the first to change.

Shekhar directed his first film, *Masoom* (Innocent), in the early 1980s. He was inspired to make *The Bandit Queen* after reading Mala Sen's (1993) biography of Phoolan Devi. He recalls the process through which he began to grapple with his attitude to violence:

> Blood, gore, sex and a sensational heroine set against the Chambal ghats: it makes super cinema. I did not then realize the socio-political dimension of the film. At that time I thought it would be great action. I had been educated in an upper-class school and I had always lived in a city. I then became a chartered accountant and lived in London. Caste and class were only a distant reality. Gender relationships were only what was played out in my, or my friends' and sisters' marriage. I never did understand all the nuances of gender till I actually began to think about the film. I was forced to shift my entire way of thinking about women and the whole question of violence while making the film.
>
> I had never grappled with my own attitude to violence. All I ever thought about was, violence was wrong and must be avoided. If I ever did hit anyone I was ashamed of it later

and most instances of my violence were spontaneous and not premeditated. As the director of *The Bandit Queen* I had to confront the issue that I could be sympathetic to somebody who might kill. It was a dilemma. Here was this woman in the image of Kali[13] out to destroy all the evils of caste and gender oppression. I began to understand her. I had to get under her skin.

My intention was to make sure that the audience understood that she was victimized again and again. That she was always at the receiving end. I wanted to make the message as stark as possible. Perhaps that is why some people feel the film was voyeuristic. I did not show the actual rape at all when Phoolan was serially raped. I just showed the door opening and closing and the feet of all the men. But it was a violent scene nevertheless. The violence was implicit. I tried to understand Phoolan, not exploit her. I succeeded because there was an upper-caste outrage against my film.

Shekhar was surprised, however, at what he calls a "feminist outcry":

What I did not bargain for was the feminist outcry. I thought the film was a statement against violence on women — how violence traumatizes and dehumanizes people. I still believe that Phoolan, in spite of her accusations against me, asked people to watch her film during the campaign. Could the film be exploitative of her if she herself asked people to see it? Yes, it is traumatic to see your life bared on 70 mm but I had spoken often to her about it and even paid her a fair sum of money for the rights to her life story.

I feel feminists exploit other women too — to promote their own cause. Some feminists in Delhi, who have few clues of rural India or the caste structures in our society, interpreted my film in a very simplistic way. They manipulated Phoolan into their way of thinking. Phoolan is smart. She got more money and publicity out of it. I do not mind that because the film was a bigger hit and made more money than she anticipated. Phoolan was scared to acknowledge the film publicly for fear of retaliation from the upper-castes against her community — the Mullahs. After the film was released there had been threats to her family. How can the elite feminists of Delhi understand the fear of caste oppression? I have no grudge against Phoolan for saying some scenes were exaggerated. Films do make images look bigger than life.

Making the film apparently changed the director's relationship with women in his own life:

I was the average insensitive urban Indian male. I thought I had liberal values but now I realize that the values were liberal because I was never forced to test them. Everything anyway went my way. I naturally assumed that the big family home in Delhi would be inherited by me and the little flat in the suburbs of Bombay [would go] to my sister. When I lived in Bombay I just moved into the flat without her permission, though she stayed in a pokey little flat in Bombay with her husband. My complete acceptance of having first prerogative over our parents' property shows my attitude to women.

Both my sisters went through troublesome marriages, but I never supported them in their break-ups. I was very friendly with their husbands, a lot of male bonding. I used to take my wife for granted too. She was the homemaker and I was the jet-setting executive. Our relationship could not stand the strain of my schizophrenia towards women. It broke up. I am married again and this time my marriage works because I am much more sensitive.

My attitude to my nieces has changed too. I respect the fact that they want to live as air hostesses in Hong Kong. Earlier I hated the idea. Then the lambasting by the feminists of

Delhi made me re-assess my own situation vis-à-vis women. I was outraged, angry and I began to feel these women were like Nazis. I wanted to lambaste them. But later I realized I would provide fuel for the anti-women's empowerment point of view if I did that and so I wrote a poem on urban hypocrisy.

Shekhar's view of violence has also changed:

I look at violence as a process now, not as a single act. It produces anxieties, uncertainties, fear, retreat, anger and passion. It is the undermining and violation of a women's right to be an individual on every step of her way. What happened to Phoolan was stark. But against most women, there is nuanced violence — deprivation of their childhoods, [being] forced to work as nurses, cooks and do other household chores. They are also deprived of their rights to education and food. They are forced to sit correctly, speak softly and stay in the background. Sons are sent off to American colleges and girls are educated at home. There is discrimination all the time and this is violence. . . . Men feel it's a role obligation to be dominant. That is violence. . . .

He proposes that education and awareness of gender equality be used to combat violence against women:

To combat the helplessness women and girls feel. The constant feeling of humiliation gives them a radically lowered feeling of self-worth. The blows to their self-esteem must stop. Only then will they stop reshaping their eyebrows or changing their hairstyles. Their self-esteem will come from within. But the change has to be cultural. Our feudal attitude to women has to change. The cumulative effect of daily blows to the woman's self-worth has to be countered. Their consciousness of being second-class citizens must be changed. Only then can their apathy, chronic discontent or rebellious rage be used productively for society. . . .

This can be done through the mass media and also through films, theatre and songs. Films create role models. So do TV serials. This would energize both men and women to change their lives and that of people around them. . . .

We need a media policy for women — their image in TV serials, films, books, even textbooks. All these have a gender bias and feed stereotypes of the women. Look at our advertising campaigns. They completely commodify the woman. They should be made to feel that they can participate in their own futures by being creative, assertive and independent. They don't have to be thin and made-up for men to respect them.

I am a film maker, not an activist. But I am a sensitive film maker. I would like to break the gender stereotypes in my film and also show men and women grappling with their identity and women successfully creating a space for themselves.

To Grapple with Identity

As we have seen, others agree with Shekhar's call for a media policy. It is another question whether or not they, and we, are brave enough to be as honest as he is about equality in private life and to "grapple with identity," as he does. The men in this chapter have all done so. Their examples, like Shekhar's, are models for new masculinities in response to new femininities. Both are needed to end gender violence at all levels of society. Gender roles and relations, which have been constituted in various ways in different times and places, can be re-examined, deconstructed and reconstructed, depending on what kind of future people want for their children and society.

The next part of the book takes up possibilities for ending gender violence in different aspects of life, and thus calls upon both women and men to re-examine their identities and behaviours if they want to go beyond the stereotypes and the patriarchal system described above.

Endnotes

1 Interview for this book arranged by UNICEF ROSA in cooperation with UNICEF Nepal. Name used by agreement. He has since followed his wife to her new job in another country.

2 Lord Ram and Sita are the archetypal male and female figures in the *Ramayana*; Radha and Krishna are famous as lovers — she a shepherdess and he a god.

3 Devi-Bhagwati can be described as a deity who "is ascetic in nature and who grants boons to those who perform asceticism" (see Kinsley 1987, page 63).

4 Anjana Shakya, of INHURED in Nepal, cautions that this assumption may not be true. Instead, she says, the girls are likely to become mistresses (personal communication, New York, November 1999).

5 Interview arranged by UNICEF ROSA in cooperation with Dr. Mabelle Arole of Jamkhed, Maharashtra, and the UNICEF India country office.

6 The Manaswini Women's Project focuses on the plight of rural women in India (see also *www.jps.net/govil/proj01.html*).

7 Interview for this book arranged by UNICEF Sri Lanka; pseudonym given by interviewer.

8 Interview for this book arranged by UNICEF Bangladesh; name of interviewee withheld. *Bai Sab* means "big brother" in Bengali.

9 Interview for this book arranged by UNICEF ROSA in cooperation with UNICEF Pakistan; name used by agreement.

10 This refers to a class structure wherein very few people control most of the land and permit others to live on it in exchange for work, over generations of their families.

11 Interview for this book arranged by UNICEF Afghanistan. Pseudonym used by request.

12 It is interesting to note that it wasn't only the reluctance of these men but also that of the interviewers that produced these results. They simply tended not to ask men about personal relations. I noticed this tendency early in the interview process in Nepal: the interviews with men by a man had far less personal information than others, and questions about child-rearing were hardly covered, if at all. So I discussed the ways in which gender-role stereotypes can influence even the questions an interviewer covers. To correct for any bias away from men's personal lives, I then had a woman in Nepal also interview men and emphasized the importance of her getting information on men's personal lives. But the bias remains in interviews from other countries, despite the effort to overcome it by stressing to offices involved that it was important to get men's views on child-rearing and to discuss family life and its influence on them.

13 Goddess of destruction and vengeance, worshipped by many as a protectress.

Girls and boys meditating in school, Sri Lanka.

Towards Solutions and Gender Peace

PART III

Towards Gender Peace

Instead of gender violence let there be gender peace. That seems to be the ultimate goal of a number of interventions designed to transform roles and relationships of women and men, girls and boys, so that exploitation and abuse based on gender are not part of their daily lives. Some campaigns strive to create a consensus that no gender violence at all should be tolerated; they also look for ways to prevent it in the first place. From outside South Asia, "Creating Violence-Free Families" (Bahai International and UNICEF/UNIFEM 1994), "Zero Tolerance for Violence to Women and Girls" (see, for example, Golfarelli 1998 and Eriksson 1997) and "Gender Justice" (see, for example, Okin 1989 and Fisher and Mackay 1996) are examples. Awareness is also growing that in armed conflicts and war the horrific gender violence — like rape as a systematic weapon of war, sex slavery and the rejection or even murder of women who are raped — emerges from the limited views of girls' and women's place and value that are all too typical before armed conflict even begins.

It is crucial to work for gender peace in families, whether there is armed conflict or not. Campaigns like "Violence-Free Families" are needed to encourage parents to raise children without reinforcing gender-role stereotypes and to use negotiation rather than aggression as the way to solve problems.

At the community level, Viji Srinivasan's (1995) approach at village level in rural Bihar, India (discussed in Chapter 3), is a good illustration of the creative initiatives for gender peace in the region. Villages in which she works join campaigns to rid themselves of prejudice and violence against girls. Each participating village that achieves its goals then lights a lamp for peace to mark its progress and to encourage the movement to spread to other villages. Another initiative in India, Project Z, promotes the idea that absolutely no gender violence of any kind should be accepted at any level of society (see Gorhe 1997). A successful example of a related community effort to control violence against women, and ethnic violence, is that of the Mohalla Committees in Bhiwandi, India (see Khopade 1998; and summary in UNICEF 1998b, page 88).

Promoting awareness about the importance of gender equality and peace; working with children and youth as well as adults; changing culture itself as well as institutions — all are required if initiatives for gender peace are to succeed. Also necessary is the recognition and fulfilment of human rights in everyday circumstances, in humble ways, not only in courtrooms or committees that depend on, laws international treaties and legal expertise.

Drawing on insights from South Asian activists and research, this chapter describes some interventions that are building gender equality and peace between boys and girls, men and women, in everyday life, with zero tolerance for gender violence. These involve socialization and re-socialization processes that go on throughout life, in the family, school and community, as well as through popular culture and interpretations of religion.

Basic and Interrelated Curricula on Gender

It is useful to think of at least three curricula in life from which we actually learn about gender roles and relations. These take place in the family, the school and the community. "Curriculum" refers to a set of activities in a certain order from which one learns. In school, the arrangement of activities is formal; in life outside the school walls, it is more happenstance, but it is instructive all the same. It is not written out. There are no formal exams. But in the course of daily life, activities and social positions are typecast as more or less appropriate for male and female. There often are negative consequences for those who do not meet the standards, with rewards for those who do.

Learning about gender, then, occurs through a process of socialization that continues throughout life. Yes, it begins at home, in the curriculum taught by daily life in the family. For those who attend school, the classroom also teaches socialization about what it means to be male and female in a particular culture. It comes from the way boys and girls, men and women are depicted in study materials, but it is also influenced by the way teachers behave towards boy and girl students, the interaction of men with women teachers (if there are any), and so on.

The content of both the family and school curricula is, of course, influenced and reinforced by community life and the nature of various institutions and interest groups, in what one can think of as "the community curriculum." Popular culture and the media carry messages about ideals, norms and sanctions for behaviour of women and men, girls and boys. Where many people are illiterate these messages can be particularly persuasive. One can think of these as part of the community curriculum, or even as a separate public or popular curriculum.

Religion provides yet another set of ideas about women's and men's roles and relations. These may feature strongly in the community curriculum, as well as in the school and family. Various interpretations of religion regarding gender roles, not always made by people with deep knowledge of religion or with pure motives, are stirring debate and politics in South Asia. This is all the more significant because some of those involved, in the name of religion and outside established legal means, pronounce and have carried out sentences against those women and girls whom they say do not act as women and girls should.

In a sense, the larger process of socialization about being female or male never ends. There are opportunities to reconsider views and attitudes about gender roles, to learn again as adults. But it is far easier to learn about equality and disavow violence against women and girls from early on in life. Article 29 of the Convention on the Rights of the Child (CRC), on the aims of education, provides important guidance; it speaks of "preparation for responsible life in a free society, in the spirit of understanding, peace, tolerance, equality of sexes and friendship among all people [along with] development of the child's personality talents and mental and physical abilities to the fullest extent, and respect for parents and culture."

It Starts at Home: The Family Curriculum

Some of the activists, like Kiran Tewari from Nepal (whom we met in the last chapter), try very hard in their own lives to create families where girls are as valued as boys. Some, like Rani Padamsee from Bangladesh (featured in Chapter 6), clearly have the advantage of having grown up in families where gender equality was taught by example. Whether they come from such a background or not, the activists would very likely agree that family life is better for the kind of socialization and learning about gender relations that will help end gender violence and create gender peace. For example, they say:

It is OK to accept that men and women are different, but that does not mean one is superior to the other. When a family is more even and respectful, there is less violence. . . . We should target the young who could become better parents.

— *Pakistani woman, journalist[1]*

We need changes in the family. One thing I really respect about my mother: she made sure, if I'm washing clothes, my brothers are also washing clothes; if I'm working in the kitchen, my brothers are also working in the kitchen; if I'm washing dishes, my brothers are also doing the same. There was no difference between what the boys and the girls did in the kitchen, with dishes or clothes or in other activities. Now my sisters-in-law are very happy because my brothers are helping in the houses and treat the boys and girls equally. In this way, violence goes down. We have to stop boys from having an upper level and girls being on a lower level in the family, or there will be violence. If the boys think themselves that they are better than the girls, they will look down on them to treat them without respect. — *Nepali woman, lawyer*

If the discrimination between the boy and the girl children could be removed from the mind of the children themselves during their childhood, then they are likely to be vocal against violence when they grow up. If a boy child could be given good orientation at the boyhood, then he is likely to develop a favourable attitude towards women's rights.

— *Bangladeshi woman, writer*

We boast of our culture but unless we change our cultural attitude to women, our children will never learn the values which sustain and nurture society.   — *Indian NGO member*

Since everything starts in the family — and society is a collection of families — it is vital that from childhood, children are made to value their own bodies/spaces/property. In addition, parental responsibilities would be shared. There should be mutual respect between spouses because they are the role models for children who could end up being either the perpetrators or victims.   — *Sri Lankan woman, activist, researcher, lawyer*

If all the family are educated, there will be discussions. . . . In my family it is very much like that . . . I play the domination role but everything is [based on] discussion. I tell my children that you never accept anything I tell you. If you have a question, you have to ask me why and why and why. So that I have to explain to you and I have to convince you or maybe . . . you can convince me that I am not right. . . . I have said I am very

sorry [to his wife]. Even I will tell my children, if I make a mistake, I still say I am sorry,
it was a mistake. . . . I am a human being.   — *Afghani man, health worker*[2]

The statements above illustrate recurring suggestions for socialization in the family
about gender, including these:

- Model equality between women and men; treat each other with respect.
- Avoid teaching about men's supposed superiority and women's inferiority.
- Children should learn about equal rights by example.
- Parents should share responsibility for childcare.
- Children, whether girls or boys, should share responsibilities, chores and rewards.
- Listen to each other's views and resolve questions and conflicts peacefully, through discussion.
- Do not tolerate gender violence.
- Teach children to do the same.

Many of these messages are summarized well in a series of useful and charming songs
in Hindi that Kamla Bhasin of India composed for parents and their children. The
songs, with accompanying drawings, depict girls and boys, men and women in non-
stereotypic ways, as this one does:

Brother, stop shouting,
Learn something,
Do something.
If you wear clothes, naturally you mend them,
If you create mess, you have to learn to clean it.
If you want to drink water, you have to fetch it. . . . etc.[3]

The song booklets have been distributed in India by UNICEF. They represent the kinds
of innovative materials that are vital for parent education if attitudes towards gender
roles are to change in ways that should diminish violence against women and girls.

Forms and Functions of Families

Many scholars have elaborated on the various forms that families take and the functions
that families have. A study for the United Nations International Year of the Family (UN
1996a, pages 42–43) lists the following functions of the family (adapted and not in
order by priority):

- Establishment of bonds between spouses
- Procreation and sexual relations between spouses
- Giving names and status
- Basic care for children — and other dependent members (elderly, disabled)
- Socialization and education, of children and even of the parents
- Protection of members
- Emotional care and recreation of members
- Exchange of goods and services

The authors of the UN study note that inequality in marriage is still institutionalized
in most of the word, as only 22 countries at the time had "granted equal rights to
both sexes in matters of marriage, divorce and family property" (page 43). And although

some countries have rewritten criminal laws to make offences of various forms of violence in the family, "examples of the awakening sensitivity to the measure of power within families are still rare. . . . Violence is an abuse of power and emerges from the desire to dominate, possess and control. In the long run, the promotion of human rights, better education and an improvement in the status of women are needed as well as public education to change attitudes towards the domination or humiliation of other human beings" (pages 50–51).

The motto for the 1994 UN International Decade for the Family was "Building the smallest democracy at the heart of society." To distinguish families that are more or less democratic, Janae B. Weinhold and Barry K. Weinhold use the terms "partnership" and "dominator" for very different models of families. The first is synonymous with a democratic family; the second, with features of "a hierarchical system in which those who are more powerful use violence and threats of violence to exploit, victimize and control those who are weaker" (UN 1996a, pages 171–172).

The Weinholds point out that dominator-family structures are "so common in many parts of the world that they are regarded as the only acceptable parenting model and are often accepted as the healthy and appropriate way of organizing a family" (page 172). However, they also point out that domestic violence and other dysfunctional aspects are associated with this type of family. The fact that family violence is generally not recorded in statistics obscures its extent.[4] Equal rights and flexible gender roles are inherent in partnership families.

The capacity of parents themselves to control in their lives and families any impulse towards revenge — the "talonic impulse," as it is called — will influence children's development into people who do or do not respect the rights of others.

In the UN study, Weinhold and Weinhold (page 181) point out that "Laws protecting the sanctity of the family were also used to keep society from interfering with abusive practices in the home unless they disturbed the public tranquility. . . . The dominator culture that supports the dominator family clearly pays only lip service to the basic rights of children" — and of women, it would seem. Without the rule of law to protect children and women within the family as well as outside it, the talonic impulse and dominator families will likely prevail, along with high levels of violence in the family.

Some CRC and CEDAW Curricula Basics

The activists' ideas — recommendations, really — parallel and bring to life some of the most important content from CRC and CEDAW as it applies to learning and teaching about gender peace in the family. Without such vital efforts, the words of the conventions would not echo truths on the ground. Family and community life and the content of the conventions obviously need to be linked.

Each convention indicates there should not be discrimination between girls and boys or women and men. The basic articles are Articles 1 and 2 in CRC and Article 2 in CEDAW; the principle of non-discrimination is to be understood as applying to the content of all the other articles in the conventions.

In addition, CEDAW includes a direct and uncompromising article that is revolutionary for family, as well as for school and community:

Article 5

States Parties shall take all appropriate measures:

a) To modify the social and cultural patterns of conduct of men and women, with a view to achieving the elimination of prejudices and customary and all other practices which are based on the idea of the inferiority or the superiority of either of the sexes or on stereotyped roles for men and women.

It is immediately followed by a call for men to share in nurturing of children:

b) To ensure that family education includes a proper understanding of maternity as a social function and the recognition of the common responsibility of men and women in the upbringing and development of their children, it being understood that the interest of the children is the primordial consideration in all cases.

And CRC makes it clear also that children are entitled to the care of both parents:

Article 18

1. States Parties shall use their best efforts to ensure recognition of the principle that both parents have common responsibilities for the upbringing and development of the child. Parents or, as the case may be, legal guardians, have the primary responsibility for the upbringing and development of the child. The best interests of the child will be their basic concern.

So far as direct gender violence is concerned, CRC states in **Article 19**:

States Parties shall take all appropriate legal, administrative, social and educational measures to protect the child from all forms of physical or mental violence, injury or abuse, neglect or negligent treatment, maltreatment or exploitation, including sexual abuse, while in the care of parent(s), legal guardian(s) or any other person who has the care of the child.

In addition, CRC gives added emphasis to the prohibition of sexual abuse of any kind, as stated in Article 34, which begins: "States Parties undertake to protect the child from all forms of sexual exploitation and sexual abuse." It also prevents, in Article 35, the sale, trafficking and abduction of children.

CEDAW, on the other hand, was formulated to stress equality, and it was assumed at the time that this would make it automatically apparent that gender violence was unacceptable. However, because countries did not tend to address the issue when reporting on implementation of CEDAW, the committee responsible for country reviews made a very detailed recommendation (19) on gender violence for countries to take into account. Thus both conventions are concerned with violence. CRC's concern is stated directly about a specific type, while CEDAW's concern is not stated directly but is brought out through Recommendation 19, which is broad and understood as dealing with any kind of gender violence.

Do the Conventions Matter for Individuals, Families and Communities?

CRC and CEDAW are treaties signed by States Parties, not communities, families or individuals. Still, they need the support of people as well as governments before the content will be compatible with real life, whether as a guide or a reflection, or both. At the family or community level, do people even know or care that the treaties exist and that their countries have signed them? What difference do they make for the three basic curricula under discussion here?

Any given country that is a party to one of these conventions is expected to report periodically on implementation. An international committee, composed of "honourable" individuals participating in their own right who are experts in the subjects concerned, review and comment on the official reports. These are submitted by governments, sometimes with parallel NGO reports. Committee members meet with government delegates in New York or Geneva and discuss the reports in sessions that are later summarized in written reports from the committees. The review committees, which have few resources, are more and more behind in trying to keep up with the flow of country reports, even though these are often late as well. And comments on reports, once made, have no real "musts" because the committees have no authority, no sanctions they can invoke should their views not be taken. In this context, the monitoring progress can lead to weak results at the national level, unless a country is deeply committed to improving the protection and fulfilment of human rights for women and girls as well as men and boys.

Committee reports do provide information, insights and some leverage to groups in civil society in any given country. The role of community groups and NGOs to promote the rights summarized in convention articles is thus extremely important, as is their contribution to monitoring. When countries do have prior commitments to improvements in protection of rights — based on traditional values, law or history — as outlined in the conventions, they probably already have a constituency that promotes the fulfilment of the conventions. In such cases, the constructive response to any critical committee observations is most likely, and both civil society and government will help put recommendations into action. The point is that the conventions are not only useful for review and discussion at the international or national level, or to stimulate harmonization of laws with their content. The truly important review process may be that which can be organized within each country, with the support and mobilization of communities there, reflecting and reinforcing local values and practices of equality. In short, the conventions can and must be brought into debate and to life in local forums, with both women and men, with both girls and boys.

The United Nations did not invent nobility of human thought and purpose. The United Nations would not have come into being if that were the case, as no one would have been ready to agree with its tenets. There already was fertile ground. Why, then, should "culture" only be assumed to be a limiting factor so far as possibilities for equality between women and men are concerned? In any case, "culture" is not a reified, set thing. Its content constantly changes as the circumstances and challenges of human life change. Culture can be understood as a tool for human adaptation to different environments. The pre-existing patterns of life and societies permit people to live without having to think every moment, "What should I do?" As circumstances change, however, some of that thinking is both necessary and useful. In the global village, as technology changes, as threat to human security increase, it is particularly timely to re-examine traditions and cultures. And already there surely are traditions that honour and reflect gender equality. Surely there are individuals, families and communities that do so without reference to the United Nations and its conventions. These indigenous efforts need to be found and featured, learned from and multiplied. That is part of the intent of this book. The lives and lessons of South Asian activists for gender peace are part of the three curricula, in fact. Their positive examples and best practices may now be exceptions but they can become the centre of a new tradition being constructed from and for the global village.

The conventions' articles against discrimination include sex as one of a long list of attributes that should not be used to deny rights. Biological sex is one of the attributes most basic to categorizing people and is not easy to change compared to occupation or even religion. Women's and men's social differences are considered by some as determined by biology alone, rather than by biology and culture, which makes it hard to overcome the prejudices. The point is that when one challenges prejudice against girls and women, one is challenging the whole structure of society built on hierarchy, exploitation, domination, control and denial of rights as seemingly justified by arguments about biology. Gender peace may or may not be a true prerequisite for other groups besides women to have their human rights fulfilled, but it will definitely contribute to the process because its realization will weaken the patriarchal structure. This is one reason why patriarchal forces do not want gender violence to end. Doing so would open and unleash groups of men and women seeking and expecting equality on yet more grounds, which would affect the whole social and political order as it now stands.

The process of working towards gender peace and equality for all can and must start at home — but it must not end at home. Ending domestic violence is profoundly political in its implications. It anticipates a time when all citizens truly matter in all the structures of society, including the home. In this light, CRC and CEDAW are political documents that can promote profound change by citizens at all levels of society. They are part of the basic curricula for democracy.

Learning First-hand about Democracy, or Not

"The world's smallest democracy." That sums up Eleanor Roosevelt's famous view of the family, the way it should be, not the way it always is. In a family, children will learn first-hand about any unequal relations between men and women, boys and girls, and about any discrimination based on gender. Human prejudices of various kinds are set as early as four years of age, as pre-school teachers can readily observe. These include ideas about any difference in the "worth" of males and females and about what little girls and boys should and should not do to become "normal" men and women. Children's expectations about what are "normal" gender roles are also influenced by what they learn at school, from play with other children, from teachers and from the kinds of activities and toys to which they are exposed and guided with reference, explicit or implicit, to what is appropriate for girls or boys. When the school system itself accepts or models sexist attitudes and behaviours, it may even "re-socialize" those children who haven't learned such attitudes at home.

There is a rich research tradition on the ways in which socialization at home and in school shapes different behaviours for girls and boys. Such findings could be used as a guide for parents and teachers about what they should and should not do if they want to treat boys and girls equally and encourage more respect and less violence between them in their childhood and later life. For example, a new line of research, at least in the United States, is investigating how socialization contributes to making boys aggressive and whether there are ways to change that, for the benefit of society as a whole (Rosenfeld 1998). This is not to say that boys and girls have the same "hard-wiring" built into their neurological characteristics. In fact, some research suggests that they probably do not. (See, for example, Pinker 1997; Kimura 1999; Lahn and Jegalian 1999.)What differences there are, and exactly how and why these affect behaviour, is not yet clear.

Any prejudices learned as a child from less than enlightened parents and teachers can surface later in life, even in an educated person. These include prejudices about gender. To avoid gender violence, prevention will be more efficient than re-socialization in later life. To date in South Asia, very little attention has been given to what can be done in the home and school for socialization of future citizens who will, in fact, promote gender peace through the way they live.

Some of the reasons for this lack of attention to socialization are as follows:

- Parenting is not a subject that is formally taught.
- Gender and conflict resolution, if taught formally, are only introduced at the university level or in special training courses for professional groups, not in the context of the family.
- Women's groups that have taken up the issue of gender violence tend to have focused on what happens to women when they try to enter public spaces, leaving their traditional roles behind; thus, rape and harassment at work have been of more interest than even domestic violence.
- Child-rearing is a topic perhaps too closely associated with women's traditional role to have attracted much attention yet as a priority area for work towards ending gender violence.
- Concepts of childhood in South Asia have not been adequately studied or addressed, but need to be.

Overall, very little attention has been paid to traditions that have honoured gender equality and how these are taught in the family and community. Rediscovering these could contribute a great deal to gender peace at home.

And if men, along with women, come to understand child development better, to know the early critical periods for development of various kinds, they will find that better childcare is in their self-interest, as it increases the likelihood of good outcomes for their progeny and families. The quality of care in early childhood, then, can be understood as a priority, along with the knowledge and well-being of the caregivers, both women and men. Through such a series of steps in their thinking and awareness, men in Jamkhed, a rural community in India, came to the conclusion themselves that women's empowerment, along with new gender roles for both women and men, girls and boys, was vital for the family and community. The inspiring stories from Jamkhed will be featured later in this chapter.

Much more can be done to highlight the ways in which socialization, understood broadly, contributes to gender violence or gender peace. More work can and should be done on the various economic, social and cultural antecedents to attitudes and practices compatible with gender equality and peace, for social change, whatever the setting (see analyses of various social facts in Agarwal 1994a and Dube 1997).

Clearly, skills need to be taught at home and at school for non-violent resolution of conflict, in general and between males and females in particular. Otherwise, the "might makes right" approach means that males learn early that they can and should get their way simply because they are male. Being that kind of man does not demand much awareness, education or skill.

For example, if men and women know that babies and young children can be permanently affected by beating of pregnant women, or even by witnessing violence at home, they may think twice before they let it happen. Even simple handouts like the one in Box 7 could be effective.

Those who work with small children should be especially aware of the potential long-term negative effects of messages, intended or unintended, about the different value of boys and girls and greater power and privilege for boys.

When asked what changes she would suggest in family environment and in society to reduce violence against women, Sahyogini Madhu, who works with the NGO Mahila Samakhya in Uttar Pradesh, replied:

> We should also have meetings with men. Try to change their attitude towards women. Not pamper boys but punish them for their small mistakes, too. Generally, boys in our society have everything to their advantage — they are given the best to eat, to wear, the property is in their name, they get away with whatever they do — good or bad. . . . [T]hey should be checked and made responsible.

> Secondly, girls should be educated, not just academic education, but about sex, their rights, laws, etc. We should treat them as friends and caution them about possible dangers as soon as they grow up. They should be encouraged to share everything, for example, incidents of pinching, teasing by boys, men, etc., which later lead to rape, incest, etc.

> Girls should be raised like boys. Courage and self-confidence should be instilled in them. They should have a wider exposure. For example, when someone dies, even boys of four and five years accompany the funeral procession and see the cremation. This builds their courage. Girls and women keep crying. . . .

Will the Family Support Education for Girls?

The importance of formal education, rather than early marriage, for girls in South Asia is another recurring theme. Parent education may be needed on the importance of education and its possible benefits for them as well as for their daughters. For example, an Indian man, a lawyer interviewed for this book, said:

> Discrimination which starts within the family is what makes me suffer most. When there is a girl and a boy child at home, it is the male child who gets all the priority and all the facilities. If someone has to choose as to who will get better health or education, it will always be the male child. The girl child is always deprived from early childhood; she has to leave school in preference to the boy, [she is] made to feel inferior even at home to her brother and that she is born to serve and has no rights of her own. These things disturb me most. There may be some exceptions in some families, but by and large this is the case throughout India and in Bangladesh, Pakistan and other Asian countries, which I have seen myself.

Parents sometimes see girls as less suited for education than boys are. This can be because of fears that "too much" education will make a girl less suitable for marriage or simply delay it too long. They may be worried that girls away from home and without close parental supervision may be sexually attacked, and thus ruined altogether for

Box 7	**What Parents Need to Know About Domestic Violence**
	How Children Are Hurt When Mothers Are Hit[25]

Even in Pregnancy . . .
- Pregnancy does not mean freedom from battering by the husband or partner. Unfortunately, battering of pregnant women happens around the globe. In the developing world, it is reported that 20% to 65% of battered women are also beaten during at least one pregnancy (Shrader Cox 1994, in Davies 1994, page 124).
- Abuse during pregnancy occurs more often than some other routinely screened complications, but it is not usually screened. It is a risk factor for both mother and child (WHO 1999a).
- Increased risk of beating in pregnancy is associated with young age of the mother, unwanted pregnancy and shorter intervals between pregnancies (UNFPA 1998c).
- Beating and battering in pregnancy may kill the mother. In rural Bangladesh, for example, almost 14% of maternal deaths are due to injury/violence (N. Huq 1997).
- Battered pregnant women who live are twice as likely to miscarry and four times as likely to have a low-birthweight baby (Heise 1991, in Davies 1994, page 124).
- Babies of battered pregnant women are 40 times more likely to die in the first year of life (Heise 1991, in Davies 1994, page 124).

How Babies and Young Children Suffer
- Just watching hurts; even babies are disturbed by violence around them, not only as it happens but even afterwards. Babies, exposed to violence at home as in war, do not sleep or eat as they would otherwise. They may be more inactive, or have crying fits. Their health can suffer. They have post-traumatic stress disorder.
- Caregivers who are beaten may suffer from depression. The depression can limit their energy and good care of children. Happy women and girls free from fear are better caregivers (Bhatti et al. n.d.).
- Children of women who report frequent beating may tend to be small for their age, both in height and weight (HMG/N, NPC and UNICEF 1997).
- Children in a home where women are beaten also face the risk of being beaten. Some research shows that up to 50% of men who beat their wives also beat their children (WHO 1999a).

Risks for School-Age Children Include:
- beatings, sexual abuse, rape, incest
- early pregnancy with or without child marriage
- not being sent to school
- problems at school, with peers, teachers and in their work
- dropping out of school
- running away from home
- child labour
- recruitment into prostitution
- HIV/AIDS
- aggressive behaviour towards others
- drug use/crime

In Later Life:
- drug use/crime
- sexual problems
- low self-esteem
- health problems
- increased risk of violent behaviour in their own families

Solve problems without beating and battering at home.
"Toxic violence" at home prevents a peaceful society (Knapp 1998, page 355).

marriage. Parents are sometimes reluctant to give up a girl's help at home. There is often the belief that any costs for a girl's education will be wasted because the girl really belongs to another family anyway. In addition, parents likely expect that girls will not help them in old age to the same extent boys will.

A study about primary education in Nepal, where there are some 20 per cent fewer girls than boys enrolled in grades one and two, cited reasons like these that parents gave as to why they did not educate girls:

> Daughters when they grow up go to another man's house. When they grow up they will not support us. That is why I haven't sent my daughter to the school. . . . I send only the son to school because the daughter should work in the house. If the daughter is also educated, there may be difficulties in marriage because for an educated bride the groom may demand more dowry. . . . What to do by sending the daughter to school? After all, they go with their man and must perform all the household jobs. It is better to teach her all the household jobs than to send her to school. (NPC 1996, pages 20–21)

At the same time, there are other voices, such as these:

> Daughters, if educated, will be able to get a job. They will have knowledge regarding various things and won't be as ignorant as us. Even after their marriage, nobody can dominate them. In this way, they will have a good future.

> But if we educate our daughters too, they can fight the injustice happening over them because after they are educated they know what is just and fair. They will also know what must be done to maintain dignity in "the society." (NPC 1996, page 21)

A 20-year-old Bangladeshi social worker, who has been helped to get work and custody of her son after she left an abusive husband (whom she had married at 14, when he was 50), said:

> In order to increase awareness of women's rights, girls need to be educated and receive skills-development training. This will enable them to earn money for their families, as well as support themselves. In addition, parents should be told to treat their male and female children equally. Sons and daughters should be given equal opportunities for education. Parents should not try to get their daughters married early. They must become physically and mentally mature enough to handle difficult situations that arise in marriage.[5]

Not only do girls have the right to education, but without it they are more vulnerable to harmful traditional practices like early marriage, to health problems associated with early pregnancy, to beating in pregnancy — which appears to be a greater risk for younger wives or partners — and for pregnancies at shorter intervals and unwanted pregnancies. While a girl's or woman's education does not prevent her from being a victim of domestic violence (found in all classes), it can give her information and skills to help her negotiate — or to find alternatives to an intolerable situation. All the same, much depends on the norms in a community. And it depends on attitudes of males, not only education of females. For example, a review by Koenig et al. (1999) of a variety of studies of domestic violence (not all from South Asia) found that "One of the most consistent relationships reported has been an inverse association between women's education and reported violence. . . . Studies have also generally found a consistent inverse relationship between husband's education and reported violence . . ." (page 4). An exception was a study in South India by Rao (1997), which actually showed that violence increased with the higher level of the husband's education and was not related to wife's education. The authors conducted their own research to look more closely into the relationship between educational status and domestic violence, following some 8,000 representative households, with all 10,368 women from them included in the study. In both study areas, the higher a woman's educational attainment, the less likely she would suffer from domestic violence. But the authors also noted that in the more culturally conservative area, individual women's increased mobility and autonomy predicted greater levels of violence.

What does this tell us? Unless the norms about women's expected behaviour change, even if more women appear in "male space," there is "little protective advantage to individual women" (Rao 1997, page 23). This is a very important finding because it points out that community norms need to be changed to accompany education, mobility and autonomy for individual women. To avoid possible backlash against girls and young women who are being educated, it could therefore be valuable for parents, communities, teachers and fellow students to learn about the possible benefits for all that girls' education could bring

Women's Status and Literacy Influence Decisions to Send Girls to School

Women's status and literacy are likely to influence community and family attitudes about sending girls to school. Women's literacy and education should be encouraged for that reason, as well as to benefit the women directly concerned. Both ideas, one notes, are in line with Article 10(e) of CEDAW:

> The same opportunities for access to programmes of continuing education, including adult and functional literacy programmes, particularly those aimed at reducing, at the earliest possible time, any gap in education existing between men and women.

Traditionally, in most of South Asia girls were trained at home to become wives and mothers in another household. The training was in the form of household chores from which the parents benefited until the girl left home. The idea that education will make girls unsuitable as wives and mothers still persists in some places, as does a perceived need for their help in the house. If a mother has herself departed from the norm, there is already a precedent for the girl to do so. Indeed, a recent study of factors that predict girls' education, conducted partly in Nepal, has found that literacy of the mother is one of the strongest factors.[6] Other studies have shown similar results. For example, a study in Kalat, Pakistan (CIETinternational 1997), shows that a girl in urban areas with a literate mother is 11 times more likely to go to school; a rural girl whose mother is in favour of education is twice as likely to school. Mothers' opinions have an even stronger effect on girls going to school than do those of local religious leaders (although the two may be interrelated). The Kalat report states: "If all rural mothers favoured education, 18% more girls would go to school" and "if all rural communities had a Pesh Imam [religious leader] in favour of girls education, 14.6% more girls would go to school" (page 7).

Wherever educated girls gain employment, make good marriages, or both, parents are more likely to support girls' education — particularly if the girls will help look after the parents. Some parents are starting to complain that after expensive education for sons, they are not providing for the parents, whereas the daughters might have done so if they had been educated. Changing attitudes are heralded by a woman from a very poor area, who said that before she wanted to have land to assure her future, but now she wanted to educate her daughter. Still, parents will weigh whether to forgo needed household help now for the chance of help later. They want to see what happens in the community, not only in the school, with regard to new gender roles: Will there be attitudes of resistance, acceptance or even approval?

Education for Equality and Gender Peace? It's Not So Easy

The better a woman's education, the less likely she is to face violence from men at home or where she may work — but only up to a point, it seems. Higher education does not ensure a woman's freedom from gender violence, although she may be better able to find remedies for it. For many men, even educated ones, the prospect of women getting ahead is like a goad that makes them act to put women down, to reassert their own masculine power and status. This phenomenon is noticed both in education and the world of work — wherever women seem to be getting ahead, departing from traditional roles. Promoting and measuring progress in girls' and women's education are sorely needed. These are not enough, however, to prevent gender violence. Prevention will depend on improving relations between women and men, girls and boys, getting rid of stereotypes about their inferiority or superiority and finding innovative ways to do so through the school, as well as in the family and the community.

A case in point is Sri Lanka, renowned for having a much higher level of education and status of women than does the rest of the South Asia region.[7] Still, domestic violence, sexual harassment and violation of women are facts of life there, although until recently they have tended to be hidden.[8]

A priority for action in Sri Lanka is the elimination of "ragging." That's the name for a form of student hazing that occurs even before university. At university level it includes extremely harsh treatments from which both girls and boys suffer. For girls, ragging seems to focus on their supposed inferiority, and in very degrading ways. Ragging can take extreme forms. It has led to the death of some students and caused others to leave university or to curtail their student activities. Young men use ragging to intimidate and shame girls, letting them know that whatever their educational or professional ambitions, girls are *Baduwa*, sexual objects to be used, and are under control of and threat from male power. This is the opposite of what one would want and expect for an educated woman in Sri Lankan society, as elsewhere.

Excerpts from some accounts in a series of interviews on ragging, collected for this book, reveal a deep resistance to education as a route to equality between men and women, even where education for women is widely promoted. The fact that the interviews come from Sri Lanka makes them particularly disturbing. One would like to believe that where education and employment opportunities are better for girls and women, attitudes about male superiority would be both weaker and less acceptable.

In general, the South Asian women and men interviewed for this book knew the limitations of formal education as a vehicle to free women from threat and violence on the basis of gender. They considered education for girls as a vital but insufficient step towards ending gender violence. Again, they saw the basic problem as cultural values and attitudes that define women as lesser beings than men and give men power over women. Some prescribed more confidence and courage for women as a prerequisite to end gender violence, along with greater opportunities for them to earn income and be economically independent. More knowledge about rights was also seen as useful for women to resist gender violence. Of course, girls' education contributes to all the above. But these prescriptions alone would put all the burden for change on the women, the targets of gender violence, leaving alone the perpetrators and systems that accept — even feature and support — gender violence, often deeming it too "trivial" to matter. That is a way to maintain the status quo. The accounts on ragging show how urgent it is for institutions of learning to help lead the change process towards gender peace rather than dismiss the problems of gender violence.[9]

Sriyani's Story

This account shows how much the formal education system itself must change if it is to contribute fully to the broad socialization process for gender peace. Obstacles exist at all levels of the system. "Sriyani" is a pseudonym for one of three girls interviewed,[10] all of whom entered the University of Peradeniya[11] between 1991 and 1993. Sriyani described one of her worst experiences when a group of male seniors made her their "prisoner" during ragging:

> When I was hesitant to answer their questions, they became very aggressive, threatening and used loud voices. I felt weak with terror. . . . [They said,] "Tell the truth, you devil. You cannot escape by telling us lies. Tell us whether you had a boyfriend in the village." They threatened me.

When she admitted that she had a boyfriend, the boys called her a devil, demanded to know what she and her boyfriend did together and became very vulgar: "You devil, you are trying to be a baby, didn't you kiss him. He sucked your lips, didn't he? Was it tasty? Tell the truth!" one senior asked. Sriyani was very embarrassed but the boys would not stop harassing her:

> "You bitch, look at our faces and tell the truth. Don't try to deceive us. Didn't he use your thighs? You have good thighs. Look at her." He pointed at my thighs. Even though I felt weak with terror, I kept my face up.

> Then another senior brought his face close to mine and said, "Did you see his penis? Is it small or big? You stroked it, didn't you? Haven't you licked it? You should taste it." They went on with similar vulgar suggestions using obscene language.

After about two and a half hours, the seniors escorted her back to her hall. On the way they made her kneel down and worship two halls of residence for men.

Another day, about 15 to 20 senior boys took Sriyani and some other girls to the common room in the evening after classes. Things started in a tame way but soon shifted to women as the inferior sex, in no uncertain terms. Sriyani described what happened when she started to cry:

> Then a senior asked, "Are you having your menses today?" I didn't reply. Then he ordered us to write down the menses dates on a piece of paper. Then he said, "You are a disgusting species. Other devils also get menses, not only you. We will not allow you to escape!" They forced me under a table. After a while I passed out. When I regained consciousness, I was in the health centre. . . .

Sriyani said that ragging continued for about three months. She described other incidents, equally if not more disgusting, that happened during the three months. She was forced to draw genitalia and describe their functions. A student threatened to hit her in the face. A school warden happened to pass by, so the seniors released her. She didn't tell the warden, or her parents, who would not have let her stay at school.

Sriyani concluded, "Physically, we were not abused during the ragging. However, we were subjected to deep humiliation and derogation for being women."

Her girlfriends' experiences were similar. One girl described the severe effect that ragging had on her and her education: She left university, was taken by her family to a psychiatrist and returned to university "engulfed with a deep sense of disappointment about university life" only for lectures and at the end of the ragging period.

> Due to the shocking experiences I underwent, I was not able to participate in any social activities in the university for the rest of the three-year period I stayed in the university. I was afraid to join any student organizations and take part in their activities. I associated only with a few selected students and tried to avoid social activities in the university. If not for the disturbing situations I faced in the beginning, I feel that university life would have been more fruitful, useful and enjoyable.

Another girl said,

> My only hope is that others like me should not fall prey to such cruel treatment. I have a fear that when I get married the memory of these traumatic experiences would haunt me and ruin my married life.

Activists against Ragging

There are some activists against ragging at the University of Peradeniya. One male faculty member, whom we will call "Jayawardene," described an experience when he once stopped male seniors who attempted to remove clothes of some first-year girls. He said they were found guilty and punished, but they organized demonstrations and strikes and got the punishments reduced.

Jayawardene received threats for his efforts to stop ragging:

> When I started taking steps against sadistic and vulgar ragging, I had to face from students and teachers various threats, insults, petitions, anonymous letters, false accusations, etc. Once, when I caught students who participated in ragging and were given punishments, I even received death threats. Also, they threatened to burn my car. . . . There are few other teachers like me who work for the prevention of ragging, but they are only a minority in each faculty. Efforts should be made to rectify this situation in the university. Otherwise, it will contribute to the general decline of the university and to the breakdown of the very fabric of a decent society. To produce people who only hold degrees is not sufficient.

"Wickramathilake," another male activist at the university, confirmed that there are many problems to be overcome before ragging could be stopped:

> We have to face several obstacles when we work for the benefit of women. The lack of enthusiasm and support from administrators is one obstacle. Even though there are rules and regulations in the university, these are not taken seriously. There are occasions when

students are caught taking part in ragging, they are not given adequate and justifiable punishments and are allowed to go free. As a result, ragging increases gradually .

Even though universities are called autonomous bodies, this is not so in reality. The few of us who work for the prevention of ragging and violence are defeated and made inactive by pressures exerted by the Government, students and politicians with ulterior motives. Also, there are no staff development programmes or training programmes in the university. In such an environment, the proper duties of teachers are not obtained and carried out in the university.

His aim is clear, but difficult to achieve. He pointed out the gaps between words that ensure equality on the one hand and the reality of discrimination on the other.

The chief aim of my fight against discrimination and violence against women is for the creation of a society where there is equal opportunity for both men and women. Although our Constitution enshrines equal rights for women, in reality there is no proper environment in the society for them to enjoy these rights. It is our aim to build up within and outside the university an environment where anybody, especially women, will be able to live happily without fear of harassment.

Wickramathilake traces the origin of his concern with gender issues to his early upbringing in a truly egalitarian environment at home. There were five boys and five girls in his family. His experience offers an example of the way in which the basic curriculum of family life leads to expectations about what should characterize the environment of formal education. He recalls,

My mother assigned various household and other duties to us without any discrimination. Unlike some families, we were also given freedom without consideration of our sex. Due to this equal status in our home environment, I was drawn to think about women's issues and also became sensitive to gender issues.

Between them, the students and activists who were interviewed made many practical suggestions to end ragging:

- They wanted more public attention to ragging, with discussion groups about its incidence and negative consequences, as well as ways to avoid it; they suggested that formal orientation programmes be organized.
- They called for psychological counselling, conversation groups and sex education programmes — "to help women victims and to inculcate gender sensitization into the socialization process of the university."
- They encouraged clear rules and regulations against ragging, with punishment for those who did it. They thought student complaints should be called for and that programmes would be useful with the Lawyers Association and some NGOs to disseminate legal information pertinent to violence and violence against women.

Professor Kamala Liyanage,[12] who helped document the ragging incidents, called for organized involvement of all faculty against ragging and organization of students who are anti-rag to form an anti-rag movement. She said it should have support of teachers, administrators, students, graduates, scholars from outside and parents, as well as religious leaders. None of this will happen if the ragging is considered trivial or if in fact the majority of male faculty members actually welcome it as a way for female students to be put in their place and for male power to be exalted.

For prevention, new policies backed by university administration and the State, teacher training and changes in formal curriculum content are all needed at earlier levels of the education system. Steps should also be taken to ensure that there is no ragging or sexual harassment. Otherwise, students may continue to arrive at university with sexist attitudes.

Politics, Education and Equality

The experiences summarized above portray both those who work for gender equality and those who would undermine it. Early socialization about what is expected of boys and girls, men and women clearly influences adult attitudes about appropriate relations between males and females. At the same time, peers are an important influence in the re-socialization process. Ragging is an unfortunate example of male students' attempts to have power above and beyond that of school authorities. Some forces can overwhelm even those with the most positive backgrounds and outlooks on gender issues. For political reasons, inequality between the sexes can be exaggerated and made part of the curriculum and school atmosphere, with threats to back it up. This can prevent students, teachers and NGOs from working effectively against gender violence in schools. An example from Pakistan was described at a regional meeting in 1997 (see UNICEF 1998b regarding the meeting):

> One [problem] is our curricula, the general ideology, which governs our educational system and the way our curriculum is organized . . . and our textbooks, [at all levels] now encourages and promotes prejudice and hatred and fear of our neighbours and contempt towards minorities,. . . and also certain negative attitudes, hostile attitudes, towards women. And this is now very aggressively promoted by our governments and pressure groups — religious pressure groups or so-called patriotic pressure groups. . . .

> I, as a father, really feel so helpless sometimes and so angry when my own son is expected not only to read those textbooks, memorize those anti-human messages and then also sit in an exam and get failed if he does not say what he is expected to say. So that is one side of it which actually is creating . . . young men and young women who are fashioned, the frame of mind is such [that], whatever we are discussing here [about gender roles and the need to and violence] will not really touch them — they have such defences built around them that these messages will not get to them.

> [Second, there is the problem of] political atmosphere in these campuses. Most campuses are controlled by fanatic armed groups. There are religious groups mostly but also there are groups based on ethnic affiliation. They are armed to the teeth, they are either supported by the government, or at least the administration is aware that they are controlling the campuses and is not willing to do anything or unable to do anything or they just look the other way. So these groups have ensured that nothing which is related to human values and prejudice-free atmosphere where two sexes can at least sit together and be educated could exist. So in some of the campuses women are so frightened of these groups that they would come to the class with their heads covered and almost invisible and then rush straight back to their hostels or homes. And there are gangs roaming around to ensure that no boy talks to no girl. So that kind of hostility and that kind of fear are inculcated both in young men and women . . . so I thought I should share these problems with you and maybe we can find some way out of it.

Working with younger children and their parents may be part of the answer. In addition to formal education, strong advocacy with communities and government authorities is also needed for emphasizing equality in and through the family and society. Work with various segments of society, including youth groups, is vital. Leadership and mobilization are essential if there is to be impact on any scale.

Formal Education for Gender Peace? Some Changes Are Needed

Most formal education, especially in the primary grades, does not include anything explicit on gender roles and relations. If it did, more people might be alerted at an early stage about the possibilities for both personal and political exploitation inherent in stereotypes for gender roles and relationships, and might not tolerate them or those who promote them.

What children learn first about men's and women's relationships comes from more than formal lessons; it comes through examples, at home for sure, but also at school. Are there both women and men teachers, do they teach the same subjects, have the same roles as educators, treat each other with respect? Are girls and boys treated differently, with lower expectations for girls? Are the two portrayed in stereotypic ways in textbooks and teaching materials? What about their mothers and fathers — are they educated equally, do both share at home and outside in a variety of responsibilities? These are the questions that guide part of what a young child learns about gender from the text of life.

To combat gender violence and promote gender equality within the education systems suggestions can be made, based on the activists' experience as well as South Asian research, about the following areas: policy, teachers, equal access, curriculum content, zero tolerance for ragging, sexual abuse or rape, advocacy with parents, status and literacy of mothers.

Policy Level

First of all, a policy is needed in favour of girls' education, with laws against discrimination. School officials at all levels need to know, acknowledge and support these policies. They also need to be aware of the benefit of girls' education for the girls themselves, their families and for development.

In both CRC and CEDAW, education is included in both conventions as a right.[13]

The most difficult situation for girls' education is obviously where authorities are officially against it, as is the case in Afghanistan with the Taliban. In general, girls there are not allowed to attend school with boys or to learn anything other than religious instruction, if that, and then only until a certain age and most likely in home schools. Even these are sharply controlled. UNICEF's decision not to support education projects in Afghanistan where these officially discriminate against girls (UNICEF 1995b) was followed by a surprising amount of controversy, even within the United Nations system.[14] At official meetings and informally, Afghans sometimes call for education of boys anyway, on the grounds that otherwise they will tend to be uncivilized and that fighting would therefore continue. However, there is not any evidence that education only for boys would be such as to lead to peace and gallantry.

Teachers' Attitudes towards Girls' Education

Where girls have access to school, their education does not always come with the respect and equality the conventions envision. Teachers, not only male students, may have negative attitudes about girls and their abilities (see, for example, MYWAS and UNICEF 1995). Teachers everywhere must be helped to become aware of any such prejudices and eliminate them, at least from their professional behaviour. Their teaching performance and advancement should be judged accordingly. After all, to discourage girls from achieving their full potential should not be a purpose of the education system and its employees, nor one for which the Government and parents are paying. Any sexual abuse by teachers of students cannot, of course, be tolerated.

Female Teachers, Too

A study on basic primary education in Nepal (NPC 1996) showed that the presence of female teachers was significantly associated with higher attendance and lower dropout and repetition rates for both boys and girls. (The reason is not clear.) However, the ratio of male to female teachers in the country was nearly 3 to 1. More information is needed in the region about the gender make-up of teaching staff and the impact of having more women teachers. Already, there are some important and suggestive findings, in addition to those from Nepal. A study (CIETinternational 1997) from Kalat, Pakistan, of 1,233 households and 25 schools indicates that a girl who has a male teacher is four times more likely to drop out than a girl who has a female teacher. Some 37 per cent of girls live in communities without access to female teachers, however. Although parents tended to criticize poor habits of teachers rather than their gender, the behaviours they complained about are more characteristic of males than females in Nepal. For example:

> Some mothers complained teachers always entered the classrooms after drinking alcohol.
> Others said teachers are always chatting with each other, do not care about teaching
> classes and sometimes go to an isolated place (forest) to play cards. (NPC 1996, page 33)

Too much physical punishment of students was also criticized. Increasing the presence of female teachers would not only provide a good model of women's advancement for both male and female students, it would very likely also decrease those behaviour of teachers to which parents object. And male teachers could be held more accountable for their behaviour if they want to keep their jobs. Reductions in drop-outs and repetitions would also follow.

Important as the ratio of female to male teachers is for girls' education, no regional study has been undertaken about this in relation to girls' enrolment and educational achievements, or concerning attitudes between boys and girls.

Equal Access to Resources and Facilities

Even those girls who are enrolled in school may still find themselves discriminated against in a number of ways, some more subtle than others. For example, access to the time of teachers, to textbooks and classroom materials, to facilities — even to toilets — should be the same for both girls and boys at school in South Asia, as elsewhere (see CEDAW Article 10). Teachers should be trained to treat all children equally. Girls in separate classes should have the same kinds of opportunities for leadership and rewards for accomplishment that boys have in their classes, as well as in extracurricular activities, including sports. Again, CEDAW is pertinent here; see Article 10(g).

Having textbooks is very important for girls to stay in and do well at school (CEDAW Article 10b). The study from Pakistan notes that "a child who has a complete set of textbooks is 2.5 times more likely to stay in school than one who does not" (CIETinternational 1997, page 5). It also points out that, at least for those in the study area, "giving a full set to all girls would mean 18% more of them would stay in school in each class." Where providing textbooks and school materials is the parents' responsibility, parents should be encouraged to do so for girls as well as boys. If that is not economically feasible, and lack of textbooks is a bar to girls' education, then the government should be made aware and encouraged to provide textbooks to overcome any related gender gap in education. The study on primary education in Nepal (NPC 1996) reports that with a full set of textbooks, children (girls) "have only a tenth the risk of having dropped-out [compared to] those without a full set." It is also noted that the relationship may be spurious because drop-outs may relinquish their textbooks when they leave school (page 29). It also shows that some 22 per cent of girls without a full set of textbooks have dropped out of school, compared to only 10 per cent of boys in the same circumstances (page 29).

The study from Kalat, Pakistan, indicates that availability of toilets can be of particular importance if girls are to attend school (CIETinternational 1997, page 11). The study predicted that some 59 per cent more girls might go to school in the study area if all girls' schools had toilets. No other factor was likely to make such a difference, according to the study. (The study found that toilets were even more important than was a boundary wall around the school — for girls to be sent to school with privacy and security.)

When I visited a girls' school in Baltistan, Pakistan, in 1995, I found that the toilet block was being used for storage. The older girls, at least, were expected to go home if they needed to use a toilet. At the boys' school, although the toilet block was out of order, a traditional type of communal latrine was provided behind the school. The importance of privacy and security for girls at school is too often overlooked. A recent UNICEF representative in Pakistan, however, made it his priority to stress the importance of providing toilets for girls if they were to stay in school.[15] He was right.

Non-Stereotypic Curriculum

Articles 5 and 10(c) of CEDAW, already cited, are very pertinent here.

A Nepali male activist[16] against gender violence shared his strong views about the need to revise curricula so that they will not perpetuate gender-role stereotypes:

> To eradicate violence against women, we have to dig out the crux of the problem; education. . . . Learners are taught that women are inferior. It is there; maybe the curriculum designers haven't noticed it, but we have. I can give you one example. The first lesson for Class I talks about family. It says that Father goes to office and brings money. . . . blah . . . blah . . . blah. Father goes to town and buys clothes and brings sweets. Father is great . . . blah . . . blah . . . blah. There is something about Mother as well. The jobs specified for her are cooking, fetching water, fetching grass for the cattle and looking after the family members. There is one interesting thing. Her duty is also to look after the sick members of the family. Those are her specified duties. The chapter never spells out who will take care

of her if she falls sick. This is a minor point, but if you take the whole concept, the whole thinking of society, changes are necessary. The whole school curriculum must be revised, from the beginning to the university level.

In Nepal, one of my colleagues shared the following story about what happened to her son in a test at school, apparently based on the same text as quoted above.[17] The little boy, when asked about what mothers and fathers do, answered in terms of his own family, not the stereotypes in the book. His mother goes to work and earns money, as does his father. He flunked the lesson. His parents complained. Stereotypic materials should indeed be eliminated from the classroom. More than that, positive images can be introduced.

In particular, images of violence against girls and women should be omitted. Yet, the draft report of the India Women's Movement (August 1999) found:

> Current assessments of education cite the 1988 study of textbooks by Kalia (surveying books regularly used by schoolchildren in five northern states) which revealed that men routinely abused and violently beat women in many lessons and texts, and over 100 female characters were victimised as a result of their sex roles. What values of equality could teachers or lessons convey to their pupils with such books? (page 110)

In addition to eliminating such images, positive ones can be introduced. A leading Indian woman activist for gender equality,[18] Kamla Bhasin, has written many songs on the subject. In the early 1990s, a woman principal of a girls' school in Bihar came to New Delhi to receive the President of India Award for the Best Teacher. The teacher had read some of Kamla's articles and songs in a Hindi magazine, *Sabala* (Strong Woman). Finally, someone told her how to meet Kamla. When they met, the teacher told Kamla, "One of your songs, I have introduced it as a morning prayer in a thousand girls' schools in Bihar."

"Imagine," Kamla said to me, "a thousand schools, seven to eight hundred students in each school . . . several hundred thousand girls. And that is the most radical song I have written. I mean, the song says:

> This *dupatta*[19]
> You should make a flag of liberation.
> Why are you looking down all the time?
> Just look up,
> And show your anger."

Kamla was amazed:

> I could not believe that this was possible. And that woman! Now she had this spark! Later on she was in charge of the school library. I got an order for 200 copies of *Patriarchy,*[20] 200 copies of *Feminism.*[21] She is now distributing these into every school in Bihar, in the secondary schools. I mean, we could not even imagine that things like this can happen. But there is so much scope. . . . So this woman now has also started a magazine; she has started campaigns against violence against women in Bihar; she has a full-time job as a teacher-trainer; she has a magazine called *Jago Bahen*, meaning "Wake up Sisters." Last year she wanted to go to Beijing on her own; she raised herself some money, then I helped. . . . And these are our resources. God knows what has created a woman like this, she is part of the feminist movement.

Two years later, in Bihar, India, by chance I finally met the woman teacher concerned, Dr. Shanti Ojha; indeed, her creative and constructive energy and its positive influence were palpable.

For Pakistan, an impressive account about the feasibility of negotiating change in textbooks so they are more gender-sensitive comes from Vina Mazumdar. She tells about a workshop on introducing women's studies at school level in Pakistan, for which she was invited as a resource person from India. Several suggestions were readily accepted. Mazumdar describes one textbook chairman's reaction to a proposal that "the reality of rural women's lives" be introduced in the textbooks. He admitted the need for change and "asked in wonder — 'Is this what you mean by women's studies?' So we have been imposing a *purdah* model of the family on rural kids whose mothers are really active peasants?' " (Mazumdar n.d., page 312).

Non-traditional images of men are also important to include in formal curriculum at all levels: images of men caring for children, questioning aggression as a means to settle problems, supporting women's roles outside the home, working to end gender violence. All can contribute to a change in attitudes at an early stage.

Showing girls in new ways — and giving them new experiences in real life — can make a difference, too. In Nepal, a generation of young city schoolgirls in Kathmandu is going to school riding in front of their fathers on motorbikes, or walking with their fathers to school. Even changes like these help transmit the message that girls belong in school, and traditions change.

Organized efforts to show men in new roles that promote gender peace are also under way. For example, both UNICEF Bangladesh and UNICEF Nepal have collected stories about men who are working to end gender violence. The idea is to feature these in materials suitable for school children. And a film project supported by Save the Children [UK] and UNICEF on new masculinities is also intended for use in the schools (SCA and UNICEF 1998).

Gender and Gender Violence as Subjects of Study?

One approach is to avoid stereotypes of boys and girls, men and women, in the curriculum. Another, more ambitious one is to take up the subjects of gender, gender violence and gender peace, to present models for a range of "masculinities" and "femininities," and even to deal with subjects like non-exploitative relationships versus abusive ones and how to try to solve problems without violence. This could be particularly difficult yet very important where patriarchal values are strong, and patrilineal kinship systems prevail with marriage patterns that take a young bride into the heart of her husband's family and property, controlled by the men there.

Two of the three Sri Lankan activists against ragging have undertaken research on women's issues (see original interviews in Wijayatilake et al. 1997a). Although courses on gender and gender violence are fairly new to the region and are usually limited to the university level or for special training, they could be useful in the lower grades as well. Teachers and administrators would also benefit from them by becoming more aware of discriminatory attitudes they may have and the basis for overcoming these.

Dealing with Sexual Abuse

Srijata Sanyal of Sakshi, an NGO in New Delhi, is working in the schools in a new programme (started in early 1996) to facilitate discussion of gender violence with schoolgirls and young adults from class five to class seven.

"We realized that most of the abuse cases started in childhood," she explained. "As a result . . . the ability to say no to abuse was taken away and there was a repeated cycle of violence."[22]

The four- to five-hour sessions start with the topic of self-esteem. Srijata says,

> Now it inevitably comes back to sexual abuse. . . . The aim is to allow for free space to talk about gender violence, to talk about sexuality and sexual abuse, because that space is not given either in the family or in the immediate environment. So, we stress the importance of talking and questioning certain rituals, norms, customs and thinking.

Permission from the schools is necessary, of course, and sometimes difficult to obtain. In colleges and universities, sessions are more readily accepted.

The Indian NGO Sakshi is planning new work with boys on gender violence, for which male facilitators will be found. They encourage work about self-esteem with still younger girls, in grades one and two, and are developing a manual or module that teachers can use. Srijata explained that after working with groups of various ages, it seemed that it would have been better to encourage younger children to understand prejudices that can affect them, and how to say no. She wants to encourage their "understanding of certain biases, imbalances, prejudices and — in a very simple language — talking about body comfort and discomfort. . . . I feel, after working with all these groups, it's more effective if addressed at an earlier age and then the input can be varied according to the ability to internalize."

Professor Seshadri (whom we met in Chapter 3), like Srijata, also feels that similar work with boys is essential and has done related workshops. He says,

> [I]nstead of starting with the whole issue of masculinity, we start with abuse of boys and then talk about what they feel about sexuality and go into the whole business of their addressing masculinity from the perspective of tenderness, of caring and of the legitimacy that men and women, boys and girls have to explore their own sexuality and, therefore, make informed choices.[23]

Zero Tolerance for Gender Violence, from Ragging to Rape

The ragging described at the University of Peradeniya could be prevented, at least in part, if throughout the educational system, discrimination, disparagement, harassment and abuse were not tolerated. Education about both gender and sex could lead to more mature attitudes and relations. Where prevention doesn't work, criminal acts should be recognized and dealt with as such.

School has to be a safe place. Sexual abuse and rape at school are problems to which insufficient attention is given. An example from Sri Lanka is a case in point. In her study "Violence against Women," Nandini Samarasinghe (1994, page 21) writes, "sexual harassment is prevalent even within the sanctified walls of educational institutions." She describes a Sri Lankan newspaper account ("Divaina," 29 June 1992, cited in Samarasinghe 1994) of a married schoolmaster who ordered a teenage female student to come to an empty classroom "to harass her sexually" (the meaning is not altogether clear); the girl would not return to school again. Samarasinghe (page 22) says that the news report "is one of the few which reached the mass media. Most such incidents are shielded from publicity due to the damaging impact on the victim's education opportunities and reputation" (not to mention the influence of the teacher or administrator).

She observes that the situation is much the same at secondary or tertiary level and cites a study from the University of Delhi ("Manshui," in Samarasinghe 1994, pages 20–21) that shows that student suicides followed sexual demands by instructors there, as well as a study in Sri Lanka of sexual harassment at universities (Udagama 1991). No punishment of perpetrators of sexual harassment, abuse or violation in schools is well documented, so far as I know.

What "sexual harassment" means in the schools, and the responsibility to prevent it, needs to be determined if it is to be admitted, monitored and stopped. That was the lesson in the United States in a 1999 Supreme Court case that ruled that schools can be held liable for damages for failing to stop a student from sexually harassing another student; the decision may be as thought-provoking for policy makers in South Asian educational institutions as it is for those in the United States.[24] Again, it points to the importance of attitudes about equality at all levels of society, and how these may need to change — along with practices — if girls' rights are to be fulfilled and gender violence is to end.

The Community Curriculum: Jamkhed

The story of Jamkhed, India, shows that re-socialization and changes in attitudes in the community — through interventions with groups of men and women — can lead to appreciated and effective non-sexist human and community development. It also shows the importance and feasibility of informal education for adults. Drs. Mabelle and Raj Arole have spent over 20 years in Jamkhed on community self-managed health care as a means for change, which has also changed the local perception and attitudes towards women and children. Theirs is a story of community curriculum, a set of planned and evolving activities that, over time, has moved lives towards gender peace (see Arole and Arole 1994).

On my way from Kathmandu to visit Mabelle and Raj, I was driving from Bombay through the Maharashtra countryside when I was startled by a dramatic shift in the human scenery near Jamkhed. Men as well as women were carrying big jugs of water alongside the road. Little boys as well as little girls were washing plates in front of the houses there.

Later, when attending a community meeting with Mabelle and Raj, I was surprised again. Women and children were seated in the front with the men, not only at the back as is often the case. They asked questions and made comments, just as the men did. The topic was the possibility of starting new savings and credit schemes. All agreed that women should have the leadership in these, that they needed to control the money for the benefit of the family and for community development. How did this happen? I wondered.

Early in their work in Jamkhed, the Aroles trained older women, widows, lower-caste women — many of whom were considered to have little value in the community — as facilitators and mobilizers. The improvements they brought to the village came to be valued by all. Their new, visible, successful roles helped to change attitudes towards women and girls, along with relations between women and men, girls and boys, within the family and the community.

From remarks he made at a meeting session in Kathmandu (UNICEF 1998b) on community action against violence to women and girls, Raj Arole recalled his motivation and method for community work. It depended for its success on new roles for and relations between men and women:

> I am a surgeon by profession and as a surgeon I would not like to treat the symptoms of a patient, I'd rather go to the root cause of it. And I feel violence against women . . . is a symptom. The root cause of violence is a deep-seated prejudice against women.

In his office he found that injuries and burns were "very often" not accidental but "almost of homicide intentions," and for "trivial reasons," like "the bride wanted to see her mother and the husband did not want to let her go or she did not cook properly." He also saw other signs of prejudice and abuse:

> [W[omen going to fetch water from long distances,. . . girls becoming blind because nobody cared to feed them properly. All these things made me think it is not enough just to sit in the hospital, but I must go to the community. There were two or three principles on which I began to work:
> 1. How to get participation of people
> 2. Integration, that is, what happens in health is really an effect of what happens in the community
> 3. Empowerment of people.

In Jamkhed, he started with men's groups and devised some non-sexist activities for them.

> Because women are often considered as properties and because they have no status, they live in constant fear. We therefore began to organize men's groups. These men were involved in collecting information about children, and they began to [help us] weigh children. . . . We showed them how the weights of girls were always less than those of the boys. "What can be done?" I said to the young men.

He also told them their wives should be fed properly if even their sons were to be well taken care of, and exhorted them to tell their mothers that they must feed daughters-in-law properly, and then and only then could "the light of the generation" — the grandson — be cared for properly and become a good man. Daughters were to benefit, too, as their mothers' status improved. He says:

> This brought many changes in the young men. They began to look after the health of their wives and feed them properly. They also began to help the wife in her work and looking after the children. I then said to the men, "Would it not be better if a woman in your village could be trained to take care of mothers and children?" Women at that time were not allowed to leave the house, they were not allowed to socialize even with other women, and with great reluctance they allowed the women to form what we call a *Mahila Mandal*, a mothers' group. Here we said, "How do we get rid of the fear of these women?" We took them to the jails, to the police stations, to the courts; we called the police officers to talk to them and share a cup of tea with them, and they began to see that the world is not unfriendly as they imagined.

Raj talked about the slow but steady process of change in women's lives and benefits for them and the community as men and women changed their views about gender roles, and saw benefits of doing so:

> Women are purposely kept in poverty. Even a wife of a rich landlord is poor. So we started some income-generating activities for these women. They began to go to the banks. They had many difficulties. . . . But through this experience of new information, new skills, they began to get respect in their villages. They saved lives of children; they saved lives of mothers, . . . and this enabled the women to have respect of their families and their husbands. Also the income generated, which helped the family to have a better life, got the respect of their husbands.
>
> And in this way they were able to have their own say. They began to look at the different social aspects — the dowry, the dowry deaths, the drunken husbands. They were able to confront the drunken husbands. . . . When the man came home drunk, the woman was able to stand up to him and say, "Why are you beating me? I can also beat you back." The *Mahila* group would come to support her.
>
> They began to go to the courts and the government offices and get their names written down as the co-owners of their fields, as the co-owners of their houses. It was not easy because the men in the offices did not like the idea, because they wondered what would happen to them if their wives also demanded the same thing. But the openness came to these women. . . .

He was optimistic about the future possibility of ending gender violence, especially if more skilled professionals would work in rural areas, organizing the people to bring about change.

> About 10 days ago, I was visiting a village. There were about two hundred people. There were fathers, sons, mothers, daughters-in-law, all in the village, and I asked the older people if they beat their wives and they said they all beat their wives. . . . That was a way of showing power. I asked the sons the same question. They replied, "Of course not. We've learnt better." So, [by] empowering women through income generation, through having respect for themselves, giving them skills and organizing them together in the form of men's groups, women's groups and children's groups, we have brought many changes. There are more girls in schools in those villages than boys. Couples are opting for family planning operations after one or two daughters [and no sons]. Therefore, there is a great hope that violence against women will diminish if I as a doctor, who has access to everybody's bedroom and kitchen, leave this pedestal and go to the villages and organize these committees and help these women.

In Jamkhed, then, the whole community has discovered that women's roles are extremely important and that women can contribute outside as well as inside the home. They have also found that the ways in which infants and young children are treated, and who cares for them, are vital issues worthy of both men and women. Men didn't know before that the early years of life are extremely influential for a child's future character and ability. Infancy and early childhood had been thought of primarily as a period of life when physical survival was in great jeopardy and physical needs, rather than psychological ones, were paramount. Men, therefore, waited to spend time only with male children who survived and who were old enough to start learning work skills, alongside their fathers and other men. New ideas about child development came up naturally once women's roles were looked at in an open-minded way. This influenced men to suggest themselves that girls and boys be treated more equally, that both should have similar responsibilities at home and outside it, that women should have more education and participate in public life, while men should help with home responsibilities, including childcare.

Much more needs to be done in parent education concerning the nature of childhood and child development about girls' and boys' capacities and rights, as well as women's equality.

Shahaji Patil, a male social worker from nearby Ghodegoan, described his involvement in the Jamkhed project. His experience confirms that the Aroles' vision has influenced deep and real change in gender roles.

> In my village, *Mahila Mandal* was established and a progressive view and respect regarding women was started. . . . Now I see them participating equally with men in some kind of income-generation activity. Maybe 25 or 30 rupees only, but she is earning and that adds to our day-to-day activity and now we know her value. We have really tortured the woman; even when we were going out, we ask her to put our shoes on our feet. We never tried to look into her mind and see how she feels, but now we have decided that now we are going to treat her as our equal.

He was particularly moved by the situations of widows.

> When the son is born she is his mother, but when the father dies, she is being shaved and the son is not even allowed to see her face. I just cannot think how humanity can be so cruel to a woman. Yet we are.

> Then I thought, this should stop somewhere and I am not in a poor economical condition, so instead of earning money I should awaken my mother, my sister-in-law and sisters in the community and remove their superstitions. Violence and atrocities are carried out in the name of religion, and the woman is suppressed under that, and I want to make her stand with pride. Then I got the opportunity through the project to organize women into women's clubs and these organizations make women to understand who she is.

> Another atrocity is that when a son is born, sweets are distributed and band is hired. If the girl is born, only the mother knows it and the whole family behaves as if a shadow or calamity has happened. If two or three girls are born, the husband remarries even up to [a] third wife.

> All the estate is in the name of male folk. The land owned by my grandfather will go to my father and then to me, but nothing will go to a woman. She has no savings in the bank and she has to work day and night for the family, but she could not claim a single piece of her property. Yet it is she who works on the land.

> It was such a dreadful state for women. At least I thought educated people should start doing something exemplary against violence to women. So I registered the land in the name of my wife, that was a start. Many men in this area have done this. If the social workers start doing something ideal like this, people will follow them. Mahatma Pule, the social reformer, educated his wife. Maybe people will take time to follow him. Maybe it took 50 years — but people did follow him. We also have an example of this doctor couple [the Aroles] who started the project. They work together, give importance and respect to each other.

"You have to take the community with you." I remembered what Mabelle Arole had told me, based on over 20 years of work with her husband in Jamkhed. That is what they have done, changing attitudes to women, all the while showing that re-socialization is possible, even with adults.

Still, working directly on attitudes at an early stage and in youth groups will serve to prevent the kind of practices and attitudes that the Aroles address and that undermine the usefulness of formal education. When the discussion on community was summed up at the 1997 Kathmandu Regional Meeting (UNICEF 1998b), it was recommended that, "So one would only say that if we want to bring about changes, if there has to be any kind of attitudinal change . . . it begins with children, it begins with adolescents, it begins with young adults, and let us begin there and not wait for a person to become an adult and then start changing the mind set of the adult."

As the Jamkhed-experience shows, there is room for effective work with adults, too. Given that early socialization processes shape gender identity and ideas about one's self-worth and appropriate behaviours toward others, interventions with parents are sorely needed. But so far, lamentably, little work is being done with either youth or parents against gender violence. The need for both is urgent and can be effective.

Parents may not otherwise understand the impact on children of their behaviours during episodes of domestic violence. They may not know that there is a risk for repeated violence in the next generation

WHO (1999d) points out that it has been possible to reduce the prevalence of child abuse "when parents are provided training in parenting skills before and after birth in a supportive environment by nursing personnel and/or community health workers. These programmes work best if they are child-centred, family-focused and community-based."

Working with youth is appropriate, too, given the multitude of risks that adolescents face from gender-based violence, including physical and sexual abuse, HIV/AIDS, early pregnancy, battering and injuries to both young mothers and their children. An initiative in South Asia looked for examples of successful interventions with youth against gender-based violence but found few (UNICEF 1999e).

The examples and words in this chapter call for a change, and soon, to bring about more involvement of youth as well as adults to stop violence against women and girls. Otherwise, gender violence will remain and grow, one of the many expressions of the patriarchal system that influences all the curricula of life; one of the many expressions of the politics of hate, discrimination, exploitation.

The next two chapters review related problems and efforts in the world of work and in the legal system. They make it all the more clear that a change of attitudes towards girls and women is sorely needed if there is to be gender peace in real life, not only in the promise of conventions, laws and policies.

Endnotes

1   Interviews in this chapter, as elsewhere, arranged by the respective UNICEF offices in these countries.

2   Interview arranged by UNICEF Afghanistan.

3   English translation as done by Kamla Bhasin during the interview; see Bhasin (1997).

4   The authors summarize characteristics of dominator and partnership families in a list too long to include here.

5   Interview arranged for this book by UNICEF; name withheld to protect privacy.

6   Personal communication with Sara LeVine, Nepal, 1997; also see LeVine and LeVine (1997).

7   For example, in Sri Lanka, the mean for years of schooling for males and females ages 25 and above, in 1990, was 7.7 and 6.1, respectively. This compares favourably with the situation in other countries in the region, both for mean years of schooling and the gender gap. Among the countries covered in this book, Pakistan was reported to have the lowest mean for years of schooling for females age 25 and over in 1990, 0.7, in contrast to 3.0 for males. For males, the mean for years of schooling is more than four times the mean for years of schooling for females. This is the widest gender gap in the region. The Sri Lanka mean years of schooling for females age 25 and over in 1990 is almost nine times greater than that for females in Pakistan; also, mean years of schooling for males in Sri Lanka is less than one third more than the mean for females. This is the lowest gender gap for the countries discussed in this book. Figures for Bangladesh and Nepal are similar to those for Pakistan, although slightly higher for both males and females.

In India, the means for males and females are 3.5 and 1.2, respectively (UNFPA/CST 1993, Table C.1, page 47). As for the gross enrolment ratio at primary levels, again the figure for girls is highest in Sri Lanka, 90 per cent, and lowest in Pakistan, 28 per cent; this is in comparison with figures for boys in those countries of 89 per cent and 53 per cent, respectively. Gross enrolment ratios for girls in the other countries covered in this book are all 80 per cent or more. Primary school completion figures for males and females combined range from 30 per cent (Nepal) to 48 per cent (Pakistan) for the countries concerned other than Sri Lanka, for which the figure is 95 per cent. It can be expected that in general the drop-out rate for females will exceed that for males. See UNICEF (1997h), pages 58–59.

8   For example, see Deraniyagala (1992); Wijayatilake et al. (1997a, 1997b); Samarasinghe (1994); Harendra de Silva (1996); Fernando (1995); Dias and Fernando (n.d.); Sonali (1992).

9   See *Davis v. Monroe County Board of Education*, decided 24 May 1999.

10   Interviews for this book arranged by UNICEF Sri Lanka.

11   The University of Peradeniya is the oldest residential university in the country. It has about 10,000 full-time undergraduates, some 65 per cent of whom live on campus in hostels (of which there are nine for males and three for females). Women comprise about 45 per cent of the total university population. In 1997, only when the girls had already graduated, were they interviewed about their ragging experiences by Dr. Kamala Liyanage, a Professor of Political Science at the University of Peradeniya.

12   Professor of Political Science at the University of Peradeniya.

13   See CRC, Article 10, and CEDAW, Article 28.

14   For example, at the International Forum on Assistance to Afghanistan, held in Ashgabat, Turkmenistan, 21–22 January 1997, which I attended, Under-Secretary Akashi of the Department of Human Resources of the United Nations announced that there was not a unified position regarding the situation of women. The ensuing discussion clarified that indeed there was a UN position, as had been enunciated by the United Nations Secretary-General. (See UN 1996b, which outlines the official position of the Secretary-General on equality.)

15   Personal communication from James Mayrides, 1996.

16   Interview for this book arranged by UNICEF Nepal.

17   Personal communication from Anjali Pradhan, 1997.

18   Personal communication from Kamla Bhasin, 1997.

19   A long scarflike cloth worn over a girl's or woman's clothing for additional modesty. Girls and women's dress are often scrutinized and judged as indicating their acceptance, or not, of "proper" roles prescribed for them. (See Bose 1996, page 65.)

20   Bhasin's book *What Is Patriarchy?* (1993).

21   *Some Questions on Feminism and its Relevance in South Asia,* by Bhasin and Khan (1986).

22   This and other quotes from Srijata Sanjal are from discussion during the 1997 Regional Meeting on Ending Violence against Women and Girls in Kathmandu (UNICEF 1998b).

23   From an interview for this book arranged by UNICEF ROSA.

24   *Davis v. Monroe County Board of Education*, decided 24 May 1999.

25   Based on Knapp (1998), unless otherwise noted.

Work and Gender Violence

O ne would like to think that women who are abused at home could escape gender-based violence by becoming economically independent, but that is not so easy for women in South Asia. In the first place, many men do not want their wives or daughters to work, lest it detract from their own status or the honour of the woman or girl. Furthermore, men from outside the family do not welcome the competition and usually do not respect women who are on their own without a visible male protector, and who are thus seen as challenging the status quo of unequal power relations between men and women. Women who try to work anyway, or who are already on their own and must work, very likely face gender violence at work, as well as from men in the family. In any case, there are discriminatory and exploitative conditions for most women workers that deny them equal remuneration, benefits and treatment. Some would count these as forms of gender violence. It can thus be said that women who continue in abusive marriages while also working outside the home are in double jeopardy of physical, sexual or psychological violence against them at home and at work, with "economic violence" added. They neither receive a fair wage nor maintain control over their earnings after they return home. For working women, the risk of being beaten at home can increase when they do not control their earnings (Koenig et al. 1999).

An anecdote told by an Indian government official helps convey a sense of part of the violence that some working women experience. He asked a group of women labourers how many had been beaten in the last 24 hours. (He didn't ask whether it was at work or at home.) They all put up their hands.[1] As a woman participant in a meeting in India said, "There is one bastard in the house, but hundreds of bastards outside" (Forum against Oppression of Women 1995, page 61).

How is the issue of gender-based violence related to the world of work treated in international conventions and declarations regarding violence against women? CEDAW and Recommendation 19, taken together with the Declaration on the Elimination of Violence against Women, with regard to women's right to work and concerns expressed about equality in employment, reveal the quandary for women who are not economically independent.[2] "Lack of economic independence forces many women to stay in violent relationships," notes Recommendation 19 (paragraph 29, page 74), while CEDAW, in Article 11 on employment, calls for the elimination of "discrimination against women in the field of employment" to ensure a variety of rights.

Recommendation 19 makes it clear that "gender-specific violence, such as sexual harassment in the workplace [paragraph 17, page 74] and sexual harassment [paragraph 18, page 74] are considered unacceptable." Article 2 of the Declaration includes "sexual harassment and intimidation at work" as forms of violence against women (page 87), as it does many forms of discrimination that affect the right to work itself. Article 3 of the Declaration refers to women's "right to just and favourable conditions of work." And CEDAW directs attention to "the particular problems faced by rural women" (Article 14, page 38) and by those forced into prostitution (Article 6), which is itself considered a form of violence against women according to Article 2 of the Declaration (page 87). The Declaration also calls for particular attention to the needs of those groups of women especially vulnerable to violence, including those in rural communities, migrant women, destitute women and female children (IWRAW and Commonwealth Secretariat 1996, page 86).

This chapter looks briefly at some of the problems of gender violence faced by women workers in South Asia, along with the related solutions suggested and attempted by the activists interviewed for this book. The chapter begins with brief descriptions of some of the most exploitative and violent situations women workers can face in South Asia, such as bonded labour, domestic servitude and prostitution, and then takes up, in turn and briefly, some aspects of work for women in the informal sector, factories and the professions. Attention is given to both sexual harassment and gender-role expectations that affect women's experiences at work. The interplay of violence and gender discrimination at work and at home is discussed. The review is meant not to be comprehensive but to give examples and to encourage possible solutions on the basis of the experiences and insights of activists.

Some of the most impressive themes that emerge from these interviews — and that will be evident in the cases below — are:

1. The almost constant concerns that women workers and activists express about possible exploitation of their children, especially their daughters. What will happen to them? How can their lives be made better than those of their mothers?

2. The success of women's groups and women's solidarity as a source of strength and confidence as well as credit, training, etc., for exploited and harassed women.

3. The important and positive roles men can and do play to help end gender violence against women.

4. The ways in which supporting the rights of girls and women also translates into good economic sense and quality development.

There is also an obvious need for government and international organizations, as well as NGOs, employers and women themselves, to support implementation of national laws and international treaties that will eliminate gender-based violence from women's places of work — including the home.

The Most Exploited Women Workers

There are groups of women and girl workers who are especially vulnerable to exploitation and violence. These are bonded labourers, the very poor, migratory workers, domestic workers and those who are trafficked. Some of the activists interviewed for this book have worked with or currently represent these groups. Their accounts are chilling as well as inspiring. It is unnerving but important to remember that for some there is little choice in their lives, little chance of escape from situations like those that will be described. For those who do have choices, possible exploitation away from home and family may seem better than certain abuse or death at home.

Take the unfortunate case of a young bride in the state of Gujarat, India, as recounted in the Indian documentary video *The Hills Are Shaking* (1988).[3] The young bride complained to her husband that his father had tried to rape her. Her husband responded with fury towards her. He held her down on the kitchen table and cut off her nose to punish her for dishonouring his father. Through a long series of events, and assisted by press exposure and free legal and medical help, the girl finally won a very small maintenance award and was given plastic surgery on her nose (photos showed what looked like a lump of clay). Asked if she would marry again, she said she preferred to be a migrant labourer, on her own.

Releasing Women from "Triple Oppression": Shakil Ahmed Pathan

There are some clear cases of unadorned slavery in which women suffer sexually as well as physically, psychologically and economically. A man who knew this all too well was Shakil Ahmed Pathan, who was in charge of the Human Rights Commission of Pakistan's Special Task Force in Sindh when he was first interviewed in 1997.[4] We met in Kathmandu later that year. He thrust his newspaper clippings and photo albums into my hands and asked me to tell others about his work and its message. He talked about the "triple oppression" of rural women who face violence from the family, the village *Wadera* (leader) and his *Ramdars* (servants).

> The *Wadera* and his *Ramdars* exploit them sexually. In 1992, when the Bonded Labour (Abolition) Act was passed, we sought release of workers from *Wadera*'s prisons. These workers were there for many years. We were horrified to learn that all women and girls in these prisons had been victims of sexual violence committed by the *Wadera* and his servants. . . . [N]ormally they [the women] don't realize that it is a crime. For them it is a routine.

When negotiating the release of some workers from another local prison, Shakil Pathan found a woman whose sad case he shared with me:

> She had been raped by the *Wadera*'s son for many years, and she also had a son from him. The *Wadera* had the baby boy killed. At the same time, the woman's two sisters . . . had also been constantly used by *Wadera*'s other sons and his servants.

About another case, he said:

> The people were literally chained and they were working in the fields under very strict vigilance by armed men. It was so inhuman and horrible that even today when I recall that, I feel a chill.

He said there were men, women and children in chains. "Bonded labour has reduced to some extent. Ninety per cent of the cases of women and girls raped as bonded labour are dealt with by us."

As to the main obstacles in his work, he remarked:

> Our state institutions are all under control of feudals or their families. Bureaucracy is also loaded down by these people. The same people make laws. This way, they themselves are always above the law. Their thinking and their attitude towards women is very degrading. Apparently they look well educated and well mannered, but they treat women as their property and as an object for sex. These are the people who are a major obstacle in repealing or changing discriminatory laws. They also have the sympathies of religious people who twist religious arguments to justify violence against women. These people are using all tactics to maintain this orthodox system. Due to this religious and societal pressure, sometimes even our very close friends are unable to help us openly in this work. I often receive threats from *Waderas*, or other influential people, vowing to kill me or my children. Sometimes they declare us foreign agents, and sometimes we are termed as non-believers.

He gave credit for his inspiration to a well-known leader of the human rights movement in Pakistan:

> A personality who inspired me the most is Asma Jahangir. Her struggle for women's rights is very inspiring. . . . When people were afraid to speak against religious, societal and governmental oppression, . . . especially Asma has done remarkable work for women's rights, and she was the one to force the government to make a law against bonded labour.

At the regional meeting in Kathmandu on ending violence against women and girls, he left me with an important question:[5]

> I'm trying to highlight the issue of bonded labour not only in Pakistan but to the whole world. To liberate and rehabilitate the bonded labour — this is an open appeal. At this meeting, when we talk about women and children, why not [talk] about the bonded child?

Shakil Pathan said he was often threatened by feudals because of his work and his stand for human rights of bonded children and women. He told me about an attempt to murder him once when he fell down because of a physical disability due to a stroke. He said his attackers must have thought a bullet had felled him because they left the scene. He persisted with his work even knowing he might be killed for it; he simply wanted us to care about and act for the rights of bonded labourers.

Bonded Labour, the Usual Version

For those in slavery, and for bonded labourers, the usual situation is virtual imprisonment of families over generations, with scarcely any chance for freedom. Debt is inherited, and quotas to work it off can be impossible to meet, even with the whole family working. I remember, for example, seeing four generations of a family working in the hot sun near Islamabad at a brick kiln. There was an old woman, said to be 80 or 90, who was very bent, watching a tiny baby in a sling at the end of a charpoy near enough to where she worked that she could rock it with her foot now and again, while her hands never faltered at the endless and voracious task that consumed her life, as it would lives of others. Across the way, a small girl about age 10 or so was among the children and women swinging pickaxes to dig out clay, which boys and girls were pushing in wheelbarrows to where other family members used moulds to shape it into bricks and then line these up in the sun on the baking, barren ground.

The kiln owner sat in the shade under a lovely tree nearby, drinking tea with some friends, all looking comfortable and cool in their spotless light-coloured shirts over matching trousers. For our benefit, the kiln owner called some children together, mostly boys, and told us they were in his school for a few hours each day. He invited us to take a group picture. I asked about the debt, how many bricks were produced in a day, and so on. It was clear that the debt would still mount, that there was no other future here for the children, show of school or not. We talked to the kiln owner about the Convention on the Rights of the Child, about related laws and about his opportunity to be a model for others by reducing the debt, employing people properly, making less economic profit but being a good Muslim who did not exploit women and children. He was polite but seemed puzzled that we would even try to suggest a different order of things, international convention, government commitment and religious teachings or not. We — in a UNICEF mission — had no success.

Class and Caste Injustice: Bhagwati Devi

Poor women work because they need money. Yet, precisely because they are poor and uneducated, they are likely to earn very little. Also, they don't know their rights and can easily be exploited. For instance, one Indian woman recalled:

> So when I was married at age 14, I worked as a stone crusher. I earned eight annas a day for five mounds of stone. I would work even when I was pregnant. I would get paid less then. That is what I term as violence. Even in late pregnancy I was forced to crush stone. If I knew of my rights, I would not have worked for such low wages or as a daily contract worker.

This is the voice of Bhagwati Devi, who was elected to the *Lok Sabha* (Lower House of Parliament in India) shortly before her interview for this book.[6] She tells a story about her mother that makes it clear that exploitation based on caste and gender makes for horrendous violence for women in some situations:

> Upper-caste Thakurs in my village subjugated my family for years. . . . We were so poor that we had to catch field rats for food. That is how the caste got its name: "Mushars." My mother, as a woman and low caste at that, had no status at all. She was regularly used by the overseers for sex. She died from a severe beating by the overseer, who accused her of stealing a handful of rice.

In such circumstances, it is not unusual for mothers to teach their daughters to expect and accept abuse, rape and assault by landlords, overseers and those they influence, including police. Resistance is not usually recommended.[7] Bhagwati, however, heard a speaker in her village in 1951, Dr. Rammanohar Lohia, a social democrat. She remembers:

> He spoke of land for the landless and how women were the most vulnerable victims of caste and class wars. They had to stretch small incomes and limited food to sustain and nurture their families. They also had to bear the brunt of their husbands' frustrations arising out of poverty, oppression and hunger.

As part of Lohia's movement, she went to prison three times. "Jail gave me freedom," she says.

> I got out of the narrow confines of domestic work and bonded labour and learnt that violence against women was interlinked with the subordinate status of women in society. With my politicization came confidence and awareness. I agitated for equal wages. I refused to provide the overseer sex. And my husband began to share in the bringing up of the children. I have now got two *bighas* (approximately two acres) of land. . . . I farm this land with my children, but they could not complete their education as they had to earn a living. They are farmers, too.

Many rural women seek property rights precisely so that they will not be taken as property themselves and can say "No" to intimidation and violence, to which they are more vulnerable when they have nothing of their own.

More Attention to Inter-Caste Violence Needed

Shakil Ahmed Pathan and Bhagwati Devi are among the few interviewees who brought up the problem of inter-caste violence and its particular affects on women and children. Neelum Gorhe[8] has since told me how much more attention this subject deserves. Stripping lower-caste women and forcing them to walk naked through the community, rape and exploitative labour practices are all a part of the picture that needs to be brought out more clearly.

Since the 1920s in India, so-called untouchables in the caste system, calling themselves *Dalits* instead, have been fighting "untouchability," casteism and economic exploration. As descendants of India's original inhabitants, *Dalits* are calling on government and the international community for more attention to their human rights. A Web site for the movement has brought attention to the plight of *Dalit* women in particular: "Dalit women are alienated on the basis of their class, caste and gender. The Dalit women have to grapple with discrimination due to caste hierarchy and 'untouchability' on the one hand, coupled with political, legal and religious culture discrimination" (see *http://www.dolis.org/memo.htm*).

Once a Domestic, Always a Domestic, or Worse

Most domestic workers face repetitious days with scarcely any economic gain and are overworked in poor conditions, with risks to their health, and limited time, if any, for their own families.

Cases of women domestic workers that have caught public attention are primarily those of women who have migrated to the Persian Gulf to work as domestics, rather than women who are domestics in their own countries. For example, it has been reported that, from the liberation of Kuwait in 1991 up to 1997, some 2,000 women domestic servants working there from India, Bangladesh, Sri Lanka and the Philippines

> have fled the homes of abusive Kuwaiti employers and sought refuge in their embassies. This mass exodus of maids is the culmination of a long-standing problem of abuse of Asian domestic servants . . . while not all domestic servants in Kuwait suffer at the hands of their employers, a significant and pervasive pattern of rape, physical assault and mistreatment of Asian maids takes place, largely with impunity. (Beasley 1994)

There have been widely publicized cases of punishments meted out to women domestic workers accused of various crimes abroad. There is more interest now in the situation for domestics in their own countries.

Rural women and girls who become domestics for families from their own communities are little more than slaves while at work. Poor working conditions, food and negligible pay are standard. However, they are free to go back home when the work is done. The long hours mean relative neglect of their own families. Their husbands are likely to be angry because their wives are gone so much yet bring home little money. They may also be suspicious about what can happen to their wives when working in other men's homes. Daughters would rarely be sent to school because they often help their mothers at work or home.

In her path-breaking article, "Women's Paid Domestic Work and Rural Transformation: A Study in South Gujarat," Uma Kothari (1997) describes conditions for paid domestic work of lower-class girls and women from landless households in South Gujarat, India, who work for newly prosperous farmers nearby. She points out that rural paid domestic work is an important source of employment but is very little studied, both because it is not always defined as "productive" work and because there is a notion that it is rare in rural areas. She says the demand for rural domestic workers is actually growing, as "previously small farmers amass wealth." Of particular note is the way in which the workers' daughters are trained also to become domestics, through being expected to help their mothers:

> The remuneration paid to women sometimes includes the labour of daughters, so that young girls work as a component of their mother's wage. Tasks that a domestic labourer is required to carry out are often divided between mother and daughter and change in time, with increasing responsibility being placed on the daughter. They are both clothed and fed, but the daughter never receives a cash payment.

Kothari describes how the mother may go home earlier, leaving her daughter to finish the work. One mother, for example, receives one meal a day, one sari a year and Rs. 10 a month, while her daughter gets three meals a day and clothes once a year, but no cash. She has never been to school. Parents may be grateful to have in-kind contributions for their daughters, which reduce the costs of raising them. Kothari points out that it is considered a "good investment to look after labourers' daughters in the hope that this will guarantee their and their husbands' labour in adulthood."

One would expect there to be less physical exploitation of women and girl domestics who don't live in the households where they work and don't have to travel far to get there — so they are never really among strangers. Rules of class, caste and gender are such, however, that domestics are likely to be abused, even by people they know and on whom they are not completely dependent. In cases where a girl has been taken in by a family after being violated or abandoned, it is understood that she is a servant with absolutely no life of her own and therefore the family can do what it wants with her.

Prostitution: The Next Step?

Rural women and girls who become domestics in the cities often find that prostitution is the next step. After being raped by an employer or tricked by a boyfriend who turns out to be a pimp, women may feel that there isn't much more to lose. Indrani Sinha, who founded the NGO SANLAPP to work with prostitutes and their children in Calcutta, says that those who are being recruited include very young wives, housemaids, school drop-outs who migrate to town with friends and refugees. For example, she says:[9]

> Grooms go to source areas to ask for young girls to marry them. They pay money, rather than demand dowry. Early marriage is encouraged and polygamy allowed, so the girls and families are happy to have marriages without cost.

And about housemaids, she says:

> There are groups of young girls from 24 *parganas* [districts], who come to work as housemaids every day. Hence I found out that many of these girls starting out as maids disappear into the red light area, . . . and we know a big gang of girls who come to work in Jadavpur, Ballygunge areas of Calcutta as housemaids, etc. Once they start coming out of their houses, they fall prey to easy money. Sometimes they are abused at home or even in the place of work. There are also agents around who spot them when they come to work in the train, etc. They befriend them, take them out for a ride, to movies, feed them, etc., and then rape them or sell them off. Also, once the girls have been raped, or bodily/sexually used, they don't have any compunctions. They feel that for a housemaid's job, I get only a few hundred rupees, whereas here I can earn Rs. 2,000 or so. The gap is so wide, and the demand is there, so they succumb easily.

The example of families who receive money from their working daughters inspires others to send their girls to become housemaids and then prostitutes, according to Indrani:

> When someone comes and says, "I'm working as a housemaid in Calcutta and . . . am able to send back some money every month," . . . then the parents say, "Let's send one of our girls to work." Some of the parents know and still send or sell off their children.

Girls who are school drop-outs are another group from which prostitutes emerge:

> This is around the time they are 12 or 13, and nobody pays much attention to them. The mother also doesn't insist on school, since she thinks that anyway the girl will get married, so let her learn to help in the house and kitchen; the mother can then go out to catch fish or do some work, etc. But the girl, if not given in early marriage, . . . finds someone coming to work in Calcutta and joins them and ends up in this area.

Indrani says that the girls who work as housemaids are mostly illiterate. Their lack of sex education makes them particularly vulnerable to exploitation. She sees an important role for NGOs in preventing trafficking: awareness and sex education for the young, uneducated girls, in both rural and urban source areas:

> It is only non-governmental organizations who can make them aware. NGOs also have to reach people who keep in touch with these girls, like clubs and little groups in villages, and make them aware about problems in this field, give them also sex education. All the HIV/ AIDS/STD intervention projects only think of red light areas; they don't think of spreading awareness in the village also. It is a very difficult area.

As for the government, Indrani says attitudes are improving towards her work:

> Today, after so many efforts, I feel some people in the government/Social Welfare Department look at my programmes/schemes a little more constructively than before; whereas earlier they used to shoo us away, even before we asked for anything, especially funds. So there are changes.

She says that the police, too, have become more cooperative:

> Police are cooperative, if you can take them on the right footing — you have to stand up to them and tell them that you might as well come with us. Earlier, we had found a lot of harassment from the police in the red light areas or while identifying families of trafficked women where we were working. Now the police have understood that they can't take these women for a ride. These are some of the organizations for which we have to give a little space. So I think things are changing.

One of the most encouraging things that has happened is that Indrani has 178 women working with her. She says, "It is a good beginning because these 178 women have been allowed to work in the red light areas by their families (husbands, parents, etc.) in what was earlier a taboo area, even three years ago." They spread awareness about problems to do with trafficking and HIV/AIDS, for prevention, and they also work to rehabilitate women involved, training them in other ways to earn income so they can escape prostitution.

As for physical violence against the women, Indrani says that her legal aid department gets about 25–30 cases every month. She stresses the need for shelters for women who are beaten. She talks about problems of rape, abortion, alcoholism, depression and suicide among the women.

She also talked about the prostitutes' deep concern for their children, with whom SANLAPP is also preoccupied:

> When we first went over there . . . we thought it would be very easy. We would open drop-in centres and the women would come and talk and cry on our shoulders. But nobody came to start with. Instead they came and said, "First you start programmes for our children." Then, when we started with the children, they gradually came, after they found out that we really wanted to help them and do something meaningful. Now they have opened up, and some of them are really very strong and work with us.

Indrani became interested in working against trafficking after her experience with flood relief in West Bengal and then in a material aid programme with a US organization. She was struck by the idea that "this giving away of alms made women and children beggars. So I started thinking of how to recognize and give some training to make them help themselves."

Her next job, with Oxfam, was on women's issues. She then took a degree in personnel management and in social work, "since I thought I need to train myself also." She travelled widely in India.

> I was the first woman project officer with Oxfam. Here I came face to face with many projects working on women and violence, and I also came in contact with women who had been in violent situations and needed help.

She became part of the women's movement and started SANLAPP with some like-minded friends in 1987. In 1989, they did a study on sexually abused girl children in West Bengal, which led to her decision to focus on women and children in red light areas.[10]

As for her priorities, she says,

> I don't believe that all these girls and millions of women who are prostituting are going to come out one day and say, "Give me a job — I want to start life anew." But at least if we can

help to stop the girls — newer and younger entrants — then we can say we won't have, [we] didn't allow second-generation prostitution. Then we can seriously take up rehabilitation of prostitutes' children and children forced into prostitution — that is another area of change where we would work.

For her, alternate sources of income for established and older prostitutes can help prevent recruitment of girls into the trade. She says, "If they are not rehabilitated, or if they are not given alternate income or any other financial help, they will bring in a small girl and start sub-letting her a room; thus, one more girl enters the profession, and they take the benefits from her."

She described some of what happens in trafficking, and why she is determined to contribute to stopping it.

So these young girls are brought here and sold in the area. Nowadays, if we find out or get the information as soon as they are sold, we intervene. Also, we try to rescue some of them, and/or if the police rescue [them] they contact us and we are taking custody of these children. When they go to court, the false parents come there. The magistrate also gives them custody, and they go back to the profession. The violence on these children is astounding. They are raped and beaten if they don't listen. A 10- or 11-year-old is expected to take on 10 to 12 customers a day. It is worse than rape. She knows that if she protests, she will get more clients — and also beaten up over and above all this. So she doesn't make a noise and meekly accepts. So these are some of the worst kinds of violence that are taking place regularly. I cannot dream of anything worse. I feel, along with others, including some of the girls, that somehow this has to be stopped, eliminated and eradicated totally. One cannot let trafficking of children happen. Because of the fierce want and emotion within us to somehow stop this, we have taken certain steps and it is working.

For this, we are going to the police and we talk to them — to find if the children are arrested; go to the courts, etc. Now we also have to find out what is done to the people who are doing this and if they are caught — how they are dealt with. The police let them off and usually complain about lack of witnesses. We have to see that they are taken to court and given stringent punishment. We also need to network with organizations working in Nepal, Bangladesh, even the rural areas or villages of India — the source areas.

So what is needed is socio-economic development projects in these areas and an early detection that the girl has become vulnerable and to find out the reasons — Is she a school drop-out? Is there poverty? Or violence, etc.? And how can we help?

Her idea is that the village *Panchayat* (locally elected officials), the school teachers and the local people from the community should all be involved in prevention.

Trafficked Girls and Women

With HIV/AIDS spreading in the region, it is sometimes said that younger and younger girls are sought as prostitutes, because of an alleged belief that sex with a virgin can cure the disease (see, for example, O'Dea 1993, page 29). Whatever the reason, the average age of girls involved in trafficking from Nepal to India dropped from between 14 and 16 in the 1980s to between 10 and 14 in 1994 (Human Rights Watch 1995, pages 230–2131, fn 67). This in line with the observation that more and more virgins are being sought in the trade.

One large study from 1991–1992 in India, also reported by Human Rights Watch

(1995), found 70,000–100,000 sex workers in six cities; 15 per cent of the Bombay brothel population alone was reported as being under age 15 at their entry into sex work, with 25 per cent between ages 16 and 18.

Some parents may truly believe that their daughters are going off for respectable work in another country in return for money they take from middlemen, but as Indrani Sinha has observed, others knowingly send their daughters, and even their wives, into prostitution, expecting a good financial return.

Shri Manahendra Mandal is a lawyer and activist for women who heads Social Legal Aid, a non-governmental and charitable organization in Calcutta, which he founded in 1982.[11] Among the organization's many activities are programmes for sex workers. He said that he had seen cases where

> women are being sold — by their own husband, by their relations, to brothels . . . even as
> minors. . . . We have also studied the problems of sex workers when we train them on
> human rights. Many of these women complained that they were trapped into prostitution
> by their friends and family, promising them good jobs, fake marriages, etc. Unless the
> attitude changes in the family, not much change can come about.

The Human Rights Watch Global Report for 1995 also observed the role of family members and friends as trafficking agents. In fact, six of the seven trafficking victims interviewed in 1994 for the report had been trafficked with the involvement of close family, friends or relatives (page 238).

As for route, and the compliance of authorities along the way, "The main trafficking routes are said to be Nepal to India; Bangladesh and India to Pakistan; India and Sri Lanka to the Gulf. There are no exact figures for the numbers involved, but estimates have been given, such as 200,000. Nepali girls primarily in India, with 5,000–7,000 trafficked per year (Forum for Women, Law and Development 1999, page 10). Officials aren't usually portrayed as taking the problem very seriously. In fact, the police are said to be directly involved much of the time (see, for example, Human Rights Watch 1995, pages 231–232). For instance, one unconfirmed account of trafficking women into Pakistan from Bangladesh, through India, has police keeping some women for several days at particular border crossings, raping them first, before letting them go on. Whether or not the women believed they were going as wives or for legitimate work, or were simply dragooned from the start seems besides the point after the women have been raped and brought into Pakistan (see also Mujtaba 1998, page 30–31.)

There, the legal system is likely to condemn the women, should they even find the opportunity to complain. This is due to the nature of the *zina* laws, which deal with sex outside of marriage and make women rape victims into potential criminals, likely to be charged and jailed for fornication or adultery due to the difficulty of proving rape — which requires testimony from four male Muslims in good standing who were witnesses to penetration, an unlikely circumstance. Renowned Pakistani lawyer Hina Jilani (1992, page 71) observes, "the prison population of women has tremendously increased since the enforcement of this law [and] is evidence of the fact that it has affected the lives of a vast number of women." In Pakistan, trafficked women are dissuaded from trying to escape their situation by both *zina* laws and threats that they could be imprisoned for being in the country illegally. Jilani describes the situation like this:

> The injustice of this law [*zina*] is apparent in cases of trafficking of women. Women from Bangladesh, and sometimes India, are abducted or brought to Pakistan on the promise of employment. Once in Pakistan, they are sold into prostitution and are exploited by instilling in them the fear that they are illegal entrants into Pakistan and can be arrested if they expose their captors. Although some brothels have been raided and women have been rescued, these women have not been treated as victims. Instead, they have been charged under the zina law and are awaiting trial in various jails of Pakistan. (1992, page 73)

It seems that most of the incarcerated women in Pakistan have in fact been charged under these laws. There is a concern that women just disappear in the jails, languishing there for years with little prospect of legal counsel or justice. All the while, custodial rape is a risk (see Ahmad 1998).

One of the more infamous places from which girls are trafficked with family involvement is Sindhupalchowk, near Kathmandu. Many NGOs and the police are working there to change local attitudes and limit the supply of girls, rather than trying to fight trafficking in the cities at the brothels, with madams, pimps and customers. The reader has already been introduced briefly to a Nepali man lawyer who is challenging trafficking, from Sindhupalchowk and similar places, by trying to change some fathers' views of their daughters as commodities. Historical factors also predispose some communities to accept trafficking in Nepal. For example, the Deuki caste traditionally provided entertainment, including sex, for royalty and others. Even today, they may train their young girls to provide sex to male visitors, in preparation for a life in prostitution or as a mistress. Some former prostitutes, however, are trying to promote other ways that women from their groups can earn a living. Activists in South Asia are concerned that macroeconomic policies have so increased consumerism and exploitation that trafficking has increased as well.

Becoming Part of the Paid Labour Force: Problems and Solutions

The ratio of women to men in the paid labour force in South Asia in 1995 was only 28 per cent, the lowest in the world (Sivard 1995, page 12).[12] Furthermore, Sivard (pages 43–45) includes data that show that women's formal participation in the money economy, as a percentage of men's, declined in South Asia between 1960 and 1995 by 11 per cent. This decline is more than five times that in the Middle East (2 per cent). As for other regions, sub-Saharan Africa shows the same 11 per cent decline. In the rest of the world there was an increase from 3 per cent in Eastern Europe and the former Soviet Union to 20 per cent in North America. In other words, the outlook for women seeking employment in South Asia is grim and getting worse in comparison to that for women elsewhere. The reasons are not clear as to why the picture should be so much worse for women in South Asia than elsewhere, although Sivard (1995, page 12) notes that,

> at the low end of the activity range are two regions where cultural and religious traditions limit women's work outside the household. In South Asia the ratio of women to men in the labour force is only 28 per cent and in the Middle East 32 percent. Tradition may not only limit women's access to gainful employment, but also the acknowledgement and recording of the paid work that they do.

The attitudes about women's roles, which may influence the relatively low participation of women in the paid labour force of South Asia, can be expected also to limit women's equal treatment at work and their control of earned income.

Primarily, women of South Asia are found in the informal sector, as casual labourers, petty traders, street food peddlers, craft producers or as doing piecework at home. Exploitation of these women is commonplace, in economic as well as sexual terms, especially when the women lack education and have nowhere to turn for help. For example, Shri Manahendra Mandal, the lawyer activist mentioned earlier who fights for the cause of women, recalls an incident when he evaluated the work of some social organizations in a district of Tamil Nadu in South India around 1980–1981.

> There we found that most of the people — both men and women — used to work in a stone quarry nearby. The men were paid Rs. 22–24 per day in those days, whereas the women were paid only 14–15 per day, and so I asked through the interpreter why such a discrimination was there and the answer was prompt: "Because they are women." I repeated the question, and they got angry in a sense, as if to say, "Don't you understand, they are women and are to be paid less." There I felt they were neither aware of the fact that there is a law called Equal Remuneration Act in the country and that by no means could they be discriminated while they are working for the same number of hours and same kind of work. When I asked the questions again, my interpreter also got irritated and said, "Please understand that this difference is because they are women." And for home-based production, women's time is likely undervalued and there are major difficulties about credit, quality control, marketing, debt and cash flow, as well as constant control by male relatives.

Women's Solidarity as the Basis for Economic and Social Advancement

Given women's economic needs and the problems they face in the labour market, one finds outstanding organizations have developed to help poor self-employed women organize, save and obtain credit and services. Among these are the Grameen Bank and the Bangladesh Rural Advancement Committee (BRAC) in Bangladesh and the Self-Employed Women's Association (SEWA) in India.[13] These are indigenous organizations started by people from South Asia who are now famous for their achievements: Professor Mohammed Yunus, Fazle Hasan Abed and Ila Bhatt, respectively. These organizations have increased women's status and influence, as well as their incomes, through the formation of and support for women's groups, which provide members with credit on a rotation basis, as well as skill-training and group solidarity.

In Bangladesh, women's needs after the war with Pakistan influenced the formation of BRAC. To identify appropriate productive activities, studies were made of women's and men's time use. The extent of women's economic activities became clear. The BRAC programme was one of several to support women's economic role after the war. It has demonstrated that production, not just reproduction, is a traditional activity for poor rural women, and also that they are successful in both savings and credit schemes. The women in the organizations have been encouraged to stand up with and for each other against both domestic violence and abuse or exploitation in work-related institutions. This has worked primarily because of the power of group action by the women themselves. The founding organizations' good names and connections with political and legal powers, as well as the media, have also helped.

It has not always been easy. For example, Chen (1986, pages 172–175) describes patterns of interference in rural Bangladeshi villages. These include, first, rumour campaigns against the women and their households claiming that the women have broken purdah, have bad morals, are associated with strange men or will likely be tricked by BRAC and sent to work in the Middle East; second, ridicule is used; and third, threats of various kinds are made, for example to be "banished from society," denied the use of the road or permission to take water from the tubewell, even to have their bones broken if they try to work in the fields. There is also the threat to be "banished from the religion" — mullahs refuse to pray or officiate in functions for them, or a salish to judge the women may be called. Fourth, they may be denied resources, or group funds or goods may be stolen. For example, when I visited Bangladesh in the mid-1990s, I was told by some BRAC staff that mulberry trees for a silk production project had, indeed, been destroyed.[14]

Patterns of resistance have depended on group and family support to ignore or challenge interference and get on with income-earning activities based on group loans.[15] Against this backdrop, the achievements of organizations like BRAC, Grameen Bank and SEWA seem even more admirable.

Self-Employed Women's Association (SEWA)

Just before she retired in 1996, SEWA founder Ila Bhatt looked back over her years with the organization:

> Through their faith in organising for their rights to protect their livelihoods and to
> safeguard their rightful place in the economy, self-employed women have made their mark.
> They are now more visible, articulate and self-confident. Twenty-four years ago, people
> didn't even recognise them as a group nor their significant contribution to our country.
> Today there is a growing recognition of their immense leadership potential and abilities.
> (SEWA 1996, page 5)

According to Bhatt, some 94 per cent of the female labour force in India is in the unorganized sector, from which SEWA draws its membership (SEWA 1996). SEWA began in Gujarat in 1972 with about two dozen women labourers from the unorganized sector (head-load carriers and cart pullers), who asked Bhatt, then head of the Women's Wing of the Textile Labour Association, for advice. They wondered if they could get some of the advantages union members had. She told them to organize. With her help, they did. Diverse groups of other women workers joined in. Consider some of SEWA's accomplishments: In 1996, it was the biggest union in Gujarat, with a membership of over 160,000 (Rose 1992; SEWA 1996). The SEWA 1996 report shows an all-India membership of over 200,000.

SEWA has been a movement as well as an organization. In addition to union activity, it includes rural development, farmers' groups, social security activities, bank activities (including savings associations), child-care groups and housing services, 71 cooperatives and an academy. There are SEWA branches in different states.

For example, SEWA-Lucknow produces and markets *chikan* embroidered products, based on a type of traditional embroidery . The organization was started after a 1979 study,

> revealed that the women and children working in the chikan industry were more cruelly
> exploited than in any other craft in the unorganised sector. To break out of the

stranglehold of middlemen, they needed a viable and sustainable production system with direct access to ready markets. (SEWA n.d. a)

By 1984, SEWA-Lucknow had been registered. It began with only 31 women. Kamla Bhasin, whom we met briefly in Chapter 8, told me that about one third of the original women had suffered from serious beatings at home. She had made up songs with them against violence and for better lives (some of which she said were still being sung in 1997, at work in the mornings, to encourage self-respect and group support). At first, organizing the women was very difficult, because many were in purdah. As a local report describes it:

> Such women are a captive and easily exploited labour force. Organising such women was an uphill task, to say the least. In the early years of SEWA's group formation, it was the perseverance of the lead team, which went from home to home talking to the women, bearing the brunt of their men's anger, which resulted in the present empowerment of 5,000 women who are confident and who are now ready to take on any problem. (SEWA-Lucknow n.d. b, page 7)

SEWA-Lucknow has made a special effort to reach rural as well as urban women. Both Hindu and Muslim women are members, about 30 per cent and 70 per cent, respectively, even though *chikan* is traditionally a craft done by Muslim women.[16]

There have been some obstacles, in addition to purdah, which reflect gender-role stereotypes for women. For example, a SEWA-Lucknow organizer told me about an incident from her early days with SEWA, which I recall like this: One afternoon a young man came to see her. He had a gun and threatened to kill her if she didn't stop trying to organize women to work outside their homes. She calmly offered him a cup of tea but asked him to sit outside since that would be more proper for both of them. She told him that he could kill her, but that there were many other women like her who would come and take her place. She explained to him the nature and benefits of SEWA's work for the women they organized, many of whom were destitute, as well as for their families; then she asked him about his own sisters, his mother, his daughters, and what would happen to them if he were arrested. What if they had no one to support them? He admitted that he had been sent to threaten her, but that he did not want to hurt her. He didn't come back.

A less dramatic obstacle, but a key one to overcome, was the fact that block-printing of the pattern to be embroidered is traditionally the work of men, of master printers, in fact. Sebha Hossain recalls,

> They all refused to print for us. There was only one sympathetic printer, but he was afraid of reprisals by the powerful mahajans.[17] We used to take our garments to him in the dead of night, using the back lanes so no one would see us. Before the crack of dawn, we would steal away with a week's supply of work for our members. (SEWA n.d. a)

By 1997, when I visited, men's attitudes were very different. For example, in my discussions with co-founders Sebha Hossain and Runa Banerjee, I was told that requests were being received from men in Lucknow asking for a parallel organization, Self-Employed Men's Association, to be set up. It was being considered. Also, I learned that SEWA-Lucknow and its members had achieved such good standing in the community that many families wanted "SEWA girls" as brides. In addition to good credit and savings programmes, SEWA had developed informal training programmes and health, water and education schemes for members and their children.

Women also supported each other about their social problems, which they discussed at work. For example, a group of women would go to the home of a group member who had been beaten, to confront the husband and ask him to change his behaviour. They used the tactic of shaming the perpetrator rather than the victim of gender violence. Also, the husband likely knew that SEWA's connections in the community were good enough that the police might come to talk to him if he persisted. The importance of women's group solidarity and visibility at the community level — as a deterrent to domestic violence — is confirmed, in fact, by Koenig et al. (1999), based on their study of antecedents to domestic violence in two areas of Bangladesh.

In another chapter of SEWA in India, SEWA-Bhopal, group organizer Vijaylaxmi Vankande works closely with some 700–800 families. She links violence against women members with alcohol abuse by men in their families. She explained:[18]

> Recently, we started a drive against alcohol, and women in these families supported us. They want to eradicate this problem, because it is a menace to them and to society. . . . First of all, we talk to their husbands (when they are sober) and try to put some sense into them. We explain how it is not right for one person to cause tension for the whole family. Men are informed about a treatment centre nearby. Legal action is a last resort.

Vijaylaxmi believes that when women are economically independent, they have a better chance to "deal with these problems." Her message to women is,

> women should never consider themselves weak — if they have initiative and courage and have set their minds on achieving something, they can do it. An ordinary man will never let a woman move forward, but she can be successful if she is determined. I would like all women to be independent.

Her co-worker Archana Sapre commented, "If we stop atrocities against women, then the future of their children will be secure."[19]

The future of their daughters is a primary concern to many women working in SEWA. Should they, too, expect to work at SEWA? In Lucknow, for example, should they be trained in *chikan* embroidery? Printing? Accounting? Or should they aim even higher? There were plans to have at least 1,200 children of SEWA-Lucknow workers enrolled in primary and middle school at two SEWA community education centres, for which SEWA also selects and trains teachers. There was to be a special programme for motivating and retaining girls who had dropped out of the school system.

New Industries: "Women's Advancement Makes Economic Sense"

In addition to the informal sector and self-employment, new industries are an evident niche for women working in South Asia. Many take young women workers with the idea that they will work only a few years before another batch comes in. The garment industry in Bangladesh and the free-trade zones in Sri Lanka are both examples. Gita Sen (1997) makes the interesting point that conditions in export-processing zones, which may not be attractive to men, offer women workers "the potential to earn higher incomes than in their traditional jobs, and to break away from the hold of traditional patriarchal structures" (page 22). She adds the very interesting footnote, highlighted here: "Indeed, one reason for the backlash from fundamentalist patriarchs is the growing ability of women to escape their hold under the strictures of economic compulsion" (page 26).

Because they are more educated than many women workers but are still young, the girls employed in new industries can be expected to learn new skills quickly yet remain docile compared to older women. However, the girls are vulnerable to sexual as well as economic exploitation, all the more so on the way to or from work, or even in hostels where they may live without adequate protection or supervision.

An example of a company with enlightened practices for women's employment and advancement is a shoe factory in Bangladesh that we will call the "Alpha Shoe Factory" and described by an executive, whom we will call "Mr. Rehman,"[20] to Naila Sattar in an interview for this book. He said that in 1997, the company employed some 900 women, out of a total of 1,000 employees. Some are in management, and more are sought. Mr. Rehman emphasized that Alpha's practices on behalf of women workers make economic sense. His account seems too good to be true. The ideas are certainly laudatory, even if some of them may prove to fail.

> We are a very quality-focused industry; we make shoes for Japan and Italy. We have found through experience that our women are definitely more quality conscious than men. In 9 out of 10 cases, women follow instructions more accurately than men. Secondly, it makes more sense to have a woman supervising other women. A woman manager can get them to speak to her about personal and family problems. So now what we have is not only 900 women working at the floor level, but 13 women who work as supervisors and 3 who work as production officers. They are part of the top management team of the factory.[21]

He noted that, "The reason we do this is primarily economic, and secondarily we can say that we focus on women's rights. These are interrelated."

Mr. Rehman explained that Alpha supported education, health and other benefits for its workers, to attract and keep them in what he sees as an increasingly competitive market. For example, with regard to health care he says:

> Health care is something we focused on very early on. Again, because it made economic sense. Initially, we had very high absenteeism and very high turnover. We found a high level of malnutrition, so we contracted with a local NGO called Concerned Women for Family Planning to provide basic health care services. . . .

This worked so well that he hired full-time nurses, doctors who come two times a week, and set up a clinic at work. According to Mr. Rehman, Alpha offers free family planning counselling services, which is somewhat controversial especially since some 60 per cent of the women workers are unmarried. Other health benefits include three months of maternity leave. A crèche is being considered.

He put it into economic terms:

> We have a lot of women who are starting to build families, and if we lose these women just because they are going to have to look after their children, after all the training we have invested in these women, we are going to lose. So that's something we want to do.

Mr. Rehman wonders if he will be able to keep his women workers:

> So we're pioneers, and there will be 20 factories coming up in the next four years. And the first thing they'll do is target our people. They'll try to headhunt people away from us.

He offers benefits, then, to keep his women workers, long-term as well as short-term. It seems to be working, at least so far as absenteeism is concerned:

> Overall, our absenteeism, for example, is less than 10 per cent, which in Bangladesh for a thousand people is pretty good. Our attrition level last year was 2 per cent, which is pretty good. So economically it makes sense.

Domestic abuse was also seen as a factor in absenteeism, which makes it a concern for the company. He explained:

> We have a lot of cases where women will come in bruised: they don't come in for two or three days, and they don't have a very good excuse for why they were not there. . . .
>
> I think if you are ever going to get out of this, you are going to have to give a certain amount of economic power for the woman to be able to say, "I will not put up with this. I have an independent income." No woman could actually wish to be abused. But as an option to get out of that, she has to have a place to go. The family that she came from won't want to accept her because of the social stigma that she is leaving her husband. Secondly, it is an economic burden. You are bringing back the daughter and her children. Whereas, if we provide some kind of income generation for this woman, then there is a third option. Which is not to put up with this, not to go back to the parents, but to live independently.

The company has set up dormitories, with a guard service, so women workers who are intimidated by violence at home, as well as those whose homes are far away, have an alternative living arrangement. He says,

> At present, we have about 40 per cent of our people living in these dormitories. Now again, we had a lot of local opposition initially — why are you taking people away from their families? But we make it very clear that this is not mandatory.

Mr. Rehman gave great importance to women knowing about their rights, as well as having education and income, if domestic violence is to lessen:

> So, coming back to violence, we don't actually see that much, but we see some of it. Very few women here are actually aware that they have any rights. That's the basic problem, an educational problem. And men don't want to acknowledge that the women have any rights because they see the women as completely dependent on them for sustenance and living. Once you change that, you will see some significant change in domestic violence.
>
> Everybody in our factory can read and write, at least read and sign basic forms. That's very important for our quality-control system, as well as for the women, at least for a sense of empowerment. That they can sign for their paycheck instead of giving a thumbprint. We do not give the paycheck to anybody else. She has to sign for her paycheck. Again, this is economic power, because in a lot of garment factories I have seen where the woman is the one working 24 or 31 days a month, 12 hours a day, but on the 31st or the 1st, there's a man there to collect the paycheck. I don't know if that's effective, because then the decision-making on how to spend that money is wrested away from the woman. . . .

Mr. Rehman said that Alpha encourages women workers to speak out and influence decision-making at work just as he hopes they do at home. Women are also encouraged to move up at Alpha, Mr. Rehman explained. As for the men's attitudes to women supervisors, Mr. Rehman's view was optimistic. He also explained how the company insists on a fair chance for women to advance. Later in the interview, however, Mr.

Rehman gave more details about his difficulties with men factory workers, especially those in management, over the question of women supervisors:

> But about 40 per cent of people that I work with, management, still think this is hogwash. They will say that we are asking for trouble. They will say that women cannot supervise. Even today they will say that. Because they [the women] are too soft, they are not strong enough, they cannot do overtime. And that's something again that takes time.

According to Mr. Rehman, family opposition to women's advancement can be even more of a problem than internal opposition. He told about one family that came to him and said,

> "What do you think you are doing? You are putting ideas into their heads. They think they are equal to men." And we said, "We are really not doing anything like that. We are telling them how to make shoes and how to work in a factory, and whatever else they pick up along the way, we take no responsibility for that."

He had, however, had the opportunity to discourage an early marriage arrangement for a very promising woman employee.

> You have to say, "Let's look at it this way. Maybe she's not ready yet. And she's doing well. And we have these plans for her. We think she can become senior management, and in that case she can get a better class of husband. She does not have to marry the next Tom, Dick or Harry. She can marry an engineer." And they say, "OK. Maybe that's an option we hadn't thought of."

Mr. Rehman did see that traditional gender-role expectations for women and men didn't always fit well with the new economic opportunities for women. He put it this way:

> It's clear that, even for Alpha women employees who are doing well, their parents or husbands may want them to stop working after a few years, given concerns about family and male status. In general, these seem to be greater where women are less independent.

He tries to make the families more comfortable about the working conditions for women at the factory. Mr. Rehman is concerned, and understandably so, that Alpha's policies on women workers, even if economically sound, will not be sustainable if family opposition remains or increases.

> We are not going to get anywhere as long as 51 per cent of our population is not working or cannot work. If you go to countries like Thailand, the workers are primarily women, whether you are in the airport or in a hotel or in a factory making T-shirts, I think, from the floor level up to manager. I think if we can create an environment in which women can still work and support and sustain a family — which means don't lock them up for 14 hours a day, seven days a week, to make sure they also have time to give to their families — more and more men will have to face the fact that women work simply for economics. It's very hard to live on one income in Bangladesh anymore. So you are going to have to have two-income families. At the same time, women are going to have to bring up the children. That is the truth for 99 per cent of the population. She has to balance the two, so you'll have to cater to that need.

Because he believes that women need to be able to balance work and family life if they are going to have family support for women to work, Mr. Rehman says he is in favour of innovations like "flexitime" and subcontracting for job work, to be supported with loans for equipment needed for production and with quality control by roving supervisors. The bulk of production could then be done by women at home, rather than in a factory.

But this approach, if implemented, would seem to contradict all that Mr. Rehman has actually been achieving for women's advancement. And women doing piecework at home, as the women of Lucknow did before SEWA was established there, would work more as isolated individuals than as part of a well-integrated production team, with direct access to senior management. They would probably have more difficulty to maintain control over their income and would be more susceptible to domestic violence. This would be especially true with no dormitory as a retreat, should the home situation prove overbearing. The idea of piecework for women working outside the factory doesn't seem to fit either with Mr. Rehman's idea that women at home are not likely to have economic independence. For example, he described the general economic position of women in Bangladesh like this:

> The woman is still economically dependent on the male, so she is totally confined to the house or the greater confines of the house. She can go to the market, but not much farther beyond. She does not have purchasing power because the money is not given to her. The money is kept by the man, and he gives her a certain amount for household purchases. That creates dependence. That allows the men to establish predominance over the women. . . . I think if you are ever going to get out of this, you are going to have to give a certain amount of economic power for the woman to be able to say, "I will not put up with this. I have an independent income."

Mr. Rehman also calls for more policy support and enforcement of laws that would support women workers in his factory:

> I think a lot will depend on better enforcement of the laws. The laws are all there. We have some of the best policies in the world. As long as we leave it completely up to the discretion of the employer, just because there is such massive underemployment, people will still take advantage and exploit labour. And so it's not going to happen just on its own. There has to be economic and policy forces driving that. But there has to be enforcement of the law. On a basic level if we do that we will see a lot of changes.

Trying to Organize Women Workers: Yousuf Khan

"Yousuf Khan" was working in the garment industry, where he tried to change the unfair conditions for women co-workers:

> When I realized that women were getting less than the minimum wage, because they were women, I, along with 80 others, asked my employer for their rights. He refused. Some of the other workers dropped out, scared of losing their jobs. I went ahead, went to labour court on behalf of the women in the factory, and won.

But when he started a factory labour union, he says his employer "reacted with open hostility." Yousuf finally left the firm after more legal battles with the employer. Two women involved in the struggle for equal wages left also. One died soon thereafter, he thinks because of effects on her health from work in the textile factory. He continues to struggle for women's equal rights at work. He is haunted by his co-worker's death and that of his mother, herself a garment factory worker who was dismissed from work after co-workers complained to management about unfair labour practices towards her. She had collapsed at work after selling her blood to earn money to feed her three children.

Yousuf's is the only account I have from the working world in South Asia that talks about women's fear as part of the violence against them, as evidence of intimidation and its toll on working women. He is surprised at how afraid women workers are to join him: "How can somebody not know how to get angry?" he asks.

> Even now they are scared to unionize. The fear is part of the violence perpetrated against them. To deal with violence, we have to deal with this fear first. That is what I have to do first, I have to get rid of this fear.[22]

Sexual and Gender-Role Harassment: You Are Asking for It If . . .

For women workers who are not organized in groups with the support of strong women's organizations like SEWA, or who do not have workplaces with policies like those Mr. Rehman describes for Alpha, or someone like Yousuf encouraging them, it can be very difficult to overcome the negative attitudes and practices towards working women.

The attitudes, and insulting behaviour to match, may come from people on the street, at work or at home. The meaning is often something like this:

> You are asking for it if you aren't home under a man's control; you aren't a real woman fit to be a wife and mother; you aren't even a real human being. We can do what we want to — ignore you, hurt you, or worse. After all, your father or husband are weaklings, or you wouldn't be here. We'll do what they didn't to control you, and use you, because we are real men and you are not where you belong.

This section looks at examples of two distinct kinds of harassment of working women — sexual harassment and what I call "gender-role harassment." The first is widely discussed and easily recognized, whether in its mild or more potent forms. Still, many women hesitate to complain about it. The second is a new concept. A lot of harassment against working women is in terms of what men think they should be doing instead — staying home, or working at some job that isn't in the so-called man's world. Gender-role harassment is to keep women limited to stereotypic activities.

Sexual Harassment

A definition of sexual harassment was made by a Supreme Court order in India in 1997. It

> has widened the definition of sexual harassment [there] to include physical contact and advances; sexual favours; sexually coloured remarks; showing of pornography, and any other verbal or non-verbal conduct of a sexual nature that is unwelcome or humiliating to the woman. The court puts the onus on the employers to provide a safe working environment for their employees. (Pail and Agarwal 1997, in *Sunday Times of India*, 24 August, 1997, page 19)

Instead of taking examples for India about sexual harassment, first we will turn to Sri Lanka, where the standing of women in employment as in education statistics is higher. One would hope, then, that sexual harassment would not apply in either case. However, interviews[23] reveal a problem with sexual harassment, despite the fact that

Sri Lanka, with India, is the only country in the region with a law against it (see Gomez and Gomez 1997 and Meindersma 1998).

On the Way to Work

Working women who use public transportation begin and end the day with the risk of sexual harassment on the way to work. An exceptional woman who stood up to her tormentors is "Latha" from Sri Lanka.[24] She travels some 20 miles to and from work each day as a commuter into the capital where she works.

> One day when I was travelling alone, I got an aisle seat on the bus. A man came and stood near me and started leaning against me. I told him to please move aside, but he wouldn't. Then I pushed him. Then he told me that if I wanted to travel without being touched, I should buy a car and travel in comfort. . . . Another woman who was close by told the man that there is enough space for him to stand and to please move away from me.

> I told him that if women can stand on their own two feet without leaning on others, why can't he, a man, do the same? This altercation took place for a few minutes. The bus came to a halt where I had to get off and when I got up I noticed that the sleeve of my blouse was wet. I loudly called him a *paaharaya* [dog] and told the other travellers to see what he had done to my dress. I was very angry at what I had had to go through.

Another day it was a man about 70 years old who leaned against Latha in the bus, wrapping a leg around hers. She asked him to move away, but he refused. Latha says,

> Then he started to abuse me verbally, saying that he had 45 years of experience travelling by bus and no one had said anything like this to him before. I told him that I am surprised that no other woman had said anything to him if this is the way he has travelled before, and that I, too, have experience travelling by bus and that in my experience it is people like him who need to be controlled.

> He moved his leg, but started to be more abusive and said that women don't want to be touched by men but they go and sleep with men, etc. . . . I addressed the old man as *seeya* [grandfather] and told him that if he wants to talk about his experience of 45 years he can publish a book about it or teach it in a class, but I am not prepared to put up with his behaviour. Other people in the bus laughed. One woman congratulated me and said that most women don't speak out and that is why this kind of thing happens.

She continued,

> On the rare occasions when someone like me protests, sometimes other men also criticize the culprit. I have found that these days, most of the bus conductors are young men, and they are more likely to be sympathetic towards women who protest than [are] the older bus conductors, . . . but as far as the travelling male public is concerned, nothing seems to have changed. Everyday there are hundreds of such incidents of sexual harassment in the buses and trains which go largely unrecorded.

She thinks that they should be made public, that women should be encouraged to let men know they do not have the right to harass them sexually and that it is a crime to do so. (In Sri Lanka there is a law against harassment of women.) Latha explains her own forthrightness as coming from her work with women's groups: "I am able to speak out and have done so on many occasions because I work with women's groups and I don't feel intimidated by men who do such things to women."

At Work

Even once "safely" at work, women employees may be subjected to degrading attitudes and behaviours, which are extremely difficult to overcome. From Sri Lanka, "Nanda" tells her story:[25]

> About two months after I started work at this office, I noticed that my immediate boss appeared to have a very familiar attitude with the other women.
>
> One day, as when I was walking home after work, along with two male colleagues . . . , the boss, who was in a vehicle, stopped them on the road and offered them a lift. As my two colleagues got into the vehicle, I too got in. But after they got out, the boss opened his bag and showed me some photographs of nude women, which he said he had got on one of his frequent visits to Bangkok. Then, he had asked me what I thought of these photographs. . . . I replied that I am aware that women are used in degrading ways and proceeded to explain to him that it is morally and socially wrong to use women in such ways. The man had then told me that he was not interested in such facts; he wanted to know what I felt when I looked at the photographs. I told him that what I had said earlier was exactly how I felt. After this discussion, he dropped me home.

Several times after that the boss offered her a ride home. She always refused. And to deter him even more, she told him she had a boyfriend who dropped her at home after work. Then, she says, things started to change at the office.

> Gradually, I noticed that he would make uncalled-for criticism of me. The other women in the office started making remarks about my appearance and behaviour, and I generally found that I was being sidelined in the office. Whenever I had to get a letter signed by the boss, he would keep me waiting, standing a long time, before he would look at my request. He would send the office peon to instruct me to do or not to do various things in relation to my work. I also learned that he had visited my boarding house and had enquired about me from the landlady as well as some neighbours. In order to keep my job, I put up with the harassment. But the boss would not let up and would have me followed and would follow me from work. I felt increasingly that it was difficult for me to work in this environment.
>
> When I visited my parents in Colombo, I confided in them as to what was happening and decided that I would leave this job. . . .When I informed the boss that I was leaving and gave him my letter of resignation, he asked me to come to the office to hand over my keys to him. I went one day with my brother to do this. The boss refused to take over the keys, which would have amounted to him accepting my final resignation, and told me that I must come alone to hand over the keys. I went the next time with my father. Once again, the boss refused to accept the keys, insisting that I must hand these over by myself. Finally, I went to court and complained to the magistrate that the boss was not accepting the keys although I had sent in my resignation. The magistrate requested the boss to present himself in court, and finally the man was compelled to accept the keys and finalize my resignation.

She also credits her work on women's issues and support of other women as the source of her courage:

> I feel that my work with the women's magazine and my friendship with women who belong to women's organizations helped me enormously in having the courage not to be harassed into submitting to the demands made by the man who was my immediate boss in that office. I am very keen that other women who are subjected to such oppression should also

be encouraged and empowered, so that men who think that women are sexual objects will not be able to behave in such ways.

In protest, some women like Nanda speak up, and even resign if necessary. However, men employers who sexually harass their women employees apparently think they will likely give in and keep quiet to stay employed.

Things are changing in India and receiving wide publicity. In Florence, Italy, on 29 December 1998, I saw a CNN report by Anita Pratak from New Delhi. She described the results of a national survey just released on the sexual harassment of working women in India. Some 50 per cent indicated they suffered from sexual harassment at work. Some women said they were forced to look at pornography, others said they couldn't even stay at their desks and work because men harassed them so much, proposing sex and making insulting remarks. Some companies, it was reported, are giving gender training courses, so both men and women employees will know what the standards are for treatment of women workers — and the consequences, I hope. Surely these would include negative points for perpetrators. For the company, greater efficiency and production — economic sense — would be the happy outcome of reduced sexual harassment. For women? Yes, greater productivity and the fulfilment of the right to work without gender violence.

Gender-Role Harassment at Work

If not harassed sexually, women at work can still face the attitude that because they are female, they don't really belong there, or they should only do certain kinds or work. This gender-role harassment is probably even more commonplace than sexual harassment. It affects highly educated professionals as well as others. Two examples follow.

"Go back, go home, you are wasting your time." A Pakistani woman lawyer describes what happened when she first started working at the High Court in Islamabad:[26]

> I don't know if it is sexual harassment . . . what I feel is people aren't generally rude to you or they don't generally say bad things to you, but they just tend to ignore you: that is one thing I have noticed here. They just have this attitude that you don't exist, so they don't even pay any attention to you. And I think that makes me feel really bad, worse than if they would abuse me. That is one thing I experience all the time. Basically, they don't take you seriously.
>
> I think that it was the first day when I went to the High Court, I was on the lift and I asked this person where this judge's court was, and he just looked at me and said, "What are you doing here? Go back, go home, you are wasting your time." That was the first thing I heard at the High Court. And people do generally have that attitude, that being a woman you won't stay for long, that you are going to leave. Now I know why women quit, because it is not that work is very hard, they don't have the staying power or that the timings are really long, but it is the general attitude of the men. Basically, working in the court is like it is the gentlemen's club, and they cooperate with each other and you feel very left out, and if you need to know something, then you have to ask people all the time. No one ever tells you, no one ever gives you voluntary information, which happens when a new guy comes into the court and joins the profession, people are, like, all out to help him, giving advice and all that. But being a woman I do feel excluded, and I think at times people want to talk to you, but they feel, if they do, others are going to talk. Because if you talk to the same man

maybe thrice in the same week, then [it is said that] you are having an affair with him. . . . Here I do find it hard; it is a very male-dominated profession.

"Motherhood" can mean "Quit!" A woman editor from India pointed out that men tried to get her to quit her job once she was pregnant, because of the stereotype that mothers should stay home. She describes how she resisted.[27]

> I entered the profession as a married woman, and they said, "You are married, and you are going to get children." And once I got my child, I took a long . . . nine-month break, which the Working Journalists Act of Leave clause allows. But they said, "No, now you won't be able to concentrate." They tried their best to get rid of me by saying, "You become a freelancer, now you have a child." This happens in all the offices. Just because you become a mother, your body is undergoing so many physical changes, as well as so much is happening inside, emotional, your hormones go awry, everything is happening and you feel slowly, "Will I be able to do it — this new responsibility at home?" A little bit of depression catches up. But that's the time they try to hit you. I am talking about 17 years ago. But if you quietly say, "No, I am here to stay, with baby or no baby," they get the message.

Today she is the chief of a news bureau with both men and women working under her.

Extreme gender-role harassment: "You cannot work." The most extreme form of gender-role harassment is practised by Taliban authorities in Afghanistan. On the basis of the idea that women should stay home, unless accompanied and protected by a male relative, women workers have been dismissed around the country from development projects, from schools, from hospitals. Girls cannot go to school, women doctors cannot practise, and so on. The rights of girls and women are denied, development is set back, all in the name of what is considered the appropriate, stereotypic female role, as claimed and sanctioned by religion.

One of the women interviewed in Afghanistan for this book described the way the situation affects her educated sister, a doctor, who does not go to the hospital to work. If she tries to,

> her family will fight with her everyday. The outside people will know. The neighbours, the families will know about her, that she is not a good person. She has a lot of problems outside and inside [the house]. Because of that she says, "OK, I am a housewife, and I don't want to work outside, and [I'll] be quiet for the family."

Women's and children's increased economic hardship under these circumstances and the effects on health are frequently reported in anecdotes from both development workers and women in the country. Despair and suicide is said to be increasing among women as a result of denial of their human rights and fundamental freedoms under the current regime.

Childcare and Women's Work

Women's work is clearly more than childcare. And it should not be women's preoccupation any more than men's, ideally. CEDAW, we recall, addresses maternity as a social function, with men and women equally responsible for childcare. Nonetheless, throughout the developing world and in many of the so-called developed countries, it appears that society still depends on women for most childcare, and both women and men tend to accept this. Employers in South Asia, as elsewhere, reflect this idea when they use maternity, present or predicted, as a reason to block employment or career opportunities for women and do not themselves provide childcare for workers' children. As things are, the State and employers, by reinforcing childcare as "women's work" rather than a benefit that all employees should have, save themselves the expenses that providing childcare would otherwise incur. Employers or the State would face considerable expense for providing childcare were there to be a strong challenge to the norm that it is women alone — not men also or even society — who are responsible for children. An uneducated mother in Nepal saw things in a more straightforward and logical way. She said, as though it were a simple matter anyone could see and accept, that the government should provide a child-care centre for the village so that children (girls) would be free to go to school regularly (NPC 1996, page 38).

Nonetheless, whatever their work, South Asian women are mindful that they are usually expected to take care of children and they try to do so as best they can. The arrangements they make vary widely. They may call on older children in the family, especially girls, to look after younger children , thereby ending the older one's chances for further education. Or working mothers may simply leave their children with relatives, with the risk of neglect and abuse. For example, in Sri Lanka, it is not uncommon for newspapers to report incidents about sexual or physical abuse of the children of migrant mothers who have had to leave them behind. Some children are at work with their mothers, but not in crèches. For example, children of bonded labourers are likely to be doomed to the same life as their mother. Children of women in new industries, such as carpet manufacturing, may be with them. Children of prostitutes have horrendous experiences, even with their mothers taking on customers in their presence. As we heard from Indrani Sinha, many prostitutes very much want their children to have a better life than their own.

It is very rare for proper child-care facilities to be provided at work in South Asia. On this point, some of the examples above are particularly praiseworthy. In many cases, SEWA has helped to organize childcare for its members. The Alpha Shoe Factory's reported provision of health care and its intention to provide a crèche seem extraordinary. And the work of SANLAPP with prostitutes in Calcutta features childcare.

Good Mothers Do Not Just Stay Home

In fact, most women who work do so because they need money to support themselves and their children; yet, there is a stereotype that women are somehow bad mothers if they are not at home. Whoever said that part of motherhood isn't to help provide for a child? And what about the fathers? They may have deserted the women and children, which is part of the reason why the women must work. Or the men may be poor, yet still many are able to buy alcohol, cigarettes or tickets to movies even when food, clothes, housing, health care and education are wanting for their children and wives. CEDAW's Recommendation 19 notes, "The abrogation of their family responsibilities by men can be a form of violence and coercion" (IWRAW and Commonwealth Secretariat 1996, paragraph 23, page 74).

Aggressive marketing of alcohol and cigarettes in South Asia makes the point. For example, a report by Bhadra and Thapa (1995) on Nepal indicates that considerable revenue was expected from alcoholic beverages. The authors make the following comment:

This indicates that still a considerable amount of alcohol has been produced and sold in the market. So, in spite of favourable trend in not licensing new factories, there still exists the risk of women being exposed to violence due to alcoholism. (page 6)

Indeed, rural women in parts of Nepal and India have organized campaigns against the sale of alcohol accordingly. As one woman activist pointed out, there isn't water available in the village, but alcohol is for sale in even the most remote areas. As it and cigarettes draw income away from the household, the well-being of children and women suffers, along with the health of the men, who are primarily the ones indulging.

When poor women earn money, their children are apt to benefit. It is sometimes said that working women are more likely than men to spend more of their money on food, health care and education. This is probably even more true for the women's daughters, as compared to what their fathers would spend on them. Here, let us recall that sex ratios skewed in favour of males predominate in some parts of the region, as has been noted in particular across the north of India. Agnihotri (1997a) has analysed how female labour-force participation and what he calls "female-friendly" versus "male-centred" social structures account for the differences in the female-to-male ratios for various ethnic groups and in various parts of India, for both the zero-to-four and the five-to-nine age groups. (The idea is that children do not migrate out for purposes of work as adults do, so that missing females in the younger age groups can more confidently be taken as evidence of truly missing cases, due to differential care and access to life-supporting services, such as nutrition and health care.) Agnihotri concludes that the "female-friendly social structure" accounts for more of the variance than does female labour-force participation, but that where the social structure is male-centred, female labour-force participation is more important as a corrective factor to what he considers an aberration rather than the norm for India, that is, low female-to-male sex ratios.

This strongly suggests that where patriarchal structures and ideologies are strong, daughters will benefit wherever female labour-force participation is higher. That is because the value placed on women can be assumed to increase as their economic contribution is counted as greater, which is more likely when there is monetary remuneration for their work outside the home. Working mothers of daughters in patriarchal societies may be the best protection the daughters could have, at least with regard to attitudes about whether or not they should have health care and proper food.

Without specific reference to the economic and social effects on daughters having working mothers, Amartya Sen (1993b, page 47) sees a definite benefit for women's status from working outside the home:

Evidence suggests that the ability of women to earn an income and to enter occupations, especially in more skilled jobs, outside the home, enhances their social standing and in turn influences the care they receive within the family. Working outside the home also gives women exposure to the world and sometimes, more of an opportunity to question the justice of the prevailing social and economic order. Literacy, education, land ownership and inheritance can also improve the overall status of women.

He points, for example, to Kerala, which has all of the above and a female-to-male ratio of 1.04. The problem enters for daughters when one considers what work the mother does. If it is exploitative, one needs to guess whether or not the daughter will follow her mother into it. If so, the daughter may have a short-term gain from her mother's work — better care — only to be followed by a long-term loss through exploitation. Still, this usually compares favourably with death.

Husbands of Working Women

Greed as well as shame or jealousy are among the negative reactions husbands show when wives work. Although many do not want their wives to work, lest they themselves lose status, other husbands see and take the benefits. They may try to control the income that a wife earns and the assets she accrues; to reduce their own responsibility for child support; or to influence men at the wife's workplace by encouraging their sexual relations with her.

In extreme cases, a husband's behaviour may even become pathological. For example, an activist whom we will call "Fajida" describes how a woman doctor's husband reacted to her success.[28] He started by monitoring the mileage on his wife's car every evening after she came home from the clinic and making accusations against her:

> And he would say that from home to clinic, it is 1.5 km; if the car runs even 1.7 km she would have hell to pay that night. And if she keeps the clinic open till 9:30 in the night, he would come and sit outside and ask the local medical shops whether there were lots of men who came with prescriptions, or did women come with men, or did men come alone, etc., and she had to be home by 9:30; afterwards she would be locked out of the house for hours. . . . Then it was systematic cutting off of her friends. They were told that their husbands were making passes at the lady doctor, and that the police would be called in. After about a year, none of her former friends were willing to talk to her.

> One day, a neighbour the woman doctor didn't know came and advised her not to commit suicide, that with her profession and three children she had a lot of reasons to live. The woman doctor was shocked and told her neighbour that she was not planning suicide. She then learned that her husband had already made a complaint to the police (where the neighbour's husband worked) that you are getting to be a psycho case, you are all upset, and that should you commit suicide, he should not be held responsible.

The woman doctor realized where things might be going: the husband had bought a flat with her earnings, in his name; he had all her jewellery in a safety-deposit box, in his name. She said to Fajida, "I had this horrible feeling that I was becoming redundant for him, and he would put away with me." She contacted a lawyer to help her with her own complaint to the police; they helped her take her things from the house, and she left her husband.

Some husbands regard women's earnings as so important that they, in effect, agree to whatever sexual exploitation of their wives may go with her job. For example, Fajida also told this story of an extreme case:

> A lady married her two daughters to her sister's two sons. Both the boys started ill treating the girls, even though they were first cousins. It took me almost two hours of questioning to find out from the girls what their problem was. Finally, I gathered that the husbands wanted their wives to become prostitutes.

In less extreme situations, the important question about a working woman's husband remains: Who controls and benefits from the women's income? Who decides what it is for? Unless a woman has control of her income, her employment is not an indicator of her empowerment. One hopes that Firdoor Azim, a university professor from Bangladesh, is right when she says, "I don't know whether women working is better for women, but at least it means a little more economic freedom, power for women."[29]

There is the insistent message from men that working women should remember they are inferior to men and that they really belong at home under their control. Childcare should remain their responsibility even when they have a heavy work burden at home and outside. Men in the family should still be served when and as they want. The women may not be allowed to decide about the use of what little money they can earn. Whether at home or away from home, men who want to show their power see working women as easy targets for economic exploitation, as well as physical, sexual and psychological violence, which can yield economic returns as well as social status to men.

The Home: A Dangerous Workplace for Women

When women must die while they are cooking dinner at home, whether because of a faulty stove or simply a hostile family, something is very wrong with the working and living conditions of the home. If people really believed that the deaths are mostly accidental, and if they really cared, they would be busy redesigning kitchens and kitchen equipment to save lives rather than to prevent smoke. That is not happening.

Even when working conditions at home are not lethal, they can be perilous. The hours are very long, longer than those that men work. The compensation is poor — the poorest food eaten last, the least health care. And certainly no consideration is given for time off for pregnancy and lactation. The care of children is obviously considered women's work and not important enough for men's attention — unless the woman lets the child cry or do something else that the man does not like, then he can hit her and the child if he wants. So men as supervisors at home often feel they have the right to treat their women workers abominably. When men admit that they beat their wives because the dinner isn't ready on time,[30] the home cannot be considered a safe place for women to work. And there is no hope for advancement (except to become the mother-in-law in due course, perhaps to contribute to some violence against other women but to be blamed for even more than is appropriate given the studies that show men as the main perpetrators).

The extent to which women are isolated in the home will increase their vulnerability to any violence there, and will limit their possibilities for seeking help solidarity with other women and for employment or migration as a means to economic status or even independence, if need be.

Here lower-caste women *(harijan)* may have some advantage, at least for the time being: There is evidence from India that lower-caste women have more freedom of mobility than other castes in some areas, and that their status is consequently higher as their economic productivity outside the home is valued (George, Haas and Latham 1994).

In fact, the study in Bangladesh by Koenig et al. (1999) of determinants of domestic violence found a statistically significant inverse relationship between women's mobility and wife-beating — so long as the community was not too conservative.

Macroeconomic Policies and Violence against Women

Mies (1986) and others have written at length on this subject, connecting patriarchy writ large expressed through the global economy with exploitation and suffering of women in the developing world. Vandana Shiva (1991, 1993, 1995) has equated nature with women and described the relentless exploitation of and violence to both through "development," which she sees as more destructive than not. Her viewpoint, shared by many others, is important to take into account. It suggests that the processes and institutions in globalization, which affect women's changing work roles, are themselves patriarchal and exploitative.

Vina Mazumdar summarizes related concerns from a 1994 international conference on gender and development, which discussed implications of globalization for women at the grassroots level. Among the negative effects brought out were "increases in migration, poverty, exploitation, prostitution, violence and drugs, reduction in social support, changes in cultural norms which affected women adversely and globalisation of elites" (Mazumdar n.d., page 321).

Bhadra and Thapa (1997) take what they call "a feminist perspective" to describe how macroeconomic policies are not really "gender neutral," but lead to economic deprivation for women in particular. They argue that the market-oriented liberal economic system has the potential to unleash violence against women. Their analysis of change in Nepal as it shifts from a subsistence to a market economy shows that women's status has declined in the agricultural sector and their role as unpaid labourers has increased. Women's decision-making roles in rural as well as urban households are reported to have declined from 1978 to 1992, based on a survey by Shtrii Shakti as reported by economist Meena Acharya (1997). They are said to have less control over income and expenditure in commercial agriculture compared to subsistence agriculture, in addition to being displaced from land and community resources (Bhadra and Thapa 1995).The authors note the heavy burdens women have in the house and community, which lead to poor health and a tendency to keep girls out of school to help at home. They also highlight a trend for girls and young women (ages 10 to 22) to enter the manufacturing sector, especially in urban areas. Many women workers are in unhygienic situations. They may have to bring newborn and very young children to work where women are migrants and childcare is lacking. Furthermore, an estimated 38 per cent of labourers in the carpet factories are girls: "They become easy victims of sexual exploitation and harassment." Women's crafts have also been put out of production in the market economy.[31] Women are reported to be only 0.4 per cent of the employers.

Bhadra and Thapa (1995, page 6) recommend that the government take the social impact of private enterprise into account as they deregulate the economy for economic growth:

> [B]lind deregulation may lead to loss of opportunity and loss of control of certain section of the population (mostly women). This is going to be against the policy of sustainable economic growth and poverty alleviation . . . the government should develop mechanisms to screen private enterprises (before licensing and during operation) in terms of their impact on women, so that women can be protected.

Their conclusions sum up the views of many women who lament the negative impact of the market economy and so-called development on women's control of resources and decision-making, along with women's vulnerability to gender-based violence of various types:

> Unless there is a change in macroeconomic perspective, women will remain as objects to be taken for granted to carry out the functions of "reproductive economy" no matter how change in "productive economy" will affect them. They will remain as objects with legitimacy to be exploited and violated both within the household and the workplace. Until patriarchal culture [no longer] dominates the macroeconomic policy formulation and reform, the potential of 50 per cent of the human resources (i.e. women), their resource base (or lack of one) and their critical role in major development issues will remain invisible and excluded. It is time to realize that inclusion of women as major and principal actors in macroeconomic policies does not stem from patriarchal "welfare approach". So, mainstreaming women in the whole policy process is an economic imperative. (National Planning Commission, HMG/UN/UNIFEM 1995, cited in Bhadra and Thapa 1995, page 8)

Indeed, Gita Sen (1997) sees an important and necessary role for women's groups to transform the State and government, as well as to reform the Bretton Woods institutions and transnational companies.

Some Achievements and Ideas for Change

The achievements of activists cited in this section are all the more remarkable, given the many difficulties and negative attitudes in South Asia about women who work and the acceptance of various forms of gender-based violence against them. The activists' examples should inspire even more thought and corrective action.

Some general points about priorities for action to improve the lot of women workers, making it violence-free, and to ensure their rights, as well as those of their daughters, are worth highlighting here. I have indicated from which interview or research the idea comes. If nothing is said, then the suggestion is something that follows logically from concerns the activists mentioned.

1. Policy-Level Changes

Review and revise economic policies that otherwise lead to exploitation of women and children, denial of their human rights and even physical violence against them (see Bhadra and Thapa 1995). Transformation of the development paradigm itself is needed from concern with profit to refocus on benefits for peoples who wish to improve the quality of life.

2. Provision of Childcare

Childcare provided by employers or the State for working women and men (as contemplated by Mr. Rehman of the Alpha Shoe Factory) would ease the burden on working mothers, as would campaigns to promote men's roles and responsibilities in childcare as Bhagwati Devi managed in her own household (as in Article 5b of CEDAW).

3. Priority on Daughters of Exploited Women Workers

Education for girls should be made a priority, with special attention to the daughters of the most exploited working women, so that they will have more opportunities for economic well-being in life and will be able to stand up to gender violence (based on the obvious need, given the experiences recounted above, to prevent a future in which the daughters of the most exploited women workers repeat the experiences of their mothers).

4. Prevention of Recruitment of Girls into Prostitution

Efforts to prevent recruitment of girls into prostitution are crucial, including information campaigns in rural and urban source communities about what may await girls who drop out of school, accept marriage proposals from grooms who are strangers, become housemaids away from home and lack sex education or support groups. Also, alternatives for older prostitutes are necessary to prevent their recruiting girls to help them (see Indrani Sinha's experience with SANLAPP described previously.)

Sex education and support groups for such girls (as above) are also necessary.

5. Recognition of and Support for Women's Groups

Provide support for working women through women's groups as receiving mechanisms for credit, training, savings and support groups against gender-based violence of various types (as is characteristic of the experience of BRAC, SEWA, SANLAPP and Latha).

6. Prevention of Sexual and Gender-Role Harassment

Campaigns to stop harassment and violation of women on the way to work and at work are needed. (As Latha says, harassment should be publicized as a crime, something that is being done in India.)

Gender sensitization courses for women workers, their male relatives, their employers and co-workers are also needed (as reported by Anita Pratak).

Make the concept of gender-role harassment more well known so as to promote action against it (as in the case of the High Court in Pakistan in which the woman lawyer was uncertain how to categorize what had happened to her).

7. Attention to Men's Roles

Men should be held responsible for rape and violence connected with the workplace, as elsewhere, and shamed publicly for these acts. Girls and women should not be blamed, discarded or exploited further (see the example of SEWA-Lucknow).

8. Making the Home a Safe Place to Work

Campaigns to make the home a safe place for women to work could make a difference. (With reference to the problem of stove-burning, see Jilani 1992.)

Also useful is support for the idea of including the value of women's work at home in national accounts (see CEDAW).

9. Showing that Change Is Possible

Identify, feature and reward those who make a difference against the gender exploitation of and violence toward working women. Too often publicity is given to the problems, not the solutions.

10. Using the Law

Review, revise, use and increase public knowledge of national laws to foster equal working conditions and benefits for women workers, in line with CEDAW. (Shakil Ahmed Pathan, Mr. Rehman, Hina Jilani, Yousuf, Shri Manahendra Mandal and Bhagwati Devi all know and are implementing the law.)

11. Criminalization of Violence against Women at Home and at Work

Greater dissemination and discussion of CEDAW and its significance for working women, especially Articles 4, 5 and 11, and improvement of national laws accordingly, are important steps.

A word on Article 11, on employment, is in order. As is the general case for CEDAW articles, there is nothing at all in Article 11 that is explicitly about violence against women at work and women's need for protection from violence in the workplace. The closest is "(f): The right to protection of health and to safety in working conditions, including the safeguarding of the function of reproduction." Reading it, even with the benefit of Recommendation 19 (see Chapter 1), one feels a long way from the realities of women's experiences of gender violence at work — realities that need far more attention from women activists, employers, governments and the United Nations to eliminate violence and inequity from all of women's workplaces.[32]

12. Challenging the Commodification of Women

Women as objects from which economic gain can derived — that is the message inherent in the way women are sometimes portrayed in advertising for goods in the global market place. Whether partially inspired by such images or not, there apparently is an alarming trend in South Asia towards the commodification of women and girls. For example, the practice of dowry is spreading, the "price" is escalating, there is extortion-like pressure for it to be paid and more cases of bride-burning follow.

How will this problem be successfully addressed? Activists are concerned that development itself exploits women. Guidelines for improved attention to gender issues are proliferating in UN and other development agencies, which may prevent some problems. Reinforcing women's and girls' inherent dignity and rights, listening to them and helping to provide economic and political opportunities can also help. Questioning patriarchal structures and values at all levels will be fundamental for prevention of even more commodification of women and girls. But is that enough? Where development is based on the profit motive rather than sustainability and people's participation, it is strongly criticized for commodification and exploitation of women and girls as well as the poor and the environment. Women are leading the way towards re-examination of the development paradigm for a more people-oriented approach. The situation of women and girls is an indicator of the extent to which development benefits or exploits the people it would serve.

Endnotes

1 Heard by the author at the Strategy Review Meeting for the Government of India/UNICEF Programme of Cooperation, New Delhi, 1996.

2 This discussion is based on information in IWRAW and Commonwealth Secretariat (1996), which contains the text of CEDAW, Recommendation 19 and the Declaration on the Elimination of Violence against Women.

3 I reviewed this in 1997 but do not recall the name of the NGO that produced it.

4 As arranged through War Against Rape, Lahore, in cooperation with UNICEF Pakistan and UNICEF ROSA. In August 1999 at a regional meeting in Kathmandu I learned by chance that Shakil Ahmed Pathan had passed away in 1998 in an accident. His wonderful spirit and tremendous contributions will be very much missed.

5 From an interview by Thomas Kelly for this book, arranged by UNICEF ROSA, 1997.

6 She was interviewed by Ruchira Gupta, Indian woman journalist, as arranged through UNICEF India, in cooperation with UNICEF ROSA.

7 Writer Rohinton Mistry's account of caste violence in his recent novel *A Fine Balance* (New York: Knopf, 1996) presents chilling scenes about what happens when a lower-caste man tries to escape his lot.

8 Personal communication, Kathmandu, August 1999. Neelum was summarizing NGO views on violence against women and efforts to end it, for a regional post-Beijing meeting.

9 The interview for this book was arranged by UNICEF India.

10 This study was funded by the Netherlands Embassy.

11 Interview arranged by UNICEF India for this book.

12 For comparison, some figures from other regions are as follows: 32 per cent in the Middle East, 55 per cent in sub-Saharan Africa, over 70 per cent in North America and 100 per cent in Eastern Europe and the former USSR.

13 See, for example, Chen (1986) and Rose (1992).

14 Personal communication from Ms. Nuzhat Shahzadi, then working with BRAC.

15 According to Anjana Shakya, questions are being asked about the amount of interest paid over time for these loans (personal communication, New York, October 1999).

16 Personal communication with a SEWA official during a visit to SEWA-Lucknow, February 1997. Name withheld for protection.

17 Very wealthy and powerful people who lend money and take interest.

18 The interview for this book was arranged by UNICEF India.

19 The interview was arranged by UNICEF India.

20 Interviewed for this book by Ms. Naila Sattar, a Bangladeshi who was a graduate student at Princeton University at the time, and in cooperation with UNICEF Bangladesh. The interviewee asked to remain anonymous to protect his company from any harassment or unfair competition.

21 Apparently, about 10 per cent of management are women.

22 A woman activist in Dhaka had put him in touch with Ila Bhatt, so he might have the opportunity to learn how women's solidarity through group formation can help overcome women's fear and exploitation at work.

23 As arranged by UNICEF Sri Lanka.

24 The interview for this book was arranged by UNICEF Sri Lanka; all interviewees were given pseudonyms.

25 The interview for this book was arranged by UNICEF Sri Lanka; all interviewees were given pseudonyms.

26 The interview for this book was arranged by UNICEF Pakistan; name withheld.

27 The interview for this book was arranged by UNICEF India; name withheld.

28 Interview arranged by UNICEF Pakistan. Name withheld due to the sensitivity of the material.

29 Interview arranged for this book by UNICEF Bangladesh.

30 For example, Afsana (1994).

31 See Hossain et al., *No Better Option* (Dhaka: Upd, 1990) for information on the situation in Bangladesh.

32 The International Labour Organization (ILO) has long had a priority to help improve the situation of women workers and rural women. Recently, the ILO study *The Sex Sector* (1998) has attracted wide attention to a problem too long neglected.

Using the Legal System to End Violence against Women and Girls

Questions about Legal Implementation

U sing the legal system: nothing has seemed more promising yet proved so generally disappointing as a reliable means for the remedy and prevention of violence against women and girls in South Asia. Legal remedy is even more distant when that violence occurs in the family and is backed by both tradition and stereotyped attitudes to women's role and responsibilities in the family as reflected in gender bias in the community and among legislators and policy makers. To be sure, many legal measures are available. Since colonial times, laws have been introduced against harmful traditional practices and other forms of gender-based abuse and violence. The most recent examples of such laws, introduced in one or more countries of the region, are about acid-throwing, incest and sexual harassment. In addition, laws are being sought in some countries of the region against domestic violence itself and also for equal property rights.[1]

Measures other than laws are also being promoted to try to ensure justice for abused women and girls. These include: women's police cells intended to handle women's complaints more effectively; training on gender issues for police and judiciary; and establishing special bodies, such as national commissions on women or human rights, with mandates related to women's situation that include investigative powers in some cases. Legal awareness, legal literacy and legal advocacy efforts by women's groups, primarily with and for rural women, are also ongoing.

Even with all this, effective use of the legal system to end violence against women and girls in South Asia remains a major problem. Why?

Primary reasons include:

- the apparent unwillingness of the State and its agents to act in favour of women victim-survivors, rather than males accused of violent acts;
- the notion that what happens in the family is private even if it leads to abuse of rights and death;
- emphasis on custom and tradition rather than national and international norms for equality of rights;
- the possibility of conflict between different legal systems within the same country; and
- risks for women who bring charges in cases of gender-based violence.

Each of these deterrents to justice is introduced briefly below, before this chapter looks more closely at the nature of the legal system and the State's implementation of it or not in cases of gender violence. Some initiatives for improvement and lessons learned are also covered. Throughout, illustrative examples are given; it is not possible here to be comprehensive: any effort to do so would require a separate book.

Throughout this chapter, the reader is encouraged to imagine being a woman victim-survivor of gender-based violence who might consider making a complaint: Would you do so or not given the problems involved? Are there particular problems ahead for a woman who tries to use the legal system for remedy in cases of violence against her in the home? What would have to change to make it more worthwhile for women victim-survivors to bring those and other cases? How can such changes be achieved? Among the existing modalities to seek legal remedies in cases of violence, what are the most promising ones? If women are reluctant to bring criminal cases, do available civil remedies provide the needed relief?

Some Deterrents to Using the Law against Gender Violence

Apparent Unwillingness of the State to Act on Behalf of Women Victim-Survivors

Comments from India and Pakistan illustrate this first point.

Kirti Singh, Supreme Court advocate in India, strongly challenges the objectivity and effectiveness of the legal system there so far as women's interests are concerned:

> One of the main problems is that, though many changes have taken place in the criminal laws, through the ceaseless efforts of women's groups and others, government has made little effort to implement the laws. These laws have either remained unused or been flouted with impunity, often by the law and order machinery itself. In fact, where a woman victim of violence goes to a police station, she comes face to face with a police force that is corrupt and inefficient, and that basically has an anti-woman attitude. If the woman is poor, the police are very likely to throw her out on the street or mistreat her themselves. (Singh 1994, pages 389–390)

From Pakistan, the Report of the Commission of Inquiry for Women (1997)[2] also refers to government's hesitation to enforce laws to protect women against violence based on gender. The Commission, in making its remarks, takes into account that there have been three such commissions before that have made recommendations, but

> in practical terms, little was achieved.[3] The governments concerned often lacked the will, vision or self-confidence, or all of these, to accept most of these reforms. Even the few that were accepted suffered in the implementation because the drive and seriousness were quickly spent in the face of the habits of centuries, the iron-hold of the system, and the opposition of the orthodoxy. Also, although most people recognized how abominable the status quo was, few felt the compulsion and the urgency to organize the effort needed to break it. Women did not have a strong enough lobby, nor were they sufficiently organized themselves to make an issue of their rights. They were in fact inured to their status of subordination, their legacy of generations. (page ii)

The Hudood Ordinance has been of particular concern to legal experts in Pakistan. For example, a member of the Human Rights Commission of Pakistan[4] made this comment:

Hudood Ordinance on *zina* [extramarital sex, adultery] has been questioned since its promulgation. Its capacity to punish a man and a woman involved in illicit relations is another issue, but its inability to win justice for a woman dishonoured — a woman raped — and rather implicate her into the offence of *zina* is disgusting. Without going into the details, just look at its simple implication. If a woman accuses someone of rape and is unable to prove so, she is booked for *zina*! All legal experts in the country have expressed their dismay over this law. Most of the women in jail today are there because of this *zina* ordinance.

Discriminatory laws of various types, not only dealing with blatant violence, may also be found in most countries of South Asia. Unless the State is actively trying to change these laws, obviously, women will be less likely to expect justice from the legal system. Yubaraj Sangroula, a lawyer and NGO leader in Nepal, gives an example about the situation in his country:

It is a pity that there are more than 25 discriminating laws still incorporated in the National Civil Code, the *Muluki Ain*. . . . Nine parliamentary sessions have been completed yet none of the parliamentarians has brought the motion to repeal the discriminating laws against women. . . . We are working on that.[5]

Are Legal Norms Applied to Women and Girls in the Family?

As for this second point, the Commission of Inquiry for Women in Pakistan (1997, page ii) notes: "Why is it that in family disputes, the concerned girl or woman almost always finds herself unable to get a fair deal from the prevailing system?"

And Bangladeshi lawyer Sara Hossain (1994) remarks:

Every state in South Asia is bound to the norm of equality and non-discrimination between men and women as defined by international human rights instruments. The norm of equality is also reflected in domestic law, in entrenched and justifiable provisions of national constitutions. In its domestic application, however, the norm is severely impaired by unjustifiable deviations in the sphere of women's rights within the family. (page 465)

The absence of a law against domestic violence itself seems to reflect State reluctance to recognize the extent of the problem and to take adequate measures against it. There are, of course, some sections of the penal code in each country that can be used, but they were not framed with the domestic sphere in view. Remarks by a Nepali human rights activist and a Bangladeshi plastic surgeon about the need for a law on domestic violence illustrate the difficulties for women that follow from the lack of such a law:

Domestic violence against women is not being considered a crime, but it is a crime. If you beat someone or kick someone or torture someone, you will definitely be brought to justice. But when a husband beats his wife, kicks or batters her, or intimidates her, it is considered a family matter. . . . No impunity [should be allowed]. . . . It [domestic violence] should be the concern of the whole community and the local administration, . . . and I say it is a crime against humanity.   — *Nepali human rights activist*[6]

According to my opinion, there should be specific laws regarding violence against women, and the trial should be impartial. If the victims were to get justice and the culprits punished, then this could help reduce the incidence of [violence against women].

                                                                    — *Bangladeshi plastic surgeon*[7]

Just as special efforts to protect women's human rights proved useful in international law, so they would at the national level to protect women's human rights in family matters. Women who are beaten and battered within the family do not usually report it. A paper prepared for the International Year of the Family Secretariat observes that "Even where laws protect women and children from abuse in families, evidence suggests that only about one in 10 cases is ever reported and few of those result in the punishment of the offender" (Weinhold and Weinhold, in UN 1996a, page 173). In South Asia, given the patriarchal culture that predominates, it is likely that the proportion of cases reported is even less. Recall, for example, that in the study done in Pakistan of battered women outpatients, only 1 in 51 went to the police (Bhatti et al. n.d.).

Emphasis on Custom and Tradition

This third point refers to custom and acts in the name of religion that may be evoked to justify violence against women by family members. Legal norms are often ignored. A well-known case that shows the conflicts in the name of tradition or religion with legal norms is that of Roop Kumar, an 18-year-old whose brother agreed, apparently under pressure, to her being burned to death on her husband's funeral pyre in 1987, despite the existence of laws prohibiting the practice of *sati*.[8] The UN Special Rapporteur on violence against women observes:

> What is the point of all these laws if the people do not believe that putting an 18-year-old woman on a funeral pyre and denying her life is not a violation of the most basic fundamental right — the right to life? What is the point of all the Constitutional protection if "ethnic identity" is an acceptable justification for reducing the status of women according to diverse cultural practice? (Coomaraswamy 1994a, page 50)

A 1999 case in Pakistan shows the extent to which custom can be sanctified by the State under the law, even though doing so condones murder of women and girls by their relatives. According to early accounts circulated through women's networks from Sisterhood Is Global Institute, Saima Sarwar was murdered on 6 April 1999 "by a hit man hired by her family" when she was in the law offices of the AGHS Legal Aid Cell in Lahore, Pakistan. Attorneys Hina Jilani and Asma Jahangir were assisting Sarwar in a divorce case she initiated because of domestic violence (*http://www.sigi.org/Alert/pak0499.htm*, 15 April 1999). The gunman also fired at Hina Jilani. According to the Sisterhood Is Global Institute, "The fact that no arrests have been made in this case illustrates the willingness of the Pakistani Government authorities to grant impunity for the crime of honour killing."[9] (Also see Stewart 1999 on this case and the reaction among human rights activists.)

Less than four months passed before the introduction of a resolution in Parliament to condemn such killings. It was suppressed, on the grounds of "custom." As a result, some critics have stepped forward to say the State — then under the leadership of Nawaz Sharif — was surely compromised in the matter (see, for example, Stewart 1999).

There could easily be many quotes from the region about gender bias in the application of the law and in the claims in the name of custom or religion that reinforce it. The subject is taken up in more detail later in the chapter. The main point is constant: Simply making or changing laws about violence against women is not enough.

So long as negative attitudes against women remain unchecked or are cornerstones of some political arrangements or policies, the legal system will not work in favour of most women and girls who are violated.

Women in South Asia know all too well, as comments throughout this chapter show, that agents of the State themselves often obstruct women's legal rights. In addition, there are bodies that make judgements in the name of religion, which all too frequently take women's lives without due process. For example, Sigma Huda, an eminent lawyer from Bangladesh, shares an example from her country:

> In the villages of Bangladesh the "Fotwa"[10] relating to the punishment of women is given and carried out at times by the local leaders and the "peer" moulana or Imam of the mosque working together. The press media has been giving considerable coverage of "Fotwa" as a mode of committing violence on women. Just one case study is sufficient to illustrate: Married [refers to her marital status] Nurjahan of a Faridpur village developed love relationships with one Farid of neighbouring village and they both left their homes and they were untraceable. Nurjahan's husband filed a case following which Nurjahan was found out and brought back to the village. The influential parents and uncles of Farid kept Nurjahan confined for 12 days. The verdict of the shalish was to spill "Kerosin" oil upon Nurjahan's body and burn her alive. The verdict was carried out at dead of night. (Huda n.d. a, page 1; see also Alam and Ahmed n.d. for a discussion of such cases)

Although in the case of Nurjahan, the State did act against those who killed her, it took a major effort by Sigma Huda to help bring about that justice. One gets the impression that all too often groups like that which condemned Nurjahan act with impunity. The State turns a blind eye to the problem.

Siddiqi (1998, page 215) describes the growing "culture of the fatwa" in Bangladesh as a probable reaction to the growth of NGO activities, many for women's empowerment and equality, often in rural areas. Sizeable funds for development so channelled are said to make NGOs a force that can disrupt or consolidate local patronage systems. In response, funds "to strengthen Islamic values" are also forthcoming. Accordingly, NGOs, particularly those with foreign ties, sometimes become targets of both rhetoric and action. For example:

> On several occasions, horrifying forms of punishment — including stoning, caning, and burning at the stake — were sanctioned or condoned by men claiming to represent Islam and tradition. . . .
>
> Particularly in more remote regions, the groundwork has been laid for the dispensation of justice through newly reconfigured networks of power. Thus, for instance, the *shalish*[11] has taken on a new life as arbitrator of Islamic morality and justice. (Siddiqi 1998, page 217)

Siddiqi sees the *shalish* as a means through which local religious leaders are not only "reformulating their legitimacy" but also "supplanting judicial authority." The focus on control of women's sexuality, honour and behaviour is said to be a constant (see also Weiss 1998).

Studies of fatwas and their content, such as that done by Shourie (1995) about India, can provide a more complete picture about the role of local religious courts and judgements regarding women's lives.

Conflicts between Different Legal Systems within the Same Country

Among the different systems of law in South Asia are personal laws, which are applied to the so-called private sphere and vary according to the religion of individuals. For example, the substance of personal laws with regard to divorce depends on the religion of the individual seeking it. Christian personal law in India forbids divorce, but Hindu personal law permits it. The right to sue for divorce may also vary for men and women, as may the difficulty of obtaining a divorce; for instance, under Muslim personal law in India and Pakistan, a man is entitled to divorce his wife simply by pronouncing "*talaq*," whereas a woman's right to initiate proceedings is usually not recognized in fact, even where it is recognized in law (Commission of Inquiry for Women 1997).

Hossain (1994, page 465) describes the complex world of personal laws in South Asia and how these laws conflict with the norm of equality reflected in domestic law based on national constitutions. She notes:

> Rights within the family are determined by personal laws, based on religious traditions, customs and practices. These personal laws sanction discrimination between men and women and between members of different religious communities. . . . They violate fundamental rights to equality and are inconsistent with the secular basis of most national constitutions in South Asia. . . . [T]he state's accommodation of orthodoxies whose agenda involves the control of women's autonomy, and in particular women's subjugation within the family, has resulted in its continued resistance to challenging personal laws. Thus blatant and pervasive inequalities have been entrenched in the arena in which most women's lives are spent. (pages 465–466)

Questions are also asked about the "fit" of personal law with constitutional law. For example, in the case of Muslim personal law in Bangladesh, Meindersma (1998, page 30) observes that "Lawyers have wondered whether this law overrides the equal rights clause of the Constitution and whether this law would be deemed void to the extent of inconsistency with the fundamental rights under the Constitution."

On this point, Radhika Coomaraswamy, the UN Special Rapporteur on violence against women, elaborates:

> The dilemma extends to issues such as . . . Shariah-type[12] punishment. Many states fail to end such practices because they do not want to antagonize their minorities. This is particularly true in the multi-ethnic states of Asia where a pattern of "live and let live" has come to guide communal action. As a result, the applicable personal law differs for women depending on the [religious] community to which they belong. Marriage, divorce, custody of children, inheritance, maintenance and so on are decided by that community, not by the national status. Many of these laws violate basic tenets of the Women's Convention [CEDAW]. (In Meindersma 1998, page 31)

Article 15 of CEDAW includes the following:

> 1. States Parties shall accord to women equality with men before the law.

> 2. States Parties shall accord to women, in civil matters, a legal capacity identical to that of men and the same opportunities to exercise that capacity. In particular, they shall give women equal rights to conclude contracts and to administer property and shall treat them equally in all stages of procedure in courts and tribunals.

In fact, CEDAW Article 16 commits States Parties to:

> take all appropriate measures to eliminate discrimination against women in all matters
> relating to marriage and family relations and in particular shall ensure, on a basis of
> equality of men and women [rights at all stages of marriage and in all matters]. (See
> Appendix for complete text.)

In a bold and telling statement, Kirti Singh (1994, page 393) sums up the implications she sees for Indian women from the conflict between the Constitution, which recognizes equal rights of men and women, and any laws — such as personal laws based on religion — which limit rights of women:

> The state is bound by the provisions of the Constitution to which it owes its existence, but
> by consistently listening to the most orthodox and obscurantist sections of the Indian
> population, namely, the religious leaders and their allies who are interested in preserving
> patriarchy, the state is perpetuating a fraud on the women of India.

And on girls. In addition to the ways in which the above examples may affect them, there is the problem of child marriage. Most countries have laws defining this as an offence for boys and girls of certain ages. However, under customary law or due to interpretations in light of religion, no age limit may be applied. For countries that are States Parties to CRC or CEDAW (as all in South Asia are), this is in conflict with their obligations under international law, as well as national law.

CEDAW Article 16.2 is clear:

> 2. The betrothal and the marriage of a child shall have no legal effect and all necessary
> action, including legislation, shall be taken to specify a minimum age for marriage and to
> make the registration of marriages in an official registry compulsory.

In fact, Article 16 commits States Parties to "take all appropriate measures to eliminate discrimination against women in all matters relating to marriage and family relations. . . ."

Risks to Women Who Seek Legal Remedy to Gender Violence

Humiliation, beating, desertion or divorce; loss of her children or responsibility for their care but without financial assistance from the father, the natal family or the State; nowhere to go and no employment opportunity; shame and poverty; rape[13] and outright death: these are some of the risks for a woman who seeks legal remedy to gender violence against her. We will never know how many "dowry deaths" or deaths from "stove-burnings" hide stories about women who might otherwise have gone to the police, or should have had the right to do so in anticipation of justice under the law.

Even very well-educated and prominent women may be threatened when they try to use the law. Consider the following. A Nepali woman's case for her property rights under *Muluki Ain* went to the Supreme Court.[14] As the law requires for a woman to inherit from her father, she is over 35 and unmarried. She is also a well-known lawyer who has been active in government. After her father died, she did not receive any inheritance so she took her claim to court. She says her brother threatened, in front of a judge, to have her killed if she did not drop the case. She wondered what chance other women have for inheritance, if even she, a prominent lawyer who fits the criteria of the restrictive law, could not manage to claim her rights through the legal system. Similarly, a woman may fear retribution if she brings a complaint against an abusive husband.

· The case of Saima Sarwar, discussed earlier in this chapter, speaks for itself about risks to those who seek legal remedy to gender-based violence in the family. Also, some risks for women who would seek justice are actually built into the law, as in the Hudood Ordinances, as already described.

More Attention Needed to Legal Implementation

Given problems and issues like those above, Rekha Pappu of India calls for attention right from the start to questions of legal implementation, not only the conceptualization of laws. She makes it clear that more analysis needs to accompany activism regarding women's use of the legal system:

> The experience of the women's movement has amply demonstrated that the premise "let's at least have the laws first and then fight for or urge its implementation" is a very chancy one. My point is not that we should now totally refuse engagement within the state or the legal system but that we need to develop a better and more critical understanding of the nature of the state and the legal system as also the mode of engagement we seek with them before we take it upon ourselves to draft laws. (Pappu 1997, page 52)

The Legal Framework

Pappu's comment directs our attention to the nature of the legal system and the State's enforcement of it, or not, with regard to offences against women. Of course, where the normal functioning of the State is disrupted by military priorities — as in Afghanistan — the situation for women can become particularly difficult, and legal remedies virtually impossible concerning gender violence and restoration of human rights. A report from Physicians for Human Rights (1998) describes the situation like this:

> Today, under the Taliban, there is no Constitution, rule of law, or independent judiciary in Afghanistan. In the absence of an independent judiciary, many municipal and provincial authorities use the Taliban's interpretation of *Shari'a* and traditional tribal codes of justice. The Taliban reportedly have Islamic courts in areas under their control to judge criminal cases and resolve disputes. . . . Decisions of the court are reportedly final.
>
> . . . Due process is absent; the Taliban's *Shari'a* courts operate arbitrarily, and authority is maintained through tyranny and terror.
>
> . . . But the aspect of Taliban rule that most deeply affects the life of women is the Taliban's idiosyncratic interpretation of the holy *Qur'an* with regard to the role of women. Their interpretation of *Shari'a* forbids women to work outside the home, attend school, or leave their homes unless accompanied by a husband, father, brother or son. (pages 27, 31, 32)

The legal framework, as described by Meindersma (1998) for countries under more normal circumstances, includes international, regional and national legal instruments. Her report covers the various routes and legal remedies potentially available at the national level for the use of substantive law:[15]

- Criminal law, which can lead to the conviction of the person charged and resultant imprisonment or fine;

- Civil law, through which the victim sues the perpetrator, with compensation as the aim;
- Constitutional remedies, which are sought in public interest or individual cases and are filed before the Supreme Court when fundamental rights in a constitution are violated;
- Alternative forms of dispute settlement, which are aimed at reaching a compromise rather than imposing criminal sanctions;
- Various national commissions, depending on their mandate and power, may also investigate cases;
- International human rights instruments, which can be used to provide standards for legal judgements within a country that is a party to them.

Some quotations from interviewees, governments, researchers and activists help portray the possibilities for a woman to seek legal remedies.[16] How do women perceive the appropriateness of using one or the other? It is particularly important to ask this about cases of physical domestic violence, since so many go unreported.

Criminal Remedies

Women victim-survivors of violence at home apparently hesitate to bring criminal cases against a husband or other male relative. Anecdotal reports, such as this one from Chuda Bahadur Shrestha, a police superintendent in Nepal, reveal that sometimes women would like police only to threaten or chastise a perpetrator rather than to arrest him:

> [A] woman came to my office one day. I guess she'd heard that I was a sympathetic sort of policeman. She wanted to show me the bruises her husband had inflicted on her face. But she also told me that she didn't want a case against her husband, just wanted him "ticked off" [given a warning].[17]

Since police usually see their role as dealing with criminal offences, complainant and police are likely at cross-purposes unless charges are made in domestic violence cases under criminal law, for offences like assault or battery. Indian lawyer Colin Gonsalves[18] observes that this is feasible, but that there are also limitations:

> The normal laws apply. There's no doubt about that. If a man beats a woman, it's assault and so on. Except that you need more specific laws for domestic violence [defined broadly] because you [a man] may not actually beat your [his] wife, you [a man] may prevent her from leaving the house. So you need special laws for domestic violence. But in terms of assault and hurt and battery, the normal laws apply. But they're not used. That's different. The police don't intervene and women themselves don't want to enforce those [criminal] laws.[19]

A 1999 Human Rights Watch study uncovered the extent to which physical domestic violence can be neglected under existing laws:

> We found that despite the staggering levels of intrafamily violence against women, it is widely perceived by the law enforcement system and society at large as a private family matter, not subject to government intervention let alone criminal sanction. At present there is virtually no prosecution of crimes of assault and battery when perpetrated by male family members against women; even intrafamily murder and attempted murder are rarely prosecuted. (page 31)

Even cases where women die under suspicious circumstances, likely perpetrators can escape legal consequences. For example, "of 215 cases of women being suspiciously burned to death in their Lahore homes in 1997, in only six cases were suspects even taken into custody" (Human Rights Watch 1999, page 1).

Civil Remedies

With regard to civil remedies, women may not want compensation for a beating from a husband any more than they want to seek his conviction under criminal law. Consequently, even where a woman has a right to claim compensation from her spouse for an assault, she is apparently not likely to do so. In Sri Lanka, for example, Gomez and Gomez (1997) could not find any instance where a victim of such violence had sought compensation from a spouse in a civil case. More analysis of the reasons why would be useful for purposes of possible legal reform and education.

Constitutional Remedies

Seeking a constitutional remedy usually involves a very sophisticated procedure, which the average rural or slum woman would not likely entertain. A class action suit, organized by a women's group with legal advice, has been tried in Nepal, however (see Malla and Sangroula 1998). A group of women lawyers there brought a public interest case regarding discriminatory laws considered at variance with the Constitution. No ruling had yet been made at the time of this writing.

In India, as described by Jethmalani (1995), public interest litigation has been successfully used in a number of cases, and can be initiated even by a letter or postcard to the court (pages 127–128). Services to the court are without charge — although the number of volunteer lawyers is "woefully inadequate" (page 137). Cases of particular relevance to violence against women and girls have dealt with conditions in protective homes; prisoners — including women and children — held too long without a trial; the sale of orphaned children; investigation of dowry harassment, among others. As Jethmalani observes,

> Public Interest Litigation [PIL] has enlarged the frontiers of criminal jurisprudence to give justice to victims. The emphasis on legal aid for the accused had eclipsed the rights of those who needed it the most, i.e. vulnerable and disempowered victims. This has been redressed through PIL. (page 135)

PIL has also been used to challenge the legitimacy of some personal laws in conflict with the constitutional guarantee of equality before the law to both men and women, and to question a government declaration limiting applicability of CEDAW (see Jethmalani 1995; also see Box 8 regarding laws against domestic violence).

Alternative Mechanisms through Which to Seek Remedies

Using alternate mechanisms would seem attractive in principle, if they would lead to compromise and change. Various bodies may be empowered to hear cases of domestic violence. These include family courts, national women's commissions or human rights commissions in cooperation with the State, mediation boards and so on. Also, as has been mentioned, local groups representing self-styled religious positions often initiate action in cases against women and make severe judgements reflecting patriarchal norms that emphasize male superiority and female inferiority. These may or may not be endorsed or condoned by the State.

Family and local secular courts. Family and local secular courts are another option. Opinions about their utility to date in South Asia range from "a disaster" to "effective."[20] Sonal Sonam takes this view:

> Family courts were welcomed by people mainly as more sensitive and less time-consuming mechanisms. However, the family courts work on reconciliation as their first goal, hence offering an assessment of marriage and family condition by court-appointed counsellors. This approach ignores the fact that women usually seek judicial support only when they can no longer bear to live in their marital homes, and the court has a very similar approach to the society which sees preservation of the family as the main and perhaps the only important goal, mostly at the expense of the women. (personal communication, 11 September 1998)

A disproportionate number of cases of various kinds, including marital disputes, are handled by family and other local courts or mechanisms for conciliation or mediation. Professor Vina Mazumdar of the Centre for Women's Development Studies in New Delhi, perhaps the most senior and distinguished of all scholars on the women's movement in South Asia, recalled at a regional meeting on ending violence that the first *Lok Adalat* (conciliation or mediation tribunal), set up in Gujarat to reduce the load on the main courts, had handled some 18,000 cases about marital disputes, by far the majority of the total 20,000 some cases brought to it over a five-year period.

Family courts often handle requests for divorce (Meindersma 1998), which may follow incidents of domestic violence.[21] Divorce, however, is not, in general, regarded socially as a viable alternative to marriage or mechanisms for conciliation or mediation. Furthermore, where marriage has not been registered, divorce may not be a legal remedy. More research about the roles, problems and successes of family courts seems to be needed, along with suggestions for improvements.

Laws concerning maintenance, custody and guardianship as well as divorce are particularly important for activists to understand and try to improve. Their enforcement also needs a just hand so that women victim-survivors of violence, and their children, have more viable alternatives than life in dangerous homes.

National women's or human rights commissions. National women's or human rights commissions may also be authorized to investigate in cases of domestic violence. Such commissions actively intervene in some cases of violence against women:

> For instance, in a case [in India] of a child rape by a medical practitioner of an 8 year old, where the culprit had been sentenced to eight years but not yet been arrested, the NCW [National Commission of Women], through the State government ensured the arrest of the person. Often through direct intervention and on-the-spot investigation, the NCW has obtained disciplinary action and ensured the prompt launching of criminal proceedings against perpetrators — police, teachers, university staff, employers, custodial officers, etc . . . and obtained measures of protection for the victim, ranging from physical rescue to placement in a shelter. (Meindersma 1998, pages 103–105)

The NCW in India has also set up *Mahila Adalats* (women's courts). "Why were they considered necessary? How are they functioning? What is necessary to make them more effective?" Mazumdar has asked.[22]

Box 8	Using Laws against Domestic Violence: Some Examples*

Bangladesh:
- Domestic violence is not recognized as a separate offence under the law; however, there are a number of laws which can be used for remedy.
- Under the Penal Code, laws pertaining to murder, voluntarily causing hurt or grievous hurt, and assault can be used to address various aspects of domestic violence.
- Under Section 326 of the Bangladesh Penal Code "causing grievous hurt by means of any instrument" is an offence (Meindersma 1998, page 87).
- In response to societal prevalence, the offence of acid-throwing was added to the Penal Code. It is defined as "causing grievous hurt or death to a child or woman, by erosure, poisoning or corrosive substance" (Section 326A, Penal Code).
- Within the context of divorce law, "cruelty" has been recognized as more than physical acts and can include allegations of the wife being unchaste. However, there is no offence of cruelty under the Penal Code (Meindersma 1998, page 87).
- Incest is not recognized as a separate criminal offence (Meindersma 1998, page 43).

India:
- Domestic violence is not recognized as a separate offence under the law; however, there are a number of laws that can be used for remedy.
- Provisions in the Indian Penal Code that can be used to address domestic violence include murder, voluntarily causing hurt or grievous hurt, assault and cruelty.

Although as yet there is no law specifically dealing with domestic violence per se, the law against cruelty addresses acts committed by husbands or relatives (Section 498A of the Indian Penal Code).

- Cruelty is defined as "any wilful conduct which may drive the woman to commit suicide or to cause grave injury or danger to life, limb and health, whether mental or physical, and harassment of a woman with a view to coercing her to meet any unlawful demand for property" (Meindersma 1998, page 90).

- In 1994, the National Commission of Women introduced a bill proposing legislation against domestic violence to the Indian government. The proposed definition of domestic violence is very broad and in addition to cruelty it adds the following to the definition of domestic violence:
  1) harassment which causes distress to a woman,
  2) any act which compels the woman to have sexual intercourse against her will either with the husband or any of his relatives or with any other person,
  3) any act which is unbecoming of the dignity of the woman, and
  4) any other act or omission or commission which is likely to cause mental torture or mental agony to the woman (Singh 1997, page 91).

- Incest is not recognized as a separate criminal offence but cases are dealt with under the criminal provisions for rape or the provision against outraging the modesty of a woman (Section 498A Indian Penal Code).

Nepal:
- Domestic violence is not recognized as a separate offence under the law; however, there are a number of laws which can be used for remedy.
- Possible related laws include attempted murder, assault and rape.
- Although no specific offence against incest is recognized, sexual intercourse with close relatives within seven degrees is considered an offence under the *Muluki Ain* (Law of the Land).

Box 8: *continued*

- Unlike murder and attempted murder cases, assault is considered a non-state or private offence and falls under the National Civil Code as opposed to the State Case Act. As a result, there is no prosecution by the State and victims must pursue a remedy in civil court. In situations of domestic violence where assault is alleged, investigations are apparently not taken seriously: "police usually say it's a domestic conflict" (Forum for Women, Law and Development 1999, page 41).
- A draft bill has been proposed to amend provisions in the *Muluki Ain* pertaining to domestic violence, property rights of women, divorce and abortion (Sangroula and Malla 1998).

Pakistan:
- Domestic violence is not recognized as a separate offence under the law; however, there are a number of laws that can be used for remedy.
- Under the Pakistan Penal Code one could bring cases with regard to "offences affecting the human body" (Chapter XVI, Pakistan Penal Code).
- However, the Criminal Law Amendment Act (1997) "shifts the emphasis from hurt and murder as wrongs against society, to a matter to be resolved between private individuals" (Meindersma 1998, page 83).
- Any person accused of murder or hurt as enumerated in the Pakistan Criminal Code (Sections 332-337) may be liable to pay the victim monetary compensation and serve a prison sentence (Jilani and Ahmed 1998, page 16).
- Because of the high incidents of death or injury from stove-burnings, the Lahore High Court has issued guidelines regarding medical and investigative procedures to be followed in such cases. Unfortunately, they tend to be ignored (Jilani and Ahmed 1998, page 5, and Commission of Inquiry for Women, Pakistan 1997).

Sri Lanka:
- Domestic violence is not recognized as a separate offence under the law; however, there are a number of laws that can be used for remedy.
- Under the Penal Code, provisions on rape, hurt, grievous hurt, assault, criminal force, attempted murder and murder could be used to address acts of domestic violence (Gomez and Gomez 1998).
- The Sri Lankan Penal Code Amendment Act recognizes the offences of gross indecency and grave sexual abuse. Any act not amounting to rape that involves the "use of the genitals or any other part of the body or the use of an instrument on another's body or orifice for sexual pleasure" constitutes grave sexual abuse (Gomez and Gomez 1998, page 7). Acts of gross indecency refer to public or private acts but no further specifications are provided (Meindersma 1998, page 47).
- Recent legislation has made sexual harassment an offence (Section 345 of the Penal Code). It is defined as the "assault or use of criminal force to sexually harass another person which causes annoyance to the victim." Both words and acts can constitute harassment (Gomez and Gomez 1998, page 9).
- In a 1995 amendment to the Penal Code, incest was made an offence and prohibits sexual intercourse between persons who belong to "prohibited categories of relationships" (Gomez and Gomez 1998, page 7).

* These are limited to some forms of physical and sexual violence. There are additional laws particularly with regard to dowry death and traditional practices. Lillian Messih, a lawyer and 1999 UNICEF intern working with the author, drafted the content for this box (1999).

Police as mediators. Gomez and Gomez (1998, page 36) describe the pressure on police to help in different ways in cases of family violence in Sri Lanka. They also suggest a new role for police, to refer cases for mediation:

> At a recent seminar members of the police complained that they are being forced to play the role of family counsellors. In this situation it would be possible for the police to refer the matter to the mediation board in the area. Mediation could play an important role in the area of domestic violence where the victim does not wish to remove herself from the particular domestic context which has caused the violence.

Use of International Instruments

The use of CEDAW and CRC as international treaties with which national and state or provincial law should be in harmony has already started. In India, for example, guidelines against sexual harassment have been handed down by the Supreme Court, which has drawn on CEDAW and especially Recommendation 19, in its judgement regarding the Vishaka case (Singh 1998; Sonal Sonam, personal communication, 11 September 1998, regarding use of Recommendation 19).

In Sri Lanka, proposals are even being made for constitutional reform in line with the non-discrimination principle in CEDAW (and CRC) (Sri Lanka Women's NGO Forum 1999). Savitri Goonesekere, Professor of Law and Vice-Chancellor of Colombo University in Sri Lanka — and a member of CEDAW Committee — has pointed out that

> violence, particularly domestic violence, was never focused on in great depth till CEDAW was ratified. Though many NGOs had raised their voice, nothing much happened till the historical ratification of CEDAW and consequently violence became an issue in both the national and international arena. (UNICEF 1998b, page 19)

In CRC and CEDAW, Professor Goonesekere sees a "framework for building policy responses within the state and for holding the state accountable for violations" (page 20). (She has also emphasized that given the pattern of early marriage, many "women" in terms of the South Asian context are covered by CRC due to the issue of adolescent marriages [UNICEF 1998b].)

Professor Goonesekere calls for more women's groups and NGOs to be involved in the implementation of both conventions and explains that they must begin to engage with the State accordingly, "however reluctant they may be to do so" (UNICEF 1998b, page 19).[23]

Professor Goonesekere points out:

> These standards [in CEDAW or CRC articles] are monitored every two years, not by government to government, but by a government being accountable to the people. Through the process of the alternative report, NGOs and others can make governments accountable for what they have and have not done yet. . . . this is a vital process. (page 20)

Its effectiveness will be influenced by the knowledge that women's groups have about the nature of the State, the legal system and international law.

A backlash? Obviously, there remains the problem of traditional and cultural values at variance with human rights and legal norms as expressed at both national and international levels. More than that, there are politics that appear to exalt custom more than women's lives. Meindersma (1998, page 28) comments that "While international treaties . . . require customs and traditions at variance with human rights standards to be modified, experience in the region reveals a different picture."

She points out that there is a backlash against the universality of human rights. It emphasizes cultural relativism, and does so as part of a political position that casts UN treaties as Western ones imposed on other countries through the UN. Meindersma (page 30) goes on to make an important point about the connection with so-called identity politics with violent practices against women.[24] "Discriminatory and violent practices," she writes, "including those harmful or discriminatory to women, became a vehicle for a post-colonial sentiment that rejects the imposition of [allegedly] Western values." And Coomaraswamy (1995b) confronts this issue, pointing out the difficulty but necessity of reflection and interrogation about "certain traditional belief systems and making them compatible with international human rights" (page 213). She draws attention to a critique of Western colonial ideas from both "conservative element" and "progressive writers alike" — for whom "human rights is the benign face of the colonial encounter" (page 215). In that context, she says, they want to know whether "Special [UN] rapporteurs [like herself] and human rights activists realize that they are instruments of the Enlightenment, a project which they feel led to colonialism" (page 215).

This all undermines the implementation of some laws related to limiting violence against women and girls, constitutional guarantees of equality and the use of international law for support. It definitely undermines the fulfilment of human rights for women and girls.

As for those on the front lines, they may be exposed to considerable risk when they challenge age-old customs and habits, as well as political realities. For example, as mentioned earlier, the Pakistani attorney Hina Jilani was fired upon in her legal office, allegedly by a gunman hired by the family of her client who was seeking a divorce and was thus considered by her family to be insulting family honour. The woman client was shot and killed instantly. Both Hina Jilani and attorney Asma Jahangir, the UN Special Rapporteur on extrajudicial, arbitrary and summary executions, who shares the law office with Jilani, have been threatened, according to Lea Browning (browning@iga.apc.org, e-mail to listserv subscribers, 15 April 1999):

> Members of the Peshawar Chamber of Commerce in Pakistan and a section of religious groups have demanded that Ms. Jahangir be arrested and hanged because, they claim "she takes the small problems of Pakistan to international forums and creates a bad name for Pakistan." They also argue that she is encouraging women and girls to rebel against their families. These groups have warned that if the [G]overnment of Pakistan does not take these actions, they will kill her themselves. They have placed head money for taking her life. A meeting against Ms. Jahangir was held by supporters of Mr. Ghulum Sarwar, the president of the Peshawar Chamber of Commerce and the father of the woman killed in Ms. Jahangir's office on April 6. The police are trying to arrest Mr. Sarwar for his involvement in the murder of his daughter. (See also Hassan 1999)

For the most part, then, women and girl victim-survivors of gender-based violence in the home are left to try this and that in the legal system as best they can, with whatever assistance and solidarity they may recruit from women's groups and supporting organizations or individuals. And almost certainly they may have to face the force of traditions and culture that are being revitalized, in part through a focus on controlling and limiting women's roles in the name of custom. Protection, then, is needed along with encouragement of workers for women's and girls' human rights.

Some Laws Related to Violence against Women and Girls

In South Asia, there are a host of laws according to which various acts of commission or omission regarding violence against women and girls are considered legal offences.[25] The laws concerned may be part of a penal code or in special acts. Various kinds of violence are covered. The following categories can be used to summarize crimes related to the most blatant forms of violence against women and girls:

- sexual offences (including rape, incest, adultery, sexual abuse, unnatural offence, sexual harassment);
- dowry-related violence and death;
- "other forms of domestic violence," such as physical and psychological abuse in the home (Meindersma 1998).

These are in addition to laws against harmful traditional practices and discrimination itself.

Sexual offences. There are problems concerning definitions, evidence and attacks on the victim's character for whomsoever would use related laws. For example, one of the most vexing problems concerning narrow definitions is the definition of rape. The definition of rape does not necessarily include abuses of the vagina or other orifices other than by penile penetration. When the definition of rape is limited to penile penetration without consent, then acts like fingering, insertion and manipulation of objects such as bottles, sticks or screwdrivers in the vagina or other orifices are not considered under the law to constitute rape, no matter how extensive the damage. If ejaculation has occurred and semen is present but outside a vagina that has also suffered trauma by means other than penile penetration, complainants do not find a legal remedy since the definition for the offence of rape is not met.

Kirti Singh notes problems in definitions, with particular regard to the abuse of children:

> The definition of rape and molestation in the Indian Penal Code, does not cover the different kinds of sexual abuse that children are subjected to. For instance, since penis penetration is not [always] possible in the case of very young children [for whom the vagina is not well developed], the abuse may not amount to rape at all under the legal definition. In a case followed up by a women's group in Delhi, even though the small 6-year-old girl had been systematically fingered and made to perform sex [without full penile penetration of the vagina] over a period of time, apart from being witness to sexual orgies by her father, the Delhi High Court held that no rape had taken place. Thus, in spite of the fact that three orifices had been penetrated no rape was established under the law.
>
> In another case, a judge held that no rape had been proved, since there was no injury on the penis of the man. (1998, pages 30–32)

In Pakistan, women who bring cases of rape risk being accused of adultery under *zina* in the Hudood Ordinances. A man lawyer from Pakistan, who is involved in advocacy against rape and assistance to victims, says[26]:

UN bodies should press governments for new legislation, especially for repeal of Hudood Ordinance on *zina,* which is a faulty law. In Zia's time many laws (and taxes as well) were titled in Islamic terminology, and now amending such laws unnecessarily takes on an un-Islamic tinge — which makes such effort more difficult.

Marital rape. India and Sri Lanka are the only countries among those discussed here in which marital rape is recognized as a legal offence — but only in cases where the wife is legally separated from her husband.

Incest. A comment on incest, given the increasing concern about this in the region: For the first time in the region it was made an offence through a 1995 amendment to the Penal Code in Sri Lanka (Gomez and Gomez 1998, page 7). In Pakistan, it is said that the construction of the law is such that charges of incest are not likely to be brought (see Ahmed 1998 and Commission of Inquiry for Women 1997).[27]

Incest could, however, be pursued under other categories in most other countries. In Nepal, it is defined as "sexual intercourse with a person in a certain degree of relationship, including direct descendants, adoptive parent, grandparent relationships, sister-brother and first degree cousin relationships," and it is recognized in the *Muluki Ain*, or Law of the Land (Meindersma 1998, pages 40–41). Meindersma (page 41) also observes:

> In India, cases of incest are adjudicated as rape or molestation. However, in the absence of legal recognition of incest as a separate crime, courts' attitudes may mitigate against acknowledging and properly adjudicating incidents of incest.

One of the most recent laws in the region concerning gender-based violence is a law against sexual harassment. It was made an offence under the Penal Code of Sri Lanka in 1995. Although no case had yet reached the courts when they wrote their report, Gomez and Gomez (1998, page 12) point out that its introduction carries an important social as well as legal message:

> By criminalizing sexual harassment the law is putting outside the pale of socially permissible conduct, types of behaviour that many men, and some women, currently do not consider morally repugnant. The very statement by the law — that such behaviour is unlawful — is a powerful indictment and has the potential to shape and alter future conduct. It may shape conduct, not through prosecutions and through the deterrent aspect of criminal law, but rather by being used effectively in educational and awareness raising programmes.

Afterwards, in 1998, according to newspaper accounts, 46 cases charging sexual harassment were filed. The Sri Lankan Women's NGO Forum *Shadow Report* (1999, page 31) comments: "This low figure is noteworthy in the light of the fact that a 1996 study [by independent trade unions] found that 81.3% of Sri Lankan women are subjected to sexual harassment while using public transport."

Dowry-related violence and death. Meindersma's useful review outlines the series of acts outlawing the practice of dowry in India (The Dowry Prohibition Act, 1961, amended in 1984 and 1986), in Bangladesh (The Dowry Prohibition Act, 1980, amended in 1982) and Pakistan (The Pakistan Dowry and Bridal Gifts [Restriction] Act, 1976). Even with all these laws, results are inconsequential so far as justice or any educational effect of the law are concerned. Meindersma (1998, page 75) observes, "the Dowry Prohibition Act, 1961 [was] amended twice . . . as the first Act proved totally ineffective." Dowry still continues to be expected and paid. In fact, "marginal increase of 10.4% in Dowry Prohibition cases is reported for India in 1997 compared to 1996" (National Crime Records Bureau 1999, page 166). There are also "dowry-related offences" and "dowry death" pertaining to murder of a woman because of unmet dowry demands, in Bangladesh and India, and these are increasing. For example, the 1997 official crime statistics for India show that dowry deaths increased by 8.9 per cent in 1997 over 1996 (page 165). The phenomenon has begun to be found in other countries. It is also spreading to parts of society where it was not previously found, as the commodification of women increases (Mazumdar n.d.).

As will be seen, laws related to the practice of dowry and its abuse fail due, in part, to faulty evidence and procedure. Also, systematic bias, greed bred by consumerism and commodification of women are factors. The problems of evidence are obvious: Bodies are often burned and may then be cremated quickly. Suicide of the woman is often claimed by the defence. There are laws in most countries against abetting suicide. Women's groups would, in general, observe that many more cases than is appropriate are determined to have been suicides rather than murder; nonetheless, charges and convictions under abetting suicide would be relatively few.

Other forms of domestic violence. Since there is no law against domestic violence per se, other laws must be used to address its physical and psychological forms or a new law should be passed.

Most, if not all, physical acts that would likely be covered under a law against domestic violence could presently be reported in the various countries under other legal categories. See Box 1 for some examples of laws appropriate for bringing cases of physical domestic violence under other categories of offence. Laws against grievous hurt and injury are among those alternatives that can be used to bring charges concerning offences of "other forms of domestic violence." In Bangladesh, acid attack — which is done to women both by husbands and unrelated men — is now covered by precisely such a law, the recently introduced offence of "grievous hurt," under Section 326A of the Bangladesh Penal Code.

As for psychological violence, crimes like "Cruelty by Husbands and Relatives" include it under the law in India, for example (see Box 1). However, the extremely low conviction rate — 2.39 per cent in 1997, of some 113,181 recorded cases (National Crime Records Bureau 1999, page 167) — renders the law ineffective in practice for both psychological and physical violence.

Is a Law against Domestic Violence Needed?

As for a possible law against domestic violence, various models are available. The law in Malaysia is often taken as a model (see UNICEF 1994). The UN Special Rapporteur for violence against women includes a model for comprehensive legislation in her 1995 report (UNCHR 1995). Another very similar model has been developed by Women, Law and Development International (Institute for Women, Law and Development 1996, pages 109–125). These last two are based on the experiences of different countries, including Malaysia, as well as the content of various international legal instruments.

The related recommendations are truly comprehensive, addressing both the penal and civil codes, as well as training for police and support services. At the same time, they show how much needs to change if both law and practice are to protect women and girls in the home. If women will not bring cases of assault and battery against their husbands under criminal law, why would they do so for domestic violence as a criminal offence? Has the problem been lack of knowledge of the law, fear of the husband's reprisal, low expectations for police response, no alternative support, desire to keep the children, or a combination? Only comprehensive legislation about domestic violence, like that which the Special Rapporteur recommends, can change the legal system so that women come forward with their complaints and have some reasonable likelihood of a remedy.

Although no country in South Asia has a law explicitly against domestic violence, a bill to introduce such a law was proposed in 1994 by the National Commission for Women of India and is under review with the states (Singh 1998, pages 90–91). Kirti Singh (1998) indicates that the proposed bill defines domestic violence very broadly:

> In addition to the offence of cruelty[28] enumerated under section 498A of the Indian Penal Code, 1860, the Bill defines domestic violence as: 1) harassment which causes distress to a woman, 2) any act which compels the woman to have sexual intercourse against her will either with the husband or any of his relatives or with any other person, 3) any act which is unbecoming of the dignity of the woman or, 4) any other act or omission or commission which is likely to cause mental torture or mental agony to the woman. (pages 90–91)

In Nepal, a draft of such a law is also under way, and its legislation has been encouraged by the CEDAW Committee. Whether or not the introduction of a law against domestic violence itself would prove educational and effective remains to be seen.

Chuda Bahadur Shrestha, the police superintendent working in rural Nepal,[29] makes this telling argument for the law against domestic violence: "A few cases are reported, but not as many as are prevalent. Unlike in England, where women are encouraged to report cases or to seek help, it's not the case here [yet]." Just as the law in Sri Lanka against sexual harassment sends a message that such harassment is not socially permissible, a law against domestic violence would indicate social unacceptability for a behaviour that is infrequently questioned as wrong.

He feels that having a law against domestic violence would both encourage women to report and strengthen the police role in concerned cases:

> [A] law on domestic violence, I feel, would help. Then police, with the support of local leaders like village development committee chairmen, local women development officers, government prosecutors, would be able to act on complaints. Victims need to be encouraged to talk, they need to be aware of their rights.

The case for a separate law on domestic violence is forcefully made by the Sri Lankan NGO Women's Forum (1999) in its *Shadow Report on CEDAW*. It reviews cases of assault on women in their homes and the finding that the majority were pregnant at the time. Although most sought medical care, only one fourth of these indicated how they were hurt. "This reflects the deep sense of social shame that these victims feel, resulting in wife battering being one of our most well kept national secrets. Separate legislation dealing with domestic violence is therefore long overdue" (page 32.)

Comprehensive legislation against domestic violence could signal an important shift in attitudes on the part of the State, indicating that the State fully endorses women's right to be free from abuse at home. It could encourage women to seek legal remedies and alert men, particularly those in law enforcement and medicine, that they should give serious consideration to women's complaints of domestic violence. But problems in the use of the legal system, like those below, are likely to remain for some time.

Some Obstacles to Effective Legal Remedy in Cases of Violence against Women

Under what conditions will women in South Asia use the law or laws that are pertinent? And with what hope of success? Under what conditions will they not? Those are the diagnostic questions that can show where improvements are most needed in the legal system for it to bring remedy to women victim-survivors of various kinds of gender-based violence. The point here is that having a specific law is not enough. It is important to ask, what changes in the legal system, and what new approaches to monitoring it, are needed for women victim-survivors of violence to be able to use the law with a reasonable hope of success when their cases are legitimate? A lot needs to be improved.

Again, the reader is invited to try to look at the legal system from the point of view of a woman or girl in South Asia who might want to use it for remedy to violence against her. One can visualize the system as a kind of game board with possible obstacles and advantages along the way. What is the risk of losing, the chance of winning? A woman victim-survivor will consider a variety of likely outcomes in addition to the legal judgement: in terms of costs to her reputation, family and future, as well as in terms of the time and money of legal procedures involved. Looking only at laws is not enough. The sociology of the legal system and the potential woman user's view of it are needed to find where changes in the legal system must follow for there to be gender justice.

According to both activists and legal experts in South Asia, for women who try to use the law, there are many, many obstacles. Even illiterate women very likely will be sufficiently aware of these to be deterred from bringing cases. The main problems to be covered below are those that a woman experiences first-hand from the moment she goes to the police onwards. They include:

- problems concerning the nature of the law;
- problems about police attitudes and failures in duty;
- procedural problems;
- problems concerning medical evidence;
- problems of judicial gender bias;
- problems for victim-survivors regarding the lack of support services.[30]

Most of the examples below happen to deal with rape and incest. They were culled from interviews to illustrate points about the legal process rather than the substance of cases. As it turns out, hardly any deal with domestic violence. This no doubt reflects the reality — as remarked on earlier — that few cases of physical domestic violence are pursued under the penal code and reach the courts: "Most of the cases of domestic violence go unnoticed, unreported, or even if reported, unregistered" (Meindersma 1998, page 8). It should not be a surprise that we do not find many examples here, but it is disappointing.

Problems Concerning the Nature of the Law

A woman victim-survivor of gender-based violence may find that under the law she is not considered to have a case. That is what happens regarding many incidents of domestic violence if a woman does not want to bring criminal charges. Even when criminal law applies, as in cases of rape and incest, problems of legal definitions can severely limit a woman's likelihood of obtaining justice. Many have already been discussed and are not reviewed here. In any case, most rural women or poor urban women would be more concerned about how they will be treated by the police, in the courts and afterwards, than they would be with the substantive nature of the law.

Corroboration. An important exception is the requirement for evidence to corroborate a woman victim-survivor's story varies in the countries of South Asia. In the case of rape, for instance, the most extreme demand is in Pakistan. It is improbable that women victims of rape can satisfy the rule of evidence under the Hudood Ordinances, introduced by General Zia in 1979.[41] Four Muslim men in good standing are required as witnesses to penetration; otherwise, the complainant is likely to be charged with adultery (*zina*). The introduction of the Hudood Ordinances illustrates that, in the name of religion, both laws and rules for evidence may be changed for political reasons (see, for example, Ahmed 1998 and Mumtaz and Shaheed 1987). The legal system then becomes a minefield for women survivors of violence.[42]

With regard to India, the UN Special Rapporteur on violence against women, its causes and consequences, writes:

> Although the judiciary in India has recognized that the special circumstances of rape
> generally do not lend themselves to the presence of eyewitnesses, judges, especially in
> cases where the victim is not a virgin or is unmarried, continue to require circumstantial
> evidence, such as physical injuries, torn clothing or the presence of semen to corroborate
> the victim's story. The increasing presence of women advocates is resulting in a deviation
> from this practice. (UNCHR 1997d, pages 11–12)

Indeed, both Kirti Singh (1998) and Savitri Goonesekere (UNICEF 1998b) from Sri Lanka are active spokeswomen to change corroboration laws and practices in such cases.

Problems about Police Attitudes and Failure in Duty

Women and their legal advocates recount experiences that show a host of problems from their point of view about dealing with the police in cases of gender-based violence. Again, most examples are about rape and incest, with only a few about domestic violence or dowry death. The main point of the discussion here is that there are problems for women with police attitudes and even failure in duties; such attitudes contribute to women's reluctance to bring complaints forward.

Attitudes and manner. For example, "Kusuma,"[31] a rape victim-survivor from Sri Lanka, says:

> Police have to be given a thorough training on how to deal with this kind of crime. They
> don't even know how to talk to a woman victim. Their very tone and speech terrifies me.
> Having women police officers to deal with this type of crime is not enough. The policemen,
> too, should be given to understand that this is a crime against society.

Refusal of cooperation. A Pakistani woman lawyer[32] says:

> [T]he biggest problem we are facing is, to be very honest, not with rape laws but with the police . . . the initial hurdles really give us problems. If you [as a complainant] go to the police, they refuse to give us the FIR [First Information Report]; they refuse to give us the medical report, and by the time we manage to do all that, and even if a victim goes to the law to complain, they give her problems.

She points out that when a statement is taken, its actual content may even contradict the FIR and what the victim-survivor claims she said. The UN Special Rapporteur on violence against women, its causes and consequences has also drawn attention to discrepancies between what a woman complainant reports and what is written down (UNCHR 1997c).

Inadequate investigation and outright obstruction. The same woman lawyer from Pakistan gave this example of appalling insensitivity and laxity in a child rape case:

> Child rape cases disturb me the most, because I have personally visited a child who was six years old and she was raped in front of her three-year-old sister, and that little child that could barely talk was telling me about the rape. The six-year-old was very traumatized, and this happened during her summer holidays. She had gone to sell some samosas and pakoras [food items], and this man just pulled her in and the three-year-old told us that [he said,] "If you tell anyone this, we will chop you into little pieces and put you in a sack." Everyone was discussing the whole thing in front of her while she was sitting in a little corner.
>
> . . . The accused is known by everyone and if the police wanted to do something about it, they could have arrested him. The mother told us that a news item came in the paper stating that the guy was dead, which is a complete lie. In the area the women are giving us this really funny story that he lives with this woman and they are not married and the woman helps him to do these things. Then we asked the girls, and she said that the woman called her in and then the man raped her. But the accused have run away. In most cases that I have come across, the accused is known.[33]

Problems in the investigation of dowry-death are notorious, for example:

> The investigation of dowry-death or cases of dowry-related violence has been judicially criticized for being done callously. The Supreme Court after finding the investigation made by police in a dowry-death totally inadequate, directed two Indian states to conduct a fresh investigation by an officer not below the rank of Superintendent of Police (SP). (Meindersma 1998, pages 80–81)

Regarding outright obstruction of justice by police for women victim-survivors, Kirti Singh (1998, page 10) writes:

> Women's organizations and victims have in many cases reported that police have refused to even lodge this First Information Report of the crime. Some time after lodging the FIR the police refuse to give a copy of the report to the complainant even though they are bound to do so under the law. . . . Seven women's organizations in Delhi have pointed out that instead of accurately lodging the FIR and telling the woman victim of her rights under the law and taking her for a prompt medical examination, the police in fact acts as a major obstacle to justice.

Suspected bribery. A woman NGO leader in India[34] described such a case:

> [T]he woman had been tortured a lot physically by her husband and ill-treated. The case
> had been referred to and solved many times by the village *Panchayat* [council of locally
> elected leaders, often feudal landowners]. She also had a child.
>
> One day she came to know that early in the morning her mother had taken ill and was very
> serious. It was the next village, which meant a walk of 45 minutes, so she went there and
> came back by lunchtime so that she could prepare the husband's food, etc. When she
> came back, she was mercilessly beaten and then given poison. When she became
> unconscious, they took her to the local village hospital, Primary Health Centre, where they
> didn't accept her. Then she was taken to a hospital . . . in the same district, but admitted
> under a fake name.

When the woman's family learned what had happened to her, the woman's brother
and father went to the city to search for her, and stayed in a hospital that night, as it
was raining. They were crying. A nurse felt sorry for them and tried to help. She told
them that

> a body of a girl answering to their description was lying in the morgue. They went there
> and found it was the same, and she had died early that morning. They went to the police,
> but the husband's family somehow managed [to make] them sign on a blank piece of
> paper and released and cremated the body.
>
> The women's *Samiti* [women's group] of the village protested and surrounded the police
> station and asked for action, but the officer-in-charge pacified them and said they would
> solve the matter. But nothing was done, and the husband was moving around freely. Then
> these women [in the *Samiti*] came to the Centre and asked for advice. It was then realized
> that no written complaint was lodged and a letter was sent by registered post, upon which
> senior officers were sent to make an inquiry. But nothing came of it as the women felt the
> police had been bribed heavily. Even though a post-mortem was done, the reports were
> never given. In such cases, these reports take years to come out.

Custodial rape. A risk everywhere, custodial rape has been confirmed by Radhika
Coomaraswamy, the UN Special Rapporteur for violence against women, in a review
related to Bangladesh. It is also discussed for Pakistan by Mumtaz and Shaheed (1987),
Human Rights Watch (1995) and by E. Ahmed (1998). In E. Ahmed's paper for the
regional study on the use of the legal system to end violence against women and
girls, she writes:

> Special rules have been laid down which deal with the arrest and interrogation of women. .
> . . Despite these various provisions women continue to be abused by the police. According
> to a survey of female prisoners in Punjab 78% claimed they had been maltreated, and 72
> said they were sexually abused by the police before being brought to prison. The report
> went on to say that "sexual abuse ranged from rape, including the insertion of foreign
> objects into the vagina and rectum, to beating and mutilating of exposed genital areas, to
> stripping and public exposure." According to data collected from Lahore based
> newspapers from January-July 1997, 52 women were physically and sexually abused in
> police custody. . . . A study done in 1992 revealed that 70% of the women in police custody
> are subjected to sexual and or physical violence and not even one police officer had been
> punished. (1998, page 20)

A case reported by the NGO CLASS, Pakistan,[35] also touches on police abuse:

> Then there are these three girls who were kidnapped four months ago from Sheikhupura
> and are still missing. All indications are there that the SHO [a senior police officer] of the
> local police station knows their whereabouts, but, as he has very strong political backing,
> he is not afraid of any action against himself.

Problems clearly exist in other countries (see, for example, Forum against Oppression
of Women 1995).

Are police above the law? This is a logical question given the examples reported
here. Another such case was reported by a lawyer activist[36] in India:

> It was a gang rape, and nothing could be proved. The Court did not care for the Supreme
> Court's judgement that circumstantial evidence should be considered. Does it mean that
> for every woman who is gang-raped in this country, the accused should go about scot-free?
> Then what is the future of stopping violence against women? Judiciary has got to be
> activated and sensitized and unless we do that we won't progress. Police sensitization is
> there, but there are still a large number of custodial rapes. Nothing happens to the police,
> they are suspended for a few months and we never know the results. This should be made
> public.

Custodial rape is also a risk in other countries in the region. For instance, the
organization SOS-Torture reported on such an incident in Bangladesh about an 18-
year-old garment worker:

> Seema Chowdury was arrested . . . and taken to the Raouzan police station apparently on
> the grounds that a woman may not walk with a man to whom she is not married. While
> being held for interrogation she was allegedly raped by four policemen. . . . The Police
> apparently both failed to record the arrest and to bring the two persons before a court
> within 24 hours as are stipulated by Bangladeshi Law. (*www.derechos.org/omct/actions/
> bgd/220797.html*, 14 July 1999)

According to the report, the woman was held in "safe custody" at the police station
for several months following her arrest. She died in custody due to the negligence
of prison authorities who failed to provide her with medical assistance despite her
deteriorating condition.

Stereotypes of women police as naturally sensitive. A woman lawyer in Pakistan[37]
described how an insensitive woman officer investigating an alleged rape of a 14-year-
old girl took the accused with her, to the girl's house, when the officer went there
to get the girl's statement. She said:

> It is basically these attitudes of even the women police officers [which are problematic]. . . .
> [T]hey don't get the point, that's the main thing. . . . They think as long as they do this legal
> duty everything is OK with them.

None of the above is flattering to the police, not even to those in the women's police
cells.

There is also a problem in that reconciliation is very much emphasized by women
police officers despite the fact that women who go to the police often do so as a last
resort.[38] There are police who are very much committed to making changes in the
way women victim-survivors of gender violence are treated by them and their
colleagues. Some initiatives for improvement will be discussed further below.

Procedural Problems

Costly and lengthy process. According to Gomez and Gomez, writing about Kirti Singh (1998, page 14):

> Many facets of the legal system do not encourage a woman victim to use the system. The system is perceived of as being elitist, distant, alien, inaccessible and costly. The trial can be harrowing and the opposing counsel intimidating. There are other facets of the legal system which also hinder women's access to justice. One of the most obvious is the delay in obtaining justice.

The authors go on to say:

> In Sri Lanka it is not unusual for ten years to lapse before the "final" verdict is delivered by a court. There are several cases where the victim is married and with family by the time a case is heard and is therefore reluctant to come forward to give evidence on her behalf.

Two case examples are given. In one, *Rajaratne* v *Attorney General*, an alleged rapist of a four-year-old was found guilty in 1984. He appealed. The judgement confirming conviction was delivered in 1996, 12 years after the incident, by which time the girl was 16. In the second, *Attorney General* v *Ranasinghe*, the alleged rapist in 1982 of an 11-year-old victim had his appeal dismissed 10 years after the incident, when the girl was already 21.

Gomez and Gomez (1998, page 15) also refer to a new study on juvenile justice, as follows:

> [A] 13-year-old girl who was allegedly abused sexually by her father made 22 visits to the court in a two year period between July 1995 and June 1997. The case was still proceeding at the time the research was concluded.[39]

And in India, Meindersma (1998, page 72) reports that "it may take 12 years for [a case] to get decided." It is doubtful that a young girl or woman will bring a case under such circumstances, particularly since conditions at home might even get worse for her were she to do so.

In the material for this chapter, there are other examples of delays at various stages of the legal process:

- Bhanwari Devi states she was examined medically only 52 hours after her rape; the magistrate ordered the exam only 48 hours after the incident (see case further below);
- The arrest of Seema Chowdury in Bangladesh, who died in police custody, was not reported within 24 hours as required by law;
- Women's police stations in Pakistan are said to delay registration of First Information Reports because they need approval and assistance of male police for search and arrest;
- The report was never received on the case of the woman murdered in India after being beaten and poisoned, ostensibly because she went to see her ill mother without permission when she had a meal to prepare for her husband.

Such delays in the legal process, especially for matters where evidence is discounted as time passes, require timely attention to remove them.

The Problem of Obtaining Medical Evidence

Refusal to conduct physical examination. From an interview in Pakistan comes a report on a harrowing case of a woman, Nasreen, who was kidnapped, tortured and raped along with her two daughters after her son refused to work any longer for his feudal boss (*zamindar*), who kidnapped him and shamed the women in his family also. An activist from the NGO CLASS (Pakistan)[40] described the case like this:

> It is a rape case involving a woman and her two daughters. A face of oppression in our villages is that if a worker associated with a particular *zamindar* works somewhere else, or he by chance gets an opportunity to earn some money somehow, the concerned *zamindar* makes life difficult for him. Now, in this case, which is referred to as [the] Nasreen case, a worker refused to work for his previous employer, who kidnapped him, his mother, Nasreen, and his two sisters. Even his minor siblings were picked up from their school and beaten. We recovered the girls through a high court bailiff. These girls were 15–16 years of age. They had been brutally raped. Their mother had also been raped before she managed to escape and reach CLASS.
>
> There I must add that we have appreciable support from other organizations and in this case also CLASS was helped tremendously by War Against Rape, [the] Human Rights Commission of Pakistan and AGHS Legal Aid Cell. AGHS arranged for the bailiff to recover the girls and their father from the police station! Their son was still missing. Police refused to register a FIR, and Nasreen moved the court to order the police to register the case. When she was going from the court to SSP Office with these orders, she was kidnapped, taken to Peshawar, and there she was brutally raped and her body was burnt by cigarettes and acid. When she escaped and reached Lahore to [name withheld] Office, her fingernails were bleeding due to acid burns, and when her body was examined, it was all covered with cigarette burns. The high court ordered . . . a medical examination.
>
> Just look at the height of inhumanity that police who were ordered for medical examination said that they did not have a lady doctor and referred the victim to [name withheld] Hospital. The lady doctor at this hospital said that they would never give evidence in the case. Then we took her to [name withheld] Hospital, who refused to carry out the needful [a medical examination]; we went then to [name withheld] and were refused there as well. The police surgeon sent a letter to the high court that they did not have the examination facility, the court ordered [name withheld] Hospital for this, but still to no avail. Finally, the judges of the high court appointed a bailiff to go along with the victim and had her examined 25 days after the incident. The accused party were following us to kill the woman. We did manage to get the medical report, which was evidence enough of the high-handedness, but despite high court orders, the FIR has not been registered so far.

Limited technical capacity. Even in Sri Lanka, probably the best-equipped country in the region so far as forensic medicine is concerned, there are problems regarding the taking of evidence:

> In cases of rape and sexual violence the medical examination is a crucial aspect of the criminal justice process. The report of the medical officer who examines the victim soon after the commission of the offence would form a significant component of the prosecution's case. The level of medical expertise across the country is uneven. In some major towns the skills to conduct a comprehensive medical examination are available. In others, the basic instruments and other facilities needed to conduct such examinations are

inadequate. Very few hospitals have medical officers specially designated to handle examinations of victims of sexual abuse. Thus a victim may be forced to wait long hours in an out-patient clinic before she is examined by a medical officer. (Gomez and Gomez 1998, page 13)

Results at marked variance with FIRs. A pertinent case from Kathmandu follows:

In August this year, a mother reported the rape of her five-year-old daughter by a 45-year-old neighbour to the Women Cell of Police in Kathmandu. While the police reported traces of sperm on the girl's skirt and inflammation around the vagina and the accused confessed the rape, the medical report stated that there was no indication of rape and that the girl was "a happy and healthy girl." When inquiring into this incident, a doctor explained that doctors are generally reluctant to appear in court and therefore reluctant to note down an indication of rape. There is no provision for reimbursing expert witnesses, including doctors, for expenses incurred while testifying in court. (Meindersma 1998, page 71)

The Problem of Judicial Gender Bias

Incest, rape, dowry death and traditional practices harmful to women, particularly "honour killings", are among the offences around which judicial bias in terms of gender has been observed on the part of courts. Each is discussed below. Some problems about conviction rates and penalties are also discussed briefly.

As Kirti Singh (1998, page 91) observes about the general situation in India regarding judicial bias,

one of the main reasons why gender sensitization has to be carried out on a huge scale is that a large number of judges also believe that the woman's role is to adjust to the matrimonial house and bear whatever happens to her.

Incest. For example, Anjali Kumar (1996, page 17) comments on what she calls the "full-blown gender bias" and disregard of evidence in the matter of *Satish Mehra* v *Delhi Administration*. The complaint was incest by the father against his daughter, then four years old. Evidence against the father came from 20 specialists, yet the opening remarks by the Supreme Court were, "Some eerie accusations have been made by a wife against her husband" (WARLAW 1996, page 4). The result?

[A] judgement plagued by a disturbing lack of understanding of child sexual abuse, prejudice, and complete intolerance for a mother who complains of such abuse when it occurs within her family. (Kapoor 1996, page 14)

Kapoor comments further:

From the outset, the perspective of the Court is clear — "incestuous sexual abuse" by a husband is "incredulous" [sic]. It is this denial of reality which reaffirms public myths and misconceptions about child sexual abuse, while the incidence of such abuse in India continues to escalate. Worse still is that such disbelief ultimately governed the Court's unquestioning acceptance of one version (the father's) and unequivocal dismissal of another (the mother's). (page 14)

Rape. Consider these observations about the judgement against the plaintiff Bhanwari Devi in an alleged rape case in India, first from Bhanwari Devi[43] herself and then from a well-known lawyer in India:

The Jaipur Court had no hesitation in holding my statement as untrue. The judge said I did not report the case to the police on the day I was raped. It is true that I reported the matter to the police only the next day. But the reason is that the police station is 10 kilometres away from the village. The judge does not seem to have realized my mental state after the rape. Did he expect me to get up, walk immediately to the police station and report the matter to the police?

The judge also gave importance to the fact that I was examined medically only 52 hours after the incident. This delay was due to the red tape. The doctor insisted on the magistrate's order. That order was issued only after 48 hours. The judge did not find fault with the delay. It is shocking how the judges, too, are biased against women.

Mohan, my husband, was the only eyewitness to the incident. But the judge discarded his evidence. He wanted to know how a husband could keep quiet when his wife is being raped. I wonder why the judge did not take into account that Mohan was assaulted, too. The other observations by the judge are even more strange. The people who raped me are 40, 50, 59 and 70. The 70-year-old held me while I was raped. But the judge felt they were too old and respectable to rape me. The judge also said a Brahmin will never rape a low-caste woman. This is 50 years after independence! The entire judgement was based on a caste and gender bias. Six judges changed during the trial so the judge who recorded my case was not the same as the judge who delivered the judgement. And even though the trial was in camera, 17 men were present in the courtroom with the legitimate right of entry, and I had to describe my rape explicitly in front of them.

I had to shed all my inhibitions and narrate the event to everyone. Failure to speak in detail about the case or in great detail, both go against us. In my case, the judgement almost said a man's word is more believable than a woman's word.[44]

She also named the official who, she says, tried at a local government meeting to get her to take back her charges, which she refused.

Bhanwari lost her case. Women's groups who were following it and supporting her were outraged, particularly because the judgement was based on assumptions about religion and caste and first-hand evidence was not accepted. Rani Jethmalani observes:

The trial judge in this case acquitted the five accused on the ground that, "Rape is usually committed by teenagers and since the accused are middle-aged and therefore respectable, they could not have committed the crime. An upper caste man could not have defiled himself by raping a lower caste woman." The judge held that they were ipso facto respectable and, with one of them being brahmin, they could not have raped a lower caste woman. (WARLAW 1996, page 20)

Low conviction figures and wide variation in sentencing have been noted with regard to rape cases in particular. A report on a 1995 seminar in New Delhi, "Is Law Enough? Violence against Women and Remedial Actions," comments, "The very low rate of conviction as well as the lengthy process that accompanies it is being deemed by many as one of the reasons for the sudden increase in crimes against women" (Mahindroo 1995, page 10). Supreme Court advocate Kirti Singh[45] was of the opinion that, in general, conviction rates in India are about 10 per cent — with even lower conviction rates for crimes against women and girls. In fact, the percentage of rape cases convicted in 1997 in India is only 4.9 per cent (National Crime Records Bureau 1999, page 167).[46]

Some judgements regarding rape cases from Sri Lanka, as cited by Meindersma

(1998, page 60), show the extent to which judicial interpretation will vary. The sentences varied from 12 years to a two-year suspended sentence upon appeal; a public whipping of a 70-year-old for the rape of a five-year-old girl; and a two-year imprisonment sentence for repeated rape of an 11-year-old girl over two days, suspended for 10 years, then increased upon appeal to five years without suspension.

The death penalty has been set for rape in Pakistan and Bangladesh but is unlikely to be invoked given the difficulty there of obtaining conviction of the accused under the Hudood Ordinances. In any case, more extreme penalties are not necessarily associated with more convictions: in fact, the reverse may be true, as there is likely to be more hesitation to convict.[47]

Kirti Singh (1998, pages 30–32) has made the following pertinent observation regarding assumptions about child victim-survivors and their perpetrators:

> In *Bahadur Singh* vs *State of Madhya Pradesh*, because the young child could not explain the act or speak of coitus it was held that no offence under section 376, i.e. no rape was made out. Another problem that often arises in the case of child sexual abuse is that there is a perception among many, including some judges, that the abuser or rapist, especially when it is a close relative, is someone who is mentally sick and requires treatment. This perception tends to play down the incidence of child abuse prevailing in the country. In fact, many refuse to believe that a "seemingly normal" human being could be involved in a case of child abuse.

This is an extremely important area for public education and legal reform.

Dowry cases. Regarding gender bias in cases of dowry death, Singh (1998, page 67) sees part of the problem like this:

> The entire criminal justice administration proved to be a major stumbling block in providing justice to dowry victims. The history of cases dealing with dowry retrieval and dowry violence and indeed other forms of domestic violence is replete with examples of deliberate inaction due to gender bias, widespread corruption, apathy and poor investigation by the police. Even the Supreme Court of India and High Courts have in fact commented on this and passed strictures against the police. Many dowry murder/cruelty cases were prosecuted so badly in court that conviction was hardly likely. Not only this, the manner in which most judges dealt with the case depended to a large extent on their individual ideology or way of thinking about the role of women.[48]

Customary or traditional practices harmful to women. That is another category of offence about which the judiciary looks the other way all too often, sometimes due to those who speak on behalf of religion. For example, child marriage is an offence in Pakistan (for girls under 16), Nepal, Bangladesh (for girls under 18), India (for girls under 15) and Sri Lanka (for girls under 18)[49] (Meindersma 1998, page 93). Abuse of statutes that restrain early marriage is commonplace, as can be inferred from the fact that many girls are married below the legal age (40 per cent of 15-year-olds in Nepal, for example). For Pakistan, E. Ahmed (1998, page 25) notes:

> Most of the girls that are sold off in marriage are under the age of 16 and therefore the offenders of this crime can be dealt under the Child Marriage Restraint Act (1929). However, "What this legislation gives with one hand it takes away [with] the other."

She points out that the penalty is so minimal it does not deter marriages, and that in any case a conviction does not make the marriage null and void. Furthermore, although an under-age girl has the right to repudiate the marriage before she reaches 18, that is not permitted if the marriage was already consummated. She says, "This law has met with much resistance from the clergy who state that Islam puts no age-limit on marriages and thus the law is not acceptable" (page 25).

As for forced marriage, not accepted under the law, E. Ahmed (page 23) refers to the Commission of Inquiry for Women, Pakistan, report, which says:

> Often defended and sanctified as cultural traditions they are fiercely defended by those who practice them, shrugged off by society and condoned both by law enforcing agencies and the courts of law. As a result most of these inhuman practices continue unabated.

A system for registration of marriages, put into practice, can facilitate enforcement of laws against child or early marriage. For example, the law against early marriage is enforced in Sri Lanka but not in other countries — in part because Sri Lanka has a system for registration of marriages.[50]

"Honour killings". This is a category of particular concern. These murders follow accusations, sometimes false, of sex outside of marriage. Motives include so-called defence of family honour, but also revenge against an enemy and desire for a girl "in compensation" from another group. For example, a man may kill his sister, daughter, wife or mother, claiming she has had sex with so-and-so, his enemy, in order to justify killing his enemy or gaining compensation in the form of a girl or girls from the relatives of the accused man. In any case, judgements are swift, do not come under general law, evidence is often lacking, compensation and compromise are the aim. The Commission of Inquiry for Women, Pakistan (1997, page 61), comments:

> The Commission is concerned at the practice of some courts' taking a lenient view of what is, in their eyes, "honour" killing. This is objectionable on two counts. First, it mitigates murder. Thereby, it becomes a strong encouragement to other murders of the kind. It makes them look respectable. And thus it waters down the basic judicial prohibition against anyone taking the law into his or her hands. If customs like *karokari* are still rampant in parts of the country, it is because of this attitude.[51]

The Commission also noted that a lenient view of "honour killings" presumes guilt on the part of a person not heard by the court, without a trial. Even for murders of women that are not necessarily claimed as "honour killings", local authorities may be very lenient in their response.

From Swat, a remote part of Pakistan, a then practising lawyer, Mufti Ziauddin, reported in a 1997 interview for this book on the attitude of the court to men who murdered women in the family, as revealed in eight cases decided in seven months.[52] There was only one conviction of a boy who killed his own mother and confessed his guilt. Without a killer's confession or such a forbidden act as matricide, families see to it that the consequences to murders of wives stay under their control:

> In the other cases, involving the murders of seven women, all of them were dismissed on the basis of compromise. . . . The judges and the courts don't play any role. It's very easy to kill your wife and go to your father-in-law, just patch up with him and say, "OK, I've killed your daughter. I'll give you my own daughter." It's a matter of patch-up. They come to the court and they say, "We don't have any complaint," and the court acquits them.

In the area where Ziauddin lived and worked,[53] national laws do not necessarily apply, as deference is often given to local custom due to the Criminal Law Amendment Act

1997 (better known in Pakistan as *Qisas* and *Diyat* Law[54]) (Commission of Inquiry for Women 1997).

As the Commission of Inquiry for Women, Pakistan (1997, page 6), explains it:

> The entire law revolves around a patriarchal structure. It makes criminal offences a private matter rather than treating them as crimes against society. . . . This law will have to be revamped, so that it protects the vulnerable and is not based on tribal concepts.

Ziauddin's story is a particularly important one to tell because it shows very clearly the difficulty of changing customs, beliefs and practices that discriminate, even blatantly, against rights and lives of women; it shows that the strength of families can be directed against women and that other institutions may accept rather than challenge their doing so. He told how he came to take up cases of women falsely accused of murdering their husbands and the unsatisfactory results for the women even when he "wins" their cases.

Early in his career[55] as a lawyer, Ziauddin was asked at the last minute to help a friend present a closing argument to defend an important case. An elderly woman stood accused of abetting the murder of her husband. The principal accused (a man) had absconded. The woman's case had not been well conducted. Feudal interests appeared to be well served if she was sentenced. She was found guilty. Ziauddin was able to get her sentence reduced, but that is all. He decided that in future he would concentrate on defending women accused of murder or *zina*, where the evidence is not solid and the women cannot afford proper legal counsel.

Of more than 100 such cases, he won all but one. Even so, the women's relatives criticized Ziauddin for defending those whom they were determined to throw out of the family due to their idea that family honour was lost. They would not take the acquitted women back. The innocent women had no other place to go. They languished in jail.

Ziauddin's story illustrates how important it is to name and face what really goes on inside as well as outside families, to call for and support related changes. His story, then, is about hope as well as shock. And it is also about being realistic: while Ziauddin's efforts helped solve some problems, they revealed others, and brought new challenges.

Problems for Victim-Survivors Regarding Support Services

No option but jail. If cases involving violence against women in the family are brought and won, then what? Are there real alternatives to staying in a dangerous family or community situation, where a woman may otherwise be tortured or killed?

The lack of options for women and girl victim-survivors is of great concern to activists in South Asia. Remember the case of the girl victim-survivor of incest whose story is at the end of the opening chapter? She was still in jail a year after she brought charges against her father for repeatedly raping her. (After that, I had no more information about her.)

The problem of having nowhere to go is one faced by most abused girls and women, as the examples below also indicate.

Inadequate shelters. "Shalini," an NGO executive from Sri Lanka points out:

There must be hotlines/safe houses or shelters that women can go to in a situation like this. Particularly for people who do not have relatives or for those who might have people but who might not want to get involved. [56]

The conditions in shelters have been brought into question. Consider the report of Eman M. Ahmed, of the AGHS Legal Aid Cell, working under the supervision of Hina Jilani, one of the founders. She reports that the first *Dar-ul-Uman* (House of Peace) in Pakistan was set up in Lahore in 1963 to offer women shelter, and that the government has established such homes for women in the major cites. Women can be admitted by court order, by recommendation of newspaper editors or from those working at shrines of religious saints. She goes on to describe some of the conditions, which have departed from the intended ones. These may include denial of freedom:

Instead of being a sanctuary for women Dar-ul-Amans are repressive and used as "sub-jails". Women are kept against their wishes and are not let out of the premises even to seek employment. They are also not allowed to have any visitors. The Dar-ul-Aman personnel refuse to release a woman till she has paid the expenses incurred by the institution on her up keep. (1998, page 26)

As the women are not allowed to work to earn money, they are in effect kept prisoners. Ahmed also describes the environment in most other shelters in the country. She says the inmates report they are locked in their rooms at night, are not allowed to use the toilets and are overcrowded (it is estimated that up to 100 may share a five-bedroom house). She observes, "The atmosphere and lack of productive-constructive activity heighten their depression and force them to think of suicide as the only viable option" (page 27).

In addition, she reports:

Not only are the conditions psychologically and emotionally debilitating but the Dar-ul-Aman personnel have been known to sexually abuse the girls and also provide girls to high ranking officials. According to a newspaper report, women were taken out at night from Dar-ul-Aman for the pleasure of senior officials.

Women's Apparent Unwillingness to Seek Legal Remedies

It is more understandable after the above review that many women do not bring their cases forward, even when there are laws that cover offences of gender-based violence against them. Of course, women may not even know about laws that could help them. An activist from Sri Lanka, "Mala," comments with regard to the new law against sexual harassment:

At the moment, even though verbal and physical sexual harassment has been criminalized in this country, there is still very little awareness about the change in our law. . . . We are encouraging men and women to take the matter of sexual harassment seriously, and trying to encourage women to go to courts if they feel that they are being sexually harassed.[57]

All the same, it seems there is greater chance of failure than success for women and girls who seek legal remedy for gender-based violence against them, even with the assistance of well-trained and committed legal advocates. One cannot blame them for failing to bring cases directly to agents of the State when the reputation of same is apparently so generally low as regards treatment of women.

Many of the activists who were interviewed from the front lines in South Asia said, however, that more and more complainants are coming forward, at least to women's organizations. We have seen some powerful examples of what has to be dealt with at the grassroots level, but are the means available? For example, when I visited Patna, India, in 1997, the NGO Bago Jahen (Wake Up, Sister) organized a meeting for me with some of the women seeking help from them. One was so desperate she wanted me to take her child. She threatened to poison herself if I did not, as her husband had beaten her, she was abandoned, and she had no means to earn an income. The NGO leader told me that the list of cases of such desperate women seeking help from her organization was growing at a dramatic rate in comparison with the numbers who had called on them in earlier years.

There is an urgent need, then, for activists to connect with those in struggle and to be able to bring their cases to the attention of persons who understand how best to use the legal system for remedy. Activists should advocate for changes in laws, yes, but more than that, they need to network and build systems that "pressurize" and monitor government response so there will be responsibility, objectivity and fairness — without gender bias — on the part of authorities in the legal system. Cases such as the ones above also remind international agencies like UNICEF about the importance of advocacy and support, implemented in ways that will make a true difference for those who struggle at the grassroots level. As an interviewee in Pakistan put it:

> If the women would bring these issues to the courts, people would start taking it seriously. They would deduce that the issues of domestic violence and sexual abuse are important. They would certainly start taking it seriously. So more and more women should move the courts and they should seek the help of the organizations. They should speak about their issues and there are so many organizations which can help them.[58]

More Success Needed

Are there successful cases? One may wonder after reading all the above. Among the cases mentioned by the South Asian activists who were interviewed, there are only a few that report at least partial successes in terms of legal outcomes for the women concerned. It could be extremely useful to collect and analyse such cases. Elements that make for success could then be seen more clearly and efforts made to replicate them more systematically and widely.

Six cases that feature at least partial success for women victim-survivors are reviewed below. It is notable that four are about divorce, maintenance and child custody. Implementation of related laws will be important for activists to consider and improve if meaningful relief is to be found for those women who are so abused in a family that they dare not stay in it.

Some of the cases show how local politics can affect outcomes, usually against women's and girls' interests. It is also clear that effective interventions by women's groups with authorities can make all the difference in favour of women's claims and rights. Sometimes such groups or individuals provided refuge and support to women in intolerable situations from which there might otherwise not have been any exit but death.

Case A: Child custody for R[59] as reported by Sahodari Project, India

"R," who was ill treated and harassed by her in-laws, also had marital problems so she separated from her husband. Petty problems were magnified and R was considered talkative and stubborn. They [in-laws] abused her through words and actions and took revenge on R by separating her child from her. The client wants her daughter back but the in-laws refuse to give the child away [to her] which caused a lot of mental agony to R. She has been fighting vehemently for the custody of the child. But all the efforts to get the child were futile. The in-laws demanded R's parents to sign on a paper which read that R had planned to commit suicide and if anything happens to R at her in-laws' home, they are not responsible. So her parents are inhibited to take any further step to settle the matter. Then, as a last resort, they approached Sahodari Project for help.

The mother was interviewed. The interviewer pointed to the change in her attitudes that has come about through counselling and will help support a new life for her daughter and grandchild:

Her views on women's problems were very narrow and limited owing to her limited exposure. As she has been going to court to attend legal proceedings, she is now able to understand the magnitude of the problem, a little bit. As the mother belongs to a traditional family, she was of the opinion that a girl's place lies in the home of her in-laws only and that it is not morally right to live away from the husband. Now, seeing the extent of the harassment, the mother is keen that her daughter should get back her child so that she can lead a new life in future. The exposure and guidance that the mother has received in the past few months from the Sahodari Project has made her realize that education can help women to courageously fight for their rights. The mother is now hopeful that her daughter would get custody of her child and then she hopes to educate her daughter and her grandchild.

Case B: Beating, dowry demands and child custody — issues faced by M. B., India[60]

[T]he case [is] of a girl from their village who was beaten and tortured by her husband and mother-in-law, who continuously expected their dowry demands to be fulfilled by her parents who are quite poor. They threw her out of the house, i.e. the girl, "M. B.," along with her first child, a son, and refused to hand over the second child, also a son, aged eight months. This woman, along with the help of these women who have formed a *Mahila Samiti* (women's group), went to the local police station and with a police escort went and got back the second child from the house of the husband. Her mother-in-law tried to strangle M. B., and the police threatened to fire if she didn't stop.

The victim, M. B., was married at a very early age (about 14 years) and is now only 19. She does not want to go back to her in-laws. The women of the *Samiti* are keen on rehabilitating her, making her stand on her own feet and helping her to earn an income to support herself and her two children.

Case C: Divorce and maintenance, as told by F. B., India[61]

The other day a case came to us of a Muslim gentleman who had married for the second time. This time he has married an *Adivasi* [from a tribal background] girl and has two children by her. The first wife has 10 children, and she wants some kind of maintenance. The man is well-off, has a two-story house and used to operate trucks carrying bricks, etc. But now, with two families to support, he is not able to manage.

The first wife came and complained about him to the *Samiti* and asked for some monetary help to educate her children. When the husband came to know that she had come to the *Samiti* for help, he beat her up. Again she complained to the *Samiti* and some members advised her to beat him back if he attacked her again, and that is what happened the second time [he beat her]. Then the former husband along with some 20–25 of his supporters went to the house of the first wife. They attacked her and beat her up as well as some of the children, including the daughters. This lady came and took refuge in [a private home]. Now we are helping her to seek divorce and maintenance for the children, legally.

Case D: Maintenance for a wife who was beaten, as reported by M, India[62]

When we started giving legal aid, our first case was the case of a woman who was beaten by her husband. I still remember that all of our Committee members brought her [away from the house]. She was a maidservant and she was beaten mercilessly. The husband was a drunkard and he was living with other women. We sent her to a doctor straight away and got her stitches done and then we started a case against the husband and then we got the maintenance for her.

Case E: Avoiding exchange marriage, as reported by S. W., Pakistan[63]

Our maid, who ran away from her house in order to avoid the exchange marriage, was in my mother's custody. She asked about me when she needed support. She said that I could help her because she knew I was involved in such work. I took up her case and pursued it, from magistrate level upwards, and was able to get for her what she wanted. She was also kept at *Dastak* [shelter home] for a few days and when she returned to the village she told my mother that there were so many educated girls in that shelter home, and the women running it are very resourceful.

Case F: Release from jail, as reported by H., Bangladesh[64]

My first attempt was to take action to release a girl [who had been raped] from jail in 1988. She was there for four years. I struggled for three days before I could get her out from jail. It inspired me to stick to this field. . . . I want other women to know that rape victims are jailed. The authorities claim that it is for the safety of the victim. But it is not so. The rape victims should seek legal help instead of withdrawing the case.

Looking towards Improvements in Civil Law and Implementation

Most of these cases involved civil, not criminal, procedures. Laws on divorce, maintenance and custody were pertinent (except for the last two cases). In patriarchal systems, the rights of men tend to take precedence under the law over the rights of women, particularly in family matters.

The system of personal laws heightens the tendency for primacy to be placed on the rights of men rather than women, as these laws are grounded in different religions that tend to be interpreted as favouring men.[65] Furthermore, personal laws can deny women legal rights solely on the basis of religion, thus undermining constitutional guarantees of equality without such restriction. For example, under personal law in India, divorced Muslim women are not viewed as considered to entitled to maintenance for more than three months, although under federal law they *are* entitled to adequate maintenance. The primacy of personal law in practice regarding maintenance cases was established after the famous Shah Bano case in 1985. When her husband divorced her after 30 years of marriage, Shah Bano sought maintenance, which was awarded to her, but her husband appealed to the Supreme Court on the basis of Muslim personal law. "The Court held that the provisions [of federal law] regarding maintenance were applicable to all communities . . . and, further, that the religion professed by the party cannot have any repercussion on the application of such laws" (Singh 1994, page 384).

Then came an outcry from groups in the name of the Muslim religion. The Government then introduced the Muslim Women's Act containing all the provisions that the fundamentalists desired (page 385).

As for custody, implementation of the law appears to be in favour of men. It is necessary, however, to distinguish between guardianship and custody. Women are more likely to attain the latter than the former (which grants full rather than limited responsibility and decision-making for the child in all matters).

The details of these and related laws for civil matters need to be well known and taken into account by an abused woman alongside her options under criminal law. Otherwise, she cannot assess the game board representing the nature of the legal system, with all its possibilities and faults, in considering legal recourse. A woman victim-survivor will also be preoccupied with the shape of her life after she might bring a case. Where will she live? What will she live on? What about her children? Will she be even more limited, constrained or even exploited than she was when living with her husband and in-laws? Will she be shamed? Will she be killed? Will the group or person who helps her bring a case then leave the scene without giving her connections with others who could continue to support her challenge to the status quo and her ability to sustain herself and her children as need be?

A detailed review of answers to such questions is beyond the scope of this book. It is an important task for those who would truly assist victim-survivors, however, and identify priorities for efforts to improve the legal system to meet their needs.

The Role of the Media

The media comes in for both praise and criticism for its approach to legal cases about violence against women and girls. Familiar complaints are that cases are sensationalized in the press, that the names of victims are given and should not be, that details are often incorrect and that negative attitudes come through.

At the same time, there is a new appreciation of possibilities for gaining attention and redress for victim-survivors through the assistance of professionals working in the print and visual media. In Chapter 4, Sugani from India, for example, credits the recovery of her mother's land to helpful coverage by the press. The girl from Gujarat, whose husband cut off her nose in response to her claim that his father raped her, received help that was drawn to her through publicity of the case. In Pakistan, referrals from editors of newspapers are accepted by shelters.

Participants in the Kathmandu regional meeting (UNICEF 1998b) expressed their appreciation that people from the press, theatre and arts were there. They saw that the importance of forging partnerships with professionals in media and the arts had, in general, been overlooked, perhaps because many activists have been put off by the impression that the press often sensationalizes and exploits cases. This time, they strongly recommended forging new alliances. It is a very important recommendation.

Groups like the Women's Feature Service in India and Asmita in Nepal also deserve recognition as important positive forces for change. These feminist services undertake monitoring the press for the kinds of coverage on women and violence that appear, and publicizing results to help bring about change (see, for example, Dali 1997).

The press can also help break the silence about subjects that have been neglected or are even taboo, such as child rape and incest. Mitra (n.d.), a child psychologist, makes very useful suggestions for press coverage of child sexual abuse case. Stories in the press about various kinds of gender violence also may offer the basis for surveys about incidence and legal response. For example, studies of rape in most countries have been based on studies of articles in the press.[66] Still, coverage of rape cases is often very much criticized. An Indian woman NGO leader[67] suggests a new approach to typical news coverage of violence against women:

> When the media highlights a rape case, it is like second rape for the woman. . . . It should be covered in such a way as to highlight the people committing the crime, not the victim. Even disclosing the identity of the victim is a violation of her modesty. There are very, very few convictions for rape or dowry deaths. Victimizers go scot-free. People must know about them.

A Pakistani woman lawyer[68] feels much the same:

> [E]specially in the Urdu newspapers, there is a lot of coverage in which they expose the identity of the rape victim, every detail about her, [her] address, sometimes even a photograph. And so we started writing a bit on that. They should never expose the identity of the victim. We always try to keep that in mind. So far we are getting very negative responses from all the newspapers because that's like juicy news for them.

For 19 years, a woman who was editor of a news bureau for a major South Indian newspaper had covered court cases of dowry deaths, rape cases and molestation of women, although many of her colleagues were not willing to look at these stories. She feels writing about individual cases is an important and effective action to expose violence against women[69]:

> You have to sensationalize, you have to do it because they have to get attention . . . put [a case] in centre stage, once you make it visible, only then can you find solutions.

> . . . We have taken women's issues, especially individual cases of dowry deaths. The father or the mother comes having a story to tell. You cannot say, "Yours is only one girl and I have no space." People know that [this paper] is the one place that at least we get a sympathetic hearing. I am not saying we are able to write all these stories. Sometimes there are tricky legal matters involved, because we have to get the other side of the story. Sometimes the other person is not available to make a comment. It becomes difficult, but even then we have stuck our necks out, and we have written.

One of her stories involves Premananda, the God-man who was sexually exploiting women:

> Now the story came to me sometime in the end of 1994, through two women who had the courage to come out and say, "Look here, this guy is exploiting women." It was an explosive story that needed to be delicately handled, but it made me very angry. This guy was in the garb of a Swamijee, a God-man. It's one thing to sexually exploit women, but to use religion to do it, the crime becomes double, because in India people are so gullible. So here was this

guy who was keeping all the girls in the ashram and having sexual relationships with them and making them pregnant. Forcing sexual acts against their will and on top of that, forcing them to get abortions. It was just atrocious. And then I broke this story and the media picked it up. And everybody knows that he is behind bars and failed to get the bail.

Despite its tendency to sensationalize, the press has definitely created more awareness of violence against girls and women as a crime and has featured individual cases, sometimes with a better outcome for the victim than otherwise would have been likely.

Many Recommendations

Specific recommendations abound at international, regional and country levels for changes in the legal system so that it will be more effective for women victim-survivors of gender violence in its various forms. At the global level, recommendations in the Beijing Platform for Action and as made by the UN Special Rapporteur on violence against women are among the better-known ones. The areas they cover are similar to those in recommendations by South Asian activists at the Kathmandu regional meeting[70] (UNICEF 1998b, pages 79–81; see Appendix 2):

- Legal system/substantive law
- Enforcement of the law
- Establishment/amendment of quasi-judicial bodies
- Police/investigation level
- Country-specific recommendations
- Legal system and media
- Support services
- Training and sensitization
- Lawyers

Most of the problems identified in each of these areas have already been discussed above. Some ideas and initiatives for change follow, again based primarily on interviews with activists, along with current research.

Some Initiatives to Improve the Effective Use of the Legal System by Victim-Survivors of Gender Violence

Throughout this book is vibrant evidence of efforts being made by individuals and groups at grassroots level to deal with the injustice of domestic violence and other gender-based violence. A closer look at some initiatives being made to improve use of the legal system shows the complexities of trying to make a difference. This section takes up, in turn, some ideas and measures to improve:

- strategies for the use of the law;
- police responsiveness to cases of violence against women;
- availability and use of evidence;
- judicial objectivity;
- legal awareness, literacy and advocacy campaigns to increase rural women's use of the law;
- support services;
- linkages between grassroots and policy levels.

Strategies for the Use of the Law

Where there are narrow definitions of an offence, or particularly negative attitudes towards women who make certain complaints, lawyers may choose to bring cases under laws other than the more obvious ones. Looking for and using such options to see what works best would, of course, be in addition to efforts to broaden definitions or introduce needed legislation. At the same time, there may be other options. In Sri Lanka, for example, it has been brought out that the law against "grave sexual abuse" provides the same penalties as does the law against rape (Gomez and Gomez 1998).

Measures to Improve Police Response to Cases of Violence against Women

Here is the heart of the matter for most women and girls who consider seeking a legal remedy. Two Sri Lankan NGO members underline the importance of improving how police handle cases, and ways this might be done:

> There is also a need for some kind of system like the police desk system that they have started recently, or some other kind of support where you don't get the policemen saying, "Here, just go home, go home and try to get along," when you go to the station to report an instance of wife battery. And you [they] don't even take the statement down. (Shalini,[71] NGO executive, Sri Lanka)

And Kusuma has already been quoted about poor police attitudes and manner that she experienced as a rape victim.

Their statements anticipate two solutions proposed to police indifference, obstruction and exploitation. These are women's police stations or units, and training for police officers. Changes in the law itself are also being promoted.

Women's police stations and units. An interview[72] with the head of a woman's police station in Pakistan outlines why the idea came about of having women officers deal with cases of violence there, and how this is supposed to work. The background in other countries would be similar:

> I'd like to begin by discussing why we felt the need to have a police station run by women for women. First of all, . . . we found that women would not and did not feel comfortable explaining certain offences and crimes against them to male police officers. For example, in a case where a woman has been raped, or even abused by her husband, and consequently suffered bruises, how can she go to a male police officer, lift her shirt or trousers, and show him her injuries? How can she even feel comfortable providing him with full details of the incident?
>
> Secondly, the public has often complained that women are mistreated in police stations run by men; regardless of whether they go in to report a crime or they are locked up for one. (Incidentally, although I have been working in a male-run police station for 20 years, I have never personally witnessed a woman being mistreated.) But, we felt that if the public conceived [of something as] abuse, then their claim must be legitimate. That is why this station was founded.
>
> Now, any police agency, such as the FIA [Federal Investigation Agency] or the Railway Police, etc., that wants to interrogate a female witness or keep a female offender overnight, in a lock-up, has to bring her to this police station. Another advantage of having this station

— with its two lock-ups — is that any recovered abductee, regardless of where her case was registered, is brought here for safe-keeping.

There is important additional information from the UNICEF/UNIFEM/UNDP-sponsored regional overview[73] on the use of the legal system to end violence against women in South Asia:

A 1992 survey in Pakistan found that 70% of women in police stations were subjected to some form of sexual abuse, while not a single police officer had been punished for such behaviour. Most victims of rape are hesitant to file a complaint with the police as they fear being charged with *zina*. The police, during investigation, as well as the court, during the trial, can convert a charge of rape to one of *zina*. Since 1994, separate police stations for women have been established in a number of cities. However, inquiry into their functioning revealed that these police stations do not function independently; they have to seek approval for registration of FIRs and assistance of male police for carrying out search or arrest. Women police stations do not have detention facilities nor are they equipped for basic investigative tasks. Women police are ill-trained in registration, law, investigation and forensic issues. (Meindersma 1998, page 69)

The woman police officer from Pakistan, already quoted, also described some difficulties in her work. She said that women often want advice on family law, and that she almost always recommends reconciliation rather than divorce. [74]

[W]e can't tell every battered wife that comes to us to get a divorce (*khulla*) from her husband and go off with her children. In cases where the woman is earning a salary, this might be feasible and she may be able to bring up the children herself. But, suppose the woman is an illiterate housewife, how can we tell her to divorce her husband just because he is beating her up? We've never done this.

We also do personal favours for some women who request them. For example, they might ask us to come to their homes in unmarked cars, or without wearing our official uniforms, to prevent people from talking. So we do that also. We don plainclothes for some homes and try to talk to both parties and get them to reconcile. We often invoke doctrines of family values, cultural norms, Islamic religious dictates — anything to fortify our case — to bring about better relations between the husband and wife. When the parties reach an understanding, we get a written agreement from the husband that he will provide for his family and not fight with his wife.

One wonders how well this has worked.

Training. Training for both women and men officers is needed on how to handle cases of violence against women. Problems are not limited to Pakistan by any means. In Sri Lanka, for example:

Women's and Children's Desks [special units to focus on and deal with cases of violence against women] have been set up in 32 police stations in Sri Lanka, some of which have stopped functioning. Initial feedback as to their performance has been negative. Problems relate to the training of women police officers, and to not being equipped to adequately deal with victims of violence. Victims of rape are still being referred to the crimes branch, negating the primary rationale behind the setting up the desks in the first place. (Meindersma 1998, page 70)

Throughout the region, training for the police in gender issues is a fairly recent initiative. For example, the Government of the United Kingdom has sponsored courses in Nepal. Police Superintendent Chuda Bahadur Shrestha says some 60 women have been trained and deployed to various districts.[75] He found the concept worked well enough in the capital but not in other areas, partly because of the attitude of male supervisors:

> I can count on my fingers the number of senior officers who are really interested in the issue. The majority think it's useless training. They may disregard it as a "female problem" or laugh it off. But like I said, in Britain it took time to accept that crimes against women — rape, domestic violence, eveteasing [sexual harassment], kidnapping — were widespread.

He adds:

> The experience has made [me] a strong protester of child marriage. I think I've always been protesting against a society which dictates that a boy goes to school and a girl works at home. I'm a strong advocate of birth control and education.

As for how to challenge domestic violence, he said:

> Unless a local community support system is established, a domestic problem remains a problem between the husband and wife. If we [the police] were to intervene directly, there would be complaints of us meddling in private affairs. But if social workers or people with standing in the community initiated the process, the police could follow up. It can't be tackled alone.

At the same time, he calls for training for police:

> [T]here are 42,000 police deployed around the country who are usually the first to receive reports ranging from murder, child abuse, domestic violence — all sorts of crimes. They are the first to come into contact with the victim. They should be equipped to handle the victims.

Some training tools. Examples of possible training tools for police, wherever they are, come from campaigns against domestic violence in Bangladesh and India that were supported by UNICEF. Police were sensitized about domestic violence as a crime and how they should respond to calls (see Box 10).

The notion of cooperation between activists and police is not necessarily attractive to activists. For example, at the Kathmandu regional meeting in 1997, some participants criticized UNICEF for including the police in the meeting:

> [Y]ou must never mix human rights activists and policemen; you have a whole host [here]. . . . [I]t's insulting. I take so much offence — this notion that you can change police officers, that you can change people. Unless they have a record of being helpful or sympathetic to the movement, you don't call police officers just because they are police officers to give them a thinking. It's very wrong.[76]

His comment shows the depth of the distrust towards police and the need for their very professional behaviour in upholding the law for women as well as men if trust is to be built. Training for police in law, human rights and gender issues could be useful.

High professional standards, with consequences for dereliction. More negative publicity, with sackings, fines or imprisonment of police, have been suggested for cases where they fail in their duties in cases involving violence against women:

One of the major suggestions which has been suggested by the Law Commission and demanded by several women's organizations was to make a police officer/personnel accountable for not recording a complaint or delaying an investigation etc. The Law Commission had suggested that if a public servant disobeys any direction of the Law regulating the manner in which he should conduct an investigation to the prejudice of any

---

Box 9   **The Criminal "Cs" of Domestic Violence**

Domestic Violence

is a **Crime** but never seen that way
is **Cowardice** of the male but never exposed that way.
is committed by **Culprits** who are often close relations; therefore it is difficult to bring them to book.
is a result of **Cultural** norms and community practices which have gone unquestioned.
is a **Conspiracy** of silence, seldom questioned or debated in public.
Always has **Co-victims**. They are almost always **Children.**
Cuts across class. The rich and the poor, the educated and the uneducated resort to domestic violence.
Results in **Collusion** of the local elite: the moulavi, the police and all symbols of patriarchy gang up together.
is **Complicated** and messy. Court cases are **cumbersome**. **Complaints** are seldom registered. People are reluctant to pursue cases.
Compensation is hardly mentioned
the woman is the one **condemned**.

Courtesy of UNICEF India, Patna office.

Box 10   **Fraternal Pledge of the Friendly Bangladeshi Police**

Dear Sister,

You are a citizen of this country and you have all the rights other people have. As believers in the Almighty, the most merciful, our prime duty is to protect your rights. We will do exactly that.

We acknowledge that no one including your husband, your father, brothers, relations or any one else has the right to do any physical or mental harm to you. Anyone who does so is a criminal, and we shall do deal with them accordingly.

We know that it has taken you enormous courage to walk up to us. Usually a woman comes to the police when all other avenues have been closed. We shall do everything possible to give you justice. In doing so we shall keep in mind what is best for you and your children.

By helping you indirectly we will [be] restoring the confidence of thousands [of]other women and children in us, the police, and in the country. It is our professional and patriotic duty to do so.

We will explain to you as best we can all your rights and all the options that you have. We will facilitate the process of law that you get full and quick justice.

We will also help you to establish contact with others who can be of help to you in this your hour of need.

Courtesy of UNICEF India, Patna office, which assisted the Bangladesh office with support for this campaign.

Courtesy of UNICEF India, Patna office, which assisted the Bangladesh office with support for this campaign.

person, he shall be punishable for imprisonment for a term which may extend to one year or fine or both. The Commission had also recommended that if an officer in charge of a police station refuses to record a complaint about a cognizable offence he should be punishable with up to one year's imprisonment. (Singh 1997, page 55)

Matters of Evidence

Strengthening the medico-legal system. To highlight the importance of preserving evidence for cases about violence against women and girls, two forensic medicine specialists from the region were invited to the 1997 Kathmandu regional meeting on ending such violence. Ravindra Fernando, Professor of Forensic Medicine and Toxicology and Director of the Centre for the Study of Human Rights, University of Colombo, Sri Lanka, stressed the importance of the "medico-legal" aspects of violence to establish scientific proof. He also referred to the trauma experienced by victims of sexual abuse that resulted from the procedures they must follow in the various countries of South Asia, and he underlined the additional problems confronting girls who are victim-survivors:

> Starting with making the complaint at the police station — often involving repeatedly recounting the story — the victim is subsequently taken for an intrusive medical-legal examination, and finally has to undergo multiple cross-examinations in the different stages of court procedures. Girl-child victims face additional problems such as the lack of credibility of their statements due to their young age. (UNICEF 1998b, page 42)

He observed that "the medico-legal system has a number of undesirable features, including the non-recognition of physical violence in children." For the prevention of sexual abuse, he suggested "strengthening the individual capabilities of women and decreasing their vulnerability to violence through various interventions by the state and NGOs" and the development of a plan "to eliminate unacceptable cultural norms, . . . to challenge the legal system that favours the abusers and discourages or obstructs the victims" (page 42) His practical recommendations to implement these strategies were incorporated in the group's overall recommendations (see Appendix 2).

Child rape is a crime about which there is more and more concern. Silence about it is being broken. Much more sensitivity and care in obtaining evidence and bringing such cases to justice are needed. Incredulity among the judiciary about the prevalence of child rape and the character of rapists calls for relevant training and monitoring of cases by women's groups and others. Incest, where it comes under child rape, is a subject for which attitudes of denial and protection of men accused can be very difficult problems to overcome.

With regard to evidence needed to convict for the offence of rape, a number of recommendations are being made by various women's groups. Singh (1998) notes that corroboration of a victim-survivor's account is not required by law but is almost always sought and that convictions are lacking without it. Goonesekere (n.d.) observes that insistence on corroboration by women rape victims is discrimination, and is foreign to Sri Lankan pre-colonial practice at the community level. She says:

> For gender-equality and a violence-free society we must depart from the colonial experience, the legacy of which affects today's gender equality and the situation of

violence against women. For instance, the rules of corroboration are a heritage of the British system.[77] (UNICEF 1998b, page 44)

In Pakistan, women's and human rights groups continue to try to overturn the Hudood Ordinances, but without success to date.[78]

Some other points being raised by South Asians are that equipment to permit testing for DNA is lacking, and that procedures for medical examinations need to be improved. At present, for example, physicians may not agree to conduct a medical examination in a legal case unless the police have first requested it. From a legal point of view, the request is not necessary, but, all too often, waiting for it seems to be the practice. A legal requirement to report all injuries congruent with physical or sexual domestic violence as well as rape could be institutionalized for physicians.

Women's groups also want the definition of rape to be changed, so that more than penile penetration is considered an offence under the law. Even with penile penetration, the question of ejaculation remains. Kusuma, the victim-survivor of rape from Sri Lanka whom we met in Chapter 6, said that it was thanks to a course on legal literacy that she knew the importance of preserving evidence from her rape. Evidence is a key issue in all cases of violence against women and girls. Many are lost for want of it. Sometimes physicians refuse examinations without an order; or police do not take pains to preserve the evidence; or the culprit or aggressor destroys it; or the woman or girl victimized does not know how to preserve it.

Overcoming Judicial Bias

A forum on Judicial Education on Gender Equality Issues was held in New Delhi in 1997. The NGO Sakshi then initiated a multi-country study on judicial attitudes towards gender, with a pilot conducted by Naripokkho in Bangladesh.

> Often it is the personal lives of women, whether accused or perpetrators, that become the subject of interrogation in courts and not the reported crime or offence. It is not unnatural that the judges, who have been born and brought up in a society where male dominance and inferiority of women are socially accepted norms, will reflect these norms in their handling of cases. (Naripokkho 1997, page 2)

Naripokkho notes that judges are, by definition, thought to be objective and fair, so that the idea of special training on gender had gone unrecognized and was not always acceptable. However, an analysis of judgements in 31 cases about violence against women — along with interviews and court observations — revealed significant problems, as well as the need for more research. In fact, judicial education concerning gender issues, pertinent to violence against women cases, is under way in South Asia (see Das 1998, for example). A seemingly effective strategy is for a senior judge to lead seminars for other judges on the topic.[79]

Legal Awareness and Legal Literacy

What are legal awareness and legal literacy? Dr. Shanta Thapalia, lawyer activist in Nepal, distinguishes clearly between them, although both are often referred to together as "legal literacy," a major thrust of programmes for women in South Asia.[80] For Dr. Thapalia, "legal awareness" means that women, even illiterate women, know about their rights under the law. As Madurai Singh[81] of Saathi, an NGO active against violence towards women in Nepal, puts it:

> First and foremost, women have to know about their rights. They have to be made aware. . . . . I would not say being aware and being educated are the same thing. . . . People who are not literate are also sometimes aware. We can always take inspiration and lessons from these people. But first and foremost people have to be made aware, especially women, of their right about this violence being a social crime.

But as for details — how to bring cases, where to get support from women's groups, NGOs, government ministries, international organizations — that depends on "legal literacy." Legal awareness can be achieved with a general campaign, but Dr. Thapalia thinks much more is required for legal literacy. It also helps if the women involved are literate, so they can then add legal literacy. The materials used are often written ones.

This is the process for her work in legal awareness and legal literacy as she described it to me:

> At first we went to the villagers to raise legal awareness. We found out those coming to the meetings were already aware and they could fight for themselves. They were the conscious people. But the 90 per cent, those suffering the most, were not coming. Then we had a new strategy, a house-to-house women-awareness campaign. This was difficult and costly. We needed people with legal background. That's how we started the women's monitoring programme with women lawyers. We took 20 graduate [women] from law school and put them in training for five months. They had to learn the actual situation of women in the villages, going door-to-door, both making women conscious of their rights and listening to the problems of women. The give-and-take is what makes the programme successful. Now we have a higher level of women legal manpower, 80 have been trained.

Examples from Sri Lanka, India and Pakistan illustrate legal literacy in the more specific sense:

> One of the reasons that affect women is ignorance of the law. So we developed this project on preparing legal literacy booklets in Sinhala, Tamil and English on issues concerning women, in an easy-to-grasp format. The dissemination part of it was a bit difficult and only a few of us opted to do this. It was done through NGOs and other community-based organizations. . . . Women were quite surprised to discover their legal rights, that the law was available, and that there were legal remedies and so on. ("Kanthi,"[82] an activist/ researcher/lawyer from Sri Lanka)

In 1991, Simorgh, a well-respected NGO in Pakistan, published a booklet on rape from the survivor's viewpoint. It was in both Urdu and English and reached a wide reading public. Simorgh was proposing publishing a series of 10 booklets on a variety of subjects "to give visibility to crimes of violence against women."[83]

The Lawyers' Collective in India provides an important service through the development and dissemination of booklets and other materials regarding legal aid. Their advice appears to be very realistic, as it must be for women victim-survivors to make informed decisions. With regard to the all-important question for most women about the custody and guardianship of their children, the Lawyers' Collective concluded (1995, page 51):

> Fighting for guardianship and custody for women in courts is an uphill task. . . . [W]omen
> are often unaware of their rights and often unable to make decisions related to custody.
> This handbook has been written in the hope that it will help them make a realistic decision.
> It is not a substitute for proper legal advice. It is wise not to expect too much from the
> courts.

> Remember that while you can tide over a crisis situation with the help of the courts, you
> cannot change the patriarchal system which remains reflected in our laws.

Even if and when the law may change to permit women as well as men to have custody
as well as guardianship, it would remain to be seen how well the new law would be
implemented in fact.

There are some big questions about the likely effectiveness of legal literacy: Even
when women know the law, do they bring cases? Are they likely to win even when their
case seems a likely one for a positive outcome? And what are the reasons why women
do or do not bring and win cases once they know the law? What if the law is not
favourable? Then "legal advocacy" may be needed, as well as discussions with women
about pertinent aspects of the legal system other than the substance of the law.

Legal Advocacy

"Legal advocacy" is not a term Dr. Thapalia uses, but it is part of what she does,
promoting changes in the law to protect and fulfil women's rights. Owning property,
in her view, is basic for women to be protected from the consequences of gender-
based violence.

"Own property or be property." That sums up the thinking of women activists on
this issue in Nepal. Although the Constitution guarantees equality before the law
without discrimination by gender, the 1963 *Muluki Ain* provides inheritance for
women only if they are over 35 and still unmarried. The thinking behind this is that
a woman should not have "double inheritance." As she really "belongs" to her future
husband's family, fathers and brothers should not provide for her long-term needs. It
is also argued that family property should not be under the control of men from
another family, who have married in. (It is generally assumed that a wife's property
would be dominated by her husband; therefore, she shouldn't own it and risk its
loss from her father's patrilineage to that of her husband's.)

Dr. Thapalia talks about problems with the press and fundamentalists regarding
the proposed law:

> I'm being scolded. Damage is being done to my character in the newspaper, on the radio
> and so on. I'm tolerating it because this is my movement. We have been working in 40
> districts contacting the people in their views. We have 20 women and 22 men lawyers
> [dedicated to this cause]. We are spreading and advocating the message about women's
> property rights and motivating colleagues. Our team is doing a good job. The women [in
> general] are united for the cause except for maybe 500 [of the women]. The men are
> divided but the positive ones are in the majority. Only the fundamentalists openly oppose
> us. . . . This is a great problem for us. Wherever we go, they are there. Now we are fighting
> fundamentalists.

> The question is being considered in Parliament session. The court says, "Bring an
> appropriate bill on property rights for women." The point of discussion is what does

"appropriate" mean? There is lobbying going on. The time is very tense. The fundamentalists are very strong and influential.

Men's support is coming up now. But the orthodox are against me because I have family property. They say, "Don't be an example for others. Nobody can be like her." They say I'm against Hinduism and trying to spread Christianity. [She is not a Christian.]

In our religion, men and women are equal. I go back to the Vedas [when considering religious texts]. It is only later that discrimination is introduced. That is not proper Hinduism. Sometimes, though, I get phone calls. The fundamentalists say I'm a destroyer of society and the home. They say I have put my husband out of the home. I get these unwanted calls at night. A man told me on the phone, "You are flying too much, we will cut your wings and legs, then you will be on the ground." Once my husband was home at midnight when a call came. I had him take the call. When the man heard my husband's voice, he hung up. My husband is supportive. He warns me the fundamentalists may harm me. He asks me to avoid night parties or going out with people I don't know well. My son tells me, "Now you have so many enemies, you must be careful." I have so much support from my father and my mother. They are so happy, they praise me. My father said, "I was saying she should be married and not get more education. I have found out that if you give opportunities, the daughter can go ahead of the son."

Two years after the interview, the bill has still not passed.

Bina Agrawal has written the authoritative landmark book *A Field of Her Own: Gender and Land Rights in South Asia* (1996), which covers patterns of land rights in South Asia, how these are associated with kinship principles and economy, how women are generally marginalized and subject to violence without land.

Kamla Bhasin,[84] a leader of regional networks among NGOs on gender and development issues and co-founder of Jagori (Awake!) in India, explains how property rights law is linked with issues about violence against women:

It is extremely important to give women property rights, to give them the land. . . . You see the direct links [with less violence to women and girls] in communities where women inherit — you will never find female foeticide, you will never find that kind of disregard and devaluation of girls because they are more than equal citizens of that family, members of that family, and they remain in their own home and husbands come and live there. Now what a psychological difference it makes. So, I think it is an absolutely important and urgent issue, and it is almost an impossible issue to deal with. . . . It is going on in Maharashtra now, they have started giving women their land.

Kamla also talked about the problems for women accused and condemned as witches, especially when land rights are involved. Radhika Coomaraswamy, UN Special Rapporteur on violence against women, its causes and consequences, reports on the accusation of witchcraft and apparent quarrels over land rights:

The killing of women as witches has taken place at different times across many cultures in all regions of the world. In southern Africa and on the Indian subcontinent, for example, women are killed because they are believed to be witches. In the Singbhum district of Bihar, India, on average 200 women are murdered every year because of this belief. Most of the victims appear to be widows who own land or women with unwanted programs. (UNCHR 1997d, page 37)

Problems over land rights may increase given the growing populations in South Asia and the extent of agricultural economies under men's control.

Support Services

Hotlines. Sri Lanka, for example, has a hotline for citizens to report cases of violence against children. According to Mr. Nihal Karunaratne, Senior Superintendent of Police, Women's and Children's Desks, Colombo, Sri Lanka, it is being used more and more.[85] More such services are needed throughout the region for cases involving women as well as girls and boys.

Shelters. The general nature and problems characteristic of shelters have been discussed. Fortunately, there are some exceptions, like the one in Sri Lanka that accepts babies:

> "X," 19, stays in a shelter in Sri Lanka with her baby born after she was raped and impregnated by a neighbour. She expressed appreciation for her parent's support (but blames herself for what happened as she never expected it), for the attitude and help of other girls in the shelter, and for the fact that she is able to have her baby there with her.[86]

Counselling. Activists rarely mention this. It did come up in an interview[87] from Sri Lanka, however, which illustrates the importance of counselling the perpetrator as well as the victim-survivor.

> There was counselling by trained counsellors of the battered women who came to the Centre. . . . Sometimes the women were also able to bring their men as well. There would be joint counselling sessions when the couple would almost come to blows but were prevented because of our presence.[88]

Training for counsellors is recommended by another interviewer, who noted that the counsellor she interviewed seemed to have very negative attitudes towards the women he was assigned to help at a shelter.

Skill training and income-earning activities for victim-survivors. Shalini, an NGO executive in Sri Lanka,[89] calls attention to the need for skill training:

> And also, some kind of link to an organization which will be able to give them some kind of skill or make them employable. Without that it's pointless. It has to be all interlinked. You have to be able to fend for yourself after the divorce.

Ram Kumar Khatri, editor of *Development Review* in Nepal, comments on the need for income-earning opportunities:

> More than 100,000 [Nepali] women have been sold [in] India, and there are many NGOs working on this issue. But unless we give a good income-generating programme, this is impossible to control. Now it is necessary that we have to give skill training to women. There must be marketing for their craft, and they will earn money. Then violence will gradually stop. Education and skill training. Especially vocational training.[90]

Linking the Grassroots and the Policy Levels to Stop Violence against Women

Community involvement. Professor Savitri Goonesekere of Colombo, Sri Lanka, emphasizes the important role for NGOs to play at both local and policy levels if the use of the legal system regarding violence against women and girls is to improve. At the 1997 Kathmandu regional meeting, she spoke about the need "to strengthen law enforcement [as] law and law enforcement are not just the business of lawyers and judges, but part of the whole interdisciplinary system for investigation and effective prosecutions, so the NGOs need to be part of this through the detection of violence" (UNICEF 1998b, pages 20–21). She went on to say that "The need is for a multi-pronged approach to advocate and lobby for effective involvement to understand the complexities of institutional structures so as to use the judiciary in combating violence."

The report of the meeting describes Professor Goonesekere's speech as follows:

> She emphasized that law cannot be isolated. Community involvement in the process of monitoring and bringing justice is necessary. And it should take local needs and strengths into account while still honouring international norms. (UNICEF 1998b)

She also points out that law cannot be seen in isolation, and a change in communal attitudes needs to take place: "There is a need to recognize the problem of having two systems of justice in South Asia, and personal laws will have to be reassessed" (UNICEF 1998b, page 44).

Using the International Legal Framework of Human Rights Treaties

Meindersma (1998, page 2) summarizes the ways in which the international legal framework applies:

> The relevance of international law in South Asia and to the issue of violence against women is apparent. The respective states have assumed legally binding commitments under international law. They are involved in the formulation of regional and global initiatives to address the problem of violence against women. There is discernible interest among the professional legal and NGO community to employ human rights strategies and pursue international mechanisms to effect change in attitudes persevering in violence against women and girls. In national court procedures, arguments based on international law are frequently made, and domestic courts are more or less inclined to allow international law to influence the outcome of national proceedings.[91] (See also Sangroula and Malla n.d.)

Among other possibilities, NGOs have a role in tracing legal cases, identifying when conventions can be brought to bear, encouraging, following and supplementing national reports on the conventions, and working for the removal of reservations to the Convention and CEDAW.[92]

Goonesekere stresses the danger of cultural relativity. It will be necessary, then, for NGOs and women's groups to master the international legal framework with regard to the issue of violence against women.[93]

State Responsibility: Due Diligence

What about a nagging issue: State responsibility even for acts of gender violence in the home? Meindersma (1998, page 20) refers to the State's "due diligence" obligation to prevent and provide effective redress for violations of international obligations. She also outlines the basis for construing State responsibility for acts of violence against women committed by private persons, as follows:

1. When the international obligations as spelled out in international instruments extend to the private sphere.

2. When the state apparatus systematically fails to prevent and provide effective mechanisms of redress in situations of violence against women.

3. . . . when the state, through acts or omission, condones, facilitates, supports, or becomes complicit in the perpetration of violence against women by non-state actors.

In such situations, the state's involvement transforms the private acts into an act of state and consequently, the state incurs responsibility for the conduct of private persons as such. For instance, where the state fails to amend laws sanctioning violence or preventing effective redress or where the state does nothing to stop the application of customs and traditions that perpetuate violence against women, or justifies such practices in the name of conserving traditional patriarchal structures of society, the state's conduct would amount to state "acquiescence" in such violence and entail the international responsibility of the state. (pages 21–23)

Meindersma points out the fact that international norms may not be taken as standards for enforcement by domestic courts where they conflict with norms in national law. She says, "It follows that, to a certain extent, the system of interaction between international and national law determines the immediate practical relevance of human rights norms in the national legal context" (page 24).

It is therefore urgent that women's groups know about the national legal system and how to improve its fit with international standards.

There are already some notable success stories showing the effectiveness of women's groups in bringing about changes in national affirmations of international law and practice. In Bangladesh, NGOs and women lawyers led the effort to have the government remove its reservations to CEDAW. In Nepal, a "Shadow Report on the Initial Report of the Government of Nepal on the Convention on Elimination of All Forms of Discrimination Against Women (CEDAW)" was prepared by the Forum for Women, Law and Development in collaboration with a coalition of women's NGOs (June 1999). It refers to Nepal's unconditional ratification of CEDAW and to Recommendation 19 as the basis for the obligation of States Parties "to overcome all forms of gender based violence, whether by public or private act," and to "take all legal and other measures that are necessary to provide effective protection of women against gender based violence. . ." (Forum for Women, Law and Development 1999, page 42). The report concludes: "Thus Nepal and consequently the report is lacking in the above mentioned aspects of legislating against VAW&G [violence against women and girls]."

Several of those women lawyers who drafted the shadow report accompanied government representatives to the review session at the United Nations with the CEDAW Committee. It will not be clear until the next report by Nepal whether or not the government will heed comments by the NGOs as well as by the CEDAW Committee. In the meantime, advocacy will, no doubt, continue.

In India, which reports to CEDAW in 2000, NGO efforts to "accompany" the government report are under way. The degree of their success will indicate the extent of government concern to listen and respond to women's views about their human rights under the law.

What about Religion?

Donna Sullivan, writing for UNIFEM, provides useful guidance regarding restrictions on manifestations of religion:

> The observance of the religious norms and their embodiment in national law should be viewed as protected manifestations of religion or belief. The right to manifest religion or belief is not unlimited, however. Both Article 18 of the Universal Declaration and Article 18 of the Covenant on Civil and Political Rights permit restrictions on manifestations of religion or belief if they are necessary to protect the rights and freedoms of others and are prescribed by law. Restrictions therefore may be imposed on the application of religious law or practice where necessary to protect women's human rights and prescribed by law. (Sullivan 1996, page 13)

The question of the fit between tradition, religious belief and international law is also addressed:

> The freedom of religion or belief may not be asserted to shield religious law or practice affecting women's human rights from scrutiny. The implementation of international norms in particular cultural contexts may entail their adaptation to culturally specific institutional and legal frameworks and the identification of analogues in indigenous cultural values. However, interpretations of international norms which would undermine the objective of those norms are incompatible with the very notion of human rights, as is the substitution of religious or cultural values for international norms. (Sullivan 1996, page 13)

Gomez and Gomez (1998, page 3) describe the important shift occurring in thinking abut the interplay between international norms based on human rights and national law:

> Much of the early human rights activism revolved around political abuse and violence. The human rights movement has now realized that human rights violations encompass not only politically motivated violence perpetrated by the state but other abuse and violence — non-political — originating in a variety of contexts and locations, including the family and the workplace. These influences and changes are evident in Sri Lanka where women's groups have campaigned for legal, administrative and other reforms.

Lessons Learned

The experiences reviewed in this chapter permit us to draw some lessons learned with regard to both problems in the legal system and changes needed if there to be more equity for women victim-survivors of violence. First, four very fundamental and important issues can be highlighted based on Ziauddin's experience in Pakistan concerning "honour killings". The points also apply to other forms of gender violence and to other countries:

- Violence against women is embedded in social and political systems and in cultural values; it is not due simply to exceptional behaviour of a deviant man here or there; rather, social norms and political action sanction and protect a perpetrator's actions, which may even be considered "manly" by others in a patriarchal system.
- The same social and political order and cultural values that condone murder and other violence to women and girls within the family cannot readily provide justice for the violated. It is thus urgent to challenge what has been called "the intolerable

status quo" (Bunch 1997) within the family as well as outside it. This is not an abstract exercise. It requires advocacy with and monitoring of the State as well as support for women's and human rights groups. Otherwise, the norms that sanction asymmetrical power between men and women will regularly and easily lead to the abuse of the human rights and lives of women and girls.

- Without state intervention and provision of alternatives for victim-survivors and penalties for perpetrators, family rule and even hideous abuse and murder will prevail.
- A law against domestic violence would signal the intentions of the State to uphold the human rights of women and children in the home and to pursue good governance based on the rule of law concerning all its citizens.

Some additional lessons learned on the basis of the material covered:

- Existing national laws are often discriminatory, even where a constitution guarantees equality and a country has ratified CEDAW and CRC.
- Women seem to believe that if discriminatory laws are changed and lacunae in the laws are filled, their rights and claims will be upheld; accordingly, activists call for changes in the laws, bringing them into harmony with a constitution, CEDAW and CRC. This is necessary but insufficient.
- Custom, patriarchy, men's solidarity and vested interests can dominate and influence outcomes even in cases where the law would seem to dictate an outcome in favour of women and girls. Some discriminatory laws predict negative outcomes for women and girls but are not overturned by the State.
- Negative attitudes of the state actors and private individuals towards women and girls must be addressed, even if shielded under the rubric of "culture" and "tradition."
- Reservations/declarations related to culture and custom made on international rights treaties, such as CEDAW and CRC, anticipate more and more problems for the implementation of such treaties, and for laws in harmony with national and international norms.

As Pappu cautioned, a formalistic approach to the legal system will be insufficient to bring about effective change. While laws must be enacted taking into account the rights of all citizens, women and girls as well as men and boys, laws need to be implemented without prejudice. For this to happen, values as embodied in the law need to be shared, respected and promulgated by the citizenry and those charged with enforcement of the law. Negative attitudes towards women and girls, or any idea that they forfeit their human rights once in the home, call for correction. So does institutional violence against women and girls when they are outside the home. Workable alternatives need to be provided for women and children faced with intolerable situations. Efforts to prevent gender violence are vital.

In short, as Professor Goonesekere urges, women's groups and NGOs in South Asia must engage even more with the State if the legal system is to bring relief from violence against women and girls and attitudes about women's inferiority are to change. At the same time, men, both agents of the State and private actors, must be encouraged to re-examine patriarchal attitudes they may exhibit in their professional as well as private lives and to work to fulfil women's and girls' human rights at all levels of society. For that to happen, they need to learn more about the costs of gender violence to society, to their families and to themselves. Men who control the home as their private domain outside the rule of law are condemned thereby to lives of greater violence than would be the case if the legal system worked well for all its citizens. They also condemn their countries to greater violence and to violations of international conventions.

International bodies concerned with human rights treaties have a vital but difficult role to play. Where States Parties to conventions like CRC and CEDAW openly or tacitly support customs and attitudes that fail to protect women's and girls' human rights, they break their commitments under international law. If the advocacy and review systems for implementation of treaties are weak, they are then at risk of themselves undermining the effectiveness of international human rights treaties. Alternatively, States Parties that pursue equality of women and men through harmonization of national laws with international treaties actively discourage gender-based violence. They also encourage the rule of law to benefit all citizens in all institutions, including the family.

Endnotes

1   Without equal property rights, women may be considered even more vulnerable to violence in the family, as their alternatives for support are limited should they want to leave a marriage. On the other hand, when women do have property or stand to inherit it, violence by a family member may be used to see that the woman is killed, or controlled, with the property then benefiting the perpetrator(s).

2   Chairperson, Mr. Justice Nasir Aslam Zahid, Judge, Supreme Court of Pakistan; Members: Senator Mr. Yahya Bakhtiar; Senator Mr. Masood Kausar; Ms. Asma Jahangir; Maulana Muhammad Tuaseen; Ms. Shaheen Sardar Ali; Ms. Shahla Zia; Ms. Shahnaz Javed, Former MNA; Senator Ms. Fiza Junejo; Ms. Rehana Sarwar, Former MNA; Ms. Anisa Zeb, Advocate, Peshawar.

3   Nor have positive changes followed based on the 1997 report, which apparently was not discussed in Parliament.

4   Interview for this book arranged by UNICEF ROSA; name withheld.

5   Nepali human rights activist and NGO leader. Interview for this book arranged by UNICEF ROSA in cooperation with UNICEF Nepal.

6   Interview for this book arranged by UNICEF ROSA in cooperation with UNICEF Nepal; name withheld.

7   Interview for this book arranged by UNICEF Bangladesh.

8   Anand Patwardana's film *Father, Son and the Holy War* gives an account that links the event to religious and political pressure.

9   Human Rights Watch (1999) states, "Sarwar's mother, father and paternal uncle were all accomplices to her murder" (page 1).

10   A *fotwa* or *fatwa* is a sentence based on interpretation of the Quran by the *shalish*, a local body claiming sanctity and authority in the name of religion.

11   A local body usually made up of male leaders, which makes rules for behaviour in their community and censors same, increasingly in the name of Islam. (See Siddiqi 1998).

12   This refers to judgements made by local bodies in the name of religion: *'fatwa'* is the name of the ruling.[Both of these words have been defined earlier; we can delete this footnote.]

13   For example, in the Vishaka Case from India, the woman activist concerned was gang-raped after taking up women's issues (personal communication, Savitri Goonesekere).

14   Name withheld. Personal communication, Kathmandu, 1998.

15   "e.g. the definition of crimes and their penalties for redress" (Meindersma 1998, page 2).

16   I am particularly indebted to those eminent South Asian lawyers who participated in the "Planning and Review Meeting on the Use of the Legal System in Combating Violence against Women and Children," 27–28 August 1997, UN Conference Hall, New Delhi (as organized by UNIFEM/UNICEF). These lawyers provided country reports to me at UNICEF ROSA in 1997–1998: Bangladesh: Sigma Huda, ASK and ILD; India: Kirti Singh; Nepal: Yubaraj Sangroula and Sapana Malla; Pakistan: Hina Jilani and Eman Ahmed; Sri Lanka: Shyamala Gomez and Mario Gomez. Christa Meindersma drafted the regional overview as part of the project I coordinated. Her effectiveness will be evident in this chapter. Many lawyers in addition to those in the regional study were among the activists who were interviewed. Their interview material has proved invaluable for this chapter along with viewpoints from other activists, not necessarily lawyers, who are keenly interested in the law.

17   Interview arranged by UNICEF Nepal.

18   Mr. Gonsalves practises in the Bombay High Court and, occasionally, in the Supreme Court. He is convenor of the Human Rights Law Network and of the India Centre for Human Rights and Law, Bombay.

19   From the interview arranged for this book by UNICEF ROSA.

20   Opinions heard at the Kathmandu regional meeting, 1997.

[21] For women whose marriages are not registered, however, this option may prove impossible.

[22] From transcript (page 20) of "Planning and Review Meeting on the Use of the Legal System in Combating Violence against Women and Children," 27–28 August 1997, UN Conference Hall, New Delhi (as organized by UNIFEM/UNICEF).

[23] Professor Goonesekere has long stressed the importance of such engagement: I remember a regional meeting on violence against women held in Colombo in 1996, where we were both guest speakers. She was already well known for keeping clippings about various cases of violence against women and for encouraging women's groups to monitor them. I happened to mention some of the horrendous cases that were in the paper that day. We were disappointed that when the priorities for follow-up action were set by the groups attending, they did not include monitoring cases or even domestic violence itself. Rather, the priorities were: breaking the silence, working with men and action against "ragging."

[24] Whereby one seeks advantage in terms of one's ethnic, cultural or religious identity.

[25] A more comprehensive review of the subject, as yet unpublished, can be found in the country reports and regional studies of UNICEF ROSA, UNIFEM and UNDP.

[26] Interview for this book arranged by UNICEF ROSA in cooperation with UNICEF Pakistan; name withheld.

[27] As the reader may recall, this refers to the requirement that there be four male witnesses to penetration and that claims of rape without such evidence can lead to convictions of the girl/woman.

[28] Reported under Torture (Cruelty by Husband and Relatives), National Crime Records Bureau (1999).

[29] Interview for this book arranged by UNICEF Nepal.

[30] Many of these problems are similar to ones described by Human Rights Watch (1999).

[31] Interview for this book arranged by UNICEF Sri Lanka. All Sri Lankan interviewees were given pseudonyms by UNICEF Sri Lanka.

[32] Interview for this book conducted by UNICEF Pakistan; name withheld.

[33] Reported in interview with a woman lawyer in Pakistan, arranged by UNICEF Pakistan for this book; name withheld.

[34] Interview for this book arranged by UNICEF India.

[35] From interview for this book as arranged by UNICEF Pakistan.

[36] From interview for this book as arranged by UNICEF India; name withheld.

[37] From interview for this book arranged by UNICEF Pakistan; name withheld.

[38] Kirti Singh, personal communication, New Delhi, 1999.

[39] Meindersma (1998, page 71) comments, "One reason forwarded by researchers in Sri Lanka for the delays is the length of time taken to conclude the non-summary procedure: a pre-trial procedure conducted by police under supervision of a magistrate [and] required in cases of rape and murder."

[40] Interview for this book arranged by UNICEF Pakistan.

[41] See Zia (1994) for a detailed account about these ordinances.

[42] On a more hopeful note, the Commission of Inquiry for Women, Pakistan, comments that there have been (some) changes for the better and reminds the reader that women are guaranteed many rights under Islam, contrary to what is often thought. The report notes the "widespread misconception about the place Islam accords to women, which is not just a distortion spread in the West but it exists even among the intelligentsia in the Muslim World,

including Pakistan" (Commission of Inquiry for Women 1997, page ii).

[43] Interview for this book arranged by UNICEF India.

[44] Interview by journalist Ruchira Gupta arranged by UNICEF ROSA in cooperation with UNICEF India.

[45] Personal communication, New Delhi, 1997.

[46] The highest percentage for convictions of crimes against women in 1997 is 54.2 per cent, for cases under the Immoral Traffic (Prevention) Act; the lowest, 0 per cent, for cases under the Sati Prevention Act (National Crime Records Bureau 1999, page 167).

[47] Personal communication with Christa Meindersma, Kathmandu, 1997.

[48] In 1999, at a meeting we had in New Delhi, Singh pointed out to me that there had been an improvement, at least with regard to dowry retrieval: A Supreme Court judgement in favour of a woman complainant regarding non-return of dowry as a criminal breach of trust was followed by an increase of such cases being registered, with women asking for their dowries back and for their husbands to be punished. She said that 70–80 per cent of these have been settled in favour of the women.

[49] These ages are the youngest for which girls can legally be married even with parental consent.

[50] Personal communication, Savitri Goonesekere, February 23, 2000, and see Goonesekere (1998).

[51] Boys and men involved in extramarital sex are called *karo*; girls and women, *kari*. Thus, *karo kari* is the term for such cases that may be followed by double murder for the sake of family name and "honour."

[52] From the interview arranged for this book by UNICEF Pakistan; name used with consent.

[53] In 1999, as this book was being finalized, Mufti Ziauddin was studying in New York City.

[54] Refers to punishment, in the form of compensation, in cases of murder and hurt; by custom, the accused or his family may sometimes hand over females rather than imprisonment or another type of penalty.

[55]

[56] Interview for this book conducted by UNICEF Sri Lanka; "Shalini" is the pseudonym they used for this interviewee.

[57] Interview for this book arranged by UNICEF Sri Lanka, which used "Mala" as a pseudonym for the interviewee.

[58] Interview for this book arranged by UNICEF ROSA in cooperation with UNICEF Pakistan; name withheld.

[59] Pseudonym for case as reported in interview for this book with Sahodari Project, arranged by UNICEF India.

[60] Pseudonym for case as reported in interview with an activist, grass-roots worker interviewed for this book by UNICEF India.

[61] From same interview, as arranged by UNICEF India.

[62] An Indian man lawyer interviewed for this book as arranged by UNICEF India; name withheld.

[63] Human rights worker interviewed for this book by UNICEF Pakistan.

[64] Woman NGO leader; interview arranged for this book by UNICEF Bangladesh.

[65] The laws vary according to the religion of the individual (Lawyers' Collective 1995).

[66] It is relevant to recall that the main source for cases of rape and incest in late 18th-century England also was the press: "From 1796, the Old Bailey Court began to suppress the publication of transcripts of sexual crimes, chiefly rape and sodomy; presumably the judges wished to protect the public from exposure to such 'offensive' testimony. The suppression of 'immorality', however, has always served to obstruct women's voices and conceal their oppression, for their ability to speak out against crimes committed against them was also suppressed. To

examine rape in 19th century London, I have therefore been forced to rely on newspaper reports of sexual assault cases [heard] in magistrate's courts and quarter sessions. . . . I have collected 238 cases of sexual assault through sampling [various newspapers]" (Clark 1987, page 17).

[67] Interview for this book arranged by UNICEF India.

[68] Interview for this book arranged by UNICEF Pakistan.

[69] Interview for this book arranged by UNICEF India.

[70] These recommendations are compatible with those put forth by the UN Special Rapporteur for violence against women, its causes and consequences, as well as those promoted in the Beijing Platform for Action.

[71] Pseudonym in interview for this book as arranged by UNICEF Sri Lanka.

[72] The interview was arranged for this book by UNICEF Pakistan; name withheld.

[73] Study on the "Use of the Legal System in Combating Violence against Women and Children," as organized by UNICEF ROSA, under leadership of author, and in cooperation with UNIFEM, with support of the Swiss Government and UNDP. There were country studies for Bangladesh, India, Pakistan and Sri Lanka, as well as a regional overview conducted by Meindersma (1998).

[74] From interview as arranged for this book by UNICEF Pakistan; name withheld.

[75] From the interview arranged for this book by UNICEF Nepal.

[76] From an interview with a man lawyer arranged for this book by UNICEF ROSA; name withheld.

[77] See also Gooneseкere (1994) in her article in Alston (1994), *In the Best Interests of the Child.*

[78] Pakistan's Commission of Inquiry for Women (1997) made detailed recommendations for changes regarding this and other legal matters related to violence against women.

[79] I had the pleasure of witnessing such a seminar conducted in Nepal by a former Chief Justice of India (Kathmandu, 1997).

[80] From the interview arranged for this book by UNICEF

ROSA. Dr. Thapalia is Associate Professor of the Law Institute, Tribhuvan University, Nepal, and founder of the Legal Aid and Consultancy Centre, an NGO. Name used by agreement with the interviewee.

[81] From the interview arranged for the book by UNICEF ROSA in cooperation with UNICEF Nepal.

[82] Pseudonym in interview, as arranged by UNICEF Sri Lanka.

[83] From a letter to the author from Simorgh.

[84] From the interview conducted by the author for this book.

[85] Personal communication, during the Strategy Meetings on Gender and Violence against Women and Girls, Perspectives on the Future Role of UNICEF in South Asia, 16–18 August 1999, Godavari, Nepal.

[86] Interview for this book conducted by UNICEF Sri Lanka, which used the pseudonym "X" for this interviewee.

[87] Arranged for this book by UNICEF Sri Lanka.

[88] Interview for this book conducted by UNICEF Sri Lanka.

[89] Interview for this book arranged by UNICEF Sri Lanka, which used "Shalini" as a pseudonym for the interviewee.

[90] From the interview arranged for this book by UNICEF ROSA.

[91] Meindersma (1998, page 3) points out that in addition to the Convention and CEDAW, "a prohibition of violence against girls and women is implicit in the provisions of both the International Covenant on Civil and Political Rights (ICCPR) and the International Covenant on Economic, Social and Cultural Rights (ICESCR)."

[92] For CEDAW, those particular relevance are about non-discrimination, marriage, family life and religion (Articles 2, 13, 16 and 5).

[93] This is true outside as well as within the region. At the World Conference on Family Violence, held in Singapore in 1998, the audience was quite interested in the subject of violence against women as a human rights issue, one about which I made a presentation. However, few had considered it before. "International instruments" like the Convention and CEDAW were, in general, a new idea. The possibility of monitoring or supplementing national reports to the committees was challenging. The group had many questions and lots of important homework ahead.

Building Movements to Stop Violence against Women and Girls in South Asia

"[W]omen's movements are now active in all Asian countries, extending into all classes active in social and political agitation, and aiming to make all women conscious of their subordination within the prevailing family structures. These growing movements have taken up many issues that affect women: dowry deaths, rape, abortion, prostitution and general violence. In doing so, they expose the male domination that underlies all Asian social practice. It should be noted, however, that these movements also draw upon the strengths of earlier ones and rely on the memories and experiences of an earlier stage of feminist struggle; it is as if, after a long period of dormancy, women's consciousness has suddenly come alive again." (Jayawardena 1994, page 280)

Links with the Past

Gender Stereotypes or Rights?

The Women's situation was an issue in social reform movements during the colonial period in most of South Asia, as well as in resistance and nationalist struggles.[1] In pre-partition India, for example, some leading South Asian activists called for social reform, as did colonists, to stop child marriage, *sati* and dowry. They were mostly men, with some very important exceptions. They also were prominent among those who wanted women to fulfil their right to education. Education for girls was seen as compatible with, even necessary for, better marriages and flourishing family life, along with accelerated local and national development. The proposed changes were presented so that they did not appear to challenge prevailing gender-role stereotypes for women. Gender-role stereotypes were also apparent as guides to women's behaviour during the partition of India. Women's experiences then included being encouraged to commit suicide to save family honour after rape. This even happened to some women for whom the government forced "restoration" to the home country following their abduction and integration into the foreign culture (see Das 1995;[2] Menon and Bhasin 1998).

These and other experiences that women had during various incidents of struggle, fighting, wars and political change in the region naturally raise questions about women's roles and rights, about the relationship between their traditional and modern lives, and about their part in efforts to bring change.

The emphasis in the 1990s on human rights in the international arena makes the questions even sharper. The process of taking up women's situation over time can be seen as a struggle of patriarchal ideas about women's purity and submission in strongly hierarchical societies versus democratic ideas about the fulfilment of human rights for women as well as for men.

In the past, three main strategies appear to have been used to "solve" the problem of tensions between girls' and women's prescribed traditional roles in patriarchal institutions and the quest for fulfilment of their rights in both private and public spheres.

First, men were the ones who usually determined the degree and terms of women's limited participation in movements, in ways men saw as beneficial. That normally meant that women's participation was in terms of traditional values about and prescriptions for women's roles.

Second, women's human rights were not made the main issue for women's struggle; rather, single issues such as child marriage, dowry, polygamy or *sati* were addressed for short periods and for reasons other than women's advancement itself: "women's issues" were often a means to achieve something else.

Third, the argument was made that by extending educational and political rights to women, women's contribution to their families would be enhanced, not diminished. Thus, it was the family that should benefit rather than individual women themselves. In short, women in public spaces could be interpreted as still putting a priority on their family roles.

As Kumari Jayawardena notes, today's movements draw upon the strengths of the past. They also reflect its weaknesses and some persisting questions. Foremost among these is, "How to reconcile women's full participation in public life and fulfilment of their human rights with family life and cultural values based on patriarchy?" The apparent fundamentalist backlash today[3] illustrates the seriousness of the problem. It is centred in a commitment to maintain stereotypes for women and men that support continuation of imbalances in power between men and women in their relationships — that is, to maintain the patriarchal order of things, even at the expense of women's human rights.

Gender violence, especially physical violence in the family, has only recently been identified as a major obstacle to the fulfilment of women's and girls' rights as worthy goals in themselves. But the State has been hesitant to set and enforce strong measures against physical and psychological violence against women in the home. Then the dominance and authority of men in the family would be questioned and put under scrutiny. Political support could wane for any leaders who seriously challenged the men's favoured position. In reality, women's rights and fundamental freedoms — protected in most countries of the region by the constitutions — are limited by attitudes, custom and personal law, even where these conflict with the constitution.

How do today's women's movements approach gender-based violence? That is another important question to consider. To help answer it, this chapter features some interviews that give the reader a glimpse into women's movements in South Asia today, and in the context of earlier times and influences.

New Challenges

Government machineries for improving women's situation and involvement in development are in place in all the South Asian countries represented in this book, except Afghanistan. There is cooperation, to varying degrees, between governments and NGOs. Accordingly, all the countries both influence and respond to United Nations programmes at the global level for the advancement of women and the fulfilment of human rights. As noted earlier, all have signed, ratified or acceded to CEDAW and CRC.

But important questions remain on the table. One is whether or not movements that have often reinforced women's traditional roles can in fact succeed in challenging the most traditional one, submission in the family. Professor Savitri Goonesekere, Vice Chancellor of Colombo University and member of the Faculty of Law, has highlighted the reluctance in South Asia even to discuss the family — and the challenge to do so (UNICEF 1998b, page 20). And Professor Vina Mazumdar (n.d., page 316) has offered this important insight:

> Feminism still has to probe adequately the layers and roots of consciousness that enmesh the individual woman's relations with her conjugal and natal families and the class and generational variations in women's innate sense of dignity and degradation, or humiliation and a sense of moral worth.

Another important question is, "What women are we talking about?" How to reflect the experience and views of women from different backgrounds, by caste, class, rural or urban life?

Increasingly, rural women are taking up issues of direct concern to them in the process of development, as some examples in this book show. Rural women and poor urban women living in slums often challenge stereotypes about women's place in very direct ways. They are trying to bring their world view into the development process so that it will not exploit them any further.

Lawyer Colin Gonsalves[4] of the Human Rights Network in Bombay emphasizes the divide between elite women and those on the front lines. He says:

> Within the women's movement there is a clear-cut differentiation. There are women in struggles and women in advocacy. Women in struggle are very busy. They're organizing women at the workplace, women in slums, women in tribal areas. They're the women who are really doing change for women in society. Then you have the advocacy stuff where you travel from place to place, you speak, you do this or that, you get your contacts, you exchange your cards, you give out your little publications, etc. There's a growing gap between those who do advocacy and those who do struggle. Because those who do struggle don't get invited anywhere. They don't get heard within the entire movement. They have their own way of doing things. They're not so glib maybe. They don't know the standards or the norms. And this [divide] now: it's like the iron curtain.

There are other potential divides between those who focus on children and those who focus on women; between women and men; between those who work for human rights and those who represent the State and some of its institutions, which can act in repressive and biased ways towards women and girls, against their rights.

And will efforts be integrative — going beyond remedies only, focusing also on prevention, policy and rights?

Historical Highlights

A very brief look at some highlights about the "women question" in South Asia in the 19th and early 20th centuries sets the scene for this chapter. This historical material facilitates greater understanding of what today's women inherit and what obstacles they face as they struggle to surpass earlier achievements and to bridge divides. A description of some challenges for women's movements today then follows, with some excerpts from interviews with a few of those activists committed to ending gender-based violence. The challenge for future networks to end violence against women, especially in the home, is discussed. Some recommendations are made.[5]

First, some elements of movements for women in South Asia at the time of pre-partition India are reviewed. In the 19th century, as mentioned above, men rather than women were the ones primarily heard in public against particular practices like dowry, purdah, child marriage, *sati* and forbidding widows to remarry. For the most part, the basic rule that men are in control of women was being followed and extended from the home to the public sphere. Ram Mohan Roy, Iswar Chandra Vidyasagar, William Bentinck, Mrityunjaya Vidyalankara, Jyotibao Bhile, Bihren Malabari — these men were foremost among those working to end what were known as "certain degrading practices." According to both Kumar (1993) and Jayawardena (1994), the men's underlying preoccupation was to overcome any taint of "barbarism" associated with indigenous culture. They wanted to show that their society should be accepted as "civilized," with concomitant regard and opportunity for its "upper-caste" people. How women were treated was to be taken as an indicator and qualifier for men in South Asia to be seen and accepted as "civilized." The audience was men from another culture who controlled the access of indigenous men to new opportunities and positions from which they did not want to be excluded, marginalized in their own lands.

Those who spoke for women's education were also primarily men, with missionaries among the first to propose and establish formal education for girls. For example, Dr. Bhandahar and Justice Ranade were well-known proponents of girls' education in pre-partition India in the 19th century. In Sri Lanka, girls' education was also a central and early issue supported by men. The Dutch had started some coeducational schools in the 18th century. Again, women's rights were not the issue. The purpose was limited to supporting girls' options for marriage, as this 1912 quote shows:

> Apart from the practical value of those who want to go in for teaching, it [girls' education] improves girls' position especially to have passed a Cambridge examination, and this helps towards a better marriage settlement. That girls' education should have any higher or more lasting results than this is not, I think, a matter of general desire throughout Ceylon. (Henham 1912, page 427, quoted in Jayawardena 1994, page 121)

There were exceptions, of course. For instance, Anagarika Kharmapala, who was said to have been important in the Buddhist revival movement of Sri Lanka,

> was convinced that the subordination of women was a feature of other religious cultures, especially the Christian and Moslem, whereas Buddhism and the "Aryan" way of life allegedly followed by the Sinhalese gave freedom to women: "woman in ancient India was free. . . . Indian woman lost her individuality after the Moslem invasion of India. Woman

was not considered sacred by the Semitic races. The story of Adam and Eve made woman degraded forever." (Guruge 1965, page 341, quoted in Jayawardena 1994, page 126)

Still, his idea of "freedom" was extremely limited, and he warned, in fact, against Western education for girls, so that "a race of true Buddhists could [still] be produced in Ceylon" (Jayawardena 1994, page 126).

A. E. Builtjens, a Sri Lankan man lawyer, was one of those who actively encouraged establishment of Buddhist schools for girls. Such schools apparently had a more "nationalist-biased education, which included stress not only on Sri Lankan and Indian history and culture, but on democratic and anti-colonial movements elsewhere." It is said that many girl students who were at these schools later participated in movements for social and political reform (Jayawardena 1994, page 125).

The relatively few women who called for girls' education in South Asia included foreigners like Annie Besant from England, Helena Petrovna Blavatsky from Russia, Marie Miseaus Higgins from Germany and Louisa Roberts from England. Among the famous South Asian exceptions was Pandita Ramabai of India, who grew up in the forest where her social reformer father went to educate Pandita's mother, who was only nine when her father married her. Pandita's unusual upbringing had prepared her to carry on her father's work. Her parents died in the 1877 famine, when she was only 19. She became internationally known for the schools she set up for child widows and received financial supported from abroad. It is said that in the late 1800s she supported some 1,900 widows, some very young, even infants (Kumar 1993, page 26).

As for the issue of women's political participation, again, men were in the forefront. Only a few women spoke out, becoming famous exceptions accordingly. One was Begum Rokeya Sakhawat Hossain. In 1909 she set up a girls' school in Bengal. She herself had not been to school, but she had learned to read and write, in both English and Bengali, from her brothers, who taught her at night. Her *Sultana's Dream* (1993), first published in 1905 in the *English Ladies' Magazine* in Madras, is a fantasy about women as enlightened rulers and men in purdah. It is one of the first visions of a new political order published by a South Asian woman in modern times. (Her husband encouraged the publication.) It is exceptional, too, in that it shows a reversal of women's and men's usual roles, going against stereotypes.[6]

For Nationalism: Extolling and Breaking Stereotypes of Women

Leaders of civil disobedience in pre-partition India urged women's participation for their own purposes, without seeing any contradiction for women who were thus brought out of the domestic sphere yet were expected to return to it. They praised the very characteristics that wed women to the home but were useful in pressing for women's involvement outside the home, at least briefly. For example, Gandhi himself extolled woman for her "self-sacrificing nature," as being better suited than a man to practice satyagraha (passive resistance). Kumar (1993, page 83) writes that Gandhi "found that women adhered more closely to his creed of non-violent war, for it calls into play suffering to the largest extent, and who can suffer more purely and nobly than woman?"

She also reports that Gandhi did not accept women into his movement unless they were "chaste in thought, word and deed." Women prostitutes ready to do "humanitarian work" were excluded unless they would first reform.

Gandhi also lauded women's role as mother and spoke about how education and participation in resistance complemented women's fundamental responsibility to ensure a better future for the family and the nation. In fact, Gandhi first called for Indian women's involvement only in issues clearly related to the home, such as the use of the *charkha* (spinning wheel) and to wear *khadi* (homespun cloth). When he called for them to join civil disobedience acts outside the home, he limited their participation to actions he considered suitable, such as picketing drink and drug shops,

> not only because they suffered from their husbands patronage of such shops, but also because the issue was one of purity and morality in personal life. Salt, however, was an issue symbolizing the economic hardship Indians suffered under British rule: as such, it was an issue relating to public life, and not therefore suitable for women to take up. (Kumar 1993, page 85)

But some women were developing other ideas. For example, Kamaladevi Chattopadhyaya appealed to Gandhi to accept women in the salt satyagraha at Dandi in Gujarat in early 1930 (Kumar 1993, page 74). He and the Congress Committee agreed. Women then led satyagraha all over the country. Thousands of women from all classes joined in. Separate women's organizations were formed to mobilize women and train them for *charkha* and *khadi* and also for propaganda efforts. There were *lathi* charges[7] against women; water hoses were turned on them, and they were arrested in the thousands. "It was reported that between 1930–31, 20,000 women satyagrahis[8] were arrested and sentenced to imprisonment" (Kumar 1993, page 80). Some were shot.

A few women broke away completely from the traditional stereotypes for them and became terrorists, such as those who joined raids on the Chittagong Armory. They also used explosives in attempts to kill police, or even shot them point-blank. The names best known include Dinesh Majumdar, Anuja Sen, Shanti Ghosh, Sunita Chaudhary, Bina Das, Kamala Dasgupta and Preetilata Wadedar. Of these, Ghosh and Chaudhary are said to have acted with revenge against men in mind, to pay men back for their brutality to women, rather than for nationalist reasons (Kumar 1993, pages 85–87).

In Bengal, where many of the terrorist women originated, Kumar writes, "there was a growing opposition not only to women's activism, but also to any form of activity outside the home for them" (page 88). To sum up the mood, she quotes a passage from the end of Rabindranath Tagore's novel *Char Adhyaya*, in which a "revolutionary heroine" realizes she should not have engaged in political activities,

> a confession which was welcomed by the hero: "At last I see the real girl. . . . you reign at the heart of the home with a fan in your hand and preside over the serving of milk, rice and fish. When you appear with wild hair and angry eyes on the area where politics has the whip hand, you are not your normal self, but are unbalanced, unnatural." (page 88)

Western feminism was blamed for women's "misbehaviour" in public. Women leaders in the nationalist struggle, like Sarojini Naidu and Begum Shah Nawaz, "declared that the Indian women's movement was not a 'feminist' one like the Western movement" (page 88). What "feminism" meant was not altogether clear, but Indian women leaders sought to maintain their cultural identity, with stereotyped roles more or less intact, while they still ventured outside the home.

Jawaharlal Nehru, in a speech at Allahabad on 31 March 1928, foresaw the limitations women would face if they did not fight for their rights:

> I should like to remind the women present here that no group, no community, no country, has ever got rid of its disabilities by the generosity of the oppressor. India will not be free until we are strong enough to force our will on England and the women of India will not attain their full rights by the mere generosity of the men of India. They will have to fight for them and force their will on the men folk before they can succeed. (Jayawardena 1994, page 73)

Political Action about Women in Some New Nations

Women's right to vote was attained with men's support, despite the patriarchal character of most South Asian societies. Did this happen precisely because of patriarchy, the men self-assured that they would surely direct the women how to vote? Did the men simply accept the social reform attitude of imperialists, to appear more "civilized" in their eyes, without real concern that women would vote in ways the men didn't control? Or was the motivation more sincere?

In pre-independence India, for example, suffrage for women was proposed to the Viceroy in 1917. The Indian National Congress supported it in 1918. The issue was left to provincial legislatures to decide, as Jayawardena (1994, page 99) recounts:

> In 1921, Madras province, where the anti-Brahmin Justice Party had a majority, was the first to allow women to vote. Other provinces followed, and in 1926, women were also given the right to enter the legislature, Dr. S. Muthulakshmi Reddi becoming the first woman legislative councillor in Madras that year. Her struggle, however, to introduce legislation such as the Devdasi Bill banning temple prostitution of young girls, met with opposition and was unsuccessful. . . .

Over the years, women's political participation increased markedly. By 1991, for example, 7 per cent of the *Lok Sabha* (Lower House) and 16 per cent of the *Rajya Sabha* (Upper House) were women. That is less than the world average but more than in some Western countries (Raju et al. 1999, page 106). Since 1996, efforts to reserve one third of the *Lok Sabha* seats for women have not yet succeeded. Women at local levels, however, are more visible in politics. As indicated in the preceding chapter, considerable legislation to improve "women's situation" has been passed in India and efforts to improve implementation are under way.

The status of women in Pakistan, which became a new nation in 1947, looked to be promising, once the horrors of partition could be left behind. The speeches of Mohammed Ali Jinnah, the father of Pakistan, were among the strongest made on behalf of women's rights.

In *Price of Honour: Muslim Women Lift the Veil of Silence on the Islamic World*, Jan Goodwin (1994, pages 54–55) rightly observes that Jinnah "intended the country to be a Muslim homeland but a secular state." She goes on:

> He noted that there was no Quranic injunction for women to be confined. "We are victims of evil customs," he said. "It is a crime against humanity that our women are shut up within the four walls of their homes like prisoners.

"I do not mean that we should imitate the evils of western life. But let us try to raise the standard of our women according to our own Islamic ideals and standards. There is no sanction anywhere for the deplorable conditions in which our women have to live."

In Pakistan, the period that is most often associated with setting back women's status came 30 years later when General Zia-ul-Haque seized power from Zulfiqar Ali Bhutto in a military coup. "Promising to return the country to 'the purity of early Islam,' he issued a series of directives aimed directly at women" (Goodwin 1994, page 55).

Rukhsana Ahmad, in the introduction to *We Sinful Women* (1994, page 9), comments, however:

The military regime led by General Zia-ul-Haque is not solely responsible for the low status of women, . . . nor has his death brought it to an end. It is the result of centuries of subjugation of women in the sub-continent. His regime clearly decided to use the women's issue to control society in a much more repressive grip.

She goes on to describe the General's "programme for Islamization," which was regarded as having "potential for cementing a crumbling national identity." International criticism was averted, according to Ahmad, because the Soviet invasion of Afghanistan drew in US support. She points out that Zulfiqar Bhutto (Benazir Bhutto's father) had begun the process with laws prohibiting alcohol, declaring Friday as the working-week holiday and closing discotheques, "as concessions to the right-wing opposition in a last bid to survive." Under Zia there was a nationwide media campaign, *Chadur aur Chardiwari* (The Veil and Four Walls), as well as an "anti-pornography" campaign, "which reduced the participation of women in television and entertainment." There were also efforts to deny girls education, as well as to reduce the marriage age. A campaign for segregated universities failed for financial reasons and due to pressure from women's groups (see Ahmad 1994, pages 10–11).

One of the most far-reaching actions on Zia's part was the introduction of the Hudood Ordinances of 10 February 1979. Among other matters, these deal with *zina*, putting a complainant of rape at risk for adultery in the sharia courts. "Specially at risk were unmarried women who become pregnant and who could therefore be held guilty of unlawful intercourse" (Ahmad 1994, page 12).

According to Ahmad, rape soon became the focus of women's protests in Pakistan, inspired by two famous cases. One was the trial of Fehmida and Allah Bux. In 1982, the couple was sentenced to death by stoning for alleged adultery.[9] Shirkat Gah, a woman's pressure group in Karachi, called women's groups together about protecting women's rights. They set up the Women's Action Forum (WAF). Chapters followed in Lahore, Islamabad, Rawalpindi and Peshawar. WAF was endorsed by the All Pakistan Women's Association (APWA), many of whose members

had fought in the freedom movement alongside men and expected equal rights in the new country. The realization that even existing freedoms were now to be taken away instead of extended, shocked them. Begum Raana Liaquat Ali, the Chair of APWA, gave the resistance her blessing. . . . (Ahmad 1994, page 13)

A leading expert in Islamic jurisprudence took on the Fehmida and Allah Bux case and got it dismissed.

Then there was the rape of Safia Bibi. Her landlord and his son raped her repeatedly over a period of a few years. Under the *zina* ordinance she was punished with 15 lashes, found guilty of adultery and sentenced to three years' imprisonment and a Rs. 1,000 fine. The accused were judged "not guilty" for lack of evidence.

> Women, shocked and horrified, managed to coordinate a sophisticated media campaign, as well as a defence, which led the government into considerable embarrassment at an international level, and a prompt dismissal of the case by the Federal Shariat High Court followed. (Ahmad 1994, page 14)

The Law of Evidence, which declared that the testimony of one woman was insufficient and needed to be supported by another woman, made the value of a woman's testimony worth half that of a man's.

> The absurdity of this law and fears that it might be a step towards disenfranchising them brought women out on a march in Lahore on 12 February 1982. . . . It was, at best, a group of 200 or so but police reacted with fierce and disproportionate violence; tear gas, baton charges and arrests followed. . . . As time went on, the Islamization campaign had the effect of escalating violence against women. (Ahmad 1994, page 16)

The man Zia had thrown out of office had a daughter, Benazir Bhutto, who might mobilize political support against him. Was that a possible factor for Zia's actions? In any case, when Benazir Bhutto did take over (after Zia died in an exploding aircraft), she faced opposition from the mullahs, one of whom even "issued a *fatwa* stating that any person voting for Bhutto would be rendered non-muslim, and thereby sentenced to an afterlife in Hell" (Goodwin 1994, page 57).

Ahmad (1994, page 17) notes that Benazir Bhutto "did not change or challenge any of the legislation affecting women" during her first, brief tenure as Prime Minister. Goodwin (1994, page 60) writes that "in the election of 1993, the nation's religious parties were in her coalition." Goodwin continues, "[A]s she did during her first administration Benazir is once again expected to appease the mullahs in order to stay in office rather than concern herself with the rights of women." She was not known as a champion of women's rights during her second tenure, either.[10]

During his period in office just before Benazir's, Prime Minister Nawaz Sharif had already introduced the Shariah Bill, through which religious courts have power to overrule existing laws, if deemed incompatible with the Quran. Goodwin (1994, page 61) refers to an unnamed woman activist's concern: *"The Shariah Bill* is a means to control women and marginalize them instead of bringing them into a just order."

Founded as a homeland for Muslims but with a secular State, Pakistan changed its policy, making interpretations of the Quran into the foundation for the workings of the State. Since Zia's time, Madeeha Gauhar observes, "the women's movement has been lobbying against the discriminatory laws, the rape laws and attitudes and inequalities which prevail in the society that perpetuate violence against women" (UNICEF 1998b, page 47). Under the military command of Pervez Musharraf following the October 1999 coup, it is as yet unclear what changes, if any, might be introduced in laws and practices related to violence against women.

And elsewhere in the region?

In the war with then West Pakistan, some women in East Pakistan joined the fight for independence by carrying grenades in their food baskets, giving supplies to men freedom fighters, sending children to fight — even by taking up arms in the underground resistance of 1971 (Siddiqi 1998, page 206).

Dina M. Siddiqi (1998, page 207) observes that

> although there was no specific women's agenda in the Bengali nationalist movement, middle-class women were critical in delineating the explicitly secular content of Bengali identity. Some women were mobilized in a highly visible fashion in the name of Bengali national culture — without any corresponding interest in women's rights in general.

Siddiqi also notes that even before the war, Bengali women did not readily follow West Pakistan's prescriptions for proper behaviour by Muslim women. She describes how the slogan "Islam in danger" was used by West Pakistanis at the beginning of the war to justify a military crackdown, and she describes a fatwa from West Pakistan that "labeled Bengali freedom fighters 'Hindus' and declared that 'the wealth and women' to be secured by warfare with them could be treated as booty of war" (page 209). She describes "rape camps" in which Bengali women were detained until they were pregnant and beyond the time when termination was possible, the point being "purifying the 'tainted' blood of Bengali Muslims . . ." (page 209).

The rape and murder of Bangladeshi women has also been featured in accounts of the war. The violated woman is expected to sacrifice herself for the honour of her family and nation (Siddiqi 1998, page 209). Although the *birangona* (women war heroes) were not generally rehabilitated, development efforts in Bangladesh have often focused on women's participation and productivity.

An Emerging Concern with Economic Status in Bangladesh

In 1972, Martha Alter Chen writes in *A Quiet Revolution: Women in Transition in Rural Bangladesh* (1986, page 1),

> Bangladesh had just begun to reconstruct after the upheavals of its liberation war. The ten million refugees who fled to India during that war were returning to start life anew. They returned to war-torn homes and villages. BRAC's [Bangladesh Rural Advancement Committee] founder and executive director, Fazle Abed, who had been active in refugee work in India, also returned to Bangladesh determined to assist the refugees.

Women's productive roles outside the home were at first overlooked by BRAC. Through trial and error, a decision was taken to concentrate on "developing social consciousness of women through functional literacy and formation of women's working groups" (page 4). Destitute widows, war victims and wives of the poor learned income-earning skills, formed savings and credit groups, and flourished. Although youth cadres were originally planned to be the channel to reach the poorest in village-wide efforts, over time it was decided that "educated youth tend to align themselves with power" (page 11). But the local power structure needed to be broken if resources were to be more equitably distributed. Then, groups of poor women, separate from groups of poor men, were formed and linked in a federation. The rest of the story has been covered in the previous chapter.

Links with the past ways of looking at women's situation in the subcontinent are seen here, as are departures from it. BRAC and Grameen Bank were set up by men. The garment industry is controlled by men. But women's stereotypic gender roles are not the only ones being furthered; women have started their own organizations, ones not aligned with political parties as most were before. At the same time, women's

NGOs are becoming more successful, speaking for themselves and calling for more concerted action to stop gender-based violence.

Today, Bangladesh has one of the best-organized and far-reaching women's movements against gender violence in South Asia, as will be seen further below. The efforts for organized action at local level for women's economic opportunities helped prepare the ground for even more effective networks against gender violence, bringing in rural as well as urban women. Yet, patriarchy persists and women are still being beaten — the antithesis of equality.

Nepal's Women Challenge Patriarchy

The story of efforts to improve women's situation in Nepal is, for the most part, more recent than in other countries of the region. Multi-party democracy was introduced only in 1990, with the end of the Panchayat system of local government.

Bina Pradhan (1979, page 4), in her ground-breaking *Institutions Concerning Women in Nepal*, reports, however, that "a few women began taking an active role in bringing about social and political change as early as in 1913." She describes some early organizations of the welfare type, to help poor women or to care for child widows. She says some women were involved in underground political activities of the Congress party against the regime; another group demanded voting rights in 1948 and won them a short time later. Girls' education was sought by still another organization.

According to Pradhan, politically motivated organizations were linked with existing political movements and men leaders, to whom women activists were related. Satyagraha was used, as in India. Women were lying down in the streets to achieve their goals.[11] Except for the right to vote, however, relatively little has been gained in the name of women's rights. As discussed in Chapter 10, both a property rights law and a law against domestic violence are being considered in Nepal, as urged by women's groups. There have been delays in progress on both. Both touch on strong patriarchal interests against the rights of women. Both challenge men's control in the home. Another priority is to end girl-trafficking. Here it has been easier to get public consensus that something must be done to change the situation. Nonetheless, problems remain, and the Government has been criticized by women's groups for its disregard of women victim-survivors.[12] To their credit, women activists in Nepal are struggling to build networks among the various NGOs in the capital and with rural women. They have taken on some of the most challenging issues possible, as mentioned above, and are trying as well to use CEDAW as a standard by which cases should be decided. In short, they have quickly departed from the tradition that men represent women's interests, that women reinforce stereotypes for gender roles in the world and that women lend themselves primarily to the support of other aims, rather than those to do with women's human rights. It isn't clear yet whether the speed at which they want to move will be possible or not.

More Stakeholders Sought by Sri Lanka's NGOs

Concerning Sri Lanka, Kamalini Wijayatilake of the Centre for Women's Research (CENWOR) explains that the women's movement has "grown from the confines of small groups to a movement that is recognized nationally. Over the years it has moved from welfare and social service orientation to the nature of equality and difference" (UNICEF 1998b, page 47).

She points to changes achieved at policy level: a Women's Bureau that became the Ministry of Women's Affairs, with a Women's Charter to its credit; reforms to the penal code relating to sexual violence — in particular, she notes, to the criminalization of incest and the recognition of sexual harassment as a crime. Wijayatilake sees law reforms as only able to achieve so much "where entrenched patriarchal attitudes were still upheld" and calls for more cooperation among "the various stakeholders if violence against women is to be [successfully] addressed" (UNICEF 1998b, page 47).

Women's voices and struggle in Sri Lanka have also called for more efforts for peace; they have linked issues about human rights of women with human rights in general, democracy and peace (see, for example, Abeyesekere 1995). They have developed many strategic alliances inside the country and beyond it. As Abeyesekere observes:

> [S]truggling for women's rights in the Sri Lankan context at this stage in time has evolved into a struggle for democratization of the society as a whole and has led to a much wider recognition of the significance and impact of such a struggle on women's lives and daily circumstances. . . . The challenge of achieving an equilibrium between standing firm on women's demands and making strategic alliances lies ahead. (page 459)

As it does in all the countries of the region.

The Newest Movement

The newest women's movement in the region is faced with the greatest odds against success, given the political philosophy of Taliban, which limits women's status and freedom in Afghanistan even more than Zia did in Pakistan. The Afghan Women's Network was established in 1995 in Islamabad in response to the UN Fourth World Conference on Women held in Beijing. It focuses on rights, development and peace issues. Fear of violence is constant among women members, who hesitate to have their names used, fear publicity and have experienced disappointment at their treatment by the UN.[13]

Their movement follows a history of reform in Afghanistan that has addressed women's roles in many different ways, from the emphasis on "modernity" in the 1920s to the ideology for women to be partners in development, even if forced to do so, under the Russians from 1979 to 1992, and to women's strict seclusion in the name of Islam, under Taliban since 1995 (when Kabul fell) (for more details, see Physicians for Human Rights 1998). The current extreme control of women symbolizes a political challenge to atheist, communist, colonialist and neo-colonialist influences alike.[14] It does so at the cost of what has been called a "war against women" of such proportion that women are said increasingly to commit suicide. At the same time, initiatives continue to press for women's human rights to be respected.

Some Current Challenges, Efforts and Achievements

As for some current efforts and achievements in the region regarding efforts to end violence against women and girls, especially domestic violence, summaries from the October 1997 Kathmandu regional meeting on women's movements in South Asia provide some insights. (See UNICEF 1998b.)

India has definitely led the way in the region in trying to meet the needs and protect the rights of the girl-child at various stages of her life. And as the brief history already covered in Chapter 3 shows, women's groups in India have reacted to various abuses of women and girls, sometimes stimulated by horrifying cases of dowry and dowry death. Formulation of related laws has not seemed to produce significant changes in people's behaviour, however. As for other forms of domestic violence, noted lawyer and activist Flavia Agnes has spoken of

> her involvement with the women's movement over the years and how the issue of domestic violence came out of the shadows. But, she asked, what had it [the movement] done towards empowering women and their awareness of the issues of violence against women? (UNICEF 1998b, page 46)

By 1999, however, India had played a key part in an important and highly visible regional campaign against domestic violence, as coordinated with UNIFEM — which also contributed its results to a number of global United Nations-sponsored events and reviews. It is clear that a number of India's NGOs and women's organizations have accelerated their work against domestic violence.

In Pakistan there has been relatively little discussion of domestic violence, although in 1999 the Progressive Women's Alliance launched a well-publicized campaign against stove-burning deaths as likely murders. Also in Pakistan, challenging *zina* ordinances remains a priority for the women's movement, along with related calls for prevention of rape, more concern for victims and an end to custodial violence. Child abuse is becoming an issue, perhaps in part because of the high proportion of children who are rape victims. The women's movement in Pakistan is directly linked to advocacy for protection and fulfilment of human rights, as it has been since women activists took to the streets to challenge Zia's ordinances. The whole question of custom or crime (see Human Rights Watch 1999) has been given much more national and international attention after the murder of Saima Sarwar in an honour killing, as discussed in Chapter 10.

For Bangladesh, Ayesha Khanam, General Secretary of the women's organization Mahila Parisad, notes that "sensitizing rural people on issues of violence and lobbying for legal reforms of existing discriminatory laws" are primary activities carried out to date (UNICEF 1998b, page 45). She also says that "effective implementation of laws and lobbying with the policy makers, administrators and the media [are] part of the action needed to eliminate gender-based violence."

She sees the need for further mobilization, especially with regard to emphasizing human rights and to bringing rural women into the movement:

> there is much that needs to be done and experience has proven that a powerful women's movement and mass mobilization can make a difference to the human rights issue. More should be done to address the *Fatwa* where fundamentalists are now interpreting Islamic religious law in such a way that they endorse discrimination. The movement in Bangladesh has to develop a strong rural base, it is still a very urban movement. (page 46)

To date, Bangladesh appears to be one of the countries in South Asia that has placed the highest priority on ending violence against women (UNICEF 1998b, page 45), thanks in part to Naripokkho and other women's organizations and NGOs. Elimination of both domestic violence and attacks outside the home are priorities. Interest continues in providing economic opportunities for women. Considerable attention has also been given to the reduction of maternal mortality. Integrated efforts on all these topics are under way, linking policy and the grassroots. Efforts are also being made for exchanges between media and women's groups to build partnerships.

The UNICEF regional meeting in Kathmandu summed up achievements to date of the women's movement in South Asia:

> The women's movements in all countries in the South Asian region have contributed significantly to both identifying and highlighting violence against women as a major concern which violates human rights and the emancipation and development of women. Over the years they have managed to influence their respective governments to recognize this issue and to bring about changes in the legal system as well as to create an awareness within their countries. However, it was revealed that much more has to be done. (UNICEF 1998b, page 45)

The group's five recommendations were:

- Lobby for reforms on discriminatory laws, as well as effective enforcement of laws related to women's issues.
- Build alliances and strengthen networking within the country and within the region.
- Change socially ingrained gender discriminatory attitudes through effective interventions.
- Empower women's participation at the grassroots level.
- Conduct gender sensitization at policy level (page 48).

Building Blocks for Movements to Stop Violence against Women

To stop violence against women and girls in South Asia, women's groups and NGOs are the most likely building blocks for movements. Some have strong programmes against gender violence, though most do not. A group that takes on the question of domestic violence is even more rare. To generate a movement, there needs to be cooperation across different organizations and at different levels, inspired by shared concern and commitment. Self-conscious and purposeful efforts are being made to connect personal and emotional experiences to their social and political context and possibilities. That is one of the tenets of women's movements everywhere. Networking that crosses boundaries by sector, class and country is growing, with violence against women a shared concern, and is being promoted by some NGOs in cooperation with both government and international development agencies. Members will want to be conscious of the extent to which past characteristics of dealing with "women's situation" may limit them. For example, will the public assume they are run by men? That they are not really concerned with women's human rights but with some other political, development or personal goal? If members do not fulfil gender-role stereotypes, can they expect harsh criticism? Will there even be danger for them if they do not conform to what is considered appropriate behaviour for women according to those who interpret religion in their countries? But if they do not proceed, what hope will there be for women's human rights — and all human rights — in their countries? These are questions faced, in fact, by women in Naripokkho from Bangladesh, the NGO story that brings home the challenges women face when they work together against gender violence.

The Naripokkho Story

Shireen Huq (whom we met in Chapter 2) is a co-founder of the women's group Naripokkho[15] in Bangladesh.[16] An interview illustrates the kind of process from which a vital women's organization emerges and works forcefully against gender violence. More often than not, the process starts with what at first seems to be a personal experience, the kind that used to be hidden and hushed but now can and does become the basis for social analysis, solidarity and group action by women to change society.

From the personal to the political. Shireen recalls vividly a time when she was seven or eight and a cousin was carried into the house one evening.

> And as the story unfolded to me, it was that my cousin had been beaten up by her husband and this was not the first time. . . . My father was her maternal uncle. They were very close. So my father finally put his foot down and said, "This is enough, there is no reason why she has to stay there and put up with this day after day." And all through this [time] she was having repeated pregnancies, which was kind of finishing her off. The person who was carried in, I couldn't even recognize that was my cousin. . . . And then, the irony was that after she had stayed with us for a while, and slowly she had recovered, her face began to look like the person I knew etc., . . . then she went back to her husband! And this I remember very clearly because my mother was very upset. Because they had kind of risked [problems] by bringing her home.

Shireen says her parents were even accused of having kidnapped the girl, with a court case threatened by the husband. She remembers her mother asking, "Why do women not break away from violence?"

> So that kind of stayed with me through my whole growing up as a girl. . . . Then I realized as I was becoming more aware and getting older . . . this is not just my experience or my cousin's experience, but its actually a problem, a social problem. I think then I became very angry.

A new perspective on the commonplace. Shireen also described the incident related in the second chapter about a woman who was miscarrying but was reluctant to go to the hospital because her husband wasn't home to give permission.

She says, "All these things seem simple, but the situation was not simple, and the problem is not simple." The memories of the two incidents stayed with her. When she was in college and university, she says, she realized

> that this is a complex problem and so much needs to be changed before simple acts of violence are going to disappear . . . but people seem to be used to a certain level of violence as commonplace and accept it as commonplace.

Through reading, study abroad and making contact with other women, outside and inside Bangladesh, Shireen continued to question the commonplace.

She was among a group of women development workers at a three-day workshop in 1983. The discussion turned to problems a woman change agent faces that male counterparts do not. The women ended up wanting to change the whole approach of women in development. Up to that point, Shireen saw it as either a predictable scenario set by development agencies or one orchestrated by political parties only interested in women as potential voters.

There didn't seem to be a third position, which was women articulating their own interests, their own demands, based on their own understanding of why there is inequality, of why there is lack of justice for women. So that was for me the beginning of Naripokkho. . . . And I think for me personally it was also a very healing process, because it actually shifted me away from anger to a kind of more constructive in-depth analysis, to build bonds with other women.

Forming and continuing a group. The specific meeting that gave birth to Naripokkho was about a month later. Eighteen of the 33 workshop participants were among those who started Naripokkho. Fifteen years later, in 1999, there is still an active core group of about 30, with some 90 official members.

Shireen says,

We have been meeting every Tuesday since May '83. . . . There were days when there were only one or two people and then others when there were 20, sometimes 40 people . . . but the main thing has been, really, engaging in a process of collective discussion. . . .

Establishing a non-hierarchical structure and procedures. Naripokkho has, at different times, taken positions that have not always been uncontroversial. Says Shireen,

All these positions were taken up after much discussion through a collective process. . . . We have also been good about expanding what is called "leadership." In this country, there is a tradition that so-and-so is a leader in an organization, very hierarchical, and we were consciously trying to stay away from that. I think we have done it. Every two years we change [the Convener]. That itself, I think, forces people to take on responsibilities, which then helps build leadership. . . . We engage in a very intensive process of participation. I think we have tried to establish the belief that what each person has to say is important, and therefore, each person must be heard.

In the context of women's traditional submissive roles, this process is momentous. It portends change in acceptance of hierarchy as the basis for organization and of inferiority as the basis for women's role.

Focusing on women's issues. Coming to focus on domestic violence was also a challenging process. In 1985, Naripokkho was invited by the largest women's organization in the country to be on a national steering committee and plan a national campaign on violence against women and other social problems. However, Shireen was disappointed, to the extent that Naripokkho withdrew. Why? She says that a lot of people wanted to use the issue of violence against women simply to further their own political interests and activities. A shadow from the past? She explained:

First, [because] they continuously put men in front in this campaign (the vice chancellor of the university, famous journalists, etc., all these respectable men who get up and give speeches about their mothers and sisters). It was just unbearable, and I was fighting in the Committee to be heard, which was also very difficult, being treated like this young radical to be dismissed . . . but I was trying to say that we should give the campaign a female face, for the country to see that it is women who are fighting back. . . . And that was to me fundamental. We can have all the male supporters we need, but it is women who have to give voice to this [issue] in the country.

In historical context, hers was a revolutionary position. Shireen says that the Committee was not willing to take on the issue of domestic violence. That was her second disappointment for the prospect of a national campaign against domestic violence, with women visibly in the lead. Instead,

> they wanted to focus on the incidence of violence being committed by . . . criminal elements (thugs) and street violence. And we were saying, "What is the proportion of street violence compared to the amount of violence women are subject to, violence everyday in their own homes by people they love and depend upon?" . . . So this focus on weapons, and law and order, didn't make sense to me. Only later, I realized that is what the larger campaign would [do], take on an anti-government stance. Now we all have had our criticisms of government, etc., [but I was] not prepared to allow an issue so fundamental to women to be used that way. And we were very angry at that time.

Making issues more visible. The issue of domestic violence was unexpectedly given a boost:

> Suddenly in '94 the Bangladesh Bureau of Statistics comes out with these figures, which actually nobody noticed for years, which say that the number of women who die of what is categorized as "unnatural deaths" is actually greater than [that for] women who die from maternal mortality. Maternal mortality in Bangladesh is one of the highest in the world. And if unnatural death is even higher, then that is something to be alarmed about. Of course, in unnatural deaths, they don't list violence. It says "snake bites, poisoning, suicide, homicides, etc." But I suspect a lot of that is homicide, and death due to injuries related to violence. But we have no way of actually saying that is so. And we have no way of saying what the extent and magnitude of violence [against women] in this country is, and what is the nature of violence [against women] in this country. So for a long time we wanted to do some kind of study. And now we have started that. And it has two main objectives: to determine the nature and magnitude of violence against women in the country, and to identify the institutional deficiencies in what needs to be done.

Networking. Naripokkho is one of two groups that contributed to a June 1997 Expert Group Meeting on State Interventions on Violence against Women, called by the Ministry of Women and Children Affairs, Government of Bangladesh, with support from the Royal Danish Embassy. The meeting was based on "a process of consultation" to prepare a multisectoral programme on violence against women. The report says, "the objective of the programme is to mobilize the state machinery at all levels to deal more effectively with prevention and redress of violence against women" (S. Huq 1997a). This sounds like the Naripokkho process, gone to scale, creating an opportunity for government to hear and respond to women's own versions of their needs.

Emphasizing rights, not stereotypes, for women and men. And what's more, the National Action Plan for Women's Advancement[17] is organized somewhat according to articles in CEDAW. This brings to life another of Shireen's suggestions, to make the international rights instruments the basis for a State action plan. She has definitely wanted rights issues in the forefront, not hidden.

Shireen says, "A lot has to change, and it is not only women activists who would do that. I think the State has an important role to play . . . the men have a very important role to play. . . ." Shireen has been trying to

> demystify what is it about the relation between men and women that we should accept inequality. . . . But that is only one small part of what has to change, so much has to change. . . . There is so much to do for women who have already been subject to violence, who

have survived, and also for the families of those who have not survived. There is so much to be done, from changes needed in health services, the legal system, the criminal justice system, even getting decent attention in a hospital — it's just endless, there is so much to do. And then of course it is easy to say that everything has to change, but everything is not going to change overnight.

Naripokkho has a range of related activities:

We are beginning to find out, by interviewing women survivors of violence, what kind of treatment they face in hospitals, [by the] police. It is beginning to show up where some glaring gaps are. . . . Forensic facility in this country is absolutely appalling. They don't even have the means to do proper semen analysis. So [there is] the whole issue of evidence in cases of rape or sexual assault: its very difficult . . . very difficult to get convictions if you don't have proper evidence. . . .

She adds,

I don't want to say there is corruption, but we have been told, after somebody had done an analysis of some 130 post-mortem reports, they have found that a large percentage have been put down as suicide which they would not have been. Doctors are bought off. So there's a lot to be corrected. . . .

Towards prevention as well as remedy: fundamental changes needed. Naripokkho has helped bring to light the horrible crime of acid attack. It also works on prevention as well as redress and rehabilitation. Shireen saw several related problems. One is the need for reconstructive surgery:

In violence units which deal with the acid burning — it's again in a very dismal state. . . . I know plastic surgery is very expensive and you cannot demand reconstructive surgery, but you know what happens to a woman after she has been disfigured by acid? It doesn't matter if the person who has done it to her gets a lifetime sentence, she is lost unless she can be given a face that she can appear with. I think it doesn't matter how expensive it is, it is necessary. We do all kinds of things which are expensive . . . so that is another concrete area for activity — giving priority to acid-burn victims for plastic surgery. . . . And then one begins to talk about the criminal justice system. . . . So there is lot to be done in terms of improving institutional services to give relief to women.

Shireen has not forgotten the underlying problem, even with all the urgent needs of victims. "But again I will say, that is about relief, but what about doing something about the problem? You know no matter how small it seems, and how slow it seems, it's ultimately changing people's attitudes, how they think about this, [that is needed]." She sees the need for prevention.

Facing obstacles. Shireen also pointed out some obstacles to Naripokkho's overall success. These no doubt influence people's expectations for how "women's situation" is taken up — with women not really in the lead, not really working for women. These reflect the "links with the past," in which members, including herself, are sometimes portrayed negatively; some believe that Naripokkho is actually a group run by men for a political purpose. Shireen characterizes their questions like this:

Who is behind Naripokkho? That's one question that pushes [the idea that] it cannot possibly be a group of women who are building up this organization. There must be some male guardians, mentors, somebody behind it. Is Naripokkho part of some political party? Or is Naripokkho an NGO? Who is [behind] Naripokkho? This is the question we have heard from day one. Nobody ever wanted to accept that "No, we are just us" — a group of independent-thinking women who want to build an autonomous organization which is not linked to any political party. . . .

She says the idea that a man led the group had to be faced,

especially when we came out to protest the introduction of Islam as State religion — which is a very daring thing to have done. None of the political parties were willing to take up this agenda because it's too challenging. And we were on the streets before anybody was even ready to think about it.

Shireen notes there is some hostility from within the women's movement itself.

Sometimes, we face hostility from the mainstream movement, and that makes life difficult. I think mentally and psychologically we can tackle hostility from conservative groups and from conservative elements in society and from males, but hostility from the women's movement becomes very difficult. Because it gets painful as well, so that is something, I think, which is a problem, another obstacle we face.

Getting resources — for more power and impact. As for the future of Naripokkho, some changes are needed: The women of Naripokkho all have full-time jobs elsewhere. Shireen wants to attract more young members. There have been funding problems. Until very recently, the group relied entirely on its own resources, Shireen says, "but gradually now we can dictate our own terms; so, for example, for this violence research project, we have applied for funds. There is no way we can do it just in our free time. We need full-time people to do it."

As of February 1999 (Naripokkho1999b), Naripokkho had developed a plan to expand the network that it had developed with some 242 women's organizations to some 350, to strengthen an autonomous women's movement in the country and move forward on a broad agenda that includes even more attention to violence against women and to the fulfilment of women's human rights.

Inspiring courage. When asked what she would like others to learn from her experience and from Naripokkho, Shireen recalled a discussion in which members said in what way Naripokkho had been important for them. "[A] number of people say 'Courage,' so I suppose that is one thing we can offer."

In August 1999, I met with Shireen in Dhaka and met some of the acid-attack victims. One had such a bright smile and energetic manner that I didn't really register that her right eyelid was seared to the eye amidst the scars on part of her face. She is an advocate for prevention of such attacks and gives talks to groups of boys calling on them to refrain from acts like that which she suffered. She also counsels and encourages other victim-survivors. She even gave up her place for reconstructive surgery in Spain so that a young mother could go instead. Her turn came, however. She left for the United States in August 1999 for reconstructive surgery — although with courage she had told Shireen, "I'm used to my face now."

Reaching Rural Women

One of the most important changes in efforts against violence is that rural women are becoming more and more organized and outspoken. In many ways, they are inspiring their urban sisters.

Surely one of the most impressive shifts in the women's movements comes from communities where women's groups and NGOs hear victim-survivors' stories, find viable alternatives to their situations and obtain redress if possible, assisted by a variety of individuals and groups.

For example, an NGO leader in Uttar Pradesh, India, says:[18]

> Our workers talk to women in villages on the problems they face. . . . Violence is an issue which inevitably comes up. . . . There's not a single woman — whether the least urbanized and most poor — who has not experienced some kind of violence, incest, sexual harassment. . . . When women find a forum, where they can talk heart to heart, it comes out. Then we help women raise their voice, seek redress. . . .
>
> In rural areas, women are quicker in taking up an issue at a public forum. In urban societies, women tend to keep them covered due to middle-class morality. They come out only when it is beyond forbearance. Again, rural women exhibit more solidarity in fighting for some issue. There's more fragmentation in urban areas. Only when a lot of women are affected [there], other women join in to support. . . .
>
> First, we deal with the local community. Get support at family level, then community level, then village level. Then we mobilize support from other women's organizations, police and judiciary. We help women take out *dharnas*, rallies, processions. . . . Activist action draws response where a single voice fails. Indeed, rural women are starting to lead the way against violence in several cases.

She gave the example of working against rape in a prosperous cane belt location:

> There is a lot of upper-caste dominance. . . . Sometimes they may be doing it for kicks but at times it is definitely caste rape. Also, as we are working there, more women have become aware, conscious of their rights and reporting cases to seek redress.

She explained that in some areas of Uttar Pradesh women are considering reporting rape, despite the risks of doing so:

> The women fear more violence if they expose it. It is an unsaid tradition that tribal girls working in the fields must spend their first night with the landlord. Women are just picked up and left back after a few days. People have come to accept it. They are dissuaded by the law-and-order system as it exists. They think protesting will be of no use. . . . They won't get justice [yet] . . . at places like [name withheld], women have started feeling even if they don't get justice, at least the perpetrators will be exposed.

Rape is high on the list of types of violence that have inspired and continue to inspire group action in rural as well as urban areas. Girl-trafficking is another.

Maiti Nepal: Villages against Girl-Trafficking

A story from Nepal about struggle for community action against girl-trafficking illustrates the difficulties and the promise of serious integrated efforts for change in rural areas. Anuradha Koirala[19] is founder of Maiti Nepal, which is centred in Kathmandu and gives shelter to girls, including returned prostitutes. The organization also works for prevention at the community level. She engages the community and law enforcement; she confronts vested political interests and focuses on rights issues.

Some of the steps in the process of her work are similar to those noted in the Naripokkho story. Others are quite different. For example, Anuradha did not begin with a women's group, which could have given constant support. Instead, she wanted to mobilize community action and sought various stakeholders, including police, to help. Her programme is, however, part of a network of NGOs that work against trafficking. Because she stresses the criminality of the offender, she herself is at risk.

How did she get started? Anuradha's own problems led her to help others. She says that she turned to God when her husband suddenly married another woman after 18 years of marriage. She gave up a private school she had been running and went to the temple everyday.

> There I saw women, very healthy, begging in the street. I used to wonder what these
> women did after begging for one or two hours every day. . . . They used to say, "Who'll give
> us work?"

They all said they had been violated by the family. She learned that all worked as prostitutes after begging. She was especially concerned about those with little children who lived by the footpath. After discussing it with the women, Anuradha took her own savings and set up nine of the most destitute women with small shops, for Rs. 1,000 each, on the understanding that they would pay her back Rs. 2 every day, so that other women could also have help. She sent their children to school by persuading her friends with schools to take them in and by finding sponsors. She received some support from donors as well, but she did not agree with the idea that the women should be motivated to return home. She also set up a home for the girls.

> I started with 20 children of the nine women I first gave money to. The oldest child was 11,
> and they were being prostituted by their parents. That same year, many women came to
> me and asked me to take their daughters, too.

Anuradha got the idea that to prevent trafficking of girls, she had to take the message to the villages, door to door. That idea led her to organize a more integrated approach than the usual welfare one: "I couldn't go alone. People would think I'm mad or would try and kill me. I didn't feel secure. So, I thought I'd make a group. First, I approached the police. . . ."

She also recruited some college girls, who were not aware of the problem before. She added Bombay returnees to talk about brothel life, added nurses to tell of HIV/AIDS risks, added lawyers and journalists.

> There were about 190 of us. . . . When we went to each village, we divided up into smaller
> groups. And we had a band, police band, for each group, because we wanted to
> communicate our messages to the masses. . . . After this, we had a door-to-door campaign,
> because everywhere only a few women came to the large gatherings.

They gave out a "criminal card" for villages to identify those who bought or sold girls. The students helped the illiterate villagers with the descriptions. The number of reported cases went up. She explained that those who are arrested can be kept in police custody for only 24 days, and they are released when the girls can't be found to testify. She organized workshops for the communities, so they could plan how to solve their own problems.

She described how pimps offer money to fathers, a year's salary up front, allegedly for a girl to work, most likely in a carpet factory in Kathmandu. From there, things develop. Girls are trafficked. She invents slogans like "Girls are our pride: let's not sell them." "This really doesn't have much to do with poverty," she says, "it has to do with discrimination."

Trafficking also has to do with crime, a message that Anuradha tries to get across with banners, in discussions, through police participation and through encouragement of reporting by the press.

She involves the police but also challenges them. According to Anuradha, some police even abuse girls who have escaped from brothels in Bombay to the Nepal border.

> There, they report to the police. The police have no place for them. And no money. . . . The journey takes up to 10 days, because the police don't have money to send them to Kathmandu directly. They ask local bus drivers to take them part of the way, and the next day another bus driver takes her to the next stop. But these girls are molested and raped by police officers and bus drivers at each stop between the border and Kathmandu. The girls say, "When we reach the border we feel so happy because we've escaped from Bombay, but it is more horrible here because we feel degraded and dehumanized by our own people, our own police officers who should help us."

She wants two transit homes "so the police don't have a chance to hurt these girls," and she wants prevention camps. She teaches new skills to girls who have escaped or been rescued. She has brought legal cases and inspired the girls.

She told about one girl who was married after returning from Bombay, but who had never told her husband that she had been a child sex worker. Several weeks earlier, Anuradha explained, when she was doing her shopping, the girl saw the man who had taken her to Bombay. So, in the middle of the street, she caught him. People had gathered around, and she said, "Please call the police. He sold me to a brothel in Bombay. He must go to jail." The girl's husband left her when he heard about it. The girl said she did not care and would not withdraw her complaint. With Anuradha's help, a case has been filed against the trafficker.

By expanding her work from welfare to prevention, involving others (including the police), going with them to rural areas, engaging media and creating legal awareness and literacy, Anuradha is doing more than social work. She is breaking gender-role stereotypes and challenging vested interests in the hierarchy.

Anuradha says, "The biggest problem that I face is political pressure. . . . I'm talking about calls from political leaders."

She told about another girl who had escaped from Bombay and then identified the person who had taken her. Anuradha called the police, who caught the man and put him in prison. Anuradha said she then got a call from a Member of Parliament, who complained, "One of my workers is now in prison because you filed a case against him." She also told about getting 15 brothel owners arrested, but that all but two were released for lack of evidence. The trial for those two was delayed for more than three years, until finally they were sentenced to 12 years in prison. According to Anuradha, one said to her, "I gave the Prime Minister 50 lakh rupees. I gave another political leader 50 lakh. How much do you want? Whoever you are, I have money to pay you." Anuradha says, "The political leaders everywhere are protecting criminals because these criminals help with vote banks and even with money."

Nonetheless, Anuradha is optimistic. She wants more awareness among police about the need to stop trafficking of girls. "Only 90 went around with me," she says, "but there are 15,000 in Nepal who must be aware of these crimes." She also wants the subject taken up in school curricula and with civil servants' training. She says, "If you are dedicated and keep working, there are great prospects for change."

Rape and trafficking: Both are concerns for rural as well as urban women. On both, rural women are starting to confront some forms of violence against them.

Rural Movements against Alcoholism

What about domestic violence? There are some movements against alcoholism that also address domestic violence, even though it is not the main focus of the efforts rural women are leading. There are differing views about whether or not alcoholism really causes violence or is simply used as an excuse for it.

Heise, Pitanguy and Germain (1994, page 16) summarize a review of the relationship between alcohol use and violence against women: "Alcohol exacerbates but does not cause violence against women." Their conclusion is based on findings from 90 small-scale societies and from research in the United States. The authors conclude, "Often both men and women use the supposed disinhibiting effects of alcohol to excuse behaviour that otherwise would not be tolerated."

Enlightened activists in Sri Lanka share this view and are trying to spread it. The prevailing idea in much of South Asia, however, is that alcoholism is a cause of violence against women. For Heise, Pitanguy and Germain, as for the Sri Lankan researchers, alcoholism is an excuse for men who perpetuate violence. Nonetheless, addressing alcoholism as a cause of gender violence is a concrete way to open discussions about attitudes. Some short-term changes in men's behaviour may result. Ending alcoholism, however, will not end violence against women. That is because the basic imbalance of power between women and men, and the attitudes that accompany that dislocation, still have to change.

The extent to which women's efforts in rural areas can make a difference, even against great odds, is evident in the story of the "anti-arrack"[20] (anti-liquor) movement in India and Nepal. It started first in Andhra Pradesh, according to Dr. Rekha Pande (n.d.), a historian at the University of Hyderabad, India, who has followed the movement for five years. She describes its importance this way:

> [I]t provided a feminist way of looking at issues, especially politics, and aligning it to the larger issues. It created a public space for the articulation of a private family violence. It questioned notions about the political apathy of the suffering masses and the inability of women to take the future into their hands, without male leadership. It is through this movement that rural women of Andhra Pradesh, who had been subjected to a lot of violence in the domestic sphere, created history.
>
> These rural women [who] had been marginalised from every sphere of life, totally illiterate, exploited by landlords, targets of domestic & social violence, now suddenly rose in revolt against the mandal officer, the police officials, in fact, the chief-minister himself. They had a simple demand, "no selling and drinking of liquor in our villages". This simple demand brought forth an agitation involving the hundreds and beginning from rural areas, spread to urban areas and from an agitation turned into a movement. . . .

How had this come about? Dr. Pande emphasizes three reasons: 1) the extent of violence associated with liquor to women in everyday life; 2) literacy classes that gave women a means to speak out; and 3) a shift in marketing of liquor in sachets that brought it into the village (personal communication, 1999). She says:

> A man could now drink throughout the day in the confines of his home and this eroded the family economy because men did not go to work and subjected women to a lot of violence. Women had to sell their sarees, utensils and even "talis" (a marriage sign worn by the women like a chain on their necks) to supply liquor to their husbands. In the drunken state when men demanded more and more and women refused to part with their belongings, they were subjected to a lot of violence. Men demanded Neesu (mutton and fish) while the women were struggling to put together a simple meal of rice and pickle. The women only saw a connection between the violence in their daily life and the men drinking [not a connection between liquor and disproportionate gains for contractors or with crime and politics, which Dr. Pande also described].

Dr. Pande is of the opinion that

> [T]he State Government tried its best to sabotage the movement. The police registered a number of cases against the women. But women continued to destroy illicit liquor, attack shops and godowns storing liquor and on April 15th, 1993 the Government had to ban liquor.

> Yet, meanwhile, the Government had already sanctioned 24 new breweries and IMF (Indian made foreign liquor) continued to flood the markets.

> Women felt that their agitation had come to naught because liquor had now come through the backdoor.

> Now started a second phase of this movement and it moved into [some] urban areas. . . . The ruling Government Congress lost the elections in which prohibition had become a major issue. The opposition party Telugu Desam came to power with a majority and declared total prohibition.

The movement in Andhra Pradesh was one of many, as the stories of Harayani Bai from Haryana, India, and Rageshwori Singh from the Far West of Nepal show about women's efforts to reduce violence at home.

Harayani Bai, India. According to Ruchira Gupta, the Indian journalist who interviewed Harayani Bai[21] for this book, Harayani "made all political parties put it [anti-arrack] on their election manifests. In fact, the new chief minister has had to succumb to the pressure of the women voters in his state, and order Prohibition, banning of sale, consumption and possession of alcohol."

Harayani Bai said that she gained more confidence from taking part in the "agitation," and went on to describe what the women themselves organized to improve their lives and that of the community.

> It used to take a full day to get drinking water and do all our other jobs. Then we have to come home, cook, collect water, water the fields, etc. We have to walk miles for medical services. When we tell the nurse to visit our area she refuses. She says, "Write a complaint against me, I would like to be transferred." The same goes for the teacher. Now we — all the women in the village — have collected enough money to call our own teacher. We have insisted that all our daughters will attend schools, too. We have also launched our own credit system through which my daughter-in-law has bought a cow. Our next plan is for a tubewell.

She credits other women's support as the reason for the success and denies she is an "activist":

> Yes, the only reason I had the courage was that other women were going, too. I would like to meet women from all over India and even outside who have similar experiences. I do not consider myself an activist. I do not even want to stand for elections, but now I have the courage to challenge those in power. Maybe my granddaughter will stand for elections.

She describes how she came to be involved in the anti-liquor campaign:

> One of the major problems women face is violence from drunk husbands. I used to be beaten by my husband. My son beats his wife. My granddaughter may be beaten by her husband. My son will not share his income with his wife. Instead, he beats her when she asks for it. He drinks every day and spends most evenings with his drinking friends rather than at home. Fifty years after independence the situation has become worse for women in villages. We have to bear the brunt of the cutting down of trees and the disappearance of groundwater. We have to work longer and longer hours. What we could get from the land earlier, now has to be supplied from shops. Also, we have to wake up earlier to go the fields. As we have no forests to give us privacy now. We have to walk further to get firewood or any kind of fuel. We sometimes have to work 20 hours a day. On top of this, the lopsided government policy tries to raise revenue from liquor. The little cash men earned was spent on liquor. We have to walk three miles to get water. Liquor shops exist in places where there are no roads or schools.

> A liquor shop was being inaugurated in Rewari Jilla in April this year. We took a *padyatra* of women and got the shop sealed. This was not our first effort. The first time we protested alcoholism we met with ridicule from passers-by and shopkeepers. One day an attempted rape by drunkards enraged the villagers and drove home the evils of alcoholism. That is how women from the 50-odd villages succeeded in closing the liquor shop. The Rewari rebellion spread to other villages and today it has reached all over Haryana. That is how I became a part of the anti-liquor agitation. My daughter-in-law was even more strict. She refused to sleep with her husband if he came home drunk.

Mrs. Rageshwori Singh, Nepal. A similar movement to those in Andhra Pradesh and Haryana was started in the Far West of Nepal in mid-1997 and spread rapidly through villages there, until women from the area came to the capital to ask the Prime Minister for prohibition, to which he did not agree.

But back home in the Far West, many villages and districts had nonetheless declared themselves alcohol-free. Mrs. Rageshwori Singh, of the Alcohol Control Centre in Kailali, Nepal, tells part of her story as the organizer of a powerful movement against alcoholism:[22]

> The first and foremost reason for our movement is that Far Western region is the remotest and most underdeveloped region. And in this region most people (men) are alcoholic and they gamble. We have very few educated women, who are most of the time busy in their household work and do not know any other vocation. They are worried about their low living standard and are always looking for ways to improve their family life. They are mostly suffering from the alcoholism abuse, because most men in that region take alcohol and after getting drunk they come back home and beat up the family, including the children, and they sell the properties, whatever they could get their hands on, and

use that money for alcohol. Many men in that region have sold everything and have become homeless. When the situation got worst, I being a chairperson of the women's organization in the village, many such cases were brought to my attention. So when I saw this situation, and I myself being a victim of such a case, I decided to go around in the villages and collect the data on how many women are victimized in one village, etc.

Now the women in the village have confidence in us. They have finally realized that there are people who really care for them, and [who will] help them abolish this alcoholism in the village. They are willing to help us. After the research, they came to us and volunteered to help in whatever way they could to abolish it. In the very beginning we started in one VDC [Village Development Centre], where we have 10,000–15,000 women. We all got together, we protested against the alcoholism in that VDC, met with the officials of the VDC, gave them our petition saying that the alcoholism and gambling should be abolished and banned in the VDC. The petition was filed and it was fulfilled. Now we have covered all the VDCs in Far Western region.

When we all came together and when our appeal was fulfilled by each VDC, and when those VDCs were declared as non-alcoholic VDCs, then many other districts came to know about our work, and they sent letters to us asking us to help them also to overcome this great problem, saying, "How did you manage to get rid of such a curse, we would also like to get the same in our villages, please help us overcome this and give us some suggestions, ideas, etc." So we started to give them feedback on what we were doing and when they also succeeded in this movement then some other women came to know about it. That is how our work began to spread around. So now all the districts in Far Western region are alcohol-free districts.

The main goal is to eliminate alcoholism. By doing this, now many women are happy, at least they have a house, and children are also being fed properly. When we banned the sale of alcohol in these districts, women in the family started to save some money and now the children are being sent to schools and are happy. We have also started some kind of vocational training with the loan from the village development bank to train them to earn some money through poultry farming, etc., so that they could be independent. Now this has even started nationwide. And we are the first ones to do this and women in the village have also gained a lot from this movement.

Men in the villages have also realized that what we are doing against the alcoholism is really good. They are now experiencing how happy the family is, how the wives are saving money and educating their children, how people have stopped the robbery and theft in the village. So now most men in the village have also helped us and are still helping us.

We had a very, very hard time to achieve this success. It has been almost six years since we started this movement. We started this in 2048 B.S. [1990]. The first and foremost problem was the financial constraint. Therefore, we used to collect the money among ourselves. We spent many nights without food in remote villages, we have been through the floods and droughts and were saved by the villagers.

Mrs. Rageshwori Singh explained that the movement against alcoholism — and against wife-beating — was also improving the children's well-being:

There has been a great deal of difference in the situation of the children in the village. Even the children sometimes protest against the alcoholism in the villages. They have seen all the activities of their mothers against the alcoholism, therefore the children, too, are aware of these things. In many villages, women themselves have made the rule of charging Rs. 5,000 for buying alcohol. Whoever buys alcohol, and if these women happen to find out about it, then they charge them this money. These women even charge Rs. 7,000 each for whoever sells the alcohol. And they contribute this money to schools and colleges, or at times they give this money to the government itself. That is why the children are very much impressed by all these activities and they now know that alcohol is very bad. And they also say that we should not drink alcohol, but we should study hard, etc.

She thinks things have improved for women, too:

There are many women like me in the village who are victimized, just like me. Being an educated woman, I do understand the situation to some extent, but still I have to suffer because of the social and cultural traditions in the society. Many rural women committed suicide due to the suffering. But now we seldom hear such cases, because of our movement.

Yes, women in my village really look up to me. They follow me in everything. They support me and encourage me. I have 50,000 followers in my movement. Because they trust me and they know that I do something good for them. They don't trust the government officials because the rural women think that these governmental people don't do any developmental work, they don't take out all these [bad] social norms nor do they try to discourage [drinking]. In my view, I think we should try to change the [poor] mentality of the people. That is how they will understand all these things. If their mentality is the same from generation to generation, then no matter what you do, it will not change their attitude.

The irony is that Mrs. Rageshwori Singh's own ward had not yet been declared alcohol-free. She explained that due to all her support, she was seen as a political threat to the men in power, who did not want to have the ward declared alcohol-free lest they be undermined in the next election. She said the dealer of alcohol had filed a petition against her in the court — which is why she came to Kathmandu.

Mrs. Rageshwori Singh looked forward to being able to meet with women like herself from other countries, to share and spread experiences, to create a network in the region that includes rural women in struggle, not only the elites in advocacy. As Colin Gonsalves[23] put it:

Women's organizations as the centre, human rights organizations and NGOs surrounding that as a penumbra, and trade unions very much as part of that. Leftist political movements should also be a part. That's the way change is made.

. . . women are liberating themselves all over the country, they're struggling. That's where the emphasis should be. From women in struggle.

Analysis and Prospects

In these local movements for improving women's status through ending violence against them, women are in the lead. Some men support their leadership, while others are threatened by it. Each movement is focused primarily on one issue, just as the movements in pre-partition India were, but these bring in other issues, too. Some of the movements refer explicitly to women's rights. Even if they do not, leaders like Harayani and Mrs. Rageshwori Singh are clearly fighting to protect women's and girls' rights, without any "cover" that seems to be in men's interest. They are not pursuing someone else's cause. Nonetheless, the women leaders keep confirming and justifying how useful results will be for the family, just as women's public roles used to be justified. Traditional gender stereotypes thus seem to be somewhat reinforced, which probably thereby protects the women leaders from excessive risk. (One woman made it clear that her husband's views should not be mentioned, lest he be offended.) They are "in struggle," not just in "advocacy." Yet Harayani and Mrs. Rageshwori Singh, for example, deny that they are really activists themselves. One allows that a granddaughter might become a politician, but not she. Declarations of "feminism" are absent. So, we do see some links between women's roles and presentations of self in these movements and in those of the past. There is also change towards stronger leadership by women, a more holistic approach, and one that addresses women's roles and rights, even in the home, and engages in occasional political confrontation. The women discussed in this section all have had conflicts with men politicians or agents of the State. And these are rural women.

The question posed at the beginning of this book remains: Will domestic violence, as well as rape and trafficking, become a focal point, clearly, explicitly, for a regionwide movement? One that challenges patriarchy in the home itself?

There are several reasons why a strong movement against domestic violence is still unlikely. Many women are reluctant to face their own experiences with violence at home. Stereotypes about self-sacrificing women and dutiful wives and daughters still likely compel many women to be quiet about abuse. They need more forums where abuse can be brought out and be seen as reflecting social problems rather than personal or family shame, as Shireen Huq learned and courageously shares. The divide between the private, family sphere and what is becoming a public and very political one would still remain for many, making it even more difficult to discuss what happens at home as a truly political issue, rather than a social concern. There are political considerations if and as governments and local leaders of various sorts focus on control of women as a way to create male solidarity designed to support their own political aims.

Questions for the Future

But, change is coming, and more quickly than might have seemed possible. One can see many reasons why. More women and girls are speaking out, as examples have already shown. Men are joining women to end gender violence: What was a movement for women is now seen as beneficial to men and children also; most men try to follow rather than disrupt women's leadership, or they go in a new direction that is complementary, men's liberation. Media coverage is there; media are encouraged to be more sensitive and analytical, less sensational and exploitative.

Women's experiences with violence have started to be linked to human rights issues and to be shown as violations of human rights and international human rights instruments. State accountability is emphasized more and more. Issues about criminality, once raised, make it more difficult for the activist but also likely make it more difficult for the State and its agents to be passive about violations of the laws concerned.

Also, concern is growing about the general level of violence in society. Violence against women both reflects and feeds that. Policy-level debates, discussions, directives and budgets are needed to stop both. As the connection between violence against women at home and the expression of violence in society is better understood, more support for redress and prevention of domestic violence should be forthcoming.

Here we take up, briefly, five issues:

1) whether there is space for men in the new movement to stop violence against women;
2) how media coverage can hurt or help;
3) some connections with human rights issues;
4) the key issue of state accountability, on which the basics have already been discussed;
5) the physical safety of women activists who work against violence in the patriarchy.

Working with Men and Boys

But do women want to share their hard-won space with men? So often when men come into what was a neglected "women's field" for which there are new resources and visibility, they take it over, dominate and exploit it, redirect the resources to themselves and their interests. It is understandable, then, that some women are reluctant to work with men against gender violence. The problem is made even greater because for many women, men have been the main perpetrators. Yet, at the Kathmandu regional meeting, most women participants welcomed the presence and cooperation of men from throughout the region. A few complained privately that police were attending, as they felt police were generally abusive of women, even those they were sworn to help. And some women belittled a men's group that was represented for not doing much. Their forming a group and going public was an achievement in itself, it seemed to me. Women are inviting men to join the movement against gender violence, and men have been inspired to do so. Why?

First of all, the main cause of gender-based violence is the alleged inferiority of women and superiority of men, with unequal power relations. Still, women in the movement seem more interested in a partnership with men, not a relationship where women dominate men. Second, men, too, want a better future for women and children as well as themselves and are often tired of having aggression and violence assigned to them as stereotypic "masculine" traits. And where gender violence is seen as linked to human rights issues, it is in the interest of both women and men to work together on their common concern.

Working with the Media

The media can help or hurt the various causes that the activists pursue. Few organizations, whether mentioned here or not, seem to have built effective partnerships with media. Relations between women's groups and the press have often been adversarial, especially when cases were sensationalized by the press, as was discussed briefly in the last chapter. Also, women leading change efforts may be attacked in the press or their efforts may be described in a way that trivializes both cause and woman concerned. Some press accounts, on the other hand, have been very helpful for specific cases. And it is more and more recognized that a media policy on violence against women is needed. As Sabir Mustafa, a journalist from Bangladesh clearly sees: "The media should develop a code of ethics regarding sexual violence, and treat stories with sensitivity and seriousness, rather than in a sensational and titillating manner. At all times, the identity of victims should be protected" (also see UNICEF 1998b, for recommendations).

Activists share the view that alternative media, such as theatre, documentaries and song, are particularly important to reach the largely illiterate and rural audiences in the region. Theatre groups in Pakistan have been very important in taking the message against gender violence to rural people, as we saw in Chapter 7. In both India and Bangladesh, a variety of theatre groups perform about the need to end gender violence. NGOs throughout the region encourage skits in training courses, and a multitude of videos have been developed, for training and awareness-raising.

Connections with Human Rights

Interviewers were requested to ask activists if they were familiar with CEDAW and, if so, did they think it useful? Many activists both knew about and appreciated CEDAW and said it was useful. But Shireen Huq[24] has another view: "Not at all, I would say. This is not to dismiss CEDAW or the Declaration against Violence. . . . It is because we have not been able to make the international instruments come into life at a level that has meaning for women."

She pointed out that Bangladesh's reservations at the time on Article 2 meant that "from the legal point of view, CEDAW has no effectiveness." She outlined the work of NGOs, well before preparation for Beijing in 1995, to use CEDAW to increase social awareness, but it did not become well known until very recently. "And the Declaration is not known at all," she added. "So in themselves, I would say, they are not very effective." She proposed that CEDAW be used in a different way: "If lawyers actually start using it as a [legal] instrument, and if policy makers start taking it as a policy guideline for what kind of programmes we need to take on if we really want to remove discrimination."

Another Bangladeshi, a lawyer named Shahjahan, had similar observations about the Convention on the Rights of the Child, which would limit abuse, negligence and exploitation of girls. He asked, "Has that [CRC] done anything to alleviate the suffering of women and children in Bangladesh?"[25] He said he was proud Bangladesh had signed the Convention but ashamed that Government had done so little afterwards. For example, there had not been a report on it in Parliament and the country report was submitted late. He also called for a study to assess the impact of distributing the CRC. "No law has been promulgated," he said, "this Convention does not mean anything until it has been incorporated with the municipal law."

He called for more serious discussion and implementation efforts:

> I know it's extremely difficult to bring about the standards overnight, but people should start talking about what has been done to implement this Convention. In my opinion, nothing much. So the Convention is a very good idea, it's a beautiful benchmark for people to start working for, but I don't think much work has been done in this field. Hell of a lot has to be done!

From Nepal, Gopal Krishna Siwakoti of the Institute for Human Rights, Environment and Development adds his practical advice, along the same lines as Huq's and Shahjahan's, about what is needed to make CEDAW a more useful instrument:[26]

Nepal has ratified the CEDAW Convention. It is an international, binding, legal document. All the provisions of CEDAW must be incorporated in the national legislation. So, we cannot say: "It comes from outside, it comes from the UN. We have nothing to do with it. We have our own cultural relativity and social reality, etc., etc." No, there is no excuse at all. It must be incorporated in the national Constitution and the national legislation. That is the remedy.

He also called for political parties to incorporate CEDAW "in the manifesto of all political parties — the assurance and guarantee that all candidates will take up this issue to eradicate violence against women through both administrative and legal measures."

The Need to Hold the State Accountable

The need to hold the State accountable is clear. Activists indicate that too many agents of the State simply use their position to exploit women and girls, not to protect them. This is so despite an international legal framework, the constitution, laws, obvious abuses and local agitation. More planning, cooperation and visibility around development and human rights issues are in order within movements against gender-based violence.

Violence against women, taken as a key development and human rights issue, can bring together individuals and groups that have had many diverse interests but overlap on this issue. Savitri Goonesekere says that "if the agenda, as set out in CEDAW and [CRC], is to be carried forward, activist groups and NGOs must begin to engage with the state however reluctant they may be to do so" (UNICEF 1998b, page 19). Their doing so seems particularly important if gender violence is to end.

In fact, that is what the women's movements in both Pakistan and Bangladesh have done, with regard to Islamization. And they have connected with, even formed the heart and leadership of, human rights groups and initiatives. Violence against women, as a key development and human rights issue, can reinforce efforts throughout the region for integrative movements towards equality. The accountability of the State, as it becomes more widely acknowledged, will draw even more cooperation by those in struggle and those in advocacy, to try to end gender-based violence in the home, not only in the public space.

Safety of Women Activists against Domestic Violence

This is a new issue. As women challenge stereotypes for gender roles that, in effect, give men authority to abuse them without retribution, they likely face retribution themselves, as the accounts of Shanta Thapalia and Anuradha Koirala confirm, along with reports of threats to women activists in Pakistan — and the murder of Saima Sarwar. Who will then support the women activists? And, if no one comes forward, what does it mean about organizations and governments that have so vocally promoted human rights of women and children?

Endnotes

1   This summary is based primarily on Kumar (1993), Sarkar (1996), Jayawardena (1994) and V. Das (1995).

2   Das bases much of her account on the ongoing work of Ritu Menon and Kamla Bhasin regarding experiences of women during the partition.

3   Shireen Huq, member of the women's group Naripokkho in Bangladesh, cautions against a too ready acceptance of the idea that there really is a fundamentalist backlash. She accounts for some anti-women activities in rural areas of her country in terms of jealousy of some smaller NGOs towards BRAC and its success in "their" areas (personal communication, Dhaka, August 1999).

4   Interview arranged by UNICEF ROSA.

5   The chapter is not meant to be comprehensive. The interested reader may wish to consult some of the excellent books available on women's movements in South Asia. See, for example, Ahmad (1994), Chen (1986), Gandhi and Shah (1992), Kumar (1993), Mumtaz and Shaheed (1987), Omvedt (1990), Jayawardena (1994), Wieringa (1995) and Datar (1993).

6   See also Roushan Jahan (1995), page 108.

7   A form of crowd control, in which police beat people with batons or canes of some sort.

8   Those who practise passive resistance.

9   For an historical account of their first emergence, see Mumtaz and Shaheed (1987).

10 Although Bangladesh, India, Pakistan and Sri Lanka have all had women prime ministers, none have been known as a champion of women's rights. Each comes from a political family in which the mantle could be said to have passed to them in honour of a famous male relative whose time in power was cut short by death, violently in some cases. Bandaranaike, Bhutto, Zia and Sheikh Hasina all fit this picture. Jayawardena (1994, page 129) puts the situation like this for Sri Lanka: "The few women who have successfully contested and made a name for themselves in the political process have generally entered politics as the result of the death of a father or a husband, inheriting, as it were, the male's mantle of power, as did Sirimavo Bandaranaike, who entered politics after the assassination of her husband who was prime minister at the time."

11 Personal communication, Bina Pradhan, Kathmandu, 1997.

12 Personal communication, Durga Ghimire, of the NGO ABC, Nepal 1997.

13 This statement is based on my experience while serving as Afghanistan focal point for UNICEF ROSA.

14 Personal communication, 1 September 1999.

15 Naripokkho is especially well known for bringing to light cases of acid attack. It supports help for survivors, as well as prevention efforts. The courage of the women survivors of acid attacks is immensely inspiring for people around the world who seek to eradicate violence against women.

16 The interview was arranged by UNICEF Bangladesh for this book.

17 Government of Bangladesh, 1999.

18 The interview was arranged by UNICEF India; name withheld.

19 The interview was arranged by UNICEF ROSA in cooperation with UNICEF Nepal. Name used as agreed. Her strong views are widely known in Nepal.

20 According to Pande (n.d.), "Arrack is rectified spirits which is obtained by distilling fermented molasses. The whole process costs the Government about Rs. 1 per litre, but this is sold to the contractor after an auction usually around Rs. 10 to 11. He in turn packets them in sachets and by the time it reaches the consumers it makes a profit of Rs. 90–95 per litre. Thus, the Rs. 812 crores which the Government got as revenue per annum on liquor was only 1/6 of the total amount and a large unaccounted amount from this went into the hands of contractors and there was a close nexus between them and politics. Between crime and politics."

21 The interview was arranged for this book by UNICEF India in cooperation with UNICEF ROSA; real name used as person is identifiable from her activity and extensive coverage of it.

22 Interviewed by Glory Sodemba. The interview was arranged for this book by UNICEF ROSA. Again, activities make the interviewee identifiable. Name used as agreed by interviewer.

23 From interview for this book arranged by UNICEF ROSA. Mr. Gonsalves was extremely critical of the "Ending Violence against Women and Girls" regional meeting in Kathmandu, 1997, because it was held in a first-class hotel (although it was made available at favourable rates at the last minute when another hotel had cancelled) and because, in his view, primarily elite women and men attended. Since most of the comments on the meeting were favourable, his forthright criticisms are all the more thought-provoking and appreciated.

24 From interview arranged for this book by UNICEF Bangladesh.

25 The interview for this book was arranged by UNICEF Bangladesh.

26 The interview for this book was arranged by UNICEF ROSA in cooperation with UNICEF Nepal.

Pakistan

Conclusions

PART **IV**

Violence against Women and Girls: A Key Development and Human Rights Issue

The Need for Advocacy — and Concerted Action

S ince the 1995 Fourth World Conference on Women in Beijing (Beijing Conference) the problem of violence against women and girls has received much more attention in dialogue among governments and within civil society. There is a new readiness by many governments to consider violence against women and girls as a serious public rather than private issue, and as one directly related to both development and human rights. After all, violence against women and girls limits, in many ways, the likelihood of reaching development goals. Programmes for prevention of gender violence can thus accelerate progress towards those goals, as well as provide obvious benefits for women and girls, families and communities. As for human rights, these can scarcely be fulfilled if over half the human race is neglected in human rights discourse and practice.

And yet there is a dearth of awareness that ending violence against women and girls is a key for development and the fulfilment of human rights. For example, a government official of an important donor country asked me in 1998, "But is violence against women really a development issue?" His question represents an old-fashioned view that paying attention to violence against women is more about social work and welfare than it is about development. Fortunately, as new information and arguments about gender violence are brought forward and seriously discussed, that attitude can change.

Consider a debate about wife-beating that went from Parliament to the public in Papua New Guinea. In 1994, the Law Reform Commission presented Parliament a report on wife-beating that showed over 60 per cent of wives in rural areas and among the urban elite were beaten (Bradley 1994, page 13). Luckily, in this case, the Law Reform Commission then decided to organize discussions with hundreds of Papua New Guineans on what is wrong with wife-beating. Physical, psychological and other effects on wives, children and husbands were all brought out, as well as the negative effects on the family, community and society. In short, the open-minded discussions led to the conclusion that ending violence against women and girls had a wide range of practical benefits. The relevance of wife-beating to progress in development began to be visible.

In that same spirit, this concluding chapter reviews some of the costs to development from violence against women and girls, along with a look at how gender violence is a major human rights issue.

Some Costs to Development of Violence against Women

The consequences of gender-based violence, domestic violence in particular, include direct economic ones and lost productivity, as well as effects on children, women and the family, and obstacles to various development goals. Ten examples follow, divided roughly into economic, social and political costs, although these are all interrelated.

Direct Economic Costs

First of all, violence against women is an obstacle to the alleviation of poverty. Gender-based violence impedes equitable distribution of resources and control over them, as well as opportunities, education, work and benefits in the development process. Where women's participation in, and benefits from, development are limited, development itself is limited. For example, food production and processing, nutrition, health, child development, protection of the environment, income-generation and growth of the economy all suffer when support to women is not in line with their key roles and specialized knowledge in these areas. It is important for development that women not be subjugated by men and excluded from decision-making and control of resources by direct or indirect violence, harmful customs or traditions. Their lost human potential translates into lost development, and a setback for the alleviation of poverty.

Second, violence against women results in high direct costs for both health and legal systems, as well as in opportunity costs for development. Health services throughout the world are burdened by domestic violence and child abuse cases, whether these are so labelled or not, along with results of other forms of gender-based violence. Given the apparently high rates of wife-beating, burns, rape and sexual abuse in South Asia, actual medical and legal costs would be very high, although these have not been adequately calculated.

Cases of battering, abuse and rape are first seen in emergency and accident treatment units or gynaecology units. Referrals take place to orthopaedics, internal medicine, neurology, radiology, obstetrics and paediatrics. Hospitals set up special burns units for women patients. Forensic medicine comes into play. Legal systems process complaints. Police and the judiciary go to training programmes. Women's police cells have been established in many South Asian countries. There are hotlines, shelters and social-work services. And more of all the above will be needed as comprehensive efforts against violence to women and girls increase. Very large sums are potentially involved, as one can easily imagine, given the high costs calculated for these services in Australia, Canada, New Zealand and the United States, where there appear to be lower percentages of women beaten by intimate partners — as was discussed in Chapter 2.

Money being spent on response to violence against women and girls in South Asia, as elsewhere, would be available for other purposes if policy and prevention efforts were more effective in discouraging gender-based violence. That means opportunity costs as well as direct costs of gender violence are high. Developing countries, along with developed ones, can scarcely afford to overlook the strain on their budgets and limits on options for their use from gender violence.

Third, violence against women and girls means time lost at work. That translates into lost income for both workers and their employers, as well as their country. For women working in the informal sector, good health may be their main asset. When they are threatened or beaten, and consequently cannot work, they suffer physically, mentally and economically. The welfare of the whole family suffers, particularly in those households that depend on the woman's or girl's earnings entirely or to an important degree. For women working at home, beating and threats can mean fear, depression, illness and neglect of self and children, with more beatings as a consequence. Lost productivity and economic well-being results, in addition to physical and emotional pain.

Social Costs

Fourth, violence against women undermines important functions of the family, and threatens its viability as an institution. The family is meant to protect, shelter and nurture its members as well as to socialize children as citizens who will contribute to, rather than be condemned or deprived by, society. Society too often relies primarily on mothers to give care to family members, care that it would otherwise have to offer at considerable expense for government. It is understandable if women victim-survivors of domestic violence, anxious, depressed and injured, give less care to others than they would were they not hurt and fearful. Men who batter thus reduce the care their children would otherwise receive from their mothers. Furthermore, the type of husbands who batter would seem less likely to share parental or household responsibilities than would other men. In South Asia, domestic violence is also being noted as a cause for the break-up of marriages.

Fifth, violence against women affects children, their health, nutrition, education, psychological well-being and enjoyment of rights. Domestic violence has a deleterious impact on children and is among the reasons children leave home and go into child labour and prostitution. Yet not enough projects in South Asia study the impact of violence on children. Doing so, and designing interventions, could lead to multiple and positive results for children, accelerating progress towards existing goals, such as improved child nutrition and reduction in school drop-outs, as well as the eradication of child labour and prevention of girl-trafficking. Meanwhile, sexual abuse and incest by family members tends to be overlooked as a problem, although it is calamitous for millions of children in South Asia, as elsewhere. In short, ending violence against women could accelerate fulfilment of children's human rights and lives.

Sixth, violence against women limits women's decision-making about reproductive health outcomes, with many negative effects. Choices about number and spacing of children and for protection against HIV/AIDS and STDs are too often denied because of men's violence to women. The 1994 Cairo International Conference on Population and Development follow-up is emphasizing that violence against women should be eliminated, and equal participation of men and women in family and community life promoted (UNFPA 1994).

Political Costs

Seventh, "women's empowerment" is limited by gender violence and discrimination. It is popular to talk of and act for "women's empowerment" as a means and goal of enlightened development. This is not really credible so long as women are still being beaten and lack control over resources, let alone their own bodies. One criteria for the achievement of women's empowerment should be whether or not they are still beaten, whether or not they have alternatives and support to claim their rights. Women's political participation is also limited by negative attitudes and discrimination.

Unfortunately, the development process itself has sometimes blocked women's empowerment and perpetuated patriarchy and gender violence. When families are given information about development programmes and projects with the goal of increasing participation, it is almost always the male household head who is contacted. But such information, resources and benefits do not automatically trickle down to women and children, especially in patriarchal and abusive families. Work with female-headed households has been a corrective in some cases, but still leaves the majority of women out of direct participation and benefits in development. Working with and through women's groups is an effective means towards women's empowerment, as well as one for the efficient realization of development goals. Yet many international organizations do not yet make sufficient efforts to do so, even though their official government counterparts could and most likely would provide an interface if asked. Development programme practitioners themselves may also display negative attitudes and exclude women's direct participation. Training programmes for development planners and workers on "gender mainstreaming" have proliferated but rarely address the necessity to prevent violence against women as a development issue.

Eighth, violence against women models violence as the way to solve problems, teaches inequality between men and women, boys and girls, and perpetuates costly gender discrimination, including domestic violence itself. Exposed to violence at home, children grow up to use violence and victimization, instead of discussion, negotiation, compromise and cooperation, in problem-solving. This paves the way towards criminality, which is very costly for society and undermines democratic institutions. Gender discrimination and violence lead to loss of ambition, spirit and productivity for girls as it does for their mothers; for boys, it encourages use of physical violence and bullying to get one's way. Boys learn it is acceptable to dominate women and girls by whatever means and there are obvious links between violence against women and girls at home and gender-based violence against them in situations of conflict and war.[1]

Ninth, violence against women prevents human security. The UNDP Development Report for 1994 presented the idea of human security as a fundamental goal for development. It distinguished between security at a national level and security for people in daily life:

> For too long, the concept of security has been shaped by the potential for conflict between states. . . . For most people today, a feeling of insecurity arises more from worries about daily life than from the dread of a cataclysmic world event. (UNDP 1994, page 2)[2]

The goal of human security should apply to women as well as to men. However, the threat and reality of men's violence is a major source of fear and insecurity for millions of women. Human security can scarcely be realized so long as gender violence is prevalent both at home and in public. An additional problem is that abuse of children, in all its forms, often accompanies abuse of women. Where that occurs, a sense of human security is undermined from early in life, in the very institution that is meant to create it, the home. Research shows that children so affected are at risk of becoming more aggressive themselves, possible agents of even more violence in the family and society.

Tenth — and what about democracy? Development assistance often features strengthening democratic processes and institutions as a goal. Where, instead, it actually supports hierarchical and exploitative processes in which gender violence is not addressed, truly democratic participation and outcomes are undermined. Good governance as a development goal will be impossible to achieve unless participation and benefits are open to all without exclusion or violence based on gender and other characteristics.

Kamla Bhasin,[3] co-founder of Jagori (Awake) NGO in New Delhi, a leading proponent of enlightened development practices, puts the matter like this:

> It is absolutely fair [to say] that the main cause [of violence against women] is the devaluation of girls and women in society. . . . [O]ur fear as activists in India is not only violence against women, but increasing violence against women, and we see it linked with the present development paradigm, which is an aggressive paradigm based on competition, based on centralization of power, based on globalization, and it automatically strengthens the strong.

What Kind of Development Do We Want?

Kamla is one of the most influential spokespeople in South Asia for efforts to base development on people's felt needs and on sustainability, to stop exploitation of natural resources — and thus of people's livelihoods that depend on using them in sustainable ways — and to stop exploitation of people themselves. (See, for example, Bhasin n.d. a, 1998 and 1999.) The emphasis on competition for profit, and the entry into development of foreign enterprise interests through globalization, threatens to diminish the human worth of those whose labour and lives are exploited in the process. For Kamla, then, the focus on gender-based violence in development should raise questions about the very nature of development itself and lead to rejection of exploitative models and processes that benefit the rich and do not reflect or meet the needs of local people. Violence to women, to marginalized people, to natural resources are allied in this paradigm. One first should ask, "What kind of development?" (See A. Roy 1999 for an impassioned protest to development in India that leaves aside local people and their felt needs.)

Those who are part of the "People's Plan for the 21st Century" (PP21),[4] like Kamla, want to correct models and processes of development that are exploitative, that destroy natural resources, that marginalize poor people even further — with women and children particularly vulnerable in the process. Women are more and more treated as commodities in the process of globalization, with their traditional resources destroyed, their knowledge made irrelevant, their bodies featured in advertising campaigns for modern goods.

Violence against Women and Girls: A Key Human Rights Issue

As development focuses more and more on promotion and protection of human rights, the links between gender violence, development and rights are being made more explicit.

Violence against women has sometimes been considered as the right, even the duty, of a man. However, that attitude easily justifies denial of women's and girls' human rights and thus has had to be addressed in the international human rights movement. As the elimination of violence against women becomes a subject more firmly embedded in human rights discourse and advocacy, the human rights movement itself becomes even more effective. After all, human rights can scarcely be considered respected, protected, facilitated and fulfilled so long as women's and girls' human rights — including social, cultural and economic rights as well as civil and political ones — are denied through gender-based violence in its various forms.

It is true that women's and girls' human rights should be understood as automatically covered in generic human rights treaties, so there would ideally not have been a separate discussion of women's, or men's, human rights. From the original 1945 UN Charter and the 1948 Universal Declaration of Human Rights (UDHR) onwards, rights instruments in the international community always include a prohibition against discrimination, including by sex — which is the most fundamental division of humankind, and thus the most pervasive. Even so, as noted earlier, the United Nations saw fit to issue the Convention on the Elimination of All Forms of Discrimination against Women (CEDAW) in 1979 — years after the Charter and UDHR. Why? Its purpose is to call for more support and accountability for the equality, rights and fundamental freedoms of women because in real life their rights proved not to be sufficiently protected on the basis of earlier rights instruments, including the International Covenant on Civil and Political Rights and the International Covenant on Economic, Social and Cultural Rights.

In 1993, once again a special effort was made by the United Nations system to underscore the importance of women's human rights. The slogan "Women's Rights Are Human Rights" was widely used in preparing for and during the 1993 Vienna World Conference on Human Rights. Accordingly, the resulting Declaration on Human Rights stated:

> Again, this fact should be self-evident, since women are human beings; however, their treatment as sub-human in many societies and cultures, and all too often including that of western jurisprudence in action,[5] has required repeated explicit statements about women's human status and rights in various United Nations instruments.

Some details show the extent of effort that was needed for women to claim their rights on the international stage.

The Vienna Conference had the result it did largely due to the intense preparation by women's groups over several years, and campaigns in the two preceding years during "16 Days of Activism against Gender Violence," which linked 25 November, already proclaimed in 1981 as the International Day against Violence against Women, with 10 December, International Human Rights Day. The main purpose, as expressed in a petition during the 1991 campaign, was to influence the 1993 Vienna Conference "to comprehensively address women's human rights at every level of its proceedings" and "to recognize gender violence, a universal phenomenon which takes many forms across culture, race and class . . . as a violation of human rights requiring immediate action" (Bunch and Reilly in Schuler 1995, page 531). Moving testimonies from women victim-survivors of gender-based violence became the talk of the Conference and helped influence the positive content on women's human rights in the Vienna Declaration and Programme of Action, which the Conference issued.

Strong advocacy for women's human rights and more attention to them in the United Nations are part of follow-up efforts to the Vienna Conference (see, for example,

Bunch 1994; Reilly 1996; Schuler 1993; and Schuler 1995). The preparation for the Vienna Conference, along with the testimonies there, the Declaration and the heightened profile of women's human rights and the problem of gender violence, also motivated advocacy efforts in delegates' home countries after the Conference. For example, Charlotte Bunch (who played a major role at the Conference and continues to do so, moving forward the agenda for women's human rights)[6] cites action by GABRIELA, a women's coalition in the Philippines, which simply stated that "Women's Rights Are Human Rights"[7] in launching a campaign in 1993. As Ninotchka Rosca (in Bunch 1994, page 14) says, "They saw that 'human rights' are not reducible to a question of legal and due process. . . . In the case of women, human rights are affected by the entire Society's traditional perceptions of what is proper or not proper for women."

So, without waiting for permission from some authority to determine what is or is not a human rights issue, they declared for all to hear that so-called "women's issues" are that but much more.

Bunch (1994) sees this as a "transformative approach" (page 14) to the concept of human rights, and "from a feminist perspective so that it will take more account of women's lives . . . " (page 13). She points out that some abuses that are very specifically related to gender — "such as reproductive rights, female sexual slavery, violence against women and 'family crimes' like forced marriage" — are the very ones likely to be disregarded as human rights violations. She observes, "this is, therefore, the most hotly contested area that requires breaking down barriers between what is seen as public and private, the state and non-governmental responsibilities" (page 14).

Bunch (page 8) quotes Riane Eisler on an integrated theory of human rights:

> The issue is what type of private acts are and are not protected by the right to privacy and/or the principle of family autonomy. Even more specifically, the issue is whether violations of human rights within the family such as genital mutilation, wife beating, and other forms of violence designed to maintain patriarchal control should be within the purview of human rights theory and action. . . .

In fact, the Platform of Action of the Fourth World Conference on Women does address all these areas as part of the critical area of concern, "The human rights of women," which built on the Vienna Programme of Action. "Beijing follow-up," then, should move forward the agenda for women's — and girls' — human rights.

The Human Rights of Girls and Women: Complementarity or Conflict

Bringing the Conventions Together

The promotion of CRC and CEDAW together dates at least from 1995 when it was included in the NGO conference in Hairou, China, that ran parallel to the Fourth World Conference on Women.[8] Although "girls" are not mentioned at all in CEDAW, common sense tells us that "women" is meant to include them, wherever the context of any given article applies.[9] In practice, country reports on CEDAW often address the situation of girls. As for CRC, Goonesekere (1998b) has emphasized that it applies to many who may have been assumed to be "women" — because they are wives and mothers — but who are still legally girls.

Before preparations for the 1995 Fourth World Conference on Women, girls' interests — and references to CRC — were all too often left out when women's situation or rights were discussed. Sometimes the phrase "and girls" was simply used here and there as a token add-on, just as "and women" so often is added in discussions or texts that focus on men, to make them look more politically correct. Balakrishnan (UNICEF 1998a) makes the point that, similarly, girls' interests are not automatically covered if girls are looked at primarily as "tomorrow's women." Although it seems to be assumed that girls will automatically benefit from improvements being made in women's lives, Balakrishnan reminds us that girls are, after all, children first. They have rights when they are still children, not only rights for that time in the future when they become women. The usage of the term "girl-child"[10] signals girls' claim to their rights as children, not only as future women. Furthermore, girls have varying needs and claims at different stages of childhood.

For the Fourth World Conference on Women, "the girl-child" (Section L) was selected as one of the critical areas of concern, as were "violence against women" (Section D) and "human rights of women" (Section I). Each subject was included for the first time in the priorities for discussion at a world conference on women's issues. Naturally, Beijing follow-up efforts are meant to cover them. Their interlinkages, as well as those with other priority concerns, are being considered more than they would otherwise have been.

For Beijing follow-up, emphasis on a few key issues such as girls' education has prompted more thinking about rights of girls as well as those of women. So has concern about reproductive health of women, as it is influenced by what happens to girls even before they may become mothers themselves — as all too many girls actually do.

The topic of violence against women is one that clearly and naturally leads to concern with the situation of girls, too. In the close confines of the family, both girls and women are affected by domestic violence and what Bunch has called "family crimes" based on gender discrimination. A new interest at global level in family violence is surely opening the way, then, for rapprochement and cooperation between advocates for children's rights and advocates for women's rights.

There are many reasons to consider CEDAW together with CRC to protect girls' as well as women's rights. Some are:

- Both girls and women are subject to gender-based violence and discrimination that block fulfilment of their human rights; thus, both will gain from the eradication of gender violence. As indicated, a particularly important group for concern are "girl-women" — those who are still legally girls but are called "women" because of their sociological roles as wives and mothers. All the articles of CRC apply to them, as do those of CEDAW. These girl-women are among the most abused by gender-based violence and traditional practices in South Asia;
- Historically, women's rights have usually been taken up before children's rights[11]; the respect, protection and fulfilment of women's rights can thus accelerate the same for children's rights;
- Linking the two conventions forces questions about the scope of women's roles, and thus about men's complementary roles. For example, the assumption that a woman is primarily responsible for maternity is not supported by CEDAW, which emphasizes maternity as a social function (Article 5b). CRC also specifies the responsibilities of men as well as women in bringing up children;

- The conventions reinforce each other in many areas, lending support to a life-cycle — or rights-cycle — perspective from the female point of view; in some areas one convention goes further than the other. Together the two provide broader coverage than one alone;
- Using the two conventions together underscores the importance of prevention efforts and the continuity of state obligations over the lifespan; more attention to the girl-child's human rights also helps prevent abuse of women and their rights.

Resistance and Resolution

Just as there are reasons to consider the two conventions together, there can be resistance to doing so. First, because women themselves may not want to be automatically associated with motherhood and children but to be taken as human beings first. It is understandable that those women who fought to free themselves and their sisters from the notion that women's reproductive and family roles are primary, even inevitable, could well see the addition of children to their agenda as a step backwards for women, into stereotypic roles and their limitations[12] on women's human rights. Second, there are those who work for children's human rights who, sometimes, do not want to "dilute" their mission by also considering women's human rights. Also, they may think that adding "women's issues" would detract from issues that already are difficult enough to address.

To overcome such barriers, UNICEF, Save the Children, the Division for the Advancement of Women of the United Nations Secretariat and the International Human Rights Action Watch explored together in early 1998 reasons to address the human rights of women and children together. One important recommendation was "anyone working toward women's and/or children's rights needs to be aware that the two areas of rights are inextricably bound up with each other and are thus critically relevant to their efforts" (UNICEF/SCA/UNDAW/IWRAW 1998, back cover). A problem identified is the extent to which "[R]eligion, tradition and culture are often used to oppose women's equality and children's rights" (page 12). Indeed, some reservations to CEDAW, in particular, would appear to have interpretations of religion or supremacy of custom underlying them.

Beyond Norms for Human Rights Based on "the Male as Norm"

As for the question of consciously considering and using women's experience in human rights theory, Eisler (in Bunch 1994, page 8) comments:

> the underlying problem for human rights theory, as for most other fields of theory, is that the yardstick that has been developed for defining and measuring human rights has been based on the male as norm.

The same can be said for what has been regarded as "violence." Norms based on men's experience with violence primarily emphasize its physical aspect. Definitions and related norms are being supplemented by female experience with what Bunch has called "family crimes," including traditional practices in the home.

Still, it has been noted that review bodies for most human rights treaties are male dominated and have largely ignored women's exploitation as a rights issue.[13]

Like it or not, men stand accused of excluding women's experience from consideration in human rights theory and action. This is all the more likely where gender violence is concerned because it stems from unequal gender relations in which women are subjugated by men in patriarchal systems. At the same time, some influential commentators take care to distinguish between patriarchal systems, male society and just plain men. For example, Charlotte Bunch (1994, page 7) speaks eloquently of her optimism about the possibilities for change once female subordination is understood as political, rather than natural:

> But I do not believe that male violation of women is inevitable or natural, and I consider that a narrow and pessimistic view of men. If such violence and domination is understood as politically constructed reality, it is possible to imagine deconstructing that system and building more just interactions between the sexes.

Her views are similar to those of the Swedish writer and playwright Eva Moberg, who has written a persuasive paper, "Men Are Better than Male Society."[14] Optimism is also evident in documents and research that call for boys to be brought up in more equalitarian ways as a basis for a more just society. (See, for example, Kindlon and Thompson 1999.)

But what of the supposed cost to men, their expected loss when girls' and women's rights are fulfilled and notions of male superiority are overcome? John Stuart Mill (1989) stated bluntly that men would have to give up some of their power. This is the same idea as Ramaswamy's, already referred to in Chapter 4, that "manhood" should go (Krishnaraj 1995a). Not everyone has the vision of humanity without manhood that Mill and Krishnaraj did. Indeed, the frequently used phrase "empowerment of women" may threaten some men. But need women be empowered at the expense of others? Women's empowerment does not have to mean a loss for men. It can mean a gain for them, too.

Why? Because women can be empowered in the sense of having more of something than they had before, so their position improves compared to what it was earlier.[15] Men can also have something they didn't have before. The redistribution of power can be a win-win scenario, as limiting gender-role stereotypes are shattered and people are free to pick up and combine the pieces as suits them.[16] It does not follow that there is then disharmony between women and men, or that family life or community life are ruined. Rather, more democratic processes and outcomes should appear at all levels of society, and all stages of life. Society will be enriched because talents can be drawn on without restriction according to whether one was born male or female.

Still, many men believe that they will lose out as women gain. What will they truly lose? Maybe they can lose the fear and anxiety that they can't be strong enough, tough enough, to be in charge all the time (as discussed by Kaufman in Chapter 5). Then they can find more calm qualities within, which will let them contribute in less hostile, competitive, frustrated and aggressive ways to a world some believe they are currently making go crazily towards self-destruction. If men are freed from gender-role stereotypes, they may also become more flexible when faced with crises that do not permit them to fulfil stereotypic roles as providers. For example, suicide rates for men in Russia far exceed those for women and seem to have been increasing along with unemployment and economic crisis there (Lewis 1999). One could comment that this is partly due to lack of adaptability in terms of gender roles for men.

The men and women activists from South Asia don't seem to be worried about men's losses versus women's gains in the future. They tend to be visionaries. They see a better world to come when human rights are supported for women and men, boys and girls, on the basis of equality with benefits for all. They call on themselves and on the State accordingly.

State Accountability for Women's and Girls' Human Rights — Even at Home

Obligations and Reservations

The State is obligated by CEDAW to protect women from violations of rights at home and by individuals, not only from violations by public institutions. For example, CEDAW

> calls on States Parties to take all appropriate measures to eliminate discrimination against women by any person, organization or enterprise. . . . States may also be responsible for private acts if they fail to act with due diligence to prevent violations of rights or to investigate and punish acts of violence, and for providing compensation. (IWRAW and Commonwealth Secretariat 1996, page 73)

This challenges the tradition of regarding the family as a sacred and private sphere, where men can then do almost anything they want to family members as the *droit du seigneur* (right of the lord).

States Parties to CEDAW can, however, enter reservations (Article 28). For example, India has a reservation on Article 16 (1), to do with discrimination against women and family relations. (See Tables 1 and 2 in Chapter 1.) A number of concerns about such reservations have been expressed by the CEDAW Committee:

> The Committee has noted with alarm the number of States Parties which have entered reservations to the whole or part of Article 16 [about the family], especially when a reservation has also been entered to Article 2 [concerning discrimination], claiming that compliance may conflict with a commonly held vision of the family based inter alia, on cultural or religious beliefs or on the country's economic or political status.

> Many of these countries hold a belief in the patriarchal structure of a family which places a father, husband or son in a favourable position. In some countries where fundamentalist or other extremist views, or economic hardships, have encouraged a return to old values and traditions, women's place in the family has deteriorated sharply. In others, where it has been recognized that a modern society depends for its economic advance and for the general good of the community on involving all adults equally, regardless of gender, these taboos and reactionary or extremist ideas have progressively been discouraged. (IWRAW and Commonwealth Secretariat 1996, page 83)

As Charlotte Bunch (1994, pages 7–8) has observed,

> This raises again the question of the state's responsibility for protecting women's human rights. Feminists have shown how the distinction between private and public is a dichotomy largely used to justify female subordination in the home.

The State Is Already Involved in Family Life

As political scientist Susan Miller Okin (1989, page 131) puts it in her enlightening book *Justice, Gender and the Family*:

> The issue is not whether but how the State intervenes. False arguments about non-intervention vs. intervention in family life by the State, which already intervenes, obscure the importance of questions about what is needed to make families equitable and safe.

She notes that "In innumerable ways, the State [already] determines and enforces the terms of marriage . . ." (page 129). These include the comparative status and rights of husbands and wives regarding property, sexual relations, divorce and support — with partiality for the husband as presumed family head.

Okin (page 130) points out that state regulation of family life is evident in the relative denial of women's rights

> in the spheres of work, marketplace and politics, on the grounds that the exercise of such rights would interfere with the performance of their domestic responsibilities. All of this obviously reinforced the patriarchal structure of marriage, but the myth of the separation of the public and the domestic, of the political from the personal, was sustained throughout.

She draws attention to other flaws in the supposed dichotomy between private and public spheres, as reflected in theories of justice. These include the assumption — similar to that in most schools of economics — that relations in the family are harmonious, whereas they are actually characterized by the dynamics of power, which usually are considered as part of the political sphere. In particular, she observes that state institutions have until recently ignored violence to women in the family. Their doing so reflected the fact that violence against women used to be legally sanctioned as part of the power of patriarchy.

Fortunately, there is a change in the propensity to accept the privacy of the family as being more important than the lives and rights of its members. Family violence is now much less sanctioned or ignored than in the past. It is becoming recognized as a serious problem for social policy and state as well as private action.

> There is now no doubt that family violence, as it affects both wives and children, is closely connected with differentials of power and dependency between the sexes. . . . In addition to physical force, there are subtler, though no less important, modes of power that operate within families. . . . [I]n many respects the notion that state intervention in the family should be minimized has often served to reinforce the power of its economically or physically more powerful members. The privacy of home can be a dangerous place, especially for women and children. (Okin 1989, page 129)

Seble Dawit, an international human rights lawyer and activist from Ethiopia, put the matter very succinctly in a seminar to launch the Center for Women's Global Leadership's Campaign for Women's Rights to be recognized as Human Rights: "In the final analysis, if what goes on in families and communities is not open to scrutiny and adjudication, then no human right can be protected. This is where we are today" (Dawit, in Center for Women's Global Leadership 1994, page 39).

What to Do? A Holistic and Integrative Approach above All

The problem of gender violence is so vast, simultaneously insidious and lethal, so entwined with negative attitudes towards women, with traditional cultural values and practices, with the ideology and structure of patriarchy, as well as with the impact of the global economy, commercial values and inadequate development models and practices — not to mention the connection with discrimination and human rights — that it is a challenge to know where to begin in order to eradicate it. In the past, most efforts started out with a focus on the legal system,[17] but these were found to be insufficient (see UN 1998, par. 33).

The Platform for Action of the Fourth World Conference on Women thus calls for a holistic and integrated approach:[18]

- "[D]eveloping a holistic and multi-disciplinary approach to the challenging task of promoting families, communities and States that are free of violence against women is necessary and achievable" (UNDPI 1996, page 75).

And two of the three "strategic objectives" for the elimination of gender violence stress either the holistic approach or prevention, which depends on it:

- "Take integrated measures to prevent and eradicate violence against women" (page 78).[19]
- "Study the causes and consequences of violence against women and the effectiveness of preventive measures" (page 81).[20]

In United Nations conference-related documents, these are the first explicit references I found about the need for an integrated and holistic approach to ending violence against women, and for prevention to be coupled with eradication efforts across many fronts. If followed, these recommendations could help overcome the factors that otherwise limit the impact of other strategies. Too often, they are reactive, focusing only on symptoms or short-term consequences, not causes. They are fragmented. Allocated resources are inadequate. Values and beliefs about women's supposed inferiority and men's superiority are not tackled. The task remains, then, to challenge and change attitudes behind the practices that discriminate, violate rights and lead to physical as well as psychological violence.

Towards Changing Attitudes

In fact, "Change attitudes" is one of six main areas in which the Commission on the Status of Women (CSW) proposes action to accelerate implementation of the "strategic objectives" regarding violence against women as a critical area of concern in the Platform for Action (UN ECOSOC 1998b).[21]

This is in keeping with the Commission's earlier call for measures "to bring about profound attitude change with regard to violence, to promote the message to perpetrators that violence is unacceptable and reassure victims that they will be taken seriously and treated sympathetically" (UN 1998, par. 36), and for "comprehensive public awareness and advocacy strategies seeking to make gender-based violence against women a critical concern to everyone" (par. 38).

Specific actions, as proposed by CSW, to change attitudes are directed to education programmes, the media, policies and programmes dealing with perpetrators and legal literacy efforts. Also called for are more programmes for particularly vulnerable groups of women — those with disabilities, migrants, refugees, potential victims of trafficking. Support for men's efforts, complementary to women's, to prevent and eliminate violence against women and institutional capacity-building for more awareness and prevention of gender violence are included, too.

Some examples of proposals given regarding education and the media and to change attitudes of those who perpetrate crime and those are responsible for justice include:

- Work to create violence-free societies by implementing participatory educational programmes on human rights, conflict resolution and gender equality for women and men of all ages, beginning with girls and boys;
- Introduce and invest in comprehensive public awareness campaigns, such as "zero tolerance," that portray violence against women as unacceptable;
- Encourage the promotion in media of portrayals of positive images of women and of men, presenting them as cooperative and full partners in the upbringing of their children, and discourage the media from presenting negative images of women and girls;
- Create policies and programmes to encourage behavioural change in perpetrators of violence against women, including rape, and monitor and assess the impact and effect of such programmes;
- Conduct research on, and create policies and programmes to change, the attitudes and behaviour of perpetrators of violence against women within family and society;
- Actively encourage, support and implement measures aimed at increasing the knowledge and understanding of violence against women, through gender analysis capacity-building and gender-sensitive training for law enforcement officers, police personnel, the judiciary, medical and social workers, and teachers.

For a holistic and integrated approach to bring about the profound social change that would make domestic as well as other kinds of gender violence intolerable, there would clearly need to be extensive networking and dialogue across all sorts of boundaries — those of profession, class, the rural-urban and gender divides, as well as geographic borders. Any walls that block communication and cooperation from the grass-roots to policy levels would also need to be dismantled.

Efforts are under way to bring about change in South Asia, as elsewhere, concerning violence against women and girls Yet domestic violence in particular is still a great cause for alarm, and for even more effective measures to be taken — integrated holistic ones that aim for prevention as well as redress.

Where Does South Asia Stand?

Monitoring Progress

There are a number of bodies and networks at the international level that monitor country progress towards ending violence against women and girls and to promote more effective action. For example, the CSW reviews country reports for Beijing follow-up; committees for various conventions on human rights comment on periodic country reports[22]; networks of NGOs and professional groups — some in liaison with UN organizations[23] — take the initiative to chart progress on priority issues and "pressurize" governments; "shadow reports" are sometimes submitted by NGO groups alongside ones from government to official monitoring bodies on implementation of human rights.

Comments made by review bodies on country reports about implementation of human rights treaties are meant to be constructive and advisory rather than punitive.

They are not enforceable. Follow-up depends on the goodwill and commitment of the States Parties concerned and on developing the needed policy and programme shifts. Reviews are periodic, but are often delayed due to a backlog of reports, so that tracing and encouraging the rate of a country's progress implementing a convention can itself be a slow process.

How are review mechanisms actually being used? And do they regularly address the problem of violence against women and girls in the home, as well as in the public arena? Are results brought to wide public attention so that they will truly influence attitudes and policy? A systematic study to answer these questions would be well worthwhile, but has not yet been done.

Some examples of reports at the international level and reactions from review bodies concerning violence against women show impetus towards change, along with the complexity and difficulty involved. These are the kinds of recommendations that women's groups and NGOs can encourage through dialogue and partnership with government in the review process. Recommendations like these also help build an integrated approach and could lead to more attention to the problem of domestic violence and the attitudes that tolerate it:

- A CSW (UN ECOSOC 1997) review of country reports for follow-up on the Fourth World Conference on Women refers to one from Bangladesh, the only South Asian country mentioned. Note is taken of the intention of the Government of Bangladesh that better use be made of the media, and that relations be improved between community members and police, for reporting and follow-up on cases of violence against women.

- The Human Rights Committee, in its concluding observations on India's[24] third periodic report on 24–25 July 1997, observed that personal law, when based on religion, violates the right of women to equality before the law and non-discrimination. They recommended "that efforts be strengthened towards the enjoyment of their rights by women without discrimination and that personal laws be enacted which are fully compatible with the Covenant" (UNCHR 1997a). The Committee also recommended that "the Government take further measures to overcome these problems and to protect women from all discriminatory practices, including violence."

- On 15 June 1999, Nepal's Secretary of the Ministry of Law and Justice introduced to the Committee on the Elimination of All Forms of Discrimination against Women his country's initial report on implementation of CEDAW. Also present was a group of Nepali women representing various NGOs, which tabled a shadow report contributing to the debate (Forum for Women, Law and Development 1999).

Among the many comments experts made, two are particularly relevant here. It was noted that among the issues not addressed in the government report was domestic violence — "which non-governmental organization reports had stated was widespread in the country." An expert also asked, specifically, about "the extent to which non-governmental organizations had been involved." This query indicates the importance that the CEDAW Committee gives to NGO participation in the country review process Also, daily press releases permit one to follow the nature of the exchange during the review process. (See, for example, *www.un.org/News/Press/docs/1999 19990615*.

WOM1136.html.) Wider circles are thus made aware of the various concerns expressed and the need for follow-up.

Regional Initiatives

At the regional level, there are also some pertinent initiatives against gender violence and review mechanisms. For example, the South Asian Association for Regional Cooperation (SAARC) named the 1990s the Decade of the Girl-Child, with a number of goals related to ending gender discrimination and violence. These are periodically reviewed by SAARC member countries[25] (see, for example, SAARC 1996 and 1997). Also, SAARC has liaisons with both UN organizations and NGOs.

Before the Fourth World Conference on Women, SAARC issued a resolution that included the intention to end violence against women and girls (see SAARC 1995). And at its 4th Ministerial Conference on Children, SAARC (1996) included the following priority in the Rawalpindi Resolution:

> Strengthen further the ongoing SAARC process to assess the extent and causes of all forms of violence against children, especially the girl child, in order to galvanize legal and other interventions to prevent such violence at all levels.

To date, one of the most visible results at the regional level is a proposed convention against trafficking.[26]

Regional networks emerging among South Asian NGOs include those engaged in women's studies, such as the South Asian Association of Women's Studies (SAAWS). Ending violence against women and girls is a persistent concern for them. Initiatives for peace are also evident — peace in the home, community, State and region. (See, for example, Jagori n.d.)

Also at the regional level, a wide range of South Asian NGOs, not all in coalitions, and individuals take opportunities to promote more action to end gender violence. Still, a focus on violence against women and girls in the family is not usual.

All the more reason, then, to recall the Kathmandu Commitment (see Appendix 1): it is both holistic in spirit and calls for the family to be free of gender violence:

> While recognizing that violence against all segments of society including children is a serious and growing problem in our times and in this region, we nevertheless state that the issue of violence against women and girls has been largely ignored.

> We come from countries in South Asia with a diversity of political situations, laws, institutions, cultures and traditions. Yet the anguish of violence is a common problem that debilitates and threatens all women and girls, manifesting itself in similar and different ways, being rooted in gender inequality, discrimination, and patriarchal value systems and son preference. . . .

> We recognize that the family itself often promotes and perpetuates gender based violence, through the differential treatment given to girls and boys from conception and birth by all members of the family. We shall endeavour to promote gender equality in the family, so that this key institution in our countries becomes a source of support for its members and creates a co-operative and nurturing environment. This requires the involvement of a number of institutions in the reconstruction of the nature and functions of the family. We call upon the State to recognize its duty to protect human rights by protecting women and children against any act of violence that occurs in the family.

Moving Forward

As seen in earlier chapters, some important actions are already being taken to end gender violence, including in the family. These can be summarized according to breaking the silence, challenging custom and tradition, holding the State accountable, building new networks and featuring success. Here only some general descriptions and a few highlights are given. All contribute to bringing the various kinds of domestic violence into the light and to a more holistic approach that will include prevention as well as redress. There would be many, many more examples if a truly comprehensive account were to be made for the region.

Breaking the Silence

People are talking about the unspeakable. Legal cases. Research. Meetings. Public debate. Individual testimonies. Even when it seems that only problems are being covered, as is primarily the case for the first part of this book, the silence about violence in the family is being broken. That very act is a vital part of the solution.

The press is playing an important role in bringing the issue of gender violence in the home to public attention. True, the stories are often sensationalized.[27] Still, problems are coming to light that were not frequently discussed before. There are more surveys and studies about the extent and different forms of domestic violence in South Asia. Liaison with media, with guidelines for coverage of cases, is a priority for many NGOs. Groups like Women's Feature Service (WFS) in India and Asmita in Nepal set new standards for media coverage, as also called for by Mitra (n.d. b), with an emphasis on coverage involving violence against children.

The direct and indirect impact of domestic violence on children is becoming better understood. The South Asian studies reported earlier in Chapter 3 are evidence of this growing awareness. NGOs like CWIN in Nepal, Sahil in Pakistan and Butterflies in India are among those pointing out that better quality of family life could help prevent children from ending up on the street or entering into child labour — among other negative outcomes. With an eye to solutions, organizations like these also contribute to the new awareness of incest and child sexual abuse as social and rights problems. In some cases, as discussed in Chapter 3, schools are hosting workshops and holding lessons on bodily integrity — so children will know when to avoid certain situations if possible.

Women's groups continue to mobilize for change. Women's solidarity helps stop domestic violence against women and girls. Examples from Chapter 9, by SEWA for instance, come to mind concerning group action by women who work together. The Karvi sexual abuse case in India is an example of spontaneous action by various women's groups organizing support for a woman who had brought a case against her husband for his alleged rape of their daughter (see The Support Group for the Karvi Child Sexual Abuse Case 1999). Shelter, financial support, legal advocacy and education costs for the children were all found for her and her two daughters.

In university settings, women's studies programmes frequently draw attention to private as well as public violence against women and girls. Women's studies have been launched in most, if not all, of the countries. For example, the Centre for Women's Studies at Quaid-I-Azam University, Islamabad, Pakistan, is among five such centres opened already in 1988 as "part of the overall development efforts made in Pakistan to conduct research and gather information on the conditions and problems of women" (CWS 1993). Women's studies programmes often reach out to the community, as this one does, through forums and newsletters.[28] Family violence is a frequent topic. And SAAWS made studies of domestic violence a priority (see Jahan and Islam 1997).

The family and community — as well as physicians — are being called on to help prevent maternal mortality. For example, public campaigns for safe motherhood were launched in Bangladesh and Nepal in 1997. The need for positive family and community attitudes towards women getting medical help when at risk is being addressed. The increased attention to maternal mortality can help correct the notion that giving birth is so natural for women that they don't need or deserve any assistance.

Challenging the Patriarchy — and Patriarchal Attitudes

The patriarchy is being named and challenged as the source of intolerable attitudes and practices against girls and women. The work of Bhasin (1993) is exemplary, as is that of Kirti Singh (1998). As we have seen in Chapter 5, interlocking parts of the patriarchal system, from the family to national levels — including key institutions such as the legal and political systems — lack checks and balances to avoid unbridled use and abuse of male power and privilege. If this continues, the idea and practice of supremacy and entitlement could destroy the usefulness of the family as a place in which humans can be secure, children can be nurtured, and where women and men can truly respect and love each other and live in harmony.

Men's voices are joining those of women against the patriarchy. For example:

> We men, realizing that no sustainable change can take place unless we give up the entrenched ideas of male superiority, commit ourselves to devising new role models of masculinity. We shall endeavour to "take off the armour"[29] and move towards becoming a more developed and complete being. We urge international bodies to focus on and explore the destructive consequences of patriarchy. (UNICEF 1998b)[30]

Systematic work to target and monitor changes in the structure and expression of patriarchy is yet to be done in South Asia. Some ideas for the kinds of variables that might be considered were presented in a regional UNICEF meeting organized in 1999 in Godavari, Nepal.[31]

Demands are being made to stop harmful practices associated with patriarchal attitudes. For example, it appears the movement against abuse of sex-determination tests as a basis for selective foeticide is being revived in India: "More than 5,000 students marched in New Delhi yesterday, demanding a ban on feticide and related sex-selection tests," reported the UN Wire (17 November 1999; see *www.unfoundation.org/unwire*). The Indian Medical Association (IMA), the National Commission for Women (NCW) and the United Nations also expressed their concern about the alarming sex ratio. "What is needed is a long-term strategy to try and change the mindset of growing boys and girls so as to counter gender discrimination at an early age," said Viba Parthasarathy, president of NCW. She pointed out that foeticide "has become much more popular only in the 90s," and explained that, while high dowry demands were one factor, "many women in feudal areas don't want to have a daughter who would go through the same misery, humiliation and dependence that seem to define their own lives." The medical profession and the legal system were found wanting, according to Shardha Jain, an IMA official. "No doctor has ever been prosecuted in India for providing sex-determination service for the purpose of feticide." In line with the new emphasis on changing public attitudes, a call was made to "make people who want to indulge in such abhorrent practices really feel criminal. Indian society must change."

Gender-role stereotypes are being challenged. A good example is the development of the series of animated cartoons on the South Asian girl-child, called *Meena*,[32] which is being distributed, along with age-appropriate multimedia materials, to audiences ranging from children and parents to policy makers. The series promotes gender equality by focusing on issues such as age of marriage, dowry, sending girls to school and keeping them there, girls' workload and nutrition and teasing of girls. An episode on violence to women and girls at home is being planned. *Meena* is well-known in many parts of the region. For example, even in hard-to-reach parts of Nepal, it is being seen thanks to those who carry battery-operated video equipment on their backs up the mountain trails.

Also, a group of men film-makers from some South Asian countries have started a project, as mentioned in Chapter 5, to depict what it is like to grow up male in South Asia and to encourage boys to think about new models of masculinity. The films[33] and related discussion materials will be available for use in schools and with youth groups. (See, for example, SCA and UNICEF 1998 on alternative masculinities in South Asia.) Men's roles in parenting are being taken more seriously and supported, too. In Nepal, for example, listening groups are starting to discuss men's roles in parenting (UNICEF 1998i). Global discussion of men's roles in the family (see UNICEF 1997f and Roberts 1995) helped stimulate the Nepali initiative.

Calling on the State to Fulfil Its Obligations to End Gender Violence

Working in a rights framework. The connection between gender violence and rights violations is being made more explicit. The complementarity between CEDAW and CRC is also being brought out, to protect rights of girls and women in a life-cycle perspective. Reporting and review mechanisms are being better understood, and means are being found for more NGO involvement in the process. Advocacy for the Optional Protocol to CEDAW for reporting on violence against women is also increasing awareness about the seriousness of expectations that the State provide redress.

More attention is being paid to harmonization of national laws with the international instruments to which States Parties are committed. There already are examples from India and Sri Lanka: guidelines about sexual harassment have been issued in India, based on CEDAW and Recommendation 19 about violence against women; a call has been made in Sri Lanka for a non-discrimination clause to be added to the Constitution, in keeping with international human rights treaties, like CEDAW and CRC, to which the State is committed. And during the CEDAW Committee review of the initial country report from Nepal, an expert observed that discriminatory laws persisted in Nepal, despite its being a State's Party to the convention (Forum for Women, Law and Development 1999).

Even more consideration of how best to reflect international human rights principles in national law is likely to be forthcoming beyond the reviews of country reports by treaty committees. For example, some 100 judges and magistrates from most of the legal traditions and cultures in the world — including participants from South Asia

— took part in the innovative October 1999 "Judicial Colloquium on the Application of International Human Rights Law at the Domestic Level," organized in Vienna, Austria, by the UN Division for the Advancement of Women of the United Nations. A Communiqué (UNDAW 1999) from the participants recognized the importance of putting universal human rights principles into practice, particularly in light of the persistence of inequality and gender-based violence against women and girls in some settings. Accordingly, the participants called for judicial education so that the principles in human rights treaties, such as CEDAW and CRC, could be translated into national laws at all levels. They asked for guidance to be developed by UN community.[34]

Better use of the legal system to stop violence to women and girls is being promoted. Legal literacy; training of lawyers, police and the judiciary; women's police cells; greater cooperation between lawyers and physicians — especially in forensic medicine; cooperation with the police: all are being developed at national level. UNICEF and UNIFEM have been cooperating[35] on country studies and a regional overview on relevant improvements needed in the legal system to eliminate gender violence. Legal reform is also featured in the interagency regional campaign, led by UNIFEM, to end domestic and other violence against women and girls (see UNIFEM 1998c). As part of the 1998 campaign, thousands of posters on women's human rights, and the responsibilities for police to protect them, were distributed to police stations throughout the country. Many NGOs and women's organizations in the region have long been active working to improve the benefits of the legal system for women victim-survivors of gender violence.

Supporting the struggle. It is all too easy for international organizations to overlook what does or does not happen with and for women and girls at the grass-roots level as a result of their efforts in partnership with governments. There are ways to ensure more impact that will benefit those groups whose rights and lives are threatened by gender-based violence. These include partnerships with governmental bodies such as national commissions on human rights and on women, which have direct links with NGOs and local women's groups. Agreements can also be made with government partners about implementation with and through NGOs. Participation of women's or human rights groups in programme planning, monitoring and evaluation is essential. Including activist rural women and those from slums in consultations and meetings is also needed, even if this requires more resources and time for interpretation and exchange. Without such measures, too often only the elites will be heard or benefit, the status quo will be reinforced and the protection and fulfilment of human rights will not be advanced.

In contrast, I remember a very positive example by the Indian Association of Women's Studies, at its 1995 conference in Jaipur. It invited Bhanwari Devi, the anti–child-marriage worker who had brought a case of rape against men of two generations from a prominent Brahmin family in her community in Rajasthan. Hundreds of us who were participating waited patiently and gratefully through two levels of translation (from the local language to Hindi and then to English) to hear her absorbing account (see Chapter 10). This was an inspiring example of appropriate respect being given to women activists who are not part of the main networks and groups anchored in urban areas. Also, the press amplified her voice so that her challenge to custom and privilege was heard throughout Indian — and South Asian — society.

Building New Networks for Violence-Free Societies and Families

South Asians from many walks of life are networking to strengthen each others efforts' for a common agenda against gender violence. They do not want to be silent, inactive "passive perpetrators." For example, along with the media, men, health professionals and youth are emerging as important partners for broader networks and coalitions that are being built in South Asia.

Working with men as part of the solution is a priority. Men at the October 1997 regional meeting "Ending Violence against Women and Girls" believed in the importance of their contributions for gender peace. They negotiated to add the following statement to the Kathmandu Commitment (see Appendix 1):

> We women and men recognize that, without the active participation of men, we cannot achieve our goal of eliminating violence against women and girls. We shall strive as individuals, as parents, as educators and as opinion formers to promote new, positive models of masculinities and femininities, so that boys and young men will grow up realizing their own potential as caring human beings committed to respecting the rights of women and girls as equal partners in their families, communities and societies.

Imran Aslam, editor of the *Karachi Times*, saw partnership with men as a difficult, although necessary task. He put it this way (UNICEF 1998b, page 30):

> The paradigm that is a man, is under attack, despite attempts by tradition, customs, religion and the media to explain away the illogicality of his behaviour. To strip this man, fashioned over centuries, of his required second nature is no easy task. Layer after layer and sediment after sordid sediment has to be removed before he can be truly restored to humanity. He is, after all, a creature born of prayers and supplication, and pilgrimages made barefoot to shrines and temples. . . .
>
> He controls linkage, legacies, history and inheritance. The law is his concubine, cringing, twisting and turning at his every whim. He can conjure up fear with an arched eyebrow . . . The present unfortunately has passed him by. . . .

Ghalib Bas kehdushwar hai	The easiest of tasks
Hai Kaam ka assan homa	So difficult seem
Admi ko bhi Mayasar	Like the transition
Ahin Insaan hona	of man into a human being

And in a special feature article of the *Karachi Times*, Imran called for a men's liberation movement in Pakistan. As background, he described how he played the role of a South Asian "Tootsie."[36] He had put on the all-enveloping garb of conservative women in Pakistan and then rode the bus. "Their eyes were my eyes," he said about the men staring at him and even trying to touch him through his voluminous outfit (Aslam 1997, page 29).

Also in Pakistan, Kamran Ahmad (1998) has stimulated open-minded consideration of men's gender roles through his collaboration on a UNDP-sponsored seminar on men's issues.[37] And elsewhere in South Asia, other men and men's groups are questioning traditional norms and supporting change against gender violence.[38] For example, men have formed a group in Bombay, India: Men against Violence against Women.

In a few countries of South Asia, individual men who are active against violence to women and girls are being featured, with names and photos, as new role models in materials for school groups, youth and the general public (see, for example, UNICEF 1998e).

Men in South Asia are also taking opportunities to link with efforts by men's groups elsewhere in the world, such as the White Ribbon Campaign that originated in Canada, spread to Europe and was discussed in 1998 in South Asia for implementation there (see, for example, Kaufman 1997, 1998).[39] For additional examples of men's initiatives against gender violence, promising for linkages outside the region,[40] see Hoffman (1999), Keynan (1997), Kimmel (1997), Male Network (n.d.), Sarah (1999) and UNESCO (1997).

Health professionals begin to be more active against gender violence. The All Women's Wing of the Indian Medical Association featured the topic of "violence against women — what physicians can do to stop it" at their 1997 annual meeting in Patna (see Hayward 1997). The Pakistan Women's Health Forum took up the issue at their annual meeting the same year. Their Director, Shershah Syed, M.D., calls attention to the importance of ending violence against women and girls if they are to fulfil their right to health and life (Syed n.d. a and b). In Nepal, some 30 physicians met in 1997 to discuss how they could improve management of domestic violence, incest and child rape — new topics for them to discuss together in an open forum. And Bangladeshi authorities, supported by UNICEF, are increasing their efforts to stop maternal mortality: having physicians screen for beating in pregnancy is planned. This is part of the Women Friendly Hospital Initiative (see Ministry of Health and Family Welfare, Government of Bangladesh 1998). And in Sri Lanka, the use of forensic medicine in cases of gender violence has improved, judging from Dr. Ravindra Fernando's account (UNICEF 1998b). Still, throughout the region, there is a great need for physicians to take the incidence and trauma of domestic violence much more seriously in their work. From Sri Lanka, Professor Harendra de Silva's story, in Chapter 3, shows what can happen as they do so.

There should be more opportunities for youth against gender violence. "The young should be inculcated with the values of respect for women, which would make them consider men and women as equal in every sense of the term." So wrote Vishai Saini (n.d.), in his first prize-winning essay for a competition sponsored by UNIFEM in 1998 as part of its campaign in South Asia for the elimination of gender-based violence.[41] Yes, youth action against gender violence will depend in part on what they learn at home. But it also depends on events that invite youth participation. For example, students contributed in many ways to the above campaign — organizing an inter-college street play competition, holding an interactive workshop on "Law and the police in dealing with violence against women," sponsoring poster competitions, panels, poetry and more. "These explorations led the campaign along a path of discovery and realization — acknowledging the value of young people's opinions and perceptions and the importance of their participation in the process of social change" (UNIFEM 1998c, page 6).

Youth involvement, however, is needed in ongoing programmes as well as special events. A regional panel on the prospects for such youth involvement observed:

> It is the world of patriarchal and institutional authority that has continued to deny them [youth] the voice and role they should have, marginalising them. Young people need to be heard, as it is among the young that the abuse continues and remains unacknowledged and

denied and it is among them that solutions to combat gender violence and abuse must be found. A few steps have been taken to engage and include young people more in processes of discourse on issues of sexuality, gender and raising awareness regarding their rights. These spaces for involvement, however, need to be enlarged and expanded. Gender violence is rarely addressed. (UNICEF 1998b, page 35)

Participants in the Kathmandu regional meeting pledged, in the spirit of CRC (which includes the right to participation), to involve children and youth much more in efforts to stop gender violence.

The "Kathmandu network" contributes. Each individual made a pledge for specific action after the meeting and to support work towards realization of a non-violent society and families. The activists then agreed to network across disciplines and geographic boundaries so far as possible, calling on the United Nations system for assistance, They put forward names of additional individuals and groups for a regional network against gender violence (UNICEF 1998b). While there has not been any survey to follow up on the network, anecdotal information indicates that these activists are contributing to important regional and global events like the UNIFEM campaign, the annual 16 Days of Activism against Gender Violence sponsored by the Center for Women's Global Leadership at Rutgers University (New Jersey, USA) and follow-up meetings on the Fourth World Conference on Women.[42] In short, the "machinery" available for advocacy, exchange and monitoring about gender violence and women's and girls' human rights is complex, but activists are learning about and using it more and more effectively.

Featuring and Building on Success

That is the intent of this book, as it is of many new initiatives. Looking for "best practices" and how to support and spread these on a bigger scale are important strategies to help end violence against women and girls. UNIFEM is leading the way at global level in the use of modern technology to exchange views and successes about ending violence against women and girls. For example, on 8 March 1999 — the last International Women's Day before the new millennium — an unprecedented United Nations Interagency Global Video Conference with the theme "A World Free of Violence against Women" was held in the United Nations. As Secretary-General Kofi Annan opened the proceedings, he stressed the importance and urgency of eliminating violence against women and girls, for both moral and practical reasons. Many, many NGOs were present, along with government representatives and UN staff. Like the 1997 Kathmandu regional meeting, this one focused on domestic violence and brought together people from many walks of life to emphasize that their experiences with gender violence reflect problems in attitudes and structures of society, which need to change. Through satellite hook-up, women, girls and some men from various regions — Africa, Asia and the Pacific, and Latin America and the Caribbean — shared success stories about efforts to end gender violence. The campaigns raised public and policy awareness of violence against women as a violation of human rights; they also celebrated women's achievements in the struggle for human rights and called for more action to honour related commitments made by governments.[43]

Modern technology affords many previously isolated women opportunities to join networks for exchange of problems and lessons learned about trying to end gender-based violence. To date, mobilizing action about problem cases like the Sarwar case from Pakistan (see Chapter 10) seems to me to be more frequent on the Web than is an exchange of lessons learned or any success stories. Specific opportunities to exchange success stories are being created, however. For example, UNIFEM is developing computer server networks among activists against gender violence. Many NGOs are acquiring the necessary equipment, gaining more information about what others do well and putting forward their own examples and questions.[44] A global fund with UNIFEM for projects designed to end gender violence includes guidelines for analysing them for lessons learned: these can be disseminated widely through the Web, as indicated above.

Initiatives like these help show just how much the agenda to end gender violence has been pushed forward since the Fourth World Conference on Women in Beijing, with an emphasis on more holistic action, changing attitudes and on prevention. One would think, with all the governments committed to the Platform for Action, and with all the signatories to CEDAW and CRC, that as one millennium is ending and another opening, there would be no question that gender-based violence is a key development and human rights issue. But there is still a long way to go, particularly for violence against women and girls to be eliminated in the home.

Still More Attention Needed to Stop "the War in the Home"

How Many Are Affected?

Here we return briefly to the question of how many are affected by gender-based violence in the home in South Asia — but go beyond the percentages as reported in Chapters 2 and 3 from various studies in particular locales to make some tentative projections for the region as a whole. This perspective is important to influence policy-level changes, with increased resources, for a holistic effort to prevent violence against women and girls in South Asia.

Clearly, the scale of violence against girls and women at home is vast. There is an unrecognized "war at home." Using the studies available, reviewed in Chapter 2, as a guide, it is estimated that those affected in South Asia alone are in the millions.

Consider the following line of thinking to get a compelling sketch of the situation. There are some 609 million females in South Asia (based on Sivard 1995, page 40).[45] Some 359 million, those between the ages of 15 and 64, are the most likely to be married (not counting those who marry younger and not adjusting for those who are widowed). That can be read as some 359 million girls and women at risk for domestic violence of some sort perpetrated by husband against wife. For wife-battering alone, if one uses the most conservative figure from the 25–50 per cent likely range for incidence, as reported by WHO in its global assessment, then at least some 90 million married girls and women in South Asia are likely affected. That figure would double to some 180 million girls and women if the 50 per cent figure were used. When one takes into account that studies from South Asia generally show even higher levels of incidence, then the 180 million figure is itself conservative. And any estimates for incidence of more widespread psychological or economic violence would be even higher.

Comparisons with some national population figures. The scale of the problem and the urgency of doing more to address it is made clearer by comparing the estimate of those likely at risk of domestic violence in South Asia with some national population figures. The combined total population of France, Italy and the United Kingdom is almost 180 million (UNICEF 1998j, page 36). In Asia and the Pacific, the combined total population of Australia, Cambodia, Japan and Malaysia is almost 180 million (UNICEF 1998j, page 35). If it were known that more than the entire population of France, Italy and the United Kingdom or that of Australia, Cambodia, Japan and Malaysia were at risk of beating at home, one can presume there would be collective outrage and action to stop it.

Comparison with maternal mortality figures. A comparison with figures for and attention to maternal mortality is also instructive. The estimate for maternal mortality worldwide is some 585,000 per year (UNICEF1998c). Most of the deaths are considered preventable. Maternal mortality is already the subject of important and deserved national and international campaigns. Bearing that in mind, one more readily grasps the immense and unnecessary scale of suffering women undergo through domestic violence. One also realizes it is relatively overlooked considering its scope. Like maternal mortality, all forms of domestic violence should be regarded as preventable — even more so — and made the focus of advocacy and interventions supported by governments and international organizations on a scale at least comparable to that for reproductive health.

And How Many Children Suffer?

Then there remains the question of how many children are affected by domestic violence in South Asia: Are there truly millions as Chapter 3 foresaw? Again, a sketch of the possible regional situation:

Estimates of those affected throughout the region will vary depending on the type of violence and impact, direct or indirect, considered. Still, given that there are some 547 million children under age 18 in the countries covered in this study (calculated from 1996 or most recent figures available up to then; see UNICEF 1998j, page 34), and that 25 per cent to 50 per cent (and sometimes more) of their mothers are likely beaten, the numbers of children at risk of negative effects from witnessing violence are clearly in the millions. The numbers of children who are themselves beaten would also be in the millions if even 10 per cent (a conservative estimate) became secondary targets when their mothers were battered. If 40–50 per cent of the children were beaten, the resulting figure would be so high as to prompt its denial as unimaginable (even though the low estimate for percentage of women beaten was being used in calculations).

So far as child sexual abuse in the family is concerned, the Indian psychiatrist Sudhir Kakkar has made "an informed guess" that some 600,000 to 700,000 children in India have experienced sexual abuse, most likely by parents or relatives, said to account for about 40 per cent of the abuse according to studies elsewhere (see Kakkar 1996, page 15). Kakkar's estimate, in the hundreds of thousands, disturbing enough, still seems low. Being conservative and using it as a base to project the likely number of cases of child sexual abuse by family members in the region would still mean more than a million children were probably victims.

The possibility of a much higher incidence is indicated, however. Dr. Shekar Seshadri has observed, as reported in Chapter 3, that incidence rates of 15–20 per cent for child sexual abuse and incest in the family most likely apply in India just as they do outside the region. As there are some 382.9 million children under 18 reported for India alone (UNICEF 1998j, page 35), that would mean some 57 to 77 million children are likely victims of sexual abuse, including incest, in India. Even 40 per cent of those cases, the level Kakkar uses for abuse by parents and other family members, would still mean there are millions of children, not thousands, who are affected by sexual abuse at home.

In other countries of the region there are another 163.7 million children (see UNICEF 1998j, page 35). Using the range Seshadri gives for likely incidence of sexual abuse, including incest, means there would be another 24 to 32 million cases, or 81 to 109 million cases for the region as a whole. If even 40 per cent of those occur in the family, that means that some 32 to 44 million children in South Asia, at a minimum, could be victims of sexual abuse, including incest, at home.

If one were to consider only the children age 11 and older — since Kakkar (1996, page 15) says 11 is the usual age of onset — there are still millions at risk. If one were to consider only girls, there are still millions at risk. And all this is without any reference to the missing millions of women, as estimated by Sen (1990), who primarily die of neglect in the family when they are children.

Going to Scale

Determining the precise number of children affected by various forms of domestic violence in South Asia would call for more detailed and extensive research than is currently available. This discussion is simply to open the mind to the reality suggested by existing research and testimonials. The numbers of children, especially girls, at risk are clearly so great, we almost dare not see and admit them to consciousness, yet we must.

Campaigns as visible as those against landmines and child soldiers are very much needed to protect children from "the war in the home." For example, UNICEF (1998c) reports that "Since 1975, landmines have killed or maimed more than 1 million people, mostly civilians, a third of them children under the age of 15." That means some 330,000 children are victims of landmines. Child soldiers? It is said that "[a]s many as 300,000, some as young as eight, in dozens of countries, are directly involved in conflicts — as soldiers, porters and forced labourers — in violation of the Convention on the Rights of the Child and the 1949 Geneva Convention" (UNICEF 1998c). That's some 630,000 children, well worth the ongoing efforts for prevention and redress of children's victimization by landmines and being made combatants.

In comparison, however, is the almost complete silence about the millions of children in South Asia alone who likely suffer sexual abuse or other types of domestic violence in the "war in the home."

It is past time for any organization or individual concerned with the well-being of society, the family, women, men and children to try to go to scale with efforts against domestic violence in all forms, sexual abuse of children being one of the most odious. We do not have to wait for more and more precise figures to break the silence and to take action.

Committing New Resources against Gender Violence

Given the need for more resources to be dedicated to the elimination of gender-based violence in the home, what are the existing budgetary priorities at national level? What possible opportunity costs could there be if the State were to make a greater commitment to ending violence against women and girls? These are important questions. For example, India and Pakistan are among the world's 10 countries with the largest armies.[46] Both are preoccupied with the prospect of nuclear attack. Their military spending is disproportionately high, compared to what is spent on health and education. More demand on the State for it to support those programmes that offer women protection, alternatives to abusive families, fulfilment of their rights and services to families that women now try to provide could put the same or increased levels of military expenditures in question. In short, are discrimination against girls and son preference useful to the militaristic State? Do the existing roles of women, emphasizing self-sacrifice, permit the State to rely on women to provide many services, such as health needs in the family, which it would otherwise be called upon to provide? Is ignoring women's human rights, claims and entitlements seen as cost-effective? But is it, once the costs of gender violence itself are made clear?

Towards Non-Violence

The "Culture of Peace" (see UNESCO 1999) and non-violence are being addressed more and more in South Asia by women's groups concerned with ending gender violence and with fulfilling human rights (see, for example, Bhasin and Bhaiya 1998; Jagori n.d.), Obvious linkages come to mind about how and why women and girls are abused in their homes in situations of armed conflict within a country, and war. As the Beijing Platform for Action points out, "While entire communities suffer the consequences of armed conflict and terrorism, women and girls are particularly affected because of their status in society and their sex" (UNDPI 1996, par. 135, page 84).

Women, even where they are non-combatants, are affected harshly by the conflicts in the region — as has already been referred to briefly in the case of Afghanistan (Physicians for Human Rights 1998), Bangladesh (Chen 1986), India and Pakistan during partition (Menon and Bhasin 1998), Sri Lanka (Abeyesekere 1995). In addition to what these various observers describe, many more examples could be given, regarding everything from loss of homes, livelihood, mobility and loved ones, to rape, sexual slavery, torture and death[47].

Non-violence as a political movement came, in modern times, from pre-partition India. The movement has been adapted in other parts of the world, including by Martin Luther King, Jr., in the United States. In 1997, a group of Nobel laureates made it the basis for a worldwide campaign.[48] The South Asian activists at the Kathmandu Regional Meeting to End Violence against Women pledged to support the campaign, and saw the linkages with non-violence in the home. In its 1998 campaign, the UNIFEM Regional Office in India also took up non-violence as a theme for the family as well as the community as a basis for ending gender violence.

As South Asian activists' efforts help to reduce violence in the family, promoting equality between men and women in it and non-violent ways to settle differences, they will be laying the groundwork for a more democratic and less violent society, perhaps even a less militaristic one, in the region as well as elsewhere.

This is men's work, as well as women's. It depends in part on their taking up new roles and questioning the inevitability of men's aggression.

Taking "Gender" Even More Seriously

In this light, one is reminded that the concept of "gender" applies to the roles prescribed for men and boys as well as women and girls according to cultural norms and values. "Gender-based violence" is normally used as though it applies only to problems women face. Logically, that is an incorrect usage. Where men are expected to play predominantly aggressive roles, they too are victims of inequality, discrimination and violence against them because of a prescribed gender role. They too will gain by challenging the stereotypes that limit their own lives as well as those of women.

Fortunately, a spate of books has appeared on research about the socialization of boys for violent roles and possible interventions to change the aggressive outcomes that are proving counterproductive for individuals and society. (See, for example, Kindlon and Thompson 1999; Pollack 1998; *Scientific American* 1999.)

As work proceeds on myths about masculinity in cultures of South Asia, as elsewhere, the ground will be laid for reinforcing those socialization practices that favour equality between boys and girls, men and women, as well as for putting less emphasis on hierarchical social structures and ideas about "entitlement" to power for men.

Questioning gender-role stereotypes, the traditions and the customs that support them, lies at the heart of CEDAW. Article 5a is truly revolutionary and worth repeated reading and thought as the basis for action. It calls on States Parties to take measures

[T]o modify the social and cultural patterns of conduct of men and women, with a view to achieving the elimination of prejudices and customary and all other practices which are based on the idea of the inferiority or the superiority of either of the sexes or on stereotyped roles for men and women. (CEDAW, page 7)[49]

Related confrontations between democratic and fundamentalist forces are likely to be unavoidable if this article — along with the basic principle of non-discrimination — is to be fulfilled. Preparing to face such differences in an informed and responsible way is a necessary step on the road to full humanity and fulfilment of rights for every girl and boy, woman and man. Activists are faced with the challenge of learning as much as possible about human rights treaties and mechanisms and their relevance to ending gender violence, based on the principle of universality of rights. The implementation of CRC, CEDAW and all human rights instruments is otherwise in jeopardy, since the universality of human rights is all too often challenged on the basis of arguments about the primacy of culture and custom, particularly concerning women's and girls' human rights. As Coomaraswamy (see, for example, 1995) consistently makes it clear, these are not acceptable arguments. And the report of the 1999 judicial colloquium, referred to above, put it this way:

They [the participants] underscored the fact that these human rights principles are applicable in all countries and in all cultural contexts and emphasized that no pretext of culture, custom or religious considerations should be allowed to undermine these principles. (UNDAW 1999)

The Courage to Bring Rights Home

Action Needed at All Levels

Some memorable words (see UNICEF 1996a) of four South Asian activists call us to join them, to do more at international, national, interpersonal and personal levels for the fulfilment of human rights of women and girls as well as for men and boys.

International

> All the provisions of CEDAW must be incorporated in the national legislation. So, we cannot say: "It comes from outside, it comes from the UN. We have nothing to do with it. We have our own cultural relativity and social reality." No, there is no excuse at all.
>
> — *Nepali man, NGO leader*

National

> I want to show in Parliament that the State which tolerates violence against women at the community and family level and which does not hold accountable those responsible for the violence is guilty as its perpetrators. That is going to be my role as Member of Parliament, to highlight instances of violence and to make the state more accountable.
>
> — *Indian woman, former stone crusher, member of Lok Sabha*

Interpersonal

> Oppression has a series of faces. It can only be eliminated if we change the values of our society. This is not possible by redressing a victim or two. That is why we are into advocacy. Both man and woman have to liberate each other.   — *Pakistani man, business executive*

Personal

> I always tell them to look at me. I am not highly educated but I am standing on my own feet, I have done something for myself. It does not take that much. It just takes a little bit of courage. . . .   — *Bangladeshi woman, self-employed*

Individual Pledges Are Important, Too

South Asian activists have taught me how important it is for each individual to make a pledge about his or her own immediate action in private as well as public life if age-old attitudes and practices are to change. Pledges might include ones like these from individual participants at the Kathmandu meeting (UNICEF 1998b, page 15). They touch on changing present behaviour as well as guiding the next generation towards a more equitable world, free of violence based on gender roles:

- I pledge to keep fighting[50] the patriarchal male inside me and around me.
- I pledge that I will allow myself to remain strong and joyful as a woman and support others to be the same, whatever the challenge may be.
- I pledge to measure my masculinity in terms of equality.
- I pledge to start at home by teaching my two sons to always fight against violence.
- I pledge to speak out and break the silence whenever and wherever I can. To raise my daughter to be strong, brave, and joyful, and to lend my strength to the organization I work for to help them to fulfil their commitment to fight violence against women and children.
- I pledge to never give up.

People like these are leading the way towards new norms for women and men in daily life. Their examples are important both in South Asia and beyond. They need States Parties to CRC and CEDAW to take more seriously the present commitments to these and other conventions that are for the respect, protection and fulfilment of human rights of all citizens — including girls and women. Where the State tolerates exploitation, brutality and violence by some groups towards others, on the excuse of custom, differences in ethnicity, religion or gender, the State invites abuse within the family also. Why? Because much of social relations will be based on the principle of power and privilege, rather than that of equality and rights. It will likely feature vengeance rather than law as a means of social control.

And where the State ignores violence within the family, it predetermines that violence outside it will prevail as well.

Much more broad and sustained public discussion on why and how to end gender violence is urgently needed. This calls for much more than a strictly legalistic approach to human rights. As Coomaraswamy cautions, it is fundamental to pursue the development of community attitudes that will resonate with any laws against gender violence and in the domestic space. Otherwise, resistance and negative reactions are likely at community level. Here, recognizing and honouring precedents from the South Asian tradition, along with courageous individuals like those in this book, is very relevant and practical.

The task is particularly daunting given the extent of patriarchal values and practices associated with the predominantly patrilineal and patrilocal kinship and residence patterns as noted by Dube (1997), who commented:

> It is a peculiarity of South Asia that the female sex is denied the right to be born, to survive after birth and to live a healthy life avoiding the risks of pregnancy and childbirth. Poverty alone can not explain this. (page 144)

Support for Family Functions Rather Than Form

Fundamental for all the above will be a process of questioning assumptions about the family, and addressing how its proper functions can best be supported while ensuring human rights for its members on the basis of equality between women and men, girls and boys. This is in keeping with human rights treaties and most States' constitutions.

Unfortunately, as discussed above, stereotypes for very limited gender roles in the family flow from taking the current patriarchal family structure in South Asia as the natural and fundamental unit of society, to be protected as such.

However, if one interprets the idea of protecting the family as applying to its functions rather than to preserving a single form — the patriarchal model — then protection of the family clearly requires state intervention to ensure it is a safe and just place in which individual rights of girls and women are not overwhelmed by vested interests of patriarchal power and privilege.

A new approach is needed, one that supports the family as an institution based on equality, love and respect rather than on power and privilege for men and boys, with weakness and subservience prescribed for women and girls. There should also be shared concern and responsibility for raising children and instilling in them the qualities of tenderness and nurturance, as well as assertion, whether they are male or female.

A greater focus is needed on socialization practices that lead to equalitarian attitudes and practices, not violent ones. What are the critical periods in child development for acquisition of tolerance and respect rather than aggression? How do children best learn to negotiate rather than bully or submit when they have differences? How can parent and teacher education best be done to make a difference to end gender-role stereotypes and inequality?

Stereotypes about women and men in the family can limit concern for the fulfilment of rights for women and girls. For example, where women are thought of primarily as tender, nurturing and self-sacrificing, then arguments follow that opportunities to care for others should be enough for them. Where men are expected to be tough, their violence will be tolerated, even encouraged.

In the development process, such stereotypes must be challenged, not used as the basis for policy, programme planning and delivery. New approaches, to support processes that result in respect, protection and fulfilment of human rights for women as well as men, will be critical if violence-free families are to predominate.

As Bahai International and UNICEF/UNIFEM (1994) have said:

> Family violence must be addressed by the world community. It is not a private matter, but has become a global pandemic that the international community can neither ignore nor allow to be protected within the privacy of the family.

Risks and Possibilities in the New Millennium

There is a growing awareness of South Asians that their region, like others, must boldly do even more to address gender violence. The time has come to get beyond the frightening paradox of the dangerous family. Otherwise, whenever and wherever it is said, "We honour motherhood" or "We care about children," it will be not be true. When it is said, "Women's human rights are protected," it will not be true.

For the new millennium to be one of peace, the "war" against women and girls must end. Supporting women's efforts and promoting men's roles for gender peace are vital parts of the effort. Still, the State is accountable when it does not take action to prevent gender violence at home and beyond — that is part of the message that the mechanisms for monitoring human rights treaties are designed to emphasize. The family will be truly strengthened when it protects the lives of its members, and the fulfilment of their human rights. Any slogan for the new millennium that talks about strengthening the family, but does not invite a deeper look at the processes and outcomes involved, could do great harm to girls and women and to human rights and development. The slogan could be interpreted otherwise as a justification of values that exalt in the power of the patriarchy and exploitation of girls and women.

The way ahead is full of risks — for individuals, women's groups and NGOs, for men who dare to question the expectation that they should be in control because of their gender, for countries and the rule of law, for human rights and for the credibility of the United Nations and other international organizations. Will those who speak so much about human rights abandon or support, truly, those who act even in the face of oppression and danger?

In Nepal, on 11 August 1999 a young girl was the first to speak at a regional NGO meeting to assess progress and action needed to bring to life the commitments made for equality at the Fourth World Conference on Women in Beijing in 1995. Anjana

Shakya, human rights activist and organizer of the meeting, told me she had decided to encourage the active participation of youth "because all we are saying and doing about rights is about the future. It is about the children." She said she used to think that work for rights was more legalistic, but now she sees it as about deconstructing power and building the basis for sharing it.

Surely that same month, somewhere in South Asia, women's groups cooperated to support a mother who took her children and left home because of incest in the family; a young girl who survived an acid attack showed some schoolboys the results of acid-throwing — and asked them to control their tempers; both girls and boys called the domestic violence hotline; a young man refused to participate in a gang rape or an honour killing; a physician counselled a husband and wife about the unacceptability of wife-beating; a father decided to educate his daughter rather than marry her off at a young age. . . .

Because of the courage of the women and men, girls and boys in South Asia who are striving to claim human rights of all, the symbolic earthenware jar that suffocates and kills girls is being broken. The pieces will surely disintegrate and vanish — only dust in the wind from a time long ago when girls and women were not yet considered truly human, and so many had to struggle to claim their rights.

Endnotes

1 Guidelines for "mainstreaming gender in unstable environments" are part of the guidelines being developed by UNICEF (n.d.). Sherrill Whittington, from the Gender, Partnerships and Participation Section of UNICEF, has also developed, in conjunction with DPKO, related training materials on gender in crisis situations, for training of peacekeepers (Sherrill Whittington, personal communication, New York, 1999).

2 This 1994 Human Development Report was planned to influence the agenda for the Social Summit, Copenhagen.

3 Interview for this book arranged and conducted by author.

4 Referred to by Kamla Bhasin (1998) as "a large network... also called an Alliance of Hope. . . . The hope comes from the fact that millions are fighting for genuine democracy be it in South Africa or in East Timor, be it in Burma or in the U.S. The hope comes from the fact that women and some men are challenging patriarchy. Different people's movements for peace, democracy, environment, human rights, rights of indigenous people; the movements of peasants, farmers, fisherfolk, workers, consumers are all different names of the same struggles, dreams, aspirations" (page 11).

5 See, for example, reports from Equality Now, The Women's Action Network, New York.

6 See, for example, various publications of the Center for Women's Global Leadership at Rutgers University (New Jersey), of which she is Executive Director.

7 "There are no Human Rights without Women's — and Girls' — Rights" is a slogan developed for the 1993 Vienna World Conference on Human Rights and used by UNIFEM to promote human rights of women. See, for example, the cover of their Report of the Expert Group Meeting, "Development of Guidelines for the Integration of Gender Perspectives into United Nations Rights Activities and Programs," Geneva, 3–7 July 1995, organized by the Center for Human Rights and by the United Nations Development Fund.

8 Based on the author's personal experience as part of a panel in the NGO Forum at Hairou, China.

9 General Recommendation 19, which deals with violence against women, refers to girls only with regard to the risk of prostitution and violence or sexual exploitation when they leave the rural community to seek employment in towns. Use of the word "incest" in the Recommendation of course indicates that the risk of violence to girls at home is recognized.

10 Razia Ismail, in her work with UNICEF India, consistently, forcefully and effectively supported the use of the term "girl-child" in development dialogue and practice. Her approach fits well with the use in the paper of the term "a girl-woman" to draw attention to the fact that girls who become both wives and mothers are deprived of their childhood and of many rights, and are sometimes forgotten in both policy and action programmes.

11 Personal communication, Dr. Urban Jonsson, then Regional Director of UNICEF ROSA, Kathmandu, 1996.

12 For example, when I took my newborn baby into the classroom with me at the University of Hawaii in 1970, where I was then an assistant professor of human development, it was women from the new women's studies department who objected, on the grounds that they had worked very hard to break the association between women and children, so they surely did not welcome seeing a child brought into the new working space for women that they were helping to create.

13 In contrast, all the members of CEDAW save one have been female (IWRAW and Commonwealth Secretariat 1994).

14 Delivered in October 1997 at the regional meeting in Kathmandu (UNICEF 1998b).

15 Based on personal experience in over 20 years of work related to gender issues in development. I have stressed this in courses on gender in development organized for various agencies, including FINNIDA, DANIDA and FAO.

16 This harkens back to the ideas of the '60s and '70s in the United States expressed in the *Free to Be . . . You and Me* materials based on the book of the same name by Marlo Thomas.

17 See paragraph 2, Follow-up to Beijing Platform. The Commission on the Status of Women put forward the Report of the Secretary-General, "Follow-up to the Fourth World Conference on Women: Implementation of Strategic Objectives and Action in the Critical Areas of Concern, Thematic Issues before the Commission on the Status of Women," posted online by the Division for the Advancement of Women (DESA), which encourages its reproduction and dissemination, with acknowledgement.

18 The full text is available at *www.un.org/womenwatch/ daw/beijing/platform*.

19 See Section D, strategic objective D.1, with actions to be taken by different actors — governments at different levels and in cooperation with local organizations and women's NGOs, also with employers, trade unions and youth organizations; by the Secretary-General of the United Nations; and in cooperation among government, international organizations and NGOs.

20 The third, and last, strategic objective is "Eliminate trafficking in women and assist victims of violence due to prostitution and trafficking" (UNDPI 1996, page 81).

21 The others are: "An integrated, holistic approach; Provision of resources to combat violence against all women; Creation of linkages and cooperation with regard to particular forms of violence against women; Legal measures; Research and gender-disaggregated data collection."

22 Reports to CRC and CEDAW as well as on the International Covenant on Civil and Political Rights (ICCPR) and the International Covenant on Economic, Social and Cultural Rights (ICESCR) are particularly useful, along with comments on same.

23 Relevant networks include the International Women's Rights Action Watch (IWRAW), Asia and Pacific; Women, Law and Development (WLD) International and the FIGO/WHO. There are also Web sites related to several of these as well as ones sponsored by UNDP, UNIFEM and WHO. Ending violence against women is a priority for each.

24 India is one of 18 countries that are partners to the ICCPR and the only member country from South Asia.

25 Bangladesh, Bhutan, India, Maldives, Nepal, Pakistan and Sri Lanka

26 The Draft addresses definitions, scope of the Convention, offences, aggravating circumstances, judicial proceedings, mutual legal assistance, extradition or prosecution, measures to prevent and eliminate trafficking in women and children, care, treatment, rehabilitation and voluntary return to the country of origin of persons released from trafficking, implementation and higher measures, as well as signature and ratification, entry into force and depository (SAARC n.d.).

27 Monitoring of the press is being carried out by organizations like Women's Feature Service (WFS) in India and Asmita in Nepal.

28 This account is based on an interview with Farzana Bari, Ph.D., in Islamabad, in 1997.

29 This echoes the title of Michael Kaufman's book, *Cracking the Armour: Power, Pain and the Lives of Men*, Toronto: Viking (1993).

30 That is part of what the men participants said at the close of the 1997 Kathmandu Meeting on Ending Violence to Women and Girls in South Asia.

31 For examples of South Asian men who are questioning the patriarchy and the gender violence typical in it, see Hayward (1997b). Also see transcripts of interviews from Sakshi and Shekar Seshadri.

32 A UNICEF project supported in part by the Government of Norway.

33 Support has been provided by Save the Children Federation, UNICEF and the German Committee for UNICEF.

34 Personal communication, Sree Gururaja, UNICEF, New York, November 1999.

35 With financial support from the Swiss Government and from UNDP.

36 Refers to the lead character in a film by the same name, starring Dustin Hoffman. He played a man who pretended to be a woman, "Tootsie."

37 He has also proposed a wider research project, Raanjhan, a progressive community for dealing with men's issues.

38 See Hayward 1997b.

39 Following a session, organized by the author, with Michael Kaufman at the 1998 Singapore World Conference on Family Violence, that included Ranjan Poudyl from SCA, Nepal Regional Office, who outlined a project on new masculinities, supported by SCA, UNICEF and the German Committee for UNICEF. Michael Kaufman then travelled to Kathmandu and participated in an exchange of views and possibilities in workshops there. An important line of work on men's roles for peace has also been developed, principally by UNESCO in cooperation with a network centred in Sweden with Ms. Eva Moberg, playwright and author. It is foreseen that there will be a related meeting to take the agenda forward, also with UNICEF, probably in 2000.

40 In 1999, the importance of men's roles against gender violence was briefly recognized at the end of the UN-sponsored global video conference "A World Free of Violence against Women," held in the UN General Assembly on International Women's Day, when the White Ribbon Campaign was mentioned and material on it was distributed in a kit for participants.

41 Vishai was a B.Ed. student at the Dayalbagh Educational Institute in Agra.

42 For example, Abha Dayal produced television spots for the UNIFEM regional campaign against gender violence, inspired by the Kathmandu discussions, which she told me had changed her life; Mufti Ziauddin said he became even more determined to champion the human rights of girls and women, and contributed to a number of meetings on peace and human rights, as well as completing his study on "honour killings"; Anjana Shakya, of INHURED, Nepal, became more active in promoting work on domestic violence and youth, and told me this was due to the influence that the Kathmandu meeting had on her.

43 But I saw only about 10 men among the hundreds of people attending the session, and about a third of those seemed to come in with the Secretary-General for his speech.

44 I am indebted to Ilana Landsberg Lewis for this information (personal communication, New York 1999).

45 This does not include any data on Maldives and Bhutan, the smaller countries, which were not covered for this book.

46 See Figure 4.1 and Table 4.1, Ul Haq and Haq (1997).

47 A case in point is the death of Rajini Thiranagama, a woman activist who was killed in 1989 for her human rights activism in Northern Sri Lanka. (Personal communication, Savitiri Goonesekere, February 23, 2000).

48 See UNICEF (1998b); the appeal is also covered in the Kathmandu Commitment.

49 India has a declaration concerning Article 5a; see Chapter 2, Table 2.

50 Use of the word "fighting" or "combating" seems to persist even in the context of ending violence.

Women hold up banners during a rally against gang rape, Pakistan.

Appendices and Bibliography

The Kathmandu Commitment on Ending Violence against Women and Girls in South Asia

We women and men gathered as participants at the Meeting on Ending Violence against Women and Girls in South Asia held in Kathmandu, Nepal from 21 to 24 October 1997, organized by UNICEF, Regional Office South Asia with UNIFEM South Asia Regional Office, do hereby commit ourselves to that end.

While recognizing that violence against all segments of society including children is a serious and growing problem in our times and in this region, we nevertheless state that the issue of violence against women and girls has been largely ignored.

We come from countries in South Asia with a diversity of political situations, laws, institutions, cultures and traditions. Yet the anguish of violence is a common problem that debilitates and threatens all women and girls, manifesting itself in similar and different ways, being rooted in gender inequality, discrimination, and patriarchal value systems and son preference.

All forms of violence against women and girls, whether physical, sexual, psychological or others, including those perpetrated under conflict situations, are a gross violation of their individual human rights, as well as a major impeding factor for the equitable and sustainable development of our countries. They are an extreme manifestation of the unequal power relations and unequal distribution of resources between men and women within the family, community, work place, in the political, economic, legal and educational systems and the State.

For too long women and girls have been forced to suffer violence silently in their families and communities, in the work place, in public spaces, within public service institutions and through the legal system. They, the victims of gross violence and infringement of their bodily integrity and basic human rights are stigmatized, victimized and blamed by societies affected by violence, inequalities and contradictions. Our silence has made us accomplices of this violence, even passive perpetrators.

Our first commitment as human beings concerned to build a gender violence free society is, therefore, to end the conspiracy of silence. We vow to recognize and expose the reality of violence against women and girls perpetrated within our families, communities, work places, professions, political formations and by State action as well as inaction. It is only through such an open and participatory approach that we can bring society to deal honestly with the problem and ensure justice and support to the victims and the enforcement of the severest sanctions against the perpetrators.

We call upon our governments to honor the commitments on fundamental rights they have made in their national constitutions and as State Parties to the Convention on the Elimination of All Forms of Discrimination against Women (CEDAW) and the Convention on the Rights of the Child (CRC) and other human rights treaties. We demand that they internalize the standards that they have ratified, at the national level. We commit ourselves to using the mechanisms provided in these constitutional and international instruments to ensure the accountability of our governments to eliminate violence against women and girls and achieve equal rights between women and men in both public and private spheres. In this respect, we shall strive especially to achieve adequate protection through the legal system for women and girls who are the victims of violence and the provision of all other necessary support services. This will include lobbying for policies on compulsory education, access to health care and allocation of adequate resources for these purposes and for law enforcement. This will also include efforts to bring knowledge of legal rights to every citizen of our countries through educational strategies and giving access to justice through the legal system. Since violence against women is also exacerbated in conditions of poverty, we shall carry out proactive advocacy for appropriate policies and programmes that will help alleviate poverty and meet basic needs as entitlement.

We shall lobby with our governments to withdraw reservations to CEDAW and CRC wherever applicable and promote legal, policy and social changes that will help to internalize their standards in our countries. Recognizing that cultures and traditions are never static and that they have been transformed through the centuries, we commit ourselves to promoting positive changes in accordance with the letter and spirit of the UN Declaration on Violence Against Women, the Beijing Platform for Action and the Beijing Declaration. We shall endeavor to strengthen traditions that conform with values of gender equality and non-violence, and eliminate those which entrench gender discrimination and result in denial of the human rights of women and girls.

We also call upon the South Asia Association for Regional Cooperation (SAARC) and the agencies of the United Nations system to play an active role in advocating for a gender violence free society in South Asia and to assist governments, educational institutions, other opinion and value generating institutions and non-governmental organizations in our countries towards that end. We in particular call upon SAARC and its member countries to fulfill and build upon the commitments of the Male Summit (1997) to adopt a Regional Convention and to demand and ensure regional and bilateral cooperation for stringent law enforcement and strict prevention of cross border and in-country trafficking of women and children.

We recognize that the family itself often promotes and perpetuates gender based violence, through the differential treatment given to girls and boys from conception and birth by all members of the family. We shall endeavour to promote gender equality in the family, so that this key institution in our countries becomes a source of support for its members and creates a cooperative and nurturing environment. This requires the involvement of a number of institutions in the reconstruction of the nature and functions of the family. We call upon the State to recognize its duty to protect human rights by protecting women and children against any act of violence that occurs in the family.

As schools often perpetuate the status quo on gender relations we urge that policy makers, educators, teachers and children develop gender sensitive curriculum and teacher training methods. We recommend life skill training with special reference to gender violence and puberty related issues using participatory and interactive methods of teaching and communication. We urge that schools interact closely with the communities in which they are located.

We women and men recognize that, without the active participation of men, we cannot achieve our goal of eliminating violence against women and girls. We shall strive as individuals, as parents, as educators and as opinion formers to promote new, positive models of masculinities and femininities, so that boys and young men will grow up realizing their own potential as caring human beings committed to respecting the rights of women and girls as equal partners in their families, communities and societies.

We recognize the potential of children, both girls and boys, to interact with one another and with adults in preventing and responding to violence against women and children and we shall endeavor as parents, educators and individuals to support and develop programs to ensure the participation of children and youth to end gender based violence.

Recognizing youth as a group with distinct needs, issues and capabilities, we commit in accordance with the letter and spirit of the Convention on the Rights of the Child to promote their participation as facilitators and mobilizers for the elimination of gender based violence. We shall build and support networks of young people, encourage discussions and understanding of issues of gender violence, unequal power relations and sexuality among the youth through various ongoing training and outreach programs in schools and other institutions and through participatory research on issues relating to them.

We realize that the media is an integral part of our lives. Acknowledging its tremendous force to change mind sets and mould public opinion, we appeal to all forms of media to play a proactive, investigative and supportive role in our struggle against gender based violence. We urge responsible and sensitive handling of such events. We believe that this is only possible if media is given access to information as a matter of right and the right to privacy of victims is respected by media. We also call upon the media to promote and portray positive gender images and confront stereotypes and discrimination.

We, individually and collectively, within our countries and in the region, commit ourselves to work towards eliminating gender bias and violence in our professions and work places and creating an environment and developing competence and sensitivity that will help to build a gender violence free community and society. We also undertake to work within our professions to develop and/or enforce a professional code of ethics that will prevent and respond to the problem of gender based violence and towards this end we commit ourselves as follows:

- As **legal professionals** and those involved in the formulation and enforcement of laws, we shall advocate and contribute to the reform of discriminatory laws and to the sensitive and effective enforcement of law, promoting awareness of the law and its proactive use in countering violence against women and girls.
- As **medical professionals**, we shall advocate and work towards increasing awareness and recognition among all health personnel, about acts of violence against women and children and to take appropriate, preventive, curative, rehabilitative medico-legal action.
- As **educators**, we shall advocate and work towards education for equality, non-violence and peace, support research and training on gender violence, legal literacy, develop gender sensitive curriculum and pedagogical training.
- As **media professionals**, we shall endeavor to portray and report on issues pertaining to violence against women and girls sensitively, vividly and honestly, keeping in mind that the victim should not be further victimized through our reportage, create awareness on gender issues and the need for social action against all forms of gender violence.
- We **writers**, recognizing that we cannot be expected to write according to a certain agenda, but also realizing the power of the word and the consequences of reinforcing gender stereotypes through writings, commit ourselves to the creation of a gender violence free society and heighten awareness, through our writings, of the issues of gender violence and the value system which sustains it.
- We the **performing artists and cultural activists**, commit ourselves to promote the values of a gender violence free society and bring about attitudinal changes through our work. We also commit ourselves to forcefully resist any attempts to place restrictions on freedom of cultural expression, especially of women and cultural workers, placed by the governments or other pressure groups in any country of the region.
- We **men**, realizing that no sustainable change can take place unless we give up the entrenched ideas of male superiority, commit ourselves to devising new role models of masculinity. We shall endeavour to "take off the armour" and move towards becoming a

more developed and complete being. We urge international bodies to focus on and explore the destructive consequences of patriarchy.

We resolve to build larger alliances involving the women's movement, sensitive professionals from the media, the arts and cultural spheres, institutions of learning, the health and the legal system and political groups across our national borders and coordinate our efforts in order to build the necessary synergy to end violence against women and children in South Asia. We appeal to our governments and the UN system to facilitate and support these efforts.

We recognize the complexity of the problem of violence against women and girls and that it requires a range of interventions at the level of the family, the community and the State. We, therefore, commit ourselves to promoting the necessary laws, policies and attitudinal changes using interdisciplinary approaches that will help us to network, share and exchange, using all communication tools at our disposal, and support each other's endeavours as citizens, officials, NGOs, professionals and human beings.

PLEDGE

We the delegates and member participants in the movement of violence against women pledge that we will mobilize to the best of our ability the Youth, Media and NGOs of our region for 16 days (25 November–10 December, 1997) of intense action against gender violence.

1. A single day action in all the countries focusing on domestic violence tentatively the 27th of November using appropriate strategies.
2. As an action we propose a series of marches from different parts of the countries to respective country capitals pressing for 33% reservation of women in the parliament and other decision making position.
3. Another same day activity in all countries emphasizing Child Rights denial to girls.
4. Following intensive action building to next year's campaign we suggest building alliances and new partnerships working towards zero violence in households, communities, schools in villages cities settlements. This would involve advocacy at the ground level to the highest level.

We support and join the appeal of the Nobel Laureates

1. Gender violence to be emphasized as needing an urgent attention and collective action with the Nobel laureates' appeal for a culture of non-violence.
2. Year 2000 be declared the year of education for Non-Violence with special emphasis on gender violence.
3. Decade 2000 to 2010 as a decade of culture of non violence.

As we commit to a culture of non violence within the next three years let us build up an environment, a research database, a strategy and action plan for the decade which follows. Let us find not lowest common denominators in the region but the highest common multiple as we build the regional alliance.

Recommendations for Enhancing the Effectiveness of Legal Tools to Combat Violence against Women

"There was a strong diversity of views among the participants, due partially to the differing legal systems in the respective countries. Discussions were primarily geared towards formulating practial recommendations. The recommended steps for enhancing the effectiveness of the legal system are grouped into several categories and included:

Legal system/ substantive law

1. Gaps in the legal system must be identified before expecting justice through the legal system.
2. As a basis for combating violence against women and girls, inheritance and property rights of women should be recognised under the law and materialised. Concrete measures should be undertaken to eliminate existing discrimination in law and in fact.
3. The crime of sexual assault should be recognised in addition to the crime of rape.
4. Amendments are needed in the law relating to rape. For instance, the definition of rape and evidentiary requirements in rape cases have to change.

Enforcement of law

5. To curb violence against women, the Child Marriage Restraint Acts in various countries must be enforced.
6. The trial of rape and sexual assault cases should be in camera (excluding the public).
7. The non-admissibility of statements made before the police should be reviewed.Currently, statements made before the police are not admissible as evidence in most courts in the region. When the same person is called upon to provide evidence in court — often many years later — there is often discrepancy between the original statements and the evidence presented in court. The relevance of the case-diary should be reviewed.

Establishment/amendment of (quasi) judicial bodies

8. Legal activism should be aimed at establishing a regional judicial system in South Asia or Asia. Such judicial authority should be empowered to hear cases of violence against women.
9. Where they do not already exist, National Commissions on the status of women should be established and entrusted with the task of systematically reviewing all existing laws and regulations and forward recommendations for amendment in accordance with international standards. National commissions for women must be autonomous but embedded in the existing governmental structure.
10. Separate courts for hearing cases related to children/ juveniles should be established.

Police/investigation level

11. Hurdles related to the registration of FIRs by the police should be identified and removed.

12. There should be proper registration of all incoming cases, noting also follow-up decisison taken.

13. Girls and women victims of violence should not be kept in police custody, whether termed protective or safe custody.

14. The police must be accountable for their action or inaction at the investigation stage. Following a recommendation of the Indian Law Commission, a recent ordinance makes the police in India accountable and punishable. This example may be followed in other South Asian countries.

15. Having the police as the principle investigatory body is a problem; investigation of cases should be done by a separate investigating authority. In addition, the judiciary should be given the power to order additional investigation and the victim's lawyer should have the right to observe the investigation.

16. Women cells should be established in all police stations. They should have adequate powers and facilities to fullly handle incoming complaints of violence against women and girls.

Country-specific recommendations

17. The government of Pakistan should be urged to implement the recommendation made in the Commission of Inquiry's report.

Legal System and Media

18. Successful legal cases must be highlighted positively in the media for both awareness and sensitization.

19. The media must be sensitized not to sensationalize reporting of cases of violence against women/ girls.

20. An autonomous pressure group should be established to identify important ongoing cases and follow and encourage the legal process.

Support services

21. Family counseling centers must be established to provide counseling to families in situations of violence against women and girls.

22. Lawyers should interact with NGOs, individuals and other organizations to make the legal system work.

23. A national interdisciplinary body should be established in every country to address situations of child abuse.

Training/sensitization

24. The entire police and judicial system must be gender-sensitized.

Lawyers

25. The existing Code of Ethics for lawyers must be followed."
(UNICEF/ ROSA, 1997)

Quiz on Violence in the Family against Women and Girls

TEST YOURSELF FIRST

Instructions: Please indicate which of the following statements are true or false by circling (T) or (F).

1. The costs of domestic violence in New Zealand (police costs, etc.) are more than the earnings from the wool industry.　　T　F

2. The costs of domestic violence per year in Canada (medical care and lost productivity) are estimated at $1.6 billion per year.　　T　F

3. Research suggests that in the United States wife-beating results in more injuries that require medical treatment than do rape, auto accidents and muggings combined. Twenty-two to 35 per cent of women who visit emergency departments are there for symptoms related to ongoing abuse.　　T　F

4. A study by the World Bank shows that "gender victimization" [rape and domestic violence] accounts for as much of the global burden of health for women aged 15–44 as tuberculosis, sepsis in pregnancy, cancer or cardiac disease.　　T　F

5. Battered women are two times more likely to miscarry and four times more likely to have a low birthweight child. Their babies are 40 times more likely to die in the first year of life.　　T　F

6. Rates of beatings in female partners by their male partners over a year range from 17–75 per cent in studies from 34 countries. Generally speaking, these are lower in the developed world (17–28 per cent) than in developing countries (only 3 of 16 studies show an incidence of 20 per cent or less, while twice that number of studies show incidence over 50 per cent). Asia, 22–75 per cent; Africa, 40–60 per cent; Latin America, 20–60 per cent.　　T　F

7. In Bangladesh, 13.8 per cent of maternal mortality is reported as being due to intentional injury and violence.　　T　F

8. In Bangladesh, the Bureau of Statistics reports that a higher percentage of mortality among women is due to injury/violence than pregnancy-related causes.　　T　F

9. In Nepal, frequent wife-beating has been linked with higher risk of stunting (1.5 times) and wasting (1.75 times) for children ages 6–36 months.　　T　F

10. In Nicaragua, children of women victims of domestic violence are three times more likely to need medical care and to be hospitalized more frequently; 63 per cent more likely to repeat a grade and drop-out at nine, compared to 12 for those whose mothers are not beaten.　　T　F

11. In India, 25 per cent of all reported rapes in 1990 were of children under age 16 [15–20 per cent worldwide]; family members are primarily responsible.　　T　F

Answers: All are true.

A Summary of Some UN Milestones for Women's and Girls' Human Rights[1]

I f we look back at the way in which women's human rights were addressed first in the UN Charter and the Universal Declaration on Human Rights (UDHR), and compare it with where we stand today on various women's human rights, so far as the UN system and its treaties and declarations are concerned, these are some highlights:

- The 1945 United Nations Charter, which is the founding document of the organization, makes no special mention of women's human rights but affirms equality between women and men and prohibits "distinction" on the basis of, *inter alia*, sex.

- One of the first achievements of the UN was the adoption of the Universal Declaration of Human Rights (UDHR) in 1948. It is a statement of general standards or principles of human rights, which affirms the equal enjoyment of human rights by all human beings and prohibits any distinction on the basis of, *inter alia*, sex. Similar provisions are found in common Article 2 of the International Covenant on Civil and Political Rights (ICCPR) and the International Covenant on Economic, Social and Cultural Rights (ICESCR), which followed the UDHR and together with it form the International Bill of Rights.

- "Concerned, however, that despite these various instruments extensive discrimination against women continues to exist" (language from the CEDAW preamble), the UN adopted the Convention on the Elimination of All Forms of Discrimination Against Women (CEDAW) in 1979. The CEDAW Convention established a monitoring mechanism, namely a Committee, known as the CEDAW Committee, to whom States Parties have to report on a regular basis. (The CEDAW Convention is also sometimes called the Women's Convention, to distinguish it from the Committee, which is commonly referred to as "CEDAW.") The CEDAW Convention (treaty) has been ratified, acceded or succeeded to by 165 countries to date.

- Non-discrimination is a fundamental principle of the Convention on the Rights of the Child (CRC), adopted in 1989. The CRC has been ratified by all but two members of the UN — the United States and Somalia (which does not have an internationally recognized government at this time). Implementation of CRC by States Parties is monitored by the CRC Committee.

- The (non-binding) Declaration on the Elimination of Violence against Women (1993), calls on States to condemn violence against women and not to "invoke any custom, tradition or religious consideration to avoid their obligations with respect to its elimination. States

---

1   I am particularly indebted to Nicolette Moodie of UNICEF for her contributions to this appendix.

should pursue by all appropriate means and without delay a policy of eliminating violence against women. . . ."

- The concept of the human rights of women and girls, especially those dealing with abuses in the family and reproductive rights, only gained full international recognition through the World Conferences of the 1990s.

- The 1993 Vienna Declaration and Programme of Action embodies the agreements reached and commitments made to human rights by governments during the World Conference on Human Rights, held in Vienna in 1993. It affirms the idea that human rights are women's rights and recommends that all UN treaty bodies do more to mainstream a concern with the human rights of women, and of the girl-child.[2] It was followed by assertions in many countries that fulfilment of rights for women is a prerequisite to fulfilment of human rights in general. This new approach forces and "transforms" thinking about what is so different about women's situations that discrimination and violation of their rights were not adequately covered in practice by norms as addressed in other human rights treaties.

- The Vienna Conference was followed one year later by the International Conference on Population and Development (ICPD), held in Cairo. The Programme of Action, agreed to at the ICPD, devotes a chapter to gender equality, equity and empowerment of women. It states that "Countries should act to empower women and should take steps to eliminate inequalities between men and women as soon as possible," *inter alia,* by eliminating violence against women (para. 4.4(e)). It goes on to say that "Countries should take full measures to eliminate all forms of exploitation, abuse, harassment and violence against women, adolescents and children. This implies both preventive actions and rehabilitation of victims" (para. 4.9). In relation to the girl-child, it calls on governments to enact and enforce laws setting a minimum age of marriage (para. 4.21) and to "take the necessary measures to prevent infanticide, prenatal sex selection, trafficking in girl children and use of girls in prostitution and pornography" (para. 4.23). This chapter of the ICPD also focuses on male responsibilities.

- The Fourth World Conference on Women in Beijing in 1995 included women's human rights as critical areas of concern, as it did violence against women and the girl-child. The Platform for Action approved by the Conference therefore contains recommendations on all three areas, which also encourages cross-cutting concerns and actions. In 1998, the Commission on the Status of Women (CSW) focused its attention on these three critical areas of concern (as well women in armed conflict), and adopted agreed conclusions calling for accelerated action in implementing them.

- Through the agreements reached at Vienna, Cairo and Beijing, governments commit themselves to eliminating violence against women. Women's and girls' experience of violence in the family is therefore increasingly regarded as a public concern, not a private matter. It is frequently remarked that CEDAW is notable because it includes wording to the effect that the State has responsibility and obligations to protect, respect, promote and fulfil human rights and is accountable for violations even by private actors who are not agents of the State.

---

2 Suggestions are being made about how various forms of violence to women and girls in the family could be considered as rights abuses under various conventions. For example, it has been argued that forced marriage can be considered as a form of slavery under the Supplementary Convention on the Abolition of Slavery, Slave Trade and Customs and Practices Similar to Slavery; domestic violence can be taken up as torture under the Convention Against Torture and Other Cruel, Inhuman or Degrading Treatment or Punishment.

- Some human rights activists argue that States Parties have obligations to eliminate gender-based violence in terms of the Convention against Torture and Other Cruel, Inhuman or Degrading Treatment or Punishment,[3] which has been ratified by 118 countries to date. In South Asia, Bangladesh, India, Nepal and Sri Lanka have ratified this convention without reservation.[4]
- At the beginning of the millennium, we are in the midst of a rapidly developing movement for attention to human rights of women as human beings, not just as mothers and wives, even when they are at home. As Sullivan (1996, page 13) puts it, "deference to norms which ascribe rights to women on the basis of their relationships to others is inconsistent with the dignity and integrity of the human person."

- Organizations committed to protecting, promoting and monitoring human rights of women on the one hand, and of children on the other, are beginning to work together for the fulfilment of the human rights of both, and to focus on what happens in the family. (See, for example, IWRAW, SCA, UNDAW, UNIFEM and UNICEF 1998b; UNICEF, SCA, UNDAW and IWRAW 1998.)

- New mechanisms for monitoring, reporting and protecting human rights of women and girls, including in the home, are being pursued and obtained. The most impressive example of success is the March 1999 passage of the Optional Protocol for CEDAW, which encourages and supports women victim-survivors to bring their cases to the Committee once other means for redress at local and national level have been exhausted. On the prevention side, models have been put forward for national laws against domestic violence.

- A new global goal could be a Convention to Eliminate Violence against Women. This would provide a more direct route for presenting norms, raising issues and calling for redress than that allowed by the present clarifications and insertions of cross-cutting concerns about gender violence into other treaties and monitoring bodies (see Bunch 1994, page 74).

---

3   See, for example: Copelon, Ronda (1994), "Intimate Terror: Understanding Domestic Violence as Torture," in Cook, Rebecca (ed) (1994). Also see: Benninger-Budel, Carin and Lacroix, Anne Laurence (1999), *Violence Against Women: A Report*. World Organization against Torture.

4   Bangladesh has entered the following declaration: "The Government of the People's Republic of Bangladesh will apply article 14 para 1 in consonance with the existing laws and legislation in the country." Art 14.1 deals with compensation for victims of torture.

Bibliography

Abbas, Zaffer (1999), "Pakistan fails to condemn 'honour killings.' " *BBC News World: South Asia*, 3 August, Islamabad.

Abdullah, Rashidah, Rita Raj-Hashim and Gabriele Schmitt (1995), "Battered Women in Malaysia: Prevalence, Problems and Public Attitudes." Petaling Jaya, Malaysia: Women's Aid Organization.

Abeyesekere, Sunila (1995), "Organizing for Peace in the Midst of War: Experiences of Women in Sri Lanka." Pages 445–59 in Margaret Schuler (ed.), *From Basic Needs to Basic Rights*. Washington, DC: Women, Law and Development International.

Abitbol, Eric and Christopher Louise (n.d.), *Up in Arms: The Role of Young People in Conflict and Peacemaking*. London: International Alert.

Abram, Morris B. (1997), "The Human Rights Muddle." *Earth Times*, 1–15 May.

Abu-Lughod, Lila (1993), *Writing Women's Worlds: Bedouin Stories*. Berkeley, CA: University of California Press.

Acharya, Meena (1997), "Gender Equality and Empowerment of Women." A status report submitted to UNFPA. Kathmandu: UNFPA.

—— (1998), "Globalization Process and the Nepalese Economy: Its Impact on Employment and Income." In Madan Dahal (ed.), *Impact of Globalisation in Nepal*. Kathmandu: NEFAS/FES. Mimeo of excerpt provided by author.

ActionAid India (1994), "Violent Homes: A Study of Shakti Shalini's Experiences with Women Victims of Domestic Violence." Bangalore, India: Policy Unit, ActionAid India.

ADAPT (1997), "Confronting Violence against Women: Men as Part of the Solution." Bramly, South Africa: Agisanang Domestic Abuse Prevention and Training (ADAPT).

Adithi (n.d. a), "A Rural Experience in Eliminating Violence against Girls and Women in Ten Years." Patna, India: Adithi. Mimeo.

—— (n.d. b), "Female Infanticide in Bihar." Mimeo.

Adler, Martin (1998), "Acid Attacks in Bangladesh" (24 November). Panos. *http://www.panos.co.uk/news/acid/acid.html*.

Adler, Nancy, J. (1997), *International Dimensions of Organizational Behavior*, 3rd edition. Cincinnati, OH: South Western College Publishing.

Afkhami, Mahnaz (ed.) (1995), *Faith and Freedom: Women's Human Rights in the Muslim World*. Syracuse, NY: Syracuse University Press.

Afkhami, Mahnaz and Erika Friedl (eds.) (1997), *Muslim Women and the Politics of Participation: Implementing the Beijing Platform*. Syracuse, NY: Syracuse University Press.

Afkhami, Mahnaz and Haleh Vaziri (1996), *Claiming Our Rights: A Manual for Women's Rights Education in Muslim Societies*, 3rd edition. Bethesda, MD: Sisterhood Is Global Institute.

Afsana, Kaosar (1994), "Socioeconomic Determinants and Wife-battering in Rural Bangladesh." Pages 140–55 in UNICEF, *Fire in the House: Determinants of Intra-*

familial Violence and Strategies for its Elimination. Bangkok: UNICEF East Asia and Pacific Regional Office.

Agarwal, Bina (1990), "Gender Relations and Food Security: Coping with Seasonality, Drought and Famine in South Asia." PEW/Cornell Lecture Series on Food and Nutrition Policy, 13 November. Ithaca, NY: Cornell Food and Nutrition Policy Program, Cornell University.

—— (1994a), *A Field of One's Own: Gender and Land Rights in South Asia*. New Delhi: Cambridge University Press.

—— (1994b), *Gender and Command over Property: An Economic Analysis of South Asia*. New Delhi: Kali for Women.

Agnihotri, Satish B. (1995), "Missing Females: A Disaggregated Analysis." *Economic and Political Weekly* (New Delhi), 19 August, pages 2,074–84.

—— (1996), "Juvenile Sex Ratios in India: A Disaggregated Analysis." *Economic and Political Weekly* (New Delhi), 28 December, pages 3, 369–82.

—— (1997a), "Inferring Gender Bias from Mortality Data: A Note." Norwich, UK: School of Development Studies, University of East Anglia. Mimeo.

—— (1997b), "Workforce Participation, Kinship and Sex Ratio Variations in India." *Gender, Technology and Development*, Vol. 1, No. 1, pages 75–112.

—— (1997c), "Unpacking the Juvenile Sex Ratios in India." International Conference on Women in the Asia-Pacific Regions, "Persons, Powers, and Politics," 11–13 August 1997. Singapore: Department of Geography Southeast Asian Studies Programme, Centre for Advanced Studies of the National University of Singapore.

—— (1999), "Inferring Gender Bias from Mortality Data: A Discussion Note." *Journal of Development Studies*, Vol. 35, No. 4 (April), pages 175–200.

Ahmad, Kamran (n.d.), "Working on the Other Gender: Proposal for Funding." Mimeo.

—— (ed.) (1998), "Report on the Other Gender: A Seminar on Men's Issues" (24 March). Islamabad: UNDP.

Ahmad, Mohuddin (1999), *Bangladesh Towards 21st Century*. Dhaka: Community Development Library.

Ahmad, Rukhsana (ed.) (1994), *We Sinful Women*. New Delhi: Rupa.

Ahmed, Durre S. (1994), *Masculinity, Rationality and Religion: A Feminist Perspective*. Lahore: ASR Publications.

Ahmed, Eman M. (1998), "Violence against Women: The Legal System and Institutional Responses." Lahore: AGHS Legal Aid Cell.

Ahmed, Leila (1993), *Women and Gender in Islam: Historical Roots of a Modern Debate*. Cairo: The American University in Cairo Press.

Ahuja, Ram (1992), *Rights of Women: A Feminist Perspective*. Jaipur, India: Rawat Publications.

Akanda, Latifa and Ishrat Shamim (1985), "Women and Violence: A Comparative Study of Rural and Urban Violence against Women in Bangladesh." Dhaka: Women for Women.

Akanda, Latifa, Farah Kabir, Khalenda Salahuddin and Ishrat Shamim (1997), "Consultation Meeting: Trafficking and Prostitution." Dhaka: Centre for Women and Children Studies.

Alam, Shahidul and Rahnuma Ahmed (n.d.), "Veiling the Truth." Mimeo.

Ali, Miriam and Jana Wain (1996), *Without Mercy: A Mother's Struggle against Modern Slavery*. London: Warner Books.

Ali, Salma (1997), "Survey in the Area of Child and Women Trafficking, July to December of 1997." Dhaka: Bangladesh National Women Lawyers Association (BNWLA).

——— (1998), "Bangladesh Country Report on Trafficking in Children and their Commercial Sexual Exploitation and Other Intolerable Forms of Child Labour." Prepared for ILO and IPEC. Dhaka: BNWLA. Mimeo.

Ali, Salma, with Mominul Islam and Sameena Bary Alam (1996), "Movement against Flesh Trade" (August). Dhaka: BNWLA.

Allione, Tsultrim (1986), *Women of Wisdom*. London: Arkana.

Alpert, Elaine J., Stu Cohen and Robert D. Sage (1997), "Family Violence: An Overview." *Academic Medicine*, Vol. 72, No. 1, Supplement (January).

Alston, Philip (ed.) (1994), *The Best Interests of the Child: Reconciling Culture and Human Rights*. Oxford: Clarendon Press.

Amarasuriya, Nimala R. (1991), "Women and Technology." *Working Papers*, No. 3. Colombo, Sri Lanka: Centre for Women's Research (CENWOR).

Amnesty International (1995a), "Afghanistan: International Responsibility for a Human Rights Disaster." London: Amnesty International.

——— (1995b), *Human Rights Are Women's Rights*. New York: Amnesty International USA.

——— (1995c), "Women in Afghanistan: A Human Rights Catastrophe." London: Amnesty International.

——— (1996), "Afghanistan: Grave Abuses in the Name of Religion." London: Amnesty International.

An-Na'im, Abdullah Ahmed (1994), "State Responsibility under International Human Rights Law to Change Religious and Customary Laws." Pages 167–88 in Rebecca J. Cook (ed.), *Human Rights of Women: National and International Perspectives*. Philadelphia: University of Pennsylvania Press.

Antony, M. J. (1995), *Landmark Judgements on Dowry-related Deaths*. New Delhi: Indian Social Institute.

Apfel, Roberta A. and Bennett Simon, with Stacey Liberty (1994), *Bibliography on the Psychological and Psychosocial Aspects of Children in War and Situations of Violence*. Cambridge, MA: Working Group on Children in War and Communal Violence.

Arasanayagam, Jean (1995), *All Is Burning*. New Delhi: Penguin Books India.

Arnold, Fred, Minja Kim Choe and T. K. Roy (1998), "Son Preference, the Family-Building Process and Mortality in India." *Population Studies*, Vol. 52, pages 301–15.

Arole, Mabelle (1995), *Voices of South Asian Women*. Kathmandu: UNICEF Regional Office for South Asia.

——— (1999), *Religion and Rights of Children and Women in South Asia*. Kathmandu: UNICEF Regional Office for South Asia.

Arole, Mabelle and Rajanikant Arole (1994), *Jamkhed: A Comprehensive Rural Health Project*. London: Macmillan Press.

Arrows For Change: Women's and Gender Perspectives in Health Policies and Programmes (1995), Vol. 1, No. 3 (December).

Asian and Pacific Development Centre (APDC) (1998), *Asia-Pacific Post-Beijing Implementation Monitor*. Kuala Lumpur, Malaysia: APDC.

Asian Women's Human Rights Council (AWHRC) (1995), "Speaking Tree, Womenspeak." Asian Public Hearing on Crimes against Women and the Violence of Development, 28 January. Bangalore, India: AWHRC and Vimochana. Mimeo.

Aslam, Imran (1997), "The Story of One Man's Conversion." *The News on Sunday* (Karachi), 30 November, pages 28–29.

Augé, Marc (1995), *Non-places: Introduction to an Anthropology of Supermodernity*. London: Verso.

Badran, H. (n.d.), "Gender and Rights: Conference Linkages." New York: Gender and Development Section, Programme Division, UNICEF. Mimeo.

Bahai International and UNICEF/UNIFEM (1994), "Creating Violence-Free Families: A Symposium Summary Report." New York: UNICEF/UNIFEM.

Bajpai, Rajendra Kumari(1997), Text of Address of H.E. Dr. Rajendra Kumari Bajpai, Lt. Governor of Pondicherry, at the Inauguration of the Third All-India Women Doctors Conference Held on Saturday, 27 September, at Patna. Mimeo.

Bakht, Baidar (ed.) (1991), *The Scream of an Illegitimate Voice: Selection of Poems of Kishwar Naheed*. Lahore: Sang-e-Meel Publications.

Baldo, Tracy D. Bostwick and Anthony J. Baldo (1996), "Intrafamilial Assaults, Disturbed Eating Behaviors and Further Victimization." *Psychological Reports*, No. 79, pages 1,057–58.

Ballard, Terri J., Linda E. Saltzman, Julie A. Gazmararian, Alison M. Spitz, Suzanne Lazorick and James S. Marks (1998), "Violence during Pregnancy: Measurement Issues." *American Journal of Public Health*, Vol. 88, No. 2 (February).

Bangladesh Mahila Prasad, Bangladesh National Women Lawyers Association and Naripokkho (June 1997), "A commentary on Bangladesh's combined third and fourth periodic report for the Members of the United Nations Committee on the Elimination of Discrimination against Women." Dhaka.

Bangladesh Jatiyo Mahila Ainjibi Samity (1998), "October Special Bulletin." Dhaka: Bangladesh Jatiyo Mahila Ainjibi Samity (BJMAS) (Bangladesh National Women Lawyers Association [BNWLA]).

Bari, Farzana and Tasneem Ahmar (eds.) (1994), "Women and Family." *Journal of Women's Studies*, Vol. 1, No. 1 (December). Islamabad: Centre for Women's Studies.

Baria, Farah (1997), "Mock Justice." *India Today*, 30 June, pages 84–85.

Baruah, Bonita (1997), "Whose Fault Is It, Anyway?" *Sunday Times of India*, 24 August, page 19.

Bass-Feld, Eena R. (1997), "The Impact of Domestic Violence on Children" (21 May). *http://www.wrc-gbmc.org/violence2.htm*. GBMC Women's Resource Centre.

Basu, Amrita (ed.) (1995), *The Challenge of Local Feminisms*. Boulder, CO: The West View Press.

BBC (1997), *Women Making a Difference: Women's development in Africa: The book of the English language teaching radio series*. Dar es Salaam, Tanzania: Mkuki na Nyota Publishers.

Beasley, M. (1994), "Maltreatment of Maids in Kuwait." In Miranda Davies (ed.), *Women and Violence: Realities and Responses Worldwide*. London: Zed Books.

Bedi, Rajinder Singh (1994), *I Take This Woman*. New Delhi: Penguin Books India.

Belkin, Lisa (1999), "Getting the Girl." *The New York Times Magazine*, 25 July, pages 26–31, 38, 54–55.

Benard, Elisabeth Anne (1994), *Chinnamastá: The Aweful Buddhist and Hindu Tantric Goddess*. New Delhi: Motilal Banarsidass Publishers.

Bennett, John (1996), "Supporting Family Responsibility for the Rights of the Child: An Educational Viewpoint." *International Journal of Children's Rights*, No. 4, pages 45–56.

Bhadra, Chandra and Sangeeta Thapa (1995), "Impact of Macroeconomic Policies on Women: A Feminist Perspective." Paper presented at Looking Forward, Looking Back: In Search of Feminist Visions, Alternative Paradigms and Practices, the VII National Conference of Women's Studies, the Indian Association of Women's Studies, Jaipur, India.

Bhagat, Pamela (1999), "Kashmir's Women Scarred by Separatist Conflict: Commentary." *IPS Gender and Human Rights Bulletin* (27 September). Mimeo.

Bhaiya, Abha and Kalyani Menon Sen (1997), "Report of a South Asian Workshop on Gender and Development." New Delhi: Shtrii Shakti-Nepal, FAO-NGO South Asia Programme and Jagori-New Delhi.

Bhan, Susheela (1991), *Child Abuse: An Annotated Bibliography*. New Delhi: Northern Book Centre.

Bhandare, Murlidhar C. (ed.) (1999), *The World of Gender Justice*. New Delhi: Har Anand Publication Pvt. Ltd.

Bhasin, Kamla (n.d. a), "Some Thoughts on Development and Sustainable Development." Mimeo.

—— (n.d. b). "Gender Workshops with Men, Experiences and Reflections." Pamphlet.

—— (1993), *What Is Patriarchy?* New Delhi: Kali for Women.

—— (1994), "Let Us Look Afresh at Development, Education and Women." Talk given at the Fifth World Assembly of the International Council for Adult Education on Women, Literacy and Development Challenges for the 21st Century, Cairo, 15–23 September. Mimeo.

—— (1995), "The Goal Is Empowerment on Human Values, Challenge for Women's Empowerment and Education in South Asia." Paper presented at the International Conference on Women's Empowerment and Education organized by the Government of India in collaboration with the Royal Netherlands Embassy in New Delhi, India, 22–31 March. Mimeo.

—— (1997). "What is a girl? What is a boy?" In English and Hindi. New Delhi: Jagori.

—— (1998), "Winners and Losers of Globalisation and Can They Live Side-by-side in Harmony and Peace." Address at the 40th Anniversary Celebrations and opening of the Fastenaktion 1998 of Miscreor, Germany, on the theme "The Poor First," held at Koeln, Germany, 26 February. Mimeo.

—— (1999), "Women's Place Is in the House! This Is Why They Should be in Both Houses of Parliament: Women and Governance." Talk given at a day-long interaction by SAP Nepal in Kathmandu on the Changing Role of Women in Governance, 26 February. Mimeo.

Bhasin, Kamla and Abha Bhaiya (1998), "Towards South Asian Solidarity: A Report of a South Asian Workshop of Gender Trainers." New Delhi: Jagori, Women's Training and Research Centre.

Bhasin, Kamla and Sumeeta Dhar (1999), "Joining Hands to Develop Woman Power." A report of a South Asian Workshop on Gender and Sustainable Development, Koitta, Bangladesh, 5 November–4 December. Dhaka: The Institute for Development Policy Analysis and Advocacy (IDPAA) at Proshika, a Centre for Human Development.

Bhasin, Kamla and Nighat Said Khan (1986), "Some Questions on Feminism and its Relevance in South Asia." *Kali Primaries*. New Delhi: Kali for Women.

Bhatia, Ritu (n.d.), "India: Too Many Hazardous Abortions." *Women's Feature Service*, 17 March. New Delhi.

Bhatti, Lubna I., Nausheen Faruqi, Nausheen Haroon, Ali I. Irqam, Khurram Hussein, Fariyal F. Fikree and J. A. Razzak (n.d.), "Women Speak about Violence." Mimeo.

Bhokari, Shanaz (1999), "Perspective on Gender, and Women's Participation and Local Governance in Pakistan." Mimeo (17 August).

Bhuiya, Abbas and Mushtaque Chowdhury (1997), "The Effect of Divorce on Child Survival in a Rural Area of Bangladesh." *Population Studies*, No. 51, pages 57–61.

Bista, Dor Bahadur (1991), *Fatalism and Development: Nepal's Struggle for Modernization*. Calcutta: Orient Longman.

BNWLA (Bangladesh National Women Lawyers Association) (n.d. a), "Hindu Family Law — An Action Study on Proposed Reform of Hindu Family Law." Dhaka: BNWLA.

—— (n.d. b), "Causes and Consequences of Children and Women Trafficking: A Socio-Economic Study on Ten Villages of Bangladesh." Dhaka: BNWLA, with thanks to UNICEF for providing financial support.

—— (1997a), Special Bulletin (January). Dhaka: BNWLA.

—— (1997b), Mimeo (November). Dhaka: BNWLA.

—— (1997c), Special Bulletin (December). Dhaka: BNWLA.

Bodman, Herbert L. and Nayereh Tohidi (eds.) (1998), *Women in Muslim Societies: Diversity Within Unity*. Boulder, CO: Lynne Rienner Publishers, Inc.

Bose, Lekha (1996), "Agony of a Village Woman." *Deccan Chronicle* (Secunderabad, India), 4 February.

Boserup, Ester (1988), *Women's Role in Economic Development*. London: Earthscan Publishers.

Bradley, Christine (1994), "Why Male Violence against Women Is a Development Issue: Reflections from Papua New Guinea." Pages 10–27 in Miranda Davies (ed.), *Women and Violence: Realities and Responses Worldwide*. London: Zed Books.

Brasileiro, Ana Maria (ed.) (1977), "Women Against Violence: Breaking the Silence, Reflecting on Experience in Latin America and the Caribbean." New York: UNIFEM.

Brauer, Arlette (1995), "Women's Health." In Ruth Leger Sivard, *Women: A World Survey*. Washington, DC: World Priorities.

Breaking the Silence Group (1997), *The Noncommercial Sexual Abuse of Children in Bangladesh: A Case Study Based Report*. Dhaka: Breaking the Silence Group.

Brod, Harry and Michael Kaufman (eds.) (1994), *Theorizing Masculinities*. Thousand Oaks, CA: Sage Publications.

Brookoff, Daniel, Kimberly K. O'Brien, Charles S. Cook, Terry D. Thompson and Charles Williams (1997), "Characteristics of Participants in Domestic Violence: Assessment at the Scene of Domestic Assault." *Journal of the American Medical Association*, Vol. 277, No. 17 (7 May).

Brooks, Geraldine (1995), *Nine Parts of Desire: The Hidden World of Islamic Women*. New York: Doubleday.

Broverman, I. K., D. M. Broverman, F. E. Clarkson, P. S. Rosenkrantz and S. R. Vogel (1997), "Sex-Role Stereotypes and Clinical Judgments of Mental Health." *Journal of Consulting and Clinical Psychology*, Vol. 34, No. 1 (February 1970), pages 1–7. Mimeo (1997).

Bumiller, Elisabeth (1991), *May You Be the Mother of a Hundred Sons: A Journey among the Women of India*. New Delhi: Penguin Books India.

Bunch, Charlotte (1994), "Women's Rights as Human Rights: Towards a Re-vision of Human Rights." Colombo, Sri Lanka: Social Scientists' Association.

—— (1997), "The Intolerable Status Quo: Violence against Women and Girls." Pages 41–45 in UNICEF, *The Progress of Nations 1997*. New York: UNICEF.

Bunster-Burotto, Ximena (1994), "Surviving beyond Fear: Women and Torture in Latin America." Pages 156–76 in Miranda Davies (ed.), *Women and Violence: Realities and Responses Worldwide*. London: Zed Books.

Burke, Jason (1999), "A Witch Is Burnt in Rural Pakistan." *The Independent* (London), 30 January, page 14.

Burns, John F. (1996), "Walled in, Shrouded and Angry in Afghanistan." *The New York Times*, 4 October.

—— (1998), "A Bleak Existence for India's Hindu Widows." *International Herald Tribune*, 30 March.

Butalia, Urvashi (1998), *The Other Side of Silence: Voices from the Partition of India*. New Delhi: Penguin Books.

Butalia, Urvashi and Ritu Menon (eds.) (1992), *In Other Words: New Writing by Indian Women*. New Delhi: Kali for Women.

Byrnes, Andrew (1994), "Toward More Effective Enforcement of Women's Human Rights through the Use of International Human Rights Law and Procedures." Pages 189–227 in Rebecca J. Cook (ed.), *Human Rights of Women: National and International Perspectives*. Philadelphia: University of Pennsylvania Press.

Caldwell, Robert A. (1998), "The Costs of Child Abuse vs. Child Abuse Prevention: Michigan's Experience." Lansing: Michigan State University. Mimeo.

Camedessus, Brigitte (1997), "Domestic Violence." Mimeo (5 September).

Campbell, Jacquelyn C. (1995), "Addressing Battering During Pregnancy: Reducing Low Birth Weight and Ongoing Abuse." *Seminars in Perinatology*, Vol. 19, No. 4 (August), pages 301–306.

—— (1998), "Abuse during Pregnancy: Progress, Policy, and Potential." *American Journal of Public Health*, Vol. 88, No. 2 (February).

Carillo, Roxanna (1992), "Violence Against Women as an Obstacle to Development." New York: UNIFEM.

Carr, Dara (1997), "Female Genital Cutting: Findings from the Demographic and Health Surveys Programme." *Demographic and Health Surveys* (September). Calverton, MD: Macro International.

Carr, Marilyn, Martha Chen and Renana Jhabvala (eds.) (1997), *Speaking Out: Women's Economic Empowerment in South Asia*. New Delhi: Vistaar Publications.

Carriere, Rolf (1996), "Eliminating Violence Against Women." Paper presented at the National Workshop on Violence Against Women: Analysis and Action, CIRDAP, Dhaka, 1 September. Mimeo.

CDEG (1997), "Summary of the Plan of Action to Combat Violence against Women." Prepared by Ms. Sheila Henderson, Consultant, 4 December. Strasbourg, France: Steering Committee for Equality between Women and Men.

CEDAW (1997), "Concluding Observations of the Committee on the Elimination of Discrimination against Women, Bangladesh, 24 July 1997." Geneva: Committee on the Elimination of Discrimination against Women, United Nations.

CEDPA and UNFPA (1995), "Voices of Young Women." Washington, DC: Centre for Development and Population Activities and UN Population Fund.

Center for Reproductive Law and Policy and International Federation of Women Lawyers (Kenya Chapter) (1997), *Women of the World: Laws and Policies Affecting Their Reproductive Lives, Anglophone Africa*. New York: Center for Reproductive Law and Policy.

Center for Study of Human Rights (1994), *Twenty-five Human Rights Documents*. New York: Center for Study of Human Rights, Columbia University.

Center for Women's Global Leadership (1994), *Gender Violence and Women's Human Rights in Africa*. New Brunswick, NJ: Center for Women's Global Leadership.

Centre for Women's Development Studies (1989), *Samya Shakti: A Journal of Women's Studies*, Vol. IV. New Delhi: Centre for Women's Development Studies (CWDS).

——— (1990a), *Samya Shakti: A Journal of Women's Studies*, Vol. V. New Delhi: CWDS.

——— (1990b), *Samya Shakti: A Journal of Women's Studies*, Vol. VI. New Delhi: CWDS.

Centre for Women's Studies (1993), Newsletter. Vol. 1, No. 1 (December). Islamabad: Quaid-i-Azam University.

Chen, Lincoln C. (1982), "Where Have the Women Gone?: Insights from Bangladesh on Low Sex Ratio of India's Population." *Economic and Political Weekly*, 6 March, pages 364–72.

Chen, Martha Alter (1986), *A Quiet Revolution: Women in Transition in Rural Bangladesh*. Dhaka: Brac Prokashana.

Chernikoff, Helen (1995), "Report on Child Prostitution in India." New Delhi: UNICEF India Country Office. Mimeo (December).

CHETNA (n.d.), "Towards Empowerment of Women and Children." Ahmedabad, India: Centre for Health Education, Training and Nutrition Awareness (CHETNA).

Ching, Frank (1997), "Responsibilities and Rights." *Far Eastern Economic Review*, 13 November.

Chughtai, Ismat (1990), *The Quilt and Other Stories*. New Delhi: Kali for Women.

——— (1993), *The Heart Breaks Free and the Wild One: Two Novellas*. New Delhi: Kali for Women.

CIETinternational (1997), "Gender Gap in Primary Education, Kalat, 1995–1996: Key Findings." Kalat, Pakistan: CIETinternational. Mimeo (13 August).

Clarity, James F. (1997), "Irish Priest Gets 12 Years for Sex Abuse." *International Herald Tribune*, 26–27 July.

Clark, Anna (1987), *Women's Silence, Men's Violence: Sexual Assault in England, 1770–1845*. London: Pandora Press.

Clark, Roberta (1998), *Violence Against Women in the Caribbean: State and Non-State Responses*. New York: UNIFEM.

Commission of Inquiry for Women (1997), *Report of the Commission of Inquiry for Women, Pakistan* (August). Islamabad: Commission of Inquiry for Women.

Connors, Jane (1994), "Government Measures to Confront Violence against Women." Pages 182–99 in Miranda Davies (ed.), *Women and Violence: Realities and Responses Worldwide*. London: Zed Books.

Cook, Rebecca J. (ed.) (1994a), *Human Rights of Women: National and International Perspectives*. Philadelphia: University of Pennsylvania Press.

——— (1994b), "State Accountability under the Convention on the Elimination of All Forms of Discrimination against Women." Pages 228–56 in Rebecca J. Cook (ed.), *Human Rights of Women: National and International Perspectives*. Philadelphia: University of Pennsylvania Press.

——— (1997), "Advancing Safe Motherhood through Human Rights." Paper presented at Safe Motherhood Matters: Ten Years of Lessons and Progress, A Technical Consultation, Colombo, Sri Lanka, 18–23 October.

Cook, Rebecca J. and Valerie L. Oosterveld (1997), "A Select Bibliography of Women's Human Rights." Mimeo (21 March).

Coomaraswamy, Radhika (1994a), "To Bellow Like a Cow: Women, Ethnicity and the Discourse of Rights." Pages 39–57 in Rebecca J. Cook (ed.), *Human Rights of Women: National and International Perspectives*. Philadelphia: University of Pennsylvania Press.

——— (1994b), "Violence against Women: Causes and Consequences." In UNICEF, *Fire in the House: Determinants of Intra-familial Violence and Strategies for its Elimination*. Bangkok: UNICEF East Asia and Pacific Regional Office.

——— (1995a), "Violence against Women." New Delhi: Indian Association of Women's Studies.

——— (1995b), "Diversity, Universality and the Enlightenment Project." Pages 213–216 in Margaret Schuler (ed.), *From Basic Needs to Basic Rights*. Washington, DC: Women, Law and Development International.

Copelon, Rhonda (1994), "Intimate Terror: Understanding Domestic Violence as Torture." Pages 116–52 in Rebecca J. Cook (ed.), *Human Rights of Women: National and International Perspectives*. Philadelphia: University of Pennsylvania Press.

Corsini, Carlo A. and Pier Paolo Viazzo (eds.) (1993), *The Decline of Infant Mortality in Europe, 1800–1950: Four National Case Studies*. Florence: UNICEF International Child Development Centre and Istituto degli Innocenti.

Cotter, Holland (1999), "She's U-Mother, Warrior, Lover: Isn't She Divine?" *The New York Times*, 25 July, pages 33–34.

Coudouel, Aline (1998), "Violence against Women in Central and Eastern Europe, the CIS and the Baltics." Florence: UNICEF International Child Development Centre. Mimeo.

Council for Social Development (1995), "Girl Child in India." *Social Change*, Vol. 25, Nos. 2–3 (June–September). New Delhi: Council for Social Development.

Crossette, Barbara (1998), "When Half of Afghanistan Is Kept in Seclusion." *International Herald Tribune*, 7 April.

Cunningham, Hugh and Pier Paolo Viazzo (eds.) (1996), *Child Labour in Historical Perspective, 1800–1985: Case Studies from Europe, Japan and Colombia*. Florence: UNICEF International Child Development Centre and Istituto degli Innocenti.

CWS (1993), *CWS Newsletter*, Vol. 1, No. 1 (December). Islamabad: Centre for Women's Studies (CWS).

——— (1994), "Violence against Women." *CWS Newsletter*, Vol. 2, No. 1 (April). Islamabad: CWS.

——— (1995a), "Action, Not Just Promises." *CWS Newsletter*, Vol. 3, No. 3 (December). Islamabad: CWA.

——— (1995b), "A Day of the Women, by the Women and for the Women." *CWS Newsletter*, Vol. 3, Nos. 1–2 (April–August). Islamabad: CWS.

——— (1996), "Whose Body Is It Anyway?" *CWS Newsletter*, Vol. 4, No. 2 (June). Islamabad: CWS.

Cyberparent (1999). "The Problem of Physical Abuse in Pregnancy" (22 June). http://www.cyberparent.com/abuse/pregnancy.htm.

Dahlburg, John-Thor (1997), "France Faces the Unspeakable: Horror Stories Help to End Law of Silence on Child Sex Abuse." *International Herald Tribune*, 24 July.

Dali, Indira (ed.) (1997), "Role of the Media and an Aspect of the Independent Status: Proceedings of a Seminar." Kathmandu: Asmita Women's Publication House.

Damon, William (1999), "The Moral Development of Children." *Scientific American* (August), pages 72–78.

Dandekar, Kumudini (1975), "Why Has the Proportion of Women in India's Population Been Declining?" *Economic and Political Weekly*, 18 October, pages 1,663–67.

Das, Kamala (1988), *My Story*. New Delhi: Sterling Publishers.

Das, Manoj (1994), *Farewell to a Ghost*. New Delhi: Penguin Books India.

Das, Veena (1990), *Structure and Cognition: Aspects of Hindu Caste and Ritual*. New Delhi: Oxford University Press.

────── (1995), *Critical Events: An Anthropological Perspective on Contemporary India*. New Delhi: Oxford University Press.

Das Gupta, Monica and P. N. Mari Bhat (1997), "Fertility Decline and Increased Manifestation of Sex Bias in India." *Population Studies*, Vol. 51, No. 3, pages 307–15.

Dasgupta, Swapan (1997a), "Dynastic Appeal." *India Today*, 25 August, pages 28–29.

────── (1997b), "Freedom of Arrogance." *India Today*, 25 August, page 29.

Dastur, Aloo J. and Usha H. Mehta (1991), *Gandhi's Contribution to the Emancipation of Women*. Bombay: Popular Prakashan.

Datar, Chhaya (ed.) (1993), *The Struggle against Violence*. Calcutta: Stree.

Datta, Anindita and Sachidanand Sinha (1997), "Gender Disparities in Social Well-being: An Overview." *Indian Journal of Gender Studies*, Vol. 4, No. 1, pages 51–64.

Datta-Ray, Sunanda K. (1998), "The Task for India Is to Invest in the Quality of Its Schools." *International Herald Tribune*, 19 November.

Davies, Miranda (ed.) (1994), *Women and Violence: Realities and Responses Worldwide*. London: Zed Books.

DeParle, Jason (1999), "Early Sex Abuse Hinders Many Women on Welfare." *The New York Times*, 28 November, pages 1 and 12.

Deraniyagala, Sonali (1991), "Report on Some Observations on the Incidence of Domestic Violence in Four Locations in Sri Lanka and the Attitudes of Women towards the Violence" (December). Colombo, Sri Lanka: WIN (Women in Need).

────── (1992), "An Investigation into the Incidence and Causes of Domestic Violence in Colombo, Sri Lanka." A study prepared for WIN, Colombo, Sri Lanka.

Desai, Anita (1989), *Baumgartner's Bombay*. London: Penguin Books.

Detha, Vijaydan (1997), *The Dilemma and Other Stories*. New Delhi: Manushi Prakashan.

Devasia, Leelamma and V. V. Devasia (1991), *Girl Child in India*. New Delhi: Ashish Publishing House.

Development Dialogue (1996), "Review of Development Dialogue's Intervention towards Rehabilitation of Women Seeking Alternatives to Continuation in Sex Work." Calcutta: Development Dialogue.

Dhanda, Amita (1987), "The Plight of the Doubly Damned: The Mentally Ill Women in India." Pages 187–98 in P. Leelakrishnan (ed.), *New Horizons of Law*. Cochin, India: Cochin University of Science and Technology.

Dias, Malsiri and Deepika Fernando (n.d.), "Women Victims of Domestic Violence: A Study of Admissions to a Provincial General Hospital." Colombo, Sri Lanka: CENWOR Library. Mimeo.

Dijkstra, Bram (1996), *Evil Sisters: The Threat of Female Sexuality in Twentieth-Century Culture*. New York: Henry Holt and Company.

Dobash, R. Emerson and Russell Dobash (1992), *Women, Violence and Social Change*. London and New York: Routledge.

Domestic Violence Service, Gold Coast (1997), *Through Our Eyes: Images of Domestic Violence by Children & Young People*. Queensland, Australia: Domestic Violence Service, Gold Coast.

Doss, Cheryl R. (1996), "Testing among Models of Intrahousehold Resource Allocation." *World Development*, Vol. 24, No. 10, pages 1,597–1,609.

DPEP (1997), "The Mahila Samakhya Experience." *DPEP Calling*, Vol. 1, No. 10 (January). New Delhi: DPEP Bureau, Department of Education, Ministry of Human Resource Development.

Dreze, Jean and Amartya Sen (1995), *India, Economic Development and Social Opportunity*. Oxford: Clarendon Press.

Dube, Leela (1997), *Women and Kinship: Comparative Perspectives on Gender in South and South-East Asia*. Tokyo: The United Nations University.

Durrani, Tehmina (1995), *My Feudal Lord*. London: Corgi.

Duza, Asfia and Hamida A. Begum (1993), *Emerging New Accents: A Perspective of Gender and Development in Bangladesh*. Dhaka: Women for Women.

Economic Times (1996), "Women's Panel Seeks Protection for Bhanwari," 21 January (Bombay).

The Economist (1997), "The Bloodhounds of History," 12 April, pages 19–21.

────── (1998a), "Crime in America: Defeating the Bad Guys," 3 October, pages 35–38.

────── (1998b), "6.3 Brides for Seven Brothers," 19 December, pages 86–88.

The Economist Review (1998), "Microlending: From Tiny Acorns," 12 December, page 10.

El-Zanaty, F., et al. (1996), *Egypt Demographic and Health Surveys III*. Cairo: National Population Council and Macro International.

Equality Now (n.d. a), "Press Clippings." New York: Equality Now.

────── (n.d. b), "United States: Judicial Misconduct in the State of Maryland, the Peacock Case." New York: Equality Now.

Eriksson, Marianne (1997), "Relazione sulla necessità di organizzare una campagna a livello dell'Unione europea per la totale intransigenza nei confronti della violenza contro le donne." *Documenti di Seduta*, IT\RR\332\332189, 16 July. Brussels: European Parliament.

Espasa-Calpa, S. A. (1989), *Diccionario Manual Ilustrado de la Lengua Española. Cuarta edición revisada*. Madrid.

Esposito, John L. (1995), *The Islamic Threat: Myth or Reality?* New York: Oxford University Press.

Evins, G. and N. Chescheir (1996), "Prevalence of Domestic Violence among Women Seeking Abortion Services." *Women's Health Issues*, Vol. 6, No. 4, pages 204–10.

Falvo, Cathey (1997), "Violence against Women." New York: Health Unit, UNICEF. Mimeo.

Fauveau, V. and T. Blanchet (1989), "Deaths from Injuries and Induced Abortion among Rural Bangladesh Women." *Social Science and Medicine*, Vol. 29, No. 9, pages 1,121–27.

Fawcett, Gillian M., Lori L. Heise, Leticia Isita-Espejel and Susan Pick (1998), "Changing Community Responses to Wife Abuse: A Research and Demonstration Project in Iztacalco, Mexico." Mexico City: Instituto Mexicano de Investigación de Familia y Población.

Fazil, Nadeem (1997), "Part of the solution, not part of the problem." *The News on Sunday* (Karachi, Pakistan), 30 November, page 29.

Federal Ministry of Economic Cooperation and Development (1997), "Concept for the Promotion of Equal Participation by Women and Men in the Development Process: Concept on Gender Equality." Bonn, Germany: Federal Ministry of Economic Cooperation and Development. Mimeo (July).

Felder, Raoul and Barbara Victor (1996), *Getting Away with Murder: Weapons for the War against Domestic Violence*. New York: Simon and Schuster.

Fernando, Vijita (n.d.), "Violence against Women." Mimeo.

────── (1995), *Once on a Mountain Side*. Nawinna, Maharagama, Sri Lanka: Tharanjee Prints.

Fields, Gary (1998), "Domestic Abuse by Cops: A Hidden Crime." *USA Today*, 16–18 October.

Finkelhor, David and Jennifer Dziuba-Leatherman (1994), "Children as Victims of Violence: A National Survey." *Pediatrics*, Vol. 94, No. 4 (October).

Finn, Geraldine (1996), *Why Althusser Killed His Wife: Essays on Discourse and Violence*. Atlantic Highlands, NJ: Humanities Press International.

Firoze, Fawzia, Karim: Shoheen Akhter Munir and Salma Ali (n.d.), "Study on Women Prisoners of Bangladesh." Dhaka: BNWLA.

Fisher, Elizabeth and Linda Gray MacKay, 1996, *Gender Justice: Women's Rights Are Human Rights*. Cambridge, MA: Unitarian Universalist Service Committee.

Fitzpatrick, Joan (1994), "The Use of International Human Rights Norms to Combat Violence against Women." Pages 532–71 in Rebecca J. Cook (ed.), *Human Rights of Women: National and International Perspectives*. Philadelphia: University of Pennsylvania Press.

Flynn, Kevin (1999), "Brooklyn Puts Murder Rate Under Study." *The New York Times*, 26 July, page B1.

Forum Against Oppression of Women (1995), "The Fourth National Conference of the Women's Movements in India." Bombay: Forum Against Oppression of Women.

Forum for Women, Law and Development (FWLD) (1999), "Shadow Report on the Initial Report of the Government of Nepal on the Convention on Elimination of All Forms of Discrimination Against Women" (June). Kathmandu: FWLD.

Frederick, John (1998), "Deconstructing Gita." *Himal* (Kathmandu), Vol. 11, No. 10 (October), pages 12–19.

Friedl, Erika (1991), *Women of Deh Koh: Lives in an Iranian Village*. New York: Penguin Books.

Fruzzetti, Lina M. (1994), *The Gift of a Virgin*. New Delhi: Oxford University Press.

Gandhi, Nandita and Nandita Shah (1992), *The Issues at Stake: Theory and Practice in the Contemporary Women's Movement in India*. New Delhi: Kali for Women.

Gangrede, K. D., R. Sooryamoorthy and D. Rengini (1995), "Child Rape: Facets of a Heinous Crime." *Social Change*, Vol. 25, No. 2–3 (June–September), pages 161–76. New Delhi: Council for Social Development.

Gaudin, James M., Jr., Norman A. Polansky, Allie C. Kilpatrick and Paula Shilton (1990), "Spotlight on Practice: Family Functioning in Neglectful Families." *Child Abuse and Neglect*, Vol. 20, No. 4, pages 363–77.

George, K. M., Jancy James, Vasanthi Sankaranarayanan and Raj Kamini Mahadevan (1993), *Inner Spaces: New Writing by Women from Kerala*. New Delhi: Kali for Women.

George, Sabu M. (1997), "Female Infanticide in Tamil Nadu, India: From Recognition Back to Denial?" *Reproductive Health Matters*, No. 10 (November), pages 124–32.

George, Sabu M. and Ranbir S. Dahiya (1998), "Female Foeticide." *Rural Haryana, Economic and Political Weekly* (New Delhi), 8 August, pages 2191–98.

George, Sabu M., Jere D. Haas and Michael C. Latham (n.d.), "Health Education Can Reduce Gender Inequity in Growth of Pre-School Children in Rural South India." Ithaca, NY: The Program in International Nutrition, Division of Nutritional Sources, Cornell University. Mimeo.

Ghiglieri, Michael P. (1999), *The Dark Side of Man: Tracing the Origins of Male Violence*. Reading, MA: Perseus Books.

Ghimire, Durga (1997), "Sexual Exploitation of Nepalese Girls with Special Reference to Girl Trafficking." Paper presented at the regional seminar Girls' Rights: Society's Responsibility, Taking Action against Sexual Exploitation and Trafficking, 8–10 December. Washington, DC: Centre for Population and Development Activities.

Gil'di, Avner (1992), *Children of Islam: Concepts of Childhood in Medieval Muslim Society*. New York: St. Martin's Press.

Giles, Patricia (n.d.), "Women, Health and Violence: Government Responsibilities, Legislative, Social and Economic." Mimeo.

Gillioz, L. et al. (1997), *Domination et violences envers les femmes dans la couple*. Lausanne, Switzerland: Editions Payot.

Goldberg, Carey (1999), "Issues of Gender, From Pronouns to Murder." *The New York Times*, 11 June, page B2.

Golfarelli, Lalla (1998), "Zero Tolerance: Un Sistema di Interventi Locali." Paper presented at Conferenza Nazionale Zero Tolerance, Bologna, 15–16 October.

Gomez, Shyamala and Mario Gomez (1997), "Sri Lanka: The Law's Response to Women Victims of Violence." Colombo, Sri Lanka: University of Colombo. Mimeo.

Goode, Erica (1999), "Study on Child Sex Abuse Provokes a Political Furor." *The New York Times*, 13 June, page 33.

Goodman, Ellen (1998), "Is It Really Sexual Harassment if Nothing Happens? Yes." *International Herald Tribune*, 29 April.

Goodwin, Jan (1995), *Muslim Women Lift the Veil of Silence on the Islamic World*. New York: Penguin USA (reprint edition).

Goonesekere, Savitri (n.d.), "Violence against Women: A Critique of Some Aspects of Sri Lankan Law." Mimeo.

——— (1992), "Women's Rights and Children's Rights: The United Nations Conventions as Compatible and Complementary International Treaties." *Innocenti Occasional Papers*, Child Rights Series, No. 1. Florence: UNICEF International Child Development Centre.

——— (1998), *Children, Law and Justice: A South Asian Perspective*. New Delhi: UNICEF International Child Development Centre and Sage Publications.

Gordon, Linda (1989), *Heroes of Their Own Lives: The Politics and History of Family Violence, Boston 1880–1960*. London: Virago Press.

Gorhe, Neelam (1997), "Z Scheme: For Prevention and Eradication of Violence and Atrocities against Women and Girls." Pune, India: Stree Aadhar Kendra.

Government of Bangladesh (1997), "Combined Third and Fourth Periodic Report in Accordance with Article 18 of the Convention on the Elimination of All Forms of Discrimination against Women" (March). Dhaka: Ministry of Women and Children Affairs, Government of the People's Republic of Bangladesh. Mimeo.

——— (1998), "Statement by H.E. Mr. Anwarul Karim Chowdhury, Ambassador and Permanent Representative of Bangladesh to the United Nations, on Follow-up to the Fourth World Conference on Women." At the Forty-second session of the Commission on the Status of Women, 2 March 1998, New York. Bangladesh Permanent Mission to the United Nations. Mimeo.

——— (1999a), *National Action Plan for Women's Advancement: Implementation of the Beijing Platform for Action*. Dhaka: Ministry of Women and Children Affairs.

——— (1999b), *Implementation of National Action Plan for Women's Advancement and Strategies to Strengthen WID Focal Point Mechanism*. Dhaka: Ministry of Women and Children Affairs.

Government of India (1995), "India National Report" (September). New Delhi: Government of India.

——— (1998), "Statement by Mrs. Asha Das, Secretary, Department of Women and Child Development, Government of India." At the Forty-second session of the Commission on the Status of Women, 6 March 1998, New York. Permanent Mission of India to the United Nations.

Government of Nepal (1995), "Nepal National Report" (September). Kathmandu: Government of Nepal.

Government of Pakistan, (1995), "Pakistan National Report" (September). Fourth World Conference on Women, Beijing. Government of Pakistan Ministry of Women, Development and Youth Affairs.

——— (1998), "Statement by Mr. Munawar Saeed Bhatti, First Secretary, Permanent Mission of Pakistan to the United Nations." At the Forty-second session of the Commission on the Status of Women, 6 March 1998, New York. Pakistan Permanent Mission to the United Nations. Mimeo.

Government of Sweden (1995), "Kvinnofrid, Del" (Peace for Women, Part A). *Official Reports of the State*, No. 1995:60. Stockholm: Social Department, Government of Sweden.

Graham-Bermann, Sandra A. (1996), "Family Worries: Assessment of Interpersonal Anxiety in Children from Violent and Nonviolent Families." *Journal of Clinical Child Psychology*, Vol. 25, No. 3, pages 280–87.

Groves, Betsy McAlister (1996), "Children without Refuge: Young Witnesses to Domestic Violence." Pages 29–34 in Joy D. Osofsky and Emily Fenichel (eds.), *Islands of Safety*. Washington, DC: Zero to Three, National Center for Infants, Toddlers and Families.

Guerrero, Sylvia H. and Carolyn I. Sobritchea (1997), "Breaking the Silence: The Realities of Family Violence in the Philippines and Recommendations for Change." New York: UNICEF.

Gulbenkian Foundation Commission (1995), *Children and Violence*. London: Calouste Gulbenkian Foundation.

Gunawardena, Lakmali (n.d.), "Where No Woman Travels Alone." Colombo, Sri Lanka: Voice of Women.

Haddad, Yvonne Yazbeck and John L. Esposito (eds.) (1998), *Islam, Gender, and Social Change*. New York: Oxford University Press.

Haeri, Shahla (1995), "The Politics of Dishonor: Rape and Power in Pakistan." Pages 161–74 in Mahnaz Afkhami (ed.), *Faith and Freedom: Women's Human Rights in the Muslim World*. Syracuse, NY: Syracuse University Press.

Haj-Yahia, M. (1997), "The First National Survey of Abuse and Battering against Arab Women from Israel: Preliminary Results." Mimeo.

Hameed, Syeda S. and Sughra Mehdi (eds.) (1996), *Parwaaz: Urdu Short Stories by Women*. New Delhi: Kali for Women.

Harendra de Silva, D. G. (1996), "Child Abuse: The Gravity of the Problem and Dilemmas in Management in Sri Lanka." Karapitiya, Galle, Sri Lanka: Department of Paediatrics, Faculty of Medicine.

Harlan, Lindsey and Paul B. Courtright (eds.) (1995), *From the Margins of Hindu Marriage: Essays on Gender, Religion and Culture*. New York: Oxford University Press.

Hart, Gillian (1997), "Rotten Wives to Good Mothers: Household Models and the Limits of Economism." Pages 14–25 in "Tactics and Tradeoffs: Revisiting the Links between Gender and Poverty," *IDS Bulletin*, Vol. 28, No. 3 (July).

Hasan, Fatema Rashid (n.d.), "Study on the Possible Reforms in the Existing Muslim Family, Law and Procedure." Dhaka: BNWLA.

Hassan, Rifat (1999), "Feminism in Islam." Pages 248–78 in Arvind Sharma and Katherine K. Young (eds.), *Feminism and World Religions*. New York: State University of New York Press.

Hassan, Yasmeen (1995), *The Haven Becomes Hell: A Study of Domestic Violence in Pakistan*, August. Lahore: Shirkat Gah, WLUML (Women Living under Muslim Laws) Coordination Office Asia.

——— (1999), "The Fate of Pakistani Women." *International Herald Tribune*, 23 March.

Hawley, John Stratton and Donna Marie Wulff (eds.) (1986), *The Divine Consort: Radha and the Goddesses of India*. Boston, MA: Beacon Press.

Hayward, Ruth Finney (1995), "Reproductive Health: Choices and Challenges." Mimeo (18 July).

——— (1996), "Beyond Beijing Is Beyond Dehumanization." Mimeo (8 March).

——— (1997a), "The Impact of Domestic Violence on Children: A Cautionary Tale for Policy, Programme and Family Life." *ROSA Reports*, No. 18. Kathmandu: UNICEF Regional Office for South Asia.

——— (1997b), "Needed: New Model of Masculinity to Stop Violence against Girls and Women." *ROSA Reports*, No. 17. Kathmandu: UNICEF Regional Office for South Asia.

——— (1997c), "Violence against Women: What Will Physicians Do to Stop It?" Kathmandu: UNICEF Regional Office for South Asia.

——— (1997d), "Who Cares about Maternal Mortality If a Woman Is a Shoe to Change?" (8 March). Kathmandu: UNICEF Regional Office for South Asia.

——— (1998), "The Dangerous Family in South Asia." Florence: UNICEF International Child Development Centre. Mimeo (6 April).

Hazare, Anna, Ganesh Pangare and Vasudha Lokur (1996), *Adarsh Gaon Yojana: Government Participation in a People's Programme*. Pune, India: Hind Swaraj Trust.

Hazarika, Yamin (1995), "An Overview of Crimes against Women in Delhi, 1984–1994." Pages 41–42 in Malavika Karlekar, Anuja Agrawal and Maithili Ganjoo, "No Safe Spaces: Report of a Workshop on Violence against Women, 27–28 March 1995." New Delhi: Centre for Women's Development Studies.

Heise, Lori L. (n.d. a), "Violence against Women: Global Organizing for Change." In Jeffrey Edleson and Zvi Eisikovits (eds.), *The Future of Intervention with Battered Women and Their Families*. London: Sage Publications. Mimeo.

——— (n.d. b), "Violence against Women and Girls: Implications for International Health Programmes." Takoma Park, MD: Health and Development Policy Project. Mimeo.

——— (1995), "Gender-based Abuse and Women's Reproductive Health." Paper presented at the Donor Workshop on Implementing Reproductive Health Programmes, New York, 12–14 June. Takoma Park, MD: Health and Development Policy Project.

Heise, Lori L., Jacqueline Pitanguy and Adrienne Germain (1994), "Violence against Women: The Hidden Health Burden." *World Bank Discussion Papers*, No. 255.

Heise, Lori L., Alanagh Raikes, Charlotte H. Watts and Anthony B. Zwi (1994), "Violence against Women: A Neglected Public Health Issue in Less Developed Countries." *Social Science and Medicine*, Vol. 39, No. 9, pages 1,165–79.

Hennes, Halim M. A. and Alice D. Calhoun (eds.) (1998), *The Pediatric Clinics of North America: Violence Among Children and Adolescents*, Vol. 45, No. 2 (April). Philadelphia: W. B. Saunders Company, A Division of Harcourt Brace and Company.

Henning, Kris, Harold Leitenberg, Patricia Coffey, Tonia Turner and Robert T. Bennett (1996), "Long-term Psychological and Social Impact of Witnessing Physical Conflict between Parents." *Journal of Interpersonal Violence*, Vol. 11, No. 1 (March), pages 35–51.

Heredia, Rudolf C. and Edward Mathias (eds.) (1995), *The Family in a Changing World: Women, Children and Strategies of Intervention*. New Delhi: Indian Social Institute.

Herman, Judith Lewis (1981), *Father-Daughter Incest*. Cambridge, MA: Harvard University Press.

Herszenhorn, David M. (1999), "Alarm Helps to Fights Domestic Violence." *The New York Times*, 27 July, page B3.

Heyzer, Noeleen (ed.) (1988), *Daughters in Industry: Work Skills and Consciousness of Women Workers in Asia*. Kuala Lumpur: Asian and Pacific Development Centre.

——— (1997), "Gender, Economic Growth and Poverty." *Development*, Vol. 40, pages 126–30.

Hina, Zahida (1994), "The Earth Is Ablaze and the Heavens Are Burning." Pages 109–33 in Samina Rehman (ed.), *In Her Own Write: Short Stories by Women Writers in Pakistan*. Lahore: ASR Publications.

HMG/N, NPC and UNICEF (1997), "Early Childhood Feeding, Nutrition and Development, Nepal Multiple Indicator Surveillance, Fourth Cycle (August–November 1996): Draft Final Report" (June). Kathmandu: HMG/Nepal, National Planning Commission (NPC) and UNICEF.

Hoffman, Björn (1999), "Fatherhood Education: A Way to a Richer Life." Paper presented at Women 2000: Gender, Equality, Development and Peace for the 21st Century, at the United Nations, 4 March 1999.

Holmström, Lakshmi (ed.) (1991), *The Inner Courtyard: Stories by Indian Women*. New Delhi: Rupa.

Holtzworth-Munroe, Amy, Natalie Smutzler and Elizabeth Sandin (1997), "A Brief Review of the Research on Husband Violence, Part II: The Psychological Effects of Husband Violence on Battered Women and Their Children." *Aggression and Violent Behavior*, Vol. 2, No. 2, pages 179–213.

Honey, Jaya, Mira Kishwar and the Sihaya Group (1995), *Dance of Madness: We Indian Women*. Shimla, India: Kishwar Ahmed Shirali.

Hopper, Jim (1997), "Sexual Abuse of Males: Prevalence, Lasting Effects and Resources" (28 May). *http://www.jimhopper.com*.

Hossain, Begum Rokeya Sakhawat (1993), *Sultana's Dream*. Dhaka: Narigrantha Prabartana.

Hossain, Hamida et al. (1990), *No Better Option?* Dhaka: UPL.

Hossain, Sara (1994), "Equality in the Home: Women's Rights and Personal Laws in South Asia." Pages 465–94 in Rebecca J. Cook (ed.), *Human Rights of Women: National and International Perspectives*. Philadelphia: University of Pennsylvania Press.

Huda, Sigma (n.d. a), "Recommendations in Synopsis." Paper presented at the UNICEF-UNIFEM Conference: Planning and Review Meeting on the Use of the Legal Systems in Combating Violence against Women and Children, New Delhi, 27–28 August. Mimeo.

——— (n.d. b), "The Use of the Legal System to Combat Violence against Women." Mimeo.

Human Rights Watch (1995), *The Human Rights Watch Global Report on Women's Human Rights*. New York: Human Rights Watch.

——— (1996), *Shattered Lives: Sexual Violence during the Rwandan Genocide and Its Aftermath*. New York: Human Rights Watch.

——— (1999a), "Broken People: Caste Violence Against India's 'Untouchables'." *http://www.brw.org/report/1999/India994-11.htm*.

——— (1999b), *Crime or Custom? Violence Against Women in Pakistan*. New York: Human Rights Watch.

Human Rights Watch/Asia (1995), *Rape for Profit: Trafficking of Nepali Girls and Women to India's Brothels*. New York: Human Rights Watch.

Huq, Nasreen (n.d.), "Healing the Wounds and Living with the Scars: Naripokkho's Response to Acid Violence." Mimeo.

—— (1997), "Maternal Mortality and Violence against Women: Insights from the Women's Movement in Bangladesh." Kathmandu: UNICEF Regional Office for South Asia. Mimeo.

Huq, Shireen (1997a), "Expert Group Meeting on State Interventions on Violence against Women." Dhaka: Ministry of Women and Children Affairs. Mimeo.

—— (1997b), "A Preliminary Outline of the Project Concept Paper on Violence against Women." Dhaka: Ministry of Women and Children Affairs. Mimeo.

——(1997c), "Speech in Opening Session of Conference on Women's Rights as Human Rights, 20–21 March, Irish Council of Civil Liberties, Dublin, Ireland." Dhaka: Naripokkho. Mimeo.

Hurdec (1997), "Psyche of Female Infanticide: A Study of Some Rural Communities in North Bihar." Patna, India: Adithi. Mimeo.

Hussain, Khalida (1994), "The Fairground." Pages 94–108 in Samina Rehman (ed.), *In Her Own Write: Short Stories by Women Writers in Pakistan*. Lahore: ASR Publications.

Hyder, Qurratulain (1996), *The Street Singers of Lucknow and Other Stories*. New Delhi: Sterling Publishers.

ICRW (1998), "Domestic Violence in India." Bulletin (September). International Center for Research on Women (ICRW), the Centre for Development and Population Studies (CEDPA) and Promoting Women in Development (PROWID).

ILRR (1996), "Paternal Property: Equal Rights to Daughter and Son" (November). Kathmandu: Institute for Legal Research and Resources (ILRR).

The Independent (Kathmandu) (1997), "The Police Got It All Wrong," 20–28 August.

Indian Association of Women's Studies (1995), "Reports from the President, General Secretary and the Treasurer, 1993 to 1995." New Delhi: Indian Association of Women's Studies.

Indian Express (1997), "Law Lenient on Rapists: Inamdar," 7 February.

Indian Medical Association (IMA) College of General Practitioners (1999), "IMA Salutes Girl Child." *Family Medicine*, Vol. 3, No. 4 (July–September). New Delhi: IMA College of Annual Practitioners with support from UNICEF.

Indira, M. K. (1990), *Phaniyamma: A Novel*. New Delhi: Kali for Women.

INHURED (1996), "Strategic Workshop on Trafficking in Women and Girls: Summary Report." Lalitpur, Nepal: International Institute for Human Rights, Environment and Development (INHURED). Mimeo.

Institute for Women, Law and Development (1993), *Claiming Our Place: Working the Human Rights System to Women's Advantage*. Washington, DC: Institute for Women, Law and Development.

—— (1996), *State Responses to Domestic Violence: Current Status and Needed Improvements*. Washington, DC: Institute for Women, Law and Development.

Integrated Development Systems (IDS) (1982), "Women in Prison: Case Studies." Submitted to International Fertility Research Program, North Carolina, USA. Kathmandu: IDS.

Inter-American Development Bank (1997), "Special Report: Domestic Violence." New York: Inter-American Development Bank.

International Herald Tribune (1998a), "Dhaka Moves to Protect Women," 1 April, page 4.

—— (1998b), "Nearly Half of All Rape Victims . . .," 19 November.

International Women's Tribune Centre (IWTC) (1998), "Rights of Women: A Guide to the Most Important United Nations Treaties on Women's Human Rights." New York: IWTC.

—— (1999), *The Tribune, a Women and Development Quarterly: Women Moving Human Rights Centre Stage*, May. New York: IWTC.

Iqbal, Anwar (1997a), "Veiled Women: Where Does the Problem Lie?" *The News* (Rawalpindi, Pakistan), 29 October.

—— (1997b), "Violence against Women." *The News* (Rawalpindi, Pakistan), 29 October.

Islam, Mahmood Aminul (1997), "Curbing Gender Violence Is Basic to Women's Empowerment." Mimeo (16 May).

Islam, Mahmuda (1994), *Whither Women's Studies in Bangladesh?* Dhaka: Women for Women.

Islam, Mominal, Sudhangshu Sekhar Roy and Mohammed Shahrear Hoque (n.d.), "Prostitution — Women, Society, State and Law." Dhaka: BNWLA.

Itzin, Catherine (ed.) (1992), *Pornography: Women, Violence and Civil Liberties, a Radical New View*. Oxford: Oxford University Press.

IWRAW and Commonwealth Secretariat (1996), "Assessing the Status of Women: A Guide to Reporting under the Convention on the Elimination of All Forms of Discrimination against Women." Minneapolis, MN: International Women's Rights Action Watch (IWRAW), Hubert H. Humphrey Institute of Public Affairs, University of Minnesota and Commonwealth Secretariat.

IWRAW, SCA, UNDAW, UNIFEM and UNICEF (1998a), "Draft Conclusions and Recommendations: NGO Expert Consultation on Preventing Violence in the Family." Geneva: IWRAW, Save the Children Alliance (SCA), UNDAW, UNIFEM and UNICEF. Mimeo (9 October).

—— (1998b), "NGO Expert Consultation on Preventing Violence in the Family: The Convention on the Elimination of All Forms of Discrimination against Women and the CEDAW Committee, Geneva, 7–9 Consultation." Geneva: IWRAW, SCA, UNDAW, UNIFEM and UNICEF. Mimeo.

Jafa, Jyoti (1994), *Nurjahan*. New Delhi: Roli Books.

Jagori (n.d.) *Women against Violence, Women for Peace*. New Delhi: Jagori.

Jahan, Roushan (1994), *Hidden Danger: Women and Family Violence in Bangladesh*. Dhaka: Women for Women.

—— (1995), "Men in Seclusion, Women in Public: Roheya's Dream and Women's Struggles in Bangladesh." In Amrita Basa (ed.), *The Challenge of Local Feminisms*. Boulder, CO: The West View Press.

Jahan, Roushan and Mahmuda Islam (1997), *Violence against Women in Bangladesh: Analysis and Action*. Dhaka: Women for Women and South Asian Association for Women Studies.

Jayawardena, Kumari (1994), *Feminism and Nationalism in the Third World*. Lahore: ASR Publications.

Jayawardena, Kumari and Malathi de Alwis (eds.) (1996), *Embodied Violence: Communalizing Women's Sexuality in South Asia*. New Delhi: Kali for Women.

Jeffery, Patricia and Roger Jeffery (1996), *Don't Marry Me to a Plowman!: Women's Everyday Lives in Rural North India*. New Delhi: Vistaar Publications.

Jehl, Douglas (1999), "Arab Honor's Price: A Woman's Blood." *The New York Times*, 20 June, page A1, A8.

Jejeebhoy, Shireen J. and Rebecca J. Cook (1997), "State Accountability for Wife-beating: The Indian Challenge." *The Lancet*, Vol. 349 (March), pages S10–12.

Jethmalani, Rani (1995), "Public Interest Litigation in India: Making the State Accountable." Pages 123–138 in Margaret Schuler (ed.), *From Basic Needs to Basic Rights*. Washington, DC: Women, Law and Development International.

Jhunjhijnwala, Bharat (1997), "As Women Vanish in Statistics." *The Indian Express*, 20 October.

Jilani, Hina (1992), "Whose Laws?: Human Rights and Violence against Women in Pakistan." Pages 63–74 in Margaret A. Schuler (ed.), *Freedom from Violence: Women's Strategies from around the World*. New York: UNIFEM.

Johnson, Kevin (1998), "Survey: Women Muscled out by Bias, Harassment." *USA Today*, 25–26 November.

Jonsson, Urban (n.d.), "Children's Rights: Charity or Solidarity?" Kathmandu: UNICEF Regional Office for South Asia. Mimeo.

Jordan, Mary (1996), "In Japanese Schools, Bullies Are a Deadly Issue." *International Herald Tribune*, 17 January.

Joshi, Pushpa (1988), *Gandhi on Women: Collection of Mahatma Gandhi's Writings and Speeches on Women*. Ahmedabad, India: CWDS and Navajivan Trust.

Jung, Anees (1987), *Unveiling India: A Woman's Journey*. New Delhi: Penguin Books India.

—— (1994), *Seven Sisters: Among the Women of South Asia*. New Delhi: Penguin Books India.

Kabeer, Naila (1995), *Reversed Realities: Gender Hierarchies in Development Thought*. New Delhi: Kali for Women.

—— (ed.) (1997), "Tactics and Trade-offs: Revisiting the Links between Gender and Poverty." *IDS Bulletin*, Vol. 28, No. 3 (July).

Kabeer, Naila and Ramya Subramanian (eds.) (1999), *Institutions, Relations and Outcomes — A Framework and Case Studies for Gender-aware Planning*. New Delhi: Kali for Women.

Kabir, Kushi (1998), "Theme Paper: Exploitation of and Violence Against Adolescents." Presented at UNFPA South Asia Conference on the Adolescent, 21–23 July, New Delhi.

Kakkar, Sudhir (1996), "Incestuous Abuse: A Comment." *Kali's Yug: Women and Law Journal*, Vol. 1, No. 1 (November), pages 15–16. New Delhi: WARLAW.

Kakkar, Sudhir and John M. Ross (1987, 1992), *Tales of Love, Sex and Danger*. London: Unwin Hyman.

Kali for Women (1990), *The Slate of Life: An Anthology of Stories by Indian Women*. New Delhi: Kali for Women.

Kapoor, Naina (1996), "Janus, Thy Name Is Man." *Kali's Yug: Women and Law Journal — The Rape Issue*. Vol. 1, No. 1 (November), pages 14–15.

Kapur, Promilla (ed.) (1993), *Girl Child and Family Violence*. New Delhi: Har-Anand Publications.

Kapur, Ratna (ed.) (1996), *Feminist Terrains in Legal Domains: Interdisciplinary Essays on Women and Law in India*. New Delhi: Kali for Women.

Karim, Wazir-Jahan (1990), "Consumption, Status Production and Classes of Goods: The Gender Function." Pages 174–91 in CWDS, *Samya Shakti: A Journal of Women's Studies*, Vols. IV and V. New Delhi: CWDS.

Karlekar, Malavika (1998), "Domestic Violence." *Economic and Political Weekly*, 4 July, pages 1,741–51.

Karlekar, Malavika, Anuja Agrawal and Maithili Ganjoo (1995), "No Safe Spaces: Report of a Workshop on Violence against Women," 27–28 March. New Delhi: CWDS.

Karp, Judith (1998), "Preventing Violence in the Family: CRC's Perspectives." Paper presented at the NGO Consultation on Preventing Violence in the Family, Geneva, 7–9 October.

Kashani, Javad H., Annasseril E. Daniel, Alison C. Dandoy and William R. Halcomb (1992), "Family Violence: Impact on Children." *Journal of the American Academy of Child and Adolescent Psychiatry*, Vol. 31, No. 2 (March), pages 181–89.

Kashtakari, Sanghatana (1996), "Towards a National Coalition for Gender Justice: Proceedings of the National Workshop on Gender-just Laws held at Bombay between 30 May and 2 June 1996." Bombay: Human Rights Law Network, Lawyers Collective, Forum against Oppression of Women and Kashtakari Sanghatana.

The Kathmandu Post (1997a), "Victims of Bangladesh Child Sex Abuse Lead Traumatized Lives," 9 August.

—— (1997b), "Women Ban Liquor in Balkumari VDC," 11 November.

—— (1997c), "Routine Rhetoric on Children's Day," 21 November.

—— (1999a), "Bill on Trafficking, Yet to See Light," 1 August, page 1.

—— (1999b), "CEDAW Members Express Concern over Women's Lot," 16 June.

—— (1999c), "Govt. for Curbing Women Trafficking," 16 June.

Kaufman, Michael (ed.) (1987), *Beyond Patriarchy: Essays by Men on Pleasure, Power and Change*. Toronto: Oxford University Press.

—— (1993), *Cracking the Armor: Power, Pain and the Lives of Men*. Toronto: Penguin Canada.

—— (1998), "Working with Men and Boys to Challenge Sexism and End Men's Violence." For the World Conference on Family Violence, Singapore.

—— (1999), "The Seven P's of Men's Violence." Toronto. Personal communication.

Kaur, Naunidhi (1998), "Rights-India: Domestic Violence Needs Public Attention." *World News*, 4 November. *http://www.oneworld.org/ips2/nov98/11_38_021.html*.

Kaushik, Susheela (1993), *Women and Panchayati Raj*. New Delhi: Har-Anand Publications.

Kazmi, Nikhat (1997), "Why Women's Rights Are Always Wrong." *Sunday Times of India*, 24 August, page 19.

Kelkar, Govind (1992), "Violence against Women: Perspectives and Strategies in India." *Occasional Papers*, No. 30. Shimla, India: Indian Institute of Advanced Study.

Keynan, Hassan (1997), "Male Roles and the Making of the Somali Tragedy." From the UNESCO Expert Group Meeting, Oslo, Norway, 24–28 September. Paris: UNESCO.

Khan, Fawad Usman (1994), "Preparing for the Future: Sexual Abuse of Girls and Young Women." Lahore: War Against Rape (WAR). Mimeo.

Khan, Nighat Said (ed.) (1992), *Voices within: Dialogues with Women on Islam*. Lahore: ASR Publications.

Khan, Nighat Said and Afiya Shehrbano Zia (eds.) (1995), *Unveiling the Issues: Pakistani Women's Perspectives on Social, Political and Ideological Issues*. Lahore: ASR Publications.

Khopade, Suresh (1998), "An Essay on Mohalla Committee in Relation to Bhiwandi Riots and Their Use in Controlling Crime against Women and Girls." Mimeo from author.

Kimmel, Michael (1997), "Reducing Men's Violence: The Personal Meets the Political." From the UNESCO Expert Group Meeting, Oslo, Norway, 24–28 September. Paris: UNESCO.

Kimura, Doreen (1999), "Sex Differences in the Brain." *Scientific American*, Vol. 10, No. 2, pages 26–31.

Kindlon, Dan and Michael Thompson, with Teresa Barker (1999), *Raising Cain: Protecting the Emotional Life of Boys*. New York: The Ballantine Publishing Group.

Kinsley, David (1987), *Hindu Goddesses: Visions of the Divine Feminine in the Hindu Religious Tradition*. New Delhi: Motilal Banarsidass Publishers.

Kirpal, Viney (ed.) (1992), *The Girl Child in 20th Century Indian Literature*. New Delhi: Sterling Publishers.

Klein, Renate, Janice G. Raymond and Lynette J. Dumble (1992), *RU 486: Misconceptions, Myths and Morals*. Dhaka: Narigrantha Prabartana.

Knapp, Jane F. (1998), "Impact of Children Witnessing Violence." Pages 355–64 in Halim Hennes and Alice Calhoun (eds.), *Pediatric Clinics of North America: Violence among Children and Adolescents*, Vol. 45, No. 2 (April).

Knop, Karen (1994), "Why Rethinking the Sovereign State Is Important for Women's International Human Rights Law." Pages 153–64 in Rebecca J. Cook (ed.), *Human Rights of Women: National and International Perspectives*. Philadelphia: University of Pennsylvania Press.

Knutsson, Karl Eric (1997), *Children: Noble Causes or Worthy Citizens?* Aldershot, UK: Arena.

Koenig, Michael, Mian Bozle Hossain, Saifuddin Ahmed and Zoha Haoga (1999), "Individual and Community-Level Determinants of Domestic Violence in Rural Bangladesh." Paper presented at the 1999 Population Association of America Meeting, New York, 25–28 March. Mimeo.

Kothari, Uma (1997), "Women's Paid Domestic Work and Rural Transformation: A Study in South Gujarat." *Economic and Political Weekly*, 26 April, pages WS5–12.

Krane, Julia Elissa (1996), "Violence against Women in Intimate Relations: Insights from Cross-cultural Analyses." *Transcultural Psychiatric Research Review*, Vol. 33.

Krishna, K. P. (1995), "Girl Child and Sexual Victimization." *Social Change*, Vol. 25, No. 2–3 (June–September), pages 124–32. New Delhi: Council for Social Development.

Krishnaraj, Maithreyi (ed.) (1986), *Women's Studies in India: Some Perspectives*. Bombay: Popular Prakashan.

—— (1995a), "E. V. Ramaswamy: Why Was Woman Enslaved?" Pages 43–49 in Maithreyi Krishnaraj, *Remaking Society for Women: Visions Past and Present*. New Delhi: Indian Association of Women's Studies.

—— (1995b), *Remaking Society for Women: Visions Past and Present*. New Delhi: Indian Association of Women's Studies.

Krishnaraj, Maithreyi and Divya Pandey (1990), "Women Assist Change by Not Changing Themselves?" Pages 143–55 in CWDS, *Samya Shakti: A Journal of Women's Studies*, Vols. IV and V. New Delhi: CWDS.

Kulatunga, Sita (1993), *Dari: The Third Wife*. Colombo, Sri Lanka: Pasad Books.

Kumar, Anjali (1996), "Child Sex Abuse: Sexual Bias in Law." *Kali's Yug: Women and Law Journal*, Vol. 1, No. 1 (November), pages 16–17. New Delhi: Women's Action Research and Legal Action for Women.

Kumar, Radha (1993), *The History of Doing: An Illustrated Account of Movements for Women's Rights and Feminism in India, 1800–1990*. New Delhi: Kali for Women.

Kunwar, D. S. (1996), " 'They Had No Right to Punish Me': Rape Victim." *Times of India*, 27 July.

La Tribuna (1994), "Reclamando Nuestros Derechos!" Agosto 1994. Centro de la Tribuna Internacional de la Mujer.

La Tribune (1993), "La violence envers les femmes," March, Bulletin No. 17. Centre de la tribune internationale de la femme.

IACC (n.d.), "A Report on 'Socioeconomic and Legal Status of Women in Nepal' and 'The Survey on Women Workers in Nepal.' " Pulchowk, Lalitpur, Nepal: Legal Aid and Consultancy Centre (IACC).

Ladin, Sharon (1995), "IWRAW to CEDAW Country Reports on: Cuba, Cyprus, Ethiopia, Hungary, Iceland, Paraguay, Philippines, Ukraine, Rwanda." Minneapolis, MN: Hubert H. Humphrey Institute of Public Affairs, University of Minnesota, and IWRAW.

Lahn, Bruce T. and Karin Jegalian (1999), "The Key to Masculinity." *Scientific American*, Vol. 10, No. 2, pages 20–25.

Lall, Kesar (1994), "Proverbs and Sayings from Nepal." Kathmandu: Ratna Pustak Bhandar.

Laporte, Lise and Herta Guttman (1996), "Traumatic Childhood Experiences as Risk Factors for Borderline and Other Personality Disorders." *Journal of Personality Disorders*, Vol. 10, No. 3, pages 247–59.

Lasa, L. I. (1993), "Problems of Adolescent Pregnancy." *Libro de ponencias* (Barcelona), pages 29–53.

Lawyers' Collective (1995), "Custody and Guardianship of Minors." *Legal Aid Handbook*, No. 2. New Delhi: Kali for Women.

Lawyers for Human Rights and Legal Aid (LHRLA), Swiss NGO Programme Office and UNESCO (1997), "Regional Conference on Trafficking in Women and Children in South Asia, Summary Report." Prepared by Dr. Khalida Ghans and Nazish Brohi. Karachi: LHRLA.

Leeza, Sultana and Rachel Kabir (1998), "Marriage Registration in Bangladesh." Dhaka: Ministry of Women and Children Affairs, Government of Bangladesh, with support from UNICEF Bangladesh.

Leslie, Julia (ed.) (1992), *Roles and Rituals for Hindu Women*. New Delhi: Motilal Banarsidass Publishers.

LeVine, Robert A. and Sarah E. LeVine (1997), "Mother's Literacy and Children's Well-being, the Search for Useful Knowledge: A Memorandum to the UNICEF Regional Office for South Asia, Kathmandu, 20 November 1997." Cambridge, MA: Harvard University Graduate School of Education.

LeVine, Robert A., Sarah E. LeVine, Amy Richman, F. Medardo Tapia Uribe, Clara Sunderland Correa and Patrice M. Miller (1991), "Women's Schooling and Child Care in the Demographic Transition: A Mexican Case Study." *Population and Development Review*, Vol. 17, No. 3 (September).

Levy, Clifford J. (1999), "Pataki Proposes Tough Measure to Crack Down on Domestic Violence." *The New York Times*, 5 May, page B1.

Lewis, Paul (1999), "Road to Capitalism Taking Toll On Men in the Former Soviet Bloc." *The New York Times*, 1 August, page 3.

Lim, Lin Lean (ed.) (1998), *The Sex Sector: The Economic and Social Bases of Prostitution in Southeast Asia*. Geneva: International Labour Organization.

Lloyd-Roberts, Sue (1999), "Nepal's Abortion Scandal." *BBC News*, 8 November 1999. *http://news2.thls.bbc.co.uk/hi/english/world/south%5Fasia/newsid%5F501000/501929.stm*.

MacCulloch, Christina (1997), "Domestic Violence: Private Pain, Public Issue." *The IDB Special Report* (November), pages 1–4. Washington, DC: Inter-American Development Bank.

Madsen, Stig Toft (1996), *State, Society and Human Rights in South Asia*. New Delhi: Manohar.

Mahajan, A. (1990), "Instigators of Wife-beating." In Sushma Sood (ed.), *Violence against Women*. Jaipur, India: Arihant Publishers.

Mahajan, Amarjit and Madhurima Mahajan (1995), *Family Violence and Abuse in India*. New Delhi: Deep and Deep Publications.

Maharajan, Pankaj (1999) "Antiquated Law Hinders Battered Women." *The Kathmandu Post*, Vol. VII, No. 176 (14 August), page 1.

Maharashtra Herald (1997), "Planning Commission Urged to Champion Women's Cause" (9 February). Pune, India.

Mahindroo, Hiti (1995), "Report of the Seminar 'Is Law Enough?: Violence against Women and Remedial Actions.' " New Delhi: Centre for Social Research.

Majupuria, Indra (1990), *Tibetan Women Then and Now*. Lashkar (Gwalior), India: M. Devi.

Malenetwork (n.d.), "Statement for Men against Violence by Men." Malenetwork brochure.

Malik, Mahnaz (1993), *Hopes, Dreams and Realities*. Karachi: Royal Book Company.

Malla, Sapana and Yubaraj Sangroula (1998), "Country Report, Nepal: A Study on the Use of the Legal System against Violence to Girls and Women." Mimeo.

Manchanda, R. (1994), "Shame!" *The Hindustan Times* (New Delhi), 21 August, page 5.

Marcus, Rachel (1993), "Violence against Women in Bangladesh, Pakistan, Egypt, Sudan, Senegal, and Yemen." *Bridge: Briefings on Development and Gender*, Report No. 10 (March). The Hague: Ministry of Foreign Affairs.

Masson, Jeffrey Moussaieff (1984), *The Assault on Truth: Freud's Suppression of the Seduction Theory*. New York: Pocket Books.

Matsui, Yayori (1996), *Women in the New Asia: From Pain to Power*. Translated by Noriko Toyokawa and Carolyn Francis. London and New York: Zed Books.

Matthews Grieco, Sara F. and Carlo A. Corsini (1991), *Historical Perspectives on Breastfeeding*. Florence: UNICEF International Child Development Centre and Istituto degli Innocenti.

Mazumdar, Sudip (1995), "Power to the People." *Newsweek*, 11 December, pages 40–41.

Mazumdar, Vina (n.d.), "Women and Development: The South Asian Experience and Expectations." In *Emerging South Asian Order: Hopes and Concerns*. Mimeo from author.

——— (1994), "Amniocentesis and Sex Selection." *Occasional Papers*, No. 21. New Delhi: CWDS.

McCauley, Jeanne et al. (1997), "Clinical Characteristics of Women with a History of Childhood Abuse: Unhealed Wounds." *Journal of the American Medical Society*, Vol. 277, No. 17 (7 May).

McFarlane, Judith et al. (1992), "Assessing for Abuse during Pregnancy: Severity and Frequency of Injuries and Associated Entry into Prenatal Care." *Journal of the American Medical Society*, Vol. 267, No. 23, pages 3,176–78.

McGirk, Tim (1997), "Nepal's Lost Daughters, 'India's Soiled Goods.' " *Time*, 27 January.

Mehdi-Barlas, Zehra (1997), "Silent Screams in the Dark." *Newstrack*, November.

Mehra, Jyoti and B. N. Chattoraj (1995), "Sexual Abuse of the Girl Child." *Social Change*, Vol. 25, No. 2–3 (June–September), pages 133–42. New Delhi: Council for Social Development.

Mehta, Meenakshi (1997), "Report on the Launching of the National Anti-violence Movement." Patna, India. Mimeo (13 May).

Mehta, Rama (1996), *Inside the Haveli*. New Delhi: Penguin Books India.

Meindersma, Christa (1998), "Use of the Legal System in South Asia to Address Violence against Women and Girls: A Regional Overview." Kathmandu: UNICEF Regional Office for South Asia. Mimeo (28 February).

Menon, Ritu and Kamla Bhasin (eds.) (1998), *Borders and Boundaries: Women in India's Partition*. New Delhi: Kali for Women.

Mernissi, Fatima (1991), *The Veil and the Male Elite: A Feminist Interpretation of Women's Rights in Islam*. Reading, MA: Addison-Wesley.

——— (1993), *Women and Islam: An Historical and Theological Enquiry*. New Delhi: Kali for Women.

—— (1994), *Hidden from History: Forgotten Queens of Islam*. Lahore: ASR Publications.

Meron, Theodore (1986), *Human Rights Lawmaking in the United Nations: A Critique of Instruments and Process*. London: Clarendon Press.

Metcalf, Barbara Daly (1992), *Perfecting Women, Maulana 'Ali Thanawai's Bihisti Zewar: A Partial Translation with Commentary*. Berkeley: University of California Press.

MHSA (1995), *Men on Men*. Stockholm: Ministry of Health and Social Affairs.

Mies, Maria (1986), *Patriarchy and Accumulation on a World Scale: Women in the International Division of Labour*. London: Zed Books.

Miller, Barbara (1981a), "Variations in Indian Sex Ratios Today." Pages 68–82 in Barbara Miller, *The Endangered Sex*. Ithaca, NY: Cornell University Press.

—— (1981b), *The Endangered Sex*. Ithaca, NY: Cornell University Press.

Mill, J. S. (1989), *On Liberty and Other Writings*. Edited by Stefan Collini. Cambridge: Cambridge University Press.

Ministry of Health and Family Welfare, Government of Bangladesh (1998), *The Woman Friendly Hospital Initiative: Preventing the Tragedy of Maternal Death and Violence against Women in Bangladesh* (November). Dhaka: Ministry of Health and Family Welfare, Government of Bangladesh, with support from UNICEF.

Minturn, Leigh, with Sivaram Kapoor (1993), *Sita's Daughters: Coming out of Purdah. The Rajput Women of Khalapur Revisited*. New York and Oxford: Oxford University Press.

Mishra, Mira (1999), "Women's Studies in Nepal: An Introduction." *The Kathmandu Post*, 14 August, page 4.

Mishra, Shanti (1994), *Voice of Truth: The Challenges and Struggles of a Nepalese Woman*. New Delhi: Book Faith India.

Mistry, Rohinton (1996), *A Fine Balance*. New York: Knopf.

Mitra, Manoshi (1990), "Women in Santhal Society: Women as Property or Women and Property." Pages 213–27 in CWDS, *Samya Shakti: A Journal of Women's Studies*, Vols. IV and V. New Delhi: CWDS.

Mitra, Rajat (n.d. a), "Violence against Children at Home." Mimeo.

—— (n.d. b), "What Media Needs to Project about Violence." Mimeo.

Mitter, Swasti (1997), "Toys for the Boys." *Development*, Vol. 40, pages 106–109.

Moberg, Eva (1997), "Men are better than male society." *The News on Sunday* (Karachi), 30 November.

Moghadam, Valentine M. (ed.) (1994), *Gender and National Identity: Women and Politics in Muslim Societies*. London: Zed Books.

—— (ed.) (1996), *Patriarchy and Economic Development: Women's Positions at the End of the Twentieth Century*. Oxford: Clarendon Press.

Mookerjee, Ajit (1988), *Kali: The Feminine Force*. London: Thames and Hudson.

Mujtaba, Hasan (1998), "Among the Sand Dunes of the India-Pakistan Border . . ." *Himal* (Kathmandu), Vol. 11, No. 10 (October), pages 30–31.

Mukherjee, Bharati (1993), *The Holder of the World*. New Delhi: Viking Penguin India.

Muller, Carl (1993), *The Jam Fruit Tree*. New Delhi: Penguin Books India.

Mullen, P. E. et al. (1996), "The Long-term Impact of the Physical, Emotional and Sexual Abuse of Children: A Community Study." *Child Abuse and Neglect*, Vol. 20, pages 7–21.

Multiple Action Research Group (1996), "Within the Four Walls: A Profile of Domestic Violence." New Delhi: Multiple Action Research Group.

Mumtaz, Khawar and Farida Shaheed (1987), *Women of Pakistan: Two Steps Forward, One Step Back?* Lahore: Vanguard Books.

Murray, C.J.L. and A. D. Lopez (1996), *The Global Burden of Disease*. Cambridge, MA: Harvard University Press, Harvard School of Public Health.

MYWAS and UNICEF (1995), "Girl Child in the Maldives: A Survey Report." Malé, Maldives: Ministry of Youth, Women's Affairs and Sports.

Nabar, Vrinda (1995), *Caste as Woman*. New Delhi: Penguin Books India.

Nagi, B. S. (1993), *Child Marriage in India: A Study of Its Differential Patterns in Rajasthan*. New Delhi: Mittal Publications.

Nair, Janaki (1996), *Women and Law in Colonial India: A Social History*. New Delhi: Kali for Women.

Narasimhan, Sakuntala (1990), *Sati: A Study of Widow Burning in India*. New Delhi: Viking Penguin India.

—— (1994), "India: From Sati to Sex Determination Tests." Pages 43–52 in Miranda Davies (ed.), *Women and Violence: Realities and Responses Worldwide*. London: Zed Books.

Naripokkho (n.d. a) "Lives Not Valued, Deaths Not Mourned: The Tragedy of Maternal Mortality in Bangladesh." Dhaka: Naripokkho. Mimeo.

—— (n.d. b), "Combating Acid Violence." Dhaka: Naripokkho.

—— (1993), "Agriculture and Environment: Peasant Women in Perspective." Naripokkho/UNIFEM Workshop, Dhaka, Bangladesh, 10–14 February. Dhaka: Naripokkho.

—— (1997), "Gender and Judges: A Pilot Study in Bangladesh." Dhaka: Naripokkho.

—— (1999a), "Tanbazar alert"(updated 8 August). Dhaka: Naripokkho. Mimeo.

—— (1999b), "Networking for an Independent Women's Movement" (28 February). Dhaka: Naripokkho. Mimeo.

Nasrin, Taslima (1994), *Lajja, Shame*. New Delhi: Penguin Books India.

Nath, Madhu Bala (1994), *And Then She Stirred*. New Delhi: Har-Anand Publications.

National Clearinghouse on Family Violence, Canada (1996), "Wife Abuse — The Impact on Children." Ottawa: Health Canada.

—— (1997), "Child Sexual Abuse." Ottawa: Health Canada.

National Crime Records Bureau (1996), *Crime in India 1994*. New Delhi: Ministry of Home Affairs, Government of India.

—— (1999), *Crime in India 1997*. New Delhi: Ministry of Home Affairs, Government of India.

National Film Development Corporation (NFDC) and UNICEF (n.d.), *Sanshodan (The Amendment)*. A film by Govind Nihalani. Mumbai, India: NFDC, Ltd. (Government of India).

National Institutes of Health (1996), "Cervical Cancer: NIH Consensus Statement Online." Vol. 43, No. 1 (1–3 April). *http://www.text.nlm.nih.gov/nih/upload-v3/CDC_Statements/Cervical/cervical.html*.

Nawaz, Mumtaz Shah (1990), *The Heart Divided*. Lahore: ASR Publications.

NAWO (1997), "Supreme Court Judgement on Sexual Harassment at Work Place." *Landmark Judgement Series*, No. 1. New Delhi: National Alliance of Women.

Newar, Naresh (1998), "My Sister Next?" *Himal* (Kathmandu), Vol. 11, No. 10 (October), pages 20–29.

The New York Times (1997), "Women's Killers Are Very Often Their Partners, New Study Finds," pages B1–2.

—— (1999), "36 Percent of Female Inmates say They Were Abused as Children" (12 April), National section, p. A19

The News (Karachi, Pakistan) (1997), "Husband Arrested for Chopping off Wife's Nose," 27 September (Karachi).

The News (Rawalpindi, Pakistan) (1997), "Crisis Centre for Women in Distress Opened," 29 October (Rawalpindi, Pakistan).

The News on Sunday (1997), "TNS Special Report: Needed, Men's Lib," 30 November (Karachi), pages 28–29.

NIPCCD (n.d.), "A Report on Indian Women from Birth to Twenty." New Delhi: Women's Development Division, National Institute of Public Cooperation and Child Development (NIPCCD).

Nisbet, Richard E. and Dov Cohen (1999), "Men, Honor and Murder." *Scientific American*, Vol. 10, No. 2, pages 16–19.

NPC/HMG/N (1996), "Nepal Multiple Indicator Surveillance: Primary Education, Final Report," November. Kathmandu: Secretariat, National Planning Commission (NPC).

NSO (1993), "National Safe Motherhood Survey." Manila: Philippines National Statistics Office (NSO).

Nussbaum, Martha and Jonathan Glover (eds.) (1995), *Women, Culture and Development: A Study of Human Capabilities*. Oxford: Clarendon Press.

O'Dea, Pauline (1993), *Gender Exploitation and Violence: The Market in Women, Girls and Sex in Nepal*. Kathmandu: UNICEF.

O'Hanlon, Rosalind (1997), "Issues of Masculinity in North Indian History: The Bangash Nawabs of Farrukhabad." *Indian Journal of Gender Studies*, Vol. 4, No. 1 (January–June).

O'Keefe, Maura (1994), "Linking Marital Violence, Mother-Child/Father-Child Aggression, and Child Behavior Problems." *Journal of Family Violence*, Vol. 9, No. 1.

—— (1996), "The Differential Effects of Family Violence on Adolescent Adjustment." *Child and Adolescent Social Work Journal*, Vol. 13, No. 1 (February).

Okin, Susan Moller (1989), *Justice, Gender and the Family*. New York: Basic Books.

Omvedt, Gail (1990), "Violence against Women: New Movements and New Theories in India." *Kali Primaries*. New Delhi: Kali for Women.

Onishi, Junko (1996), "The Missing Millions of Females in South Asia: A Literature Review." Kathmandu: UNICEF Regional Office for South Asia. Mimeo (21 August).

Onta-Bhatta, Lazima (1996), "Street Children: Contested Identities and Universalizing Categories." *Studies in Nepali History and Society*, Vol. 1, No. 1 (June). Kathmandu: Centre for Social Research and Development.

Organization of American States (1994), "Inter-American Convention on the Prevention, Punishment, and Eradication of Violence Against Women (Convention of Belém do Pará)." Adopted at Belém do Pará, Brazil, 9 June 1994.

Osofsky, Joy D. (1996), "Introduction." Pages 5–8 in Joy D. Osofsky and Emily Fenichel (eds.), *Islands of Safety*. Washington, DC: Zero to Three, National Center for Infants, Toddlers and Families.

Osofsky, Joy D. and Emily Fenichel (eds.) (1996), *Islands of Safety*. Washington, DC: Zero to Three, National Center for Infants, Toddlers and Families.

Ouellette, Marcy (1998), "Louisiana Office of Public Health Domestic Violence Campaign." Paper presented at the World Conference on Family Violence, Singapore, 8–11 September.

Oxfam (1997), "Men and Masculinity." *Gender and Development*, Vol. 5, No. 2 (June). Oxford: Oxfam.

Pan American Health Organization (1993), "Violence Against Women and Girls: Analysis and Proposals from the Perspective of Public Health." 13th Meeting, Washington, DC, 5–7 April. MSD 13/6.

Pande, Rekha (n.d.), "Anti-Liquor Movement." From the report "A Women's Movement — the Anti Arrack Movement," sponsored by the Department of Women and Child Welfare, Ministry of Human Resources, Government of India 1994–1996. Mimeo (1999).

Pappu, Rekha (1997), "Rethinking Legal Justice for Women." *Economic and Political Weekly*, 10 May.

Parinita (1995), "She Is Stuffed in a Pot." Pages 20–29 in Viji Srinivasan, *If Indian Men Wish*. New Delhi: Har-Anand Publications.

Parker, B. (1993), "Abuse of Adolescents: What Can We Learn from Pregnant Teenagers?" *Awhonn's Clinical Issues in Perinatal and Women's Health Nursing*, pages 363–70.

Parker, B., J. McFarlane, K. Soeken, S. Torres and D. Campbell (1993), "Physical and Emotional Abuse in Pregnancy: A Comparison of Adult and Teenage Women." *Nursing Research*, Vol. 42, No. 3 (May–June), pages 173–78.

Paul, Sumita and Vandana Agarwal (1997), "How Her Sex Works against a Working Woman." *Sunday Times of India*, 24 August, page 19.

Peled, Einat, Peter G. Jaffe and Jeffrey L. Edleson (eds.) (1994), *Ending the Cycle of Violence: Community Responses to Children of Battered Women*. Thousand Oaks, CA: Sage Publications.

The People's Review (1997), "Scourge of dowry raising its head," 21 August (Nepal). *http://www.info-nepal.com/p-review/august97/august-21/scourge.html*

Physicians for Human Rights (1998), *The Taliban's War on Women: A Health and Human Rights Crisis in Afghanistan*. Boston, MA: Physicians for Human Rights.

Pinker, Steven (1997), *How the Mind Works*. London: Penguin Books.

Pipher, Mary (1995), *Reviving Ophelia: Saving the Selves of Adolescent Girls*. New York: Ballantine Books.

Pollack, William (1988), *Real Boys: Rescuing Our Sons from the Myths of Boyhood*. New York: Henry Holt and Company.

Population Action International (1994), "Sexual Health of Adolescents Threatened by Lack of Services" (4 April). *http://www.populationaction.org/programs/youth.htm*.

Pradhan, Bina (1979), "Institutions Concerning Women in Nepal." *The Status of Women in Nepal*, Vol. I: Background Report, Part 3. Kathmandu: Centre for Economic Development and Administration, Tribhuvan University.

Pradhan, Bina and Dudley L. Preston, Jr. (1997), "Women's Autonomy and Reproductive Health in Nepal: New Issues and Perspectives in Demographic Thinking." Paper prepared for the annual meeting of the Population Association of America, Washington, DC, 27–29 March.

Pradhan, Gauri (1996), "Violence against Women in Nepal: Realities, Challenges and Change: Domestic Violence in Nepal." Kathmandu: CWIN.

Pradhan, Sapana (n.d.), "Judicial Interpretation and Gender Discrimination." Mimeo.

Progressive Women's Association (n.d.), "Trial by FIRE." Islamabad: Progressive Women's Association.

PromPT (1996), "Dowry: Poor People's Perspectives" (October). Dhaka: PromPT.

Purewal, Jasjit (1995), "Sexual Violence and the Girl Child." *Social Change*, Vol. 25, No. 2–3 (June–September), pages 154–60. New Delhi: Council for Social Development.

Quisumbing, Agnes R. (1996), "Male-Female Differences in Agricultural Productivity: Methodological Issues and Empirical Evidence." *World Development*, Vol. 24, No. 10, pages 1579–95.

Qureshi, Asma Fazia, Narjis Rizvi, Fauziah Rabbani and Fatima Sajan (1999), "Domestic Violence: Determinants and Consequences." A study from Karachi, Pakistan. Report prepared for WHO Centre, Kobe, Japan (October). Karachi: Department of Community Health Sciences, The Aga Khan University.

Radhakrishan, Mita (1995), "Feminism, Family and Social Change: Myths and Models." Pages 179–99 in Rudolf C. Heredia and Edward Mathias (eds.), *The Family in a Changing World: Women, Children and Strategies of Intervention*. New Delhi: Indian Social Institute Delhi.

Rai, Lal Deosa (1995), *Human Rights in the Hindu-Buddhist Tradition*. Jaipur, India: Nirala.

Raikes, A. (1990), *Pregnancy, Birthing and Family Planning in Kenya, Changing Patterns of Behaviour: A Health Utilization Study in Kissi District*. Copenhagen: Centre for Development Research.

Rajasthan University Women's Association (1994), *Shakti* (January). Jaipur, India: Rajasthan University Women's Association.

Rajbhandari, Renu and Binayak Rajbhandari (1997), "Girl Trafficking: The Hidden Grief in Himalayas." Kathmandu: Women's Rehabilitation Centre.

Rajgopal, P. R. (1987), *Social Change and Violence: The Indian Experience*. New Delhi: Centre for Policy Research.

Raju, Saraswati, Peter Atkins, Narresh Kumar and Janet G. Townsend (1999), *Atlas of Women and Men in India*. New Delhi: Department for International Development, India, British High Commission and Kali for Women.

Råkil, Marius (n.d.), "Counselling Men Battering Their Partners." Oslo: Alternative to Violence. Mimeo.

Ramalingaswami, Vulimiri, Urban Jonsson and Jon Rohde (1996), "The Asian Enigma." Pages 11–17 in UNICEF, *The Progress of Nations 1996*. New York: UNICEF.

Ramanujan, A. K. (ed.) (1993), *Folktales from India: A Selection of Oral Tales from Twenty-two Languages*. New Delhi: Penguin Books India.

Ramu, G. N. (1990), " 'Men Don't Cry, and Men Don't Cook and Clean': A Study of Housework among Urban Couples." Pages 156–74 in CWDS, *Samya Shakti: A Journal of Women's Studies*, Vols. IV and V. New Delhi: CWDS.

Ranasinghe, Anne (1991), *Not Even Shadows*. Colombo, Sri Lanka: English Writers' Cooperative of Sri Lanka.

Rape Crisis Center (n.d.), "Statistics." *www.rapecrisis.org.za/statistics.htm*. South Africa: Rape Crisis Center. Mimeo.

Rao, Arati (1996), "Right in the Home: Feminist Theoretical Perspectives in Interactive Human Rights." Pages 100–21 in Ratna Kapur (ed.) *Feminist Terrains in Legal Domains: Interdisciplinary Essays on Women and Law in India.* New Delhi: Kali for Women.

Rao, Vijayendra and Francis Bloch (1993), "Wife-beating, Its Causes and Its Implications for Nutrition Allocations to Children: An Economic and Anthropological Case Study of a Rural Indian Community." Washington, DC: Policy Research Department, Poverty and Human Resources Division, World Bank.

Rauch, Mikele and John Jones (1995), "Effective Group Therapy with Male Survivors of Sexual Abuse." *http://www.yesican.org./articles/icanjj.html.*

Ravindra, R. P. (1993), "The Campaign against Sex Discrimination Tests." Pages 51–101 in Chhaya Datar (ed.), *The Struggle against Violence.* Calcutta: Stree.

Rehman, Samina (ed.) (1994), *In Her Own Write: Short Stories by Women Writers in Pakistan.* Lahore: ASR Publications.

Reilly, Niamh (ed.), (1996), *Without Reservation: The Beijing Tribunal on Accountability for Women's Human Rights.* New Brunswick, NJ: Center for Women's Global Leadership, Douglass College, Rutgers University.

Richie, Beth E. and Christine Johnsen (1996), "Abuse Histories among Newly Incarcerated Women in a New York City Jail." *Journal of the American Medical Women's Association,* Vol. 51, No. 3 (May/July).

Richters, J. (1994), *Women, Culture and Violence: A Development, Health and Human Rights Issue.* Leiden, The Netherlands: Women and Autonomy Centre.

Rimal, Sarita and Bhagirath Yogi (1997), "The Nightmare Continues." *Spotlight,* 16 May.

Roberts, Kristin (1995), "Fathers, Families, Children: A Cross-cultural Bibliography." New York: NGO Working Group on Education, UNICEF.

Rogers, Barbara (1980), *The Domestication of Women: Discrimination in Developing Societies.* London: Routledge.

Rose, Kalima (1992), *Where Women Are Leaders: The SEWA Movement in India.* London: Zed Books.

Rosenfeld, Megan (1998), "What Nobody ever Bothered to Ask about Boys." *International Herald Tribune,* 27 March.

Ross, Asirvatham V. (n.d.), *Dowry Murder.* New Delhi.

Roth, Kenneth (1994), "Domestic Violence as an International Human Rights Issue." Pages 326–39 in Rebecca J. Cook (ed.), *Human Rights of Women: National and International Perspectives.* Philadelphia: University of Pennsylvania Press.

Roy, Arundhati (1999), *The Cost of Living.* New York: Modern Library.

SAARC (n.d.), "Convention on Preventing and Combating Trafficking in Women and Children." SAARC/Summit.10/CM.20/3 Annex III. Mimeo.

——— (1995), "Dhaka Resolution on Women." SAARC Ministerial Meeting on Women: Towards the Fourth World Conference on Women in Beijing, 29–30 July, Dhaka.

——— (1996), "Rawalpindi Resolution on Children of South Asia" (22 August). Rawalpindi, Pakistan: South Asian Association for Regional Cooperation (SAARC).

——— (1997), "Declaration of the Ninth SAARC Summit." Malé, Maldives: South Asian Association for Regional Cooperation.

Saathi (n.d. a), "Breaking the Silence of Victims: A Profile of SAATHI Nepal." Kathmandu: Saathi. Mimeo.

——— (n.d. b), "Results of a Pilot Study on Domestic Violence in Kathmandu." Kathmandu: Saathi. Mimeo.

——— (1997a), "A National Survey on Violence against Women and Girls in Nepal." Kathmandu: ActionAid.

——— (1997b), "Violence against Women and Girls in Nepal." Kathmandu: The Asia Foundation.

Sabbadini, Linda Laura (1998), "Molestie e Violenze Sessuali." Rome: National Statistical Institute. Mimeo (22 September).

Safe Motherhood (1998), "Fact Sheet: Unwanted Pregnancy." *http://www.safemotherhood.org/factsheets/unwanted_pregnancy.htm.*

Saha, B. P. (1994), *Growing Violence in Rural Areas: A Sociological, Political and Economic Analysis.* New Delhi: Vikas Publishing House.

Saifullah, M. (1997), "Cruel Numbers." *Sahil against Child Sexual Abuse,* No. 5 (July–September), pages 18–19.

Saini, Vishal (n.d.), "Violence Women Face." First prize in the General Category of the Second Unnati Competition sponsored by UNIFEM. New Delhi: UNNATI Features. Mimeo.

Saltus, Richard (1998), "New Theory on Cause of War: An Overabundance of Young Men." *San Francisco Chronicle,* 3 October, page A7.

Samarasinghe, Nandini (1992), "International Trafficking and Labour Migration of Women and Children from South Asia." Paper presented at the Commonwealth Workshop on Trafficking of Women and Children and Labour Migration in South Asia, Dhaka.

——— (1993), "Rights Discourse and Gender Equality." Mimeo.

——— (1994), "Violence against Women." Colombo, Sri Lanka: Law and Society Trust. Mimeo.

Sangari, Kumkum and Uma Chakravati (eds.) (1999), "From Myths to Markets: Essay on Gender." Shimla: Indian Institute of Advanced Study; New Delhi: Manohar Publishers and Distributors.

Sangroula, Yubaraj and Sapana Pradhan Malla (n.d.), "A Study on the Use of Legal System Against Violence on Girls and Women." Submitted to Regional Office UNICEF. Kathmandu: UNICEF Regional Office for South Asia. Mimeo.

Sangwan, Soni (1996), "Minors Bear with Unwanted Motherhood." *Hindustan Times* (New Delhi), 19 August.

Santos Pais, Marta (1997), "Human Rights in Development: The Role of Advisory Services and Technical Assistance." Paper presented at the seminar The Universal Protection of Human Rights: Translating International Commitments into National Action, Salzburg, July 1997. Mimeo.

Sarah, Rachel (1999), "Getting Both Personal and Political in Male Involvement." *ICPD+5 Watch,* 26 March. Women's Feature Service.

Sariola, Heikki and Antti Uutela (1992), "The Prevalence and Context of Family Violence against Children in Finland." *Child Abuse and Neglect,* Vol. 16, pages 823–32.

Sarkar, Tanika (1996), "Colonial Lawmaking and Lives/Deaths of Indian Women: Different Readings of Law and Community." Pages 210–42 in Ratna Kapur (ed.), *Feminist Terrains in Legal Domains: Interdisciplinary Essays on Women and Law in India.* New Delhi: Kali for Women.

SCA and UNICEF (1998), "Workshop on Alternate Masculinities in South Asia." Kathmandu: Save the Children (UK) and UNICEF Regional Office for South Asia. Video.

Schuler, Margaret A. (ed.) (1992), *Freedom from Violence: Women's Strategies from around the World.* New York: UNIFEM.

——— (ed.) (1995), *From Basic Needs to Basic Rights.* Washington, DC: Women, Law and Development International.

Schuler, Margaret A. and Dorothy Q. Thomas (eds.) (1997), *Women's Human Rights Step by Step.* Washington, DC: Women, Law and Development International and Human Rights Watch.

Schuler, S. R., S. M. Hashemi and S. H. Badal (1998), "Men's Violence against Women in Bangladesh: Undermined or Exacerbated by Microcredit Programme?" *Development in Practice,* Vol. 8, No. 2, pages 145–57.

Scientific American (1999), *Men: The Scientific Truth about Their Work, Play, Health and Passions,* Vol. 10, No. 2 (summer). New York: Scientific American, Inc.

SEARCH Bulletin (1998), "Female Infanticide." *SEARCH Bulletin,* Vol. 13, No. 3 (July/Sept.). Bangalore: SEARCH.

Sen, Amartya K. (1990), "More than 100 Million Women Are Missing." *The New York Review of Books,* Vol. xxxvii, No. 20 (December), pages 61–66.

——— (1993a), "Africa and India: What Do We have to Learn from Each Other?" *WIDER Discussion Papers,* No. 19. Helsinki: UNU/WIDER.

——— (1993b), "The Economics of Life and Death." *Scientific American,* May.

——— (1995), "Mortality as an Indicator of Economic Success and Failure." *Innocenti Lectures,* No. 1, 3 March. Florence: UNICEF International Child Development Centre.

——— (1999), "Keynote Speech: A Decade of Human Development." First Global Forum on Human Development, 29–31 July. New York: Human Development Report Office, UNDP. Mimeo.

Sen, Gita (1997), "Globalization, Justice and Equity: A Gender Perspective." *Development*, Vol. 40, No. 2, pages 21–26.

Sen, Mala (1993), *India's Bandit Queen: The True Story of Phoolan Devi*. New Delhi: HarperCollins Publishers India.

Seth, Vikram (1993), *A Suitable Boy*. London: Phoenix House.

Sethu (1995), *Pandavapuram*. Madras: Macmillan India.

SEWA (n.d. a), "SEWA, the Self-employed Women's Association." Lucknow, India: SEWA.

——— (n.d. b), "SEWA at a Glance." Lucknow, India: SEWA.

——— (1996), "SEWA, the Self-employed Women's Association." Ahmedabad, India: Mahila SEWA Trust.

Shaha, Rishikesh (1996), "Human Rights and SAARC." *South Asian Survey*, Vol. 3, No. 1–2 (January–December).

Shaheed, Farida (1994), "The Experience in Pakistan." Pages 213–19 in Miranda Davies (ed.), *Women and Violence: Realities and Responses Worldwide*. London: Zed Books.

Sharabi, Hisham (1988), *Neopatriarchy: A Theory of Distorted Change in Arab Society*. New York: Oxford University Press.

Sharma, Arvind and Katherine K. Young (eds.), (1999), *Feminism and World Religions*. New York: State University of New York Press.

Sharma, Manish (1996), *When Fathers Rape: A Socio-Psycho-Legal-Global Study*. New Delhi: A.P.H. Publishing.

Sharma, O. C. (ed.) (1994), *Crime against Women*. New Delhi: Ashish Publishing House.

Sheikh, Misbah M. (1997), "Unveiling Violence in South Asia: A Priority for Action." Kathmandu: UNICEF Regional Office for South Asia. Mimeo (June).

Sherpa, Helen and Dibya Rai (1997), "Safe Motherhood: It Is a Family Responsibility." Kathmandu: Centre for Development and Population Activities Field Office.

Shirali, Kishwar Ahmed (ed.) (1995), *Dance of Madness: We Indian Women*. Shimla, India: ASK (Atma Swasthya Kendra), Psychology Department, H.P. University.

Shirkat Gah (1997), "Shirkat Gah Women's Resource Centre in Lahore, Pakistan." Lahore: Shirkat Gah. Mimeo.

Shiva, Vandana (1991), *Ecology and the Politics of Survival: Conflicts over Natural Resources in India*. New Delhi: UN University Press and Sage.

——— (ed.) (1993), *Minding our Lives: Women from the South and North Reconnect Ecology and Health*. New Delhi: Kali for Women.

——— (1995), "Women, Ecology and Economic Globalization: Searching for an Alternative Vision." New Delhi: Indian Association of Women's Studies.

Shourie, Arun (1995), *The World of Fatwas, or the Shariah in Action*. New Delhi: ASA Publications.

Shrader Cox, Elizabeth (1994), "Gender Violence and Women's Health in Central America." In Miranda Davies (ed.), *Women and Violence: Realities and Responses Worldwide*. London: Zed Books.

Shtrii Shakti (1995), *Women, Development, Democracy: A Study of the Socioeconomic Changes in the Profile of Women in Nepal*. New Delhi: Shtrii Shakti.

Siddiqi, Dina M. (1998), "Taslima Nasreen and Others: The Contest over Gender in Bangladesh." Pages 205–48 in Herbert Bodman and Nayereh Tohidi (eds.), *Women in Muslim Societies: Diversity Within Unity*. Boulder, CO: Lynne Rienner Publishers, Inc.

Sidhwa, Bapsi (1984), *The Bride*. London: Futura Macdonald.

Silver, Lee M. (1998), "A Quandary That Isn't: Picking a Baby Won't Lead to Disaster." *Time*, 21 September, page 98.

Simon, Harvey B. (1999), "Longevity: The Ultimate Gender Gap." *Scientific American*, Vol. 10, No. 2, pages 107–12.

Simons, Marlise (1998a), "Cry of Muslim Women for Equal Rights Is Rising." *New York Times*, 8 March.

——— (1998b), "Islamic Feminists Speak a Little Louder against Inequalities." *International Herald Tribune*, 10 March.

——— (1999), "Unmarried Mothers Outcasts in Morocco." *International Herald Tribune*, 2 February, page 2.

Simorgh (1990), *Rape*. Lahore, Pakistan. Mimeo.

Singh, Chitralekha and Prem Nath (1995), *Hindu Goddesses*. New Delhi: Crest Publishing House.

Singh, Khushwant (1989), *I Shall Not Hear the Nightingale*. New Delhi: Time Books International.

Singh, Khushwant and Shobha Dé (eds.) (1993), *Uncertain Liaisons: Sex, Strife and Togetherness in Urban India*. New Delhi: Viking Penguin India.

Singh, Kirti (1994), "Obstacles to Women's Rights in India." Pages 375–96 in Rebecca J. Cook (ed.), *Human Rights of Women: National and International Perspectives*. Philadelphia: University of Pennsylvania Press.

——— (1996), "Change the Rape Law." *Pioneer*, 24 July.

——— (1998), "Violence against Women and Girls in India." Mimeo.

Singh, N. K. (1997), "Judges in the Dock." *India Today*, 25 August.

Singh, Preeti and Deepali Vasudev (1996), "Tunnel Vision." *Financial Express* (New Delhi), 2 March.

Singh, Shailendra K. (ed.) (1994), *Poems by Nepali Women*. New Delhi: Book Faith India.

Sinha, Mrinalini (1997), *Colonial Masculinity: The "Manly Englishman" and the "Effeminate Bengali" in the Late Nineteenth Century*. New Delhi: Kali for Women.

Siriwardena, Regi (1994), "The Almsgiving and Other Plays." Colombo, Sri Lanka.

Sisterhood Is Global Institute (1998), *Safe and Secure: Eliminating Violence Against Women and Girls in Muslim Societies*. Bethesda, MD: Sisterhood Is Global Institute.

——— (1999), "Strategizing for Safety: Essays from the Expert Group Meeting on Eliminating Violence Against Women and Girls, 3 October 1998." Bethesda, MD: Sister Is Global Institute.

Sivard, Ruth Leger (1995), *Women: A World Survey*. Washington, DC: World Priorities.

Snively, Suzanne (1994), "The New Zealand Economic Cost of Family Violence." Wellington, New Zealand: Family Violence Unit, Government of New Zealand. Mimeo.

Sobhan, Salma (1994), "National Identity, Fundamentalism and the Women's Movement in Bangladesh." Pages 63–80 in Valentine Moghadam (ed.), *Gender and National Identity*. London: Zed Books.

Sobritchea, Carolyn I. and Lorna Israel (1997), "A Review of Conceptual Frameworks and Studies of Family Violence." Pages 13–33 in Sylvia H. Guerrero and Carolyn I. Sobritchea, *Breaking the Silence: The Realities of Family Violence in the Philippines and Recommendations for Change*. New York: UNICEF.

South Asian Declaration on Food Safety (n.d.), "The South Asian Declaration on Food Safety." Presented at international meeting in New Delhi, 1–August (no date given). Mimeo.

Sri Aurobindo Society (1978), *On Women: Compiled from the Writings of Sri Aurobindo and The Mother*. Pondicherry, India: Sri Aurobindo Society.

Sri Lanka Women's NGO Forum (1997), *Moving Forward towards the 21st Century: A Handbook on Implementing the Beijing Platform for Action on Women*. Colombo, Sri Lanka: Sri Lanka Women's NGO Forum.

——— (1999), *Sri Lanka Shadow Report on the UN Convention on the Elimination of All Forms of Discrimination against Women*. Colombo: Sri Lanka Women's NGO Forum, with the assistance of the Canadian International Development Agency.

Srinivasan, Viji (1995), *If Indian Men Wish*. New Delhi: Har-Anand Publications.

Srinivasan, Viji, Parnita Vijay, Alice Shankar, Mukul Medha and Amila Kumari (n.d.), "Female Infanticide in Bihar." Patna, Bihar: Adithi. Mimeo.

Steiner, R. Prasaad, Kaycia Vansickle and Steven B. Lippmann (1996), "Domestic Violence: Do You Know When and How to Intervene?" *Postgraduate Medicine*, Vol. 100, No. 1 (July).

Steinfels, Peter (1997), "Church Held Liable for Molestations." *International Herald Tribune*, 26–27 July.

Stephenson, Patricia (1996), "Domestic Violence: The Hidden Epidemic." For UNICEF. Mimeo (10 November).

Stevens, Lynne (n.d.), "Bringing Order to Chaos: A Framework for Understanding and Treating Sexual Abuse Survivors." Mimeo.

Stewart, Nell (1999), "Honour Killings: Human Rights Defenders Face Death Threats While Killers Walk Free."

Human Rights Tribune, Vol. 6, No. 3 (September), pages 26–27.

Stolberg, Sheryl Gay (1999), "Racial Divide Found in Maternal Mortality." *The New York Times*, 17 June.

Straus, M. and R. Gelles (1986), "Societal Change and Change in Family Violence from 1975 to 1985 as Revealed by Two National Surveys." *Journal of Marriage and the Family*, Vol. 48, pages 465–79.

Stree Aadhar Kendra (1997), "The Law Enforcement Machinery and Violence against Women," 7 February. Pune, India: Stree Aadhar Kendra.

Suárez Toro, María and Roxana Arroyo Vargas (n.d.), "Towards a Methodology for the Popularization of Women's Human Rights." San José, Costa Rica: People's Decade of Human Rights Education.

Subedi, Prativa (1999), "Women and Human Rights." *The Kathmandu Post*, 20 August, page 4.

Sullivan, Donna (1996), "Integration of Women's Human Rights into the Work of the Special Rapporteurs." New York: UNIFEM.

Sunday Pioneer (1999), "Rapist Father Gets Death," 22 August, pages 1 and 4, New Delhi.

Sunder Rajan, Rajeswari (1993), *Real and Imagined Women: Gender, Culture and Postcolonialism*. London: Routledge.

Support Group for the Karvi Child Abuse Case (1999), "Urgent Appeal Re: The Karvi Child Sexual Abuse Case." New Delhi: The Support Group for the Karvi Child Sexual Abuse Case. Mimeo (9 August).

Syed, Dr. Shershah (n.d. a), "Life Cycle of Pakistani Women." Mimeo.

—— (n.d. b), "Poverty, Women Rights and Maternal Death." Karachi: Sobhraj Maternity Hospital. Mimeo.

Tamrakar, Mandira and Mira Mishra (1995), "Social Construction of Violence in School: Notes from Kathmandu." Paper presented at VII National Conference on Women's Studies, 27–30 December, Jaipur, India.

TAMWA (1998), "Using the Media to Promote CEDAW: The Experience of TAMWA." Dar es Salaam: Tanzania Media Women's Association (TAMWA).

Thapalia, Shanta (n.d. a), "The Initiatives for Legal Literacy and Legal Awareness as an Intervention to Eliminate Violence against Women and Girls." Kathmandu: Legal Aid and Consultancy Centre. Mimeo.

—— (n.d. b), "Success Story of the Intervention Undertaken." Mimeo.

—— (n.d. c), "What Motivated Me the Most to Serve the Social Development Sector." Mimeo.

Tharu, Susie and K. Lalita (eds.) (1993a), *Women Writing in India: 600 B.C. to the Present, Vol. I: 600 B.C. to the Early 20th Century*. New Delhi: Oxford University Press.

—— (eds.) (1993b), *Women Writing in India: 600 B.C. to the Present, Vol. II: The 20th Century*. New York: The Feminist Press at the City University of New York.

Thero, Koswatte Ariyawimala (1993), *Child Care in Buddhism*. Colombo, Sri Lanka: Postgraduate Institute of Pali and Buddhist Studies, University of Kelaniya and UNICEF.

Times of India (1996a), "Women's Groups Hail Verdict," 8 August.

—— (1996b), "Court Orders FIR against Bajaj Couple," 8 August.

—— (1996c), "K.P.S. Gill Will Appeal against Verdict," 8 August.

—— (1997a), "Girl, Raped by Father, Abandoned by Family, Seeks Justice," 22 June.

—— (1997b), "PM to Make Public Scheme for Girl Child on August 15," 12 August.

—— (1997c), "NCW Members Probing Rape of Girl Attacked," 16 August.

The Tribune (1996), "Power: Converting Information Into Power! Using the Platform for Action," Newsletter 55 (September). International Women's Tribune Centre.

—— (1997), "Global/Local Strategies for Change: Women Take on the World," Newsletter 56 (April). International Women's Tribune Centre.

Turnbull, Colin (1972), *The Mountain People*. New York: Simon and Schuster.

Twin-City Home News (1997), "Pakistan Human Rights Remain Grim, Says HRCP Report," 1 April.

UBINIG (n.d.), "Nayakrishi Andolon: An Initiative of the Peasants of Bangladesh for a Happy Life." Dhaka: UBINIG.

—— (1994), "Faces of Coercion: Sterilization, Tearing apart Organs." Dhaka: Narigrantha Prabartana.

Udagama, D. (1991), "Sexual Harassment." *LST Fortnightly Review* (Sri Lanka), Vol. II, No. 29.

Ugalde, Juan Gerardo (1988), "Sindrome de la Mujer Agredida." *Mujer* (San José, Costa Rica), page 5.

Ul Haq, Mahbub and Khadija Haq (1997), *Human Development in South Asia 1997*. Karachi: Oxford University Press.

—— (1998), *Human Development in South Asia 1998*. Karachi: Oxford University Press.

UN (1983), "Indirect Techniques for Demographic Estimation, Annex 1: The Singulate Mean Age of Marriage." *Population Studies*, No. 81. New York: Department of International Economic and Social Affairs, United Nations.

—— (1988), *Human Rights: A Compilation of International Instruments*. New York: United Nations.

—— (1989a), *1989 World Survey on the Role of Women in Development*. New York: United Nations.

—— (1989b), *Violence against Women in the Family*. Sales No. E.89.IV.5. New York: United Nations.

—— (1991), "The World's Women 1970–1990: Trends and Statistics." *Social Statistics and Indicators*, Series K, No. 8. New York: United Nations.

—— (1993a), *Women's Indicators and Statistics Database, 1970–1993*, version 3. New York: United Nations. CD-ROM.

—— (1993b), "Declaration on the Elimination of Violence against Women," A/RES/48/104, 20 December. New York: United Nations.

—— (1993c), "Understanding the Problem." Pages 1–9 Miranda Davies (ed.), *Women and Violence: Realities and Responses Worldwide*. London: Zed Books.

—— (1995a), "Population Consensus at Cairo, Mexico City and Bucharest: An analytical comparison," ST/ESA/SER.R/ 142. New York: United Nations.

—— (1995b), "Population and Development: Programme of Action adopted at the International Conference on Population and Development, Cairo, 5–13 September 1994," ST/ESA/SER.A/149. New York: United Nations.

—— (1995c), "Report of the Fourth World Conference on Women," A/CONF.177/20, 17 October. New York: United Nations.

—— (1995d), "Report of the International Conference on Population and Development," 5–13 September 1994, Cairo, A/CONF.171/13/Rev.1. New York: United Nations.

—— (1995e), "Summary of the Programme of Action of the International Conference on Population and Development: ICPD '94." New York: UNDPI.

—— (1995f), *Women's Indicators and Statistics Database (Wistat)*, version 3. Sales No. E.95.XVII.6. New York: United Nations. CD-ROM.

—— (1996a), *Family: Challenges for the Future*. New York: United Nations Publications.

—— (1996b), "Secretary-General Restates United Nations Policy on Gender Equality in Response to Concerns about Status of Women in Afghanistan." Press Release, SG/SM/ 6072 AFG/70, 7 October.

—— (1997), "Report of the United Nations Interagency Gender Mission to Afghanistan, 12–24 November 1997." New York: Office of the Special Advisor on Gender Issues and Advancement of Women, United Nations.

—— (1998), "Follow-up to the Fourth World Conference on Women: Implementation of Strategic Objectives and Action in the Critical Areas of Concern: Thematic Issues before the Commission on the Status of Women, Report of the Secretary-General," 23 January, E/CN.6/1998/5. New York: United Nations.

—— (1999a), "Human Rights: Integration of the Human Rights of Women and the Gender Perspective, Violence against Women." Report of the Special Rapporteur on violence against women, its causes and consequences, Ms. Radhika Coomaraswamy, E/CN.4/1999/68/Add.1.

—— (1999b), Human Rights: "Integration of the Human Rights of Women and the Gender Perspective, Violence against Women." Report of the Special Rapporteur on violence against women, its causes and consequences,

Ms. Radhika Coomaraswamy, in accordance with Commission on Human Rights resolution 1997/44, E/CN.4/1999/68/Add.4.

—— (1999c), "Nepalese Women Suffer from Ill Health, Poverty, Legal Discrimination Women's Anti-discrimination Committee Told." Committee on Elimination of Discrimination against Women, Twenty-first Session, 434th Meeting (AM); WOM/1136. *http://www.un.org/news.*

UNAIDS (1999), "Estimated number of children newly infected with HIV during 1997." *http://www.unaids.org/unaids/graphics/1997/report97/sld008.html.*

UNAIDS and WHO, "AIDS Epidemic update: December 1998." Geneva: UNAIDS, Joint United Nations Programme on AIDS.

UNCHR (1994), "Preliminary report submitted by the Special Rapporteur on violence against women, its causes and consequences, Ms. Radhika Coomaraswamy, in accordance with Commission on Human Rights Resolution 1994/45," 22 November, No. E/CN.4/1995/42. New York: Commission on Human Rights, Economic and Social Council, United Nations.

—— (1995), "Report of the Special Rapporteur on violence against women, its causes and consequences, submitted in accordance with the Commission on Human Rights Resolution 1995/85, and addendum 2: A framework for model legislation on domestic violence." UN Document E/CN.4/1996/53 and Add. 2.

—— (1996), "Report of the Special Rapporteur on violence against women, its causes and consequences, Ms. Radhika Coomaraswamy: Addendum: Report on the mission of the Special Rapporteur to Poland on the issues of trafficking and forced prostitution of women (24 May to 1 June 1996)," 10 December, No. E/CN.4/1997/47/Add.1. New York: Commission on Human Rights, Economic and Social Council, United Nations.

—— (1997a), "Concluding observations of the Human Rights Committee: India," 4 August, CCPR/C/79/Add.81. Geneva: United Nations Human Rights Committee.

—— (1997b), "Report of the Special Rapporteur on violence against women, its causes and consequences, Ms. Radhika Coomaraswamy: Addendum, Report on the mission of the Special Rapporteur to Brazil on the issue of domestic violence 15–26 July 1996," 21 January, No. E/CN.4/1997/47/Add.2. New York: Commission on Human Rights, Economic and Social Council, United Nations.

—— (1997c), "Report of the Special Rapporteur on violence against women, its causes and consequences, Ms. Radhika Coomaraswamy: Addendum," 30 January, No. E/CN.4/1997/47/Add.4. New York: Commission on Human Rights, Economic and Social Council, United Nations.

—— (1997d), "Report of the Special Rapporteur on violence against women, its causes and consequences, Ms. Radhika Coomaraswamy," 12 February, No. E/CN.4/1997/47. New York: Commission on Human Rights, Economic and Social Council, United Nations.

UN Commission on the Status of Women (1998), Listen to Girls: A forum sponsored by the NGO Working Groups on Girls, 2–13 March 1998.

UN Division for the Advancement of Women (UNDAW) (1999), "Judicial Colloquium on the Application of International Human Rights Law at the Domestic Level: Communiqué." Vienna: United Nations Office at Vienna, Austria.

UNDP (1994), *Human Development Report 1994.* New York: Oxford University Press.

—— (1995), *Human Development Report 1995.* New York: Oxford University Press.

—— (1996), *Human Development Report 1996.* New York: Oxford University Press.

—— (1998), *Human Development Report 1998.* New York: Oxford University Press.

—— (1999), "Gender Reference Guide, Mainstreaming Gender Equality." Kathmandu: UNDP in Nepal.

UNDPI (1996a), "Women and Violence." United Nations Department of Public Information, DPI/1772/HR, February 1996, dpil 772e.htm at *http://www.un.org.*

—— (1996b), "Platform for Action and the Beijing Declaration." New York: UNDPI.

UN Economic and Social Council (ECOSOC) (1995a), "Preparations for the Fourth World Conference on Women: Action for Equality, Development and Peace," 13 January, E/CN.6/1995/2. New York: United Nations.

—— (1995b), "Follow-up to the Fourth World Conference on Women," 3 November, E/ICEF/1996/3. New York: United Nations.

—— (1997), "Synthesized Report on National Action Plans and Strategies for the Implementation of the Beijing Platform for Action: Report of the Secretary-General," 22 December. New York: United Nations.

—— (1998a), "Implementation of Strategic Objectives and Action in the Critical Areas of Concern: Thematic Issues before the Commission on the Status of Women, Report of the Secretary-General." New York: United Nations.

—— (1998b), "Commission on the Status of Women, Report on the Forty-Second Session (2–13 March 1998), Economic and Social Council." Official Records, 1998 Supplement No. 7, E/1998/27 E/CN.6/1998/12. New York: United Nations.

UNESCO (1995), "Women's Contributions to a Culture of Peace." Statement for the Fourth World Conference on Women, Beijing. Paris: UNESCO.

—— (1997), "Male Roles and Masculinities in the Perspective of a Culture of a Peace." Report of the Expert Group Meeting, Oslo, Norway, 24–28 September. Paris: UNESCO.

UNFPA (1994), "Programme of Action adopted at the International Conference on Population and Development, Cairo, 5–13 September 1994." Cairo: United Nations Population Fund (UNFPA).

—— (1995), "Statement by Dr. Nafis Sadik, Executive Director, United Nations Population Fund at the Fourth World Conference on Women, Beijing, 5th September, 1995." Mimeo.

—— (1996), "National Perspectives on Population and Development: Synthesis of 168 national reports prepared for the International Conference on Population and Development," 1994;E/4200/1995/R-1000/1996. New York: UNFPA.

—— (1998a), "AIDS Update 1998: A Report on UNFPA Support for HIV/AIDS Prevention." New York: UNFPA. *www.unfpa.org.*

—— (1998b), "Programme Advisory Note: Reproductive Health Effects of Gender-Based Violence: Policy and Programme Implications," Number 6, E/2,000/1998. New York: UNFPA.

—— (1998c), "Socioeconomic, Demographic and Reproductive Health Profiles of Adolescent Girls in SAARC Countries," South Asia Conference on the Adolescent, 21–23 July 1998. New Delhi, India.

—— (1998d), *The State of World Population: 1998 The New Generations.* New York: UNFPA.

UNFPA/CST (1993), "Population Profile of SAARC Countries with Special Reference to Women," November. Kathmandu: UN Population Fund/Country Support Team for South and West Asia.

UNICEF (n.d.), "Gender Mainstreaming: A Guide for UNICEF-Assisted Programmes, Field-Testing Draft." New York: UNICEF.

—— (1993a), "A Time for Action: Girls, Women and Human Rights." New York: Development Programmes for Women Unit, UNICEF.

—— (1993b), *"We Will Never Go Back": Social Mobilization in the Child Survival and Development Programme in the United Republic of Tanzania.* New York: UNICEF.

—— (1994), *Fire in the House: Determinants of Intra-familial Violence and Strategies for its Elimination.* Bangkok: UNICEF East Asia and Pacific Regional Office.

—— (1995a), "Children of Minorities: Deprivation and Discrimination." *Innocenti Insights.* Florence: UNICEF International Child Development Centre.

—— (1995b), "Girls' Education Is a Human Rights Issue." *Information,* 10 November, PR/GVA/95/45. Geneva: UNICEF.

—— (1996a), "Atlas of South Asian Children and Women." Kathmandu: UNICEF Regional Office for South Asia.

—— (1996b), "Violence against Women and Girls in South Asia: Prospects for Change." Kathmandu: UNICEF Regional Office for South Asia.

—— (1997a), "Children and Violence." *Innocenti Digest*, No. 2 (September). Florence: UNICEF International Child Development Centre.

—— (1997b), "Dangerous Homes: Communicators Initiative on Child Rights against Domestic Violence." New Delhi: UNICEF.

—— (1997c), "Men in Families." New York: UNICEF.

—— (1997d), *The Progress of Nations 1997*. New York: UNICEF.

—— (1997e), "The Reporting Process to the Committee on the Rights of the Child: A UNICEF Resource Guide," 1 February. New York: UNICEF.

—— (1997f), "The Role of Men in the Lives of Children." New York: UNICEF.

—— (1997g), "Statement by Ms. Carol Bellamy, Executive Director of United Nations Children's Fund on the Launch of the 1997 Edition of 'Progress of Nations,' " London, 22 July 1997.

—— (1997h), "Statistics of South Asian Children and Women." Kathmandu: UNICEF Regional Office for South Asia.

—— (1997i), "Women's Health in Pakistan: Fact Sheets," November. Islamabad: UNICEF Pakistan.

—— (1997j), "Children of Bangladesh and Their Rights," November. Dhaka: UNICEF Bangladesh.

—— (1998a), "And the Girl Child: Review of Chapter IV, Strategic Areas of Concern." Compiled by Vijayalakshmi Balakrishnan for UNICEF. New Delhi: UNICEF India Country Office. Mimeo (23 January).

—— (1998b), "Ending Violence against Women and Girls in South Asia: Meeting Report, 21–24 October 1997, Kathmandu." *ROSA Reports*, No. 23 (March). Kathmandu: UNICEF Regional Office for South Asia.

—— (1998c), *Facts & Figures 1998*. August. *http://www.unicef.org*.

—— (1998d), "The Human Rights of Women and Children: Challenges and Opportunities for NGOs in Monitoring the Implementation of the Convention on the Rights of the Child and the Convention on the Elimination of All Forms of Discrimination against Women." New York, UNICEF.

—— (1998e), Profiles of men active against violence to women and girls; Interview conducted by "Steps Towards Development" for UNICEF Bangladesh, June. Dhaka: UNICEF Bangladesh.

—— (1998f), "Recommendations to the Commission on the Status of Women, Report of the 42nd Session." New Delhi: UNICEF India Country Office. Mimeo (23 January).

—— (1998g), *The State of the World's Children 1998*. New York: Oxford University Press.

—— (1998h), "Tarrytown Document: Gender Equality and the Rights of Women and Girls." New York: UNICEF. Mimeo (10 September)

—— (1998i), "Parenting and Child-Rearing in Nepal: A Study of Knowledge, Attitude and Practice." Kathmandu: UNICEF Nepal.

—— (1998j), *The Progress of Nations 1998*. New York: UNICEF.

—— (1999a), "Foundation Inaugurated to Assist Survivors of Acid Attacks and to Counter Acid Violence in Bangladesh." Information and Advocacy Section, UNICEF Bangladesh. Mimeo.

—— (1999b), "Helping Survivors of Acid Violence and Preventing Further Attacks in Bangladesh," June. UNICEF Bangladesh.

—— (1999c), *Networks, Organisations and Individuals Working to End Violence Against Women and Girls: A Directory*. Report No, 32 (February). Kathmandu: UNICEF Regional Office for South Asia.

—— (1999d), *The State of the World's Children 1999*. New York: UNICEF.

—— (1999e), "Working with Youth Against Gender Violence." Kathmandu: UNICEF Regional Office for South Asia. Mimeo.

—— (1999f), "Reduction of Maternal Mortality and Violence against Women." Exploratory Formatic Research submitted to UNICEF Bangladesh by Expressions Unlimited. Mimeo (January).

—— (1999g), "Training Module on Management of Violence against Women, Second Draft." Dhaka: UNICEF Bangladesh. Mimeo.

—— (1999h), "Violence against Women." Swat, North West Frontier Province, Pakistan.

—— (1999i), "Transforming Private Rage into Public Action: Strategy Meetings on Gender and Violence against Women and Girls — Perspectives on the Future Role of UNICEF in South Asia." Kathmandu: UNICEF.

UNICEF, SCA, UNDAW and IWRAW (1998), "The Human Rights of Women and Children: Challenges and Opportunities," 21–22 January. New York: UNICEF, SCA, UNDAW, IWRAW and Commonwealth Medical Association.

UNICEF and UNIFEM (n.d.), "Convention on the Elimination of All Forms of Discrimination against Women: Legal Status and Legal Reality." In UNICEF and UNIFEM (n.d.), "Women's Rights are Human Rights." New York: UNICEF and UNIFEM. Mimeo.

UNICEF, UNIFEM and UNDP (1997), "Report Legal Roundtable Discussions." Kathmandu: UNICEF, UNIFEM and UNDP. Mimeo (27 October).

UNIFEM (1995), "Report of the Expert Group Meeting on the Development of Guidelines for the Integration of Gender Perspectives into United Nations Human Rights Activities and Programmes." Geneva: UN Development Fund for Women (UNIFEM).

—— (1997), *UNIFEM News*, Vol. 3, No. 2 (March). New York: UNIFEM.

—— (1998a), "Asia and the Pacific Campaign to Eliminate Violence against Women: 'A Life Free of Violence, It's Our Right'." UNIFEM. *http://www.unifem.undp.org/campaign/violence/asia.htm*.

—— (1998b), *Bringing Equality Home: Implementing the Convention on the Elimination of All Forms of Discrimination Against Women, CEDAW*. New York: UNIFEM.

—— (1998c), *A Life Free of Violence: It's Our Right*. UNIFEM 1998 Global Campaign for the Elimination of Gender-based Violence in the South Asia Region. New Delhi: UNIFEM South Asia Regional Office in collaboration with UNFPA, UN Resident Coordinator of the UN system in India, UNICEF.

—— (1999), "A World Free of Violence Against Women: United Nations Inter-Agency Global Videoconference," (International Women's Day, 8 March). New York: UNIFEM.

UNIFEM with UNICEF, UNFPA and the UN Resident Coordinator for the UN system in India (1998), "Trade in Human Misery, Trafficking in women and children," November. New Delhi: UNIFEM.

UN Wire (1999), "Women's Groups Decry Law on Rape" (22 October). *www.unfoundation.org/unwire/unwire.cfm#8.ID=91571*. New York: UN Foundation.

Uprety, Aruna and Haydi Sowerwine (1995), "Hidden Miseries of Childbirth." *The Kathmandu Post*, 30 July.

US Department of Justice (1996), "Violence against Women," February. Washington, DC: Department of Justice.

van der Veer, Peter (1996), *Religious Nationalism: Hindus and Muslims in India*. New Delhi: Oxford University Press.

Venkatachalam, R. and Viji Srinivasan (1993), *Female Infanticide*. New Delhi: Har-Anand Publications.

Vinayak, Ramesh (1997), "Victims of Sudden Influence." *India Today*, 15 December.

Vyas, Anju (1996), *Voices of Resistance, Silences of Pain: A Resource Guide on Violence against Women*. New Delhi: CWDS.

Wagar, Janet M. and Margaret R. Rodney (1995), "An Evaluation of a Group Treatment Approach for Children Who Have Witnessed Wife Abuse." *Journal of Family Violence*, Vol. 10, No. 3.

Walker, Alice and Pratibha Parmar (1993), *Warrior Marks: Female Genital Mutilation and the Sexual Blinding of Women*. New York: Harcourt Brace.

WARLAW (1996), *Kali's Yug: Women and Law Journal*, Vol. 1, No. 1 (November). New Delhi: Women's Action Research and Legal Action for Women.

WEDO (1996), *Beyond Promises: Governments in Motion, One Year after the Beijing Women's Conference*. New York: Women's Environmental and Development Organization.

—— (1997), "Lighting the Path to Progress." Paper presented at the Dialogue Session with Women at the

Fifth Session of the Commission on Sustainable Development. New York: WEDO.

—— (1999), "Risks, Rights and Reforms: A 50-Country Survey Assessing Government Actions Five Years After the International Conference on Population and Development." WEDO.

Weiss, Anita M. (1998), "The Slow Yet Steady Path to Women's Empowerment." Pages 124–43 in Yvonne Yazbeck Haddad and John L. Esposito (eds.), *Islam, Gender, and Social Change*. New York: Oxford University Press.

Whitehead, A. (1981), "I'm Hungry Mum: The Politics of Domestic Bargaining." In K. Young et al. (eds.), *Of Marriage and the Market: Women's Subordination Internationally and Its Lessons*. London: Routledge and Kegan Paul.

WHO (1993), "Violence and Health." *World Health Statistics Quarterly*, Vol. 46, No. 1. Geneva: WHO.

—— (1995), "Elimination of Violence against Women: Finding Some Responses Together." Geneva: WHO. Mimeo.

—— (1996a), "Project to Prevent Intra-family Violence Against Women." Research Protocol, "Women Affected by Family Violence: The Critical Process," April. Washington, DC: WHO.

—— (1996b), "Violence against Women: WHO Consultation," Geneva, 5–7 February 1996. Geneva: Women's Health and Development, Family and Reproductive Health, WHO.

—— (1997a), "Elimination of Violence Against Women: In Search of Solutions." Executive Summary. Geneva: WHO.

—— (1997b), "Female Genital Mutilation: A Joint WHO-UNICEF-UNFPA Statement." Geneva: WHO.

—— (1997c), "Violence against Women," WHO/FRH/WHD/97.8. Geneva: Women's Health and Development, Family and Reproductive Health, WHO.

—— (1998a) "Abortion in the Developing World." Press Release WHO/28, 17 May 1998. *http://www.who.int/inf-pr-1999/en/pr99-28/html*. Geneva: WHO.

—— (1998b), "Extracts from Executive Summary of the WHO/FIGO Pre-Congress Workshop 30-31 July 1997." *http://www.who.int/frh-whd/publications-vaw2.htm*. WHO.

—— (1999a), "Annotated bibliography on violence against women: a health and human rights concern," WHO/CHS/GCWH/99.2. Geneva: Rights and Humanity in collaboration with Women, Health and Development and the Global Commission on Women's Health.

—— (1999b), "Building the Evidence-base on Violence Against Women." Geneva: Global Programme on Evidence for Health Policy, WHO.

—— (1999c), "WHD: Women's Health and Development." *http://www.who.int/frh-whd/WHD/activities/whd.vaw.htm*. Women's Health and Development Programme, WHO.

—— (1999d), "WHO recognizes child abuse as a major public health problem." Press Release WHO/20, 8 April 1999. *http://www.who.int/inf-pr-1999/en/pr-99-20.html*.

—— (1999e), "Report of the Consultation on Child Abuse Prevention" (29–31 March). Geneva: WHO.

WHO/Nepal (1998), "Nepal Human Development Report: Measures and Indices." WHO.

Wieringa, Saskia (ed.) (1995), *Subversive Women, Historical Experiences of Gender and Resistance: Women's Movements in Africa, Asia, Latin America, and the Caribbean*. New Delhi: Kali for Women.

Wijayatilake, Kamalini (n.d. a), "Domestic Violence: A Silent Cry." Mimeo.

—— (n.d. b), "A Socio-legal Overview of Rape as a Form of Violence against Women." Mimeo.

Wijayatilake, Kamalini, Sepali Kottegoda, Kamala Liyanage, Gameela Samarasinghe and Maithree Wickramasinghe (1997a), "Activists against Violence against Girls and Women in South Asia," February. Colombo, Sri Lanka: CENWOR.

—— (1997b), "Violence against Women: Voices of Victims and Activists." *Study Series*, No. 12 (March). Colombo, Sri Lanka: CENWOR.

Wijenaike, Punyakante (1994), *Amulet*. Nugegoda, Sri Lanka: Deepani.

—— (1995), *To Follow the Sun*. Colombo, Sri Lanka: Gunasena.

Wilber, Ken (1996), *A Brief History of Everything*. Boston, MA: Shambhala Publications.

Winberg, Margareta (1999), Statement by Margareta Winberg, Minister for Gender Equality, Sweden, at Seminar on Men and Gender Equality arranged by the Governments of Germany and Sweden, 3 March, New York.

Women, Law and Development International (1998), *Gender Violence: The Hidden War Crime*, Washington, DC: Women, Law and Development International.

Women's Bureau of Sri Lanka, Ministry of Women's Affairs (n.d.), "Towards Empowerment of Women." Colombo, Sri Lanka: Women's Bureau of Sri Lanka, Ministry of Women's Affairs. Mimeo.

Women's Education and Research Centre (1993), *Nivedini: A Sri Lankan Feminist Journal*, Vol. 1, No. 1 (December). Colombo, Sri Lanka: Women's Education and Research Centre.

—— (1994), *Nivedini: A Sri Lankan Feminist Journal*, Vol. 2, No. 1 (July). Colombo, Sri Lanka: Women's Education and Research Centre.

Women's Feature Service (n.d.), "A Dossier on Violence Against Women." New Delhi: Women's Feature Service.

Women's Feature Service with Mary Khemchand, Bhargavi Nagaraj and Pamela Philipose (1999), "Advancement of Women in India 1995–1999: A Draft Report from the Women's Movement," August. New Delhi: Women's Feature Service.

Wonderlich, Stephen A., Richard W. Wilsnack, Sharon C. Wilsnack and T. Robert Harris (1996), "Childhood Sexual Abuse and Bulimic Behavior in a Nationally Representative Sample." *American Journal of Public Health*, August.

World Bank (1997), *World Development Report 1997: The State in a Changing World*. New York: Oxford University Press.

—— (1998), "Bangladesh: Country Gender Profile," 9 November. *http://www.worldbank.org/gender/info/bangla.htm*. World Bank.

Worldwide YWCA (1998), *Abstracts: World Conference on Family Violence*. Singapore: Worldwide YWCA.

Wright, Karen (1998), "Thugs in Bassinets," *New York Times*, 10 May, page 10.

Young, Richard H. and Helen Chernikoff (1996), "Trafficking of Children and Prostitution." Paper presented at the Workshop on Trafficking in Persons in South Asia, Shastri Indo-Canadian Institute, New Delhi, 26–28 February.

YWCA (1997), "Action Plan of the 1997 YWCA Asia-Pacific Conference on Violence against Women." Taipei: YWCA. Mimeo (April).

Zeanah, Charles H. and Michael Scheeringa (1996), "Evaluation of Posttraumatic Symptoms in Infants and Young Children Exposed to Violence." Pages 9–14 in Joy D. Osofsky and Emily Fenichel (eds.), *Islands of Safety*. Washington, DC: Zero to Three, National Center for Infants, Toddlers and Families.

Zero to Three (1994), "Diagnostic Classification of Mental Health and Development Disorders of Infancy and Early Childhood." Washington, DC: Zero to Three, National Center for Infants, Toddlers and Families.

Zia, Afiya Shehrbano (1994), *Sex Crime in the Islamic Context: Rape, Class and Gender in Pakistan*. Lahore: ASR Publications.

Zide, Arlene R. K. (ed.) (1993), *In Their Own Voice: The Penguin Anthology of Contemporary Indian Women Poets*. New Delhi: Penguin Books India.

Zierler, Sally, Lisa Feingold, Deborah Laufer, Priscilla Velentgas, Ira Kantowitz-Gordon and Kenneth Mayer (1991), cited in Lori L. Heise, Jacqueline Pitanguy and Adriene Germain (1994), "Violence against Women: The Hidden Health Burden." *World Bank Discussion Papers*, No. 255.

S. PAUL

*A blooming, beaming girl-child dances in a public park,
New Delhi, India.*